P9-APX-059

PEOPLE'S LAWYERS

PEOPLE'S LAWYERS

Crusaders for Justice in American History

Diana Klebanow
and
Franklin L. Jonas

M.E.Sharpe
Armonk, New York
London, England

Library of Congress Cataloging-in-Publication Data

Klebanow, Diana.
    People's lawyers : crusaders for justice in American History / Diana Klebanow and
Franklin L. Jonas.
       p. cm.
    Includes bibliographical references and index.
    ISBN 0-7656-0673-9 (hardcover : alk. paper)
      1. Lawyers—United States—Biography. I. Jonas, Franklin L. II. Title.

KF372.K58 2003
340′.092′273—dc21
[B]   2002066805

Dedication

To my parents, Irving and Ruth Klebanow, and my aunt, Ella N. Pinsker,
in loving memory
and for
my nephew, David I. Klebanow, and my students
—Diana Klebanow

To my wife, Blanche Jonas, my sons, Sheldon, Oscar,
and the late Larry Jonas,
and my grandson, Zachary Jonas
—Franklin L. Jonas

Contents

Introduction

The most famous line about lawyers comes from William Shakespeare. In *Henry VI,* Part 2, a character in the play, Dick the butcher, speaks the oft-quoted words: "The first thing we do, let's kill all the lawyers."

The authors of this study have written (with apologies to Shakespeare) a favorable book about lawyers. We have focused on ten lawyers who fought for the rights of the people and whose primary goal was to make use of the law to fight for social justice.

The book is an outgrowth of our work in American history and political science. We wanted to write about men and women who have earned their place in history because of their accomplishments, and we recognized the key role played by "people's lawyers" as crusaders for social change in American society.

The lawyers selected for this book are: Belva A. Lockwood (1830–1917); Louis D. Brandeis (1856–1941); Clarence Darrow (1857–1938); Samuel S. Leibowitz (1892–1978); Charles Hamilton Houston (1896–1950); Thurgood Marshall (1908–1995); William M. Kunstler (1919–1995); Ruth Bader Ginsburg (1933–); Ralph Nader (1934–); and Morris Dees (1936–).

In deciding which lawyers to include in this work, we drew upon both our professional and personal values. The lawyers discussed in this book reflected the professional standards and personal attributes that we deemed essential to this kind of study: they were interesting because of their eventful careers; they were intriguing and admirable in their own right; they had the fortitude to challenge the inequities in the status quo; they took on cases and championed causes that had a lasting impact upon American life; and they maintained a faith in the ability of the legal system to improve people's lives and create a more just society.

Their accomplishments were not always apparent on a case-by-case basis, but the sum total of their work led to fundamental changes in this country. In particular, they championed the rights of forgotten members of society, including the poor, the powerless, and the marginalized.

The majority of these attorneys came from modest backgrounds, but they drew on the support system provided by their family members. All of them became highly accomplished and successful in their profession. Four (Brandeis,

Leibowitz, Ginsburg, and Nader) were first-generation Americans; one (Marshall) was the grandson of a slave; three (Lockwood, Darrow, and Dees) were the offspring of struggling farmers; and three (Brandeis, Marshall, and Ginsburg) reached the United States Supreme Court.

These ten lawyers dealt with some of the most important issues before the country in the nineteenth and twentieth centuries. Lockwood championed world peace and the rights of women and Native Americans; Brandeis pioneered in the struggle against corporate privilege; Darrow was the attorney for the defense in several of the most controversial trials in America's history; Leibowitz fought for the indigent Scottsboro defendants accused of rape; Houston distinguished himself in court and trained a whole generation of black attorneys; Marshall took up the mantle of Houston in seeking to obtain and enforce equal rights; Kunstler became a household name in his defense of anti–Vietnam War protesters in the Chicago Seven trial; Ginsburg stood as the foremost advocate against discrimination based on sex; Nader led the fight for protection of the American consumer; and Dees (a millionaire turned lawyer) helped to dethrone the Ku Klux Klan as a powerful force in Southern society.

The book includes accounts of the most important cases handled by these lawyers. We also focus on the forces in their lives that shaped their passionate commitment to social justice, as well as the strengths upon which they relied to overcome the obstacles in their paths. The achievements of these men and women in the battle against entrenched interests were due not only to the spirit of the times, but to their determination to succeed, forcefulness of their arguments, and their sheer personal courage.

Each of the ten chapters in this book consists of four parts: a chronology of important events; a biographical section covering the lawyer's life and accomplishments; an account of the lawyer's most significant cases; and an annotated bibliography.

It was an inspiring book to write at this particular moment in history. At a time when the nation needs to rekindle its faith in its past and gain confidence in its ability to face the challenges of the future, the authors hope that this book will be a guide to the kinds of victories that can be achieved in the country's perpetual quest for social justice.

Diana Klebanow wrote the chapters on Darrow, Houston, Marshall, Kunstler, and Dees. Franklin L. Jonas wrote the chapters on Lockwood, Brandeis, Leibowitz, Ginsburg, and Nader.

Diana Klebanow wishes to express her appreciation to Annette Kalin, who typed her portion of this manuscript. In addition to being a cherished friend, Ms. Kalin showed great skill, unending patience, and graciousness in helping with this book.

The author had the good fortune to be able to use the wonderful resources at St. John's University for a substantial portion of her research. She acknowledges the courtesies extended to her by Toni L. Aiello, Head of Faculty and

Access Services, Rittenberg Law Library, St. John's University School of Law, and her staff. She is also grateful to John Butler, Senior Law Librarian, Queens Supreme Court Law Library, for his assistance with her research, and to the staff at the New York Public Library.

She appreciates the encouragement of her work given by Professors John Ehrenberg, Chairman, Department of Political Science, and Alfred J. DiMaio, Department of Political Science, and Division Coordinator, Social Sciences, at the Brooklyn Center of Long Island University. In addition, she expresses her gratitude to Professor John W. Brennan, former Chairman, Department of History, Long Island University; Professor Audrey Wilson, Department of Anthropology, Long Island University; Robert Grass, Esq.; and Ida K. Ellis, who kindly consented to read portions of the book; as well as to Professor Joseph P. Dorinson, former Chairman, Department of History, Long Island University, for his interest in this project. Judy Bruno, Assistant to Morris Dees at the Southern Poverty Law Center, was also very helpful in furnishing material used in this book. Ronald L. Kuby, Esq., graciously discussed the material in the Kuntsler chapter with her.

She wishes to thank four outstanding physicians—Drs. Carmel J. Cohen, James P. Gaston, Harry Weinrauch, and the late Frederick M. Marek—for their excellent care. She holds them in the same kind of esteem as the lawyers whom she was privileged to write about in this book.

Franklin L. Jonas wants to thank Lester Jackson, who graciously shared his knowledge of the United States Supreme Court with him. He would also like to thank the following: Janet Munch, Special Collection Libraries at Lehman College of the City of New York; Mike Margolis, Librarian at the Manhattan branch of Adelphi University; the staff of the library at the Rose Hill campus of Fordham University for their gracious assistance with his research; Wendy Chmielowski, archivist of the Peace Collection at Swarthmore College, and the Niagara Historical Society, for the abundant material they supplied on Belva A. Lockwood; the library staff of New York University Law School, who were generous in finding materials; Janet Fusco, Putnam Valley, New York, for her help in locating some of the law cases in this book; and Nerva Ramos for her fine work as a typist and computer expert.

His thanks are also extended to Professors John W. Brennan and Joseph P. Dorinson, both former chairmen, History Department, at the Brooklyn Center of Long Island University, for their unfailing encouragement with this project. Professor Audrey Wilson, Department of Anthropology, Long Island University, has been a good friend who has made many helpful comments. Professor Michael Klausner of the University of Pittsburgh at Bradford, Pennsylvania, and Professor Rick Shiels of the Department of Political Science at Mercy College, Dobbs Ferry, New York, read chapters of the book and made useful comments. The author's wife, Blanche Jonas, listened patiently to his ideas, read his pages, and was his best critic.

Both authors would like to thank their editor, Andrew Gyory, and editorial assistant, Esther Clark, and project editor, Henrietta Toth, of the M.E. Sharpe editorial department, for their guidance in the execution of this book.

PEOPLE'S LAWYERS

—Belva A. —
Lockwood

(Swarthmore College Peace Collection)

Chronology

1830   Born on October 24 in Royalton Township in Niagara County, New York.

1835–1845   Attended various country schools in and around Royalton.

1848   Married Uriah McNall, a farmer and sawmill operator, on November 8.

1849   Daughter, Lura, born on July 31.

1853   Uriah McNall died on April 8.

1854   Entered Genesee Wesleyan Seminary.

1857   Received B.S. with honors from Genesee Wesleyan College.

1857–1861   Preceptress of Lockport Union School, where she introduced public speaking and gymnastics classes for girls.

1861–1866   Taught at seminaries in Gainesville, Hornelsville, and Oswego, New York.

1866   Moved to Washington, D.C., where she opened a coeducational school and became active in various movements of reform.

1867   Helped found Universal Franchise Association, the first woman's suffrage group in Washington, D.C.

1868   Married Ezekiel Lockwood, a sixty-five-year-old former minister and dentist.

1869   Gave birth to a second daughter, Jessie Belva, but the child survived for less than two years.

1871   Was admitted to National University Law School.

1872   Graduated, but was at first denied her diploma.

1873   Received law degree after appealing to President Ulysses S. Grant.

1874   Refused the right to practice before the U.S. Court of Claims because she was a woman.

1876   Denied the right to practice before the U.S. Supreme Court because of her sex.

1877   Her husband, Ezekiel Lockwood, died on April 25.

1879   Played the principal role in securing the passage of the "Lockwood Bill," which permitted women to practice law before the U.S. Supreme Court; on March 3, became the first woman ever admitted to practice before the Supreme Court.

1884   "Nominated" for president of the United States by the Equal Rights Party, she toured through much of the nation.

1888   "Ran" again for president.

1885–1892   Was a popular lecturer.

1894   Daughter Lura died. Lockwood became the first woman ever licensed to practice law in Virginia.

1906   As one of the attorneys for the Eastern and Emigrant Cherokee Indians in their case against the United States, presented oral argument before the Supreme Court that helped to win award to the plaintiffs of more than $4.5 million.

1909   Received an honorary L.L.D. from Syracuse University.

1889–1914   Was a prominent activist in both the international and American peace movements.

1917   Died at age eight-six in Washington, D.C., on May 19.

Biography

On the morning of December 1, 1880, there took place a historic event at the Supreme Court building in the nation's capital when a slender, middle-aged widow rose in the chamber to become the first of her sex ever to present oral argument in a case before the high court. This was Belva Ann Lockwood, the nation's first prominent woman lawyer, who had also been the first of her sex to plead cases in the courts of Washington, D.C., and in 1884, as the candidate of the Equal Rights Party, would become the first woman ever to garner votes in a presidential election.* A cogent speaker and writer, Lockwood was throughout most of her life an activist in the woman's rights and peace movements as well as an accomplished lobbyist for reformist laws.[1]

Origins

Lockwood was born on October 24, 1830, in a log house in Royalton, New York, in the county of Niagara, about two miles from the Erie Canal. She was the second eldest as well as the second daughter among the five children born to Lewis and Hannah Bennett, both of whom had grown up in Washington County in eastern New York before settling as newlyweds in Royalton in 1827, when Lewis was twenty and Hannah was barely sixteen. For a few years, Lewis Bennett had owned a hundred-acre farm which (in advertising it for sale) he once described as "well-watered, well-timbered, . . . with every kind of fruit tree . . . and a good dwelling house." The Bennetts did not prosper, however, and in 1854, Lewis and Hannah immigrated to Illinois, taking their three youngest children with them.[2]

As a child, Belva was spirited and courageous. "I was a little dirty-faced girl," she would later recall, "not afraid of rats or snakes or nothing, as active as a boy . . . in for anything, and delighted to ride the horses after the cows." As the leader and protector of her little playmates, she would drive off and sometimes kill the snakes and rats that the others found frightening.[3]

Raised a Methodist in an area noted for the frequency and intensity of its Protestant revivals, Belva had read the whole of the Bible by her tenth birthday. At that time, she took the scriptures literally and attempted to duplicate by herself some of the biblical miracles. In trying to walk on the water of a local pond, she got all her clothes wet, including her underwear. Although Belva would later take a less literal approach to the Bible, she would always uphold traditional moral standards both from the speaker's platform and by her own conduct.[4]

---

*Victoria Woodhull, who was nominated by the Equal Rights Party in 1872, is often referred to as the first woman to run for president, but her campaign disintegrated and she was credited with no votes on Election Day.

Early Education

Belva attended various one-room schoolhouses, either at Royalton or in other nearby towns. At such schools the children were expected to "toe the mark," to step up to the chalk line at the front of the room whenever they were called on to recite their lessons. Belva was, by all reports, always the best student in any class that she happened to be in. She also read a great deal on her own, and from her books, especially those on history, she acquired high ambitions that she would later strive to fulfill. She seems from an early age to have believed that women were as capable as men of competing for success and fame. In an article that she wrote in middle age, Lockwood declared that she had never been able to believe in the laws and customs that had confined women to their limited domestic sphere. "Has God," she asked rhetorically, "given one half of his creatures talents and gifts that are but a mockery— wings but not to fly?"[5]

In 1845, the school board of Royalton hired Belva, who was then fourteen years old, to teach a small group of young children in the summer term of the very school from which she had herself just graduated, and for the next three years, she would continue to teach every summer at Royalton. On discovering that some of the male teachers were getting paid twice what she was, Belva protested bitterly to the school board, only to be told that the men had to be paid more because they had families to support. She appealed next to her good friend, the wife of the town's Methodist minister, who sadly told her: "I cannot help you, you cannot help yourself. It is the way of the world." On hearing this, Belva resolved that she would never tamely accept the subordination of women.[6]

Eager for education, Belva attended the Royalton Academy, a coeducational school for teenagers, paying her way out of her summer earnings. She was also beginning to write essays and poems, some of which were published by local newspapers while others appeared in literary journals, such as the *Western Literary Messenger*, the *Boston Olive Branch*, and the *Ladies' Repository*. Belva was eager to go on to college, but at that time scarcely any females did so. "Girls should get married," her father once told her; "only boys go to college."[7]

"There seemed only one avenue open [to me]," Lockwood would later remark—"marriage." She therefore accepted the proposal of Uriah McNall, a twenty-three-year-old farmer and sawmill operator with ambitious plans to build and sell houses. The young couple were wed in Royalton on November 8, 1848, and went to live on Uriah's farm, just outside the nearby town of Gasport. Approximately nine months later, Belva gave birth to a girl whom they named Lura. The young family's prospects were suddenly shattered when Uriah snagged his right foot in the sawmill's machinery. Severely injured, he never recovered, and after two years as a shut-in and invalid, he contracted consumption and died on April 8, 1853.[8]

Attends Genesee College

A widow at twenty-two with a three-year-old child to support, Lockwood returned to the classroom, teaching for eighteen months in a Gasport school, but the pay was too low to afford a decent standard of living. At a time when few women had well-paid jobs, it seemed to her that her one chance of adequately supporting herself and Lura was to add to her qualifications as a teacher by continuing her education. Of course, her decision to go on to college was fueled as well by her old childhood dreams of success and fame.

In the autumn of 1854, Lockwood registered for classes at Genesee Wesleyan College (which later became part of Syracuse University) in Lima, New York, and sent her five-year-old daughter to live with her parents. Adding to the anguish of the separation was the fact that the Bennett family was about to emigrate to Illinois. It would be three years before Lockwood saw her child again.

Genesee Wesleyan was actually two separate schools: a seminary for young women and a college whose student body consisted almost entirely of men. The school had recently allowed some of the best students among the seminary girls to transfer to the college, which had a demanding curriculum, in that more than half of the courses were in the natural sciences. After a single term at the seminary, Lockwood applied for admission to the college and was accepted.[9]

The regimen at the college was both demanding and somber. Students were not permitted to read newspapers nor even to converse in the dining hall. They were required to put in long hours at their studies and, whatever their religion, to attend prayers daily. Lockwood did not complain about the school's strictness, however, for she viewed her work at Genesee as her one and only chance to make something of her life. "I seized greedily," she later remembered, "every opportunity that came to me—studied in season and out of season, and while fond of my roommates and kind to them, I deliberately banished them from my room that I might not be disturbed."[10] She did, however, find time for charity work and was active as well in the college literary society. In June 1857, Lockwood was awarded with honors the degree of bachelor of science.

Preceptress and Teacher

Even before she graduated, the trustees of the Lockport Union School selected Lockwood to be their school's next preceptress (a sort of tutor and adviser to the female students), and she accepted the appointment. Lockport Union, which was one of the best-regarded high schools in the state, had over 600 students, divided about equally between boys and girls. Lockwood taught a wide variety of courses, including logic, mathematics, botany, and public speaking. She also supervised the work of three male teachers, each of whom, ironically, was paid far more than she was. At the end of her first semester at Lockport, Lockwood visited her family in Illinois, where she was reunited with her daughter, and when she returned east, she took Lura with her.

As the school's preceptress, Lockwood was expected to set its moral tone. Although she was authorized to use corporal punishment, if necessary, it seems unlikely that she ever did. In fact, her statements to the students were positive rather than punitive ones in which she urged them to view life positively and to embrace its challenges gladly. "The World Is Beautiful" was the title of one of her speeches, and another hailed a seventy-seven-year-old woman as "a model for the girls" because of her vigor, even in old age. Lockwood herself kept remarkably active in the charitable activities of the Lockport community, including its missionary society and a school for poor children that she maintained entirely at her own expense. "She also had a Bible class and an infant class," said Lockport's Methodist minister, "and was constantly doing some deeds of charity. At the time Kansas was famishing she was president of a relief society and spent much time and money in the cause."[11] (The privation and hunger among the settlers of what became known to history as "Bleeding Kansas" were an outgrowth of the violent struggle there between the advocates of slavery and its opponents.)

On the premise that girls had the same educational needs as boys (a truly radical idea at the time), Lockwood required the school's female students to participate in gymnastics and take a course in public speaking. When she encountered resistance from male staff members, she decided to teach both of the new courses herself. Some of the parents, opposing the new requirements as inappropriate for young ladies, lashed out at her as "that crazy teacher" and as "a bold woman who is unsuitable to her position." The storm soon blew over, however. As Lockwood's programs proved popular with her pupils, they soon came to be accepted by most of their parents and by the majority of the faculty as well.[12]

Lockwood was also active in the teacher organizations of her town, county, and state. It was at a meeting of the New York Teachers Association in 1858 that she first met feminist Susan B. Anthony, who had formerly been a teacher in a Rochester public school and was still a forceful advocate for change within both the teaching profession and the schools. At meetings of the State Teachers Association, Anthony would demand a larger role within the association for its female members and would call for an end to the segregation of students, whether by race or by sex.

Lockwood, who had been deeply impressed by Anthony when she had first heard her speak in Lima, New York, while attending college there, now became her ally at Teachers Association meetings, seconding her motions and defending her proposals. The male teachers who dominated the association, however, "were much disturbed," as a reporter noted, by "the eternal jangle over women's rights." Joining with the most conservative of their female colleagues, they defeated nearly all of the proposals made by Anthony and her supporters.[13]

When the Civil War began in the spring of 1861, many of Lockport's young men, including some of Lockwood's former students, enlisted in the Union army. Although stunned at the descent into violence, she now took the lead in organizing the work of both the local Ladies' Aid Society and of her own schoolgirls in sewing together uniforms and in furnishing woolen stockings, sewing kits, shirts, and other supplies that were needed by Lockport's "citizen-soldiers." Opposed to slavery since childhood, Lockwood would later hail its demise as "a grand step onward in the liberties of the world," but she deplored the war, in which her own brother, Warren, was wounded, as "a sad carnage" for which the nation had sacrificed much blood and treasure. She would later remark that the freedom of the slaves could have been purchased for a small fraction of what the war had cost. Her ambivalence toward the war foreshadows her later involvement with the American and international peace movements.[14]

Weary from the combined demands of her job and her active role in the community, and perhaps irritated by the knowledge that she was earning, at $400 annually, only two-thirds of the amount that her male "assistants" were getting, Lockwood decided to make a change. At the end of the spring 1861 semester, she suddenly resigned and was promptly hired as the preceptress of a school for girls in the nearby town of Gainesville. Here, she again introduced a program of physical exercise, including ice-skating and nature walks. This innovation led to a clash with the woman who owned the school, so Lockwood moved on after one year to a new job as principal of a girls' school in Hornelsville. In 1863, she purchased the Oswego Female Seminary, where she remained for the next two and a half years. Here, she established a liberal curriculum aimed at developing "the whole person," in which intellectually rigorous instruction was combined with physical training, nature study, and moral guidance. In taking this approach, Lockwood was clearly preparing her young charges for a fuller and more varied life than the women of that era normally enjoyed.[15]

Life in Washington

Early in 1866, Lockwood sold at a profit her Oswego school, enrolled Lura, who was now sixteen, at the Genesee seminary in Lima, and moved to Washington, D.C. Her sole purpose, she would later recall, was "to see what was being done at this great political center—this seething pot—to learn something of the practical workings of government, and to see what the great men and women of the country felt and thought." Her words demonstrate the vigor of her personal ambitions, revealing a powerful appetite for both recognition and for intellectual stimulation. (Note the reference to "the great men *and women* of the country.") Moreover, in order to improve the prospects of both of them, she had once again separated temporarily from her daughter. As Louis Filler has noted, in moving to Washington, Lockwood was "seeking a broader field of action."[16]

For the next year, she divided her time between teaching part-time at a school for girls and observing the debates in Congress and the sessions of the United States Supreme Court. She then opened a school of her own, one of Washington's first coeducational high schools. Unable to find a school building large enough, Lockwood rented the third floor of Union League Hall (also known as Temperance Hall), Washington's largest public meeting center. Converting small parts of the rented space into living quarters and an office, she located her school in one of the large meeting halls. In time she acquired two other halls and for several years made a profitable business of renting all three at night to temperance societies, suffrage reformers, Grand Army of the Republic branches, and other assorted fraternal orders that were holding meetings in Washington. Lockwood's school also flourished, and her daughter, Lura, was again living with her while teaching French and Latin at the school.[17]

Lockwood was also becoming active in movements of reform. A supporter of temperance since her days at Royalton, she attributed nearly all of Washington's crime to "spirituous liquors" and called for their "entire abolition." She hoped that once liquor was eliminated, tobacco, "that foul vilifier of heaven's pure air," would also be banned in "the onward march of progress." She also joined the Universal Peace Union and would in time play a prominent role in its agitation against war and armaments. It seems obvious that the violence of war, like tobacco and liquor, was a vice associated chiefly with men. Thus, in calling for their abolition, Lockwood was, in effect, calling upon men to mend their ways for what she regarded as the betterment of all.[18]

Her principal cause, however, was woman's rights, a movement to which she was drawn as much from her own experiences and feisty temperament as from the intellectual convictions that had resulted from her wide reading and from her personal acquaintance with feminist women, such as Susan B. Anthony. Antagonized by the failure of male reformers, such as Horace Greeley and Wendell Phillips, to support votes for women, even as they were demanding the franchise for black men, many of the feminist leaders, including Anthony and Elizabeth Cady Stanton, now formed independent organizations of their own. In May 1867, Lockwood was among the founders of the Universal Franchise Association (UFA), the Washington branch of the woman's suffrage movement, which was committed to the enfranchisement of all citizens, regardless of race or sex. Lockwood, one of the organization's four vice presidents, often presided at the weekly meetings held in the auditorium that adjoined her school in the Union League Building. From the outset, the UFA gatherings were plagued by the ridicule of a uniformly hostile press and by the presence of hecklers who would interrupt the speakers with hisses and yells. At some meetings, cooking utensils or even vegetables were rolled down the aisle. According to Lockwood, "the police when appealed to failed to keep order, seeming rather to join hands with the mob."[19]

In the meantime, she had become well acquainted with Dr. Ezekiel Lockwood, a "painless" dentist and former Baptist minister who was a veteran of the Civil War, and on March 11, 1868, they were married. Although sixty-four, twenty-seven years older than his new wife, Dr. Lockwood shared her enthusiasm for social reform, especially when it came to temperance and woman's rights. At their wedding, most of the guests were members of temperance orders, many of them in full regalia. Ezekiel now gravitated into his wife's orbit, moving into her quarters at Union League Hall and assisting her with the management of her school. He even chaired a few of the woman's suffrage meetings. Early in 1870, Belva gave birth to a daughter, Jessie Belva, but after only twenty months of life, the child became seriously ill and died soon afterward.[20]

In spite of her marriage and the death of her child, Lockwood remained active in the woman's movement. In 1869, she managed the UFA's lecture series, arranging for talks before her group of such militant woman's rights orators as Stanton, Anthony, Anna Dickinson, the most popular lecturer of her day, and Theodore Tilton, a leading New York City editor and social reformer. Early the following year, Lockwood addressed the plight of the women who were employed by the federal government. She drew up a petition that declared it "a national disgrace that just because a person wears skirts instead of trousers, she can never earn more than seventy five dollars a month." She drafted a bill, requiring that women in the federal work force receive equal pay for equal work, which was introduced in the House of Representatives on March 21, 1870, by Representative Samuel M. Arnell, a Tennessee Republican and the chairman of the Education and Labor Committee. A few weeks later, Lockwood journeyed to New York, where the two rival woman's suffrage organizations—the National Woman Suffrage Association and the American Woman Suffrage Association—were both holding conventions. She managed, with the assistance of Horace Greeley, to gather 700 signatures on petitions endorsing the Arnell Bill. Two years later, a modified version of her proposal was enacted into law.[21]

The Aspiring Law Student

By this time, Lockwood was resolved on becoming a lawyer. Even before her marriage to Ezekiel, she had acquired a passionate interest in the subject dating back to her undergraduate days at Genesee, when she had attended an off-campus series of lectures given by a young attorney. Since coming to Washington, she had been reading on her own such legal classics as Blackstone's *Commentaries on the Laws of England* and Kent's *Commentaries on American Law*. She now found herself in a small but growing category of woman's movement activists, most of them younger than she, who had decided to become lawyers because it was clear that the courts were fast becoming a crucial battleground in the struggle for woman's rights.[22]

In 1869, Lockwood applied to and was rejected by three different law schools in the Washington, D.C., area. According to John Samson, president of the district's Columbian Law School, his faculty believed that "it would not have been expedient" to admit Lockwood (who was thirty-nine and married for the second time) as she "would be likely to distract the attention of the young men." Samson's remark came to the attention of reporters for Washington newspapers, and their published stories, according to Lockwood, aroused so much sympathy for her among lawyers, judges, and politicians that Congress decided to create a new "national" law school in Washington that would admit women on an equal basis with men.[23] In 1871, the new National University Law School opened its doors. The entering class consisted of thirty men and fifteen women, one of whom was Lockwood.

The women were required from the outset to attend separate recitation sections, but were at first allowed to attend the same lectures as the men. After a few weeks, however, the male students protested and the women were excluded from the lectures as well. By the middle of the school's second year, most of the women had dropped out. Only two, Lockwood and Lydia S. Hall, completed the course.

Although Hall and Lockwood had met all requirements and passed every examination, they were neither invited to graduation nor awarded their diplomas. Hall now gave up on becoming a lawyer, got married, and left the city. "She," wrote Lockwood of Hall, "was a staid matron past 40. I suppose she became 'merged,' as Blackstone says, in her husband. I was not to be squelched so easily."[24]

Even before she had completed her law school courses, Lockwood had already begun to practice law in Washington, appearing at police and probate courts and also before justices of the peace.

In April 1872, Charlotte E. Ray, a black woman and a graduate of Howard University Law School, became the first woman ever formally admitted to the bar of Washington, D.C.; a month later, she was admitted as well to the bar of the Supreme Court of the district. At Lockwood's request, a male colleague moved that she, too, be admitted to the bar of the district's highest court. There followed a rigorous three-day oral exam, but the examining committee, finding it impossible to fail her, blocked Lockwood's admission by simply failing to report. Her appeal to the chief judge resulted in a second examination, but the same thing happened again.[25]

Lockwood was also becoming politically active. Like other militant feminists, she had adopted the argument of Victoria Woodhull and others that the Fourteenth Amendment, in providing that no state could "deny to any person in its jurisdiction the equal protection of the laws," had legally enfranchised American women. In January 1871, Lockwood filed a petition, bearing 20,000 signatures, with the newly created legislature of Washington, D.C., asking that the women of the district be permitted to vote. "We are Americans," declared Lockwood, "and as such we have been guaranteed the right to vote by the Constitution of the United States." Later that year, she was among the several dozen women in the East and the Middle West who attempted, at the urging of Woodhull, to register as voters; but, like all the others, Lockwood was denied the right to register by the local authorities.[26]

In 1872, Lockwood presented a petition for woman's suffrage bearing 35,000 signatures to Congressman Ben Butler of Massachusetts, a staunch advocate of woman's rights. In that year's presidential election, Lockwood at first supported Victoria Woodhull, the adventuress, spiritualist, feminist, and stockbroker who was running for president on the ticket of the Equal Rights Party. Lockwood was unusual among Woodhull's supporters in that she was neither a spiritualist nor a medium. A speech that Lockwood delivered in New York City for Woodhull, who had ties to labor and the Workingmen's International, was probably the most radical of Lockwood's career. In it, she called for the adoption of a single civil and criminal code for the entire country and proposed also that the federal government take over the banking system and provide employment to every jobless person. When Woodhull's campaign collapsed long before Election Day, however, Lockwood was recruited by Theodore Tilton, the editor of *Golden Age*, a reformist periodical published in New York City, both to campaign in the South for Horace Greeley, the nominee of the Democrats and Liberal Republicans, and to write articles on what she observed.[27]

With the election over and Ulysses Grant reelected, Lockwood returned to Washington to resume her struggle for acceptance and recognition as an attorney. She attended several law school lectures, first at Georgetown University and later at Howard University, but neither institution would permit her to matriculate. Fearful that she might never be allowed to practice law, she wrote to President Ulysses Grant, who was also the ex officio president of the National University Law School. "Sir, you are, or you are not, the President of the National University Law School. If you are its President, I desire to say to you that . . . I am entitled to and demand my diploma. If you are not its President, then I ask that you take your name from its papers, and not hold out to the world to be what you are not." About a week later, she received her diploma. Perhaps it was the letter, but more likely, Grant had simply signed hers as one in a pile of diplomas without any idea at all as to whose name was on it. In late September 1873, when Lockwood was at last admitted to the bar of the District of Columbia, one of the judges of the district's Supreme Court warned her that in his courtroom she would be treated just as though she were a man.[28]

Integrating the Courts

Eager to succeed, Belva Lockwood took on every case that came her way, whether civil, criminal, or equitable, and regardless of the client's ability to pay. In one of her first trials, she defended an impoverished young woman who had shot a police officer. Lockwood argued that her client had shot the policeman only because her husband, an apparent felon, had told her to load a gun and shoot the first officer who tried to force his way into the house. Pointing out that under common law wives must obey their husbands, Lockwood declared that the wrong person was on trial: "Surely you would not have a woman resist her husband." The jury brought in a verdict of "not guilty," moving the judge to dismiss it from further service, observing that the jurors had just "done a hard day's work."[29]

Another of Lockwood's early clients was Charlotte Van Cort, the widow of the inventor of a torpedo boat used during the Civil War, who in 1873 sued the federal government for $100,000, alleging that it had infringed upon her husband's patent. The required venue for a case where a United States citizen was pursuing a claim against the federal government was the United States Court of Claims, and as Mrs. Van Cort's attorney, it was essential that Lockwood gain admission to its bar.

At her request, a male colleague moved that she be admitted, but one of the judges declared: "Mistress Lockwood, you are a woman." "For the first time in my life," Lockwood would later write, "I realized that it was a crime to be a woman, but it was too late to deny the charge so I pled guilty." The case was postponed for a week, and at the appointed time, Lockwood returned, now accompanied by her husband and several friends. "Mistress Lockwood," observed Chief Justice Drake, "you are a married woman." "Yes," she replied, "but I am here with the consent of my husband." Dr. Lockwood promptly rose to his feet and bowed before the judges.[30]

Three weeks later, Judge Nott, speaking for a unanimous court, ruled that "under the Constitution and law of the United States, this court is without power to grant . . . [Lockwood's] application, and . . . a woman is without legal capacity to take the office of Attorney." Allowing women to become lawyers, the judge argued, might inflict damage upon their husbands, their children, and, conceivably, upon society at large. "It is not for the judiciary," declared Nott emphatically, "to intermeddle as to what is . . . the proper sphere of woman. It is enough for judges to know that her legal position is by an unwritten law interwoven with the very fabric of society."[31]

Despite this setback, Lockwood continued to advise and work with clients in Court of Claims cases. She was still permitted to file the cases, to take testimony outside of court, and to prepare motions and briefs for her clients to read aloud in the courtroom. The court's unwillingness to accredit her as an attorney did, however, make these cases more difficult to win. At one Court of Claims session, a client attempted to transfer his claim to Lockwood, but the judge refused to permit it, and when Mrs. Lockwood attempted to address the court, he became white with rage and demanded that she keep still. Lockwood now decided that she had no choice but to hire an attorney to plead the case (*Raines* v. *United States*). Unfortunately, the lawyer that she engaged required, according to her, "three days to say very badly what I could have said well in an hour. This was some small revenge, but he lost my case."[32]

Lockwood immediately filed an appeal to the U.S. Supreme Court, hoping that by the time the Raines case reached its docket, she would be eligible to present it herself. The high court's rule on the admission of counsel said only that they must be of good character and "of good standing before the highest court of a State or Territory for three years." In October of 1876, virtually three years to the day of Lockwood's admission to the bar of the District of Columbia's highest court, A.G. Riddle, a prominent Washington lawyer sympathetic to woman's rights, nominated her for the bar of the United States Supreme Court. But she was again rebuffed when Chief Justice Morrison R. Waite, speaking for the majority, declared, "none but men were eligible to practice as attorneys." "This," said Waite, "is in accordance with immemorial usage in England and practice in all of the states until within a recent period; and the court does not feel called upon to make a change until such change is required by statute or more extended practice in the highest courts of the states."[33]

Even as she battled to establish herself in her profession, Lockwood was again struck by personal tragedy. Her husband, who had suffered a stroke in 1874, grew progressively worse and died on April 25, 1877. After nine years of marriage, Lockwood was again on her own, but she would continue to campaign aggressively against the exclusion of women from the legal profession, a struggle in which the advancement of her own career and livelihood often coincided with the broader cause of woman's rights. "I have never stopped fighting," she would in later years truthfully boast: "my cause was the cause of thousands of women."[34]

With the Supreme Court unwilling to admit a woman attorney unless required to do so by legislation, Lockwood now attempted to get just such a law enacted by the United States Congress. At her request, Congressman Butler drafted and introduced in the House of Representatives in December 1876 a bill calling for the admission of qualified women to the bar of the Supreme Court. Butler's measure won the approval of the Judiciary Committee, but was defeated on the House floor. A second bill was introduced in early 1877, but never got out of committee.

Lockwood now drafted a bill of her own, providing that any "duly qualified woman" who had been "a member in good standing of the highest court of a State or Territory, or of the District of Columbia," and was a person of "good moral character" would be admitted to practice before the United States Supreme Court. Congressman John M. Glover of Ohio introduced "the Lockwood Bill" in the House, and Lockwood testified for it before the House Judiciary Committee, which quickly approved it without a dissenting vote. On February 26, 1878, her bill passed the House by a margin of 169 to 87.[35]

Five days later, Lockwood's bill, HR 1077, was referred to the Senate Judiciary Committee, where Senator Aaron A. Sargent of California took charge of it. Lockwood submitted a brief to the Senate in which she argued that to deny the right conferred by the bill would deprive female citizens of rights proclaimed by the Declaration of Independence and guaranteed by the Fourteenth Amendment. In spite of her arguments and energetic lobbying, the committee reported adversely on the measure, maintaining that since each federal court already possessed the authority to decide who was eligible to plead cases, there was nothing in the statutes to prevent a federal judge from allowing a woman to act as an attorney in his courtroom. In spite of the committee's ruling, Sargent managed to have the bill placed on the calendar, so that it might be voted on its merits. The session ended with no further action taken on Lockwood's bill.

In the debate on the Senate floor that took place early in the next session of Congress, Sargent drew several of his arguments from Lockwood's brief, arguing, as she had done, that the right of all qualified persons to practice law and other professions was a basic human right that could not rightfully be denied simply because the professional was a woman. To meet the criticism that the bill favored women over men, Sargent amended it to read "no person shall be excluded from practicing as an attorney from any court of the United States on account of sex."[36]

When Senator Sargent fell ill, Lockwood persuaded Senator Joseph E. McDonald, of Indiana, to take charge of the measure. At her suggestion, 160 of Washington's leading attorneys signed a petition endorsing her bill. With the end of the session rapidly approaching, Lockwood intensified her lobbying. "Nothing," she would later reminisce, "was too daring for me to attempt. I addressed senators as though they were old, familiar friends, and with an earnestness that carried with it conviction."[37]

The Lockwood Bill, as the press was now calling it, was again taken up on the floor of the Senate on February 7, 1879. Senators Sargent and McDonald, now joined by Senator George Hoar of Massachusetts, made a compelling case for its passage that its opponents made no attempt to rebut. Senator Sargent insisted that the bill was "merely a measure of justice, recognized so by the [legal] profession themselves [sic], recognized so in many of the states of the union," a reference to the states that already allowed female lawyers to practice in their courts. "The enjoyment of liberty," declared Sargent, "the pursuit of happiness in her own way, is as much the birthright of women as it is of men." Hoar redefined the issue, contending that if it passed, the Lockwood Bill would "secure to the citizen of the United States the right to select his counsel." As things now stood, he pointed out, a female lawyer who had handled a client's case in the lower courts would not be allowed to do so in the Supreme Court.[38]

Perhaps swayed by these arguments, the Senate passed the Lockwood Bill by the resounding margin of 39 to 20. On the day after the bill's passage, the women who had lobbied for its enactment sent baskets of flowers to the bill's three principal backers in the Senate and boutonnieres to every senator who had voted for it. A few days later, President Hayes, whose wife, Lucille, had made it abundantly clear that she favored the measure, signed it into law.[39]

With the passage of the law that she had devised and that had been named after her, Lockwood had now established herself as a persistent and effective lobbyist. "The credit for this victory," commented the *Washington Star*, "belongs to Belva Lockwood of this city who . . . by dint of hard work has finally succeeded in having her bill passed by both houses." The *Washington Post* pointed out that when the Lockwood Bill was first introduced, not even a quarter of the Congress would have voted for it. The decisive factor in passing it, said the newspaper, had been "the strong-minded females who held the fort from day to day and talked members and senators into believing it a just measure." Even the patrician *Nation* agreed that Lockwood's very presence at the final floor debate and vote had served to increase the margin of victory.[40]

At the March 3 session of the Supreme Court, A.G. Riddle, the official legal representative of the District of Columbia, who was well acquainted with Lockwood and her work, moved that she be admitted to the bar of the Supreme Court. "No objection was raised," wrote the *New York Times,* "and for the first time in the history of the court, a woman stands on the roll of its practitioners." After Lockwood had taken the oath, she was immediately congratulated by a bevy of well-wishers, including several of her feminist woman friends, three United States senators, and various members of the Washington bench and bar, some of them personal acquaintances, who had supported her in her campaign to open the federal courts to woman lawyers.[41]

On February 2 of the following year, Lockwood moved in turn that Samuel Lowery, a black attorney and educator from Huntsville, Alabama, be admitted to the bar of the U.S. Supreme Court. The justices admitted Lowery without any hesitation, and to some observers, such as Senator George W. Julian of Illinois, it seemed "fitting" that the first woman admitted to the Supreme Court bar should have been the one to move the admission of the first black man from the South. "Who dares say the world is not progressing," asked Lockwood's daughter, Lura, "when, on motion of *a woman, a black man* is admitted to practice in the highest court of the land? Shade of Taney."[42]*

With her admission to the bar of the Supreme Court, Lockwood could no longer be excluded from any federal court, and she became the first woman to practice law in the lower federal courts of Virginia, Maryland, and Massachusetts. She also attempted to integrate some of the state court systems of the eastern seaboard, but was often rebuffed. In 1878, while the Lockwood Bill was still pending in the U.S. Senate, Lockwood applied for admission to the Circuit Court of Prince George's County in Maryland, but Judge Daniel R.

---

* Roger B. Taney, a Chief Justice of the Supreme Court, said in a famous obiter dictum in *Dred Scott* v. *Sanford* (1857) that a Negro could never be a citizen under the United States Constitution.

Magruder ruled against her, ordered her not to speak in his courtroom, and described her and her cocounsel, Lavinia Dundore, as "two wandering women" who belonged at home "waiting upon their husbands and children. . . . I pray to God that the day may never come when women would be admitted to the bar of Maryland." Once the court had adjourned, Belva staged an impromptu protest meeting on the courthouse porch at which she linked her plight with that of all single women who must struggle to support themselves and their families and vowed to continue her battle in the Maryland courts.[43]

It was, in fact, only a matter of weeks before Lockwood was appearing for the defense at the trial in Frederick, Maryland, of three teenage boys accused of pilfering goods from a sealed railroad car. The case drew a large audience, with many local attorneys in attendance along with almost the whole student body of a nearby school for girls. When the motion was made to admit Lockwood to practice, the judge asked if there were any objections from the members of the local bar. When none was voiced, he declared "the lady" admitted. During the boys' trial, the schoolgirls would discreetly hiss whenever the prosecutor spoke harshly of the defendants. Lockwood succeeded in gaining acquittals for two of the boys, but the remaining defendant was sentenced to ten days in the city jail. The blow was softened, however, by the schoolgirls, who escorted him to the jail, saw to it that he had a good supper, and visited him often during his brief jail stay.[44]

In 1894, Lockwood applied for admission to the state bar in Virginia's highest court, the Supreme Court of Appeals. With one member absent, the court was deadlocked, with two judges voting in favor of admitting her and two opposed. Lockwood appealed immediately to the U.S. Supreme Court, asking leave to file a writ of mandamus to force the Virginia court to admit her to the practice of law in that state. In the brief that she submitted to the high court, Lockwood argued that in denying her the right to practice law simply because she was a woman, the Virginia court had acted contrary to the "privileges and immunities" clause of the Fourteenth Amendment. The Court rejected this argument, pointing out that in a previous case, *Bradwell* v. *Illinois* (1873), which had also involved an aspiring woman lawyer, it had ruled that the right to practice law in state courts was not a privilege or immunity of citizens of the United States. The Court admitted that Virginia's code of laws stated that all "persons" with the necessary qualifications were to be admitted to the state bar, but left it up to the Virginia courts to decide "whether the word person as therein used is confined to males." In short, at the very time that the Supreme Court was insisting that business corporations were always "persons" under the Constitution, it was leaving it up to the states to decide in what respects and to what extent citizens who happened to be female were persons. But three weeks later, the Virginia Supreme Court of Appeals handed Lockwood a victory in deciding that she would be allowed to practice law in that state after all.[45]

A Successful Woman Lawyer

Among the female lawyers of her time, Lockwood was by far the most successful. She often found herself handling two or even three cases a day and by the 1890s was averaging $300 a month from her law practice, far more than most male lawyers were earning. According to women's historians Eleanor Flexner and Ellen Fitzpatrick, Lockwood was the first fully successful woman practitioner of law in the United States. While a majority of her clients were women, especially in divorce and breach of promise cases, Lockwood had many male clients as well, since she accepted virtually any case that came her way, regardless of the type of law involved. In the obituary of her husband that appeared in the *Washington Post* in 1877, she was described as "well-known" and "one of the most industrious members of the bar in this city."[46]

Her principal source of income as a lawyer lay in the handling of claims against the United States government. Her law firm's stationery listed "patents, pension, bounty, and land claims" as among her specialties. In 1875, she drafted and succeeded in lobbying through Congress a bill appropriating $50,000 for the payment of the bounties owed to sailors and marines. Her list of clients included Southerners who were seeking compensation for the damage done to their property by Union soldiers during the Civil War. Author Rollin S. Kirk in his *Many Secrets Revealed; or Ten Years Behind the Scenes in Washington City,* a book published in 1885, recommended to Southerners with pending war claims that they engage a Washington attorney such as Lockwood "who is on friendly terms with all political parties, and who is esteemed throughout the nation for her sterling activities and fine abilities."[47]

More typical of Lockwood's practice were the thousands of pension, bounty, and land claims that she filed with government bureaus and the various patent and damage suits against federal agencies that she pursued before the Court of Claims. In that court, which had been forced to accept her as an attorney once she had been admitted to the U.S. Supreme Court, she became a familiar figure, winning the admiration eventually even of Judge Nott, the man who had once told her that no woman could be a lawyer in America.[48]

In 1877, Lockwood had moved into a twenty-room house at 619 F Street, a structure known to Washington residents as "the Lockwood Building," which would serve as both her residence and law office for over thirty-five years. Leaders of the peace, temperance, and woman's movements would often gather at Lockwood's house when in Washington to discuss issues and plan their activities.[49]

As her legal business expanded, Lockwood relied increasingly on her daughter, Lura, who, although a married woman with two children, continued to work at her mother's law firm. Two other woman lawyers, Marilla Ricker and Lavinia Dundore, lived for a time in the Lockwood building while working with Lockwood at the law offices on its first floor. So frequently were the trio seen together that the press in Washington dubbed them "the Three Graces." Lockwood made a point of employing only women at her law firm.

Many young woman lawyers were inspired by Lockwood's example. They would write to her and she would respond with words of advice and encouragement. Lockwood was also an active member of the Equity Club, an association of woman lawyers that had originated among the alumnae of the University of Michigan Law School, and she was an important link between the club's members and the woman's movement. As the club's rules required of each member, Lockwood wrote each year an account of her activities. Among the women who acknowledged Lockwood as their role model were two future presidents of the Women's Bar Association: Emma Gillette and Ellen Mussey.[50]

While drawing closer to her female colleagues, Lockwood was somewhat bitter toward, and sarcastic about, the male lawyers who made up the great majority of her profession. Although there were many exceptions, she believed that most members of the bar jealously obstructed the path into their profession of aspiring and deserving women. Even when a woman "through indefatigable zeal" had become an attorney, "the chilliness and uncongeniality of her surroundings have often caused her to retreat rather than to fight the unequal contest of justice for her clients, and respect for her sex." She also observed (perhaps in jest) that the American bar, meaning those accredited as attorneys, was "not the bar most popular with the male legal talent of this country."[51]

In 1890, Lockwood wrote an article in which she assessed the progress of women in the legal profession. Noting that there were roughly 300 woman lawyers in the United States, she claimed that the prejudice in the common mind against them was at last giving way, for "every substantial law firm" was seeking out female attorneys. "Women," she wrote cheerily, "are especially welcome" when it comes to drafting wills for female clients and for managing the records of the firm. Lockwood considered it progress when women were added to law firms, even if they were permitted to play only a minor or subordinate role.

Lockwood considered it essential to the well-being of women that they be well versed in the law, which involved "all of their pecuniary interests and many of their social rights and privileges." Daughters and wives, accustomed to doing as they were told by the men in their lives, would simply sign bills of sale, deeds, and wills without knowing their contents or recognizing their importance. For this reason, among others, Lockwood hailed the growing presence of women in the legal profession and predicted that it would result in "a revolution in the law of descent, the abolition of dower, and a general partnership in the marriage relation." In short, she envisaged woman lawyers as playing a key role, perhaps the central role, in the liberation of women in American society.[52]

As a woman attorney, Lockwood always strove to appear serious and dignified, avoiding alike the extremes of gaudy fashion and the "sensible shoes" and male-style trousers of the "dress-reform" feminists. In her photographs, Lockwood, who was of medium height, always looks earnest, forthright, and steady of gaze. Reporters who interviewed Lockwood found her a talkative and vivacious woman, and they usually thought her at least a few years younger than her actual age. Her clothing was almost always conventional and conservative, consisting usually of a dark-colored dress or suit, made out of either silk or satin. Whatever her personal taste may have been, the conservatism of her garb in the courtroom made it easier for male judges and lawyers to take Lockwood seriously. As Virginia Drachman has pointed out, all of the pioneer female lawyers tried to balance professionalism and femininity in their outward appearance. In Lockwood's case, she would leaven the dark colors and heavy fabrics by wearing flowers and beads in her hair, beadwork and lace on her dresses, and below her throat a golden brooch carved in the shape of a scissors and thimble, lending to the female attorney just the barest suggestion of domesticity.[53]

Lockwood was not always this staid, however. In the early 1880s, she became the first woman in Washington to take up the tricycle, viewing it as "just the thing" to convey her to and from the courthouses where she earned her living. "Why," she asked, "let the men have all the fun?" Although her vehicle had a dashboard that was specially designed to keep her skirts in place, it was alleged in the press that her bright red stockings could clearly be seen as she pedaled down Pennsylvania Avenue at the speed of ten miles per hour. "This," notes writer Julia Davis, "in a day when women were supposed to skim over the ground without appearing to use their legs, caused astonishment close to scandal."[54]

Although extremely busy with her law practice, Lockwood still found time for the woman's movement. In January 1880, she was a featured speaker at the annual convention of the National Woman Suffrage Association (NWSA). Her speech accused the nation and its political leaders of practicing "taxation without representation" in denying the vote to women, among them millions of property-owning taxpayers. Noting that the Constitution opened with the words "We, the people," Lockwood said that she had never heard of a "people" that consisted entirely of men. "There are 12,500,000 women property owners [in the United States]. Should they not have something to say about what is done with the taxes they pay? If the Constitution does not allow women to vote, then the Constitution should be amended or abolished."[55]

Later that year, Lockwood was one of the women who represented the NWSA at the Republican convention in Chicago, where she appeared before its platform committee to appeal for an endorsement of woman suffrage by the party. By adopting a prosuffrage plank, Lockwood told the platform writers, "you will not only win support from the electorate, but most important of all, you will know that you have taken the first step to right an intolerable wrong." In the end, her plea was ignored, and the Republican Party and its candidate, James Garfield, had little to say about woman's rights in their presidential campaign that fall. Four years later, Lockwood again journeyed to the Republican convention (while other suffrage advocates appealed to the Democratic and Prohibition parties) and was again rebuffed by its platform committee. Lockwood's opinion of the Republican Party sank even lower when the assembled delegates raucously booed Frances Willard, the president of the Women's Christian Temperance Union, a woman whom she greatly admired.[56]

Running for President

When Susan B. Anthony and Elizabeth Cady Stanton, the two principal leaders of the woman's movement, sent out a circular endorsing James G. Blaine, the Republican candidate for president, Lockwood refused to go along. In a letter to Marietta L. Stow, the editor of the *Woman's Herald of Industry*, a militant feminist journal published in San Francisco, she called on women to act independently in politics. "The Republican Party," she wrote, "has little else but insult for women when they appear before its 'Conventions' and ask for recognition. . . . It is quite time that we had our own PARTY, our own PLATFORM, and our own NOMINEES. We shall never have rights until we take them, nor respect until we command it." There was, she insisted, nothing in the law or the Constitution to prevent women, although themselves without the vote, from being voted for by others.[57]

In late August, Lockwood received a letter that "suddenly, like a clap of thunder from a blue sky," announced that she had herself been nominated for the presidency of the United States by the convention of the Woman's National Equal Rights Party of California. The letter, signed by Stow and three other women active in the woman's rights movement of California, explained with startling candor that Lockwood had been selected because Stanton was "too old," Anthony "too much of a spinster," Mary Livermore "too much opposed to certain classes," and Lucy Stone "too narrow." The letter closed with the statement that its authors awaited Lockwood's reply with "breathless interest."[58]

It was disclosed after Lockwood's death that the letter had been intended as a joke upon the high-minded Lockwood, which would explain the impolitic references contained in it. There was no Equal Rights Party in California and there had been no nominating convention. Stow had drafted the letter to Lockwood in collaboration with a lawyer and activist named Clara S. Foltz. In her account, Foltz claimed that after a few weeks had passed, she informed both Lockwood and various San Francisco news reporters that it had all been a hoax, but that all concerned, perhaps to save face, never publicly admitted that they had been deceived.

Unaware at first of the trick that had been played on her, Lockwood took her nomination seriously. After carrying the letter around with her for three days, she showed it in private to a courthouse clerk with whom she was friendly, who promptly remarked that it was "the best joke of the season." Undeterred,

Lockwood sent a letter of acceptance along with an eleven-point platform to San Francisco. Accounts differ as to how the press learned of the story, but within less than a week it had been picked up by the Associated Press and was appearing in newspapers throughout the nation. Lockwood suddenly found herself famous as the woman who was running for president.[59]

Her "platform" reflected both Lockwood's lifelong interest in reform and the issues of the day, but it derived as well from her genuine desire to attract votes. The candidate herself boasted in a newspaper interview that in writing her program she had "made a bid for all voters—Irish, German, temperance, monopolists and anti-monopolists, capitalists and laborers." To appease the Germans who were opposed to temperance, she said simply that "due consideration will be given to the honest, industrious, home-loving Germans."[60]

Lockwood's manifesto opened with a pledge "to do equal and exact justice to every class of our citizens, without distinction of color, sex, or nationality." Yet she nowhere proposed any new measures by the federal government to secure the rights of either blacks or women. On the question of woman's rights, the issue that was always the most important to her, she advocated neither a constitutional amendment nor federal legislation, but would merely "recommend" to the states that they give women the vote and make their laws as uniform as possible, particularly when it came to divorce and property rights. Similarly, at a time when the rights of blacks were increasingly under assault in the southern states, Lockwood, in the interest of intersectional peace, called for a proportional distribution of federal patronage and of subsidies to the South, thereby falling in with the North's continuing retreat from Radical Reconstruction.

On the subject of the Indian tribes, which was inescapably a matter of national policy, Lockwood proposed that their autonomy be ended and their members treated simply as citizens of the United States. Perhaps naively, she declared that the government should "treat the Indian like a rational human, as we have the Negro—make him a citizen, amendable to the laws, and let him manage his own affairs."[61]

On the tariff, one of the leading questions of the time, Lockwood called for a compromise that would avoid alike the two extremes of "free trade" and of high tariff "protectionism." She strongly supported civil service reform and proposed to "engraft it onto the Constitution." Her endorsement of temperance and of settling disputes between nations by arbitration reflected her longstanding commitment to these reforms. Finally, her assertion that the federal government should treat Civil War veterans and their widows more generously was derived from her own experiences as a lawyer who had handled many pension cases.

Lockwood's candidacy was supported by very few of the women who were active in the movement for woman's rights. The major figures either supported the Republican ticket or remained neutral in the election. Some of the activists accused Lockwood of making the movement look ridiculous in order to promote her law practice and collect lecture fees. Of all her critics, the harshest was Abigail Scott Duniway, editor of *The New Northwest,* who charged that Lockwood was bringing upon the woman suffrage cause "an abundance of odium and contempt at a time when it was commanding respect and enlisting help. The damage done by her and a little band of eccentric zealots in San Francisco cannot be estimated."[62]

Undaunted, Lockwood and her supporters went on with their campaign. In early October, Stow was declared the Equal Rights Party's candidate for vice president. At six feet tall, Stow made a striking appearance. She was both a feminist and a dress reformer who wore fedora hats and divided skirts. In 1885, she had run for school director of San Francisco, winning votes from hundreds of women. Their ticket complete, Lockwood and her friends managed in a few instances to persuade prominent women to head slates of Lockwood electors in their respective states. As in any other campaign, handbills and ballots were printed up and distributed and campaign buttons were given out.[63]

Stow confined her campaigning to the West Coast, while Lockwood went on an extensive speaking tour of the major cities in the East and Middle West. Lockwood's principal theme was, understandably, woman's rights. "For 100 years and more, my brothers," she declared, "you have been running the government of the United States as a gigantic, hide-bound monopoly based on sex which makes paupers of the women of the country, and checks and strangles in them at birth inspiration and aspiration." In order to bring this "senseless oppression" to an end, women must be given equal rights and their dependency on men ended by making them economically productive.[64]

In the campaign's final weeks, Lockwood placed greater stress on economic issues and took positions that went beyond her platform in calling for action by the federal government. She proposed, for example, a reorganization of the national banking system and an increase in the money supply. She also advocated that the government control the railroad and telegraph systems. Finally, in a passage that seems to foreshadow the policy of a much later time, the candidate called for "reasonable expenditures on the part of the government as well as of individuals, to give constant employment with good wages, to the laboring men and women of the country."[65]

Like any intriguing novelty, Lockwood's campaign was reported in the press, but most of what was written by the reporters and editorialists was snide and patronizing. The nation's press refused to take her seriously, suggesting that as a woman, candidate Lockwood was by her very nature concerned mainly with housekeeping, interior decorating, embroidery, clothing, and her hairstyle. In a broad parody both of Lockwood's candidacy and of how politicians deal with issues, the *New York Times* called on her to take a forthright position on the controversial and divisive issue of the divided skirt. Even the *Lockport Daily Journal,* one of her hometown newspapers, made fun of her, predicting that when Lockwood moved into the White House, "she will have a new terra cotta pug dog in the hall, and a folding mirror in each room."[66]

Contributing to the ridicule was the coverage given by the newspapers to the Belva Lockwood clubs which sprang up in a number of towns and cities, consisting of young men, clad in loose-fitting "Mother Hubbard" dresses and bonnets, who would parade though the streets carrying Lockwood placards and brooms. The "Hubbards" or "broom brigades" would sing, clang bells, bang pots, and, in general, raise a rumpus. They would sweep their brooms as though they were sweeping the streets clean of anti-Lockwood voices, and their slogan was, predictably, "a clean sweep with Lockwood." At all of their meetings, one of them would pretend to be Lockwood and deliver a "speech" consisting of nonsense.[67]

Once the returns were in, Lockwood found it difficult to get the votes that had been cast for her acknowledged in the official state tallies. Claiming that she had received over 4,000 votes distributed across six states, Lockwood petitioned the United States Congress, asking that these votes for Lockwood and Stow be officially recorded. Alleging that the electors of Indiana had at first voted for Cleveland but had then changed their minds, Lockwood's petition also demanded that Indiana's electoral vote be counted for Lockwood and Stow.[68]

To many of her critics, Lockwood's campaign had been little more than a publicity stunt. She, of course, viewed the venture in a positive light as "the first practical movement in the history of woman suffrage . . . which had awakened the women of the country." To Susan B. Anthony, the political tactician of the woman's movement, Lockwood's campaign had been of at least some value because "it served to educate the people up to the idea of women candidates for high places of public trust."[69]

Lockwood the Lecturer

Now famous, Lockwood found herself in great demand on the lecture circuit, and her work in this field amounted for a time to virtually a second career. From 1885 to 1892, she would speak almost daily for up to six months out of the year, earning on the average between $30 and $40 dollars per lecture. She spoke in dozens of cities and towns, principally in the eastern half of the country, but on occasion even in Denver and San Francisco. According to H.L. Slayton, the head of the Chicago Labor Lyceum, and Lockwood's booking agent, between March 1885 and April 1886, Lockwood spoke on more nights than the combined total of any three other lecturers in the United States.

Lockwood's lectures were well attended and sometimes filled the hall to capacity. At many of the stops along the way, one or more local newspapers covered her lecture. Although reporters occasionally criticized the loudness and nasality of Lockwood's voice and the racehorse speed of her delivery, most of their comments were favorable. Her talks were praised for their interesting content, eloquent phrasing, and occasional flashes of wit. In Beatrice, Nebraska, for example, a reporter described her discourse on "The Tendencies of Parties and Governments" as "the finest literary production, the most instructive and interesting lecture that was ever delivered in Beatrice."[70]

Lockwood lectured initially on subjects that she had long been speaking and writing about, such as temperance and woman's rights, but she soon added other topics on national politics or reporting on her travels in America and Europe. In a temperance lecture delivered before a capacity crowd at Tremont Temple in Boston, Lockwood, according to the report in the *Boston Herald,* assailed "left and right the poor, weak, sinful apostles of whiskey and to-bacco" while the women in the audience "patted their kid gloved hands to-gether with glee." In a talk entitled "The Social and Political Life of Washington," Lockwood, herself something of an "insider," graphically de-picted the nation's capital as a hotbed of venality and corruption in which great fortunes were made by clever contractors and promoters with the con-nivance of dishonest officials.[71]

While on her lecture tours, she would gather up dozens of land, pension, and other claims against the federal government and mail them to her home in Washington, where her daughter, Lura, would fill out the required forms and file them with the appropriate agencies or in the Court of Claims. Once back in Washington, Lockwood would follow through on the cases that had been filed. She had learned from experience that claims cases could be just as lucrative as other fields of law, while normally requiring fewer appearances in court.[72]

On May 15, 1888, a small group of feminist women staged a meeting in Des Moines, Iowa, at which it was announced that Belva Lockwood had again been "nominated" for president by the Equal Rights Party. Apparently with-out asking him, the party had also designated Alfred H. Love, a Philadelphia businessman and the president of the Universal Peace Union, with whom Lockwood had been acquainted for over twenty years. Although Love re-fused the nomination, Lockwood had him renominated and he was still on the ticket come Election Day.[73]

Lockwood again embarked on a long campaign tour in which she delivered speeches on themes that she had been lecturing on for the past three years. In addition to the stands on issues that she had taken in her previous campaign, she also called for the abolition of capital punishment, maintained that women ought to receive the same pay as men for doing the same work, and urged that the United States use arbitration rather than war in settling its disputes with foreign nations. Some of her remarks seem to have been calculated to attract attention from the voters, such as her observation that financial speculation, whether in stocks or grain futures, should be a felony punishable by law. On August 30, Lockwood was greeted warmly at a huge Granger picnic in Williams Grove, Pennsylvania, to which had come thousands of farmers and their families. "She delivered an address," wrote a reporter for the *New York World,* "every word of which was drunk in by her audience like so much picnic lemonade."[74]

The press remained interested in Lockwood, and two New York newspapers interviewed her respectfully and at length: the *Sun* and the *World.* The latter interview was conducted by none other than Nelly Bly, the pioneer woman reporter who was famous for having gone around the world in less than eighty days. To many in the press, however, the idea of a woman running for president remained absurd. The *Washington Morning Journal,* for example, commissioned a satirical poem, entitled "Belva Dear," which was later set to music and published as a song. One of its seven stanzas reads:

> When our votes for you are cast
> Belva Dear; Belva Dear;
> Will you tax the bustle vast,
> Belva Dear; Belva Dear?
> Will you place a tariff high,
> On the hosiery we buy?
> We await your calm reply,
> Belva dear; Belva Dear![75]

In Defense of the Mormons

In addition to Lockwood's legal career and her political activity, she also functioned as a lobbyist, representing, with little or no remuneration, some of her favorite causes and organizations before congressional committees and in other forums. A notable instance was her impassioned defense over a fifteen-year span of the Mormons of Utah, who had come under nationwide attack due to their practice of polygamous marriage. The Territory of Utah, which had given its women the right to vote in 1870, was only the second United States territory to have enacted woman suffrage, and at a time when no state of the Union had yet done so.

Amid the furor over polygamy, various congressmen introduced bills that proposed either to end woman suffrage in Utah altogether or to deprive only the parties to plural marriages of their right to vote. Lockwood now took the lead in opposing these measures, declaring both before congressional committees and in newspaper interviews that polygamy was merely the pretext for what amounted to an attack on the principle of woman suffrage itself. "I do not believe in polygamy," Lockwood told a reporter from the *Rochester Democrat,* "but I do believe in fair play." After the arrival in Utah of federal commissioners, apparently bent on ending woman suffrage there, Belva received a telegram from a group of Utah women asking her for advice. "Stand by your guns," she wired back, "and resist every encroachment on your liberties. I will do what I can to defend you."[76]

At the 1883 convention of the NWSA, she repeated her claim that conservatives in Congress were exploiting the revulsion over polygamy to deprive the women of Utah of the franchise. "That Cassidy's bill [repealing the territorial law conferring the right to vote upon the women of Utah] was a blow aimed at woman suffrage," she told the delegates, "only a fool or knave would deny. . . . [Besides] it does not matter so much what a gun is aimed at as what it hits." In this instance, the suffragist convention followed where Lockwood led, opposing the disfranchisement of the women of Utah and resolving to fight against its enactment.

In spite of opposition from the suffragists and the Mormon leadership, however, Congress passed the Edmunds-Tucker bill, which both banned woman suffrage in Utah and provided for the punishment of bigamists and polygamists residing in any territory over which the United States had exclusive jurisdiction. Lockwood and the other suffragists appealed to President Cleveland to veto the measure, but he allowed it to become law without his signature. In retaliation, Lockwood attempted to identify some bigamists in Washington, D.C., and to file these cases with the district attorney, but even though a few indictments were brought, she soon abandoned this tactic, which had attracted but little notice in the press and was ignored by the woman's movement.[77]

The rescinding by Congress of woman suffrage in Utah, in tandem with their annoyance over Lockwood's presidential campaigns, led Anthony, Stanton, and the other woman suffrage leaders to became wary of Lockwood. It seemed to the suffragist leadership that the cause of votes for women had been damaged by its linkage in the minds of many with the Mormons and their practice of polygamy. The suffrage leaders tended now to have less to do with Lockwood, who had led the charge on "the Mormon question" and had talked the NWSA into following her lead on the issue. As a result of this estrangement from its leaders, Lockwood became somewhat less active in the woman's movement and devoted herself primarily now to the cause of world peace.[78]

Lockwood and the Peace Movement

Since 1868, Lockwood had belonged to the Universal Peace Union (UPU), an organization that, since its founding in the aftermath of the Civil War, had uncompromisingly opposed all wars and all armaments. The UPU's membership was small, comprising at its peak some 400 active members, about a third of them women, and somewhere between 3,000 and 4,000 sympathizers. The organization's leader, from its founding until his death in 1913, was Alfred H. Love, a Philadelphia businessman and a devout Quaker, for whom, according to historian Peter Brock, it was his organization's mission "to remold society in a spirit of Christian love and Christian brotherhood." Lockwood, whose views were in close accord with Love's, served for nearly four decades as the UPU's vice president and corresponding secretary.[79] She also wrote numerous articles for the UPU's journal, *The Peacemaker,* and from 1889 to 1913 sat on its editorial board.

From 1889 to the outbreak of World War I in 1914, there were annual peace congresses that brought together the representatives of the principal peace organizations of Europe and the Americas, and Belva attended most of them as one of the delegates of the UPU. She delivered lectures at several of these gatherings, beginning with the Paris meeting in 1889, when she spoke in French on the principle of arbitration and was warmly applauded by the delegates. At the 1891 meeting in Rome, Lockwood spoke in favor of the resolution establishing a permanent International Peace Bureau. When the resolution carried, Lockwood was the only woman named to the new agency, and she established an American branch with its headquarters in her own home and herself as its corresponding secretary.

In 1893, in conjunction with the Colombian Exposition, the International Peace Congress was held in Chicago, and Lockwood hailed the meeting as "a peace convention of the nations of the world . . . [in which] every well-wisher of the brotherhood of man should take part." She herself was in charge of the International Peace Bureau exhibit. Ever the reformer and optimist, Lockwood predicted, "by bringing together the active thinking reformatory minds of every nation [the exposition] must advance the cause of social and moral reform in every sphere." She hoped in particular that the exposition would help bring to fruition the proposal for a permanent court of arbitration to which all disputes between nations could be submitted, and resolved without war. In 1899, after a diplomatic gathering at The Hague had created the International Arbitration Court, Lockwood hailed the new body as "the highest moral and economic advance in the recorded civilization of the peoples of the nineteenth century . . . [and] the entering wedge for the abolition of armies."[80]

Lockwood also served the UPU as its most effective lobbyist, working tirelessly against military appropriations and promoting actively both the theory and practice of arbitration, which to her, as to most peace activists in her day, offered the best hope for averting war. Lockwood was in frequent touch on peace issues with members of Congress and officials of the executive branch and had on occasion discussed these issues at the White House with Presidents Hayes, Cleveland, and Harrison. According to Merle Curti, a leading historian of the peace movement, her contacts with the peace activists of Europe permitted Lockwood to cooperate with them in "planning joint campaigns on the foreign offices and on the State Department." During the Cuban crisis of 1898, for example, Lockwood, along with other American and European peace advocates, tried, from behind the scenes, to persuade key figures in the governments of Spain and the United States to arbitrate, although they were, of course, unsuccessful in averting war.[81]

Like Alfred Love, Lockwood believed that for peace between nations to be genuine and perfect, it must begin with individuals in every country leading pure and upright lives. "We must teach our children to be kind and peace loving," she wrote, "and impress upon them the sanctity of human life." She was critical of every violent tendency in daily life, denouncing, for example, both prizefighting and hunting for sport as "barbarous relics" of a less civilized age. When President Cleveland was reported to have ordered the members of his cabinet not to permit their wives to ride bicycles in the streets of Washington, Lockwood observed that "Mr. Cleveland has perhaps forgotten that his term ends on the 4th of next March,—and that it is far more humane and civilized to ride a bicycle than it is to shoot ducks."[82]

The Eastern Cherokee Case

Although often preoccupied with her reformist causes and with her lecturing sideline, Lockwood remained an attorney, and it was from the practice of law that she earned most of her income. Her work before the Court of Claims attracted the attention of Jim Taylor, a Cherokee Indian who was about to file suit against the United States. He hired Lockwood and she pleaded his case in the Court of Claims and won it. Taylor knew of many other Cherokees with legal problems, and he and Lockwood signed a contract in which he agreed to bring her clients in exchange for a percentage of the resulting fees.[83]

The most important of her Indian cases and, arguably, the most important legal work of her career, was Lockwood's representation of the Eastern and Emigrant Cherokees in their lawsuit against the United States. The case was an outgrowth of the Indian removal policy of the 1830s, when the Cherokees, along with other tribes, were expelled from their lands in Georgia, North Carolina, and other southern states. In 1838, about 20,000 Cherokees had been forced to emigrate overland to Indian Territory (Oklahoma), and some 4,000 died during their coerced journey along the route that became known as "the trail of tears." Other members of the tribe (the Emigrant Cherokees) settled in Oklahoma after the initial migration, while a third segment (the Eastern Cherokees) never went there at all. Congress had created an interest-bearing trust fund in 1835, intending that it be used to compensate all the Cherokees for the land that they had lost, but in practice, it was only the Western Cherokees, "the old settlers," comprising about two-fifths of the tribe, who had received any payment at all from the federal government as of the year 1905.

The Cherokees whom Lockwood represented, about 6,000 in all, were descended from people who, although expelled from their homes in the 1830s, had somehow managed to avoid the forced migration to what was then called Indian Territory (Oklahoma). About two-thirds of her clients had remained in the East, often becoming citizens of southern states. The remaining third had emigrated to Oklahoma at some point after 1838, but they too had never received any payment from the Cherokee trust fund. The objective of their lawsuit was to obtain the money, both the principal and the interest that was due them under federal law.[84]

The case was a complicated one, and Belva spent years doing the necessary research on all the treaties and laws relating to the Cherokee tribe. She discovered that federal officials had drawn over $1 million from the Cherokee trust fund in 1838 to pay for the forced migration to Oklahoma, and that in doing so, they had violated federal law. According to the government's own accountants, the money withdrawn from the trust fund, when added to the interest that it would have earned had it remained in the fund, amounted altogether to more than $4 million as of the year 1900. Belva argued that to make the Indians pay for their own removal "to a country to which they did not want to go was a monstrous abuse of a treaty which they had not read, had not signed, and to which they had not in fact been parties."[85]

An act of Congress passed in March 1903 authorized the Court of Claims to adjudicate, "with a right of appeal to the U.S. Supreme Court," the claims of the three Cherokee groups against the United States. Each group of claimants had its own counsel and each filed its own lawsuit, but it was arranged that the three cases would be consolidated into one and decided jointly. The trial began in early March 1905, and at its close, the court ruled that the Indian plaintiffs were entitled to both the principal of $1.1 million and to the total amount of the interest that would have accumulated on it at 5 percent annually for 68 years. Amounting in all to over $4.5 million, this was at the time the largest damage claim ever assessed against the federal government.[86]

The government appealed the ruling to the U.S. Supreme Court and the case was heard January 16–18, 1906. On the trial's second day, Lockwood addressed the high court for the second time in her career. She had appeared before the Court for the first time in 1880, but on that occasion spoke briefly and played no significant role in the proceedings. In the Cherokee case, however, Lockwood spoke at length and figured prominently in the presentation of the case. Originally allotted only ten minutes, she actually spoke for forty-five minutes. "She apparently made a good impression on the judges," wrote one reporter, "stating her case with clearness and force and exhibiting no nervousness whatever when the court interrupted her several times with questions."[87]

Both Lockwood and Robert L. Owen, another attorney in the case, argued that the Western Cherokees, who had already been compensated by the federal government, both in money and in land, were not entitled to further compensation, and therefore that it should be only the Eastern Cherokees, as represented by Owen, and the Eastern and Emigrant Cherokees, as represented by Belva, who should benefit from the current case. Their argument prevailed with the court, which ruled that the Court of Claims award stood, but departed from the lower court's decision by ruling that the Western Cherokees were not to share in it. Because Owen had represented approximately three times as many claimants as Lockwood, his portion of the settlement came to $160,000 while she received just $50,000.[88]

Last Years

Lockwood's daughter, Lura Ormes, died in 1894, and for the rest of her life, Lura's son, De Forest Ormes, would reside with Lockwood. She continued to practice law until 1913. "My normal condition," she wrote to a friend in 1907, "is hard at work in my office at Washington without stopping, except to eat and to sleep, with about 100 unanswered business letters before me, and half a dozen law cases, waiting to be taken up." She continued to have Indian clients, journeying often to Muskogee, Oklahoma, where she argued land cases before the Court of the Five Nations. Belva also remained active in other fields of law, representing clients in divorces and in the settlement of estates, a few of them quite large.[89]

Syracuse University awarded Lockwood an honorary L.L.D. in 1909. Four years later, she announced that she was retiring as an attorney and would devote the rest of her life to her two favorite causes: woman's rights and international peace. Lockwood remained an active participant in the growing and increasingly successful movement for woman suffrage, testifying before congressional committees and participating in demonstrations in Washington, D.C. As one of the movement's aging heroines, Belva had become a symbolic figure, the guest of honor at many suffragist receptions and pageants. On May 9, 1914, there was a woman suffrage parade in Washington that ended at Capitol Hill. The parade's leaders, with Belva in front, then presented their petitions to the Congress. By 1916, more than twenty states had conceded the vote to women, moving Lockwood to observe that "suffrage is no longer an issue, but an accomplished fact."[90]

Lockwood was also still active in the peace movement and had maintained her ties to the pacifists of Europe. As a member of the International Peace Bureau, she nominated individuals for the Nobel Peace Prize. She belonged also to the World Center Society, an organization based in Rome and whose professed aim was "the creation of a world conscience." In 1914, the U.S. State Department named Lockwood to the delegation of eighteen prominent women that it sent to the women's peace conference in London.[91]

Toward the end of her life, Belva's finances crumbled. It was rumored that she had entrusted her funds to an unscrupulous "admirer" who had proceeded to lose most of her savings. The heirs of Jim Taylor, Lockwood's Cherokee friend, delivered the crowning blow to Belva's solvency. After finding a copy of their father's agreement with her, they sued her for $10,500, which, according to them, was Taylor's rightful share of the fee collected by Belva in the Eastern Cherokee case. In 1914, a judgment was handed down, ordering Mrs. Lockwood to pay $9,000 to Taylor's estate. As a result, she lost the spacious home that she had lived in for four decades and was obliged to move into a small apartment.[92]

Lockwood's last public statement was a speech that she gave endorsing President Woodrow Wilson for reelection. She was in poor health now, and in late April of the following year she became seriously ill and was hospitalized. On May 19, 1917, Belva Lockwood died at the age of eighty-six. Her funeral was attended by prominent feminists and by delegations from the Women's Bar Association and the Women's Press Association, both of which she had formerly headed. "Today," wrote the *Philadelphia Public Ledger*, "the American people will lay upon her bier their tribute of respect and admiration, and they will remember her as one who was not afraid to uphold her convictions at a time when she was in a pitiful minority."[93]

Courage, fighting spirit, and unending persistence were the dominant qualities in the life and career of Belva Lockwood. "When I wish to do a thing," she once wrote, "I know only one way, to keep at it until I get it."[94] In a nation that had barely begun to accept women in the professions, she overcame formidable obstacles to become the first successful woman lawyer, thereby opening the way for the women who would enter her profession in later generations. Moreover, in keeping with her faith that the modern world was advancing inexorably toward equality and justice, she committed herself wholeheartedly to social reform and in particular to the two great focal points of her life: the quest for international peace and the struggle for women's rights.

Notes

1. See Jill Norgren, "Before It Was Merely Difficult: Belva Lockwood's Life in Law and Politics," *Journal of Supreme Court History* 23 (1999): 16–17.

2. Quoted from Julia Hull Winner, "Belva A. Lockwood—That Extraordinary Woman," *New York History* 39 (October 1958): 324; ibid., 322–323; [Lura McNall?] "The Women Who Tried to Vote," *Lockport Daily Journal* (hereinafter cited as *LDJ*), as reprinted in Julia Hull Winner, *Belva A. Lockwood,* No. 19 of the Occasional Contributions of the Niagara County [NY] Historical Society (Lockport, NY: Niagara County Historical Society, 1969), 1–2; data from entry in McNall family Bible in Winner, *Belva A. Lockwood,* 108.

3. Quoted from a newspaper interview published in *LDJ,* August 26, 1893, 8, reprinted in Winner, *Belva A. Lockwood,* 92; [McNall?], "The Women Who Tried to Vote," 2.

4. Belva A. Lockwood, "My Efforts to Become a Lawyer," *Lippincott's Monthly Magazine,* February 1888, as reprinted in Winner, *Belva A. Lockwood,* 109–110; Virginia G. Drachman, *Women Lawyers and the Origins of Professional Identity in America: The Letters of the Equity Club 1887–1890* (Ann Arbor: University of Michigan Press, 1993), 242.

5. Quoted by Dawn Bradley Berry, *The 50 Most Influential Women in American Law* (Los Angeles: Lowell House, 1996), 19; Lockwood, "My Efforts to Become a Lawyer," 109; [McNall?], "The Women Who Tried to Vote," 4.

6. Quoted passage is from "Belva Lockwood, Lawyer, Dies at 85 [sic]," *New York Times,* May 20, 1917, 23; "Belva A. Lockwood," *Case and Comment* 24 (August 1917): 253.

7. [McNall?], "The Women Who Tried to Vote," 3–4.

8. Quoted from Lockwood, "My Efforts to Become a Lawyer," 111; entry in McNall family Bible, in Winner, *Belva A. Lockwood,* 108, 326.

9. Laura Kerr, *The Girl Who Ran for President* (New York: Thomas Nelson, 1947), 40–47; David K. Boynick, *Pioneers in Petticoats* (New York: Thomas J. Crowell, 1959), 67–68; Lockwood, "My Efforts to Become a Lawyer," 112.

10. As quoted by Winner, "Belva A. Lockwood—That Extraordinary Woman," 327–329.

11. Quoted in [McNall?] "The Women Who Tried to Vote," 5; ibid., 8–9, 11; Winner, "Belva A. Lockwood—That Extraordinary Woman," 329–330. Mary Virginia Fox, *Lady for the Defense: A Biography of Belva Lockwood* (New York: Harcourt Brace Jovanovich, 1975), 66–70.

12. Lockwood, "My Efforts to Become a Lawyer," 113–114; Winner, "Belva A. Lockwood—That Extraordinary Woman," 329.

13. Reports in Lockport's local press about the school are cited in Winner, *Belva A. Lockwood,* 7–8; Lockwood, "My Efforts to Become a Lawyer," 113.

14. Lockwood, "My Efforts to Become a Lawyer," 114–115; Winner, "Belva A. Lockwood—That Extraordinary Woman," 330–331; [McNall?], "The Women Who Tried to Vote," 9–10.

15. Michael Gulashock, "Belva Lockwood's Extraordinary Career," *Tioga County Courier*, November 27, 1988, 1, 2, 7; Winner, "Belva A. Lockwood—That Extraordinary Woman," 331–332; Lockwood, "My Efforts to Become a Lawyer," 114.

16. Quote is from Lockwood, "My Efforts to Become a Lawyer," 115; Louis Filler, "Lockwood, Belva Anne Bennett McNall," *Notable American Women, 1607–1950: A Biographical Dictionary* (Cambridge, MA: Belknap Press of Harvard University Press, 1971), vol. 2, 414; [McNall?], "The Women Who Tried to Vote," 6.

17. Allan C. Clark, "Belva Ann Lockwood," *Records of the Columbia Historical Society* 35–36 (1933): 206; [Belva Lockwood?], undated material in the possession of the Niagara County Historical Society, printed in Winner, *Belva A. Lockwood,* 96; "Lockwood, Belva A.," in Frances Elizabeth Willard and Mary A. Livermore, *Woman of the Century* (Buffalo, NY: C.W. Moulton, 1893), 469.

18. Quote is from Belva A. Lockwood, "Christmas Week in Washington," *LDJ,* December 30, 1872, reprinted in Winner, *Belva A. Lockwood,* 23; Merle Eugene Curti, *Peace or War: The American Struggle, 1636–1936.* (New York: W.W. Norton, 1936; reprint, New York: Garland Publishing, 1972), 142–143; Helena Ducie Reed, "Belva Ann Lockwood: First of Our Great Women Lawyers," *Kappa Beta Pi Quarterly* 38 (1954): 68.

19. The quotation is in Elizabeth Cady Stanton, Susan B. Anthony, and Matilda Joslyn Gage eds., *History of Woman Suffrage* (Rochester, NY: Charles Mann Printing Co., 1886; reprint, Arno and the *New York Times,* 1969), vol. 3, 809; Beverly Beeton, *Women Vote in the West: The Woman Suffrage Movement, 1869–1896* (New York: Garland Publishing, 1986), x; Clarke, "Belva Ann Lockwood," 207–210; Fox, *Lady for the Defense,* 80–85.

20. "Washington Items: An Interesting Wedding," clipping from an unidentified Washington newspaper, reprinted in Winner, *Belva A. Lockwood,* 14–15; Fox, *Lady for the Defense,* 84–90; Kerr, *The Girl Who Ran for President,* 63–64, 83–84.

21. Quotation is in Kerr, *The Girl Who Ran for President,* 79–80; Stanton, Anthony and Gage, eds. *History of Woman Suffrage,* vol. 3, 810–812; Belva A. Lockwood, "How I Ran for the Presidency," *National Magazine,* March 1903, reprinted in Winner, *Belva A. Lockwood,* 130; Norgren, "Before It Was Merely Difficult," 22.

22. Lockwood, "My Efforts to Become a Lawyer," 117; Clark, "Belva Ann Lockwood," 207; Virginia G. Drachman, *Sisters in Law: Women Lawyers in Modern American History* (Cambridge, MA: Harvard University Press, 1998), 14–16.

23. The president's comment is quoted in Lockwood, "My Efforts to Become a Lawyer," 117–118; "Diploma," Memorandum, Lockwood Papers, Series 2, Part C, Swarthmore College Peace Collection; Lockwood, "Report on Washington," 813.

24. Lockwood, "My Efforts to Become a Lawyer," 118; "Diploma," Lockwood Papers, Swarthmore.

25. Quotation is in Lockwood, "My Efforts to Become a Lawyer," 119; Lura McNall, "Our Washington Letter," *LDJ,* February 10, 1872, reprinted in Winner, *Belva Ann Lockwood,* 17–18; "Diploma," Lockwood Papers, Swathmore.

26. Stanton, Anthony, and Gage, eds. *History of Woman Suffrage,* vol. 2, 488, 587; vol. 3, 613; Drachman, *Sisters in Law,* 14.

27. "The International Society in Rochester: Mrs. Lockwood's Lecture," *LDJ,* May 24, 1872, 3, reprinted in Winner, *Belva A. Lockwood,* 19–20; Lois Beachy Underhill, *The Woman Who Ran for President: The Many Lives of Victoria Woodhull* (Bridgehampton, NY: Bridge Works, 1995), 206–207, 218; Lockwood, "My Efforts to Become a Lawyer," 119.

28. The quotation is in Lockwood "My Efforts to Become a Lawyer," 119; see also Norgren, "Before It Was Merely Difficult," 18–20; "Diploma," Lockwood Papers, Swathmore.

29. Quoted passages are in Boynick, *Pioneers in Petticoats,* 59–62; Annie Nathan Meyer, *Women's Work in America* (New York: Henry Holt, 1891), 240.

30. Lockwood, "My Efforts to Become a Lawyer," 120–121.

31. *Lockwood* v. *The United States* (1873), 9 U.S. Court of Claims 352, 355–356; "Mrs. Lockwood and the late Judge Knott [*sic*]," Memorandum, Lockwood Papers, Swarthmore.

32. Quote is from Lockwood, "My Efforts to Become a Lawyer," 122; *Raines* v. *United States* (1875), 11 U.S. Court of Claims, 648, 648–653.

33. "Law Reports. United States Supreme Court: Women Excluded from Practice in the Court," *New York Times,* November 7, 1876, 3; "A Former Lockport Lady Denied Practice in

the United States Supreme Court," *LDJ,* November 7, 1876, 4, reprinted in Winner, *Belva A. Lockwood.*

34. Quoted statement is in "Belva Lockwood, Lawyer, Dies at 85 [*sic*]," 23; entry in McNall family Bible, printed in Winner, *Belva A. Lockwood,* 108; Lockwood, "My Efforts to Become a Lawyer," 123.

35. *Congressional Record,* 45th Congress, 2nd sess., 1878, vol. 7, part 2, 1235, 1326.

36. Stanton, Anthony, and Gage, eds., *History of Woman Suffrage,* vol. 3, 106–111; Frances A. Cook, "Belva Ann Lockwood: For Peace, Justice, and President," paper submitted to Professor Barbara Allen Babcock at Stanford University Law School, May 13, 1997, *Women's Legal History Biography Project,* website <www.Stanford.edu/group/WLHP/papers/lockwood.htm>; Lockwood, "My Efforts to Become a Lawyer," 123.

37. Quote is from Lockwood, "My Efforts to Become a Lawyer," 124; Cook, "Belva Ann Lockwood," 9.

38. *Congressional Record,* 45th Congress, 3rd sess., 1879, vol. 8, part 2, 1082–1084.

39. Ibid; "Friday in Congress," *New York Times,* February 8, 1879, 1; Lura McNall, "Our Washington Letter," *LDJ,* February 11, 1879, reprinted in Winner, *Belva A. Lockwood,* 34.

40. All the quoted statements are in Stanton, Anthony, and Gage, eds., *History of Woman Suffrage,* vol. 3, 140–141.

41. Quoted from "The United States Supreme Court," *New York Times,* March 4, 1879, 5; Lura McNall, "Our Washington Letter," dated March 4, 1879, *LDJ,* March 6, 1879, as reprinted in Winner, *Belva A. Lockwood,* 35–37.

42. Lura McNall, "Our Washington Letter," *LDJ,* February 11, 1880, reprinted in Winner, *Belva A. Lockwood,* 43; Stanton, Anthony, and Gage, eds., *History of Woman Suffrage,* vol. 3, 174.

43. "Mrs. Lockwood Is Denied Admission to the Maryland Bar," *New York Times*, October 19, 1878, 3; see also Clark, "Belva Ann Lockwood," 214.

44. Belva A. Lockwood, "Women of the American Bar," *Illustrated American,* July 26, 1890, 45–46.

45. *Ex Parte Lockwood* (1894) 154 U.S. 116; Norgren, "Before It Was Merely Difficult," 31; "Victory for Mrs. Belva Lockwood," *New York Times,* June 16, 1894.

46. Eleanor Flexner and Ellen Fitzpatrick, *A Century of Struggle* (Cambridge, MA: Belknap Press, 1996), 116, 124; Drachman, *Sisters in Law,* 99; Lockwood, "How I Ran for the Presidency," 130.

47. Rollin Kirk, *Many Secrets Revealed* (Washington D.C.: 1885), as quoted in Madeline B. Stern, *We the Women: Career First in Nineteenth Century America* (New York: Schulte, 1962; reprinted Lincoln, NE: University of Nebraska Press, 1994), 365; various letters, Lockwood Papers, Swarthmore, Series 2, Part C; Leila Crum Gardiner, "Hearings, Memorials, Petitions and Resolutions by Belva Lockwood," in Winner, *Belva Ann Lockwood,* 105.

48. "Mrs. Lockwood and the late Judge Knott [*sic*]," Lockwood Papers, Swarthmore; "Lockwood, Belva Ann Bennett," *National Cyclopedia of Biography,* vol. 2, 62; Leila J. Robinson, "Women Lawyers in the United States," *Green Bag* 2 (1890): 27; Drachman, *Women Lawyers,* 57, 244.

49. Clark, "Belva Ann Lockwood, 214–215; Frances Fenton Park, "Lockwood, Belva Ann Bennett," *Dictionary of American Biography,* vol. 6, 341.

50. Filler, "Lockwood, Belva Ann Bennett McNall," 415; Reed, "Belva Ann Lockwood," 69; Drachman, *Sisters in Law,* 69–71.

51. Belva A. Lockwood, "Women of the American Bar," 45; Belva A. Lockwood, "The Present Phase of the Woman Question," *The Cosmopolitan,* October 1888, 469; Drachman, *Sisters in Law,* 60–70; Meyer, *Woman's Work in America,* 243.

52. Lockwood, "Women of the American Bar," 45, 48.

53. Clark, "Belva Ann Lockwood," 214; Drachman, *Sisters in Law,* 94–95; Frank G. Carpenter, *Carp's Washington* (New York: McGraw-Hill, 1960), 33, 230.

54. F.E.T., "Belva Lockwood at Home," *New York Sun,* August 27, 1888, 5; Julia Davis, "A Feisty Schoolmarm Made the Lawyers Sit Up and Take Notice," *Smithsonian* 11 (March 1981): 138.

55. Davis, "A Feisty Schoolmarm," 141–142.

56. Fox, *Lady for the Defense,* 129–130; ibid., 131–133; Lockwood, "How I Ran for the Presidency," 129; Stanton, Anthony, and Gage, eds., *History of Woman Suffrage,* vol. 3, 177–178.

57. Belva A. Lockwood, Washington, D.C.: "Letter to the Editor," of the *Woman's Herald of Industry,* August 10, 1884, reprinted in October 1884 issue, 4; Lockwood, "How I Ran for the Presidency," 129–130.

58. The quoted statements were printed in *LDJ,* September 5, 1884, 2, reprinted in Winner, *Belva A. Lockwood,* 50 and in *Woman's Herald of Industry* 3 (October 1884): 1; Reda Davis, *Women's Republic: The Life of Marietta Stow, Cooperator,* 176–180; Lockwood, "How I Ran for the Presidency," 130.

59. Clara Shortridge Foltz, "First Women's Presidential Candidate: Nomination in Fun by Women in Convention Assembled," *Women's Law Journal* 7 (1918): 27–28; Belva Lockwood, Washington, to Clara S. Foltz et al., San Francisco, September 25, 1884, printed in Lockwood, "How I Ran for the Presidency," 131–132.

60. *LDJ,* September 5, 1884, 2, reprinted in Winner, *Belva A. Lockwood,* 50; Davis, *Women's Republic,* 180–183.

61. The quoted statements are in Lockwood, "How I Ran for the Presidency," 132–134; handbill, "Women's Presidential Campaign," Lockwood Papers, Swarthmore; *LDJ,* September 6, 1884, 2, reprinted in Winner, *Belva A. Lockwood,* 50, 52; "Mrs. Lockwood's Political Principles," *Lockport Daily Union,* September 11, 1884, 3, reprinted in Winner, *Belva A. Lockwood,* 54–59.

62. Duniway's statement is in *Woman's Herald of Industry,* October 1884, 1; Fox, *Lady for the Defense,* 134–135; Lockwood, "How I Ran for the Presidency," 134–135.

63. Reed, "Belva Ann Lockwood," 69; Foltz, "First Woman Presidential Candidate," 28; Lockwood, "How I Ran for the Presidency," 135–136.

64. Lockwood's statement was quoted in "A Woman Can Be President," *New York Times,* October 20, 1884, 5; Foltz, "First Woman Presidential Candidate," 28.

65. Quoted by the *Louisville Courier-Journal,* October 15, 1884, reprinted in Winner, *Belva A. Lockwood,* 63.

66. "The Way of the Candidate," *New York Times,* September 14, 1884, 8; "When Belva Takes Possession," *LDJ,* October 10, 1884, 2, reprinted in Winner, *Belva A. Lockwood,* 61.

67. Kendall Haven, *Amazing American Women* (Englewood, CO: Libraries Unlimited, 1995), 79; "Fun of the Campaign," *New York Times,* November 4, 1884, 1; *LDJ,* October 13, 1884, 3, reprinted in Winner, *Belva A. Lockwood,* 62.

68. "Notes from Washington," *New York Times,* January 13, 1885, 3; Lockwood, "How I Ran for the Presidency," 136–137; Winner, *Belva A. Lockwood,* 72.

69. Anthony's statement was published in the *Rochester Post-Express,* November 17, 1884, reprinted in Winner, *Belva A. Lockwood,* 66–67; Lockwood, "How I Ran for the Presidency," 131–132, 137.

70. Quotation is from the *Beatrice* [Nebraska] *Democrat* of June 19, 1885, reprinted in Winner, *Belva A. Lockwood,* 73; Belva A. Lockwood, Washington, to Sisters of the Equity Club, April 30, 1887, in Drachman, *Women Lawyers* 56–59; H.L. Slayton to Mrs. Belva A. Lockwood, April 20, 1886, in Winner, *Belva A. Lockwood,* 74–75.

71. The *Boston Herald* story was reprinted in *LDJ,* December 24, 1884, 2; advertising handbill, "Belva Lockwood, the Eminent Barrister," reprinted in Winner, *Belva A. Lockwood,* 84; ibid., 73.

72. Drachman, *Women Lawyers,* 57–58; Filler, "Lockwood, Belva Ann," 415.

73. Winner, *Belva A. Lockwood,* 77; "The Equal Rights Leader," *New York World,* May 19, 1888, 1; Robert Wesley Doherty, *Alfred H. Love and the Universal Peace Union,* M.A. thesis, University of Pennsylvania, 1962, 139.

74. Quote is from "Belva Made Them Smile," *New York World,* August 30, 1888, 1; "Belva's Talk: The Equal Rights Candidate Appears in Brooklyn," *Brooklyn Daily Eagle,* July 27, 1888, 2; F.E.T., "Belva Lockwood at Home," *New York Sun,* August 27, 1888, 5.

75. Mignon Rittenhouse, *The Amazing Nelly Bly* (New York: Dutton, 1956), 138–140. The song "Belva Dear, Belva Dear," words and music by M.H. Rosenfeld (New York: Benjamin W. Hitchcock, 1888), is reprinted in Winner, *Belva A. Lockwood,* 79.

76. Both quotations are from *LDJ,* March 12, 1884, 3, reprinted in Winner, *Belva A. Lockwood,* 48–49.

77. Quotations are from Beeton, *Women Vote in the West,* 63; ibid., 64–78.

78. Ibid., 78–80; Filler, "Lockwood, Belva Ann," 415.

79. Peter Brock, *Pacifism in the United States: From the Colonial Era to the First World War* (Princeton, NJ: Princeton University Press, 1965), 928–930; Curti, *Peace or War,* 78; "Lockwood, Belva," *National Cyclopedia of Biography,* vol. 2, 62.

80. Both of the quotations relating to the Chicago World's Fair are in Belva Lockwood, "The Political Aspect of the Columbia Exposition, Its Peace Side," *American Journal of Politics* 3 (July 1893). The "peace convention" statement is on 110 and the "reformatory minds" reference is on 108; the "highest moral and economic advance" quote is from Kerr, *The Girl Who Ran for President,* 185; see also Belva A. Lockwood, *Peace and the Outlook: An American View* (Washington D.C.: G.W. Codich, 1899), 10–18.

81. Doherty, *Alfred H. Love,* 92–93; Curti, *Peace or War,* 106–107, 142–143; 149, 151, 156, 169, 186; Gardner, "Hearings, Memorials, Petitions and Resolutions," in Winner, *Belva A. Lockwood,* 105–107.

82. The "we must teach our children" quote is in Belva A. Lockwood, *Peace and the Outlook,* 19–20; the "Mr. Cleveland" quote is from Winner, *Belva A. Lockwood,* 95; Cook, "Belva Ann Lockwood," 15.

83. "Belva Lockwood, Lawyer, Dies at 85 [sic]," 23; Norgren, "Before It Was Merely Difficult," 42, footnotes 66 and 67.

84. Belva A. Lockwood, "The Eastern Cherokee Case," Lockwood Papers, Swarthmore; Cook, "Belva Ann Lockwood," 15; Alain M. Josephy Jr., *The Indian Heritage of America* (New York: Bantam Books, 1969), 323.

85. Quoted by Fox, *Lady for the Defense,* 152; Appellees' Reply Brief in *United States* v. *Cherokee Nation* (1906), 202 U.S. 101.

86. *Cherokee Nation* v. *United States* (1905), 40 Ct. Cl. 252.

87. Unidentified newspaper clipping, dated January 18, 1906, in Winner, *Belva A. Lockwood,* 97; Fox, *Lady for the Defense,* 153.

88. *United States* v. *Cherokee Nation* (1906), 202 U.S. 101, 101–132; "Indians Win Suit for $4,589,588," *New York Times,* May 1, 1906, 5; Fox, *Lady for the Defense,* 154; Stern, *We the Women,* 230–231.

89. Quotation is from Belva A. Lockwood to an unidentified person, November 28, 1907, in Winner, *Belva A. Lockwood,* 97–98; "Lockwood, Belva," *National Cyclopedia of Biography,* vol. 2, 62; Kerr, *The Girl Who Ran for President,* 186–188.

90. Quoted passage is from "Belva Lockwood, Lawyer, Dies at 85 [sic]," 23; Clark, "Belva Ann Lockwood," 217; Stern, *We the Women,* 232; Fox, *Lady for the Defense,* 155; Kerr, *The Girl Who Ran for President,* 190.

91. "Lockwood, Belva Ann Bennett," *Who Was Who In America* (Chicago: A.N. Marquis Company, 1943), vol. 1, 739; Kerr, *The Girl Who Ran for President,* 188–190; Fox, *Lady for the Defense,* 154–155.

92. "Belva Lockwood in Dire Need," *Woman's Journal,* April 4, 1914, 111; Stern, *We the Women,* 232; "Belva Lockwood, Lawyer, Dies at 85 [sic]," 23; Fox, *Lady for the Defense,* 155.

93. The newspaper was quoted in Clark, "Belva A. Lockwood," 219; "Belva Lockwood Dead," *Washington Post,* May 20, 1917, 13.

94. United States Postal Service, *Postal Bulletin,* May 22, 1986, 21.

Selected Cases

Bradwell v. *State of Illinois* (1873)
83 U.S. 130

A female attorney prior to Belva Lockwood, Mrs. Myra Bradwell, a resident of Illinois, applied to the justices of the Illinois Supreme Court for a license to practice law. Her application was rejected on the ground that the state's legislature had never intended that women should be permitted to practice law. In an appeal to the U.S. Supreme Court, Bradwell was represented by Matthew Hale Carpenter, who argued that the privileges and immunities clauses in the Fourth and Fourteenth Amendments assured to every citizen who could meet the learning and character requirements the right to practice law.

A majority of the Court affirmed the state court's ruling, holding that the right to practice law in the courts of a state was not among the privileges and immunities protected by the Fourteenth Amendment. A concurring opinion by Justice Bradley gave a different reason for affirming the Illinois court's verdict. "In the nature of things," said Bradley, the authors of the Fourteenth Amendment could not possibly have intended to open all occupations to women. "The natural timidity and delicacy of the female sex evidently unfits it for many of the occupations of civil life." Therefore, a state legislature may quite properly ordain the offices, positions, and callings that are to be occupied exclusively by men.

In re Mrs. Belva A. Lockwood, Ex Parte (1873)
9 Ct. Cl. 346

Belva Lockwood, who was already a member of the bar of the District of Columbia, applied in 1873 for admission to the bar of the United States Court of Claims. Her attorneys argued that according to the court's own published rules, Lockwood was fully qualified since she was universally acknowledged to be of good character and was a member of the Supreme Court of the District of Columbia, the district's highest court.

It was, maintained Lockwood's attorneys, entirely within the discretion of its judges to decide whether women would be allowed to practice law before the Court of Claims. Were this to happen, they said, it would be thoroughly in accord with "the tendency of the age to offer women new modes of livelihood and new spheres of activity." Conceding that the rules also referred to would-be counsel as "he" and "man," Lockwood's attorneys pointed out that in recent federal statutes, words of masculine gender had been interpreted as applying also to females.

Speaking for the court, Judge Nott rejected Lockwood's application. The rules of the Court of Claims, he insisted, contemplated only the admission of men. While it was true, he admitted, that masculine words in laws and statutes did sometimes apply as well to women, this was not the case when it came to the practice of law. Neither the common law derived from England nor American statutory law allowed women to qualify as attorneys. "Under the Constitution and the laws of the United States," the judge concluded, "a court is without power to admit a woman to its bar and a woman is without legal capacity to become an attorney."

Andrew J. Secor v. *Polly Secor* (1874)
Supreme Court of the District of Columbia
1 MacArth 630

In 1874, Belva Lockwood represented Andrew Secor of Lockport, New York, in a divorce action against Polly Secor, to whom her client had been married for over thirty years. The couple had three children together, all of whom were of mature years by the time of the divorce suit.

Mr. Secor claimed that even before he and Polly married, she was already experiencing periodic attacks of insanity, adding that he had not learned of them until much later. Such attacks, lasting sometimes for months, continued to afflict Polly during their marriage. When she was at home, Mrs. Secor was often irritable and used profane and violent language. As a result, claimed Andrew, he considered it dangerous to go on living with his wife.

The marriage was generally unhappy, and in April 1873, Mrs. Secor refused to live any longer with her husband or to perform any of the duties of a wife. On one occasion, Mrs. Secor tried to kill herself. When Andrew moved to Washington, D.C., Polly remained in Royalton, New York. In October 1873, the couple divided their property and no longer lived together.

Despite this history, the court refused to approve the divorce. "The alleged insanity of the wife," it ruled, "was settled too long ago by the marriage of the parties and the birth of a family. . . . A marriage after the lapse of more than thirty years ought not to be disturbed for such a cause." The judge added that since the couple was living apart, there could be no divorce on grounds of abandonment.

Webster M. Raines et al. v. *The United States* (1875)
11 Ct. Cl. 648

The hotel owned by Cynthia Raines in Eufola, Alabama, was the place of residence of a number of soldiers of the United States Army from 1865 to 1868, the period after the Civil War when most of the former "rebel" states were under military occupation. According to Raines, the government had neither paid rent nor compensated her for the damages done to her property.

In February 1874, Raines and her husband, Webster M. Raines, filed a petition in the Court of Claims against the government of the United States for rent and damages to her hotel in the amount of $11,000. Their petition assigned to Belva A. Lockwood, "for a valuable consideration had, and received during the winter of 1874," a part interest in their claim. Mr. and Mrs. Raines had taken this step in order to qualify Lockwood, who was not yet a member of the Court of Claims bar, to represent them in that court.

When the Raineses' petition was taken up by the court, Lockwood attempted to speak, but was declared out of order. The court ruled that the document purporting to transfer "a part interest" in a claim for payment against the U.S. government was too vague and indefinite to confer a legal title. Therefore, ruled the court, Lockwood had no legal interest and was not entitled to join the case as a party claimant.

By the time the case was heard in 1875, Mrs. Raines had died so her husband was the sole petitioner recognized by the court. On the merits of his case, the Court of Claims ruled that the occupation of his wife's property by Union troops in time of war was an "appropriation of property," but, according to federal law, the Court of Claims lacked jurisdiction in such cases. It therefore dismissed the petition of Mr. Raines.

Elizabeth Gordon, Widow v. *The United States* (1891) 26 Ct. Cl. 307

One of Lockwood's clients in the 1880s was a pension claimant named Jerry Gordon, who had lost both his legs while working for the Union Army in a nonmilitary capacity during the Battle of Bull Run. In 1870, Gordon was granted a pension of $25 a month by a special act of Congress. By 1878, his monthly stipend had risen to $72 a month due to the passage by Congress of general Civil War pension laws.

On May 31, 1881, the U.S. government's Commissioner of Pensions accused Gordon of filing fraudulent claims and ordered that his monthly pension payments cease. Gordon hired Lockwood to plead his case, and she petitioned the U.S. Court of Claims on his behalf. She asked the court to require the Commissioner of Pensions to again permit Gordon to receive his pension. In 1890, Gordon died and the Court of Claims permitted his widow, Elizabeth Gordon, to supplant her late husband as the petitioner of record.

After the court heard the petition, the judges rejected it. Speaking for the court, Judge Nott conceded that the petitioner's case had merit but added that the Court of Claims could not grant her request. Congress, he explained, had passed a law in 1887 that declared all federal pension issues to be outside the jurisdiction of the Court of Claims. Therefore, said Nott, his court could not rule on pension claims, not even on those like Gordon's, which had originated long before the new law was passed.

In re Lockwood (1894)
154 U.S. 116

Belva Lockwood applied in 1893 for permission to practice law in the Virginia Supreme Court of Appeals. The statutes of Virginia regarding attorneys at law included a provision that "any person duly authorized and practicing as counsel or attorney at law in any State or Territory of the United States, or in the District of Columbia, may practice as such in the courts of the State." By then Lockwood had been practicing law in the District of Columbia for over twenty years and had also been admitted to the bar of Massachusetts. These facts notwithstanding, the court, Virginia's highest, rejected her application.

Lockwood appealed next to the United States Supreme Court, asking it to require the Virginia court to admit her to its bar. The question, as earlier in *Bradwell,* was whether the right to practice law in the state courts was "a privilege or immunity" of a citizen of the United States and therefore protected by either or both the Fourth and Fourteenth Amendments. Again, as in the earlier case, the Supreme Court, speaking through Chief Justice Fuller, ruled that the right to practice law in the state courts was *not* under federal protection. The right to regulate the licensing of lawyers in state courts was, wrote Fuller, "in no manner governed or controlled by citizenship of the United States in the party seeking such license." Therefore, a state court's ruling that confined the right to practice law to males was not in violation of the U.S. Constitution.

Fuller quoted a section of the Virginia Code pertaining to attorneys at law that used the word "he" three times and the word "his" twice. It was up to Virginia's highest court, he concluded, "to determine whether the word 'person' as therein used is confined to males, and whether women are admitted to practice law in that Commonwealth."

Only three weeks after this decision was handed down, however, the Virginia Supreme Court relented and allowed Lockwood to practice law in the state courts by a margin of three to two.

Friend v. *The United States et al.* (1895)
29 Ct. Cl. 425.

On February 5, 1868, the ranch owned by John Friend in Llano County, Texas, was raided by a group of about fifteen Comanche Indians. Friend was away at the time, but his wife and son were at the ranch when the raid took place. The raiders inflicted multiple injuries on Mrs. Friend, shooting her with an arrow, stabbing her, and scalping her in two places. Temple Friend, the couple's eight-year-old son, was abducted, to be held by the Indians for nearly five years. The Comanche raiders also seized $287 in cash, along with personal property worth $60.

In 1894, Friend petitioned the Court of Claims for financial recompense
under the Indian Depredations Act of 1891. Belva Lockwood and M.B.
Eggesholl represented him in the case. There were two causes of action in the
case. The first was the property taken or destroyed by the defendant Indians.
The court awarded Friend the $887 due him, according to his claim as en-
dorsed by the Commissioner of Indian Affairs. The other cause of action was
the damage (and resulting financial costs) inflicted on Friend's wife and son
by the Indian marauders. Here, according to Judge Richardson, the law provided no remedy.

Under the statute, Friend would have been entitled to restitution for the
harm suffered by his wife and child only if he had filed suit within three years
of the raid. Judge Richardson therefore dismissed the portion of Friend's claim
relating to the suffering of his wife and son.

Cherokee Nation v. *United States* (1905)
40 Ct. Cl. 252
and
United States v. *Cherokee Nation* (1906)
202 U.S. 101

On several occasions, Lockwood represented groups of Cherokee Indians in
lawsuits against the government of the United States. In 1905, for example,
she pleaded the cause of some 6,000 Eastern and Emigrant Cherokees who
were seeking to share in the proceeds of a trust fund set up in 1838 by the
United Congress to compensate members of their tribe for the lands they had
been deprived of in the era of Andrew Jackson. What the U.S. Congress had
intended was a quid pro quo in which the government would allot funds for
the benefit of the Cherokees and the latter would agree to seek no compensation other than the earnings accumulated by the trust.

Lockwood's clients in the case were descended from Cherokees who had
been expelled from their land in the 1830s, but had somehow managed to avoid
the forced march along "the trail of tears" to Oklahoma. This group had never
received any payment from the federal government. Indeed, the only Cherokees to have been paid anything by the government were the "old settlers" (or
Cherokee Nation) who had gone to the Indian Territory during the 1830s.

Lockwood argued that it was particularly unjust that the government of the
United States had drawn on the trust fund to pay the costs of the forced migration of the Indians to Oklahoma. In effect, the Cherokees had subsidized the
carrying out of a policy that had abused and oppressed them. Fairness required, she argued, that her clients should receive payments based on the
amount of money that would have accrued had the fund been permitted to
grow undiminished over the years.

In 1905, three distinct groups of Cherokees filed lawsuits against the United
States, each with its own attorneys. The three cases were consolidated into

one by the Court of Claims. The court ruled in favor of the claimants and required the government to pay them a total of $4.5 million. The government appealed the ruling to the United States Supreme Court, but it too ruled in the Cherokees' favor.

Lockwood, representing various Eastern and Emigrant Cherokees, and Frank Owen, counsel to the majority of Eastern Cherokees, both held that the Western Cherokees had already been compensated by the government and should not share in the proceeds from the current case. Their argument prevailed with the Court, which ruled that the Court of Claims award stood, but added that the Western Cherokees were not to share in it.

Annotated Bibliography

Alumni Record and General Catalogue of Syracuse University (1899): 220. Contains several helpful details.

Beeton, Beverly. *Women Vote in the West: The Woman Suffrage Movement, 1869–1896.* New York: Garland Publishing, 1986. Unearths new material on Lockwood through a search of the files of organizations with which she had dealings.

"Belva Lockwood, Lawyer, Dies at 85 [*sic*]." *New York Times,* May 20, 1917, 23. This obituary includes some telling quotes and sidelights on Lockwood's career.

"Belva A. Lockwood." *Case and Comment* 24, no. 3 (August 1917): 252–253. A brief, competent summary of Lockwood's career.

Belva A. Lockwood Papers. Housed at the Swarthmore College Peace Collection, Friends Historical Library, Swarthmore College, Swarthmore, PA. The collection includes various writings by Lockwood, some items of personal correspondence as well as legal briefs, various memoranda by her, and newspaper clippings.

Belva Ann (Bennett) Lockwood Papers, 1881–1916. Housed at the Smithsonian Institute, National Museum of American History, Division of Political History, Washington, D.C. Consists of a few items of correspondence, various writings relating to world peace, feminism, and social reform, and clippings from newspapers.

Belva Ann Lockwood Collection, 1830–1917. Housed at the New York State Library in Albany, NY. Three boxes of material, including writings about Lockwood by various authors, various writings by her, and documents relating to her friends and associates in the woman's movement.

Belva Lockwood Collection, 1879–1880. Housed at New York State Historical Association Library, Cooperstown, NY. Collection includes clippings, pictures, and approximately 500 pages of lecture notes.

Bernard, Job. "Early Days of the Supreme Court of the District of Columbia." *Records of the Columbia Historical Society* 22 (1919): 1–35. Relates the story of one of the first courts to permit women, and specifically Lockwood, to practice law before it.

Berry, Dawn Bradley. *The 50 Most Influential Women in American Law.* Los Angeles: Lowell House, 1996. These essays, aimed at the general reader, contain many interesting facts and quotations.

Boynick, David K. *Pioneers in Petticoats.* New York: Thomas J. Crowell, 1959, 59–89. An informative and readable work of popular history.

Brock, Peter. *Pacifism in the United States: From the Colonial Era to the First World War.* Princeton, NJ: Princeton University Press, 1965. Contains a six-page account of the work done by the Universal Peace Union.

Carpenter, Frank G. *Carp's Washington,* arranged and edited by Frances Carpenter. New York: McGraw-Hill, 1960. Refers briefly to Belva's doings and provides interesting material on the Washington of her day.

Cheshire, Herbert and Maxine. "A Woman for President?" *New York Times Magazine,* May 27, 1956, 60–61. An article that briefly depicts the "campaigns" of Woodhull and Lockwood for the presidency.

Clark, Allan C. "Belva Ann Lockwood." *Records of the Columbia Historical Society* 35–36 (1933): 206–219. A well-researched article that focuses on Lockwood's involvement with her adopted city of Washington, D.C.

Cook, Frances A. "Belva Ann Lockwood: For Peace, Justice, and President." Paper submitted to Professor Barbara Allen Babcock at Stanford University, Spring 1997. *Women's Legal History Biography Project.* <http://www.stanford.edu/group/WLHP/papers/lockwood/htm.> A very good article, presenting up to date research on Lockwood's career along with a fine bibliography.

Curti, Merle Eugene. *Peace or War: The American Struggle, 1636–1936.* New York: W.W. Norton, 1936; reprint, New York: Garland Publishing, 1972. Lockwood appears frequently in these pages by a great historian, as a lobbyist and editor for the Universal Peace Union.

Davis, Julia. "A Feisty Schoolmarm Made the Lawyers Sit Up and Take Notice." *Smithsonian* 11 (March 1981): 133–150. A good article that includes key quotations from primary sources.

Davis, Reda. *Women's Republic: The Life of Marietta Stow: Cooperator.* Berkeley, CA: Point Pinos Editions, 1980. A solid biography of the woman behind Belva's 1884 "presidential campaign."

DeBenedetti, Charles. *The Peace Reform in American History.* Bloomington: Indiana University Press, 1980, 59–61. A brief survey of America's peace movements over the years, from 1776 to now.

Doherty, Robert Wesley. *Alfred H. Love and the Universal Peace Union.* M.A. thesis, University of Pennsylvania, 1962. Biography of Lockwood's longtime friend and fellow peace movement activist.

Drachman, Virginia G. *Sisters in Law: Women Lawyers in Modern American History.* Cambridge, MA: Harvard University Press, 1998. A comparative study of woman lawyers during the late 1800s that makes frequent references to Lockwood and makes clear that she was a role model for many younger woman lawyers.

———. *Women Lawyers and the Origins of Professional Identity in America: The Letters of the Equity Club, 1887–1890.* Ann Arbor: University of Michigan Press, 1993. There is a five-page segment on Belva Lockwood, who was active in the Equity Club and corresponded with some of its members.

Evans, Melinda. "Belva Lockwood and the Mormon Question." Paper submitted to Professor Barbara Allen Babcock at Stanford University, Autumn 1999. *Women's Legal History Biography Project* <http://www.Stanford.edu/group/WLHP/papers/Mevans-lockwood.pdf>. A detailed and vivid account of Lockwood's defense of the Mormons.

Filler, Louis. "Lockwood, Belva Ann Bennett McNall," in Edward S. James, ed., *Notable American Women: A Biographical Dictionary,* 6 vols. Cambridge, MA: Belknap Press, 1971. Vol. 2, 413–415. A fine summary account of Lockwood's life and career.

Flexner, Eleanor, and Ellen Fitzpatrick. *A Century of Struggle: The Woman's Rights Movement in the United States.* Cambridge, MA: Belknap Press, 1996. A survey of the history of American women.

Foltz, Clara Shortridge. "First Woman Presidential Candidate: Nomination in Fun by Women in Convention Assembled." *Women's Law Journal* 7 (1918): 27–28. Claims Lockwood's presidential "run" began as a practical joke.

Fox, Mary Virginia. *Lady for the Defense: A Biography of Belva Lockwood.* New York: Harcourt Brace Jovanovich, 1975. A well-researched account intended for school-age readers.

Friedman, Jane M. *America's First Woman Lawyer: The Biography of Myra Bradwell.* Buffalo: Prometheus Books, 1993. Biography of Lockwood's contemporary and fellow lawyer.

Goldsmith, Barbara. *Other Powers: The Age of Suffrage, Spiritualism and the Scandalous Victoria Woodhull.* New York: Alfred A. Knopf, 1998. This biography links the feminism of the time with the theory and practice of spiritualism.

Hanaford, Phoebe A. *Daughters of America.* Boston: B.B. Russell, 1883. Includes a contemporary account of Lockwood's career as teacher and fledgling lawyer.

Hardy, Gayle J. *American Women Civil Rights Activists: Biobibliographies of 68 Leaders, 1825–1992.* Jefferson, NC: McFarland, 1993. A valuable work of reference.

Haven, Kendall. *Amazing American Women.* Englewood, CO: Libraries Unlimited, 1995, 75–81. Provides a colorful account of Lockwood's run for the presidency.

Irwin, Inez Haynes. *Angels and Amazons: A Hundred Years of American Women.* Garden City, NY: Doubleday, Doran, 1933. A popular account of women's history from the 1830s to the 1930s.

Kerr, Laura. *The Girl Who Ran for President.* New York: Thomas Nelson, 1947. Written for children, but of some value for scholars.

Lockwood, Belva A. "The Benefit of Suffrage to Women." *American Magazine of Civics* 8 (June 1896): 607–609. Argues that women need the ballot to protect their interests and as "natural persons" are entitled to it.

———. "How I Ran for the Presidency," *National Magazine,* March 1903. Reprinted in *Belva A. Lockwood* by Julia Hull Winner. Her own account of the venture that made her famous.

———. "How Shall the Exposition Be Opened?" *American Journal of Politics* 1 (July 1892): 44–47. An eloquently written antiwar essay in which Lockwood opposes all military display at the World's Fair of 1893.

———. "My Efforts to Become a Lawyer." *Lippincott's Monthly Magazine,* February 1888, 215–229. Reprinted in *Belva A. Lockwood* by Julia Hull Winner, 109–125. A remarkably compressed yet very well-written essay recording Lockwood's recollection of her childhood and youth, as well as her career in teaching and law.

———. *Peace and the Outlook: An American View.* Washington, D.C.: G.W. Codich, 1899. A pacifist manifesto in which she denounces the evils attending the Spanish American War and hails the international movement toward arbitration between nations.

———. "The Political Aspect of the Columbia Exposition, Its Peace Side." *American Journal of Politics* 3 (July 1893): 107–110. Views the World's Fair as a great opportunity to promote world peace.

———. "The Present Phase of the Woman Question." *The Cosmopolitan,* October 1888, 467–470. Argues that women were being held back more by popular attitudes than by legal disabilities.

———. "Women in Politics." *American Journal of Politics* 2 (April 1893): 385–387. Hails such recent gains as woman delegates at political party conventions and membership on world's fair committees, adding that "they have come to stay."

———. "Women of the American Bar." *Illustrated American,* July 26, 1891, 45–50. This is an interesting account of the progress made by woman lawyers as of the 1890s.

"Lockwood, Belva Ann Bennett," *National Cyclopedia of Biography,* vol. 2, 62–63. A brief summary that provides useful clues to Lockwood's life and work.

[McNall, Lura?], "The Women Who Tried to Vote," *Lockport Daily Journal.* Reprinted in *Belva A. Lockwood* by Julia Hull Winner. This essay, probably by Lockwood's daughter, contains some unique details.

McNall, Lura. "Our Washington Letter." Series of articles appearing once a week in the *Lockport Daily Journal.* Reports on the Washington scene, including the doings of her mother and her friends.

Meyer, Annie Nathan. *Woman's Work in America.* New York: Henry Holt, 1891. A contemporary account of women's "progress" in the United States.

Morello, Karen B. *The Invisible Bar: The Woman Lawyer in America, 1638 to the Present.* New York: Random House, 1986, 31–36. Provides a vivid account of Lockwood's early struggles to become a lawyer.

Norgren, Jill. "Before It Was Merely Difficult: Belva Lockwood's Life in Law and Politics." *Journal of Supreme Court History* 23 (1999): 16–43. Combines painstaking research with a readable style, well illustrated with drawings and photos from the period.

———. Lockwood, Belva Ann Bennett McNall. *American National Biography,* vol. 13, 807–809. Updated biographical summary.

Park, Frances Fenton. "Lockwood, Belva Ann Bennett." *Dictionary of American Biography,* vol. 11, 341–342. Brief summary of Lockwood's life and career.

Proctor, John Clagett. "Belva Ann Lockwood: Only Woman Candidate for President of the United States." *Records of the Columbia Historical Society* 35–36 (1932): 193–205. Contains interesting anecdotes about Lockwood's life in Washington as an independent woman lawyer.

Reed, Helena Ducie. "Belva Ann Lockwood: First of Our Great Women Lawyers." *Kappa Beta Pi Quarterly* 38 (1954): 67–69. This is a brief, incisive summary of Lockwood's career.

Riegel, Robert. *American Feminists.* Lawrence: University Press of Kansas, 1963. Useful as background and includes some brief but astute comments on Lockwood.

Rittenhouse, Mignon. *The Amazing Nelly Bly.* New York: Dutton, 1956. A biography of the famous newspaper reporter.

Robinson, Lelia J. "Women Lawyers in the United States." *Green Bag* 2 (1890): 10–32. Profiles of pioneer women lawyers, including Lockwood.

Stanton, Elizabeth Cady, Susan B. Anthony, and Matilda Joslyn Gage, eds. *History of Woman Suffrage,* 6 vols. Rochester, NY: Mann Printing Company, 1886; reprinted New York: Arno and *New York Times,* 1969. Several of the volumes refer to Lockwood's feminist activities, particularly Volume 3.

Stern, Madeline B. *We the Women: Career Firsts of Nineteenth Century America.* New York: Schulte, 1962; reprinted Lincoln: University of Nebraska Press, 1994. A pioneer work that is remarkably thorough in its research and has an excellent bibliography.

Underhill, Lois Beachy. *The Woman Who Ran for President: The Many Lives of Victoria Woodhull.* Bridgehampton, NY: Bridge Works, 1995. Portrays Woodhull as an important forerunner of modern feminism.

Willard, Frances Elizabeth, and Mary A. Livermore. *A Woman of the Century*. Buffalo: C.W. Moulton, 1893, 468–469. Brief, useful summary as well as a "primary source."

Winner, Julia Hull. *Belva A. Lockwood*. Publication No. 19 of the Occasional Contributions of the Niagara County [NY] Historical Society. Lockport, NY: Niagara County Historical Society, 1969. This is an extremely valuable compilation of source materials on Lockwood, some of it autobiographical.

———. "Belva A. Lockwood—That Extraordinary Woman." *New York History* 39 (October 1958): 322–331. A solidly researched pioneer article that makes a strong case for Lockwood's historical significance.

"Women's Presidential Campaign." *Woman's Herald of Industry* 3 (October 1884): 1–4. The entire issue is devoted to the presidential "race."

—Louis D.—
<u>Brandeis</u>

Chronology

1856	Born on November 13 in Louisville, Kentucky, to Adolph and Frederika Brandeis.
1872	Awarded a gold medal for all-around excellence by the public school system of Louisville.
1877	Graduated first in his class from Harvard Law School, setting a record for academic excellence at the school that stood for over eighty years.
1879	Admitted to the Massachusetts bar and formed a partnership with his former Harvard roommate, Samuel Warren.
1880s	The firm of Brandeis and Warren flourished and added rapidly to its list of clients. Brandeis, although a Republican, supported Grover Cleveland, the Democratic candidate for president.
1888–1890	Warren and Brandeis published three scholarly articles in the *Harvard Law Review,* including "The Right to Privacy," a contribution of great future importance in American law.
1891	Married his second cousin, Alice Goldmark.
1893	First daughter, Susan, was born on February 27.
1896	Second daughter, Elizabeth, was born on April 25.
1896	Joined with Edward A. Filene and other Boston progressives in a successful campaign to prevent the West End Transit Company from controlling the subways of Boston.
1903	Joined with other leaders of Boston's business and professional classes in organizing the Good Government Association.
1904	Persuaded Boston, the Consolidated Gas Company, and the Massachusetts legislature to adopt the "sliding scale" method (increasing stockholder dividends in proportion to the decline in rates) in regulating the price to consumers of illuminating gas.
1905–1907	Proposed savings bank life insurance and orchestrated the campaign of agitation and lobbying that resulted in its enactment by the state of Massachusetts.
1907–1913	Jousted with the House of Morgan in his long but successful battle to block the merger of the New Haven and Boston and Maine railroads.
1908	Argued *Muller* v. *Oregon* before the U.S. Supreme Court and won the case. The brief used in *Muller* was the first sociological or "Brandeis Brief."

1910   Mediates a settlement of the ladies' garment workers' strike in New York City.

1910–1911   Served as cocounsel for Louis Glavis at the hearing of the Senate Judiciary Committee on the Ballinger-Pinchot dispute.

1912   Became a key adviser to Woodrow Wilson in the presidential election of 1912.

1914   Became the leader of the American Zionist movement; published *Other People's Money*.

1916   Nominated by President Wilson for the Supreme Court and confirmed by the U.S. Senate after a bitter four-month battle.

1916–1939   Served as an associate justice of the U.S. Supreme Court.

1939   Resigned from the Supreme Court on February 13.

1941   Died on October 5.

1945   Alice Goldmark Brandeis died on October 12.

Biography

On January 28, 1916, President Woodrow Wilson touched off a massive political controversy when he nominated Louis D. Brandeis to the vacant seat on the U.S. Supreme Court. There followed one of the bitterest confirmation battles in the history of the United States Senate.

Known as the "People's Attorney," Brandeis had for two decades challenged some of the nation's most powerful business and political leaders, doing battle even with J.P. Morgan himself. To many political conservatives and to most of the nation's leading lawyers, Brandeis was anathema, a gifted but unscrupulous troublemaker who had repeatedly and improperly attacked major corporations. To progressives, on the other hand, he was a heroic figure, the very embodiment of the progressive as legal advocate, and one of their movement's most important leaders. In the end, Brandeis was confirmed by the Senate, but only after four months of hearings before the Senate Judiciary Committee, during which its members had reviewed at length the many controversies arising from a legal career of nearly four decades.

Origins

Louis Dembitz Brandeis was born in Louisville, Kentucky, on November 13, 1856, the youngest of the four children, two boys and two girls, born to Adolph and Frederika Brandeis. Both parents were Jews of Germanic culture who had grown up in Prague, the principal city of Bohemia. Adolph was the son of a once prosperous cotton print manufacturer whose business had declined in the 1840s. To improve his prospects, Adolph attended the Technical School of Prague, where he studied estate management, marketing, and agriculture, graduating with distinction in 1843.[1]

In 1846, Adolph Brandeis, who was then twenty-four, became engaged to Frederika Dembitz, a lively and intellectual girl of seventeen to whom he was distantly related. Her mother had died when Frederika was twelve, and soon thereafter, her father consented to an arrangement whereby Amelia and Moritz Wehle, his late wife's sister and brother, took control of the upbringing of Frederika and her brother, Lewis. Although she attended elementary school for six months and high school for a year, most of Frederika's education came from a succession of tutors who had instructed her in geography, arithmetic, and, above all, music, art, and literature. She learned to play the piano skillfully and became a voracious reader, versed not only in Goethe, Schiller, and the other German romantics, but also in the works of Homer and Molière.[2]

Following the revolutionary upheaval of 1848, Adolph and Frederika emigrated to the United States as part of an extended family, numbering twenty-seven in all and drawn from three branches on their family tree: the Wehles, the Dembitzes, and the Brandeises. The decision to emigrate had been jointly arrived at and was due both to economic and political factors. The Wehle family included textile manufacturers for whom, as with Adolph's father, the mechanization of their industry threatened financial ruin. As Jews in the Hapsburg Empire, the three families were also compelled to pay special taxes. Moreover, economic conditions in the 1840s were so unstable that, according to Amelia Wehle, some Jewish families "went to bed worth one hundred thousand gulden and woke up worth only 20,000."[3]

The decision to go to America was also influenced by the Revolution of 1848. Liberal in their political views and sympathetic to the rebel cause, the elders of the three families must have been shocked by the anti-Semitic riots that erupted in Prague while the city was in the hands of the Czech rebels. They also realized, of course, that if the traditional authorities were to be restored, the mistreatment of the Jews was likely to become even worse. In June, forces loyal to the Hapsburg dynasty bombarded the city, and it was then that the three families decided jointly to emigrate.[4]

Intending to establish their own little community of farms in the American West, the elders dispatched Adolph Brandeis to America to prepare the way for the immigration of his relatives. After spending a few months in the Midwest, Adolph, impressed by the nation's institutions and moved by the tolerance he had encountered among its people, wrote to Frederika: "America's progress is the triumph of the rights of man." When it came to farming, however, Adolph, after visiting farms in seven states and working briefly as an agricultural laborer, decided that the work done by American farmers was too onerous and boring for city-dwelling professionals and businessmen such as the Brandeises and Wehles. They should all go, he advised, to an American city, preferably to one of the prospering river ports of the Midwest.[5]

In April 1849, twenty-six of Adolph's relatives journeyed to Hamburg, where they booked passage on the steamer *Washington* for New York. Determined to preserve their cultured ways, the three emigrating families carried twenty-seven chests of luggage, containing among other things two grand pianos, their linens and silver plate, and thousands of books. After arriving in New York, they traveled to Ohio via canal boat and then made their way by rail to Cincinnati. Only two in the party remained in that city, with the rest all following Adolph's lead in moving as a group to Madison, Indiana, a town with a population of roughly 10,000, strategically located on the Ohio River midway between Cincinnati and Louisville, Kentucky. It was in Madison that Adolph and Frederika were wed on September 5, 1849, and it was also there that Fanny, their first child, was born. The young couple soon wearied of Madison, however, and in 1851 moved on to Louisville, where Adolph soon established a thriving business as a grain and produce merchant. In the next five years, Frederika gave birth to three children: Amy, Alfred, and Louis.[6]

Childhood and Education

By the 1850s, the nationwide clash over the future of slavery was intensifying and the Brandeises' adopted state of Kentucky was one of its many battlegrounds. Politically liberal, Adolph and Frederika, along with virtually all of their kinsmen, were firmly in the antislavery camp. In 1860, Frederika's brother, Lewis Dembitz, was a delegate to the Republican National Convention, where he voted to nominate Abraham Lincoln for the presidency. With the outbreak of the Civil War, the Brandeises, like many Louisville families, were Union sympathizers. Louis Brandeis would later recall accompanying his parents at the age of five to the Union camp outside the city, where they would distribute coffee and sandwiches to the soldiers.[7]

During the war years, Adolph Brandeis made a fortune selling grain to the Union armies. As a result, he was able to move his family to a larger house in a more prosperous section of Louisville where he and Frederika could raise their children in secure affluence. The family now owned a stableful of fast horses and employed a number of servants, including a coach driver. They also traveled, going on vacation often to New York and Newport and, on occasion, as far as Niagara and Canada. The family owned and operated a flour mill, a tobacco factory, an eleven-hundred-acre farm, and a river freighter, the *Fanny Brandeis*.[8]

The Brandeises were a cultured family who never talked of business or money matters at the dinner table, discussing instead a wide array of subjects pertaining to history, politics, and culture as well as to their daily experiences. Raised on German culture, Louis would always love, and frequently quote from, the works of Goethe and Schiller, while Beethoven and Schumann were always among his favorite composers. He had learned to love literature from his mother, and throughout his life Louis always remained an avid reader. He was also given violin lessons and even performed with an amateur orchestra in Louisville.[9]

For the young Louis Brandeis, his Jewishness seemed merely an accident of birth, since he and his brother and sisters were raised with no formal religious training of any kind. At Christmas, the Brandeises exchanged gifts. In later years, after he himself had become a husband and father, Louis Brandeis even had a Christmas tree; but to him the holiday was always a purely secular occasion. While rejecting organized religion, Frederika and Adolph raised their children to be high-minded idealists. "I believe," wrote Frederika, "that only goodness and truth and conduct that is humane and self-sacrificing toward those who need us can bring God nearer to us. . . . I wanted to give my children the purest spirit and the highest ideals as to morals and love. God has blessed my endeavors."[10]

Louis's formal education began at six at a small private school. Two years later, he moved up to the German and English Academy of Louisville where he attended for six years, impressing his teachers with his brilliance and diligence. From the autumn of 1870 to the spring of 1872, Brandeis attended Louisville Male High School, where he scored the highest possible grades given at the school in every subject, save only foreign languages, an area in which he was judged merely "excellent" rather than, as in his other subjects, "without fault." When he was sixteen, the Louisville University of the Public Schools awarded Brandeis a gold medal for "excellence in all his studies."[11]

With the economic downturn of the early 1870s, the business of Adolph Brandeis became less profitable, and he decided to sell off his business assets and take his family to Europe for an extended stay. After sightseeing with his family for over a year, Louis journeyed on his own to Dresden, where he resumed his education at the *Annen Realschule*, an exacting private academy where he studied for three terms, again receiving the highest grades given by the school in every subject except foreign languages. Brandeis would later credit the rigorous training that he received at the *Realschule* with teaching him how to think.[12]

At Harvard Law School

Louis returned to the United States in June 1875, resolved on becoming a lawyer. He chose the law as his life's work largely out of admiration for his uncle, Lewis Dembitz, a frequent visitor to the Brandeis household, whom he idolized for his wide learning and skill in debate. In September 1875, Brandeis was admitted to Harvard Law School, which was then in the midst of the academic revolution begun by Dean C.B. Langdell, the pioneer of the "case method" in legal education, in which students, instead of memorizing textbooks, would examine individual cases, studying for themselves the actual court records. Brandeis took readily to the new methods and immediately made his presence felt through his contributions to class discussions as well as in the moot court debates that were staged at the Pow Wow Club, an association of law students to which he belonged. "Mr. Brandeis," recalled one of his classmates, "had hardly taken his seat before his remarkable talents were discovered and his claim to immediate distinction allowed." Brandeis was stimulated by his studies and also by the cultural life of Cambridge and Boston, where he attended concerts and the theater and where he heard lecture such literary giants of old New England as Holmes, Longfellow, and Emerson.[13]

Despite a shortage of money and problems with his eyesight, Brandeis completed his law degree in two years. He ranked first in the graduating class of 1877 with an average of 97, setting a record at Harvard Law that stood for eight decades. Since he was not yet twenty-one, he required a special waiver from the president of Harvard, Charles Eliot, to graduate with his class. "Those years," Brandeis would later write of his period at Harvard, "were among the happiest of my life. I worked! For me, the world's center was Cambridge."[14]

A Young Lawyer

After graduation, Louis stayed on at Harvard for an extra year, which he devoted to reading law and improving his finances by tutoring other law students. In November 1878 he accepted a job with the law firm of James Taussig in St. Louis, and it was there that he filed his first brief and published his first law review article. After the brilliance of Cambridge and Boston, however, St. Louis seemed a cultural backwater, and after seven months of thoroughly minor casework, Brandeis decided to accept the offer of Samuel Warren, his Harvard roommate, that he return to Boston as Warren's law partner. The two young lawyers had been close friends at Harvard, where Warren had ranked second in the class of 1877 to Brandeis's first. A key factor in Louis's decision was the business and social prominence of Warren's family, which he knew would be of value in bringing in clients.[15]

Within a few weeks of his return, Brandeis was appointed law clerk to Horace Grey, the chief justice of the Massachusetts Supreme Law Court, remaining in that post for two years. Late in July, he was admitted to the Massachusetts bar without taking an examination, an occurrence that, as Louis wrote to his brother, was "contrary to all principle and precedent." The speed with which he was admitted probably was due to his high standing with his former professors at Harvard Law as well as to the influence of Chief Justice Grey.[16]

The new law firm soon flourished, gaining clients not only in Massachusetts but in several neighboring states as well. Their former professors referred a number of clients to the two fledgling lawyers. Of great importance in the partnership's early years was the account of Warren's own father, a leading paper manufacturer in Boston. Their other clients consisted chiefly of middle-sized business firms, especially paper and shoe manufacturers and merchants in various lines. Of the latter, many were ethnically German and several were German Jews. "If Warren could work Brahmin Boston," notes Brandeis biographer Philippa Strum, "Brandeis could do his bit with Boston's German-Americans."[17]

Although always more of a consultant and adviser than a trial lawyer, Brandeis was also a capable litigator who reveled in the challenge of the courtroom. "There is," he wrote to his brother, "a certain joy in the exhaustion and backache of a long trial which shorter skirmishes cannot afford." In 1889, Louis pleaded for the first time before the U.S. Supreme Court as the eastern counsel of the Wisconsin Central Railroad. The suit involved taxation of the railroad's land grant, and Brandeis won it. According to Alfred Lief, Brandeis's first biographer, Chief Justice Melville Fuller was so impressed by Brandeis's presentation that he would soon afterward call him "the ablest attorney he knew of in the East."[18]

In taking on business clients, Brandeis would set two major conditions: first, that he would never have to deal with intermediaries, but only with the person in charge, the firm's chief executive; second, that he must be permitted to offer advice on any and all aspects of the firm's affairs that seemed to him relevant to its legal problems. He saw himself as truly a "counselor at law" rather than as merely a strategist in lawsuits. The idea was to help the client to avoid lawsuits, strikes, and other crises by timely advice that considered legal problems within the total context of the client's business affairs. "I would rather have clients," Brandeis told Ernest Poole in 1911, "than be somebody's lawyer." He took particular pride in his own ability with figures, gleaning valuable findings on points at issue from the study of corporate records.[19]

Brandeis was unusual among lawyers because he refused to serve in a cause that he considered bad. If he believed a client to be in the wrong, either he would persuade his clients to make amends to those with legitimate grievances against them or Brandeis would withdraw from the case. On one occasion, he even switched sides, at first representing the United Shoe Machinery Company but, later on, counseling a group of shoe manufacturers in their struggle against United and testifying against his former client before a congressional committee. On another occasion, he referred to himself as "attorney for the situation" although he was in fact serving as counsel to a particular client. "The position that I should take if I remained in the case," Brandeis advised the client, "would be to give everybody a square deal." In a memorandum found among his papers, Brandeis reminded himself to "advise client on what he should have, not what he wants."[20]

A Mugwump Reformer

Given his idealism and his strong conscience, it is not surprising to find Brandeis in the ranks of the mugwump reformers. (The term "Mugwump" referred originally to the Republicans who backed Grover Cleveland, the Democratic presidential candidate in 1884. But the same label was also applied to the political independents of both major parties who stood for "honest government" and civil service reform.) Major campaign issues in 1884 were "character" and the record of Republican candidate James Blaine, which was too blemished with scandal and corruption to be acceptable to gentlemen of "virtue." Besides, Brandeis agreed with Cleveland on the issues of the day. Like him, he wanted the tariff reduced and the appointive offices filled through competitive examinations. In the 1880s and 1890s, Brandeis joined a number of reform organizations, including the Civil Service Reform Association, the American Free Trade League, and the American Citizenship Committee.[21]

Brandeis collaborated with his law partner, Samuel Warren, on three scholarly articles that were published in the *Harvard Law Review* from 1888 to 1890. In all three, they expressed the firm faith in the common law that they had acquired at Harvard along with a corresponding mistrust of legislative activism. The first two articles, dealing with the law of ponds, argued that the owners of land must be compensated when their water is drawn off to meet the needs of nearby cities. "All the restraints imposed by the Constitution and the courts are needed," wrote the two lawyers, "to protect property from the encroachments of the legislature."[22]

Their third article, "The Right to Privacy" was by far the most important, later credited by the noted legal scholar Roscoe Pound as having accomplished "nothing less than add a chapter to our law." According to Warren and Brandeis, the development of the modern newspaper and of snapshot photography had resulted in the publication of photographs of private persons and also of their words and statements without their consent. These actions, they argued, had done serious injury to the feelings of many individuals and, in exceeding the bounds of decency, had weakened the moral standards of society as a whole. In their search for a principle of law that would protect privacy, Warren and Brandeis contended that since individuals may under the common law normally decide (as in copyright law) whether to communicate to others their thoughts, sentiments, and emotions, it followed that a right to privacy already existed. "The cases referred to show that the common law has for a century and a half protected privacy and to grant the protection now suggested would be merely another application of an existing rule." When the victims of prying journalists sue, judges should feel free to grant them "substantial compensation" even as they would do in cases of slander and libel. In protesting against these abuses, Brandeis and Warren were reacting to the then emerging phenomenon of modern journalism like the true gentlemen of the old school that in fact they were.[23]

In 1889, the legal career of Brandeis entered a new phase when Samuel Warren withdrew from their partnership to take charge of his family's paper company following the death of his father, who had managed it for many years. The firm of Warren and Brandeis had over the years recruited as associates promising recent graduates of Harvard Law School. With Warren's departure, Brandeis would learn to rely on these young colleagues. He tried fewer and fewer cases himself and, after 1897, when his public career absorbed most of his energies, seldom took part in active court trials. Two of the firm's young recruits evolved into full partners, and in 1897, the name of the firm was changed to Brandeis, Dunbar, and Nutter. Joseph Eastman, another of the bright young lawyers employed at the Brandeis firm, would go on to a great career as a government regulator and administrator.[24]

Brandeis's first victory as a public man came in 1891, when, through a series of adroit maneuvers and a masterful redefinition of the issue, he persuaded the legislature of Massachusetts to make the liquor laws less restrictive on the manufacturers and distributors and thus, in his view, more reasonable and enforceable. In the midst of an impassioned debate between the forces of temperance, bent on impeding the sale of alcoholic beverages in the name of virtue, and the liquor dealers, demanding that they be treated simply as property owners and businessmen, Brandeis managed to devise a viable middle course. In moderating the regulation, he told the lawmakers, they would at a single stroke deprive the liquor dealers of their incentive to violate the laws and to corrupt through bribery the politics of Massachusetts. The legislature was won over by Brandeis's arguments and the regulations were changed. Now it would no longer be necessary to order a meal to buy a drink lawfully in Massachusetts.[25]

Marriage and Family Life

In 1890 Brandeis, who had previously found little time for flirtation and court-
ship, became engaged to his second cousin, Alice Goldmark of New York
City, the daughter of a physician who had emigrated to America from Austria
following the collapse of the Revolution of 1848, in which he had been an
active participant. On March 23, 1891, Louis and Alice were married at the
home of her parents in New York City in a civil ceremony conducted by Felix
Adler, the founder and head of the Ethical Culture Society, who also happened to be Alice's brother-in-law. The newlywed couple moved into a modest house that Brandeis had bought at the foot of Beacon Hill in Boston. The
couple had two daughters; Susan, who was born in 1893, and Elizabeth, who
arrived three years later.[26]

The Brandeis family lived well but without extravagance. Like virtually all
upper-class people of their day, they had servants, employing a cook, a "second girl," and a nurse. The daughters attended Windsor School, a respectable
private school in Boston, and the family rented and later bought a vacation
cottage in the upper-class suburb of Dedham, where they would typically spend
their weekends and the entire month of August. They shunned the more luxu-
rious ways of their class, holding few formal dinner parties and avoiding the
luxury hotels when they traveled. Brandeis would never fit the stereotype of
the wealthy man. Although he belonged to a polo club, he never played polo.
He owned no yacht, just a canoe that he would paddle by himself on the fast-
flowing river that adjoined his cottage in Dedham.[27]

Even as he and his family were living frugally, Brandeis was adding steadily
to his wealth. By 1907, he had become a millionaire, and in future years his
net worth would continue to grow in spite of his generous contributions to
charity and to causes he believed in. He would always remain a cautious in-
vestor who almost always avoided the stock market, preferring to invest in
high-quality bonds that would yield a fair but safe return. "Take [in your busi-
ness] all the risk that you think it prudent to take," he advised his brother, "but
risk only there."[28]

With their finances secure, Alice and Louis resolved that he should devote
more of his time to public causes. In 1894, Brandeis became counsel for Alice
N. Lincoln, a Boston philanthropist and crusader for the poor, at public hearings held by Boston's Board of Aldermen to investigate conditions in the public poorhouses. Lincoln, who had been visiting the poor-houses for over three
years, charged that the inmates were dwelling in misery and that the temporarily unemployed were being thrown in together callously with the mentally
ill and the hardened criminals. In fifty-seven public hearings in the ensuing
nine months, Brandeis interrogated a long series of witnesses, most of whom
bore out Lincoln's charges. At the close of the hearings, Brandeis appealed for
a new policy that would not only care for the poor but also prevent and even
cure pauperism itself. The poor, he declared, would be redeemed if housed

and fed better, exposed to entertainments of an uplifting kind, and the able-bodied among them required to work. "Men are not bad. Men are degraded largely by circumstances. . . . It is the duty of every man and the main duty of those who are dealing with these unfortunates to help them up and let them feel that there is some hope for them in life." As a result of the hearings, the aldermanic board decreed that the administration of the poor law should be completely reorganized.[29]

From Mugwump to Progressive

It was in the early 1890s that Brandeis began to reevaluate his views on the industrial order in America. Well aware that there were now giant firms capable of dominating whole industries, he began to lose faith in the idea that the economic system could be adequately regulated by an evolving common law. Although not as convinced as he would be later that bigness in business was a "curse," he denounced "cut-throat competition" and fretted over the dangers of monopoly. A book that had an impact on his views was *Wealth Against Commonwealth,* by Henry Demarest Lloyd, an 1894 best-seller that exposed the tactics used by John D. Rockefeller in building the Standard Oil Trust. Brandeis found Lloyd's account convincing, and he hoped that it would open the eyes of the American public to the sins of Rockefeller and other major capitalists.[30]

Brandeis was also influenced toward progressivism by his friendship with Mary Kenney, a prominent labor organizer, and her husband, John F. O'Sullivan, president of the Boston Central Labor Union and a reporter on labor matters for the *Boston Globe.* The O'Sullivans made Brandeis more aware of the plight of workers and more sympathetic to the labor movement.[31]

Brandeis and the Battle for Municipal Reform

These modifications of his basic views were accompanied by a series of campaigns of resistance to the designs advanced by the public service and transportation corporations of Boston. Late in 1896, Brandeis was sought out by progressive businessman Edward A. Filene to handle the legal end of the fight that Filene was leading against the bid of the West End Transit Company to secure concessions from the state legislature that would have given it a stranglehold on the city's emerging subway system. After some initial setbacks, the company's opponents formed the Public Franchise League (PFL), with Brandeis as one of its founding members. There followed a nonpartisan mobilization of public opinion, which in 1900 succeeded in winning a citywide referendum, rejecting another proposal from the transit company that would have reduced the role of the city in the management of its own transit system.

Another company measure was actually passed by the state legislature in 1901, but Brandeis persuaded Governor Winthrop Crane to veto it. Still another company proposal was introduced in the legislature the following year, as was a rival PFL bill that had been drafted by Brandeis. In hearings held by the legislature's Committee on Metropolitan Affairs, Brandeis, as counsel for the PFL, clashed repeatedly with the transit company's lawyer, Albert Pillsbury. In the course of the struggle, Brandeis demonstrated his ability to sway the opinion of both elected officials and the general public. He urged on Filene as the publicity director of the PFL to get the members to flood the newspapers with letters, to plant editorials in friendly newspapers, and to secure supportive endorsements from trade unions who were to be asked to repeat them as often as possible. In the end, it was Brandeis and the PFL that prevailed. The legislature enacted Brandeis's bill, approving the construction by Boston of a new subway line that would be leased to the company for twenty-five years at an annual rental of 4.5 percent of the cost of construction. Due in large part to Brandeis's influence, the city would continue to combine municipal control with private operation.[32]

The transit franchise struggle revealed that many of Boston's politicians had placed "friends" and ward heelers on the payrolls of the Elevated Railway Company and other public service corporations. One alderman alone had found work in this way for 200 of his followers. In Boston, as in other American cities, such abuses were part of a larger pattern of corruption in which graft and bribery were commonplace. Convicted felons would return from prison terms to resume their political careers.[33]

Always the moralist, Brandeis declared in March 1903 that "misgovernment in Boston had reached the danger point." He now joined forces with progressive businessmen and professionals to organize the Good Government Association (GGA), with the objective of electing good and honest leaders. The association, Brandeis announced, would keep a ledger "impartially recording the good and bad deeds," thereby making the record of Boston's politicians accessible to all the city's voters. In the face of repeated defeats for the "good government" forces at the polls, Brandeis persevered, plotting strategy for the GGA and contributing funds to its coffers. He urged the association's secretary, Edmund Billings, to send out speakers to every organization that would give them a forum and delivered many speeches for the cause himself. In some of his addresses, he achieved a soaring eloquence. "We want a government," he told one reform gathering in 1903, "that will represent the laboring man, the professional man, the businessman, and the man of leisure. We want a good government, not because it is good business but because it is dishonorable to submit to a bad government. The great name, the glory of Boston is in our keeping." In 1906, Brandeis and the reform movement in Boston won a modest victory when the state legislature enacted an anticorruption measure that he had drafted and publicly advocated for three years. This measure made it a crime punishable by a fine of $200 for a public official to solicit a job from a regulated public utility or for an officer of such a company to offer such favors.[34]

Meanwhile, Brandeis had also become involved with the battle to rein in the rates charged in Boston for illuminating gas. A loud controversy erupted in 1904 when the leaders of the newly organized Consolidated Gas Company proposed to the Utilities Commission that the company be valuated at more than $24 million while the Public Franchise League insisted that the figure be set at only $15.1 million. The dispute was important because, under Massachusetts law, the permissible rate for gas was linked to the assessed value of the company supplying it. As in their other municipal battles, Brandeis and the progressives launched a major campaign to sway public opinion. There were public meetings, letter-writing campaigns, and planted editorials, some of which Brandeis wrote himself.[35]

Brandeis was in reality seeking a solution to the problem that would be fair both to the public and to the company, whose stockholders, he maintained, deserved a fair return. Rejecting municipal ownership, he proposed that Boston follow the example of London's city government by adopting the "sliding scale" principle, in which the dividends of regulated utilities are permitted to rise in proportion to the decline in the rates charged to the consuming public. At a private meeting between Brandeis and James L. Richards, the president of the Consolidated, the two agreed on the sliding scale, a valuation of $15.1 million, and an initial dividend of 7 percent. In addition, the maximum price of illuminating gas in Boston was to be set at ninety cents per thousand feet. Their accord was worked into a bill that Brandeis presented to the Public Franchise League, where, although a wide majority endorsed it, both the bill and Brandeis were denounced by some of the more militant members. A foe of the plan suggested that there could be a second vote on it later, moving Brandeis to snap "Don't cry, baby," a response that so angered PFL activist Edward Warren that in 1916, he opposed the confirmation of Brandeis for the U.S. Supreme Court at the hearings held by the Senate Judiciary Committee.

The sliding-scale bill now went to the legislature where, after a spirited debate, it passed by a comfortable margin. After conferring with Brandeis and a handful of others, Governor Curtis Guild signed the measure into law. "I succeeded in running this campaign," Brandeis wrote to his brother, "mainly by putting others on the firing line. As your daughters would say, 'the man behind.'" Initially, the rates charged for gas did go down, but there were no further reductions thereafter even though the gas rates were declining in other cities. By the end of the decade, virtually everyone had given up on the sliding scale in Boston and it was repealed by the legislature. Lewis J. Paper contends that the measure failed due to inflation in the nation's economy, unforeseen developments in technology, and the need to reward company managers, not just the stockholders, for the efficiencies achieved.[36]

"The People's Lawyer"

Brandeis had begun to evolve into "the people's lawyer." He was no longer accepting remuneration for "the public interest" cases that he was pleading before judges, legislative committees, and administrative agencies. He had become involved also with the development of public opinion by writing magazine articles, making speeches, and joining with others to form interest groups. He was also developing ties with noted journalists, such as Lincoln Steffens and Norman Hapgood, and granting numerous interviews that were published in newspapers in both Boston and New York.[37]

Brandeis would again battle powerful interests in his successful campaign to establish savings bank life insurance in Massachusetts. He first became involved with questions of life insurance in March 1905 when he became counsel to the New England Policy-Holders' Protective Committee, a newly organized group of affluent policyholders who were concerned that their insurer, the scandal-rocked Equitable Life Assurance Society, might be descending into bankruptcy. As had by now become his standard practice in all public interest cases, Brandeis insisted on serving without pay so that he would be free to address the wider issues involved rather than confine himself merely to the case at hand. After some heated discussion with members of the committee, they agreed to his terms. Over the next year, he devoted every available moment to the study of life insurance, reporting his findings in speeches and articles, which on many points corroborated the recent findings of the Armstrong inquiry into the life insurance industry in New York State. Initially, Brandeis made harsh accusations against the insurance companies, at one point describing some of their practices as "legalized robbery." On reflection, however, his basic optimism about the motives of businessmen and lawyers led him to depict the insurance industry as inefficient rather than immoral, as caught up in a system to which its leaders were clinging out of ignorance rather than greed.[38]

According to Brandeis, life insurance as of 1906 was simply a bad bargain for the vast majority of policyholders due in the main to the inefficiency of the industry. Roughly 70 percent of all the policies issued were in the "industrial" category, meaning that they had been sold door to door in working-class areas. Such policies insured the lives of poorly paid breadwinners for small amounts, typically from $150 to $350. The premiums, usually fifty cents or less, were collected weekly at the policyholder's door. Should a payment be missed, the policy was often cancelled, a fact that the sellers of such policies would usually not mention. As a result, most industrial policies lapsed, so benefits were actually paid out to only one policyholder out of every eight. Moreover, industrial policyholders were charged twice as much per dollar of insurance as the holders of regular policies. Industrial policies were highly profitable, however, accounting for most of the earnings realized by the nation's top three insurance companies.

The objective, Brandeis wrote, should not be to sell insurance to people who neither wanted it nor could afford it, but simply "to furnish a good article at a low price." He now launched a campaign of organization and education, which, in spite of the united opposition of the insurance industry and of most of the state's savings banks, succeeded in creating a groundswell in Massachusetts for savings bank life insurance. Acting through surrogates, Brandeis created the Savings Bank Life Insurance League, consisting of progressive businessmen, social reformers, and many of the trade unions of Massachusetts. Brandeis soon found himself speaking six times a week for his new cause and keeping a set of dinner clothes at his law office so that he would always be ready to attend the social functions at which he would be a featured speaker. Enlisting the aid of friendly newspapers, he gained wide and favorable publicity for his ideas. By March 1907, the Savings Bank Insurance League had 70,000 members and Brandeis's face and name were appearing regularly in newspapers throughout the state.[39]

After several conferences with Brandeis, the governor of Massachusetts, Curtis Guild, stated in his annual message that he commended to the legislature "the study of plans to be submitted to you for cheaper industrial insurance that may rob death of half of its terrors for the worthy poor." In December 1906, Brandeis persuaded a former governor, a Republican, to become the president of the Savings Bank Insurance League and a second ex-governor, a Democrat, to become its vice president. Late in February 1907, Brandeis drafted his own bill, circulating copies to the members of the Massachusetts legislature and also to the state's financial institutions and trade unions. At the bill's first legislative hearing on March 21, the committee room was thronged with the bill's supporters. When the hearing was resumed twelve days later, an impressive array of labor leaders, industrialists, ministers, educators, and prominent political figures of both major parties all testified in support of the bill. As the lead witness, Brandeis testified that the bill was clearly in the public interest and that it was opposed only by the chronically pessimistic and by insurance company officials "whose selfish interests prompt them to oppose the measure."[40]

After the hearings ended, Brandeis and his supporters kept up the pressure on the members of the legislature, inundating them with letters supporting the bill. On May 28, the House Ways and Means Committee approved the measure and on June 3, it gained the approval of the whole House by a margin of 146 to 23. The final obstacle was now the Senate, but it too passed the bill by a surprisingly one-sided vote of 23 to 3; and on June 26, 1907, the savings bank insurance measure was signed into law in Massachusetts by Governor Guild. Against the odds and over the opposition of powerful interests, Brandeis had prevailed. Seasoned legislators complemented him on the skill with which he had organized and led his forces.[41]

With his bill enacted, Brandeis was eager to see it carried out. Within a few days, he sent to Governor Guild a list of prospective trustees for the new system. Although the Massachusetts banks were slow in setting up departments of insurance, the new program was given credit by some observers for the fact that within two years of its creation, the major insurance companies had reduced the premiums on their industrial policies by over 20 percent. Brandeis always considered savings bank life insurance to be one of his greatest achievements and, like a proud parent, he kept a watchful eye on it, sounding the alarm through letters, speeches, and interviews whenever the insurance companies attempted through political influence to limit or restrict the program. Although savings bank life insurance would eventually spread throughout the nation and ultimately become a useful alternative to the policies of the major insurance firms, it never became what Brandeis had hoped it would, a mechanism for protecting working-class people from all the recurring hazards of life.[42]

The New Haven War

Even while still immersed in his battle for savings bank insurance, Brandeis had become involved in yet another of his public interest campaigns: the struggle to prevent the New York and New Haven, New England's largest and most important railroad, from gaining control of its chief competitor, the Boston and Maine. His foes this time were the most powerful that he had yet encountered. The stock of the New Haven was widely owned among New England's most affluent families and it also enjoyed solid support both within Boston's legal establishment and among the powerful State Street bankers, such as H.L. Higginson, who had already become an enemy of his.

Since the 1890s, the New Haven had been under the control of J.P. Morgan, the most powerful of all American bankers and probably the most dominating figure in all of American business. Bent on making the New Haven into a single unified network of transportation that would service most of New England, Morgan pursued a policy of acquiring many of the line's competitors, including not only railways, but also trolley and shipping companies. To carry out his policy of expansion, Morgan selected the veteran railroad executive C.S. Mellen to be the New Haven's president, and Mellen (in violation of a Massachusetts law) moved quickly to acquire a number of Boston's traction and ferry lines. In 1906, Mellen began his campaign to gain control of the Boston and Maine.[43]

As with most of his other public interest cases, Brandeis became involved initially by accident. In June 1907, he was engaged as counsel by two major stockholders of the Boston and Maine who were bent on blocking the merger of the two lines. Once again, as had become his custom in public interest cases, Brandeis insisted on serving without payment, leaving him free to act as he thought best. In this instance, he decided on his own initiative to pay $25,000 to his law firm so that his partners and associates would not suffer financially by his participation in the case.[44]

After doing extensive research into the financial condition of the New Haven, Brandeis published a seventy-seven-page pamphlet in which he argued that the company's recent acquisitions had overextended it financially; he predicted that within a few years, it would either become insolvent or be compelled to cut its dividend. Scarcely had his pamphlet been published than Brandeis found himself under attack not only by the officers of the New Haven, but also by many newspapers and periodicals, by chambers of commerce, Boston bankers, and even by certain college professors who were supposedly expert on railroads and their finances. (It was later revealed that several journalists and a Harvard professor had received payments from the New Haven.) "I have made," wrote Brandeis cheerfully to his brother Alfred, "more enemies [this time] than in all my previous fights together."[45]

Unfazed, Brandeis now joined with other high-minded citizens to form the Massachusetts Anti-Merger League, a citizens' lobby, which included many of the same people who had been active in the Savings Bank Insurance League. This time, however, there was less of a response from the public than in the insurance battle. The issue of the railway merger seemed perhaps more complex and certainly less clear-cut than the other struggle. To many New Englanders, the New Haven's goal of consolidating the region's transportation media seemed reasonable and perhaps even desirable (as in fact some historians now believe that it was). Brandeis spoke frequently to groups of citizens, warning them that the New Haven sought to monopolize the transportation of New England and raising the prospect of alien control. "We must not," he declared before an audience of merchants in February 1908, "entrust the determination as to what our welfare demands to the decision of persons who may be influenced by considerations other than the interests of Massachusetts."[46]

Although Governor Guild, formerly an opponent of the merger, switched sides in early 1908 and urged the legislature to pass a promerger bill. The merger cause was in that year dealt several stunning blows. First, the Massachusetts lower house rejected the merger bill after the Senate had approved it. Then, the Massachusetts Supreme Court ruled that the company had acted illegally when it had acquired its Boston transit and ferry holdings. Finally, after Brandeis had met twice with President Theodore Roosevelt, the U.S. Department of Justice filed on May 22, 1908, an antitrust suit against the New Haven.[47]

With the merger seemingly blocked, Brandeis turned his attention elsewhere, but the New Haven had only begun to fight. It retaliated with a series of audacious maneuvers that caught its foes, including Brandeis, napping. In July 1908 the railroad sold its Boston and Maine holdings to an obscure Connecticut coal dealer named John A. Billard who, with an estate worth only $30,000, had somehow managed to borrow from an obliging bank the $14 million needed for his "purchase." Soon thereafter, the newly elected governor, Eben Draper, after conferring with the New Haven's officers, persuaded the legislature to create a holding company for the sole purpose of acquiring the securities of the Boston and Maine. Billard now sold his B. and M. stock to the new holding company, which was in fact controlled by the chief officers of the New Haven. It was later revealed that Billard had reaped a profit of $2.7 million without risking a single cent of his own money. The way had been prepared for these maneuvers by the decision of President Taft's new administration to drop the antitrust suit against the New Haven.[48]

The scene of battle now shifted to Washington, D.C., where Senator La Follette delivered a fiery speech on the floor of the U.S. Senate in which he denounced the management of the New Haven, the legislature of Massachusetts, and especially old J.P. Morgan himself, whom he described as "a beefy, red-faced, thick-necked financial bully, drunk with wealth and power [who] bawls his orders to stock markets, courts, governments and nations." Brandeis had supplied many of the facts (but not the rhetoric) for La Follette's speech. Meanwhile, Brandeis continued to attack the New Haven via the press, giving interviews to at least half a dozen newspapers in Boston and New York and secretly writing editorials against the merger for the *Boston Journal* and the *New York Press*. At a hearing of the Interstate Commerce Commission that was held in Boston, the New Haven's president admitted that the railroad had maintained a floating slush fund that was used to make "donations" to politicians who cooperated.[49]

In 1913, the battle over the merger entered its final phase. First, the New Haven's finances came undone just as Brandeis had predicted they would. Afflicted now by the heavy debts resulting from its acquisition of new properties, the railroad was forced to cut its dividend in half. Morgan died in early 1913 and the directors of his bank forced Mellen to resign. In the year's final quarter, the stockholders of the New Haven, for the first time in forty years, received no dividends at all. In the spring of 1913, the Department of Justice launched a new investigation of the New Haven; in July of the following year, the Interstate Commerce Commission announced the findings of its own investigation, charging the New Haven with extravagance and political corruption and its board of directors with dereliction of duty. The New Haven now gave up the struggle, disposing of its Boston and Maine stock and selling off its trolley and shipping lines. Thus, after a nine-year battle against a powerful corporation that had enjoyed the backing of J.P. Morgan himself and in the face of a long, bitter campaign of personal abuse and vilification, Brandeis and his cause had again prevailed.[50]

The Muller Case

In taking on public interest cases, Brandeis was acting on his belief that the changes in American society resulting from the growth of industry and the rise of big business made it imperative that lawyers play a more evenhanded role. As things then stood, the nation's best lawyers functioned as "mere adjuncts of great corporations" whose principal activity was to shield their clients from regulation by the state. "We hear a great deal about the corporation lawyer," said Brandeis in a speech addressed to a group of Harvard law students in 1905, "and far too little about the people's lawyer." To creatively and constructively participate in the emerging industrial order, lawyers must become knowledgeable about social conditions and thoroughly aware of the "dangers to liberty" posed by the corporation and the factory. In urging upon the young law students the path of personal independence, evenhandedness, and the ongoing study of society, Brandeis was, in effect, inviting them to follow his example.[51]

A notable instance of his own work as "people's lawyer" was his representation of the state of Oregon in the famous Muller case, which was heard by the U.S. Supreme Court in January 1908. The question at issue in *Muller* v. *Oregon* was whether it was constitutional for a state to limit by law the hours that female workers could work. The state and federal courts had in the preceding twenty-five years usually ruled against such wages and hours legislation, finding it to be an "unreasonable" infringement of freedom of contract. In studying the case law, however, Brandeis noted that in several of the cases that had reached the Supreme Court, a majority of the justices had conceded that a state might constitutionally limit liberty of contract if it could be shown that the measure in question had "a real or substantial relation to public health or welfare." He decided that the way to win the case was to present facts that would demonstrate a clear connection between the health and morals of female workers and the hours that they worked. To accomplish this, he filed a new kind of brief (soon to be known as the Brandeis, or sociological, brief) in which legal argument took up only a few pages but was supplemented by more than a hundred pages of data drawn from the reports of social workers, commissioners of hygiene, and factory inspectors, all attesting that when women worked long hours, it was destructive to their health and morals.[52]

The strategy worked. The Oregon Ten Hours Law was upheld, and in his majority opinion, Justice David Brewer mentioned Brandeis by name and credited his brief with demonstrating "a widespread belief that woman's physical structure and the functions that she performs . . . justify special legislation restricting or qualifying the conditions under which she should be permitted to toil." After Muller, Brandeis became the leading defender in the courts of protective labor legislation. He continued to file sociological briefs, some of which were as long as six hundred pages. He won a major victory in 1914 when the U.S. Supreme Court affirmed the constitutionality of Oregon's minimum wage law.[53]

Brandeis and the Trade Unions

By the early 1900s, Brandeis was thoroughly in favor of unions, and he urged his business clients to work with them as both the best means of dealing fairly with workers and as an emerging reality with which business would have to cope. The workers, he noted, were thinking long and hard about their condition, and their unrest was increasing. Strong unions were needed both as a check on the power of the employer and as an outlet for worker discontent. "We must avoid industrial despotism. . . . Some way must be worked out by which employer and employee, each recognizing the proper sphere of the other, will each be free to work for his own and for the common good."[54]

Although favorable to unionism, Brandeis was forthright in denouncing lawbreaking and industrial violence by union members and advocated that labor organizations incorporate so that they would be liable financially for the harm done to business resulting from their violations of the law. He also denounced as "un-American" the policy of the closed shop, which excluded nonunion workers from unionized shops, and warned that in the long run such a practice must prove destructive of both capital and labor.[55]

Despite these and other disputes with union leaders, Brandeis was still viewed by many union members as friendly to their cause. In late June 1910, he was asked by leaders on both sides to assist in settling the general strike of the women's garment workers on New York's Lower East Side. Then in its third week, the conflict was both economic and ideological because a considerable number of the strikers were militant socialists who believed, at least in theory, in class warfare. There was also an ethnic, Jewish dimension to the conflict since the great majority of the shop hands in the industry as well as virtually all of their employers were Jews. Although many of the manufacturers were from Eastern Europe, the most prominent and successful of the garment center employers were highly assimilated Jews of Austrian or German descent. Brandeis's first move as mediator was to call a conference that was attended by ten union leaders and ten members of the Manufacturers' Association. Within a week, the conference had broken up over the insistence of the union leaders on the closed shop. Brandeis returned to Boston, but other "peacemakers," including the financier Jacob Schiff and the lawyer Louis Marshall, the leader of the Jewish community in New York, arranged a meeting between the attorney for the manufacturers and the legal representative of the union at which a settlement of the points at issue was worked out. Marshall labeled the agreement "the Protocol" in the hope, as he privately admitted, that "neither group will know what that means."[56]

Central to the settlement was its adoption of the preferential union shop, a concept that had been originated by Brandeis as his own solution to the problem of hiring (and firing) in the workplace. He rejected the open shop as destructive of unions and as protective of employer tyranny, but he was also, as we have seen, opposed to the closed union shop. In contrast to the other two arrangements, the preferential union shop was a compromise that left the decision of whom to employ with the employer but required of him a pledge that he would give "preference" to union members so long as they were equal in skill and efficiency to other job applicants. "The preferential union shop," wrote Brandeis in 1910, "seems to offer a solution consistent with the American spirit and traditions as well as with justice and the strengthening of the unions."[57]

In order to prevent lockouts and strikes in a chaotic industry prone to sudden outbursts of labor trouble, the Protocol created three joint boards, on each of which sat representatives of the manufacturers, the unions, and the public. A seven-member Board of Sanitary Control was to impose uniform standards with regard to working conditions in the shops. A Board of Grievances was to deal with disputes that had not been resolved at the shop level. Should the latter fail, the dispute was then to go to a three-member Board of Arbitration, which would have the final say.[58]

Since no one else was as acceptable to both sides, Brandeis was persuaded to become chairman of the Board of Arbitration. Over the next several months, similar protocols were established in two more of the garment trades following brief strikes, and Brandeis was induced to head their arbitration panels as well. Initially, some headway was made in improving conditions and averting strikes, but before long there were again bitter disputes and work stoppages, with each side blaming the other and each condemning the Protocol as a well-meant but futile arrangement. In April 1916, a lockout in the cloak and suit industry was followed by a general strike. Three months later, an agreement was negotiated that abandoned the preferential shop and, with it, the rest of the Protocol. The attempt by well-intentioned outsiders to create a new, harmonious, and cooperative order of labor relations in the garment industry, in what Brandeis termed "the spirit of get-together," had failed.[59]

The Ballinger–Pinchot Dispute

Brandeis attained national fame in 1910 when he served as legal counsel in the congressional investigation of the controversy between Richard Ballinger, the Secretary of the Interior in the Taft administration and Gifford Pinchot, the head of the forestry division in the U.S. Department of Agriculture. The dispute between the two men had begun in the previous year over a conservation policy. Ballinger announced that certain public lands that had been withdrawn from sale during the administration of Taft's immediate predecessor, Theodore Roosevelt, would again be up for sale to private purchasers. Pinchot, who had helped to develop Roosevelt's conservation policies, denounced Ballinger's innovations in several public speeches.

In August 1909, Louis Glavis, the commissioner of the Federal Land Office, confided to Pinchot his belief that Secretary Ballinger and his underlings at the Department of the Interior had deliberately obstructed Glavis's investigation of the claims filed by one Clarence Cunningham to public land in Alaska that contained much timber and coal. Glavis alleged further that the Cunningham claims had been fraudulently filed through the use of "dummy" claimants and that wealthy capitalists, including the Guggenheims and J.P. Morgan, were conspiring with Cunningham, Ballinger, and others to gain control illegally of Alaska's most profitable resources. At Pinchot's urging, Glavis took his complaints against Ballinger to President Taft, handing the president a written report in which he presented his allegations in detail. After looking into the matter, Taft, convinced that his secretary of the interior had done nothing wrong, authorized him to dismiss Glavis; and Ballinger promptly did so.[60]

With the secret encouragement and assistance of Pinchot*, Glavis retaliated by sending his report (which he had written for Taft) to *Collier's Magazine,* which published it in November 1909 as an article entitled "The Whitewashing of Ballinger." The magazine displayed on its cover a drawing of Ballinger in the grip of a giant hand above a caption that asked: "Are the Guggenheims in charge of the Department of the Interior?" Amid the uproar that followed, a joint congressional committee was created to investigate the roles played in the affair by, respectively, the Department of the Interior (headed by Ballinger), the federal land office (headed by Glavis), and the forestry service (led by Pinchot). The committee that was chosen consisted of six senators and six members of the House of Representatives, of whom eight were Republicans and four were Democrats. Brandeis was persuaded to become co-counsel for Glavis by his friend, Norman Hapgood, the editor of *Collier's,* who was fearful that Ballinger might sue the magazine for libel if the committee were to absolve him of wrongdoing.[61]

At the hearings, which required nearly four months to complete, Brandeis took the lead in interrogating both Glavis and major officials of the Taft administration. He was especially aggressive in interrogating and cross-examining Secretary Ballinger, repeatedly impeaching both his ethics and his truthfulness. Brandeis was able to show that Ballinger had, in fact, as secretary of the interior dealt with land claims filed by former clients of his Seattle law firm. Unable to find convincing evidence of the conspiracy that had been alleged by Glavis, Brandeis demonstrated instead that both Taft and his attorney general had rushed to exonerate Ballinger without ever inquiring seriously into the charges against him.

Under Brandeis's relentless probing, Ballinger admitted that a Justice Department official named Oscar Lawler had prepared a memorandum on the case that had been delivered in Ballinger's presence to the president. The turning point came when a Department of the Interior stenographer, L.S. Kirby, came forward with detailed information about the memorandum, testifying that it had been prepared in secret and its rough drafts burned. At first, Taft denied that he had ever seen such a document, but when Attorney General Wickersham, unaware of Taft's statement, released a copy to the committee,

*In January 1910, Taft dismissed Pinchot from office after the latter had written a letter to Senator Owen Dolliver (R-Iowa), in which he supported Glavis's allegations.

the president was forced to retract. Taft now issued a statement to the press, conceding that he had instructed Lawler to draft a summary and response to Glavis's charges "as if he [Lawler] were president" and had later drawn on it in writing the public letter in which he had exonerated Ballinger and authorized the dismissal of Glavis.[62]

At the close of the hearings, the joint committee found Ballinger blameless by the predictably partisan margin of seven (all Republicans) to five (four Democrats and one Republican progressive). It was clear, however, that Taft's credibility had been damaged and his administration weakened. In his private letters, Brandeis observed that the administration's wounds had been largely self-inflicted, arising from its attempted cover-up and its lack of candor about its conservation policies. "If they had brazenly admitted everything," he wrote, "and justified it on the ground that Ballinger was at least doing what he thought best, we should not have had a chance. Refusal to speak the truth is the history of many a downfall." The truth-telling of Glavis and Kirby, on the other hand, offered a heartening example of dedicated public service and demonstrated that "America has among its young men, happily, men of courage . . . in whom even the heavy burden of official life has not been able to suppress manliness."[63]

The hearings had brought out Brandeis's fighting qualities and, at least in the eyes of some observers, revealed in him a streak of vindictive cruelty. Even his brother Alfred had asked during the hearings whether Louis was going too far in his baiting of Ballinger and in his sweeping charges against the Taft administration. In reply, Louis had vowed that he would "follow the trail of evil wherever it extends." Brandeis, who sometimes transformed what some had viewed as moral questions into practical ones, was clearly made intensely angry at the sight of high officials who abused their offices. In March 1911, Ballinger resigned, ostensibly for health reasons, but some observers blamed Brandeis for the personal and political decline of the man whom he had called "unfit for the office that he holds."[64]

To succeed Ballinger, Taft chose Walter L. Fisher, a dedicated conservationist whose selection was applauded by progressives of every section. Brandeis had by now become interested in conservation issues and, as was his practice when taking up a new subject, had spent several weeks reading everything he could find on the subject of Alaska. He recommended to Secretary Fisher and to congressional progressives that the federal government build and own a railroad and other public utilities in Alaska. Although he usually preferred private sector activity to governmental activism, he urged federal action in Alaska in order to ensure that the new wealth that would result from development would go to the actual settlers of the territory and to the American people as a whole rather than to predatory capitalists and corporations. As Philippa Strum has pointed out, Brandeis in devising his plan for developing Alaska "rejected the approach that had typified much of American land and resources policy." To Senator La Follette he proposed as a slogan for progressives: "Alaska, the land of Opportunity, Develop it by the People, for the people. Do not let it be exploited by the Capitalists, for the Capitalists."[65]

Brandeis and the Corporations

As his views on Alaska suggest, Brandeis had become increasingly conscious of and hostile to the powerful corporations and to the trend toward bigness in American industry and finance. As early as 1895, he remarked in a private letter that Americans needed to awaken to the harm that great corporations were doing to their competitors, to their customers and above all, to ordinary workers. His legal career coincided with the formative period in the history of big business in America, the era of the so-called trusts, corporations so large that they threatened to dominate whole industries. By the 1880s, mammoth firms had emerged in various industries that seemed to threaten the well-being of millions of Americans.[66]

In 1890, Congress enacted the Sherman Anti-Trust Act, which declared it to be a federal crime, and punishable by law, to "conspire to restrain trade." It was not until after 1900, however, under Presidents Roosevelt and Taft, that there was a major effort to apply the Sherman law. During their presidencies, the federal government filed more than 100 antitrust suits. The results of the policy were mixed, but in some cases at least, the trusts that were sued were forced to divest some of their holdings—to combine less and to compete more.[67]

By 1910, however, various leaders in thought and politics, including Theodore Roosevelt, were questioning the value of the antitrust policy. Some "progressives," such as Roosevelt and Charles Van Hise (the president of the University of Wisconsin and a leading expert on the problem of industrial concentration), contended that there was nothing that could prevent the continuing concentration of industry and therefore, like it or not, big business was here to stay. Other "progressive" leaders, such as William Jennings Bryan, who on three occasions was the Democratic Party's candidate for president, and Robert M. La Follette, a Republican senator from Wisconsin, continued to believe that the big business trend could and should be slowed or even reversed. While virtually all progressives, Roosevelt included, thought that the industrial order required regulation, they differed over how far it should go, what forms it should take, and, most important, over what its goal should be. As Brandeis formulated it, the issue pitted those, like himself, who favored "regulated competition" against those who called for "regulated monopoly."[68]

His wide reading and, above all else, his experiences as a commercial lawyer had convinced Brandeis that the great trusts were neither inevitable nor desirable. He believed that the largest of the concentrations of wealth and power were not "natural" developments but had resulted from the suppression of competition, "either by ruthless practices or by an improper use of inordinate wealth and power." He denied that the trusts were more efficient than the smaller firms that they had absorbed or driven out of business. In

fact, they were less efficient. He claimed, for example, that monopolistic enterprises were less innovative than other companies because "their secure
position frees them from the necessity which has always been the mother of
invention." A trust was also inefficient because its chief executive would never
be able to learn and consider carefully everything that a person in charge
needed to know in running a huge, unwieldy company. "There is a limit to
what one man can do well." Once a trust drove out its competition, the quality
of its products tended to decline while the prices charged for them tended to
go up. The trusts were like clumsy dinosaurs, which, if they ever had to face
real competition, would collapse of their own weight.[69]

Most serious of all was the harm that the great corporations were doing to
their own workers, which in embittering them had helped to provoke violence. "You cannot," declared Brandeis, "preserve political liberty unless some
degree of industrial liberty accompanies it." He was convinced that the trusts
were the most autocratic and exploitative of employers. In the steel industry,
for example, the standard work schedule was twelve hours per day, seven
days a week. By increasing hours while cutting wages, trusts such as U.S.
Steel "have stabbed industrial liberty in the back." The resulting unrest had
done great damage to business in provoking both strikes and illegal acts of
violence. The resort by certain laborers to acts of terrorism and sabotage reflected their belief "that the wage-earner, acting singly or collectively, is not
strong enough to secure substantial justice."[70]

Brandeis and the New Freedom

The question of the trusts carried over into the presidential campaign of 1912,
in which it became the central issue and part of a larger debate over the future
of the economic system and the role of the national government in American
life. As the year began, Brandeis was backing his friend and ally, Senator
Robert La Follette of Wisconsin, in the latter's ill-fated bid to wrest the Republican Party's presidential nomination from the grip of President Taft. After
Theodore Roosevelt declared his candidacy, nearly all of La Follette's supporters (but not Brandeis) deserted him for T.R., who was still a compelling
and popular figure. Although Taft was renominated by the Republican Party,
Roosevelt remained in the race as the candidate of the newly organized Progressive (or Bull Moose) Party. Meanwhile, the Democratic Party's national
convention adopted a progressive platform and gave its presidential nomination to Woodrow Wilson, the reform governor of New Jersey.

There were now two progressive candidates in the presidential race with
contrasting approaches to the problem of the trusts and other national questions. Roosevelt and his Progressives called their agenda the New Nationalism. To them, the trusts were the inevitable, natural outgrowth of economic
development and therefore an irreversible reality that would now have to be
thoroughly regulated by the federal government. There was also a paternalis-

tic streak in the new party, which called for welfare measures to assist working-class Americans, primarily at the local level but, if need be, at the federal level as well. In contrast, Wilson and the Democrats viewed the trusts as the result of the immoral, at times illegal, practices of certain ruthless business-men and of the special favors done for these men by obliging, often corrupt politicians. Under the banner of the New Freedom, Wilson and the Democrats proposed to destroy the trusts by ending the special privileges (such as the protective tariff) and the unfair business practices that had made them pos-sible. Were their program carried out, they argued, opportunity would be re-stored and there would be little need for social insurance or any federal role in providing it.[71]

To Brandeis, the foe of bigness in both business and government, the ap-proach of the Democrats seemed infinitely preferable to that of the new party. Soon after La Follette's withdrawal from the race, Brandeis began to urge his friends and associates to fall in behind Wilson. Following a friendly exchange of letters, the two men met on August 28 at Sea Girt, New Jersey, where they conferred for three hours on economic issues. As Mason has written, Brandeis had found "his captain." He came away from Sea Girt a confirmed admirer of Wilson, whom he described in letters to his friends as possessed of a remark-able mind and likely to make "an ideal president." As for Wilson, the meeting seems to have altered his basic approach to the trust question. Where previ-ously he had stressed the enforcement of the antitrust law, he now began to refer to "regulated competition," a concept that Brandeis had developed, as the essence of his program.[72]

Brandeis both spoke and wrote in Wilson's cause. In September and Octo-ber, he delivered more than two dozen speeches in the Northeast and Mid-west, addressing primarily labor groups and associations of professionals. His talks drew attention in the press and were replied to by rival partisans. In one of his speeches, he accused the Progressive Party of trying to serve both God and Mammon because he deemed it impossible for the Progressives to be both the party of social reform and of big business. In a speech delivered before the Massachusetts branch of the American Federation of Labor, Brandeis charged that Roosevelt's new party had accepted and defended the trusts, whose policy remained "the extermination of organized labor." When Roosevelt was wounded by a would-be assassin's bullet on October 14, Brandeis used the incident to advantage, arguing that it was a symptom of the declining respect for law and that the trust policy of Roosevelt's new party was adding to that tendency by proposing to "legalize that which had grown up illegally." The Roosevelt camp, understandably, cried foul, and it seems clear that Brandeis's fierce will to win when combined with his intellectual brilliance and lawyer's subtlety made him a formidable foe, whether in the courtroom or in a political campaign. Brandeis also attacked Roosevelt and his party through a series of articles published as unsigned editorials in *Collier's Magazine,* which was edited by Brandeis's friend, Norman Hapgood. When Robert Collier, who was trying to keep the magazine neutral in the election, learned that it was Brandeis who had written the editorials, he fired Hapgood.[73]

Of even greater importance to the Wilson campaign was the Boston lawyer's role as a source of ideas and advice. Late in September, Wilson asked him to "set forth explicitly the actual measures by which competition can be effectively regulated." In reply, Brandeis made two major suggestions: that the federal government should remove the uncertainties of the Sherman Act and that a commission be set up to investigate violations of the antitrust law and to assist in prosecuting those who violated it.[74]

Brandeis and Wilson's Presidency

Wilson won the election but fell well short of a majority of the popular vote. "You were yourself," he wrote to Brandeis, "a great part of the victory. It now remains for us to devote all our strength to making good." Wilson considered Brandeis for the post of attorney general and, a few weeks later, for secretary of commerce, but the loud outcry against the Boston lawyer made the president-elect hesitant about appointing him. Brandeis was called an enemy of business by corporation executives he had opposed in court, and was denounced as untrustworthy and unscrupulous by conservative Boston attorneys. The leaders of the regular Democratic organization in Boston, and in Massachusetts generally, also warned Wilson against appointing a man with so little loyalty to party. Although puzzled by the vehemence of the Boston lawyer's foes, Wilson finally concluded that Brandeis was simply too controversial a figure to appoint to his cabinet.[75]

Although passed over for the cabinet, Brandeis would exert considerable influence both within the administration and in Congress, where he continued to work closely with leading progressives. In the first year of Wilson's presidency, he played a key role in shaping the Federal Reserve Act. Since 1907, when a panic on Wall Street had nearly caused a financial collapse, it had been widely acknowledged that the nation's currency and banking systems needed reform. Early in 1913, Senator Carter Glass, a conservative Democrat from Virginia, who had studied the problem for several years, proposed a central banking system in which the president of the United States would choose six members of the central board, and private sector bankers would select the remaining three. In addition, the private banks would issue the currency. Wilson tentatively endorsed the Glass bill, but his secretary of state, William Jennings Bryan, the leader of the Democratic Party's progressive wing, denounced the measure as a betrayal of the platform on which Wilson had been elected. True to his Nebraska populist past, Bryan insisted that the president must appoint *all* the board members and that the government, not the banks, must control the supply of money and credit.

With the leaders of his party divided, Wilson turned for advice to Brandeis, whose economic expertise he respected. Brandeis sided with Bryan on the issue, maintaining that to restore competition, the power of the "money trust" must be broken, and claiming that the enactment of the Glass proposal would only strengthen the great banking houses. The aims of the financial interests, Brandeis argued, were incompatible with those of the administration. Therefore, to offer them concessions would be futile, and to follow their advice would be politically unwise as well as damaging to the cause of small business. According to Arthur Link, an outstanding authority on Wilson's presidency, Brandeis's arguments were decisive in breaking the deadlock on the banking issue. Wilson endorsed the Bryan-Brandeis approach, and in enacting the Federal Reserve Act, Congress adhered closely to the president's guidelines.[76]

In 1913, Brandeis wrote a series of articles for *Harper's Weekly* that analyzed the money trust and suggested ways of curbing its power. The material for the articles was drawn partly from the transcripts and final report of the investigation in 1912 of investment banking by a congressional committee headed by Arsene Pujo. Brandeis found in the hearing transcripts much that confirmed ideas on the trusts that he had already expressed in articles, speeches, and testimony before legislative committees and regulatory commissions. In 1914, the ten articles were brought together as a book entitled *Other People's Money—and How the Bankers Use It*. It received a mixed reception from reviewers, some of whom argued that Brandeis had neither demonstrated the validity of his criticisms of industrial bigness nor proven that there was in fact a money trust that was actively promoting economic concentration by denying to small business the credit that it needed to survive and prosper. Historian Lewis Paper contends that Brandeis raised more questions than he answered in *Other People's Money* and presented few concrete facts in arguing his case. Brandeis himself seems, at least temporarily, to have become disenchanted with the book, writing in a letter to his wife in 1915 that *"Other People's Money* seems pretty stupid now."[77]

In the later months of 1913, Brandeis, like most progressives, was urging the Wilson administration to develop and present to Congress its proposals for new antitrust legislation. The president, offering his antitrust agenda in an address before a joint session of Congress in early January 1914, announced, "the antagonism between business and government is over." Shortly thereafter, three of Wilson's proposals were combined into a single measure that was introduced in the House of Representatives by Congressman Henry Clayton, an Alabama Democrat. Brandeis was delighted that several of the bill's provisions related to points that he had made in his writings and speeches over the previous four years and had also mentioned to Wilson during the 1912 campaign. As originally drafted, Clayton's bill specifically permitted private parties to cite government findings when suing a firm for damages resulting from anticompetitive practices. It also banned interlocking directorates of all kinds and outlawed "tying clauses" in business contracts (in which a supplier requires, as a condition of doing business, that his customers agree to buy products of the kind that he makes or sells exclusively from him). Brandeis had learned of the latter tactic through personal experience in the course of his law practice and had, of course, strongly denounced interlocking directorates in *Other People's Money*. Unfortunately, the version of the bill that was enacted by Congress in October 1914 was far weaker than the original measure, due to the numerous amendments and qualifiers that had been added by the Congress. For example, instead of simply banning interlocking directorates, the actual statute banned them only "where the effect may be to substantially limit competition."[78]

Wilson's January message had also endorsed the concept of an interstate trade commission, and a bill of which Brandeis was the principal draftsman was soon written, calling for a commission that would investigate the practices of American business while assisting the Department of Justice in enforcing the antitrust laws. To many progressive, however, a mechanism of this sort seemed far too limited to be able to tame, or even to cope with, the trusts. George Rublee, a young lawyer who had worked with Brandeis in other legal battles, prepared an alternative measure, the Stevens bill (named after its legislative sponsor, Congressman Raymond B. Stevens, a Democrat from New Hampshire). This measure called for a basic strengthening of the commission, replacing Brandeis's catalogue of "anticompetitive" offenses with a broad statement that prohibited "unfair practices" without trying to name them all. The commission was also to be granted the power to issue "cease and desist" orders that would have the force of law. On June 10, Wilson conferred at the White House with Rublee, Stevens, and Brandeis. After Rublee had explained his bill, Brandeis declared it superior to his own and Wilson pledged that he would make it the cornerstone of his antitrust policy. After more than two months of strenuous lobbying by Brandeis and Rublee and of "arm-twisting" and partisan appeals by Wilson, Congress enacted the Federal Trade Commission (FTC) bill largely in the form that Rublee had given it.[79]

Within less than a year, Brandeis, Rublee, and progressives generally were thoroughly disappointed by the performance of the FTC. Brandeis blamed the agency's poor showing on the fact that Wilson had named chiefly businessmen to the commission who regarded it as their proper role to work with businessmen rather than criticize or discipline them. When Wilson attempted to add Rublee to the FTC, the U.S. Senate rejected the nomination.[80]

The fact is that Brandeis was far more critical of big business than Wilson was. To the president, corporate wrongdoing was due chiefly to the sins of individuals. If the excesses of the trusts and the monopolists were curbed, then enterprising and talented individuals would again be able to prosper and to advance. To "the people's lawyer," however, it was not so much individuals who were at fault as it was a system, which structured their behavior in antisocial and destructive ways. "The important thing," he told a congressional committee, "is to prevent rather than to punish . . . industrial crime is not a cause, it is an effect—the effect of a bad system."[81]

By the autumn of 1914, Wilson believed that the basic agenda of the New Freedom had been accomplished. The president was now drawing closer to the business community, appointing, for example, private bankers to the Federal Reserve Board, a policy Brandeis disliked. With the structural reforms of the New Freedom in place, Brandeis found that his influence on the administration was no longer as strong as it had been during its first year. The two men remained on good terms, however, and during Wilson's second term, he sought Brandeis's views on issues relating to diplomacy and, specifically, on questions relating to the League of Nations.[82]

Brandeis Joins the Court

In 1916, Wilson demonstrated his faith in Brandeis in nominating him to the Supreme Court, a decision that was, as we have already seen, bitterly contested and denounced. Spearheading the opposition to Brandeis's nomination were conservative Republicans, both in and out of office. Senator Henry Cabot Lodge, representing Brandeis's home state of Massachusetts, wrote dozens of letters in opposition to his joining the Supreme Court. So did former president Taft, who remembered with bitterness how in the Ballinger-Pinchot affair the attorney had called into question Taft's own credibility and damaged his administration politically. "He is a muckraker," wrote Taft to a friend, "an emotionalist, a socialist . . . a hypocrite, a man of infinite cunning, of great tenacity of purpose and in my judgment, of much power for evil."[83]

Much of the opposition came from the legal profession. Seven former presidents of the American Bar Association, including Taft and Senator Elihu Root of New York, joined in declaring Brandeis unfit to serve on the Supreme Court. Prominent attorneys from Boston asserted that Brandeis was regarded in that city as a good but untrustworthy lawyer. Old cases were dredged up in which it was claimed that he had betrayed the interests of his clients.

What Brandeis's opponents most objected to was his "radicalism." "In all the anti-corporation agitation of the past," declared the *Wall Street Journal,* "one name stands out . . . where others were radical, he was rabid." Somewhat more reasonably, the *New York Times* noted that Brandeis was essentially a reformer and therefore a partisan rather than a judge. Such a man could not possibly possess, argued the *Times* and other newspapers, the dispassionate temperament that is required of a judge.[84]

Although a few of the opponents of confirmation did engage in anti-Semitic slurs, Brandeis's Judaism seems to have played only a minor role in the battle. Certain conservative Jews, such as Jacob Schiff, in fact, were privately opposed to confirmation though publicly in favor of it. Moreover, Brandeis's foes were fearful that his Judaism might actually work in his favor because those opposed to confirmation would be in danger of being thought anti-Semitic.[85]

Those in favor of confirmation were at least as numerous and, arguably, just as influential as their foes. Many lawyers, social workers, and reformers with whom Brandeis had worked testified eagerly in his behalf. Roscoe Pound, a professor of law at Harvard, remarked to the committee that Brandeis was "one of the great lawyers" and predicted that he would one day rank "with the best who have sat upon the bench of the Supreme Court." The lawyers who favored him pointed out that Brandeis had angered some of his clients by his conscientious striving to be fair to both sides in a case, that, in fact, his approach to the law had always been judicial rather than one-sided.[86]

Politically, President Wilson stood firmly behind his nominee, pressuring the Senate Democrats and quietly lobbying for the support of the progressive Republican bloc led by Bob La Follette. Newspapers and periodicals of the progressive persuasion, in some of which Brandeis had earlier published articles, also rallied to his support. On the whole, however, the advocates of Brandeis were forced to wage a defensive battle in answering the charges that had been raised by their opponents. Although he was active behind the scenes, Brandeis said nothing publicly and in fact was persuaded by his friends to stay out of Washington while the hearings were going on. It was the strategy of the Brandeis forces to play down both the Jewish and progressive aspects of the nomination struggle. They emphasized instead that the selection of Brandeis for the high court was the stand in an election year of a Democratic president, and it therefore deserved the support of Democratic senators.

On June 2, after four months of controversy, the Judiciary Committee voted ten to eight along strictly partisan lines to confirm the nomination of Brandeis to the Court. Had even one of the Democrats on the committee defected, Brandeis would have been kept off the Court. On June 10, the Senate officially confirmed the nomination by a vote of 47 to 22. With the exception of Senator Newlands, every Democrat who was present voted to confirm, as did three Republican progressives: La Follette, George Norris of Nebraska, and Miles Poindexter of Washington.[87]

The elevation of Brandeis to the Supreme Court brought to a sudden close the second phase of his career, when, as the "people's lawyer," he had been a leading figure in the nationwide movement of reform. A brilliant lawyer, he had evolved also into an effective writer, lecturer, and organizer of reformist coalitions. He became as well a creative theorist of reform, originating savings bank insurance, the preferential union shop, and the "Brandeis brief," and was an architect of the New Freedom second in importance only to Wilson himself. In joining the Court, he embarked on a new career in which he would become one of the most famous and influential figures ever to serve on it.

Brandeis and the Court

As a member of the Supreme Court, Brandeis preached and usually practiced a policy of judicial self-restraint. The Court, he maintained, should normally presume that new legislation was constitutional, and the burden of proof should be placed on those who challenged a law's validity. Moreover, the Court should usually base its rulings on the common law and on enacted statutes, dealing with constitutional questions only when that was essential to deciding the case before it.[88]

Brandeis advocated judicial restraint in part out of a desire to strengthen the power of the states. There must be latitude for experimentation, he argued, if the law was to cope effectively with economic and social change. In *Liggett* v. *Lee* (1933), for example, Brandeis dissented when the Court declared unconstitutional a Florida law that taxed retail stores more heavily when they were part of a multistore chain than when they were individually owned and independent, and more heavily still when the retail chain to which the store belonged operated in more than a single county. Not only did Brandeis vote to sustain this openly discriminatory law, but he also made it clear that he approved warmly of its purpose: to place a limit upon the size of companies engaged in retailing in Florida. "The State . . . may prefer," he wrote, "the way of cooperation which leads directly to the freedom and the equality of opportunity, which the Fourteenth Amendment aims to secure."[89]

The same Brandeis who thought it essential (as well as constitutional) that government have the power to regulate business believed that public agencies lacked the power under the Constitution to restrict freedom of speech or assembly except in cases of "clear and present danger." The latter phrase is, of course, the principle first stated by Justice Oliver Wendell Holmes in *Schenk* v. *United States,* a 1919 decision with which Brandeis had concurred. In various cases during the 1920s, however, he sought to limit the ability of government to restrict free expression. In his *Gilbert* v. *Minnesota* dissent in 1920, he suggested that the Fourteenth Amendment might be used to secure basic civil liberties against the states. In 1927, Brandeis wrote a concurring opinion in *Whitney* v. *California* in which he redefined "clear and present danger" as a threat to the public safety that was both "serious" and "imminent." Anything short of that standard, according to him, could never justify measures of repression under a Constitution whose authors "believed that freedom to think as you will, and to speak as you think, are means indispensable to the discovery and spread of political truth."[90]

In *Olmstead* v. *United States* (1928), Brandeis wrote another memorable dissent in which he objected to the invasion of privacy by unauthorized wiretapping. In this case, federal prohibition agents had used a wiretap to gather evidence against a group of convicted bootleggers without physically entering any of their homes or offices. Brandeis warned that future breakthroughs in technology might permit government to spy on even the most private aspects of people's lives. The Constitution, he declared, confers on every citizen "the right to be let alone—the most comprehensive of rights and the right most valued by civilized men."[91]

With his ascension to the Court, Brandeis decided that it would be improper for him to remain active as a publicist, lecturer, and writer. Although he no longer participated publicly in politics, he continued to exert influence behind the scenes. During Wilson's second term as president, Brandeis advised him secretly on various issues, and in the 1930s, he fed ideas to President Franklin Roosevelt through their mutual friend, Dean Felix Frankfurter of the Harvard Law School, and the scores of young lawyers that the latter recruited for the New Deal. It is now well known that Brandeis gave Frankfurter thousands of dollars over the years so that his friend could afford to remain at his influential post at Harvard rather than go into private practice.[92]

Brandeis and the New Deal

Brandeis had mixed feelings about the programs inaugurated by Roosevelt's New Deal in the 1930s. Like the New Dealers, he believed that the nation's economy should be reformed by national legislation, but he opposed national planning as beyond the capacities of the government and its officials. As the onetime people's attorney, he found it easy to support the regulation of financial institutions and securities markets. (*Other People's Money*, his 1914 exposé of investment banking, was widely read by New Deal officials.) Brandeis's favorite New Deal measure was the Tennessee Valley Authority. He appreciated its localized approach and its expressed intention of applying a "yardstick" to the rates charged by privately owned public utilities. Brandeis was also sympathetic toward such New Deal innovations as Social Security, unemployment insurance, and expenditure for public works, all of which addressed problems in which he had long been interested.[93]

During Roosevelt's first term, the Supreme Court nullified several New Deal measures, but Brandeis voted to strike down only two: the National Industrial Recovery Act (NIRA) and the Frazier-Lemke Act. The NIRA was a national planning measure that attempted to stabilize industrial conditions by setting up codes of fair practice to limit within each industry the intensity of competition. In *Schechter Brothers* v. *The United States* (1935), the Court voted unanimously to declare NIRA unconstitutional on the grounds that it gave to the president "an unfettered discretion" to make whatever laws he thought were needed for economic recovery.

In *Louisville* v. *Radford,* announced on the same day as the NIRA decision, Brandeis, speaking for a unanimous court, declared the Frazier-Lemke Act unconstitutional. This law had attempted to prevent struggling farmers from having the mortgages on their farms foreclosed. Under it, foreclosures could be halted for five years and farm mortgages taken over by bankruptcy courts, which would then set a schedule of repayment for the farmers they assisted. Brandeis maintained that the Frazier-Lemke law violated the Fifth Amendment because it deprived the mortgage-issuing banks of their property without due process of law. "The Fifth Amendment," he declared, "commands that, however great the Nation's need, private property shall not be thus taken over without just compensation."[94]

Brandeis was also opposed to Roosevelt's court reorganization bill, which proposed to add one additional justice to the Supreme Court for every sitting member who had reached the age of seventy without retiring. This was, of course, a thinly veiled attempt to change the decisions of the Court by adding new members who were supporters of the New Deal. Brandeis, who revered the Court, was not alone in thinking that Roosevelt's scheme threatened the integrity of the institution. Although he did not speak out publicly against the measure, Brandeis helped nonetheless to bring about its defeat. He suggested to Senator Burton K. Wheeler, a Democrat from Montana, who led the opposition to the Court plan in the Senate, that he ask Chief Justice Charles Evans Hughes to comment on the president's claim that the present Court could not keep up with its workload. Hughes's letter contradicting the president's statement (written, Hughes claimed, with the concurrence of Justices Brandeis and Willis Van Devanter) helped to turn the tide against the bill. On May 18, 1937, the Senate Judiciary Committee rejected the court-packing plan, and by the summer the proposal was dead.[95]

Brandeis's last important judicial opinion proved to be one of the most significant of his career. In *Erie Railroad Co.* v. *Tompkins* (1938), a resident of Pennsylvania had sued the railroad for negligence after one of its passing railway cars severed his right arm while he was walking along the railroad's right of way. This case furnished the occasion for a decision that overruled the doctrine of *Swift* v. *Tyson* (1842) that in lawsuits where the parties are from different states, federal judges are free to exercise an independent judgment based on "general law" rather than follow the common law as practiced in a particular state. Speaking for the court, Brandeis ruled that the ninety-six-year-old doctrine of *Smith* v. *Tyson* was fundamentally in error. There was in fact, he insisted, no such thing as federal general common law. In cases such as *Erie* v. *Tompkins,* the federal courts should apply the law of the state in which the accident took place, in this instance, Pennsylvania. This ruling fits in well, of course, with Brandeis's goals of strengthening the states and reversing the long-term trend toward centralization and bigness.[96]

In February 1939, Brandeis retired from the Supreme Court, and on October 5, 1941, he died following a heart attack. He had lived to see many of the ideas that he had championed become the law of the land. Wages and hours legislation were now accepted as constitutional, and the right of labor to organize was protected by law. The federal government was beginning a system of old-age pensions under Social Security, while at the state level there were new and expanding programs of social welfare and unemployment insurance. Although the nation has not reversed its long-term drift toward bigness in industry and government, these trends have been increasingly criticized in recent years. Finally, Brandeis's spirited, eloquent defense of free speech and the right to privacy have had a continuing, powerful influence upon the Supreme Court and, ultimately, upon the life of the entire nation.

Notes

1. Alpheus Thomas Mason, *Brandeis: A Free Man's Life* (New York: Viking Press, 1946), 11–12; Philippa Strum, *Louis D. Brandeis: Justice for the People* (Cambridge: Harvard University Press, 1984), 1–2.

2. Stephen W. Baskerville, *Of Laws and Limitations: An Intellectual Portrait of Louis Dembitz Brandeis* (Rutherford, NJ: Fairleigh Dickinson University Press, 1994), 38–40; Mason, *Brandeis*, 13–14; Strum, *Louis D. Brandeis*, 2–5.

3. The quotation of Amelia Wehle is in Baskerville, *Of Laws and Limitations*, 32.

4. Ibid., 33–35; Mason, *Brandeis*, 15–16.

5. The Adolph Brandeis quote is in Mason, *Brandeis*, 16; Baskerville, *Of Laws and Limitations*, 35–36; Alfred Lief, *Brandeis: The Personal History of An American Ideal* (New York: Stackpole Sons, 1936), 16.

6. Lewis J. Paper, *Brandeis* (Englewood Cliffs, NJ: Prentice Hall, 1983), 8–9; Strum, *Louis D. Brandeis*, 6–7; Mason, *Brandeis*, 23.

7. Paper, *Brandeis*, 20; Lief, *Brandeis*, 17–18.

8. Mason, *Brandeis*, 23–25; Lief, *Brandeis*, 15.

9. Lief, *Brandeis*, 18; Baskerville, *Of Laws and Limitations*, 49–53; Mason, *Brandeis*, 26–27.

10. The quotation of Frederika Brandeis is in Mason, *Brandeis*, 28; Allon Gal, *Brandeis of Boston* (Cambridge: Harvard University Press, 1980), 72; Strum, *Louis D. Brandeis*, 9–10.

11. Paper, *Brandeis*, 11; Strum, *Louis D. Brandeis*, 10; Lief, *Brandeis*, 18–19.

12. Paper, *Brandeis*, 12; Lief, *Brandeis*, 18; Baskerville, *Of Law and Limitations*, 51, 58–59; Mason, *Brandeis*, 28; Strum, *Louis D. Brandeis*, 11–12.

13. Quotation is from Mason, *Brandeis*, 47; Louis Brandeis to Otto Wehle, March 12, 1876, in Melvin I. Urofsky and David Levy, *Letters of Louis Brandeis* (cited hereafter as *Letters*) 5 vols. (Albany, NY: State University of New York Press, 1972–78), 1, 5–6; Louis Brandeis to Alfred Brandeis, 28 June 1878, *Letters*, 1: 24; Lief, *Brandeis*, 20–21.

14. Brandeis quoted in Mason, *Brandeis*, 47; Paper, *Brandeis*, 14–17.

15. Louis Brandeis to Samuel D. Warren, May 30, 1879, *Letters*, 1: 35; idem, 36, footnote 1; Mason, *Brandeis*, 54–55.

16. Louis Brandeis to Charles Nagel, July 12, 1879, *Letters*, 1: 39; Louis Brandeis to Alfred Brandeis, July 31, 1879, *Letters* 1: 44.

17. Strum, *Louis D. Brandeis*, 33; Gal, *Brandeis of Boston*, 31–43.

18. Quoted from Louis Brandeis to Alfred Brandeis, March 21, 1887, *Letters* 1: 72–73; the Fuller quote is in Lief, *Brandeis*, 28; Edward F. McClennen, "Louis D. Brandeis as a Lawyer," *Massachusetts Law Quarterly* 33 (1948): 14.

19. Quote is in Mason, *Brandeis*, 86; Strum, *Louis D. Brandeis*, 40, 159–60; Mason, *Brandeis*, 183–184.

20. The "square deal" statement is quoted in Mason, *Brandeis*, 233; see also 220–229, 235–237; Strum, *Louis D. Brandeis*, 40; McClennen, "Louis D. Brandeis as a Lawyer," 3.

21. Mason, *Brandeis*, 89; Melvin I. Urofsky, *A Mind of One Piece: Brandeis and American Reform* (New York: Scribner, 1971), 12–13; Gal, *Brandeis of Boston*, 9–14.

22. Samuel D. Warren and Louis D. Brandeis, "The Watuppa Pond Cases," *Harvard Law Review* 2 (1888): 211.

23. Samuel D. Warren and Louis D. Brandeis, "The Right to Privacy," *Harvard Law Review* 4 (1889–1890), reprinted in Louis D. Brandeis, *The Curse of Bigness*, ed. Osmond K. Frankel and Clarence M. Lewis (Port Washington, NY: Kennikat Press, 1965), 309, footnote 40.

24. McClennen, "Louis D. Brandeis as a Lawyer," 17; Paper, *Brandeis*, 49–52; Mason, *Brandeis*, 82–86.

25. Baskerville, *Of Laws and Limitation*, 119–129; Lief, 34–37; Mason, *Brandeis*, 89–90.

26. Louis Brandeis to Amy Brandeis Wehle, January 2, 1881, *Letters* 1: 62; Mason, *Brandeis*, 72–78; Lief, *Brandeis*, 46–47.

27. Strum, *Louis D. Brandeis*, 45–49; Mason, *Brandeis*, 79–81; Lief, Brandeis, 47, 107; Gal, *Brandeis of Boston*, 38–40.

28. Quoted from Louis Brandeis to Alfred Brandeis, July 28, 1904, *Letters* 1: 262–263; Gal, *Brandeis of Boston,* 26; Paper, *Brandeis,* 53–54.

29. Quoted by Paper, *Brandeis,* 39–40; Lief, *Brandeis,* 52–54; Baskerville, *Of Laws and Limitations,* 128.

30. Louis Brandeis to Edwin Doak Mead, November 9, 1985, *Letters* 1: 121–123; Baskerville, *Of Laws and Limitations,* 114–116.

31. Gal, *Brandeis of Boston,* 56–58; Strum, *Louis D. Brandeis,* 94, 226; Paper, *Brandeis,* 64, 163.

32. Brandeis to Edward A. Filene, June 1, 1901, in *Letters* 1: 169–170; Strum, *Louis D. Brandeis,* 57–61; Paper, *Brandeis,* 55–62; Gal, *Brandeis of Boston,* 47–49; Lief, *Brandeis,* 64–69; Mason, *Brandeis,* Chapter 7.

33. Lief, *Brandeis,* 70; Paper, *Brandeis,* 63–64.

34. Quoted in Mason, *Brandeis,* 121; Lief, *Brandeis,* 69–75; Strum, *Louis D. Brandeis,* 65–66.

35. Mason, *Brandeis,* 125–127; Paper, *Brandeis,* 69–71; Strum, *Louis D. Brandeis,* 67–68.

36. Louis Brandeis to Alfred Brandeis, May 27, 1906, *Letters* 1, 438; Paper, *Brandeis,* 70–79; Strum, *Louis D. Brandeis,* 68–73.

37. Mason, *Brandeis,* 148, 158; Paper, *Brandeis,* 51; Urofsky, *A Mind of One Piece,* 30–31.

38. Strum, *Louis D. Brandeis,* 76–77; Mason, *Brandeis,* 153; Louis D. Brandeis, "Life Insurance: The Abuses and the Remedies," a 1905 speech, reprinted in Brandeis, *Business: A Profession* (New York: Augustus M. Kelley, 1971), 108–153; Louis D. Brandeis, "Wage-Earners' Life Insurance," a 1906 article reprinted in Brandeis, *The Curse of Bigness,* 3–17; "Savings Bank Insurance," 1907 article, reprinted in Brandeis, *Business: A Profession,* 163–165.

39. Quote is from Brandeis, "Wage-Earners' Life Insurance," 12; Gal, *Brandeis of Boston,* 97–98; Paper, *Brandeis* 88–89; Mason, *Brandeis,* 164.

40. Quoted by Mason, *Brandeis,* 166; Strum, *Louis D. Brandeis,* 85–87.

41. Lief, *Brandeis,* 102–104, Paper, *Brandeis,* 89–91; Mason, *Brandeis,* 166–171.

42. Louis Brandeis, "The Road to Social Efficiency," a 1911 article reprinted in Brandeis, *Business: A Profession,* 51–64; Mason, *Brandeis,* 172–177; Strum, *Louis D. Brandeis,* 87–93.

43. John L. Weller, *The New Haven Railroad: Its Rise and Fall* (New York: Hastings House, 1969), 41–52; Paper, *Brandeis,* 93–95; Mason, *Brandeis,* 177–179.

44. Mason, *Brandeis,* 177–180; Lief, *Brandeis,* 119–120; Strum, *Louis D. Brandeis,* 159; Paper, *Brandeis,* 92–98.

45. Louis Brandeis to Alfred Brandeis, January 2, 1908, *Letters* 2: 61; Mason, *Brandeis,* 185–188; Paper, *Brandeis,* 97–100.

46. Quoted statement is from Louis Brandeis, "The New England Transportation Monopoly," in Brandeis, *Business: A Profession,* 268; Strum, *Louis D. Brandeis,* 159; Paper, *Brandeis,* 100–101; Mason, *Brandeis,* 187–188; Lief, *Brandeis,* 117–123.

47. Mason, *Brandeis,* 188–193; Paper, *Brandeis,* 101–102.

48. Mason, *Brandeis,* 193–198, 205; Paper, *Brandeis,* 102–105; Lief, *Brandeis,* 151–155.

49. Weller, *The New Haven Railroad: Its Rise and Fall,* 49–154; Lief, *Brandeis,* 154; Mason, *Brandeis,* 199–203; Paper, *Brandeis,* 105–108.

50. Paper, *Brandeis,* 105–111; Mason, *Brandeis,* 203–214; Louis D. Brandeis, "The New Haven—An Unregulated Monopoly," a 1912 article reprinted in Brandeis, *Business: A Profession,* 279–305.

51. Quoted passage is in Louis Brandeis, "The Opportunity in the Law," reprinted in Brandeis, *Business: A Profession,* 321; see also "The Living Law," in Brandeis, *The Curse of Bigness,* 316–326.

52. Strum, *Louis D. Brandeis,* 120–121; Mason, *Brandeis,* 248–250; Paper, *Brandeis,* 161–165.

53. Paper, *Brandeis,* 165–166; Mason, *Brandeis,* 250–253.

54. Quotation is from Louis D. Brandeis, "The Employer and Trades Unions," a speech delivered before the Boston Typothetae on April 21, 1904, reprinted in Brandeis *Business: A Profession,* 17.

55. Ibid., 14–16, 22–27; Mason, *Brandeis,* 142–143, 301.

56. Marshall quote is in Mason, *Brandeis,* 300; Moses Rischin, *The Promised City* (New York: Corinth Books, 1962), 251–252; Irving Howe, *The World of Our Fathers* (New York: Simon and Schuster, 1976), 307–308.

57. Louis Brandeis to Lawrence Abbott, September 6, 1910, *Letters*, vol. 2: 371–372.

58. Lief, *Brandeis*, 188–190; Paper, *Brandeis*, 140–141; Howe, *The World of Our Fathers*, 301–303.

59. Howe, *The World of Our Fathers*, 303; Paper, *Brandeis*, 141–144; Strum, *Louis D. Brandeis*, 177–178.

60. Mason, *Brandeis*, 254–256; Paper, *Brandeis*, 111–117; Lief, *Brandeis*, 157–158; Strum, *Louis D. Brandeis*, 132–133.

61. Mason, *Brandeis*, 256–258; Lief, *Brandeis*, 158–159.

62. Mason, *Brandeis*, 271–275; Strum, *Louis D. Brandeis*, 134–137; Paper, *Brandeis*, 130–131; Lief, *Brandeis*, 164–172.

63. Lief, *Brandeis*, 175; Strum, *Louis D. Brandeis*, 137–138; Paper, *Brandeis*, 130–131; Mason, *Brandeis*, 279–281.

64. Paper, *Brandeis*, 127, 131; Baskerville, *Of Laws and Limitations*, 157; Louis Brandeis to Alfred Brandeis, May 1, 1910, in *Letters*, 2: 332.

65. Strum, *Louis D. Brandeis*, 139–144; Paper, *Brandeis*, 133–134; Mason, *Brandeis*, 287–289.

66. Louis D. Brandeis to Edwin Doak Mead, November 9, 1895, *Letters*, 1: 121–123.

67. George Mowry, *The Era of Theodore Roosevelt and the Birth of Modern America* (New York: Harper and Row, 1958), 121–134, 286–290.

68. Ibid., 293–294; Baskerville, *Of Laws and Limitations*, 168, 182–183; Louis D. Brandeis, "Shall We Abandon the Policy of Competition?" a 1912 article reprinted in Brandeis, *The Curse of Bigness*, 104–105; Louis D. Brandeis, "The Solution of the Trust Problem," a 1913 article reprinted in *The Curse of Bigness*, 129–131.

69. "Improper use" quotation is in Brandeis, "Shall We Abandon the Policy of Competition?" 105; see also Louis D. Brandeis, "Competition," a 1913 article reprinted in Brandeis, *The Curse of Bigness*, 112–124; Mason, *Brandeis*, 354–356.

70. Quoted by Donald R. Richberg, "The Industrial Liberalism of Justice Brandeis," *The Brandeis Reader*, ed. Ervin H. Pollock (New York: Oceana Publications, 1956), 216–217; "wage-earner" quote is in Brandeis, "Shall We Abandon the Policy of Competition?" 107.

71. Arthur S. Link, *Woodrow Wilson and the Progressive Era, 1910–1917* (New York: Harper and Row, 1954), 1–24; Lief, *Brandeis*, 248–253.

72. Paper, *Brandeis*, 176; Lief, *Brandeis*, 250–251; Mason, *Brandeis*, 375–377; Baskerville, *Of Laws and Limitations*, 183; Strum, *Louis D. Brandeis*, 198–199.

73. Paper, *Brandeis*, 177; Lief, *Brandeis*, 251–252; Strum, *Louis D. Brandeis*, 200–201.

74. *Letters*, 2: 688–694; Strum, 198–199; Baskerville, 185–187.

75. Quoted in Lief, *Brandeis*, 257–258; Ibid., 259–261; Strum, *Louis D. Brandeis*, 206–208; Paper, *Brandeis*, 179–180; Mason, *Brandeis*, Chapter 25.

76. Albert S. Link, *Wilson: The New Freedom* (Princeton, NJ: Princeton University Press, 1953), 28–31; Lief, *Brandeis*, 274–275; Paper, *Brandeis*, 184–185; Louis Brandeis to Woodrow Wilson, June 13, 1913, in *Letters* 3: 113–116.

77. Strum, *Louis D. Brandeis*, 211–214; *Letters*, 3: 185–186, 259: Paper, *Brandeis*, 187–188; Baskerville, *Of Laws and Limitations*, 315–316; Lief, *Brandeis*, 282–286; Mason, *Brandeis*, 408–421.

78. Link, *Woodrow Wilson and the Progressive Era*, 67–72; Lief, *Brandeis*, 287–292; Mason, *Brandeis*, 400–401; Paper, *Brandeis*, 190–191.

79. Mason, *Brandeis*, 401–404; Lief, *Brandeis*, 287–290; Paper, *Brandeis*, 191–193; Link, *Woodrow Wilson and the Progressive Era*, 71–74.

80. Mason, *Brandeis*, 406–407; Lief, *Brandeis*, 335–337; Link, *Woodrow Wilson and the Progressive Era*, 71–74; Paper, *Brandeis*, 191–194.

81. Quoted in Mason, *Brandeis*, 402; idem, 403, 406–407; Strum, *Louis D. Brandeis*, 212–216; Paper, *Brandeis*, 193–194.

82. Strum, *Louis D. Brandeis*, 216–218; Link, *Woodrow Wilson and the Progressive Era*, 78–80.

83. The Taft quotation is in Mason, *Brandeis*, 470; idem, 465–469; Paper, *Brandeis*, 212–214; Alden L. Todd, *Justice on Trial: The Case of Louis D. Brandeis* (New York: McGraw-Hill, 1964), 55–86.

84. Quoted in Todd, *Justice on Trial*, 73; Mason, *Brandeis*, 470–475, 489; Strum, *Louis D. Brandeis*, 297.

85. Strum, *Louis D. Brandeis,* 294; Paper, *Brandeis,* 214.

86. Quoted in Todd, *Justice on Trial,* 208; idem, 52.

87. Strum, *Louis D. Brandeis,* 298–299; Mason, *Brandeis,* 491–508; Paper, *Brandeis,* 233–238.

88. Philippa Strum, "Brandeis and the Living Constitution," in Nelson L. Dawson, ed., *Brandeis and America* (Lexington: University Press of Kentucky, 1989), 122–124; Baskerville, *Of Laws and Limitations,* 239–242; Mason, *Brandeis,* 576–581.

89. *Liggett Co.* v. *Lee* (1933), 288 U.S. 517, 579.

90. The quotation is from Brandeis's concurring opinion in *Whitney* v. *California* (1927), 274 U.S. 357, 375; see also *Gilbert* v. *Minnesota* (1920), 254 U.S. 325, 335–338; see Mason, *Brandeis,* 564–566.

91. *Olmstead* v. *United States* (1928), 277 U.S. 438, 478–479.

92. Leonard Baker, *Brandeis and Frankfurter: A Dual Biography* (New York: Harper and Row, 1984), 241–244; Bruce Allen Murphy, *The Brandeis/Frankfurter Connection* (New York: Oxford University Press, 1982), 10–11, 41–44; David J. Danelski, "The Propriety of Brandeis's Extrajudicial Conduct," in Dawson, ed., *Brandeis and America,* 21–29; Nelson L. Dawson, "Brandeis and the New Deal," in Dawson, ed., *Brandeis and America,* 41–50.

93. Philippa Strum, *Brandeis: Beyond Progressivism* (Lawrence, KS: University of Kansas Press, 1993), 90–96; Dawson, "Brandeis and the New Deal," 44–50; Mason, *Brandeis,* 615, 620.

94. Lief, *Brandeis,* 465–466; Mason, *Brandeis,* 615–620; Strum, *Louis D. Brandeis,* 351–353.

95. Dawson, "Brandeis and the New Deal," 50–53; Paper, *Brandeis,* 366–371.

96. Paper, *Brandeis,* 378–385; Melvin I. Urofsky, "The Brandeis Agenda," in Dawson, ed., *Brandeis and America,* 144; *Erie Railroad Co.* v. *Tompkins* (1938), 304 U.S. 64, 69–80.

Selected Cases

Muller v. Oregon (1908)
208 U.S. 412

This famous case originated on February 19, 1903, when the Oregon legislature passed a law limiting to ten the hours that could be worked in any given day by a female employee in a factory, mechanized workshop, or laundry. In 1905, Curt Muller, the owner of a large laundry in Portland, was convicted of violating the statute and fined ten dollars. Muller appealed to the Oregon Supreme Court, which affirmed his conviction. He then appealed to the United States Supreme Court on a writ of error, and it agreed to hear the appeal.

The attorneys for both sides agreed that every person under the constitution had the right to purchase someone's labor and to sell his or her own. It was also agreed that these rights were not absolute, but could be restricted where necessary to protect the health, safety, or morals of the community and/or the individuals of which it was composed.

The issue over which the two sides clashed was whether the Oregon ten-hours law was in actual fact protective of the community's physical and moral health. Muller denied that there was any connection between the hours worked by female tailors and the well-being of the wider community. According to the plaintiff's lawyers, the Oregon measure was simply an arbitrary and unreasonable infringement by the state of people's rights under the "due process" and "privileges and immunities" clauses of the Fourteenth Amendment.

The National Consumer's League secured the services of Brandeis, and the Oregon authorities agreed to put him in charge of the Muller case. He decided to document as thoroughly as possible the harm done by excessive hours to female workers and, as a result, to society at large. The legal reasoning in his brief took up less than three pages. The remainder of the brief, comprising more than 100 pages, consisted of factual data.

Among the facts presented were the laws limiting the working hours of women that had been enacted by eighteen states and five European nations. The brief also excerpted many reports by legislative communities, bureaus of statistics, and other official agencies, all of which indicated that long hours of labor were harmful to women. (Brandeis would later characterize his Muller brief as "what everyone knows.")

Speaking through Justice David Brewer, the Court, in a unanimous ruling, found the Oregon law constitutional. Mentioning Brandeis by name (a rarity in Supreme Court decisions), Brewer observed that his brief had demonstrated that many legislators and officials believed that the health and morals of woman workers were injured when their hours of toil were excessive. Moreover, the difference between the sexes in physical structure, according to Brewer, justified a difference in legislation. "She is properly placed," he wrote, "in a class by herself and legislation for her protection may be sustained, even when like legislation is not necessary for men and could not be sustained."

Ritchie v. Wayman (1910)
224 Ill. 508

In 1895, the Supreme Court of Illinois in *People* v. *Ritchie* declared invalid the law limiting to eight hours the workday of female manufacturing workers. The Illinois court found that the eight-hour statute was in conflict with both the state constitution and the Fourteenth Amendment to the U.S. Constitution.

After the Muller decision, however, Illinois and several other states enacted new maximum hour legislation for women. In September 1909, an Illinois court issued an injunction against the enforcement of the state's new ten-hours law. It was W.C. Ritchie, the same man who had successfully challenged the eight-hours act of the 1890s, who had obtained the court order and was now challenging the constitutionality of the new law.

The National Consumer's League asked Brandeis to defend the challenged statute in the Illinois courts. As in the Muller case, Brandeis's brief contained only a few pages of legal argument and many more of factual data. Drawing on information provided by the National Consumer's League and developed in particular by his cousin, Josephine Goldmark, his brief comprised some 600 pages of material gleaned from official archival sources in both America and Europe.

In April 1910, the Illinois Supreme Court upheld the validity of the Illinois ten-hours act. According to Brandeis, the difference in the outcome of the two *Ritchie* cases was that in the first case the court had relied on abstract conceptions, but in the second the court had "reasoned from life." In other words, in the second *Ritchie* case, the court had taken notice of the facts that demonstrated the need to limit the hours of working women. "In the light of this evidence as to the world's experience and beliefs, it proved impossible for reasonable judges to say that the legislature of Illinois had acted unreasonably and arbitrarily in limiting the hours of labor."

Ex Parte Hawley (1911)
85 Ohio 495
and
Anna Hawley v. Walker (1914)
232 U.S. 718

In 1911, the Ohio Manufacturers Association challenged the constitutionality of the state's law establishing a fifty-four-hour workweek for women. This statute set ten hours as the maximum number in any one day that a woman would be permitted to work. The state's attorney general invited Brandeis to lead the legal defense of the state's law, and he accepted the offer.

Brandeis drew up the brief, took the leading role in oral argument, and prevailed in Ohio's highest court. The Ohio manufacturers appealed next to the U.S. Supreme Court. Brandeis again prepared one of his lengthy "sociological" briefs and also made the case for the Ohio statute in oral argument before the court. On February 25, 1914, the Ohio Supreme Court ruling was affirmed by the Court upon the authority of *Muller* v. *Oregon* (1908) in an unwritten *per curiam* opinion. "This," noted one editorial page writer for the *New York Times*, "is in harmony with the earlier decision in the same court, concerning a similar law passed by the Oregon legislature, and it would seem to make further controversy on the subject impossible" ("Topics of the Times," *New York Times*, February 26, 1914, 8).

New York v. *Charles Schweinler Press* (1915)
214 N.Y. 395

In 1911, a fire in the Triangle Shirtwaist Factory in lower Manhattan claimed the lives of 150 women workers. This disaster let to heightened concern in New York State and elsewhere as to all aspects of industrial working conditions. The New York State Legislature created a Factory Investigating Commission, and its report led to the passage of much new labor legislation. One of the new measures outlawed the employment of women in factories for "night work" between the hours of 10 P.M. and 6 A.M.

In 1907, the New York State Court of Appeals in *The People* v. *Williams* (189 N.Y. 131) had rejected as unconstitutional a virtually identical "night work" ban. The new law was quickly challenged in the New York courts by an employer who argued that it violated the Constitutions both of the state and of the United States by unjustly discriminating between different classes of citizens, thereby depriving them of the equal protection of the laws.

Once again, Brandeis headed the defense of a protective law, and he produced another of his sociological briefs prepared, as always, with the assistance of the National Consumer's League. The brief contained detailed statistics regarding night work by women and described the numerous laws that had been passed both in the American states and in Europe that attempted either to regulate or to ban the practice. Once again, Brandeis's side prevailed in court. On March 26, 1915, the Court of Appeals sustained the new law, thereby overturning its adverse verdict in the Williams case. The court credited the facts unearthed by study and investigation with having changed its mind about the validity of banning night work among female workers. In 1924, in the case of *New York* v. *Radice,* the U.S. Supreme Court unanimously upheld the New York law.

Bunting v. *Oregon* (1917)
243 U.S. 426

In 1913 Oregon enacted as "a health measure" a new ten-hours act that was to apply equally to both sexes. This law stated that no person was to be employed by a manufacturing establishment or mill for more than ten hours in any one day. Certain exceptions were allowed for, however, including a provision for up to three hours of overtime in one day to be paid for at the rate of time and one-half of the regular wage.

Franklin O. Bunting, the owner of the Lake View Flour Mill, was charged by Oregon authorities with having violated the new statute by employing one of his workers for thirteen hours in a single day without paying him overtime. Since Bunting freely admitted that he had done what he was accused of, he was tried, found guilty, and fined $50. He appealed his conviction to the Oregon Supreme Court on the ground that the ten-hours law was invalid because it violated both the Fourteenth Amendment and the Oregon Constitution. The judgment against Bunting was confirmed, however, by Oregon's highest court, and he then filed an appeal to the United States Supreme Court.

As soon as Bunting had begun to challenge the ten-hours act in the courts of his state, the authorities there had put Brandeis in charge of the law's defense. Once again, he compiled a lengthy, highly factual brief, running this time to more than 900 pages. By the time the case was first heard by the U.S. Supreme Court in April 1916, however, President Wilson had already nominated Brandeis for a seat on that very court. For that reason, Brandeis withdrew from courtroom advocacy and was replaced in *Bunting,* as in various other labor cases, by Felix Frankfurter.

The case was reargued in January 1917 and decided on April 9 of that year. The Court affirmed the decision of the Oregon courts and the conviction of Bunting by a margin of 5 to 3. Once again, Brandeis recused himself due to his major role in the preparation of the brief, nearly all of which he (in collaboration with his cousin, the social worker Josephine Goldmark) had written.

In his opinion for the majority, Justice Joseph McKenna identified the point at issue as whether the Oregon law was in accord with the Fourteenth Amendment. This depended in turn upon whether the statute was a proper exercise of the police power of the state. Were it a bona fide health measure, there could be little doubt, according to the Court, of the Oregon law's validity. McKenna noted the plaintiff's contention that the law's true purpose was not to protect the workers' health, but to raise their wages and their employers' expenses. But the court rejected Bunting's claim as unproven and as belied by the stated purpose of the act. As to the claim that the law was neither necessary nor useful in preserving the health of the workers covered by it, McKenna said there were no facts in the case record that supported this assertion and against it stood "the judgment of the legislature and the [State] Supreme Court."

Stetler v. *O'Hara* (1917)
243 U.S. 629

In 1913, the Oregon legislature passed a law establishing an Industrial Labor Commission (ILC). This official body was charged with investigating and, where necessary (for health, safety, or welfare), regulating the working conditions, wages, and hours of everyone employed within the state. Soon after its creation, the commission promulgated a minimum wage for all women employed by factories and stores. F.C. Stetler, a Portland box manufacturer, applied immediately for an injunction against the commission's order on the grounds that the law creating it was unconstitutional. After his challenge was heard and rejected by a lower court, Stetler appealed to the Oregon Supreme Court. The ILC brought in Brandeis to defend its minimum wage order (and the law that had authorized it). He did so successfully before the state's highest court in March 1914.

Stetler appealed the decision to the U.S. Supreme Court, where Brandeis again defended the Oregon law. He filed another of his sociological briefs, presenting 390 pages of evidence to back up his claim that the commission's ruling had been reasonable. His brief noted that it was widely held among official bodies and legislatures both in America and in Europe that minimum wage laws were needed and were beneficial to society at large. Brandeis also urged the court to show "restraint" by permitting the states latitude for social invention. So long as it was possible that a state law might remedy the defects of meager wages, he argued, the Court should not interfere.

There followed a lengthy silence from the justices on the issue. More than a year went by and still *Stetler* v. *O'Hara* remained undecided. Late in 1916, the Court asked for reargument on the issue of whether minimum wage laws for women were constitutional. By then, Brandeis had joined the Court, and Felix Frankfurter, Brandeis' protégé and himself a future justice of the Supreme Court, presented Oregon's case. With Brandeis recusing himself, the court split evenly on the issue, thereby preserving the Oregon statute, but leaving unresolved the question of whether the minimum wage was constitutional.

Olmstead v. *United States* (1928)
277 U.S. 438, affirmed. Justice Louis Brandeis, dissenting.

Roy Olmstead, Charles S. Green, Edward H. McInnis, and others were convicted of a conspiracy to violate the National Prohibition Act (27 U.S.C.A.) by unlawfully possessing, transporting, and importing intoxicating liquors and subsequently selling such intoxicating liquors. The convictions were affirmed by the Circuit Court of Appeals for the Ninth Circuit and their cases were granted certiorari by the United States Supreme Court on the question of whether the use of evidence of private telephone conversations between the defendants and others, intercepted by means of wiretapping, violated the defendants' rights under the Fourth and Fifth Amendments to the Constitution.

The defendants objected to the admission of the evidence obtained by wiretapping on the ground that the government's wiretapping constituted an unreasonable search and seizure in violation of the Fourth Amendment. The defendants further argued that the use of the evidence of the conversations overheard through such wiretapping compelled the defendants to be witnesses against themselves, in violation of the Fifth Amendment.

The Court majority held that the Fourth Amendment did not forbid what the prohibition officers had done in procuring the evidence in this case. The Court maintained that Congress could through legislation protect the secrecy of telephone conversations by making wiretap evidence inadmissible in federal criminal trials. In the absence of such measures, for the Court to simply declare wiretap evidence inadmissible in courts of law would be to enlarge and therefore distort the meaning of the Fourth Amendment. There was no search or seizure and the language of the amendment could not be extended or expanded to include telephone wires. There would be no justification in enlarging the "language employed beyond the practical meaning of houses, persons, papers and effects, or so to apply the words search and seizure as to forbid hearing or sight."

Justice Brandeis dissented from the majority's opinion, insisting that the Constitution also afforded protection against the latest means of invading individual security. He emphasized that the progression of science and technology would shortly be furnishing the government with advanced means of espionage that would go well beyond wiretapping. "Time works changes," he warned, "brings into existence new conditions and purposes. . . . In the application of a Constitution, therefore, [the court's] . . . contemplation cannot be only of what has been but of what may be. Under any other rule, a Constitution would indeed be as easy of application as it would be deficient in efficacy and power. Its general principles would have little value and be converted by precedent into impotent and lifeless formulas. Rights declared in words might be lost in reality."

Brandeis pointed out that one day a means might well be developed that would permit the government access to "the most intimate occurrences of the home." Or a device might be developed that "without removing papers from secret drawers, . . . [could] reproduce them in court, and . . . enable [them to be] expose[d] to a jury."

Brandeis subscribed to the court's decision in *Boyd* v. *United States,* 116 U.S. 616 (1885), stating that it was a case that would be remembered so long as civil liberties were found in the United States, especially in its review of the Fourth and Fifth Amendments to the Constitution. "The principles laid down in this opinion affect the very essence of constitutional liberty and security . . . they apply to all invasions on the part of the government and its employees of the sanctities of a man's home and the privacies of life. It is not the breaking of his doors, and the rummaging of his drawers, that constitutes the essence of the offense; but it is the invasion of his indefeasible right of personal security, personal liberty and private property, where that right has never been forfeited by his conviction of some public offense—it is the invasion of this sacred right which underlies and constitutes the essence of . . . [the] judgment. . . . Any forcible and compulsory extortion of a man's own testimony or of his private papers to be used as evidence of a crime or to forfeit his goods, is within the condemnation of that judgment. In this regard, the Fourth and Fifth Amendments run almost into each other."

Brandeis held that the ordinary meaning of "search" and "seizure" does not apply when referring to a defendant required to produce documents in the orderly operation of court procedure. The protection guaranteed by the Constitution and Amendments is much broader in scope. The framers of the Constitution attempted to secure conditions favorable to the pursuit of happiness and liberty. "They conferred, as against the government, the right to be let alone—the most comprehensive of rights and the right most valued by civilized men. To protect that right, every unjustifiable intrusion by the government upon the privacy of the individual, whatever the means employed, must be deemed a violation of the Fourth Amendment. And the use, as evidence in a criminal proceeding, of facts ascertained by such intrusion, must be deemed a violation of the Fifth. . . . Experience should teach us to be most on guard to protect liberty when the government's purposes are beneficent. Men born to freedom are naturally alert to repel invasion of their liberty by evil-minded rulers. The greatest dangers to liberty lurk in insidious encroachment by men of zeal, well-meaning but without understanding."

Decency, security, and liberty alike demand that government officials shall be subjected to the same rules of conduct that are commands to the citizen. In a government of laws, existence of the government will be imperiled if it fails to observe the laws scrupulously.

"To declare that the government may commit crimes in order to secure the conviction of a private criminal would bring terrible retribution. Against that pernicious doctrine, this court should resolutely set its face."

Liggett Co. v. Lee (1933)
288 U.S. 517

In 1931, the Florida legislature passed a law that imposed annual license fees on all the state's retail businesses. The new law provided that the fee per store was to rise in proportion to the number of units owned, so that each chain store branch would pay a higher license fee than an individually owned business, and the larger the chain the higher the fee. Finally, the retail chain operations that did business in more than one county were to pay higher fees than the multiple-store businesses that were entirely within a single county.

The Liggett Company, which had stores in several of the state's counties, applied for an injunction to halt the enforcement of these regulations on the grounds that it was being denied the equal protection of the laws as required by the Fourteenth Amendment. The Supreme Court of Florida rejected the company's claims, so Liggett appealed its verdict to the U.S. Supreme Court, which agreed to hear the case.

By a five-to-four vote, the Court overturned the challenged section of the Florida statute. It was arbitrary and hence invalid, declared the Court's majority, to impose a heavier license fee when the multiple stores of a single owner are located in more than one county than when one man or company owns several stores but all are in a single county. In its discrimination against the Liggett Company, the Court ruled that Florida had violated the Fourteenth Amendment. It therefore reversed the ruling of the Florida Supreme Court and ordered it to reconsider the company's request for an injunction against the enforcement of the challenged section of the law.

Brandeis dissented from the ruling on the ground that there was nothing in the case record to indicate that the complained-of provision of the law was unreasonable. Without such evidence, he maintained that the Court should exercise self-restraint by presuming the constitutionality of the legislation. Plunging into history, he noted that many of the early restrictions upon corporations in America had given way over the years. The result, he argued, had been a growing concentration of power and wealth that had done much harm to the American people. Given these trends and the present economic emergency, it was not unreasonable for Florida to assist small business by imposing a financial burden upon chain stores. Indeed, should the Legislature of the state choose, it could even eliminate chain stores altogether. According to Brandeis, there was nothing in the Constitution to preclude them from doing so.

Brandeis incorporated into his dissent an eloquent and fiery restatement of his ideology. "The excessive power of the few over the many," he said, had, in the Great Depression, "paralyzed individual effort and initiative, impaired creativity, and lessened human happiness. It is only by releasing from corporate control the faculties of the unknown many . . . that confidence in our future [can] be restored and the existing misery overcome." In subjecting its intrastate corporate chain stores to discriminatory taxation, the people of Florida were trying to curb the power of Big Business, and he was aware of nothing in the federal constitution that "precluded them from doing so. . . . To that extent, the citizens of each state are still masters of their destiny."

Erie Railroad Co. v. Tompkins, 90 F.2d 603, *certiorari granted*, 304 U.S. 64 (1938), Reversed. Justice Louis Brandeis delivered the majority opinion of the court.

The federal constitution assigns jurisdiction to the federal courts in cases where the rival parties are from different states. The issue in *Erie* v. *Tompkins* was whether in deciding a "diversity of citizenship" case, a federal court could ignore the rulings of the state courts. Was there, in fact, a federal common law for cases in which the plaintiff and the defendant were from different states?

On July 27, 1934, while walking along a footpath on the Erie Railroad Company's right of way in Hughestown, Pennsylvania, Harry Tompkins, a citizen of Pennsylvania, was struck by something protruding from a passing freight train, causing his arm to be severed. Tompkins claimed that the accident occurred as a result of the negligence in operation and/or maintenance of the train. He subsequently brought an action against the Erie in federal district court for Southern New York, which had, he claimed, jurisdiction because the railroad operated under a corporate charter issued by New York state. Under New York law, if the railroad was aware that members of the public were often using a footpath adjacent to its tracks, then it was liable for any negligence by its employees that resulted in harm to pedestrians on that path.

The railroad replied that the federal courts should follow in this case the judicial precedents of Pennsylvania where the accident occurred. Under the state's common law, maintained the Erie's attorneys, Tompkins was a trespasser for whose safety the railroad was in no way responsible, if unaware of his presence near its tracks. Since the accident took place after dark, argued the railroad, there was no way for its employees on the train to know that Tompkins was walking along the Erie's right of way. Therefore, argued the railroad, it was not liable for the injury to Tompkins and owed him no restitution. Tompkins's attorneys disputed this version of Pennsylvania law and its implications for Tompkins's case.

The federal district court in New York found in favor of Tompkins and awarded damages for negligence. The Erie appealed the decision to the Second Circuit Court of Appeals (again in New York) where it was affirmed. The circuit court held that it was unnecessary to consider the common law (the non-statutory, judge-made law) of Pennsylvania because the question was not one of local, but one of general law. "Upon questions of general law," said the decision, "federal courts are free, to exercise their independent judgment as to what the law is; and it is well settled that the question of the responsibility of a railroad for injuries caused by its servants is one of general law."

In finding for Tompkins, the circuit court cited *Swift* v. *Tyson,* 16 Pet. 1, 18, 10 L.Ed. 865, a decision handed down by the U.S. Supreme Court in 1842. In *Swift,* the court had ruled that a federal court sitting in diversity was required to apply as rules of decision only state statutes, not the judge-made common law of the state courts.

The railroad appealed the Second Circuit Court's ruling to the U.S. Supreme Court, which accepted the case, and ultimately reversed the decision. In his opinion for the Court, Brandeis linked the Court's reversal of the circuit court's ruling in the *Erie* case with his broader argument that *Swift* v. *Tyson* had been wrongly decided and should be overturned. In doing so, he addressed an issue that had not been raised by either of the contending parties in the case. Brandeis contended that the decision of the High Court in *Swift* had misinterpreted the Rules of Decision Act §34 of the Judiciary Act of 1789. According to him, recent research had shown that the Rules of Decision Act had in fact required federal courts sitting in diversity that they apply the unwritten common law of the forum state in addition to the written state statutory law.

Brandeis maintained that in allowing U.S. courts to create a federal common law, *Swift's* construction of §34 had given to the federal judiciary a power that was inconsistent with the U.S. Constitution. "There is," Brandeis wrote, "no federal general common law. Congress has no power to declare substantive rules of common law applicable in a State whether they are local in their nature of 'general' be they commercial law or a part of the law of torts. And no clause in the Constitution purports to confer such a power upon the federal courts."

Therefore, concluded Brandeis, the Circuit Court of Appeals had erred when it declared the past rulings of the Pennsylvania courts irrelevant in deciding *Erie* v. *Tompkins.* He declared the ruling of the Second Circuit Court of Appeals reversed and remanded the case back to it for further consideration. Moreover, four other justices voted with Brandeis in declaring invalid the old ruling of the High Court in *Swift* v. *Tyson.* In striking down this venerable precedent, the majority, speaking through Brandeis, was attempting to restore to the state courts a power that had been exercised for nearly a century by the federal judiciary.

Annotated Bibliography

Abrams, Richard M. *Conservatism in a Progressive Era: Massachusetts Politics, 1900–1912.* Cambridge, MA: Harvard University Press, 1964. Abrams views the Progressives as conservatives and he considers Brandeis a prime example.

Acheson, Dean. *Morning and Noon.* Boston: Houghton Mifflin, 1965. A personal and highly original view of Brandeis is conveyed in chapters 3 and 5 of this memoir, by one of Brandeis's law clerks who later became a notable secretary of state.

Baker, Leonard. *Brandeis and Frankfurter: A Dual Biography.* New York: Harper and Row, 1984. A readable book that compares the two men's careers while telling the story of their friendship.

Baskerville, Stephen W. *Of Laws and Limitations: An Intellectual Portrait of Louis Dembitz Brandeis.* Rutherford, NJ: Fairleigh Dickinson University Press, 1994. This interpretive study of the development of Brandeis's ideas also deals briefly with the key events of his life.

Bickel, Alexander. *The Unpublished Opinions of Mr. Justice Brandeis: The Supreme Court at Work.* Cambridge, MA: Belknap Press of Harvard University, 1957. Provides eleven of Brandeis's unpublished opinions and analyzes various aspects of his thought.

Brandeis, Louis D. *The Brandeis Guide to the Modern World,* ed. Alfred Lief. Boston: Little, Brown, 1941. An anthology of Brandeis quotations arranged alphabetically.

———. *Business: A Profession.* Boston: Small, Maynard, 1914. Reprint, New York: Augustus M. Kelley, 1971. In essays dealing with various economic issues, Brandeis urges businessmen to work for social justice.

———. "The Constitution and the Minimum Wage." *Survey* 33 (February 6, 1915): 521–524; reprinted in Brandeis, *The Curse of Bigness,* 52–69. This was originally the oral argument by Brandeis before the U.S. Supreme Court in *Stettler* v. *O'Hara* (1914), 243 U.S. 269.

———. *The Curse of Bigness: Miscellaneous Papers of Louis D. Brandeis,* ed. Osmond K. Frankel and Clarence Lewis. New York: Viking Press, 1934; Port Washington, NY: Kennicat Press, 1965. Provides many of Brandeis's most important articles as well as a bibliography, topically organized, identifying where other writings can conveniently be found.

———. "The Harvard Law School." *Green Bag* (January 1889). Brandeis's reminiscences of his law school days.

———. "The Living Law." *Illinois Law Review* 10 (February 1916): 461–471; reprinted in Brandeis, *The Curse of Bigness,* 316–326. A speech in which Brandeis argues that the public's dissatisfaction with law and with lawyers would be eased only if attorneys became versed in the social sciences, more knowledgeable about people's lives, and more committed to the public good.

———. "The Opportunity in the Law." *American Law Review* 39 (1905): 555–563; reprinted in Brandeis, *Business: A Profession,* 313–327. A speech in which Brandeis calls upon law students to become "people's lawyers" who would represent fairly the interest of the public at large, not just the interest of the rich.

———. *Other People's Money—And How the Bankers Use It.* New York: Stokes, 1914. In this attack on the money trust, Brandeis accuses the big bankers of gaining huge profits by artificially encouraging the dominance of giant firms.

———. *Papers.* Housed at Harvard Law School, Cambridge, MA. Most of the collection relates to Brandeis's work as a justice of the Supreme Court.

———. *Papers.* Housed at University of Louisville Law Library, Louisville, KY. Contains correspondence organized according to Brandeis's various spheres of activity.

———. *Public Papers.* Housed at the Brandeis University Library, Waltham, MA. Consists mainly of eight rolls of microfilm relating to his legal concerns.

———. *The Social and Economic Views of Mr. Justice Brandeis,* ed. Alfred Lief. New York: Vanguard, 1930. A topically organized collection of Brandeis's views on social and economic questions.

———. "Wage-Earners' Life Insurance." *Collier's Weekly,* September 15, 1906: 16–17, 28–30; reprinted in Brandeis, *The Curse of Bigness,* 3–17. Brandeis's angry exposé of the insurance industry.

Brandeis University. *Guide to a Microfilm Edition of the Public Papers of Louis D. Brandeis,* compiled by Abram L. Sachar and William L. Goldsmith. Waltham, MA: Brandeis University, 1978. Includes an introduction that summarizes Brandeis's life and career.

Burt, Robert A. *Two Jewish Justices: Outcasts in the Promised Land.* Berkeley: University of California Press, 1988. Burt argues that the unifying element in Brandeis's career was his "outsider's" view of himself as an advocate in the courts for the oppressed and the neglected.

Danelski, David. "The Propriety of Bandeis's Extrajudicial Conduct." In Dawson, ed., *Brandeis and America,* 11–37. Danelski views Brandeis's secret political involvements while a member of the Court as ethically questionable, and in some respects improper.

Dawson, Nelson L., ed. *Brandeis and America.* Lexington: University of Kentucky Press, 1989. Essays on the various aspects of Brandeis's career by leading historical and legal scholars. Excellent commentary and bibliographies.

De Haas, Jacob. *Louis D. Brandeis: A Biographical Sketch.* New York: Bloch, 1929. Deals primarily with Brandeis's activities as leader of the American Zionist movement.

Frankfurter, Felix, ed. *Mr. Justice Brandeis.* New Haven, CT: Yale University Press, 1932. A collection of essays by lawyers and scholars on various aspects of Brandeis's thought.

―――. *Of Law and Men.* New York: Harcourt Brace, 1956. Includes a brief interpretive essay on Brandeis's character that was written immediately after his death in 1941.

Freund, Paul A. "Mr. Justice Brandeis: A Centennial Memoir." *Harvard Law Review* 10 (1957): 769–792. This article is by a major legal scholar who had long studied Brandeis's career.

Gal, Allon. *Brandeis of Boston.* Cambridge, MA: Harvard University Press, 1980. Stresses the role of ethnic and Jewish factors in the shaping of Brandeis's outlook, political stance, and legal career.

Garraty, John A. *The New Commonwealth, 1877–1890.* New York: Harper and Row, 1968. Provides useful material on national events and trends during Brandeis's lifetime.

Goldmark, Josephine C. *Fatigue and Efficiency.* New York: Russell Sage Foundation, 1912. Contains summaries of various Brandeis legal briefs in welfare cases.

―――. *Impatient Crusader: The Life of Florence Kelley.* Champaign: University of Illinois Press, 1953. Brandeis's sister-in-law and sometime collaborator describes his activities for the National Consumers League and provides useful material on most of the early "Brandeis Brief" cases.

―――. *Pilgrims of '48.* New Haven, CT: Yale University Press, 1930. Contains numerous references to the family and youth of Louis Brandeis.

Gross, David C. *A Justice for All the People: Louis D. Brandeis.* New York: E.P. Dalton, 1987. A biography for grade school readers.

Hapgood, Norman. *The Changing Years.* New York: Farrar and Rinehart, 1930. Chapter 13 sheds light on the Ballinger-Pinchot dispute and on Brandeis's connection to Wilson.

Kolko, Gabriel. *The Triumph of Conservatism: A Reinterpretation of American History, 1900–1916.* Chicago: Quadrangle Paperbacks, 1963. Alleges that Brandeis was antilabor and insists that his stress upon efficiency could not possibly have tamed the great corporations.

La Follette, Bell Case, and Fola La Follette. *Robert M. La Follette.* New York: Hafner Publishing, 1971. Makes frequent reference to Brandeis as a friend and ally to the senior La Follette and his family.

Levy, David. "The Lawyer as Judge: Brandeis's View of the Legal Profession." *Oklahoma Law Review* 22 (1969): 374–391. Analyzes Brandeis's unusual view of the lawyer's role in society.

Lief, Alfred. *Brandeis: The Personal History of an American Ideal.* New York: Stackpole Sons, 1936. A lively account that draws heavily on Brandeis's speeches and articles, supplemented by details furnished by Brandeis to the author.

Link, Arthur S. *Wilson: The Road to the White House.* Princeton, NJ: Princeton University Press, 1947. Discusses Brandeis's role in the 1912 presidential campaign.

―――. *Wilson: The New Freedom.* Princeton, NJ: Princeton University Press, 1953. Describes Brandeis's contributions to Wilson's administration.

―――. *Woodrow Wilson and the Progressive Era, 1910–1917.* New York: Harper and Row, 1954. Provides historical background on the New Freedom and the battle over Brandeis's appointment to the Supreme Court.

Mann, Arthur. *Yankee Reformers in the Urban Age*. Cambridge, MA: Harvard University Press, 1954. Makes several passing references to Brandeis, viewing him as one of Boston's leading progressive reformers.

Mason, Alpheus Thomas. *Brandeis: A Free Man's Life*. New York: Viking Press, 1946. The classic work on Brandeis. A great achievement in biographical research and writing and the starting point for all subsequent research on the subject.

———. *Brandeis: Lawyer and Judge in the Modern State*. Princeton, NJ: Princeton University Press, 1933. An appraisal of Brandeis's contributions to the law.

———. *The Brandeis Way: A Case Study in the Workings of Democracy*. Princeton, NJ: Princeton University Press, 1938. A study of Brandeis's role in the development (and promotion over the years) of savings bank life insurance.

McClennen, Edward F. "Louis D. Brandeis as a Lawyer." *Massachusetts Law Quarterly* 33 (1948): 1–28. Brandeis's former law partner provides here an admiring portrait of him as an attorney whose goal was fairness to all sides rather than victory for his clients.

McCraw, Thomas K. *Prophets of Regulation: Charles Frances Adams, Louis D. Brandeis, James M. Landis, and Alfred E. Kahn*. Cambridge, MA: Belknap Press of Harvard University, 1984. McCraw is highly critical of Brandeis's economic views and feels that several of his triumphs had either meager or negative results.

Mersky, Roy M. *Louis Dembitz Brandeis, 1859–1941: A Biography*. New Haven, CT: Yale Law School, 1958. A useful guide to the literature on Brandeis.

Mowry, George. *The Era of Theodore Roosevelt and the Birth of Modern America*. New York: Harper and Row, 1958. Provides a short but authoritative account of Progressive Era politics, including the New Nationalism–New Freedom debate in which Brandeis played a major role.

Murphy, Bruce Allen. *The Brandeis/Frankfurter Connection: The Secret Political Activities of Two Supreme Court Justices*. New York: Oxford University Press, 1983. A controversial work that is critical of Brandeis for his secret political activities while a sitting member of the Court.

Paper, Lewis J. *Brandeis*. Englewood Cliffs, NJ: Prentice Hall, 1983. By interviewing his family as well as his friends and coworkers, Paper dwells more on the personal side of Brandeis's story than have other biographers.

Peare, Catherine. *The Louis D. Brandeis Story*. New York: Crowell, 1970. A popular account of Brandeis's life and career.

Penick, James L., Jr. *Progressive Politics and Conservation: The Ballinger-Pinchot Affair*. Chicago: University of Chicago Press, 1968. Penick thinks Brandeis in the wrong in the Ballinger-Pinchot controversy.

Pollock, Ervin H., ed. *The Brandeis Reader: The Life and Contributions of Mr. Justice Louis D. Brandeis*. New York: Oceana Publications, 1956. Includes some of Brandeis's most important essays and judicial opinions and also analyses and tributes written by others.

Poole, Ernest. "Brandeis: A Remarkable Record of Unselfish Work Done in the Public Interest." *American Magazine*, February 1911, 481–493. A revised version serves as the introduction to Brandeis, *Business: A Profession*, ix–lxi. A good biographical summary that deals briefly with Brandeis's public battles up to 1914.

Purcell, Edward A., Jr. *Brandeis and the Progressive Constitution: Erie, the Judicial Power, and the Politics of the Federal Courts in Twentieth Century America*. New Haven, CT: Yale University Press, 2000. Contends that Brandeis's majority decision in *Tompkins* demonstrates both his greatness as a judge and his continuing commitment to the progressive ideals of the early 1900s.

Richberg, Donald R. "The Industrial Liberalism of Justice Brandeis." In *The Brandeis Reader*, ed. Ervin H. Pollock. New York: Oceana Publications, 1956, 214–226. A well-documented analysis of Brandeis's views on labor issues.

Staples, Henry Lee, and Alpheus T. Mason. *The Fall of a Railroad Empire: Brandeis and the New Haven Merger Battle*. Syracuse, NY: Syracuse University Press, 1947. Staples and Mason view the New Haven War as a power grab by J.P. Morgan's lieutenants blocked by a heroic Brandeis.

Strum, Philippa. "Brandeis and the Living Law." In Dawson, ed., *Brandeis and America*, 118–132. Lexington: University of Kentucky Press, 1989. Strum credits Brandeis with having a coherent judicial philosophy that was based, according to her, on his unchanging views on human nature.

————. *Brandeis: Beyond Progressivism.* Lawrence, KS: University of Kansas Press, 1993. Argues that in his writings, Brandeis was groping his way toward a new social contract that would be founded on industrial democracy.

————. "Brandeis, Louis Dembitz." *American National Biography.* ed. John A. Garraty and Mark C. Carnes. New York: Oxford University Press, 1999, vol. 3, 418–422. An updated summary by a Brandeis biographer.

————. *Louis D. Brandeis: Justice for the People.* Cambridge, MA: Harvard University Press, 1984. Regards Brandeis's thought, including his economic ideas, as still relevant for our time.

Teitlebaum, Gene. *Justice Louis D. Brandeis: A Bibliography of Writings and Other Materials on the Justice.* Littleton, CO: Fred B. Rothman, 1988. An updated list of works by and about Brandeis that is comprehensive and well-organized.

Todd, Alden L. *Justice on Trial: The Case of Louis D. Brandeis.* New York: McGraw-Hill, 1964. A lively, well-researched account of the battle over Brandeis's appointment to the Supreme Court in 1916.

Urofsky, Melvin I. "The Brandeis Agenda." In Dawson ed., *Brandeis and America,* 133–149. Lexington: University of Kentucky Press, 1989. An essay that briefly surveys the literature on different aspects of Brandeis's life and work, and also notes where further research is needed.

————. *Louis D. Brandeis and the Progressive Tradition.* Boston: Little, Brown, 1980. Provides a well-written summary of Brandeis's career.

————. *A Mind of One Piece: Brandeis and American Reform.* New York: Scribners, 1971. Argues that Brandeis's greatness as a lawyer and judge lay in his ability to apply old moral values to the new conditions wrought by industrialism.

————. "Wilson, Brandeis and the Trust Issue, 1912–1914." *Mid-America* 49 (1967): 3–28. Urofsky credits Brandeis with altering the course of Wilson's presidential bid in 1912, and of his thinking about the Trusts.

Urofsky, Melvin I., and David W. Levy, eds. *The Letters of Louis D. Brandeis.* 5 vols. Albany, NY: State University of New York Press, 1972–1978. This is a major work of scholarship that is of great value to students of modern American history.

Warren, Samuel D., and Louis D. Brandeis. "The Right to Privacy." *Harvard Law Review* 4 (1889–1890), 193–220; reprinted in Brandeis, *The Curse of Bigness,* edited by Osmond K. Frankel and Clarence M. Lewis, 289–315. Port Washington, NY: Kennikat Press, 1965. This article introduces a concept of great importance in modern American law.

————. "The Watuppa Pond Cases." *Harvard Law Review* 2 (1888–1889), 1995–211. An article that defends the property rights of pond-owners against the claims of the state.

Weller, John L. *The New Haven Railroad: Its Rise and Fall.* New York: Hastings House, 1969. Weller's version of the New Haven's history is critical of the role that Brandeis played in its affairs.

—Clarence—
<u>Darrow</u>

(Illinois State Historical Library)

Chronology

1857   Born on April 18 to Amirus and Emily Eddy Darrow in Farmdale, Ohio.

1873   Graduated from Kinsman Academy, Kinsman, Ohio.

1874   Completed freshman year at Allegheny College, Meadville, Pennsylvania; taught at a local school in Kinsman.

1877   Entered law school at the University of Michigan.

1878   Left law school to read for the bar under a local lawyer in Youngstown, Ohio; passed bar examination and admitted to the bar; practiced law in Kinsman.

1880   Married to Jessie Ohl, his teenage sweetheart; left Kinsman to practice law in Andover, Ohio.

1883   Birth of Paul Darrow, his only child.

1884   Moved to Ashtabula, Ohio, to practice law.

1887   Moved to Chicago, Illinois, to practice law.

1889   Named as special assessment attorney to Mayor Dewitt C. Cregier of Chicago

1890   Served as corporation counsel for the city of Chicago.

1892   Became general attorney for the Chicago & Northwestern Railway.

1894   Left job as railroad attorney to defend Eugene V. Debs and other members of the American Railway Union against charges of violating an injunction and conspiring to obstruct interstate commerce.

1896   Ran unsuccessfully for the United States House of Representatives from Chicago.

1897   Divorced from Jessie Ohl Darrow.

1898   Defended Thomas J. Kidd, general secretary of the Amalgamated Woodworkers' International Union, on charges of conspiracy.

1902   Elected to a two-year term in the Illinois State Legislature; became chief counsel for the United Mine Workers in hearing before an arbitration commission called by President Theodore Roosevelt.

1903   Marriage to Ruby Hamerstrom, a Chicago society journalist.

1907   Defended William D. ("Big Bill") Haywood and two other members of the Western Federation of Miners on charges of conspiring to murder Frank Steunenberg, former governor of Idaho.

1911   Defended James B. McNamara and his brother John J. McNamara on charges of conspiring to blow up the *Los Angeles Times* building in 1910; the explosion killed twenty men.

1912   Indicted, tried, and acquitted of the attempted bribery of George Lockwood, a prospective juror in the McNamara case; indicted and tried for the attempted bribery of Robert Bain, the first juror to be sworn in the McNamara case, but jury was unable to reach a verdict and prosecution decided not to retry the case.

1920   Defended Benjamin Gitlow and other New York radicals indicted under state sedition laws for subversive activities.

1924   Defended Nathan Leopold Jr. and Richard Loeb, two affluent teenage boys who pleaded guilty to the "thrill" killing of fourteen-year-old Robert Franks.

1925   Defended John T. Scopes, a Tennessee high school teacher, accused of violating the state's law prohibiting the teaching of evolution; defended Ossian H. Sweet, a black physician accused of killing a member of a white crowd who tried to storm his home in Detroit, Michigan.

1926   Defended Henry Sweet, the brother of Dr. Ossian H. Sweet, on charges of conspiring to kill a member of a white crowd who tried to storm Dr. Sweet's home in Detroit, Michigan.

1927   Defended Calogero Greco and Donato Carillo on charges of stabbing two Fascists to death outside a New York subway station.

1932   Defended United States Navy Lieutenant Thomas H. Massie and three other defendants for the murder of a Hawaiian man who allegedly raped Massie's wife; published his autobiography, *The Story of My Life*.

1938   Died of heart disease on March 13 in Chicago.

Biography

Clarence Seward Darrow, the most famous courtroom lawyer in the United States, made a striking appearance in court. He wore baggy pants held up by midnight blue or fireman red suspenders; looked perennially unkempt; suffered few qualms about appearing in his shirt sleeves in warm weather; liked to be seen slouched down in his chair; possessed an unruly lock of hair which periodically fell over his forehead; and had a deeply lined face that looked like it bore all the burdens of humanity upon it.[1] Although he could be vain about his liaisons with attractive women (both during and in between his first and second marriages), he regarded his wrinkles as a badge of honor. In 1907, the fifty-year-old Darrow returned to Chicago after a hard-fought victory in court and gave explicit instructions to photographers not to retouch his pictures. "Don't wash out the lines, boys," he said. "I worked too hard to earn them."[2]

In the forty-year period from the 1890s until the 1930s, Darrow towered over the legal profession. Two of his cases—the Leopold-Loeb case and the Scopes "monkey trial"—were among the most famous trials of the century. Known as the "Defender of the Damned," he thoroughly earned his reputation as a fearless advocate of unpopular causes, and he estimated that nearly half of his more than 2,000 clients never paid him a fee. Among his clients were confessed murderers, gangsters, labor radicals like Eugene V. Debs and William D. ("Big Bill") Haywood, and a variety of society's outcasts and obscure citizens who often had no one else willing to take up their cause.

It was a treat to see Darrow perform in court, and he left his persona on every case he tried. Blessed with a melodious baritone voice that he could modulate as the occasion demanded, Darrow was in complete control of the courtroom and was known to make jurors weep, as well as himself. Attorney Arthur Garfield Hays described Darrow's courtroom performance in the following manner:

> Darrow would arise, shrug his shoulders. His posture, his quiet demeanor, his force of personality would immediately center the attention of the expectant audience. He was not merely a lawyer discussing the case; he was a philosopher discussing life. He would refer to the strange and inexplicable behavior of human beings, moved by unpredictable forces and sudden emotions. He would make only slight reference to the particular facts of the case. He would rather show the factors that had brought the defendant to his present predicament—his heritage, his bringing up, his way of life, the vise closing him in—all those elements that control a man almost without his knowledge. Darrow would talk of man's inhumanity, the misery of the unfortunate, of the danger of sitting in judgment, of the intolerance of human beings. He not only placed the facts before the jury but presented those facts in their own setting. Soon every man on the jury was inclined to lean backwards in an effort not to do an injustice.[3]

Checkered Career

It is hard to realize that the real Clarence Darrow—as opposed to the legend-ary figure—had a checkered life. There was little indication in his early years that he would have such a great impact on his profession over so long a period of time. An indifferent student, he went to college for only one year and left law school after his first year to study in a lawyer's office for the bar.

His career was anything but a straight path to success. His law practice nearly came to an abrupt end in 1912, when he was accused of bribing a witness. In an incident that was not widely publicized, Darrow toyed with the idea of committing suicide when he was about to be indicted for bribery.[4]

In spite of his reputation as the "Defender of the Damned," he had a public career that was marked by three distinct stages: He represented the city of Chicago and large corporations from 1888 to 1894; he took up the cause of trade union leaders from 1894 to 1911; and he became a criminal defense attorney in the period after 1912 until his death in 1938. Although one of his admiring biographers began a book about Darrow with his giving up his lu-crative job as a corporation attorney in order to represent Debs,[5] Darrow actu-ally defended as many rich clients as poor ones in all three stages of his career.[6]

Nor was he immune to the pleasures of money. Writer Brand Whitlock, who knew him personally, maintained that Darrow "was corrupted by the awful compulsion of the age, to make money."[7] In later years, Darrow re-sorted to speculating in the stock market to support the lifestyle he had ac-quired after his second marriage. On one occasion, he was asked by a client, "Oh, Mr. Darrow, how can I ever thank you enough for all you've done?" He replied, "Madam, ever since the Phoenicians invented money, there has been an answer to that question."[8]

For all his brilliance in court, Darrow had violent mood swings and could be terribly erratic. His office was just as disorderly as his appearance. He never kept notes, records, or files; he had all of the facts of a case in his head. His desk was always a shambles, but he refused to let anyone touch it. He would sometimes disappear from his law office, as when he left during "Big Bill" Haywood's trial in 1907 in order to go off and watch a ball game.[9] This pattern of behavior led one of his law associates to remark that "he had a lazy streak, and wouldn't work on a case until the last minute, until he had to. Most of the legal preparation was done by others."[10]

A Passion for Writing

It is equally surprising to realize that Darrow periodically dreamed of leaving the law to become a writer. Although he never realized this dream, his literary outpourings include an autobiographical novel, *Farmington* (1904), seven other books, and hundreds of essays and short stories in both mass-circulation maga-zines and obscure journals. It has been estimated that a bibliography of books and articles by him and about him would exceed two hundred pages.[11] His literary work was considered important enough to be the subject of a book, *Clarence Darrow and the American Literary Tradition* (1962) by Abe Ravitz. Although Darrow was long regarded as a loner, a trove of 450 of his personal letters discovered in the early 1990s revealed that he corresponded with such writers as Theodore Dreiser, Sinclair Lewis, H.L. Mencken, progressive reformer Brand Whitlock, in addition to architect Frank Lloyd Wright, labor activist Mary Harris ("Mother") Jones, sociologist W.E.B. Du Bois, and Presidents Woodrow Wilson and Franklin D. Roosevelt.[12]

Several of the writers he knew were initially surprised at his knowledge of literature. When Whitlock met him in 1895, he was astonished to learn the extent to which Darrow was well-versed in literary matters. "Darrow had read books other than those of the law," wrote Whitlock, "and for an hour we talked of Tolstoy and other great Russians and of Thomas Hardy, and of Mr. [William Dean] Howells."[13] His vast knowledge was also a source of admiration to his attorney friends. "Darrow studied philosophy, psychology, biology, and history," remarked Hays, "while other lawyers studied law."[14]

An Inherited Love of Learning

Clarence Darrow inherited his love of learning from his parents, Amirus and Emily Eddy Darrow. He was born in the small village of Farmdale in northeastern Ohio on April 18, 1857, the fifth of seven surviving children. Both his parents had come from lower-middle-class families who had earlier settled in Connecticut before moving to Ohio. As children, Amirus and Emily stood apart from their families because of their interest in books. When Amirus met Emily in the early 1840s at Ellsworth Academy in Amboy, Ohio, it seemed as if fate had drawn them together.[15]

But fate conspired to make Amirus Darrow the perennial outsider in a land consumed by the desire to realize the American Dream. Following his marriage to Emily in 1845, he took his bride to Meadville, Pennsylvania, in order to attend Allegheny College, which was affiliated with the Methodist Church. However, Amirus soon had a change of heart about Methodism on account of the schism that developed over the issue of slavery, and he transferred to a Lutheran seminary. By the time he had completed his studies there, he once again lost his faith and a chance to earn a steady living as a minister. He would spend the rest of his working years as an ill-paid carpenter and as an undertaker.

Amirus did take one year off from his work in 1864 to attend law school at the University of Michigan, but dropped out the following year. In 1865, he took his family to the town of Kinsman, Ohio (population: 400 to 500). Clarence, who was eight at the time, remained there until he was twenty-three.

Both Amirus and Emily were formidable people in their own right. Firmly committed to abolitionism, they made their home available to the Underground Railroad during the 1850s. When Clarence was born, he was given the middle name of Seward in honor of New York senator and abolitionist William Henry Seward. Although Darrow had few recollections of his mother, who died when he was fourteen, he recalled that she took time out from her household chores to read her beloved books whenever she had an opportunity. Unlike other women in the community, she supported woman's suffrage.[16]

A Son Charts His Own Course

Darrow inherited his father's agnosticism. "My father," wrote Darrow, "was the village infidel, and gradually came to glory in his reputation. I cannot remember that I ever had any doubts that he was right."[17] This agnosticism was never allowed to overshadow Amirus's equally compelling interest in his children's education. Every night the children sat around the kerosene lamp and studied their lessons. When they felt they had learned them, they recited them to their father. Darrow recalled that his father "watched our studies with the greatest care, and diligently elaborated and supplemented whatever we absorbed in school. No one in town had an education anywhere so thorough."[18]

The young Darrow did not always take kindly to his father's strict ways. He was a disciplined student only when he liked what he was doing. As he later admitted,

> I was none too industrious, and I have never loved to work. In fact, strange as it may seem, I have never wanted to do the things that I did not want to do. These activities are what I call work. I liked to do certain things no matter how much exertion they required; I liked to play baseball, no matter how hot the day. I liked to read books that I liked to read. I liked debating in school and out of school. I liked to "speak pieces" and was always keen to make due preparation for that, no matter what the subject might be. I always preferred diversions to duties, and this strange taste has clung to me all through life.[19]

Among the books to which Amirus introduced his children were the works of Charles Darwin, John Stuart Mill, Herbert Spencer, and Thomas Paine; the political satire of Voltaire; the *Odyssey* of Homer; and the *Republic* of Plato. While Darrow admired his father and acknowledged the intellectual stimulation that Amirus provided, the son was keenly aware of his father's inability to make money. Darrow would later recall:

> One of my earliest recollections is the books in our home. They were in bookcases, on tables, on chairs, on the floor. The house was small, the family large, the furnishings meager, but there were books whichever way one turned. How my father managed to buy the books I cannot tell. Neither by nature nor by training had he any business ability or any faculty for getting money.[20]

In his adult years, Darrow would also have books strewn about his home, but his love for ideas was always tempered by the need to be practical and self-sustaining. Despite his radicalism, iconoclasm, and nonconformity, Clarence Seward Darrow was one of the shrewdest lawyers ever to grace an American courtroom. In contrast to Amirus, Darrow always played to win.

A Choice of a Profession

Another influence in Darrow's early life was Kinsman, the town in which he grew up. The one social event of the week in Kinsman was the Saturday night debate, held either in the schoolhouse or in a large barn. Darrow took part in nearly every debate and enjoyed arguing against a popular position. While working on his lessons could be a chore for him, he had endless patience when preparing a speech and committing it to memory. He soon gained the reputation of being "the best young speaker in these parts."[21]

After his graduation from Kinsman Academy in 1873, Darrow followed in the footsteps of his father, older brother Everett, and sister Mary, by attending Allegheny College. Darrow's stay there was confined to one year because of his father's precarious financial situation as a result of the Panic of 1873, and he returned home to accept a job teaching at a local school.

It was while he worked as a teacher that he began to think about becoming a lawyer, spending a considerable amount of time reading his father's law books. In later years, Darrow remarked, "I am not sure what influenced me to make this choice. I knew that I had never intended to work with my hands, and no doubt I was attracted by the show of the legal profession."[22] Darrow's aversion to manual labor stemmed from the hot summer day when his father found a job for him hoeing potatoes on a nearby farm. Darrow would later refer to this incident as instrumental in his decision to study law. "After I worked hard for a few hours," he remarked, "I ran away from that hard work, went into the practice of law and have not done any work since."[23]

In the autumn of 1877, Darrow entered law school at the University of Michigan. His studies were made possible by the financial help of $50 that he received from Everett, a high school teacher, and Mary, who taught in grade school. His school fees amounted to $25 for tuition and an additional fee of $25 as an out-of-town student.[24]

At that time, the usual course of law studies at Michigan was two years, but Darrow reasoned that he would save money by leaving school at the end of his first year and reading for the bar under a lawyer's direction. He took a job in a law office in Youngstown, twenty miles from Kinsman. At the end of the year, Darrow presented himself to a committee of lawyers in Youngstown who "did not seem to take it as seriously as examiners do today. I was not made to feel that the safety of the government or the destiny of the universe was hanging on their verdict."[25] He passed this examination (along with eleven other students who also presented themselves that day) and was admitted to the bar in 1878.

Law Practice, 1878–1887

For the next two years, Darrow practiced law in Kinsman. His cases mainly involved bad debts, actions for the recovery of stolen goods, and defending clients accused of such "crimes" as watering their milk supplies and selling liquor. It was a modest start, for Darrow wrote that the townspeople "could not conceive that a boy whom they knew, and who was brought up in their town, could possibly have the ability and learning that they thought was necessary for the practice of law."[26]

In 1880, the twenty-three-year-old Darrow married Jessie Ohl, his teenage sweetheart whose well-to-do family owned the local gristmill in Kinsman. He took his bride to Andover, which was located twelve miles north of Kinsman. His average income from his law practice in Andover was between $50 and $60 a month.[27]

After three years in Andover and an unsuccessful stab at politics by running for state senator and for prosecuting attorney, Darrow concluded that he had outgrown the town. In 1884, he moved twenty-five miles away to Ashtabula, a town of 5,000 people in the northeastern part of Ohio. The move was sparked by a desire to make more money, coinciding with the birth in December 1883 of his son, Paul, who would be his only child.

Darrow's career blossomed in Ashtabula. His legal work before the Court of Common Pleas so impressed Judge Laban S. Sherman that the judge helped Darrow when the latter ran successfully to become the town's city solicitor. The position paid $75 a week and gave Darrow the right to take his own cases as well.[28]

The job security enabled Darrow and his wife to save $500, and in 1896 they decided to apply it toward a down payment on a $3,500 house owned by a couple in town. Darrow drew up the deed of purchase and agreed to pay the balance in installments, but the owner's wife refused to sign it, presumably because she did not think that Darrow would be able to make the payments. When confronted with the news, Darrow blurted out, "All right, I don't believe I want your house because—because—I'm going to move away from here."[29]

A Move to Chicago and a Mentor, 1887

It took Darrow another year to make good on his promise, but by 1887 he had moved to Chicago and opened a law office. The move was a major undertaking for the thirty-year-old lawyer, who had never ventured far from his birthplace. Fortunately, his older brother and sister were teaching in Chicago, and they offered to help.

Darrow speculated that his life would have been different if the owner's wife had signed the deed.[30] On the other hand, it is not implausible that he would have made this move on his own initiative. Although Darrow would maintain throughout his life that man was not the master of his fate—he once remarked that "instead of being the captain of his soul . . . man isn't even a deck-hand on a rudderless ship"[31]—his own life was a firm refutation of that belief.

Although it might have seemed that this fledgling country lawyer was out of his depth in Chicago, Darrow was well prepared for city life. By the time he had arrived in Chicago, he had read extensively in political economy and was a devotee of the determinist ideology of Herbert Spencer. Darrow's thinking was further crystallized by two books he was given by a banker and by a judge in Ashtabula: Henry George's *Progress and Poverty* (1879), which attacked the capitalism of the era, and John Peter Altgeld's *Our Penal Machinery and Its Victims* (1884), a criticism of the criminal justice system in America for its failure to come to grips with the causes of crime.

While Darrow sympathized with many of the radical groups in the city, he was always more comfortable as a philosophical radical than as an adherent to any particular movement. Although he was attracted to socialism, he never joined the Socialist Party. Instead, he became active in Chicago's Democratic politics and was a frequent speaker at the city's Henry George Club. He also sought out Altgeld, who would be subsequently elected governor of Illinois in 1892. Altgeld took him under his wing and became Darrow's mentor.

A Meteoric Rise in Chicago, 1889–1892

Using his political connections to Altgeld, Darrow had a meteoric rise in Chicago and entered mainstream respectability: He was named to be a special assessment attorney by Mayor Dewitt C. Cregier in 1889 at a salary of $3,000 a year and became corporation counsel to the city during the following year. It was a remarkable achievement for a young man so recently removed from Ashtabula, which he promptly renamed "Asstabula."[32]

His work as corporation counsel in the early 1890s and the political skills that he displayed in dealing with city agencies marked him as a young man of considerable promise. In 1892, he accepted a position as general attorney for the Chicago & Northwestern Railway. His decision to work for the railroad displeased many of his radical friends, but Darrow maintained that he had not betrayed his ideals. In a rather specious argument, he insisted that by virtue of working with Ralph Richards, the railroad's claims agent known to be sympathetic to working class people when they had actions pending against the company, he and Richards were able to "help a great many people without serious cost to the road."[33]

The Debs Case

Darrow first gained national prominence in 1894, when he quit his railroad job to represent labor leader Eugene V. Debs. His decision to give up this secure position has been emphasized by many of his biographers, but Darrow did not sever his ties to corporate management. At the urging of Marvin Hughitt, president of the railway, Darrow agreed to continue his connection on a retainer basis. The retainer lasted for many years, and Darrow and Hughitt remained good friends until the latter's death in 1920.[34]

Debs, who had founded the American Railway Union (ARU) in 1893, first ran into trouble with the federal government when he ordered a boycott of the cars of the Pullman Palace Car Company following a strike by the Pullman workers in 1894. On July 2, 1894, federal judges Peter S. Grosscup and William A. Woods obtained an injunction against Debs and his three chief ARU officers from interfering with any trains carrying the mail. On July 10, they were also indicted on the charge of criminal conspiracy in connection with their role in the Pullman strike.

One week later, Debs and the three union officials (as well as four other ARU officers) were arrested for violating the injunction of July 2. In December 1894, Judge Woods found the eight defendants guilty of contempt in the injunction proceedings. Debs was sentenced to the maximum sentence of six months in jail, while the other seven defendants received three month terms. The men were released from jail on January 21, 1895, pending the outcome of Darrow's application to the United States Supreme Court for a writ of habeas corpus.[35]

In the meantime, Debs and the other defendants were to be tried for criminal conspiracy in January 1895. In order to prepare for the case, Darrow virtually abandoned his law practice. He rented a small office, surrounded himself with law books, and spent weeks reviewing the history of labor unions and the conspiracy laws.

The conspiracy trial began on January 25, 1895, and Darrow (assisted by S.S. Gregory, the former city solicitor of Chicago) employed a strategy that was used by him in other labor cases: He attempted to turn the tables by putting the capitalist system on trial rather than the defendants. As Darrow presented the case, the federal government and the Pullman Company were the real conspirators because of their efforts to destroy the lives of the workers and to crush their labor unions.[36]

In referring to Debs and the seven other accused conspirators, Darrow made a strong argument to the jury in support of their right to strike:

> These men are not conspirators—these men are not criminals. You and I may disagree with them, may say that what they did was unwise, but when the record is made up, that of men laying down their tools out of sympathy for their fellow man . . . [their action] was one of the proudest sublimest spectacles in the world. Men have a right to strike; these men did nothing more.[37]

Darrow had hoped to call George Pullman, president of the company, to the stand, but the latter disappeared before he could be served with a subpoena. Darrow had earlier put Debs on the witness stand and turned the embattled labor leader into a sympathetic hero by deftly drawing out details of Debs's life and his dedication to the cause of labor.[38]

The trial came to an abrupt end when one of the jurors became ill. Although the jury could have been reconvened, the judge adjourned it on February 12, and the government subsequently dropped the case. At the time that the trial ended, Darrow was informed by one of the jurors that they had stood eleven to one in favor of acquittal.[39]

The matter did not end with the conspiracy trial. Darrow and fellow attorney Lyman Trumbull had appealed the contempt citation to the Supreme Court. The Court denied the appeal in May 1895, and Debs used the other defendants returned to jail.

Midlife Conflicts

Following the Debs case, Darrow returned to his private law practice, which now included a large number of rich clients. When Ellen Gates Starr of Chicago's Hull House, a settlement house she cofounded with Jane Addams to provide services to immigrants, expressed dismay in 1897 at the dishonesty of some of his affluent clients, Darrow pointed out that society should neither condemn a physician who treats a criminal nor a lawyer who represents one.[40] He further explained his actions to Starr in the following way:

> I have taken their ill-gotten gains and have tried to use it to prevent suffering . . . I have defended the poor and weak, have done it without pay, and will do it again. I cannot defend them without bread, I cannot get this except from those who have it, and by giving some measure of conformity to what is.[41]

Although his explanation may have placated Starr, Darrow was not completely satisfied with his work. He turned out a substantial number of articles and novels at this time in the hope of establishing himself as a writer, but eventually concluded that he would be unable to make a comfortable living as a man of letters.

Another option that Darrow considered was a career in politics. He ran unsuccessfully for the House of Representatives from Chicago in 1896, but had better luck in 1902, when he was elected to a two-year term in the Illinois State Legislature. At the end of the term, he concluded that it was futile for an independent man to continue in politics.[42]

The Debs case had put Darrow into the national limelight, and for the next twenty years he continued to add to his stature as a labor lawyer. But his growing fame helped to wreak havoc in his personal life. His burgeoning career and his celebrity status put him in great demand as a public speaker in Chicago, and he chose to spend less time with his wife and his son, Paul.

Darrow's wife, Jessie, who never fully adjusted to life in Chicago, gave him a divorce in 1897. She later married a local judge who practiced in Ashtabula, where the couple resided with Paul Darrow. The son did not follow in his father's footsteps as an attorney, but had a successful career as a businessman. In later years, Darrow maintained a close relationship with Paul and his children.

Following Darrow's divorce, he became involved with a number of beautiful young women who found him attractive in spite of his rumpled appearance.

In 1903, the forty-six-year-old Darrow married Ruby Hamerstrom, who was sixteen years his junior. She had worked as a society journalist in Chicago before their marriage, but gave up her career when she became Mrs. Clarence Seward Darrow. His new wife was bright and well read, and catered to him more than many of the "new women" with whom he had been romantically involved before his remarriage.[43]

Unfortunately, marital fidelity was not one of Darrow's virtues. In 1908, he met thirty-year-old Mary Field, a Hull House social worker and an aspiring writer. Their affair began immediately, and he later helped her with her career when she went to live in New York. They saw each other sporadically over the next several years and met again in Los Angeles in 1911, when he defended the McNamara brothers and she covered the trial for a magazine. She eventually married Lemuel Parton, a San Francisco newspaperman, wrote her autobiography (which was never published, but is a valuable source of information about her famous lover), and remained friends with Darrow until his death.

His wife, Ruby, knew about this affair and asked writer Irving Stone to leave Mary Field Parton out of his biography of her husband on the grounds that if Stone included Mary, he would have to refer to her husband's other "ladies-in-waiting." Stone acquiesced in this request.[44]

Darrow's second marriage led to a change in his lifestyle. He and his wife took a spacious apartment on Chicago's north side, and he began to buy expensive clothes, such as silk shirts and black satin ties. At the same time, his friends recognized a growing cynicism in his remarks, which may have reflected a certain disillusionment with his own life. In spite of his success as a savvy big-city lawyer, Darrow never completely outgrew his country-boy outlook. His ambivalence in his later years was noted by writer J. Anthony Lukas in the following manner:

> The irony of Darrow's midlife predicament lay in the contrast between, on the one hand, his thriving law practice, his distinguished friends, and the esteem in which he was increasingly held by the press and public and, on the other, the acute distaste he felt for the life of a lawyer, the craving for a higher, more aesthetic vocation, the inner doubts bordering on self-contempt at the compromises he felt compelled to make.[45]

The Defense of Thomas Kidd, 1898

After the Debs trial ended, Darrow's most notable client was Thomas J. Kidd, the general secretary of the Amalgamated Woodworkers' International Union, whom he defended in 1898. Kidd's trial was held in Oshkosh, Wisconsin, and it was Darrow's first trip away from Chicago.

Kidd was tried along with two other leaders of a strike called against the Paine Lumber Company, which employed 1,600 workers in Oshkosh. The defendants were charged with conspiracy for leading the workers in a strike for higher wages. In his moving appeal to the jury, Darrow asked it to put aside the allegations made by the prosecution against his clients and to concentrate instead on the evidence he presented attesting to the exploitive practices of the Paine Lumber Company.

Darrow's summation to the jury lasted for two days. He spoke without notes and held the jurors in rapt attention. It took the jury only fifty minutes to return a verdict of "not guilty."[46]

For his defense of Kidd, Darrow received only $250. It was a pittance in comparison to his substantial earnings from his law firm, now known as Darrow, Thomas & Thompson. As explained by Kevin Tierney, Darrow's decision to defend Kidd came from a mixture of motives:

> In spite of Brand Whitlock's impression at the beginning of 1898, Darrow was not completely under "the awful compulsion of the age"; the fact that he took the Kidd case in the fall of that year proved that his conception of success was not wholly mercenary. Had he been a hard-nosed lawyer on the make financially, he would never have bothered with Kidd, whose pitiful defense fund did not equal the profit from even a week of office practice with Darrow, Thomas & Thompson. On the other hand, neither could it be claimed that Darrow's entry into the case was born of pure altruism. If he had merely wanted to practice philanthropy, literally dozens of chances to aid the faceless poor emerged in Chicago every week, most of which he ignored. The truth was that his pay in the Kidd case was the assurance of public attention: he liked money, but he preferred fame.[47]

The Trial of "Big Bill" Haywood

Darrow added to his fame as a labor lawyer in the fall of 1902, when he accepted an invitation from the United Mine Workers (UMW) to be its chief counsel in hearings before an arbitration commission called by President Theodore Roosevelt to settle the anthracite coal strike. The hearings before the commission were begun in Scranton, Pennsylvania, in November and lasted three months. Darrow produced 241 witnesses to speak on behalf of the UMW and the strikers. When the time came for him to make his summation (it lasted eight hours and was extemporaneous, as usual), a crowd gathered to hear him.

Darrow's efforts proved to be successful as the commission handed down a settlement largely favorable to the UMW. His role in these proceedings was unique for him. It marked one of the few times in his life that the cause he supported met with the approval of the public.[48]

Before he was compelled to abandon his career as a labor lawyer, Darrow represented William D. ("Big Bill") Haywood and the McNamara brothers. The trials were similar insofar as they both took on the aspect of the kind of sensational criminal trial that attracted so much attention in later years. But the Haywood trial ended in a hard-fought win for Darrow, while events in the McNamara trial drove him to a suicide attempt and nearly ended his career.

The trial of Haywood revealed some of the deep divisions between capital and labor that haunted American society in the late nineteenth and early twentieth centuries. It had all the elements of a full-scale drama: the murder of Frank Steunenberg, the former governor of Idaho; the kidnapping of Haywood and the two other defendants; the prosecution's use of James McParland, America's most famous detective; the planting of spies on the defense team by the prosecution; the subornation of perjury by the defense; and the court-room battle between two magnificent public orators, William E. Borah for the prosecution and Clarence Darrow for the defense.

The intensity of the drama did not go unnoticed. The trial was covered by some of the leading journalists throughout the nation and has been referred to as "the first courtroom spectacular in American politics."[49]

The events in question began on December 30, 1905, when a bomb exploded as former governor Frank Steunenberg opened the gate to his house in Caldwell, Idaho. It was widely believed that his murder was an act of revenge by a group of radical union members for Steunenberg's antilabor activities as governor.

A short time later, local authorities arrested a miner named Harry Orchard for the murder and hired James McParland of the Pinkerton Detective Agency to question Orchard. McParland, who had gained fame thirty years earlier by helping to break up the terrorist labor society known as the Molly Maguires, was convinced that Orchard was acting on behalf of the Western Federation of Miners (WFM), one of the most radical unions in the country.

McParland secured a confession in which Orchard said he had been a hired assassin for the inner circle of the WFM: Haywood, secretary-treasurer (he held the same post in the newly established militant union, the International Workers of the World), Charles H. Moyer, president, and George A. Pettibone, who was active in the union. This confession was suspect in union circles because Orchard gave the incriminating statement only after McParland held out the promise that, if Orchard cooperated with the authorities, "you will not be hung." Besides obtaining this confession, McParland further assisted the prosecution by arranging for the money to finance the case and later planting undercover spies known as "Operative 21" and "Operative 28" to work on the defense team.[50]

The fact that Haywood, Moyer, and Pettibone were living in Colorado at the time of Steunenberg's murder, posed a problem for the prosecution. The laws of extradition prevented the removal of the men because they were not fugi-tives from justice in Idaho. Accordingly, the matter was solved in February 1906 when the enterprising McParland arranged for the men to be kidnapped: they were arrested in Denver, kept in jail all night, and then put on a chartered train (provided by E.H. Harriman's Union Pacific) bound for Idaho. Once there, they would be tried separately as accomplices in Steunenberg's murder.[51]

Haywood was the first to be tried. Recognizing the importance of securing local counsel, Darrow obtained the services of Edward Wilson and Edmund Richardson to work with him. It took the defense over two weeks to select a jury. Darrow had long ago turned jury selection into an art form, and he sel-dom was surprised at a juror's reaction to the events of a trial.[52]

The trial began on May 10, 1907, in the District Court of Ada County, Idaho. For his appearance in court, Darrow cast aside his newly acquired, expensive clothes to don some of his old tweed suits and a clumsily tied necktie dangling at mid-waist. Journalist J. Anthony Lukas, in his book dealing with the Haywood trial, criticized Darrow's contrived demeanor and suggested that a close observer at the trial could detect "a whiff of the bogus, sensing behind this artfully constructed rustic the guile, cunning and cynicism of a big-city fixer."[53]

The depiction of Darrow as a "big-city fixer" was well earned. In the course of his defense of Haywood, Darrow apparently had few qualms about winning at all costs, particularly when faced by a prosecution that he believed had repeatedly breached the established standards of legal ethics. Using the proceeds of a $350,000 defense fund raised by popular subscription from the ranks of labor, Darrow allegedly paid $25,000 to get a witness to change his story and $50,000 to the uncle of this witness for his role in getting the nephew to recant. There were also rumors in town that persons pretending to be book salesmen or peddlers had visited families of the jurors in order to remind them that it would be dangerous to go against the interests of the mine workers.[54]

Darrow prepared for the trial by leaving nothing to chance. His closing argument lasted a total of eleven hours and fifteen minutes. In telling the jury that "I speak for the poor, for the weak, for the weary," Darrow argued that the moral righteousness of the defendant's cause was the paramount issue, regardless of whether or not he was actually guilty as charged.[55]

The Haywood trial concluded in July 1907, when the jury returned a verdict of "not guilty." Ironically, the decision had more to do with the judge's instructions to the jury than to Darrow's defense. The judge told the jurors that "under the statutes of this state, a person cannot be convicted of a crime upon the testimony of an accomplice, unless such accomplice is corroborated by other evidence." One of the jurors later stated that "all the jurors thought Haywood guilty," but there was insufficient corroborative evidence to warrant a conviction.[56]

The verdict took Darrow by surprise. Fearing that the sentiment in the community was clearly against acquittal, he was in the midst of apologizing to Haywood for losing the case when the jury announced its decision. Darrow, who had spent nearly two years of his life on this trial, also helped obtain an acquittal for Pettibone, and the case against Moyer was dismissed. He received a fee of $50,000 for his efforts.[57]

Darrow never admitted to wrongdoing—either then or in the aftermath of the McNamara trial—but did acknowledge that underhanded tactics were needed to prevail in the fierce battle with foes of organized labor. "Do not the rich and powerful bribe juries, intimidate and coerce judges as well as juries?" he once asked a colleague. "Do they shrink from any weapon?"[58]

Darrow's own raison d'être was expressed in an interview he gave in 1918 to the Illinois Historical Society when he alluded to John Peter Altgeld, his beloved mentor:

> He would do whatever would serve his purpose when he was right. He'd use all the tools of the other side—stop at nothing—but always with an end in view—to do good for the poor man. He was perfectly unscrupulous in getting ends, but absolutely *honest* in those ends.[59]

The Case Against the McNamaras, 1910–1911

At the conclusion of the Haywood trial, Darrow returned to Chicago and re-established his law practice. His next major labor case—the defense of the McNamara brothers in 1911—became the last case he was ever asked to take by organized labor. It ended with a guilty plea for his clients and two subsequent trials for perjury in which Darrow was the defendant.

The case against the McNamara brothers stemmed from an act of violence. On October 1, 1910, the *Los Angeles Times* building was blown up by dynamite and twenty men were killed. The newspaper was regarded as rabidly antiunion, and it blamed labor for the incident.

The bombing occurred in the midst of smoldering relations in the city's construction industry between the National Erectors Association (NEA) and the Structural Iron Workers Union (SIWU). A general strike had been called by the city union in support of the closed shop, a move which was vehemently opposed by the *Times*.

Following the bombing, William J. Burns, of the detective agency that bore his name, was hired by the NEA to investigate the bombing. Burns narrowed down the investigation to a handful of suspects, including James B. ("Jim") McNamara and Ortie McManigal, both members of the SIWU. On April 14, 1911, he arrested them in Detroit on charges of safe blowing. Both men were moved without warrants to Chicago, where they were extradited to Los Angeles. Two weeks later, Jim's brother, John J. ("J.J.") McNamara, who was secretary-treasurer of the SIWU, was arrested at a union meeting in Indianapolis and extradited to Los Angeles.

McManigal confessed to the *Times* bombing and implicated the McNamara brothers. He also accused J.J. of masterminding a series of other bombings in the Los Angeles area and stated that Jim had personally placed the dynamite in each instance.[60]

In the wake of McManigal's confession, Darrow was asked to take the case by Samuel Gompers, the respected head of the American Federation of Labor (AFL). Despite the confession, Gompers apparently believed that the men had been framed. At the time he was approached by Gompers, Darrow knew about the case only from its extensive coverage in the press. The reports convinced him that the brothers were guilty, as he confided to his friend Ernest Stout of the Central Press. In a conversation with Stout prior to accepting the case, Darrow stated that he felt Burns had absolute proof of their guilt, and that he did not want to take a case which "he had no chance of winning."[61]

Why did Darrow take the case? The reason was that Gompers maneuvered him into taking it. Gompers, a shrewd observer of human nature, had concluded that Darrow could be coerced. "You will go down in history as a traitor to the great cause of labor," he told Darrow, "if now, in our greatest need, you refuse to take charge of the McNamara case." His threat was combined with an offer of a $50,000 fee and an ample defense fund. In the end, Darrow acquiesced.[62]

Darrow's apprehensions proved to be correct. Although there was a possibility that McManigal had turned state's evidence to save his own life, he had nevertheless told the truth, and virtually every detail of his story could be corroborated by other witnesses.

The McNamara trial opened on October 11, 1911, in Los Angeles. Buttressed by the acclaim he had received from organized labor for undertaking to defend the brothers, Darrow planned his strategy. In order to devote his unwavering ardor to the defense of his clients, he had long ago learned to refrain from asking them if they were guilty, and this case was no exception.

Part of Darrow's strategy may have been to bribe members of the jury. One of the first things that he did when he took the case was to hire Bert Franklin, a former detective on the staff of the county sheriff and an ex-deputy United States marshal, to gather information from "The Wheel," a revolving list of prospective jurors. On November 28, 1911, Franklin was arrested at the corner of a busy Los Angeles street after attempting to bribe prospective juror George Lockwood with $4,000 for his assistance in bringing about either a hung jury or an acquittal. Lockwood had notified the district attorney on November 14, after Franklin had first approached him, and the police were waiting to arrest Franklin at the appointed time.

Shortly before the arrest was made, Darrow received an anonymous telephone call in his office. A voice he did not know said, "Darrow? If you want to save your man Franklin, you'd better hurry. They're onto him. If he passes that money at Third and Los Angeles, you're all for it."[63] Darrow arrived at the time that Franklin was about to be arrested, and one of the policemen later testified at Darrow's first bribery trial that he heard Darrow exclaim, "They're onto us, Bert." The statement was disputed by another policeman, who stated that Darrow told Franklin, "They're onto you, Bert." A third policeman, who was also on the scene, said he was unable to hear the conversation.[64]

Three days after Franklin was arrested, Darrow changed the "not guilty" plea for the McNamara brothers to a "guilty" plea. Darrow, who would later state that a plea bargain had been negotiated before Franklin's arrest, justified his action on the grounds that the evidence against the brothers had been overwhelming and that Jim McNamara had actually confessed to him in the course of being prepared for trial. But the district attorney and the judge presiding at the McNamara trial suggested that the change of plea was made only after

Franklin was arrested. Their view was shared by many members of organized labor who believed that Darrow had betrayed the McNamaras: he entered the guilty plea in order to show that he would have had no motive to bribe jurors in a case that had already been settled.

The McNamara brothers were sentenced on December 5. Jim received a life sentence, and J.J. was sentenced to fifteen years in jail. Later in the month, Darrow paid a visit to Mary Field, who was then working as a journalist and staying in Los Angeles to write about the McNamara trial. When Darrow arrived at her apartment, he took her by surprise by taking out a bottle of whiskey from a pocket in his coat, pulling a gun out of his other pocket, and announcing that he was going to kill himself. "They're going to indict me for bribing the McNamara jury," he told her. "I can't stand the disgrace." Field spoke to him for hours until she finally hit upon an argument that worked: if he killed himself, the public would always believe that he was guilty, and his legacy could be ruined.[65]

State of California v. Darrow, 1912–1913

Darrow correctly surmised what was going to happen to him. In January 1912, Franklin pleaded guilty to the attempted bribery, paid a $4,000 fine (the same amount as the alleged bribe), and swore that Darrow had directed him to bribe another prospective juror, Robert Bain. Shortly thereafter, Darrow was indicted on two counts of attempted bribery. Each case would be tried separately.

The Lockwood trial began in May 1912 and lasted three months. Darrow was defended by Earl Rogers, regarded as the most skilled defense attorney in Los Angeles. Ironically, Rogers had been previously hired by the McNamara prosecution team to investigate the *Times* bombing. He agreed to take this case without his usual up-front fee of $25,000, and his family later charged that Darrow failed to pay him more than $27,000 for legal expenses.[66]

It was agreed that Rogers would defend Darrow in court, and the latter would be allowed to give his own closing statement. In spite of the fact that Rogers gave a brilliant performance in court, Darrow looked like a broken man throughout the trial. But his mastery returned when he needed it most, and he made one of the most persuasive summations in his entire career. In a particularly compelling part of his summation, Darrow posed a question to the jury. "Suppose I am guilty of bribery?" he asked. He then declared that there were many crimes infinitely worse than perjury and presented himself as a martyr to the cause of justice:

> I am not being tried for having sought to bribe a man named Lockwood. There may be, and doubtless are many people who think I did seek to bribe him, but I am not being tried for that. . . . No man is being tried upon that charge. I am tried because I have been a lover of the poor, a friend of the oppressed, because I have stood by labor for all these years, and have brought down upon my head the wrath of the criminal interests in this country. Whether guilty or innocent, that is the reason that

> I have been pursued by as cruel a gang of cutthroats as ever pursued any man since the world was born.[67]

His summation lasted nearly two days. By the time he had finished, his face was streaming with tears, and the jury was weeping. Even the court stenographer had cried. The summation has been referred to as "one of the great all-time performances ever seen and heard in any courtroom since Cicero."[68]

It took the jury only twenty-seven minutes to deliberate before returning a verdict of "not guilty." As tumultuous rejoicing filled the court, the judge made his way to the defendant. He grasped Darrow's hand and said, "There will be hallelujahs from millions of voices through the length and breadth of this land."[69]

In late January 1913, Darrow was tried for bribing Robert Bain, acting as his own attorney. On March 8 the jury announced that it was hopelessly deadlocked. At that time, it stood eight to four for conviction. The prosecutors decided not to retry the case, and Darrow once again returned to Chicago to resume the practice of law.

Was Darrow innocent of the charges? His lawyer, Earl Rogers, believed him to be guilty, as did Mary Field. As his earlier career suggested, Darrow was not averse to using any means necessary to win in the struggle against the powerful interests of the day. "Do not be surprised at any thing you hear," he wrote to his son from Los Angeles. "As for me, I don't care much. My mind and conscience are at ease."[70]

The Birth of a Criminal Attorney

Despite the two acquittals, Darrow was shunned by many of his friends and scorned by the leadership of the AFL. His corporate and civil clients largely deserted him, but an entirely new field was opened up to him by clients seeking his help when they were defendants in criminal cases. For the first time in his thirty-eight years of practice and at a time when retirement was an option for a man of his age, Clarence Seward Darrow began to think of himself as a criminal attorney.[71]

His work in criminal law turned out to be one of the most fascinating and fulfilling experiences in his life. As he wrote:

> Strange as it may seem, I grew to like to defend men and women charged with crime. It soon came to be something more than winning or losing a case. I sought to learn why one man goes one way and another takes an entirely different road. I became vitally interested in the cause of human conduct. This meant more than the quibbling with lawyers and juries, to get or keep money for a client so that I could take part of what I won or saved for him; I was dealing with life, with its hopes and fears; its aspiration and despairs.[72]

His greatest glory lay ahead. From the time he was sixty-seven until he reached the age of seventy-five, Darrow represented several high-profile criminal defendants, including Nathan Leopold Jr. and Richard Loeb (1924);

Dr. Ossian H. Sweet (1925); Henry Sweet (1926); and Thomas H. Massie (1932). Among his lesser-known clients were Benjamin Gitlow and other New York radicals indicted under state sedition laws in 1920 for their allegedly subversive activities, and Calogero Greco and Donato Carillo, two Italian immigrants falsely accused in 1927 of stabbing two Fascists to death outside a New York subway station.

Although he became a legend in his own time following his victories in the Leopold and Loèb case and the famous Scopes trial in 1925, Darrow remained one of the most controversial men in America. One afternoon in the 1920s, he was invited to lunch at the home of H.L. Mencken in Baltimore and had to climb a flight of steep, narrow stairs in the critic's house. "Be careful, Clarence," Mencken told him. "If you fall and kill yourself in my house, the public will crucify me." Darrow had another thought on the matter. "No, they won't," he replied. "They'll canonize you."[73]

The Leopold-Loeb Case, 1924

The Leopold-Loeb trial was a prime example of the dichotomy in the public's mind about Darrow. On one hand, the "Old Lion" was deified for his brilliant defense of the teenage murderers and his fervent plea against capital punishment. To his critics, Darrow had sold out to the rich families of the defendants by accepting what was incorrectly termed "a million-dollar defense fund."[74]

Nathan ("Babe") Leopold Jr., eighteen, and Richard ("Dickie") Loeb, seventeen, were unlike any clients Darrow had ever defended. Babe, a Phi Beta Kappa graduate of the University of Chicago, was the youngest student to graduate from that university, and Dickie was the youngest student ever to graduate from the University of Michigan. Both came from prominent Chicago families, and they had been involved in a homosexual relationship—a fact that remained muted in the course of the trial. In 1924, they began to plan a random thrill killing with the intention of kidnapping and murdering a victim, demanding ransom, gaining notoriety, and committing the perfect crime. All their goals were realized, except the last one.[75]

Their "thrill" killing took place on May 21, 1924, when Dickie and Babe gave a ride to fourteen-year-old Robert ("Bobby") Franks, on his way home from school. The boys later contacted Bobby's father and demanded a ransom of $10,000. Before the ransom could be paid, Bobby's mutilated body was found in a marshlands drainage on the far south side of Chicago. A pair of eyeglasses with an unusual rim was left at the crime scene and was later traced to Babe. Within ten days after Bobby was murdered, the police had cracked the case. They arrested Dickie and Babe, who confessed to the murder.[76]

Under Illinois law, the prosecutor could ask for the death sentence, and Robert E. Crowe, the chief prosecutor and a former Cook County circuit judge, made his intentions known from the beginning. "I have a hanging case," he announced. "The state is ready to go to trial."[77]

The distraught Loeb family prevailed upon Darrow to take the case. Although the promise of a substantial fee and the opportunity to participate in a sensational trial may have made his decision easier, Darrow had long expressed his antipathy to the death penalty. In *Crime: Its Causes and Treatment* (1922), Darrow had reiterated his earlier views that no personal blame could be attached to crime because the behavior of human beings was dictated by their environment and heredity.

In accepting the case, Darrow hoped to prevent his clients from being executed. "No client of mine ever had been put to death," he wrote, "and I felt that it would almost, if not quite, kill me if it should ever happen."[78] But he was aware that public sentiment was strongly against the boys because of its revulsion at this senseless crime, and he doubted if either of these two brilliant boys could meet the legal definition of insanity. Accordingly, two days before the trial was scheduled to begin, he startled the prosecutor by changing the plea to "guilty" and waiving the right to a jury trial.

The trial, which began on July 23, 1924, was tried without a jury before Judge John Caberly, chief justice of the Criminal Court of Cook County. The defense consisted of Darrow and attorneys Benjamin and Walter Bachrach, two brothers who were distant cousins of Loeb. As allowed by Illinois law, they offered evidence in mitigation of punishment, and Darrow called several psychiatrists (then called "alienists") to testify to the mental abnormality of the boys. It was a much more flexible concept than the insanity defense and was subject to considerable interpretation.[79]

The sensational nature of the trial drew both the national media and the public to the crowded Chicago courtroom, which held only three hundred seats. Mounted police guarded the building in order to keep the crowd from stampeding into the court. Several persons in the courtroom fainted from the intense heat, and on one occasion a court attendant had his arm broken as the spectators stormed their way into the proceedings.

On August 22, Darrow began his final presentation. It took two days and lasted over twelve hours. He reminded the judge that

> Your Honor stands between the past and the future. You may hang these boys; you may hang them by the neck until they are dead. But in doing it, you will turn your face toward the past. In doing it you are making it harder for every other boy who, in ignorance and darkness, must grope his way through the mazes which only childhood knows. In doing it, you will make it harder for unborn children. You may save them and make it easier for every child that sometimes may stand where these boys stand. You will make it easier for every human being with an aspiration and a vision and a hope and a fate.
>
> I am pleading for the future; I am pleading for a time when hatred and cruelty will not control the hearts of men, when we can learn by reason and judgment that understanding and faith that all life is worth saving, and that mercy is the highest attribute of man.[80]

When Darrow finished, there was a stunned silence throughout the courtroom. One of the many reporters covering the trial noted that Darrow's eyes were "dimmed by years of serving the accused, the oppressed, the weak, [and] were not the only ones that held tears."[81]

Judge Caberly, who was one of the people who wept in court that day, announced his decision on September 10, 1924. He sentenced each boy to ninety-nine years in prison for Bobby Franks's murder and ninety-nine years for kidnapping. Darrow's clients escaped the death penalty, and he again became a national celebrity.

His "million-dollar defense" actually netted him only $70,000, which he had to share with his law firm.[82] Fame also had come with its own price, for the case had drained him emotionally. He later noted that "when I closed I had exhausted all the strength I could summon. From that day, I have never gone through so protracted a strain, and could never do it again, even if I should try."[83]

The Scopes Trial, 1925

Darrow's fame rose to new heights the following year, when he defended John Thomas Scopes in the famous "monkey trial." It marked the first—and only—time in Darrow's life that he volunteered to take a case. While the trial took on some of the aspects of a farce rather than a serious courtroom drama, it signified a clash between two major currents in American thought: religious fundamentalism versus the teaching of evolution.

On March 21, 1925, Tennessee became the first of several states to enact a law prohibiting the teaching of evolution by making it unlawful for any teacher in the public school system to teach "any theory that denies the story of the Divine creation of man as taught in the Bible, and to teach instead that man has descended from a lower order of animals." As soon as the law was passed, the American Civil Liberties Union (ACLU) took out advertisements in newspapers throughout the state announcing its intention to challenge the law and offering to pay for the defense of any public school teacher who would violate it. The ACLU, which had been founded in 1917 to protect civil liberties in the country, viewed the Tennessee law as a flagrant violation of the rights of free speech in the classroom.

The advertisement caught the attention of civic leaders in the town of Dayton (population 1,800), including George Rappelyea, a thirty-one-year-old mining engineer, who opposed fundamentalism, the view that every statement in the Bible be accepted as literally true. He also believed that a trial held in Dayton on this issue would attract national attention and bring needed business to town. Rappelyea immediately contacted the ACLU to confirm that it would really finance the defense in the event that such a trial took place. The ACLU wrote back that it would guarantee all expenses, including a $1,000 fee to each of the attorneys.

On May 5, 1925, a fateful meeting took place in Robinson's Drug Store in Dayton. Rappelyea approached John Thomas Scopes, a good-natured, twenty-four-year-old high school football coach, who had briefly taught evolution when he substituted as a biology teacher. Rappelyea told Scopes that he wanted to bring a court action against him for having taught evolution. When Scopes agreed, Rappelyea swore out a warrant for the teacher's arrest, and Scopes turned himself into custody.[84]

The trial took on national prominence later that month when it was announced that William Jennings Bryan had volunteered to join the prosecution in *State of Tennessee* v. *Scopes*. Bryan was a three-time Democratic presidential candidate, an avowed fundamentalist, and one of the greatest orators in America.

A week before he learned that Bryan would represent the prosecution, Darrow, who was both an agnostic and an evolutionist, conferred with leaders of the ACLU in New York about the upcoming litigation. They agreed that it would be better for a local attorney to head the defense, but the announcement of Bryan's entry into the case changed the dynamics of the situation.

Darrow was in Richmond, Virginia, when he learned that Bryan would prosecute Scopes. Although he had twice supported Bryan in his presidential campaigns, he had come to regard him with disdain. "I would like to meet Bryan in this case," Darrow told a friend. "I believe I could down him. I would be willing to do it without charging Scopes any fee."[85] He then wired the ACLU and offered to enter the case. After some hesitation because of the suspicion that the controversial Darrow wanted to use the trial to enhance his star-studded reputation, the Executive Board of the ACLU accepted the offer.[86]

The ACLU sent Darrow and attorneys Arthur Garfield Hays and Dudley Field Malone to Dayton. Their strategy was to admit the guilt of Scopes (who had already confessed) and to argue that the antievolution law was unconstitutional.

The trial, which began on Friday, July 10, 1925, in the Eighteenth Tennessee Court of Rhea County, would rival the Leopold-Loeb case as the media event of the 1920s. Telegraphic facilities hastily put up in lofts over stores were inadequate to handle the 2 million words that were filed in the course of the twelve-day trial. Spectators included fundamentalists from the mountain areas of Tennessee who were curious about the trial, and well-dressed evolutionists from nearby cities who were eager to see the legal battle between Bryan and his famed adversary.[87]

The tone of the trial was set when the two lead attorneys exchanged hostile remarks in the courtroom shortly before Judge John Raulston commenced the proceedings. "The trial uncovers an attack for a generation on revealed religion," Bryan proclaimed. "A successful attack would destroy the Bible and with it revealed religion. If evolution wins, Christianity goes." Darrow, vehemently disagreeing with this statement, snapped back: "Scopes isn't on trial; civilization is on trial. The prosecution is opening the doors for a reign of bigotry equal to anything in the Middle Ages. No man's belief will be safe if they win."[88]

The defense had assembled a team of scientists and biologists to discuss evolution, but Judge Raulston refused to let them testify. Since the jury was unable to hear this testimony, the defense decided to call Bryan to the stand on Monday, July 20, as an expert witness on the Bible. The defense's theory was that it could embarrass Bryan by encouraging him to express fundamentalist views of the Bible as the literal truth, thereby weakening the prosecution's case. In a bizarre twist, Judge Raulston allowed Bryan to testify.

Darrow's two-hour cross-examination of Bryan became the most famous part of the trial. Although Bryan did not do as poorly as has been alleged, he was subjected to public humiliation. As one attorney later noted:

> There was something cruel about the proceedings. Bryan appeared trapped, like a dumb animal. The truth was that he was too far removed from the modern world, from intellectual exercise, to put up a decent fight. He was used to popular adulation, and had grown flabby. Darrow, accustomed to adversity and fighting public opinion, had grown strong—and hard.[89]

The next day, Judge Raulston ordered that Bryan's testimony be expunged from the record. In order to prevent Bryan from making a comeback in his closing statement, Darrow pleaded Scopes guilty and waived the defense's right to a closing speech. Under Tennessee law, the prosecution was thus precluded from delivering its own closing statement.

The jury obliged Darrow by taking nine minutes to return a verdict of "guilty." The judge then fined Scopes $100 for teaching evolution, and the "monkey trial" was over. The verdict was a pyrrhic victory for Bryan, who was physically exhausted from the ordeal. He died in his sleep five days later.

In 1926, the Tennessee Supreme Court overturned the verdict on the grounds that the jury—rather than the judge—should have imposed the fine. Although the state chose not to prosecute Scopes again, the antievolution law remained on the books in Tennessee until 1967, when it was repealed. The next year, the Supreme Court declared in *Epperson* v. *Arizona* that a similar antievolution statute in Arkansas was unconstitutional.[90]

A Varied and Fulfilling Life

For Darrow, life did not turn out to be anticlimactic, even after Scopes. His three most famous cases in subsequent years involved racial intolerance. In 1925, he defended a black physician, Ossian H. Sweet, and eleven other defendants accused of killing a member of a white mob who allegedly tried to storm Sweet's home in Detroit. Following a mistrial, he defended Dr. Sweet's brother, Henry Sweet, in 1926 on the same charge. Darrow retired in 1928, but journeyed to Hawaii four years later to defend Thomas H. Massie, a Navy lieutenant charged with killing a Hawaiian man who had participated in the gang rape of the lieutenant's wife. In each of the cases, he gained freedom for his clients.

Darrow spent the last years of his life lecturing throughout the country, traveling in Europe with his devoted wife Ruby, and venturing into and out of retirement. In 1931, he was asked by the National Association for the Advancement of Colored People to help in the representation of the Scottsboro defendants (nine black boys and young men accused of raping two white prostitutes), but subsequently withdrew from the case when he became convinced that the Communist Party intended to use the trial to advance its own political agenda. He later served as head of a commission appointed by President Franklin D. Roosevelt in March 1934 to assess the operation of the New Deal's National Recovery Administration, and he spent the next four months working up to fourteen hours a day on the job. He was then seventy-seven years of age.[91]

As always, he made time to write. His autobiography, *The Story of My Life* (1932), became a best-seller and has been reissued in subsequent years. The book continues to inspire the public, attorneys, and would-be attorneys, and various movies and plays have been based on his life or on one of his famous trials.

In a memorable passage from *The Story of My Life,* he recalled a troubling incident from his early days in Chicago and noted the vicissitudes of life:

> After the meeting at the West Side hall, I was in gloom amounting almost to despair. If it had been possible, I would have gone back to Ohio; but I didn't want to borrow the money, and I dreaded to confess defeat. I did not then know the ways of Fate, I did not know that Fortune comes like the day, sometimes filled with sunshine, sometimes hidden in gloom. I had not then learned that one must accept whatever comes along without regret; that he must not take either gratification or disappointment too seriously. I did not know, as Bret Harte put it, that the only sure thing about luck is that it will change. And luck can change as suddenly as daylight and darkness on a tropical land.[92]

Darrow died of heart disease on March 13, 1938, shortly before his eighty-first birthday. He undoubtedly would have been pleased that the fame that he sought so assiduously has continued to grow in the years since his death. Although his armor has not been unblemished, his courtroom work remains unsurpassed.

Notes

1. See J. Anthony Lukas, *Big Trouble: A Murder in a Small Western Town Sets Off a Struggle for the Soul of America* (New York: Simon and Schuster, 1997), 327–328.

2. Quoted in Irving Stone, *Clarence Darrow For the Defense* (New York: Doubleday, Signet Books, 1971), 291.

3. Arthur Garfield Hays, *City Lawyer: The Autobiography of a Law Practice* (New York: Simon and Schuster, 1942), 215–216.

4. Geoffrey Cowan, *The People v. Clarence Darrow: The Bribery Trial of America's Greatest Lawyer* (New York: Times Books, 1993), 3–5.

5. Stone, *Clarence Darrow,* 11–16.

6. Ray Ginger, "Clarence Seward Darrow, 1857–1938," *Antioch Review* 13 (March 1953): 52–66.

7. Quoted in Cowan, *The People v. Clarence Darrow,* 7.

8. Quoted in James W. McElhaney, "The Trial of Henry Sweet: Clarence Darrow Confronts the Issues of the Day," *ABA Journal* 78 (July 1992): 73.

9. Cowan, *The People v. Clarence Darrow,* 194; Stone, *Clarence Darrow,* 96–97.

10. Quoted in Lukas, *Big Trouble,* 602.

11. Bennet L. Gershman, review of *The Story of My Life,* by Clarence Darrow, *Trial* 33 (April 1997): 80.

12. Henry J. Reske, "A Lawyer's Letters: Clarence Darrow Papers for Sale," *ABA Journal* 81 (March 1995): 18.

13. Brand Whitlock, *Forty Years of It* (New York: D. Appleton, 1941), 84–85.

14. Hays, *City Lawyer,* 216.

15. Miriam Gurko, *Clarence Darrow* (New York: Thomas Y. Crowell, 1965), 3.

16. Clarence Darrow, *The Story of My Life* (New York: Charles Scribner's Sons, 1932; reprint ed., with a new introduction by Alan M. Dershowitz, New York: Da Capo Press, 1996), 1–21; Stone, *Clarence Darrow,* 29–30.

17. Darrow, *The Story of My Life,* 14.

18. Ibid., 19–20.

19. Ibid., 31–32.

20. Ibid., 8.

21. Quoted in Stone, *Clarence Darrow,* 29.

22. Darrow, *The Story of My Life,* 28.

23. Stone, *Clarence Darrow,* 29. A similar version of this story can be found in Ginger, "Clarence Seward Darrow," 54.

24. Arthur and Lila Weinberg, *Clarence Darrow: A Sentimental Rebel* (New York: G.P. Putnam's Sons, 1980), 26.

25. Darrow, *The Story of My Life,* 30.

26. Ibid.

27. Stone, *Clarence Darrow,* 35.

28. Darrow, *The Story of My Life,* 34.

29. Ibid., 39.

30. Ibid.

31. Quoted in Abe C. Ravitz, *Clarence Darrow and the American Literary Tradition* (Cleveland: Press of Western Reserve University, 1962), 35.

32. Lukas, *Big Trouble,* 306.

33. Darrow, *The Story of My Life,* 57.

34. Ibid., 62. In his account, Darrow spelled Hughitt's name as "Hewitt."

35. William Moses Kunstler, *The Case for Courage* (New York: Morrow, 1962), 205–235.

36. Stone, *Clarence Darrow,* 71–73.

37. Quoted in Weinberg and Weinberg, *Clarence Darrow,* 62.

38. Kunstler, *The Case for Courage,* 227–228.

39. Darrow, *The Story of My Life,* 66.

40. Arthur and Lila Weinberg, "The Massie Trial: Darrow's Last Case," *Trial Diplomacy Journal* 11 (Fall 1988): 22.

41. Quoted in Lukas, *Big Trouble,* 315.

42. Darrow, *The Story of My Life,* 119.

43. Weinberg and Weinberg, *Clarence Darrow,* 118.

44. Cowan, *The People v. Clarence Darrow,* 65; Weinberg and Weinberg, *Clarence Darrow,* 156.

45. Lukas, *Big Trouble,* 301.

46. Cowan, *The People v. Clarence Darrow,* 41–42; Weinberg and Weinberg, *Clarence Darrow,* 78–79.

47. Kevin Tierney, *Darrow: A Biography* (New York: Thomas Y. Crowell, 1979), 147.

48. Ibid., 186.

49. See Joann Wypijewski, review of *Big Trouble: A Murder in a Small Western Town Sets Off a Struggle for the Soul of America,* by J. Anthony Lukas, *The Nation* 265 (October 13, 1997): 27.

50. Mark Sullivan, *Our Times: The United States, 1900–1925,* 6 vols. (New York: Charles Scribner's Sons, 1927), vol. 3: *Pre-War America,* 481–490; Lukas, *Big Trouble,* 433–458, 536–537, 629.

51. Sullivan, *Our Times,* 487–489.

52. Weinberg and Weinberg, *Clarence Darrow,* 137.

53. Lukas, *Big Trouble,* 328.

54. Ibid., 335.

55. Quoted in Arthur Weinberg, ed., *Attorney for the Damned* (Chicago: University of Chicago Press, 1957), 486.

56. Sullivan, *Our Times,* 494.

57. Lukas, *Big Trouble,* 329.

58. Ibid., 325.

59. Quoted in Cowan, *The People v. Clarence Darrow,* 29–30.

60. Stone, *Clarence Darrow,* 295–298; Weinberg and Weinberg, *Clarence Darrow,* 162–170, 272–275.

61. Quoted in Cowan, *The People v. Clarence Darrow,* 123.

62. Ibid., 121–122.

63. Quoted in Adela Rogers St. Johns, *Final Verdict* (Garden City, NY: Doubleday, 1962), 386.

64. Ibid.

65. Cowan, *The People v. Clarence Darrow,* 4.

66. Gerald F. Uelmen. "What's Happened in California Law for Past Century? Top 10 Legal Stories Prove That History Tends to Repeat Itself: The Journal Turns 100," *Los Angeles Daily Journal,* April 6, 1988, 1.

67. Quoted in Edward Mosk, "Darrow on Trial," *California Lawyer* 3 (March 1982): 34.

68. Tierney, *Darrow,* 267.

69. Quoted in Cowan, *The People v. Clarence Darrow,* 431.

70. Quoted in Reske, "A Lawyer's Letters," 18.

71. Stone, *Clarence Darrow,* 395–396.

72. Darrow, *The Story of My Life,* 75–76.

73. Quoted in Stone, *Clarence Darrow,* 559.

74. Tierney, *Darrow,* 223.

75. Ibid., 321–322.

76. Weinberg and Weinberg, *Clarence Darrow,* 297–298; Stone, *Clarence Darrow,* 435–442.

77. Quoted in Weinberg and Weinberg, *Clarence Darrow,* 298.

78. Darrow, *The Story of My Life,* 232.

79. Paula S. Fass, "Making and Remaking an Event: The Leopold and Loeb Case in American Culture," *The Journal of American History* 80 (December 1993): 931.

80. Quoted in Weinberg, *Attorney for the Damned,* 86–87.

81. Quoted in Tierney, *Darrow,* 341.

82. Ibid., 350.

83. Darrow, *The Story of My Life,* 242.

84. Frederick Lewis Allen, *Only Yesterday: An Informal History of the Nineteen-Twenties* (New York: Harper Brothers, 1931), 201–206.; Sullivan, *Our Times,* vol. 6: *The Twenties,* 641–644.

85. Quoted in Stone, *Clarence Darrow,* 487.

86. Ibid.; Edward J. Larson, *Summer for the Gods: The Scopes Trial and America's Continuing Debate Over Science and Religion* (New York: Basic Books, 1997), 101–103.

87. Sullivan, *Our Times: The Twenties,* 442–443.

88. Quoted in Stone, *Clarence Darrow,* 493.

89. Tierney, *Darrow,* 365.

90. Weinberg and Weinberg, *Clarence Darrow,* 329.

91. Gurko, *Clarence Darrow,* 261–262.

92. Darrow, *The Story of My Life,* 45–46.

Selected Cases

United States v. Debs (1894)
64 F. 724

Eugene V. Debs, president of the American Railway Union (ARU), ordered a boycott of the Pullman Palace Car Company following a strike by the Pullman workers. On July 2, 1894, federal judges Peter S. Grosscup and William A. Woods obtained an injunction against Debs and three other ARU leaders to prevent them from interfering with any trains carrying mail. They were arrested later that month (along with four other officers of the ARU) for violating the injunction.

At the time the injunction was issued, Darrow was general attorney for the Chicago & Northwestern Railway. He resigned his railway job in order to serve as Debs's attorney.

In September 1894, Darrow, assisted by S.S. Gregory, represented Debs at the contempt trial for violating the injunction. Gregory, who in later years would become a president of the American Bar Association, was regarded by Darrow as one of the smartest lawyers he ever knew.

Edwin Walker, counsel for the Chicago, Milwaukee & St. Paul Railroad, was appointed special attorney for the government. He was assisted by United States District Attorney Thomas E. Milchrist. The case was heard in Chicago before the United States Circuit Court, with Circuit Judge William A. Woods presiding. The judge (along with Peter S. Grosscup) earlier had been one of the two federal judges enjoining Debs and other ARU officials from prolonging the Pullman strike.

The prosecution opened the case by assailing Debs for being guilty of a conspiracy to starve the country, cripple its industries, and destroy its economic system. Darrow, who was advised by Gregory, countered the argument and took a whole month to tell the jury about the history of labor unions and the conspiracy laws.

Judge Woods announced his decision in December 1894. He found all the defendants guilty of violating the injunction and sentenced them to jail. On January 8, 1895, Debs began his six-months term at the McHenry County jail at Woodstock, Illinois. The seven other defendants were sentenced to three months each at the same facility. However, they were released from jail on January 25, pending the outcome of Darrow's application to the United States Supreme Court for a writ of habeas corpus.

United States v. Debs (1895)

In January 1895, Eugene V. Debs, president of the American Railway Union (ARU), was tried for conspiracy to obstruct the United States mails in connection with the 1894 Pullman boycott. His trial began sixteen days after he started his prison sentence of six months for violating an injunction issued against him in the Pullman case.

Debs, who was represented by Darrow, was tried in Chicago before Federal Judge Peter S. Grosscup. The judge (along with William A. Woods) earlier had been one of the two federal judges enjoining Debs and other ARU leaders from prolonging the Pullman strike. In order to attend his trial, Debs traveled fifty-five miles to Chicago to spend the day in court. He returned each evening to his jail in Woodstock, Illinois.

The distinguished-looking Debs appeared in court dressed like a corporate attorney, while his attorney was clad in a rumpled suit. Darrow, who showed his contempt for the proceedings by slouching down in his chair throughout the trial, had a disdainful expression on his face.

At the trial, Darrow used the techniques that were to become his trademark throughout his legal career: turning the tables on the prosecution by putting it on trial, stirring up compassion for the defendant, and expounding on the inequities in the American economic and social system.

In a bold move, Darrow put Debs on the witness stand. By deftly questioning him about his work for the ARU, Darrow turned Debs from a so-called irresponsible union leader into a highly sympathetic man. Darrow was less successful in getting George M. Pullman, president of the Pullman Palace Car Company, to testify. Pullman managed to disappear and could not be served with a subpoena.

The trial came to an abrupt end on February 12, 1895, when one of the jurors became ill and the judge adjourned the trial. At the time, the jury had been eleven to one in favor of an acquittal. The government decided not to retry Debs, and the conspiracy charge against him was dropped.

In re Debs (1895)
158 U.S. 565

Following the conviction of labor leader Eugene V. Debs in 1894 for contempt in violating an injunction issued by the United States government in conjunction with the Pullman boycott of that same year, the defense appealed the decision to the United States Supreme Court on a writ of error, which was denied. However, a hearing was held on a writ of habeas corpus.

The case was argued by attorney Lyman Trumbull and Darrow. Trumbull argued that it was not against the law to delay the mails or interfere with interstate commerce. Darrow maintained that the Sherman Anti-Trust Act did not apply to unions and stated that the government had no right to apply for an injunction to restrain interference with private property of the railroads.

On May 27, 1895, a unanimous court ruled against Debs. In some respects, the decision was a crushing blow to organized labor. It sanctioned the use of injunctions against labor and established the precedent that the government had the right to interfere with the rights of strikers in order to prevent interference with the rights of employers. Nevertheless, Darrow did not regard the Debs verdict as a defeat. It focused national attention on the struggles of the working masses and enabled labor to learn from its past experiences.

As a result of the verdict, Debs served out his remaining time in jail. But the case helped to establish Darrow as the leading labor lawyer in the country.

State of Wisconsin v. Kidd (1898)

Thomas J. Kidd, general secretary of the Amalgamated Woodworkers' International Union, and George Zentner and Michael Troiber were accused of "criminal conspiracy" against the Paine Lumber Company in Oshkosh, Wisconsin. Zentner and Troiber were residents of Oshkosh who acted as picket captains during the union's fourteen-week strike.

The owner of the company was George W. Paine. He paid his male employees ninety-six cents for a ten-hour day, women were paid at the daily rate of eighty cents, and children received sixty-five cents for the same working day. At one point, he decided to replace the men with women and children. While Wisconsin law set fourteen as the minimum age for child labor, Paine was able to coerce desperate fathers to sign false age affidavits for their children. As a result, many of the children working at the Paine factory were no more than ten years of age.

In 1898, Kidd called a strike. Paine retaliated by hiring nonunion workers and tried to obtain an injunction forcing the strikers to return to work. The Oshkosh court refused to grant the injunction, holding that the workers had a right to strike. Therefore, Paine availed himself of other options. He got the district attorney in Oshkosh to arrest Kidd, Zentner, and Troiber for conspiring to injure his business.

The Woodworkers' Union saw this action as more dangerous than the lawsuit against Eugene V. Debs and the American Railway Union in 1895, when an injunction had been sought against the union for interference with interstate commerce. The union feared that in the event the Wisconsin court were to rule that the woodworkers' strike was criminal, the decision could be cited by other states in similar situations.

Darrow was asked to take the case by the Woodworkers' Union. He had gained fame for his defense of Debs in 1895 and vehemently opposed the use of injunctions against organized labor.

The trial was held in the Municipal Court in Oshkosh. Darrow was assisted by local lawyers Harry I. Weed and Earl P. Finch. The prosecution was represented by Oshkosh's district attorney, H. Quartermass, and F.W. Houghton, a special counsel appointed to assist him.

In the course of his presentation to the jury, Darrow gave a summary of labor's fierce struggle for justice, described Paine's treatment of his workers in the harshest possible terms, and argued that a victory for the company would cripple the union movement. He told the jury that he intended to go well beyond the facts of the case and depicted the struggle between the union and Paine as a struggle in the battle for human liberty.

The trial began in October and ended on November 2. After deliberating for fifty minutes, the jury returned a verdict of "not guilty."

Darrow's summation had lasted two days, and writer William Dean Howells called it "as interesting as a novel." It was subsequently printed and distributed all over the world.

People v. Haywood (1907)

In 1905, former Idaho governor Frank Steunenberg was killed by a bomb as he opened the gate to his home in Caldwell, Idaho. Evidence left at the crime scene led the police to arrest Harry Orchard, a miner who had been living in Caldwell under the name of Tom Hogan. When the authorities were unable to obtain a confession from Orchard, they hired James McParland of the Pinkerton Detective Agency to question him. McParland obtained a confession, in which Orchard said that he was involved in the murder. However, he insisted that he was acting at the behest of three leaders of the Western Federation of Miners in retaliation for Steunenberg's antiunion activities during his governorship. The leaders named by Orchard were William D. ("Big Bill") Haywood, secretary-treasurer; Charles H. Moyer, president; and George Pettibone, who had been active in the union. The three of them had been living in Colorado at the time of Steunenberg's murder and were unable to be extradited to Idaho because they were not fugitives in Idaho. But McParland arranged for the men to be kidnapped in Denver, and they were put on a train bound for the penitentiary in Boise, Idaho.

At the time of Orchard's confession, he also named union member Steve Adams as an accomplice in Steunenberg's murder. Adams was represented by Darrow in a trial in connection with another matter, which was held in Wallace, Idaho, in February 1907.

Darrow had entered the Haywood case (the three defendants were to be tried separately) in 1906, and the trial was finally set for May 10, 1907, in the District Court of Ada County, Idaho. Darrow was assisted by Edmund Richardson of Denver, John Nugent and Edgar Wilson of Boise, and Fred Miller of Seattle, Washington.

Famed orator William E. Borah, senator-elect from Idaho, represented the prosecution. In addition to Borah, James H. Hawley (who had earlier prosecuted the Adams case), Owen M. Van Duyn, and Charles Koelsche served on the prosecution's team.

Prior to the start of the Haywood trial, the prosecution attempted to gain public sympathy for Orchard, its chief prosecution witness, and the governor of Idaho permitted pretrial interviews of him. His confession was printed in *McClure's Magazine.*

Darrow made effective use of the press interviews. He organized a small army of investigators to check Orchard's story, and they provided him with valuable information. When the trial began, Darrow called nearly one hundred witnesses to the stand in an attempt to discredit many of Orchard's statements. Several witnesses also claimed that Orchard had threatened Steunenberg's life on several occasions in anger over the latter's forcing him to sell his share in a lucrative mine in 1899. The testimony had the effect of not only impeaching Orchard as a witness, but giving him a motive for the murder.

Darrow's summation to the jury lasted over eleven hours and was considered to be one of the best in his career. As usual, he spoke without notes.

In July, the jury returned a verdict of "not guilty," which took Darrow by surprise because of the hostility to the union in the community.

Darrow later defended Pettibone, who was acquitted, and the case against Moyer was dropped. In another trial, Orchard was found guilty of Steunenberg's murder and sentenced to death. The sentence was later commuted to life imprisonment, and Orchard spent nearly fifty years in prison until his death in April 1954.

Idaho v. *Adams* (1907)

When Harry Orchard confessed in 1905 to the murder that year of former Idaho governor Frank Steunenberg, he named Steve Adams as an accomplice. Adams was a member of the Western Federation of Miners (WFM), which was cited by Orchard as the force behind the killing. Orchard had claimed he was acting under orders from three prominent members of the WFM: William D. ("Big Bill") Haywood, secretary-treasurer; Charles H. Moyer, president; and George Pettibone, who had been active in the union.

At the time of Orchard's confession, Adams was living in Oregon. He was arrested by local officials for Steunenberg's murder, denied a lawyer, and put on a train to the penitentiary in Boise, Idaho. The only person he was allowed to see was fellow prisoner Orchard, who told him he would be hanged unless he agreed to back up the story that the murder was committed at the instigation of the union.

When Adams balked at confessing, the authorities sent John McParland of the Pinkerton Detective Agency to obtain a confession. McParland informed Adams that the only way he could gain his freedom was to sign a confession implicating the union. This time, Adams confessed.

The confession was short-lived. Darrow, who was to represent Haywood in the trial for Steunenberg's murder, persuaded an uncle of Adams to visit him in the penitentiary. The uncle informed Adams that Darrow would represent him if he recanted his confession. As a result of the meeting, Adams recanted.

When the state prosecutors learned about the recantation, they brought charges against Adams for the murder of Fred Tyler. Tyler, who had taken land belonging to a friend of Adams, was allegedly killed in the northern Idaho town of Wallace in August 1904.

Adams's trial was held in Wallace and began in February 1907. Darrow traveled 2,000 miles in order to appear in court on behalf of Adams. He was assisted by Edmund Richardson of Denver. The prosecutor was James H. Hawley.

In his defense of Adams, Darrow proceeded to put the prosecution on trial and passed over questions pertaining to the innocence or guilt of his client. He argued that the state had charged Adams with Tyler's murder solely to coerce him into supporting Orchard's story about the role of the WFM in Steunenberg's death.

The trial lasted three weeks. It ended in March, when the jury was unable to reach a verdict. The jury had been split seven to five in favor of an acquittal. Adams later was held for retrial and was consequently unable to be a state's witness in the trial of Haywood, scheduled to begin in May 1907.

Following Haywood's acquittal in July, Adams was tried for a second time in Rathdrum, Idaho. That trial also ended in a hung jury, and the count stood ten to two in favor of an acquittal.

Adams was later extradited to Colorado and tried for the shooting of the manager of a mine in Telluride during a strike. This time, he was acquitted and was finally a free man.

People v. McNamara (1911)

On October 1, 1910, the *Los Angeles Times* building was blown up by dynamite, and twenty people were killed. The dynamite actually had been placed not in the building but in Ink Alley, an adjacent roofed-over alley in which barrels of printing ink were stored. When the dynamite went off in Ink Alley, it ignited gas that was leaking from defective pipes and set off the explosion that rocked the *Times* building.

The bombing came at a time when unions in the city were involved in a bitter fight to make Los Angeles a "closed town"—a move designed to bar nonunion members from competing with union workers for jobs. The owner of the *Los Angeles Times* was General Harrison Gray Otis, who was fiercely antiunion and an ardent supporter of the "open shop."

Otis blamed the unions for the explosion, and they accused him of dynamiting the building in order to implicate them and collect the insurance money. In the midst of these smoldering tensions, the National Erectors Association (a powerful group of construction owners) hired detective William J. Burns to investigate the bombing.

Burns gathered enough evidence to implicate John J. ("J.J.") McNamara, secretary-treasurer of the Structural Iron Workers Union (SIWU), his brother James B. ("Jim") McNamara, and Ortie McManigal. Both Jim and McManigal were members of the SIWU.

On April 14, 1911, Jim and McManigal were arrested in Detroit, Michigan. At the time of their arrest, detectives found a large supply of dynamite and percussion caps in their possession. Two weeks later, J.J. McNamara was arrested at a union meeting in Indianapolis, Indiana. The three of them were taken into custody and brought to Los Angeles.

McManigal quickly confessed to a series of bombing plots in California and implicated the McNamara brothers. As to the *Times* bombing, he stated that Jim had put the dynamite in Ink Alley, under orders from his brother. In the wake of McManigal's confession, Jim remained silent. But J.J. McNamara issued a statement in which he urged the public to reserve judgment until he and his brother received a fair trial.

Organized labor rallied in support of the McNamaras. Samuel Gompers, president of the American Federation of Labor, vowed to help them gain their freedom and persuaded Darrow to represent them. Darrow was reluctant to take the case because he had doubts about the innocence of the brothers. Nevertheless, he bowed to Gompers's pressure when he became convinced that he would hurt his own career as a labor attorney by turning down the case. Gompers's offer was also made more attractive by a $50,000 fee for Darrow and an ample defense fund.

Upon his arrival in Los Angeles, Darrow hired a large investigative staff to travel throughout the country in an attempt to find evidence refuting McManigal's confession about the numerous acts of violence allegedly committed by him and the McNamaras. However, the investigators found that virtually every statement in McManigal's confession could be corroborated by other witnesses. At the same time, Darrow learned from his visits to his clients in jail that Jim was indeed responsible for the dynamiting of the *Times* building. Jim told Darrow that he had planted only a small amount of dynamite in an attempt to scare the owners; the fatal explosion was a freakish accident. He insisted that he had not intended to take the life of anyone.

The trial was scheduled to begin in Los Angeles in October 1911, and Darrow entered a "not guilty" plea on behalf of the brothers. On December 1, he was in the middle of picking a jury when he changed the plea to "guilty." The change in plea came as a surprise, and Darrow would be blamed by organized labor for selling out the McNamaras. Darrow justified his action by stating that he had become convinced in the course of preparing for trial that the McNamaras were guilty and that he persuaded them to change their plea in order to avoid a death sentence.

The brothers were sentenced four days later. Jim received life imprisonment, and J.J. McNamara was sentenced to fifteen years. Darrow was never again asked by organized labor to serve as an attorney for the defense.

The trial led to unforeseen consequences. As the settlement was being discussed by Darrow and law enforcement officials in November 1911, Bert Franklin, one of Darrow's investigators, was arrested on charges of trying to bribe a juror. Franklin claimed that he was acting on behalf of Darrow, whom he also accused of trying to bribe another juror. The following year, Darrow would be tried on charges of jury tampering.

State of California v. *Darrow* (1912–1913)

In the course of representing the McNamara brothers in *People* v. *McNamara* (1911), Darrow was accused of attempting to bribe two jurors. In January 1912, he was indicted on two counts of attempted bribery. The cases, which were brought by the State of California, were tried separately.

A key figure in both trials was Bert Franklin, a Los Angeles detective and former federal deputy marshal, whom Darrow had hired to gather information on prospective jurors for the McNamara trial. On November 28, 1911—three days before Darrow changed the plea in the McNamara case from "not guilty" to "guilty"—Franklin was arrested on charges of attempting to bribe George Lockwood, a prospective juror.

The timing of the guilty plea became a matter of controversy. Darrow's detractors contended that he entered the guilty plea as a way to indicate that he had no reason to bribe a juror. On the other hand, Darrow's defenders maintained that he previously had concluded that his clients were guilty and that plea bargain was the only way they could escape the death penalty.

At the time that Darrow was indicted, Franklin pleaded guilty to attempted bribery, paid a $4,000 fine (the same amount of the alleged bribe), and swore that Darrow had also directed him to bribe Robert F. Bain, the first juror to be sworn in for the McNamara trial. Franklin further accused Darrow of attempting to influence five prospective jurors. Darrow faced a one- to ten-year prison term on the bribery charge and not more than five years or a fine of $5,000 on the charge of jury tampering.

The Lockwood bribery trial was the first to be held. It began in May 1912, and lasted three months. The state was represented by Los Angeles district attorney John D. Frederick, in addition to Joseph Ford, Arthur Keetch, and Asa Keyes. Darrow, who would play a prominent part in his own trial, retained the services of Earl Rogers. The latter, one of the leading criminal defense attorneys in the country, had served as special prosecutor in the McNamara investigation, and had indicted the brothers. Rogers was assisted in the defense by Harry Dehme, Horace Appel, and Jerry Giesler.

Judge George H. Hutton of the Superior Court of the State of California was the presiding judge. The trial was held in Los Angeles County.

The chief witness for the state was Bert Franklin. Lincoln Steffens, who had participated in the plea bargain negotiations, appeared as a defense witness. A number of leading citizens, including a former president of the Illinois State Bar Association, were character witnesses for Darrow.

The strategy of the defense was to argue that Darrow had been framed by Franklin and the prosecution as a vendetta against him and the labor movement. At the end of the trial, Darrow made his own summation to the jury, and it was a masterful performance. At its end, nearly every member of the courtroom was weeping, including the judge.

It took the jury only twenty-seven minutes to deliberate, and it returned a verdict of "not guilty." The crowd in the courtroom became hysterical upon learning the news, and a number of jurymen shouted. One of the first persons in the room to congratulate Darrow was Judge Hutton.

In January 1913, the state brought charges against Darrow for the alleged bribery of Bain. It was a more difficult trial for Darrow because the alleged bribe was offered prior to the incident involving Lockwood.

The case was heard by Judge William M. Conley of the Superior Court of the State of California. The defense team remained the same as in the earlier trial, except that former judge O.W. Powers of Salt Lake City, Utah, replaced Horace Appel, who had another commitment. Earl Rogers appeared briefly for the defense at the beginning of the trial. Darrow, assisted by Jerry Giesler, handled most of his own defense.

The trial ended on March 8, 1913, when the jury was unable to reach a verdict. At the time, the count stood eight to four in favor of conviction. Darrow appeared to have undermined his own case in his summation by concentrating on the defense of the McNamara brothers instead of dealing with the accusation of bribery against him.

The state did not retry the case and dropped all charges against Darrow nine months later.

People v. *Lloyd* (1920)

In 1920, twenty members of the newly formed Communist Labor Party in America were arrested in Chicago and charged with violating the espionage act of 1919. The act had made it a crime to advocate the overthrow of the government of the United States by force.

The members had been arrested in one of the raids of Attorney General A. Mitchell Palmer, who was responsible for what became known as the "Palmer Raids." The targets of these raids were suspected members of radical groups operating within the country.

The twenty defendants were intellectuals who were sympathetic to the goals of communism. Many of them were well-to-do native-born Americans, including William Bross Lloyd, a Winnetka, Illinois, millionaire businessman who was the son of Henry Demarest Lloyd, author of *Wealth Against Commonwealth* (1894), a book critical of the economic order.

The defendants were charged with encouraging a general strike in Seattle in 1919 in an attempt to take over the political control of the city. Ole Hanson, a former mayor of Seattle, was the chief witness against them.

Darrow represented the defendants. He did not defend their ideology, but insisted on their right to express their beliefs. He pointed out to the jury that a general strike was legal; in the event that such a strike resulted in violence, the jury would have the right to punish the violence, but nothing else. He also attempted to persuade the jury that Hanson was an unreliable witness and that the evidence for the prosecution had been obtained illegally because the police had entered Lloyd's apartment without a search warrant.

The trial lasted ten weeks, and Darrow was assisted in the case by William S. Forrest. Their arguments failed to convince the jury, and all defendants were found guilty. Their sentences ranged from terms of one to five years, in addition to fines. Lloyd received a one- to five-year sentence and was fined $2,000.

The case was appealed to the Illinois Supreme Court, which affirmed the opinion of the lower court. Darrow sought executive clemency and was successful in his efforts. In 1922, the governor of Illinois pardoned sixteen of the defendants.

State of Illinois v. Nathan Leopold Jr. and Richard Loeb (1924)

In the beginning of 1924, the future looked very promising for Nathan ("Babe") Leopold Jr., eighteen, and Richard ("Dickie") Loeb, seventeen, who were brilliant boys from wealthy Chicago families. Leopold, the son of a retired millionaire box manufacturer, was a Phi Beta Kappa graduate of the University of Chicago and the youngest student ever to graduate from the university. Loeb, the son of a vice president of Sears, Roebuck & Company, was the youngest student to graduate from the University of Michigan. Leopold was enrolled at the University of Chicago Law School, and Loeb was making plans to enter law school.

Four years earlier, Loeb had decided he wanted to commit a perfect crime for the thrill of it and told Leopold about his plan. Leopold, a shy and hypersensitive youngster, idolized the outgoing and popular younger boy and persuaded Loeb to enter into a homosexual relationship with him in return for helping to commit the crime.

The crime took place on May 21, 1924. Their victim was a fourteen-year-old boy named Robert ("Bobby") Franks, who, coincidentally, was a distant relative of Loeb. Bobby Franks was chosen at random from a number of boys who attended the exclusive Harvard Preparatory School, located across the street from Leopold's home in South Side, Kenwood.

Leopold and Loeb picked Bobby up from school and offered him a ride home. As soon as the car moved away, Loeb struck Bobby on the head several times with a chisel. Bobby was then gagged with a rag soaked in hydrochloric acid, and his body was wrapped in a rug. Later in the day, Leopold and Loeb dumped Bobby's body in a culvert under a railroad crossing on the far south side of Chicago.

On the evening of the killing, Leopold made a call from a pay telephone one block from his home. Using the name of "Johnson," he spoke to Bobby's father. Leopold told him that Bobby was safe and would not be harmed if the police were not called. After the call, Leopold went with Loeb to mail a special delivery letter to Bobby's father demanding a ransom of $10,000. The letter arrived the next day.

On May 23, Bobby's father was making plans to pay the ransom when he received a telephone call from the police. The body of his son had been found and identified. A few days later, the police found a pair of horn-rimmed eyeglasses with unusual hinges and traced them to Leopold. On May 30, the police picked up Leopold, but he told them he was with Loeb on the day of the murder. Loeb, picked up for questioning, confessed to the murder on May 31 and stated that it was Leopold who had killed Bobby with the chisel. Stunned by Loeb's assertion, Leopold also confessed, but denied that he was the one who had killed Bobby.

Darrow, who was asked to take the case on June 2 by Loeb's father, represented both boys in what became known as the "thrill" killing and "the crime of the century." A staunch opponent of capital punishment, Darrow sought to save his clients from being sentenced to death. Since he took pride in being a "people's" lawyer, Darrow drew widespread condemnation for his "million-dollar defense."

In the course of preparing for trial, Darrow reasoned that a defense of insanity would be difficult to prove because of the brilliance of his clients, and he convinced them to plead guilty to the murder to which they had already confessed. Feeling that a jury would be decidedly unsympathetic to the boys, he waived the right to a jury trial.

The trial, which began on July 23, 1924, was heard by Judge John Caberly, chief justice of the Criminal Court of Cook County. The defense team offered evidence in mitigation of punishment and called several psychiatrists (then called "alienists") to testify to the mental abnormality of the boys. It was a more flexible concept than the insanity defense, and was subject to considerable interpretation.

The sixty-seven-year-old lawyer gave his memorable final summation on August 22. It took two days and lasted over twelve hours. In the course of the summation, Loeb dug his fist in his eyes, while Leopold unsuccessfully tried to hold back tears. Darrow's impassioned plea to spare the lives of the boys brought tears to many of the spectators in court, as well as to the judge. The chief prosecutor for the state was Robert E. Crowe, a former Cook County Circuit Court judge, who also spoke for two days when delivering his summation.

Judge Caberly announced his decision on September 10, 1924. Each defendant received ninety-nine years for the murder, plus ninety-nine years for kidnapping. Nevertheless, their lives were spared.

Although Darrow had been criticized for his "million-dollar defense," he actually received only $70,000 for his work and had to share it with his law firm. The boys went to Joliet Penitentiary in Illinois. Loeb was killed in a prison fight in 1936. Leopold became a model prisoner and was paroled on March 13, 1958, the twentieth anniversary of Darrow's death.

State of Tennessee v. John Thomas Scopes (1925)

The Scopes trial, or the "monkey trial," involved the teaching of evolution in the public school system in Dayton, Tennessee. Pitted against each other in the courtroom were two of America's most famous attorneys: William Jennings Bryan for the prosecution and Clarence Darrow for the defense.

On March 21, 1925, Tennessee became the first of several states to enact a law prohibiting the teaching of evolution in its public school system. The law stemmed from the state's rejection of Charles Darwin's theory of evolution, which held that all life had evolved from the simple to the complex and that man was descended from the apes. The teaching of evolution ran counter to the thinking of the fundamentalists, who believed in the literal interpretation of the Bible and accepted the story of the creation of Adam and Eve as told in the Bible.

The Tennessee law attracted the attention of the American Civil Liberties Union (ACLU), which had been founded in 1917 to protect civil liberties in the United States. Accordingly, it took out advertisements in newspapers throughout the state announcing its intention to challenge the law and offering to pay for the defense of any public school teacher who would violate it.

The advertisements caught the attention of George Rappelyea, a thirty-one-year-old mining engineer, who opposed fundamentalism and believed that antievolution law was unconstitutional. He also thought that a test case in Dayton would bring business to the town.

At a fateful meeting on May 5 in Robinson's Drug Store, located on the main street in Dayton, Rappelyea approached John T. Scopes, an unmarried, twenty-four-year-old high school football coach who had briefly taught evolution when he substituted as a biology teacher. Scopes opposed the antievolution law and agreed to be the defendant in a case challenging the Tennessee statute.

When William Jennings Bryan learned of the pending lawsuit, he volunteered his services to the prosecution. A three-time candidate for president on the Democratic ticket, Bryan was an avowed fundamentalist and one of the greatest orators in the country.

The entry of Bryan into the case prompted Darrow to do something he had never done before: volunteer his services for a lawsuit. The ACLU accepted his offer, and Darrow joined the defense team. In addition to Darrow, the ACLU sent attorneys Arthur Garfield Hays and Dudley Field Malone to Dayton.

Spectators swarmed into Dayton from all parts of Tennessee, and the trial attracted the attention of the national media. Western Union installed twenty-two telegraph wires in the city for the use of the more than twenty newspapermen covering the trial. Revival groups set up tents, and hot dog and lemonade vendors assembled makeshift stands in the area surrounding the courthouse; a circus atmosphere pervaded the town.

The trial began on July 10, 1925, in the Eighteenth Tennessee Court of Rhea County and was presided over by Judge John Raulston. The jury consisted of twelve men, eleven of whom were churchgoers. Six of them were Baptists, four Methodists, and one a member of Disciples of Christ.

Judge Raulston refused to let expert witnesses assembled by the defense team testify on evolution. At this point in the proceedings, many newspapermen, concluding that the trial was over, left town. But in a surprise move, the defense called Bryan to the stand as an expert witness on the Bible.

Bryan took the stand on July 20, and Darrow's two-hour cross-examination of him became the most famous part of the trial. Toward the end of the questioning, Darrow asked Bryan about the six days of Creation. In an answer that horrified his followers at the trial, Bryan stated that he did not think the term "day" necessarily meant a day of twenty-four hours. Instead, it could mean a period rather than a literal day, and Creation could have gone on for a million years.

The next day, Judge Raulston ordered that Bryan's testimony be expunged from the record. In order to prevent Bryan from making a closing statement, Darrow pleaded Scopes guilty and waived the defense's right to a closing statement.

The jury returned a verdict of guilty, and Judge Raulston fined Scopes $100 for teaching evolution. In 1926, the Tennessee Supreme Court overturned the verdict on the grounds that the jury—rather than the judge—should have imposed the fine. The antievolution law remained on the books until 1967, when it·was repealed.

People v. *Sweet et al.* (1925)

Ossian H. Sweet, a black graduate of Wilberforce College in Ohio and Howard Medical School, opened an office to practice gynecology in Detroit, Michigan, in 1921. The following year, he married Gladys Mitchell, the daughter of a black musician, and studied abroad for three years. He returned to Detroit in 1925 with his wife and baby daughter, who had been born in Paris, and purchased a house for $18,500 in a middle-class white neighborhood in Detroit. The house had been previously owned by a white woman married to a light-skinned black man who had passed for white. When the neighbors learned that the home had been sold to a black family, the Water Works Park Improvement Association was formed for the purpose of keeping black people out of the neighborhood.

Dr. Sweet moved into his new home on September 8. Anticipating trouble, he requested police protection. In addition, he asked nine male friends and relatives to accompany him. They brought nine guns and ammunition with them. The group included Dr. Sweet's two younger brothers: Otis, a dentist, and Henry, a student at Wilberforce. Gladys Sweet accompanied her husband to their home, but their daughter had been left with the child's grandmother.

On September 8, a crowd gathered outside the Sweet home. Approximately nine policemen were present to guard the premises. However, the crowd was relatively quiet and dispersed.

The next night, the crowd was much larger and more unruly, with shouts of "Niggers!" and "Get the damn niggers!" Several people in the crowd threw rocks at the Sweet home, breaking a few windows. The occupants of the house were prepared, and shots were fired in rapid succession from several windows on the second floor. One of the shots hit Leon Breiner, a white man, in the back and killed him. Another white man was shot in the leg.

The police were initially unaware that anyone had been hit. Police Inspector Norman Schuknecht knocked on the front door to speak to Dr. Sweet, who told him that the shooting would stop. But when Schuknecht was later informed that two men had been hit, he returned to the house accompanied by five policemen and arrested the occupants of the house, including Mrs. Sweet. The arrested parties were indicted and charged with conspiracy to commit murder in the first degree. Henry Sweet was the only defendant who admitted firing a gun, but it could not be shown whether a bullet from his gun had killed Breiner.

At the behest of the National Association for the Advancement of Colored People, Darrow became chief counsel for the defendants. He handled the case with Arthur Garfield Hays of New York and four attorneys (three of whom were white) from Detroit. The prosecutor was state's attorney Robert M. Toms, assisted by Lester S. Moll and Edward J. Kennedy.

The trial began on October 30, 1925, before Judge Frank Murphy of the Record's Court in Detroit. In later years, Murphy would become an associate justice of the United States Supreme Court.

The all-white jury heard the defense contend that its clients used their constitutional right of self-defense to protect themselves from the crowd and that there was no conspiracy to hurt anyone in the crowd. The defense blamed the police for failing to disperse the crowd before it became unruly and the Water Works Park Improvement Association, whose members had given "pep" talks at meetings held prior to the night of the killing about the need to prevent the Sweet family from taking up residence in their home.

The prosecution argued that there had been no agitation from the crowd on the night of the killing and relied on a Michigan law that took a narrow view of the right to self-defense. Its case was bolstered by the fact that the defendants had made conflicting statements to the police on the night of their arrest and that Breiner, who had been shot in the back, may not have been inciting a riot.

Darrow worked at crossword puzzles while the prosecution brought witness after witness to testify that no mob had gathered outside the Sweet home. He was particularly effective when he got a fifteen-year-old prosecution witness to reveal that he had been coached in his remarks about the size of the crowd by the prosecution before the start of the trial. In addition, he told the jury to put themselves in the place of the defendants and asked them how they would have reacted during such a terrifying experience.

Darrow's effectiveness as counsel for the defense may have prevented a guilty verdict. The first trial ended on November 27, 1925, when Judge Murphy declared a mistrial. They jury had been out for forty-six hours and was unable to reach a verdict. The final count had been seven to five in favor of conviction on manslaughter.

People v. Henry Sweet (1926)

After *People* v. *Sweet* (1925) had ended in a mistrial, the defense asked that each defendant be tried separately if the prosecution chose to retry the defendants. The prosecution opted for a retrial. In view of the fact that Henry Sweet was the only defendant to admit that he had fired his gun on the night of September 9, 1925, it decided that he would be the first defendant to be retried.

The trial began in April 1926. Darrow once again served as lead counsel. Arthur Garfield Hays, who had a previous commitment, was replaced by Thomas Chawke, a prominent black attorney.

It was assumed that the trial might be easier for the defense than the first one because tensions in Detroit had eased in the interim. Yet the prosecution also believed that it had a good case. Although it had been unable to link the gun fired by Sweet to the fatal shot, it maintained that he had either killed Breiner or aided and abetted the man who committed the crime.

As he did in the first trial, Darrow continued to blame the Water Works Park Improvement Association for Breiner's death. He received a break in the case when he elicited from a state witness that "action" had been advocated at a meeting of the association held prior to the night of the murder.

In lieu of calling Henry Sweet as a witness, Darrow and Chawke put Dr. Ossian H. Sweet on the stand as the main witness for the defense. During prosecutor Lester S. Moll's summation to the jury, he referred to Dr. Sweet as a "quasi-intelligent" witness and maintained that the Sweet home was under no threat.

Darrow's closing statement lasted seven hours. He asked the jury to imagine what would have happened if the situation had been reversed and eleven white people had killed a black man in the course of protecting their home. He suggested that the whites would have not only been set free, but received medals for their actions.

On May 19, 1926, the jury returned a verdict of "not guilty." In July of the following year, the prosecutors moved to dismiss all charges against the defendants.

At the end of the trial, the Sweet family did not choose to return to their home, and they lived elsewhere in Detroit. The next two years were tragic ones for Dr. Sweet. Both his wife and little daughter died of tuberculosis, the disease that would kill Henry Sweet fourteen years later.

In 1930, Dr. Sweet did move back into the house and remained there for twenty-one years. He remarried twice, was divorced twice, ran unsuccessfully for the Michigan State Senate in 1934, and for the United States Senate in 1950. In later years, he suffered intense pain from arthritis. His life ended in March 1960, when he committed suicide.

People v. Massie et al. (1932)

On Saturday evening, September 12, 1931, Thomas H. Massie, a United States Navy lieutenant stationed at Pearl Harbor, Hawaii, and his wife, Thalia Fortescue Massie, attended an informal officers' dance held at the Waikiki Beach Section of Honolulu. Thalia Massie, a twenty-one-year old socialite from Washington, D.C., decided to take a walk before the dance ended. She went only a short distance before she was grabbed by two men, who dragged her to a car. Three other men had remained in the car, and they drove to an isolated area, where she alleged that she was raped. The evidence for rape later turned out to be inconclusive, but she was beaten severely enough to have broken her jaw.

The men left her along the side of a road, and she was able to flag down a car. She told the driver that she had been raped by a "gang of Hawaiians." In actuality, two of the men were Hawaiians, two were Japanese, and one was Chinese.

The next day, Thalia Massie identified four of the men. On October 12, 1932, they were indicted for rape and assault. The trial began in November, and the case was submitted to a local jury on December 2. It ended in a mistrial four days later when the jury was unable to reach a verdict. The men were released on bail and instructed to report to court daily until a date had been set for a new trial.

Before the new trial took place, Lieutenant Massie beat up one of the alleged assailants and forced him to confess. But the assailant had pictures taken of the welts and bruises on his back, and the lieutenant's lawyer advised that this "confession" would never stand up in court.

In the meantime, Grace Fortescue, the mother of Thalia Massie, arrived in Hawaii from Washington, D.C. When she learned about the assault on her daughter, she was certain that the men were guilty. Determined that they be found guilty at the second trial, she persuaded Massie and two American sailors under his command to kidnap Joseph Kahahawii, one of the alleged kidnappers, and force him to confess. The sailors were Albert O. Jones and Edward J. Lord.

Kahahawii was seized and taken to the house where Grace Fortescue was staying on the island. According to the story told by the defense at the trial, Massie pointed his service revolver at Kahahawii, demanding that he confess. When Kahahawii stated, "Yeah, we done it," the enraged lieutenant killed him with one shot.

While Lieutenant Massie stayed in the house, Grace Fortescue and the two sailors put the body in the trunk of a car and hastened to dispose of it. The car was stopped for speeding, and the body was discovered.

On January 26, 1932, Massie, Fortescue, Jones, and Lord were indicted by a grand jury for second-degree murder. Although Darrow was seventy-five years old and had retired in 1928, he was asked by the defense to represent them. When he decided to take the case for a fee of $25,000, he was criticized for "selling out" to the rich.

The trial began in April, and many spectators lined up outside the courthouse to hear Darrow present his case. Darrow was assisted by George Leisure, a New York lawyer. John C. Kelley, a former Butte, Montana, attorney, was the chief prosecutor. Charles S. Davis, a native New Englander who had been raised in Honolulu, served as judge.

Darrow had insisted that he would represent the defendants on condition that he would not base his plea on race, but on the causes and motives that led to the killing. He admitted the guilt of his clients, but pleaded with the jury to understand the mental anguish of Fortescue and Massie. Early in the trial, he called an expert witness who stated that Lieutenant Massie had been brought to a dangerous emotional state by the attack on his wife and his feeling that her attackers would not receive justice.

Darrow's statements to the jury drew a sharp rebuke from the prosecutor. He argued that Darrow had presented a defense based on sympathy and had ignored the facts of the murder.

At the conclusion of the trial, Judge Davis instructed the jury to convict the defendants if they were responsible for the murder, regardless of the provocation. The jury returned a verdict of manslaughter, but recommended leniency.

The defendants served one hour in custody. At the end of the hour, Lawrence M. Judd, the governor of Hawaii, commuted their sentences. The attorney general of the island asked Darrow for help in retrying the alleged assailants, but he refused, noting that he had never represented the prosecution in his life.

It would be Darrow's last case.

Annotated Bibliography

Allen, Frederick Lewis. *Only Yesterday: An Informal History of the Nineteen-Twenties.* New York: Harper and Row, 1931. Overview of the 1920s; section on Scopes and Leopold-Loeb trials.

Arnold, Thurman. "Review of Clarence Darrow's *Story of My Life.*" *Yale Law Review* 41 (April 1932): 932. Discussion of Darrow and his autobiography.

Babock, Barbara Allen. "Defending the Guilty." *Stanford Lawyer* 18 (Spring 1984): 4–9. Transcript of lecture given at the Cleveland Marshall College of Law on April 5, 1983, about lawyers, including Darrow, and their defense of clients known to be guilty.

Baillie, Hugh. *High Tension.* New York: Harper and Row, 1950. Chapter on relationship between Darrow and Earl Rogers, the attorney who defended him at his perjury trial.

Burns, W.J. *The Marked War: The Story of a Peril That Threatened the U.S. by the Man Who Uncovered the Dynamite Conspirators and Sent Them to Jail.* New York: George H. Doran, 1913. An account by detective William J. Burns of his part in the events leading to the conviction of the McNamara brothers in 1911 for their part in the dynamiting of the *Los Angeles Times* building the previous year.

Cargill, Oscar. *Intellectual America: Ideas on the March.* New York: Macmillan, 1941. Segment on Darrow's career as a writer.

Chroust, Anton-Herman. *The Rise of the Legal Profession in America.* 2 vols. Norman: University of Oklahoma Press, 1965. Discussion of the legal profession and its place in American society.

Conlin, Joseph R. "The Haywood Case: An Enduring Riddle." *Pacific Northwest Quarterly* 59 (January 1968): 23–32. Discussion of the complexities in the 1907 trial of William D. Haywood.

Connolly, C.P. "Protest by Dynamite: Similarities and Contrast Between the McNamara Affair in Los Angeles and the Moyer-Haywood-Pettibone Trial in Boise." *Collier's,* January 13, 1912, 9–10, 23. Review of two of Darrow's most famous cases.

———. "The Saving of Clarence Darrow: Factors and Motives That Led to the Dramatic Close of the McNamara Case." *Collier's,* December 23, 1911, 9–10, 22. Commentary on the reasons for Darrow's change of plea in the McNamara case.

Cowan, Geoffrey. *The People v. Clarence Darrow: The Bribery Trial of America's Greatest Lawyer.* New York: Times Books, 1993. Account of the trial of Darrow on charges of bribing jurors in the McNamara case.

Craddock, Ashley. "Hidden Treasure: Letters Reveal a New Side to Clarence Darrow." *Los Angeles Daily Journal,* February 9, 1995, 4. Discussion about reflections made by Darrow in his previously unpublished letters.

Darrow, Clarence. *Clarence Darrow on the Death Penalty.* Evanston, IL: Chicago Historical Bookworks, 1991. Darrow's debate with Judge Alfred Tailey on capital punishment, and his closing argument in the Leopold-Loeb case.

———. *Crime: Its Causes and Treatment.* Montclair, NJ: Patterson Smith, 1979. Darrow's discussion of the sociological aspects of crime, and his objections to capital punishment.

———. "Evolution of a 'Crime.'" *Los Angeles Daily Journal,* January 18, 1982, 4. Reprint of remarks made by Darrow during the second day of the Scopes trial in 1925.

———. *Farmington.* Chicago: A.C. McClurg, 1904. A fictionalized account of his childhood: the book went through seven editions under the imprints of five different publishers during the course of Darrow's lifetime.

———. *The Story of My Life.* New York: Charles Scribner's Sons, 1932; reprint ed., with a new introduction by Alan M. Dershowitz, New York: Da Capo Press, 1996. Darrow's account of his life and work.

———. "Why I Have Found Life Worth Living." *The Christian Century: A Journal of Religion* 45 (April 19, 1928): 504–505. Reflection by Darrow on the rewarding aspects of his life.

"Darrow Admirers Commemorate 50th Anniversary of His Death." *Chicago Daily Law Bulletin* (March 14, 1988): 1. Remarks on the contributions of Darrow to the legal profession from people who gathered to mark the fiftieth anniversary of his death.

De Camp, L. Sprague. *The Great Monkey Trial.* Garden City, NY: Doubleday, 1968. Discussion of the Scopes trial and its impact on the American scene.

Eaton, Walter. "C.D.: Crusader for Social Justice." *Current History* 35 (March 19, 1932): 786. Commentary on Darrow's work on behalf of social justice.

Fass, Paula S. "Making and Remaking an Event: The Leopold and Loeb Case in American Culture." *Journal of American History* 80 (December 1993), 919–949. Conflicting approaches to famous murder trial.

Foner, Philip Sheldon. *History of the Labor Movement in the United States.* 4 vols. New York: International Publishers, 1965. Account of the struggles of organized labor and the attitudes of the United States government toward the movement.

Ford, Patrick H., ed. *The Darrow Bribery Trial with Background Facts of McNamara Case and Including Darrow's Address to the Jury.* Whittier, CA.: Western Printing, 1956. Collection of writings about McNamara trial and Darrow's subsequent trial for jury bribery.

Gershman, Bennett L. Review of *The Story of My Life,* by Clarence Darrow. *Trial* 33 (April 1997): 80–81. Review of Darrow's autobiography.

Gertz, Elmer. "Clarence Darrow As I Knew Him." *Trial Diplomacy Journal* 10 (Summer 1987): 29–33. Personal recollections by a friend.

Giesler, Jerry, as told to Pete Martin. *The Jerry Giesler Story.* New York: Simon and Schuster, 1960. Segment dealing with Darrow's bribery trial.

Ginger, Ann Fagan. "Watching Darrow Work a Jury." *Criminal Justice Journal* 8 (Winter 1985): 29–46. Discussion of the techniques and strategies employed by Darrow in the trial of Donato Carillo and Calogero Greco, two anti-Fascists, for the murder of two Fascists in New York in 1927.

Ginger, Ray. "Clarence Seward Darrow, 1857–1938." *Antioch Review* 13 (March 1953): 52–66. Overview of Darrow's life and his contributions as an attorney for unpopular and politicized clients.

———. *Eugene V. Debs. A Biography.* New York: Collier Books, 1962. Biography of the labor leader, who was defended by Darrow in 1894 and 1895.

———. *Six Days or Forever? Tennessee v. John Thomas Scopes.* Boston: Beacon Press, 1958. Analysis of the Scopes trial and its implications.

Goldstein, Nicole. "Panel Examines 'The Celebrity Lawyer.'" *New York Law Journal* (April 23, 1998): 2. Discussion of the work of Darrow and his influence on the legal profession.

Gompers, Samuel. *Seventy Years of Life and Labor.* 2 vols. New York: E.P. Dutton, 1925. Discussion by one of the early leaders of the American Federation of Labor of his life and the history of the union; account of Darrow's role in the trial of the McNamara brothers in 1911.

Gurko, Miriam. *Clarence Darrow.* New York: Thomas Y. Crowell, 1965. Concise account of Darrow's life and famous cases.

Harrison, Charles Yale. *Clarence Darrow.* New York: Jonathan Cape and Harrison Smith, 1931. First bibliography of Darrow; author had the cooperation of both Clarence and Ruby Hamerstrom Darrow.

Hawley, James. "Steve Adams' Confession and the State's Case Against Bill Haywood." *Idaho Yesterday* 7 (Winter 1963–1964): 16–27. Account of Haywood trial of 1907.

Hays, Arthur Garfield. *City Lawyer: The Autobiography of a Law Practice.* New York: Simon and Schuster, 1942. Autobiography of the famed civil rights lawyer; discussion of his professional association with Darrow.

Higdon, Hal. *The Crime of the Century: The Leopold and Loeb Case.* New York: G.P. Putnam's Sons, 1945. Study of the Leopold and Loeb trial and Darrow's role as attorney for the defendants.

Howe, Scott W. "Reassessing the Individualization Mandate in Capital Sentencing: Darrow's Defense of Leopold and Loeb." *Iowa Law Review* 79 (July 1994): 989–1071. Discussion of Darrow's arguments against capital punishment in his defense of Nathan Leopold Jr. and Richard Loeb.

Jenkins, Philip. "The Radicals and the Rehabilitative Ideal, 1890–1930." *Criminology* 20 (November 1982): 347–372. Account of theories of criminal behavior, including discussion of the views of Darrow.

Jones, Stephen. "Clarence Darrow, A Sentimental Rebel." *Oklahoma Bar Journal* 52 (April 25, 1981): 989. Review of *Clarence Darrow: A Sentimental Rebel*, by Arthur and Lila Weinberg.

Kornstein, Daniel J. "Honest, Frank, Fearless Advocacy." *New York Law Journal* (September 10, 1984): 1. Tribute to Darrow's defense of unpopular clients.

Kunstler, William Moses. *The Case for Courage.* New York: Morrow, 1962. Discussion of ten lawyers who represented unpopular clients; chapter on Darrow's defense of Eugene V. Debs.

Kurland, Gerald. *Clarence Darrow: Attorney for the Damned.* Charlotteville, NY: SamHar Press, 1972. Analysis of Darrow's most important cases.

Larson, Edward J. *Summer for the Gods: The Scopes Trial and America's Continuing Debate Over Science and Religion.* New York: Basic Books, 1997. Account of the Scopes trial in terms of the clash between science and religious belief.

Lukas, J. Anthony. *Big Trouble: A Murder in a Small Western Town Sets Off a Struggle for the Soul of America.* New York: Simon and Schuster, 1997. Study of the trial of William D. ("Big Bill") Haywood in 1907; detailed examination of Darrow's career and his famous defense of Haywood.

Macgill, H.C. "Darrow." *Connecticut Law Review* 12 (Winter 1980): 410–426. Discussion of Darrow's place in the legal community.

McElhaney, James W. "The Trial of Henry Sweet: Clarence Darrow Confronts the Issues of the Day." *ABA Journal* 78 (July 1992): 73–74. Commentary on Darrow's defense of Henry Sweet, a young black college student who was acquitted of murder in Detroit in 1926.

McKernan, Maureen. *The Amazing Criminal Trial of Leopold and Loeb.* New York: New American Library, 1957. Study of the trial of Leopold and Loeb, and Darrow's role as attorney for the defendants.

Mosk, Edward. "Darrow on Trial." *California Lawyer* 3 (March 1982): 32–35. Account of Darrow's trial for allegedly attempting to bribe a juror in California in 1912.

Paine, Donald F. "*State of Tennessee* v. *John Scopes Revisited.*" *Tennessee Bar Journal* 32 (May–June 1996): 32–34. Discussion of the Scopes trial and Darrow's presentation of the case.

Ravitz, Abe C. *Clarence Darrow and the American Literary Tradition.* Cleveland: Press of Western Reserve University, 1962. Analysis of Darrow as a literary figure.

Reske, Henry J. "A Lawyer's Letters: Clarence Darrow Papers for Sale." *ABA Journal* 81 (March 1995): 18. Notation of sale of several letters written by Clarence Darrow to his friends.

Review of *The Story of My Life*, by Clarence Darrow. *Georgia Bar Journal* 2 (April 1997): 41. Review of Darrow's autobiography.

Rintels, David W. *Clarence Darrow: A One-Man Play Based Upon Irving Stone's* Clarence Darrow for the Defense. Garden City, NY: Doubleday, 1975. Adaptation of Stone's biography for the stage.

St. Johns, Adela Rogers. *Final Verdict.* Garden City, NY: Doubleday, 1962. Reminiscence by journalist and daughter of Earl Rogers, Darrow's attorney in his bribery trial; segment dealing with the trial.

Scopes, John T., and James Presley. *Center of the Storm.* New York: Holt, Rinehart and Winston, 1967. Reflection on the "monkey trial" of 1925.

Steffens, Lincoln. *Autobiography.* New York: Harcourt, Brace, 1931. Recollections by the reformer, including commentary about the McNamara trial of 1911.

Stein, Jacob A. "The Capacity to Rebel." *Washington Lawyer* 8 (March-April 1994): 44. Account of Darrow's stands on unpopular topics.

———. "Haywood Found Not Guilty: 1905 Murder Trial Where Defense Lawyer Was Clarence Darrow." *Litigation* 12 (Summer 1986): 45–47. Discussion of the Haywood trial and Darrow's role in Haywood's acquittal.

Stone, Irving. *Clarence Darrow For the Defense.* New York: Doubleday, Signet Books, 1971. A popular biography based primarily on Darrow's private correspondence, family documents, manuscripts, legal briefs, notebooks, and published memoirs sold to the author by Darrow's second wife, Ruby Hamerstrom Darrow.

Sullivan, Mark. *Our Times: The United States, 1900–1925.* 6 vols. New York: Charles Scribner's Sons, 1927. Overview of the significant developments in American history during the early decades of the twentieth century.

Tierney, Kevin. *Darrow: A Biography.* New York: Thomas Y. Crowell, 1979. A study of Darrow based on extensive research and unpublished correspondence.

Uelmen, Gerald F. "What's Happened in California Law for the Past Century? Top 10 Legal Stories Prove That History Tends to Repeat Itself: The Journal Turns 100." *Los Angeles Daily Journal,* April 6, 1988, 1. Discussion of famous California cases, including Darrow's defense of the McNamara brothers in 1911.

Weinberg, Arthur. "The Sweet Case: Detroit, 1926." *American Journal of Trial Advocacy* 9 (Summer 1985): 67–97. Story of Darrow's defense of Dr. Ossian Sweet, a black physician, for conspiracy to murder, and his younger brother, Henry Sweet, a college student, for murder.

———, ed. *Attorney for the Damned: Clarence Darrow in the Courtroom.* Chicago: University of Chicago Press, 1957. A collection of many of Darrow's most famous speeches in court, with notes accompanying the presentations.

Weinberg, Arthur, and Lila Weinberg. *Clarence Darrow: A Sentimental Rebel.* New York: G.P. Putnam's Sons, 1980. Well-documented biography, with focus on Darrow's own trial for jury bribery; authors made use of previously unpublished Darrow letters.

———. "Darrow: Scopes Revisited." *Trial Diplomacy Journal* 8 (Winter 1985): 14–17. Discussion of trial of John T. Scopes in 1925.

———. "The Massie Trial: Darrow's Last Case." *Trial Diplomacy Journal* 11 (Fall 1988): 22–28. Account of Darrow's defense in 1932 of Thomas Massie, a Navy lieutenant charged with killing a Hawaiian man who had participated in the gang rape of Massie's wife.

Whitlock, Brand. *Forty Years of It.* New York: D. Appleton, 1941. Recollections by the writer; account of his friendship with Darrow.

Wise, Stuart M. "Remembering Clarence Darrow." *National Law Journal* (April 1, 1985): 43. Reflections on the life of Darrow and his contributions to the legal system.

Wright, Theon. *Rape in Paradise.* New York: Hawthorn Books, 1966. Account of the Massie trial and Darrow's role as attorney for the defense.

Wypijewski, Joann. Review of *Big Trouble: A Murder in a Small Western Town Sets Off a Struggle for the Soul of America,* by J. Anthony Lukas, *The Nation* 265 (October 13, 1997): 25–28. Discussion of Lucas's book and conditions in Idaho at the time of the trial of William D. ("Big Bill") Haywood in 1907.

– Samuel S. –
<u>Leibowitz</u>

Chronology

1893	Born on August 14 in Jassy, Rumania, to Isaac and Bina Lebeau.
1897	The three Lebeaus came to the United States; after a few years, Isaac Lebeau changed the family name to Leibowitz.
1911	Samuel Leibowitz graduated from Jamaica High School in the borough of Queens.
1915	Received his law degree from Cornell University; admitted to the New York bar.
1919	Opened his own law office; married Belle Munves on December 25.
1920s	Represented and won acquittals for defendants of every kind, including prominent gangsters, such as Al Capone.
1929	Won an acquittal for Harry Hoffman, who had been accused of murdering a Staten Island woman.
1930	Defended the convict Max Becker, on trial for the murder of a guard at Auburn Prison, and obtained a verdict of "not guilty."
1931	Accused and indicted for suborning perjury.
1932	The indictment was dismissed when Chile Mapocha Acuna, Leibowitz's accuser, died of cancer.
1933	The International Labor Defense (the ILD), an organ of the American Communist Party, retained Leibowitz as chief counsel for the defense of the Scottsboro Nine.
1933	Both the first and the second trials of Haywood Patterson at Decatur, Alabama, resulted in verdicts of "guilty."
1934	Leibowitz broke with the ILD after its failed attempt to bribe chief prosecution witness Victoria Price became public knowledge. Helped organize a rival organization to influence public opinion, raise funds, and, in general, act on behalf of the Scottsboro Nine.
1935	Argued *Norris* v. *Alabama* before the U.S. Supreme Court and won, forcing Alabama and other southern states to include blacks on their jury rolls and winning new trials for Haywood Patterson and Clarence Norris.
1937	The Alabama authorities suddenly dropped all charges against four of the Scottsboro defendants, and Leibowitz hurriedly conveyed them to New York; the other five were released one at a time during the 1940s after spending additional years in jail.

1939   Salvatore Gatti, the 140th defendant in a murder trial to be repre-
            sented by Leibowitz, is convicted of murder in the first degree
            and is executed, becoming the only one of his clients ever sen-
            tenced to death.

1940   Nominated by the regular Democratic Party organization for a
            seat on the Kings County Court, one of the nation's busiest crimi-
            nal courts; Leibowitz won a huge majority.

1949   Initiated from the bench a grand jury probe that uncovered a
            corrupt connection between gambling kingpin Harry Gross and
            several high-ranking police officials.

1953   Nominated for mayor of New York by the Fusion Party, he with-
            drew from the race on August 1, due to his inability to raise suf-
            ficient funds to make a serious run.

1962   Became a justice of the New York State Supreme Court for Kings
            County.

1970   Retired from the bench.

1978   Died on January 11, following a stroke.

Biography

Of the attorneys who have come to be known as people's lawyers, there have been some who did not start out that way. The career of Samuel S. Leibowitz is a case in point. His first dozen years as a lawyer were a study in ambition rather than idealism. A masterly tactician in the courtroom, he was quite willing to use trickery, if necessary, in order to win acquittals for his clientele. Most of his clients in these years were petty criminals; a few were major gangsters, including Al Capone, Abe Reles, "Bugsy" Siegel, and Vincent Coll; and a growing number were ordinary citizens who had been indicted for a major crime, usually for the first time in their lives. Although most of his clients had done what they were accused of, Leibowitz succeeded in winning acquittals in the great majority of his cases. Of the 140 men and women whom he defended over the years against the charge of homicide, all but a handful were acquitted outright and only one was ever executed.

It was through his representation of the defendants in the Scottsboro cases of the 1930s that Leibowitz became involved for the first time with a cause that transcended his own ambition. In this famous cause célèbre, two young white women accused nine black youths of raping them on a moving freight train in Alabama. As the young men's attorney, Leibowitz received death threats and found himself up against the flagrant racial biases of Alabama prosecutors, juries, and judges, who were urged on by inflamed mobs. In the end, none of the nine defendants was executed, and this was due in no small measure to Leibowitz. Four of them were released when the charges against them were dropped in 1937, and gradually, one by one, the remaining five would gain their freedom over a period of some thirteen years.

The attorney's most significant Scottsboro victory came in 1935, when he pleaded successfully before the U.S. Supreme Court that the systematic exclusion of qualified blacks from jury service had deprived the black defendants of their constitutional rights. Thereafter, blacks were of necessity listed on the jury rolls of every state, including those in the South. The Scottsboro case was thus a key landmark in the struggle of American blacks for equal justice, and the legal talent and fighting spirit of Leibowitz had helped to make this victory possible.

Origins

Samuel Leibowitz was born on August 14, 1893, in Jassy, a small town in the northern Moldavia region of Rumania, the only child of Isaac and Bina Lebeau. The family's livelihood came from the dry goods business that Isaac carried on near the railway station at the center of the town. The Lebeaus were Jewish, and in Rumania, as in much of Eastern Europe, Jews were second-class citizens who paid special taxes and served in the army, but were permitted neither to vote nor to own land. In 1895, the Rumanian government heaped added abuse upon its Jewish citizens by authorizing and promoting the Anti-Semitic League, which agitated openly and aggressively against them.[1]

The Lebeaus were now thinking seriously about moving to America. After corresponding with relatives and friends who were already living in New York City, they decided to emigrate. They journeyed to Antwerp, where they embarked on February 27, 1897, aboard the S.S. *Kensington,* bound for New York. At first, the voyage went smoothly, but as the ship neared the English Channel, a hurricane struck, flooding the cabins and very nearly disabling the ship's steering mechanism. Four-year-old Samuel was constantly seasick and spent virtually the entire voyage in sick bay. Adding to the discomfort of the Lebeaus and the 150 other Jewish families among the ship's steerage passengers was the absence of kosher food, which forced them to make do on little more than tea and biscuits. After twelve dreary days at sea, the *Kensington* finally docked in New York harbor on March 11.

Upon arrival, the Lebeaus and the other immigrants among the passengers were taken to Ellis Island, where they were examined and processed by immigration officials. After nearly a week on the island, they were formally admitted and immediately took the ferry to the Battery. The Lebeaus' first residence in New York was a tiny two-room apartment on the fourth floor of a congested tenement at 66 Essex Street along New York's Lower East Side, the district that housed the largest enclave of Jews in the world. As in many of the tenements of this era, there were neither bathrooms nor bathtubs. On each floor, there was a single water-tap and a water closet that was shared by six families. In the winter when the pipes would freeze, the tenants would have to walk downstairs to the outhouse in the yard. In some ways, however, even their crowded, plumbing-poor tenement was an improvement on what they had known in Jassy. At least there was (usually) running water and one did not have to gather firewood to light the stove.[2]

At first, Isaac Lebeau earned his livelihood by selling dry goods and notions from the pushcart that he tended on Orchard Street. At the urging of a fellow peddler who had been in America ten months longer than he, Isaac "Americanized" the family name, or so he believed, by changing it legally from Lebeau to Leibowitz. By the end of their third year in America, the Lebeaus had amassed enough capital (some $150) for Isaac to open his own dry goods shop on Second Avenue near 107th Street in Manhattan, while housing his family in the two rooms at the rear of the shop.

For the next six years, Sam attended a public school on 110th Street where he encountered children from a wide variety of ethnic backgrounds. He was not then a very diligent student, preferring sports to homework. "To you," complained one of his teachers, "Bull Run is a cow pasture, instead of a battlefield." His favorite school subject was elocution, for he loved to recite famous speeches and poems, many of which he learned by heart. After school, Sam behaved like a typical city boy, playing stickball in the streets, chasing fire engines, swimming with his friends in the East River, and taking a precocious interest in the burlesque and vaudeville shows that were staged in Manhattan theaters.[3]

In 1906, Isaac Leibowitz closed his Harlem store and opened a new and bigger one along Fulton Street in Brooklyn. He now bought a house for his family in the East New York–Cypress Hills section of Brooklyn, that was then a comfortable, tree-lined neighborhood with fine playgrounds and little crime. Sam attended the local public school and, at fourteen, moved on to Jamaica High School. Although he belonged to the school's baseball and track teams, he had become far more serious about his studies and was now receiving excellent marks. As in grade school, his favorite subject was elocution, which allowed him to express a theatrical streak that would later prove useful to him in the courtroom.[4]

At the insistence of his father, Sam, who had been leaning toward a career in engineering, agreed to study law. He enrolled in 1911 at the Cornell University Law School in Ithaca, New York. To make ends meet, he waited on tables and washed dishes at a nearby boys' school. At Cornell, Leibowitz was a hard-working and successful student, but he also found time for team sports and was the first Jewish student ever admitted to the Dramatic Society, performing in featured roles in several of its productions.

Sam also excelled in debate. As a member of the debating society, he was required to take whichever side of a question was assigned to him and, no matter how indefensible it might seem, make the best case that he could for it. In his senior year, Leibowitz made the varsity squad of the Debate Team and was president of the Cornell Congress, a student organization that debated public issues.[5]

Although he was performing well at an outstanding law school, Leibowitz felt that as an immigrant's son, it was unrealistic for him to aspire to one of the high-prestige law firms. He therefore decided on a career in criminal law, a field that appealed to his sense of drama and in which, he believed, it would be easier to obtain clients, even if at first many of them were penniless. When he described his plan to the dean of the law school, the latter exclaimed: "Not criminal law, Sam—anything but that."[6]

From Student to Lawyer

In June 1915, Sam graduated from Cornell and immediately took the bar exam in Rochester, New York, scoring the highest grade in a field of 600. He worked briefly at two law firms in Manhattan, but he quit both when denied a small raise in pay. In April 1916, he was hired by Michael F. McGoldrick, a prominent Brooklyn attorney with a largely Irish-Catholic clientele. Sam proved popular with McGoldrick's clients, who called him "our Roman Jew." McGoldrick allowed the young lawyer to draw up legal documents, research and write briefs, and to involve himself in general with every aspect of the firm's activities except for the pleading of its cases in court.[7]

After two years with McGoldrick, Leibowitz was determined to become a courtroom advocate and to acquire clients of his own in his chosen specialty of criminal law. It was only, he was sure, through actual trial experience that a lawyer learned his trade. He therefore volunteered to represent indigent defendants free of charge. His first client was Harry Patterson, a middle-aged drunkard and small-time crook, who was accused of having broken into a saloon and stealing seven dollars from the cash register along with a bottle of whiskey. This rather trivial case appeared open and shut because Patterson had confessed and, when asked how he had gotten into the bar, had produced a skeleton key. With his case coming to trial, however, Patterson now insisted that he was innocent. At his trial, in April 1919, Leibowitz, rejecting the advice of McGoldrick and other senior attorneys, entered a plea of "not guilty," thereby accommodating the wishes of his first client while astonishing the prosecutor and Judge Howard Nash. The prosecution's case rested on the confession and the key. The fledgling lawyer undermined the former by pointing out (truthfully) that Patterson had only confessed because the police had beaten him with a rubber hose. On the issue of the skeleton key, Leibowitz requested the judge to order the jury to the crime scene so that its members could see for themselves whether Patterson's key would open the door of the burgled saloon. His gamble paid off. With a full schedule of cases to try, the prosecuting attorney replied that he would not waste the time of the court by agreeing to such a demonstration and promptly closed his case. Four minutes later, the jury pronounced Patterson "not guilty." His first victory in hand, Leibowitz proceeded to try out the key and found that it opened every locked door at the courthouse.[8]

His Early Law Practice

Soon afterward, hoping to appear older, the aspiring attorney bought three elegant suits, a frock coat, and a pince-nez that he fitted with ordinary glass. He then quit his job and opened a small law office at 50 Court Street in Brooklyn in May 1919. It was a month before he had his first paying client, a successful pickpocket known professionally as "Izzy the Goniff," who, while admitting that he had lifted many a wallet in his career, insisted that he was innocent of the particular charge on which he had been indicted. Known to the police as "the millionaire pickpocket," Izzy demonstrated his prowess by picking the lawyer's pocket clean of the $100 bill he had handed him as his retainer. At the trial, Leibowitz decided on a strategy of candor. Acknowledging that his client was indeed a professional pickpocket and would, if acquitted, undoubtedly remain one, he declared that he was too good at it, too professional, to be caught in the act by an ordinary citizen on a Coney Island boardwalk. Perhaps amused by the effrontery of the lawyer's argument, the jury acquitted the pickpocket.

The minor felons of Brooklyn knew legal talent when they saw it, and Leibowitz soon found himself with a growing clientele, consisting mainly of petty criminals, many of whom could not afford to pay him. In one such case, a hat had fallen off the perpetrator's head while he was stealing chickens from a poultry market, but Leibowitz argued that his client was not the man who had lost the hat. The jury acquitted the defendant, but as they were leaving the courtroom, he asked Leibowitz in a whisper if he could get his hat back.[9]

Leibowitz was also beginning to represent ordinary citizens who found themselves in the unaccustomed position of being tried for a crime. In the fall of 1919, he defended his first murder case, a rather routine one, in which he won an acquittal for a bartender, Angelo Clementi, who had in apparent self-defense shot and killed a pistol-brandishing hoodlum and ex-convict. For this trial Leibowitz received a fee of $300.[10]

The most important case in this initial phase of his career was *The People* v. *Gallender,* which came to trial in 1920. The accused man was a sculptor who, billed as "the Great Gallando," had performed on the vaudeville stage by instantly making clay models of people in the audience. In April 1920, an eighteen-year-old resident of an orphan asylum, identifying herself as Minnie Gallender, the sculptor's daughter, accused him and his third wife, her stepmother, of having cruelly and systematically tortured and abused her. According to Minnie, her father, his recent wife, and their assorted offspring had, among other things, starved her, left her virtually naked, held her prisoner, stuck her with safety pins, struck her repeatedly with planks and other solid objects, and had even stabbed her with a heated knife. A medical examination done at the office of the district attorney found fifty-one scars on her body. Gallender was immediately arrested and charged with felonious assault. On May 20, he hired Leibowitz to conduct his defense.

In his search for an alternative explanation for Minnie's lesions, all of which were on the left side of her body, Leibowitz turned to the psychological literature and then consulted with a neurologist. The latter also appeared as an expert witness for the defense at the trial, testifying that Minnie Gallender suffered from "hysterical amnesia," a rare ailment that had both mental and physical symptoms. One of its effects was the development of insensible patches on the skin along one side of the body, "separated from the other [in this case, the right side] by a perfectly sharp line of demarcation." Those in this condition, asserted Leibowitz's expert witness, also experienced losses of memory, hallucinations, and a form of self-hypnosis. Apparently unimpressed, the jury deliberated for only a few minutes and found Gallender guilty. This was not the end of the story, however. A few days after the trial, Minnie Gallender recanted. Her wounds, she now said, had been self-inflicted. She could not say why she had harmed herself, but claimed that after her father's trial, she had gradually remembered what had happened. In any case, Leibowitz had (at least in the end) prevailed in his first important case.[11]

In his personal life, Leibowitz was ardently courting Belle Munves, the daughter of a pharmacist in the Bronx, who was studying piano at the Institute of Musical Art (later known as Juilliard). He had first met the highly attractive Belle, who was then eighteen, at a vacation resort in the Catskills during the summer of 1918. He immediately decided that he was going to marry her and, in the face of numerous rebuffs, launched a campaign to win her over that was both persistent and ingenious. First, he set out to charm her parents and soon succeeded in gaining their support. By taking along a third party, an older man with a gift for conversation, he persuaded the reluctant Belle to go out with him on weekly dinner dates. His persistence paid off, and after a few weeks, no chaperone was needed. On December 25, 1919, they were married. Belle immediately became pregnant, giving birth to twin boys, Robert and Kenneth, on September 10, 1920. In May of the following year, the family moved into a new nine-room one-family house in the Midwood section of Flatbush. A daughter, Marjorie, their third and last child, was born in 1926.[12]

In 1923, Leibowitz defended Raffel Meyer, a Williamsburg butcher, who was accused of burning down his butcher shop for the insurance money. In examining the premises of the burnt-out shop, fire investigators had found rags, including a butcher's apron that, to their experienced noses, seemed to smell of kerosene. In cross-examining these men, Leibowitz set out to establish the unreliability of their sense of smell. With the aid of a chemist, he prepared a number of vials, each containing a different substance. He then asked the investigators to smell each vial in turn and identify its contents. In handing each witness the kerosene vial first, the attorney insured that their nasal sensors would be saturated with the pungent kerosene odor, and as a result, all of them testified (wrongly) that every one of the vials contained kerosene. The attorney then invited the jury to smell the contents of the vials, but reversed the order, giving the jurors the water vial fist, then the gasoline vial, and so forth, but saving the kerosene vial for last. As a result, the jury concluded that the investigators were incapable of distinguishing the odor of kerosene from that of other substances. Needless to add, Mayer was acquitted.[13]

Between 1919 and 1923, Leibowitz was the defense lawyer in more than 1,000 criminal trials and gained acquittals in more than 800 of them, winning 46 jury trials in a row. His fee for a felony case as of 1923 was $2,500. Prosecutors were by then trying to avoid cases in which Leibowitz was appearing for the defense. The young lawyer's remarkable success was due partly to the public's awareness that, in New York and other cities, the police were routinely beating confessions out of arrested suspects. Consequently, juries in criminal cases, as well as the wider public from which the jurors were drawn, were highly skeptical of confessions that had been obtained by the police at their station houses. Leibowitz played effectively on these doubts, alleging in case after case that his client had been beaten into confessing.[14]

His Gangster Clients

Leibowitz's courtroom success was attracting new clients, many of them gangsters who could afford to pay their attorneys well. After 1925, he represented literally dozens of big-time criminals, including such well-known underworld figures as Ben "Bugsy" Siegel, Abe Reles, "Pittsburgh Phil" Strauss, and Albert Anastasia, whom he defended in three different murder trials. Leibowitz would later maintain that he had never socialized with gangsters, boasting that none of them had ever slapped him on the back. "Such vultures of our society," Leibowitz remarked, "were as repulsive to me as . . . they are to all decent citizens." The lawyer compared his attitude toward his gangster clients to that of the doctor "who takes every precaution not to become infected by the germs of his patient."[15]

One of Leibowitz's highest-paying clients was Al Capone, the nation's leading bootlegger and racketeer. While residing in Brooklyn for a few weeks in 1925, he had become the ally of the Italian gang of waterfront toughs, headed by the Terranova family, that was then engaged in a violent power struggle with a rival Irish gang known as the White Hand. On Christmas night, Capone visited a speakeasy in the company of several members of the Terranova gang. Shortly after midnight, a White Hand gangster insulted the Italians, and then the lights went out. When they came back on, it was discovered that three members of the Irish gang had been shot to death. Later that morning, police officials ordered the arrest of two of the surviving White Hand gangsters and seven of their Italian rivals, including Capone.

At a conference held at Leibowitz's home with Capone and the other Italian suspects, the lawyer agreed to represent all nine of the wanted men. Determined to prevent his clients from being beaten into confessing, he arranged with a Brooklyn police captain for five of the suspects to turn themselves in with the proviso that they would be immediately arraigned. In turning the suspects over, Sam warned Captain John Ryan that there were witnesses who would testify that they were handed over in good condition. "Don't dare try any funny stuff with them," he said.

There followed an elaborate game of cat and mouse in which the lawyer obtained four different writs of habeas corpus and had them served by a messenger on a motorcycle. "Each writ," wrote Alva Johnston in his profile of Leibowitz that appeared in *The New Yorker,* "was served just in time to prevent the police from interrogating Al and his pals with blunt instruments." When the police rearrested the suspects on a charge of assault against a fourth White Hander who had been wounded on the night of the shootings, Leibowitz was ready. He visited the man in the hospital and got him to sign an affidavit stating that strangers had shot him and that none of Leibowitz's clients were to blame. With this affidavit in hand, he successfully petitioned the court on January 1 to release his clients on bail, and the charges against Capone and his friends were dropped the following day. That night, there was a banquet of celebration at which Capone and the Terranova crowd repeatedly raised their glasses amid gleeful cries of "Viva Leibowitz."[16]

Leibowitz dealt with Capone a second time in 1931, when the Chicago gang leader was faced with a federal indictment for the evasion of income taxes. The lawyer journeyed to Chicago, where he spent several days in an exhaustive review of Capone's financial documents. Impressed by the weight of the evidence against Capone, Leibowitz warned him and his lieutenants that he might well be sentenced to a prison term so long that "he will look like Rip Van Winkle when he gets out." This could be averted, he advised the assembled crooks, only by threatening to unmask the government officials to whom they had paid "protection" over the years. When Capone and his men rejected his suggestion, Leibowitz decided that the case was unwinnable, and although Capone offered to pay him whatever he asked, he withdrew as counsel and returned to New York. Soon afterward, Capone was convicted of tax evasion and sentenced to Alcatraz, where he died eleven years later.[17]

Although the guilt of many of his clients was apparent, Leibowitz seemed at times to hypnotize himself into believing in their innocence, irrespective of who they were or what they had done in the past, and prosecutors would sometimes denounce him for using his talents to shield his criminal clients from the law. According to his son Robert, Leibowitz claimed that if a client insisted that he was innocent, "regardless of my personal belief as to his guilt, I would defend him with every ounce of ability that I possess." Yet he knew that many professional criminals lie to their attorneys, particularly on the matter of their guilt or innocence. In his own defense, Leibowitz contended that incorrect jury verdicts were caused far more by the errors of prosecutors and judges than by the stratagems and deceptions of defense lawyers. Moreover, since even a criminal was a citizen, he was as entitled to his day in court as anyone else. In protecting the right to due process of even hoodlums and racketeers, the criminal lawyer was in the end safeguarding the rights of all citizens. "The important thing," he told Quentin Reynolds in 1950, "is that the rights they [his clients] represented were of greater consequence to me than the individuals themselves."[18]

On the other hand, there were times when even a gangster client would turn out to be truly innocent of the charges against him. One of Leibowitz's clients was Vincent Coll, the young leader of a brutal gang of killers. On October 28, 1931, a botched gang slaying in Harlem resulted in the accidental wounding of five children and the killing of a baby boy. Coll came under suspicion and was promptly arrested. At his trial, the chief witness was one George Brecht, who claimed that he had seen Coll and a second gunman spray machine gun bursts from a moving car along East 107th Street. Through his aggressive cross-examination, Leibowitz was able to undermine Brecht's credibility totally. When asked how he earned his living, Brecht had answered that he sold Eskimo pies. Leibowitz then sent out for fourteen of the ice cream bars and, after giving them out to the judge, the prosecutor, and to each member of the jury, proceeded to quiz Brecht about the wrappers, how the bars were made and prevented from melting, and so forth. Brecht was quickly shown to know nothing at all about Eskimo pies. Further questioning revealed that he had lied about his past and was in fact an ex-convict who had been a "professional witness" at trials in another state. With the only witness against Coll discredited and with no other evidence linking him to the Harlem shootings, the judge dismissed the case.[19]

In Defense of the Accused

In addition to his criminal clientele, Leibowitz also had a growing practice among ordinary men and women, most of them accused of murder and facing trials at which their lives would be at stake. In most such cases, a normally law-abiding citizen had committed a single act of violence that had resulted in the taking of a life. At the trial, Leibowitz would argue that such a defendant had been "temporarily insane" and that, therefore, the killing had been unintentional since an insane person is without free will. "Forces over which he has no control," said Leibowitz of one such defendant, "compelled him to a violent act which he would never have committed under normal conditions." Leibowitz would attempt to account for what his client had done by portraying (as vividly as possible) the stresses and strains that had driven him or her to the shedding of blood. He would note in particular the harm that had been done to the defendant by the person killed. When the fatal gunshot or knife thrust was delivered, argued Leibowitz, it came as an act of desperation due to a temporary mental breakdown. The defendant had in fact been simply the instrument of violence. It was "the hand of God" that had actually delivered the fatal blow.[20]

Over the course of his career, Leibowitz handled twenty-five cases in which women were on trial for murder, and in virtually every one, the victim had been a man. One such client, Angelina Miceli, labeled by the tabloids as "the grandmother slayer," who was put on trial in 1928 for the murder of her son-in-law, was, at age sixty-seven, the oldest person ever tried for murder in New York State up to that time. Leibowitz gained her an acquittal by arguing that her son-in-law had constantly abused her verbally and had threatened to evict her from her own home. One morning, according to Leibowitz, her fear was so great that "everything went black," and she shot him to death. His other female defendants were much younger than Miceli and the men they killed were either their husbands or their lovers, but in every instance, the accused was acquitted. In the case of one woman who had borne her husband seventeen children, he had rewarded her by breaking her nose fifteen times. In summing up for the defense, Leibowitz asked the jurors if, after looking at that nose, there could be "any doubt about what kind of beast her husband was? Can there be any doubt that she had a right to protect herself?"[21]

The Hoffman Case

The defense of Harry Hoffman, in which Leibowitz decisively refuted a great mass of incriminating evidence to win the freedom of a clearly innocent man, was probably his greatest single performance as a lawyer. Hoffman, a resident of Staten Island, had been found guilty of murder in the second degree by a local jury in 1924 for the slaying of Maude Bauer, a housewife of thirty-five, and was sentenced to Sing Sing for twenty years to life. This verdict was overturned on a technicality three years later, and, at the second trial, in which the noted attorney Leonard Snitkin defended Hoffman, the jury was unable to agree on a verdict. Before his third trial could begin, Snitkin died, and so Hoffman, in desperation after nearly five years in jail, sent a postcard to Leibowitz, declaring his innocence and pleading with him to take his case. His money was gone and his wife had divorced him. "This," he wrote, "is the last desperate appeal of an innocent man." When the attorney visited Hoffman in jail, he became convinced that he was innocent and agreed to defend him, free of charge.

In interviews with the press before the trial opened, Leibowitz described Hoffman as "the most glaring object of persecution in the history of this country." He charged that the prosecution knew that Hoffman was innocent, and he promised to reveal the identity of the actual murderer in court. Even as the jury was being selected, Leibowitz injected the name of one Horatio Sharrett into the proceedings. In his opening remarks, he pointed out that Sharrett, the brother of an important political figure, had on the night of the murder been driving near the scene of the crime in a car that was the same make and model as the one in which Maude Bauer had been slain. Yet Sharrett had been only superficially investigated, because, charged Leibowitz, the district attorney had interceded for him with the police.

The most impressive of the evidence against Hoffman at the first trial was the testimony of three ballistics experts that the bullet that had killed Bauer had come from a .25-caliber pistol owned by Hoffman. In order to counteract this finding, Leibowitz studied ballistics for three months and then consulted three of the leading firearms experts in the nation. After making exhaustive tests, all three reported, and afterward testified in court, that the fatal bullet could not possibly have been fired from Hoffman's gun. At the trial, a comparison microscope was set up in the courtroom and Leibowitz invited members of the jury to compare for themselves the markings on a bullet fired from Hoffman's pistol with those on the bullet removed from the body of Maude Bauer. In order to insure that the jury would be able to grasp the ballistic evidence, Leibowitz had seen to it that seven of its twelve members had a technical background.

At the first trial, two witnesses, a thirteen-year-old schoolgirl and a policeman, had identified Hoffman as the driver of the car in which Bauer was last seen alive. Leibowitz attacked the credibility of these witnesses, noting that neither had identified Hoffman until more than three weeks after the slaying and that the policeman had not even mentioned seeing either the car or its driver until a reward of $8,000 had been announced.

Hoffman had also been incriminated by his own behavior in the days following the murder. With the aid of a friend, he had concocted a false alibi, and he had tried to conceal that he owned a .25-caliber pistol by mailing it to his brother in the Bronx and then burning the holster. In his closing statement to the jury, Leibowitz argued that the ultimate source of Hoffman's odd behavior lay in the fact that he was by trade a motion picture projectionist who had been exposed to hundreds of hours of crime melodrama in which it was commonplace for innocent men to be "framed." It was not, as the district attorney claimed, "the consciousness of guilt" that had caused him to lie to the police but his "overweening fear" that he might, like the hapless men in the crime movies, find himself arrested, tried, convicted, and sentenced for a crime that he did not commit.

Near the end of the trial, Leibowitz dropped a bombshell on the prosecution by revealing for the first time that his client was left-handed, having him demonstrate it in court by threading a needle and hammering a nail, each time with his left hand. He had previously drawn from the county coroner the admission that it was almost certainly a right-handed man who had shot Bauer. To clinch the point, when Hoffman took the stand, he testified that he had never fired his pistol because its safety catch, which was on the right side, made it hard for him to use.

In his summation, Leibowitz reminded the jurors that "for five years, this man has been caged like a wild animal, from dungeon to dungeon." Once a healthy man, he had become increasingly emaciated and was now "little more than a bag of bones." Hoffman had told a lie and had been brutally and excessively punished for it. "I do not believe any jury would convict a dog on the evidence presented here," Leibowitz stated. "I leave the verdict in your hands." It took the jury just a little over four hours to bring in a verdict of "not guilty." Now convinced of Hoffman's innocence, the New York newspapers called on the police and prosecutors to be less hasty in their investigations in the future. The case also attracted the attention of national magazines, giving Leibowitz his first glimmer of recognition beyond the confines of New York City. [22]

The Becker Trial

Before the Scottsboro trials of the 1930s, the case that Leibowitz considered his most difficult was that of Max Becker, a twenty-six-year-old inmate of Auburn Prison in upstate New York, who was on trial for the murder of George Durnford, the prison's principal keeper (chief guard), during an uprising among the inmates in December 1929. In the weeks before the trial, Leibowitz interviewed Becker and every other potential witness at Auburn and granted a series of interviews to the local press in which he pointed out that Becker was no hardened killer, but in fact just a small-time burglar whose specialty was robbing houses when their owners were not at home.[23]

To both the prosecution and the defense, the makeup of the jury was of critical importance, and each side made full use of its peremptory challenges. For his part, Leibowitz probed the talesmen as to whether they could credit, or would always discount, the testimony of convicts. In all, it required seven days in which 250 panelists were interrogated before the twelve-man jury was finally in place.[24]

The witnesses for the prosecution consisted of several guards, the foreman of the prison's woodworking shop, and Warden Edgar S. Jennings. The warden and two of the guards said that they had seen Becker among the rebels and had heard him boast that the inmates meant business and had plenty of ammunition. By far the most damaging witness was one of the guards, Claude Dempsey, who, in relating how Becker had shot Durnford, was far more detailed than the other witnesses. In his cross-examination, Leibowitz accused the guard of lying. He pointed out that while Dempsey could not with certainty name any of the other convicts at the scene, yet, when it came to Becker, he was always "Johnny on the spot," locating precisely the whereabouts and movements of this one convict in the minutes that preceded the taking of Durnford's life. "By the way, Mr. Dempsey," asked Leibowitz, "did you ever tell a lie in your life?" (This was a device that Leibowitz frequently employed in order to cast doubt on prosecution witnesses.) When during redirect questioning by the district attorney, after more than two hours on the witness stand, Dempsey rested one foot on the rail of the witness box, Leibowitz saw his chance. "I ask the court," he interjected, "to instruct the witness to remove his foot from the rail. He acts as though he were in a barber-shop or bar-room." Aware that Dempsey's lounging posture had probably alienated the jury, the prosecutor immediately excused his own star witness.[25]

The witnesses for the defense consisted of Rabbi David Friedman, the Jewish chaplain at Auburn, and five convicts. According to them, Becker had only gone to the pantry, the place where the mutiny had begun, to attend the meeting of some Jewish inmates who were raising money for the celebration of Passover at the prison. This, argued Leibowitz, was how Becker had come to find himself in the vicinity of the rebelling convicts and their hostages. He was then caught in the cross fire between Durnford's revolver and the gun of the inmate who was the principal keeper's actual killer. Becker's story, he pointed out, had been backed up by two other inmates who had testified that the man who had shot Durnford was himself slain later that day when the National Guard had stormed the prison.[26]

In his summation, Leibowitz claimed that there were "100 reasons for reasonable doubt." "Tell me," he challenged the jurors, "that you are citizens of the United States with a love of justice and fair play for Jew and gentile, saint and sinner." Pointing to Becker's mother (who had sat, often weeping, in the first row of the courtroom throughout the trial, dressed in black and wearing a veil), he pleaded with them not to send her boy home to her "a burned corpse." In his own summation, District Attorney James J. Hosmer dismissed the story told by the defense witnesses as "the real frame-up." The jurors must either believe the warden and guards or "this unreasonable story told by burglars, stick-up men, and convicts." He called upon the jury to "stand by the state of New York, by the guards of Auburn and of every other prison" by finding Becker guilty as charged.

After deliberating for twenty-two hours, the jury delivered a verdict of "not guilty." Leibowitz, who had eaten little during the preceding week and had gone without sleep while the jury was out, fainted when the verdict was announced. He had salvaged Becker from execution against the odds, a claim that is strengthened by the fact that three other participants in the Auburn uprising were found guilty of murder and executed.[27]

The Science and Art of Swaying Juries

His success in the courtroom was based in part on the extraordinary thoroughness with which Leibowitz prepared for each one of his cases. Before a trial began, either he or his assistant, John "Terry" Capozucca, would interview every possible witness of whom they were aware and would check and re-check the basic facts in the case. Leibowitz also granted numerous interviews to the local newspapers in order to sway the opinion of the public from which the jury would be drawn. Jury selection, according to Leibowitz, was one of the most important functions of a criminal lawyer, and in many of his cases he made maximum use of his right to challenge in order to bring onto the panel as many as possible of the type of jurors he thought most likely to vote his way. While engaged in a difficult legal battle, he went over the case records until early in the morning, often sleeping no more than two hours a night. He would not only develop his own arguments, but attempted to anticipate the arguments of his opponents. "When I went into the courtroom," boasted Leibowitz in 1950, "I had an answer for every bit of evidence the D.A. would use against me." He would also do careful research into specialized fields of knowledge that related to his cases. For the Becker case, he had studied ballistics, but in other instances, it was aspects of medicine or psychology, or even of Nietzsche's philosophy, that he looked up and mastered, so that he might then explain them effectively to a jury.[28]

His ultimate purpose in all this, of course, was to sway the jury, and Leibowitz reveled in his ability to take most juries wherever he wanted them to go. "It's an emotion I've always gone through," asserted the veteran attorney, "an exultation in the knowledge I was making the jury cry, molding it like clay." This had, he acknowledged, its theatrical side. "A criminal lawyer," he said, "has to be a combination of a Belasco [a then-famous theatrical producer], a Barrymore, an Einstein, and an Al Smith [the colorful governor of New York during the 1920s]." In criminal trials, observed the journalist Alva

Johnston, perhaps with some exaggeration, victory normally goes to the best showman, and he regarded Leibowitz as "a triple threat," capable of winning a case through dramatic surprise, or by sentimental appeals to the emotions, or by simply making a jury laugh.[29]

A good example of how Leibowitz used humor to win cases was *Santangelo* v. *New York,* which came to trial in April 1931. Viscenzo Santangelo claimed that he had been working in a fish market while the crime that he was on trial for was taking place. To refute his alibi, the prosecutor had a basket of fish brought into the courtroom. Holding up each fish, he asked Santangelo to identify it. Out of twenty-one fish, he was wrong twenty-one times. Thinking quickly, Leibowitz protested that the prosecuting attorney was trying to fool the jury. Of the fish that he had asked his client to name, not one was of a kind used in making *gefilte fish.* The defendant, he pointed out, had worked in a Jewish fish market, so how could he be expected to know about Christian fish? The jury roared, as did nearly everyone else in the courtroom, and Leibowitz had won another case.[30]

In spite of his courtroom triumphs, Leibowitz's career was suddenly put in jeopardy in 1931 when he was accused of suborning perjury. On September 29, he was indicted, arrested, handcuffed, fingerprinted, and forced to spend an indignant night in jail. The charges against him were the outgrowth of his defense of five vice squad policemen at trials conducted by the New York City Police Department during the first few months of 1931. These men were among the fifty vice squad members who had been accused by Chile Mapocha Acuna, a police informer and sometime procurer, of falsely arresting women for prostitution and then extorting money from them. Leibowitz discredited Acuna and won acquittals for his clients through the testimony of two women, one of whom testified that Acuna was her procurer and that she did not even know any of the five defendants. Six months later, the two women declared before a grand jury that, at the urging of Leibowitz, they had lied on the witness stand. District Attorney William F.X. Geoghan and Leibowitz were old adversaries and disliked one another, and this probably played a role in the district attorney's pursuit of the case. When Acuna died of a brain tumor in June 1932, Geoghan decided to drop the charges against Leibowitz and his assistant, John Capozucca, conceding that even had Acuna lived to testify against Leibowitz, Geoghan was not at all certain that a jury would have believed Acuna. In dismissing the indictment, Judge Nova remarked that "to ruin and stain a lawyer's reputation . . . take away his right to practice upon the word alone . . . of an admitted disreputable prostitute, is carrying it a bit too far."[31]

By the end of 1932, Leibowitz was clearly at the top of his profession. He had by then defended seventy-eight people for murder during his career, of whom seventy-seven had been acquitted outright and none had been found guilty. For several years, he had managed not to lose even a single jury trial. "Samuel S. Leibowitz," wrote Frances Fink in the magazine of the *Evening Graphic* in January 1932, "has probably broken the hearts of more [district attorneys] than any one attorney for the defense." Other news reporters referred to him as "a magician" and as "a miracle man." He was in such demand that he could pick and choose his clients now and employed three young lawyers at his newly opened offices at 225 Broadway in Manhattan.[32]

The Scottsboro Case

In 1933, Leibowitz's career entered a new and strikingly different phase when he became chief counsel for the defense of nine black boys and young men who had been accused and convicted of having raped two white women on an Alabama freight train in 1931. The criminal lawyer, whose practice up to then had been confined almost exclusively to New York City, now found himself doing battle with southern segregationists in Alabama courtrooms, then appearing for his first and only time before the U.S. Supreme Court, addressing rallies, and setting up new organizations on behalf of the Scottsboro defendants. He was in this instance not only a lawyer bent on the acquittal of his clients, but also an opponent of racial injustice. In the process, he would become a hated man in the South and the recipient of countless death threats, but he would also attain national recognition as one of the country's best criminal lawyers.

The Scottsboro tragedy had begun on a freight train during its run from Chattanooga, Tennessee, to Huntsville, Alabama, in the late morning and early afternoon hours of March 25, 1931. There happened to be on board nineteen or twenty hoboes (people who rode freight trains without paying), some of them white, but the majority of them black. As the train crossed into Alabama, a fight broke out in one of the freight cars between a group of white youths and a larger group of young blacks. The whites got the worst of it, and six of them either jumped or were forced from the train, which was beginning to gather speed. The white hoboes, some of whom had been injured, complained to the stationmaster at the nearby railway station in the town of Stevenson, who telephoned ahead to the sheriff's office at Scottsboro, but the train had already passed by. As it pulled in at the next scheduled stop at Paint Rock, Alabama, the train was boarded by a posse of armed deputies who arrested the nine black hoboes still on board, ranging in age from twelve to twenty. Also on the train were three white hoboes, a nineteen-year-old white male and two young white women who, like the others, were clad in overalls and workman's caps.

The two women, Victoria Price, twenty-one, and her friend, Ruby Bates, who was seventeen, were both from Huntsville, where they were employed part-time in a textile mill. Within twenty minutes of their arrival in Paint Rock, the two women told the deputies that following the expulsion of all but one of the white boys from the train, both of them had been raped by six or more of the blacks, and that all of the black hoboes had taken part in the attack. Shortly afterward, the nine black youths and young men and their two accusers were driven to Scottsboro, where they were all placed in the town jail.[33]

It was only after they had been in jail for over two hours that the nine youths were told of the rape charges. They knew that in Alabama, as in the

South generally, the mere charge of rape by a white woman against a black male was often all that it took to get him lynched. "I knew," recalled Clarence Norris, one of the nine, "if a white woman accused a black man of rape, he was as good as dead."[34]

By nightfall, a large crowd of angry white townsfolk and farmers had gathered around the rickety jailhouse, calling loudly for the sheriff to turn his prisoners over to them. Yet the mob never attacked the jail, perhaps because the women who said they had been raped were from outside the community. By midnight, Alabama's governor ordered the National Guard to surround the Scottsboro jail, and the threat of a lynching abated, at least for the time being. In the days and weeks that followed, the newspapers of Scottsboro intensified the rage of local whites by publishing blatantly one-sided news stories and editorials that simply assumed or declared the guilt of the accused youths, referring to them as "savages," "brutes," and "gorillas" and to their supposed act as the most heinous and atrocious crime ever recorded in Alabama.[35]

Four of the accused were a group of friends from Chattanooga who had been on their way to Memphis in search of work. The remaining five were all from Georgia, three of whom had not known either one another or any of the other youths prior to their arrest at Paint Rock. None of the defendants had more than a few years of schooling, and one of them had attended school for just three months. None of them could have been described as of 1931 as more than semiliterate. One of the accused youths was 90 percent blind, and another so painfully afflicted with syphilis that he could walk only with a cane. None had ever been in serious trouble with the law before. Isolated from their homes and families, and in fear for their lives, they began to accuse one another of having raped one or both of the women.[36]

The first four Scottsboro trials took place between 9 A.M. on April 6 and 5 P.M. on April 9, 1931. Within the span of these four days, four different trials were held and completed, each with its own jury, until all nine of the defendants had been put on trial and convicted. The hostility in Scottsboro toward the accused youths was so palpable and intense that the authorities found it necessary to place machine guns to either side of the courthouse entrance and to house the defendants in the jails of nearby communities that were sturdier than the one at Scottsboro.[37]

Two rather mediocre attorneys, one court-appointed and the other a white lawyer hastily retained by the black community of Chattanooga, handled the case for the defense, but neither proved effective, refusing in the end to argue any of the four cases before the jury. At each one of the trials, the star witness for the prosecution was Victoria Price, who, after identifying the defendant or defendants as among those who had attacked her, would give a spirited, detailed account of how she and Ruby had fought long and bravely against men armed with knives and guns before the two women were both overpowered and repeatedly raped. "One was holding my legs and the other had a knife to my throat while the other [third?] one ravished me," she said. The next witness was Ruby Bates, who told much the same story but more hesitantly, less graphically, and in much less detail. A Scottsboro doctor, one of two who had examined the girls an hour and a half after they left the train, now testified that he had "found their vaginas were loaded with male sperm." In other respects, however, the testimony of neither doctor corroborated that of Victoria Price. Unfortunately, neither defense lawyer made any attempt to question the doctors about the medical evidence.[38]

Eight of the defendants were found guilty and were sentenced to die in the electric chair. In the case of the ninth defendant, Roy Wright, who had just turned thirteen, the state had called for life imprisonment, but his jury became hopelessly divided over whether that was sufficient punishment, compelling a reluctant Judge Alfred E. Hawkins to declare a mistrial. Following the verdicts, the eight who had been sentenced were placed immediately on death row at Kilby Prison in Montgomery, Alabama.[39]

The trials and their outcomes aroused widespread protest that often took the form of public rallies and demonstrations in cities in both the South and the North as well as in Europe. Angry letters full of bitter charges now inundated the offices of Alabama judges and officials. The International Labor Defense (ILD), an organization often described as the legal arm of the Communist Party, played the leading role in the agitation. The National Association for the Advancement of Colored People (NAACP), the mainstream civil rights organization, tried to take control of the case but failed to persuade either the accused boys and men or their parents to abandon the ILD. In early January 1932, the NAACP withdrew from the case.[40]

In 1932, the ILD retained Walter L. Pollak, a leading constitutional lawyer, to handle the appeal of the Scottsboro verdicts to the U.S. Supreme Court. In November, the Court, by its decision in *Powell* v. *Alabama,* overturned the verdicts and ordered new trials for the defendants on the grounds that by denying them the time needed to obtain adequate counsel, in a case punishable by death, the Alabama courts had violated their right to "due process" under the Fourteenth Amendment.[41]

Leibowitz Joins the Scottsboro Defense

In January 1933, William L. Patterson, the executive director of the ILD, asked Sam Leibowitz to become chief counsel in the coming trials of the Scottsboro defendants. Since the lawyer was in no sense a radical or even a reformer, it was obviously his record as a courtroom lawyer that led Patterson to make the offer. Moreover, by appointing an attorney who had never lost a client to the death house, the ILD was deflating the claim that it was in the case not to save the defendants but only to advance the cause of communism. In the exchange of letters between Liebowitz and Patterson, it was agreed that the Brooklyn lawyer would have a free hand in the conduct of the defense and that he would receive neither fees nor any reimbursement for his expenses. "We do have this to offer you," wrote Patterson—"an opportunity to give your best in a cause which for its humanitarian appeal has never been equaled in the annals of American Jurisprudence." Not only were the boys and men innocent, said Patterson, but their case was also linked inseparably with the cause of their people, the 12 million oppressed African-Americans in the United States.[42]

Leibowitz decided to take on the case, at least in part, because after reading the transcripts from their Scottsboro trials, he was convinced that the defendants were not guilty, but he was influenced also, in the words of his son Robert, by "a compelling desire to add to the realm of his renown." As historian Dan T. Carter remarks, however, "the relationship between Leibowitz and the ILD was a marriage of convenience, never of preference." A mainstream Democrat, Leibowitz held views about the South that, to some of his friends and, still more, of course, to the Communists, seemed remarkably naive, even romantic. "If it is justice that black men be adjudged innocent," he wrote to Patterson, "I cannot believe that the people of Alabama will be false to their great heritage of honor and to those brave and chivalrous generations of the past in whose blood the history of the state is written."[43]

In early March, Leibowitz and two of his associates traveled from New York City to Alabama by automobile, a journey of a thousand miles that marked the first time that he had ever been in the South. He was shocked and his optimism about the case shaken by what he was told in the diners and gas stations along the route. Virtually every white person he met as he continued southward wanted the Scottsboro defendants hanged, irrespective of their guilt or innocence, if only to "keep the niggers in their place." Leibowitz still clung, however, to the hope that, even in Alabama, an all-white jury would acquit the defendants once it realized the flimsiness of the state's case. Toward that end, he insisted that he was no Communist and, to prove it, he released to the press the full text of the letters that he had exchanged with Patterson. "I am coming here," he told interviewers in Alabama, "simply as a lawyer to try a case."[44]

Prior to Leibowitz's arrival in Alabama, the defense team had requested a change of venue to Birmingham, but their motion was denied. Instead, Judge Hawkins decided to shift the case to Decatur, a city of 18,000, the seat of Morgan County and fifty miles to the west of Scottsboro, which it closely resembled in social attitudes and in the makeup of its population. The first of the nine defendants to be retried was Haywood Patterson, originally from Chattanooga, whose trial was scheduled to start on March 27 when he would be just twenty years old. The presiding judge was James E. Horton and the prosecution was led by Thomas Knight, the attorney general of Alabama, both of them from old and important families.

The First Decatur Trial

Leibowitz opened the pretrial proceedings by moving to quash the indictment on the ground that the grand jury that returned it had been "illegally constituted." In omitting all Negroes from its jury rolls, Leibowitz maintained, Jackson County had deprived Haywood Patterson of his right to equal protection of the laws under the Fourteenth Amendment. To demonstrate his point, the New York lawyer put on the stand a county official who, after a bit of prodding, candidly admitted that in choosing jurors, "Negroes was never considered." When Attorney General Knight argued that the rarity of blacks on jury panels was due to careful selection rather than exclusion, Leibowitz replied by putting "living exhibits" on the stand, calling a series of black witnesses, all of whom were employed, married, and well-spoken, and none of whom had ever been arrested. Each testified that he had never been summoned to jury service and had never heard of a black man who had been.[45]

When Knight refused to concede that there were no Negroes on the rolls, Leibowitz threatened to subpoena every man on the Jackson County list "even if it takes twenty five years." After a day and a half of bitter argument on the issue between the two lawyers, Judge Horton denied Leibowitz's motion. Continuing his attack on the jury system of Alabama, Leibowitz immediately responded with a second motion, challenging the all-white jury pool in the current trial. With the issue still deadlocked, Leibowitz also moved that the juror lists of Morgan County be brought into the courtroom and examined, and to everyone's surprise, Judge Horton granted the motion. The defense lawyer's next move was to draw up a list of prominent Negroes from Decatur in order to determine whether any of their names could be found on the alphabetically arranged juror lists. After several dozen of the names had been called with none of them appearing on the jury rolls, Horton called a halt. He denied Leibowitz's motion, but ruled that the defense had made a prima facie case that blacks had been unlawfully and unconstitutionally excluded from the jury rolls of Morgan County. Leibowitz was now confident of prevailing in the U.S. Supreme Court should Patterson be found guilty at Decatur.[46]

Victoria Price, again the state's principal witness, told essentially the same story as she had at Scottsboro, after pointing out the defendant as one of the men who had raped her. In his cross-examination of Price, which went on for more than three hours, Leibowitz attacked her credibility, pointing out that she was a woman of loose morals who had served brief prison terms for vagrancy and adultery and was known to have dabbled in prostitution in her hometown of Huntsville under the name of "Big Leg." Although uneducated and often evasive on the stand, Price proved a difficult witness who resisted Leibowitz at every turn. "Her testimony was full of holes . . ." historian James Goodman has observed, "yet she herself was hard to shake."[47]

Price testified that she and her friend Ruby had on March 24, 1931, spent the night in Chattanooga at the boarding house of Callie Brochie, which was located on Seventh Street, three blocks from the railway station. Leibowitz told her that Seventh Street was actually two miles from the station, that it contained no boarding houses, and furthermore that there was no such person as Callie Brochie in Chattanooga. "By the way," added the defense attorney,

"Callie Brochie is the name of a character in a series of stories that appeared in the *Saturday Evening Post*. Isn't that where you got the name?" Unfortunately, Leibowitz's rough treatment of Price on the witness stand violated southern customs about how white women were to be treated and seems to have weakened the chances of gaining an acquittal for Patterson.[48]

Another witness for the prosecution was Dr. R.R. Bridges of Scottsboro, who had examined the two women shortly after they had been taken off the train and had testified at the original trials in 1931. As in the earlier trials, Bridges testified that he had found semen in the vaginas of both women. Under cross-examination, however, the doctor revealed much that was helpful to the defense. He acknowledged that the amount of semen he found in Price was quite small, that it was dry, and that it contained no living spermatozoa, all of which, he admitted, would be highly unusual in a woman who had been raped by six men less than two hours before. He also testified that both women had a normal pulse and seemed in relatively good spirits. Neither was bleeding and both had only a few scratches on their bodies. Victoria Price had claimed that she had been struck on the head with the butt of a pistol, but the doctor had seen no head injury of any kind.

On the trial's second day, the state called five more witnesses, but four of them added little if anything to the prosecution's case. One of the witnesses, however, did serious damage to the defense when he testified that he had found a penknife on one of the Scottsboro Nine—he did not remember which one—who had "said that he took it off the white girl, Victoria Price." The statement stunned everyone in the courtroom, including Leibowitz. Attorney General Knight was so delighted that he leaped from his seat and slapped his hands together. Leibowitz angrily moved for a mistrial. "That," he shouted, "is something I haven't seen in fifteen years at the bar."

Knight quickly apologized and Judge Horton told the jury to disregard the prosecutor's conduct, but he refused to declare a mistrial.[49]

Now it was the turn of the defense. Leibowitz called to the stand the conductor of the train, who testified that he had found the snuffbox belonging to Victoria Price in the fourth gondola (an open flatcar) from the engine (car number 13), which was sandwiched between two other gondolas. This testimony cast serious doubt on Price's claim that her attackers had leaped onto the open gondola from atop a neighboring boxcar. The train's fireman testified that he had seen two women at Paint Rock who were running in the opposite direction from an approaching posse. Another witness, a resident of Chattanooga, identified Victoria Price as the young woman he had seen and talked with at the Chattanooga rail yard at 6 A.M. on the day of the alleged rapes. At the same time, he said, he had also seen a second young woman, whom he identified from a photograph as Ruby Bates, and a couple of hours later, he again saw both women at the rail yard, but now in the company of a young man. Unfortunately for the defense, the latter two witnesses were both black, and so had little credibility with a southern jury.[50]

It was, of course, even easier for the Decatur jurors, as well as other white southerners, to disregard the testimony of the Scottsboro boys and men themselves, but Leibowitz nevertheless put six of them, including Haywood Patterson, on the witness stand. To a man, they now insisted that they had not even been aware that there were women on the train and that none of them had raped anyone. When the prosecutor quoted from their testimony at the Scottsboro trials, they replied that they had testified against one another only because their lives had been threatened and they were frightened. "You were tried at Scottsboro," Knight said to Patterson. "I was framed at Scottsboro," replied the defendant.[51]

With his usual flair for the dramatic, Leibowitz had saved his two most important witnesses for last. These were Lester Carter, one of the six whites forced off the train, and Ruby Bates, both of whom had been in New York City for several weeks while the prosecution was searching for them in Alabama and Tennessee. Carter testified that he had first become acquainted with Price and Bates through his friend, Jack Tiller, whom he had met in jail. Shortly after meeting Ruby, Carter had sexual relations with her in the Huntsville hobo jungle, while, less than three feet away, Tiller was having sex with Victoria Price. On the following morning, March 24, 1931, according to the young hobo's story, he rode with the two women on a freight train to Chattanooga, where they spent the whole day in the hobo jungle adjoining the rail yards. That night, he again slept with Ruby Bates and he was positive that Victoria also spent the night in the hobo jungle. On the morning of the 25th, Carter joined the two women and a young hobo named Orville Gilley in hopping a freight train bound for Huntsville. When the fight broke out in an adjoining car, Carter was one of the six white youths forced off the train, but he testified that Gilley, the only white male hobo still on the train, later told him that there had been no rape.[52]

As Ruby Bates entered the courtroom, there was a gasp of surprise from the spectators, and her former friend, Victoria Price, glared angrily at her. Ruby's testimony corroborated Carter's in claiming that Victoria Price had made up her story about being raped and had demanded that Ruby go along with it because she feared that, unless they lied, they would both go to jail for having crossed a state line for immoral purposes. Bates also corroborated the claim of the accused blacks that on the day of the alleged rape, they had saved Orville Gilley from falling under the wheels of the train. This was a point for the defense, for, if the nine black men had intended to rape the women, why would they rescue the only witness? Unfortunately for the defense, Ruby Bates was reduced to tears and forced into repeatedly contradicting herself by the skillful cross-examination of Thomas Knight. He demanded to know where she had gotten the fine clothes that she was wearing at the trial and suggested that both she and Carter, who had also come to court wearing new, expensive clothing, had been bought and paid for by the Communists of New York City.[53]

Following the testimony of Carter and Bates, sizeable crowds gathered at rallies where angry speakers called for the lynching of the nine blacks and the

tarring and feathering of their lawyers. A pamphlet appeared under the title
"Kill The Jew From New York." Amid rumors of impending violence, there
were rallies of the Ku Klux Klan at which crosses were burned and violence
threatened. Judge Horton now thought it necessary to warn the spectators in
the courtroom that he had instructed the National Guardsmen who were on
duty at the trial to shoot to kill if anyone attempted to attack either the defendant or his lawyers. Leibowitz persuaded his wife, Belle, to return to Brooklyn. So hostile was local sentiment that nine National Guardsmen were
instructed to keep the hotel where the northern lawyers were staying under
round-the-clock surveillance.[54]

County Solicitor Wade Wright began the state's summation with an address to the jury laden with anti-Semitic rhetoric. "Show them," he shouted,
"that Alabama justice cannot be bought and sold with Jew money from New
York." Leibowitz again asked for a mistrial, but was rebuffed. In his own
summation, he described Wright as saying, in effect, "Come on boys, we can
lick this Jew from New York." It was, he said, "an appeal to prejudice, a
hangman's speech." Leibowitz again dismissed the testimony of Victoria Price
as "one long outrageous lie." He pleaded with the jury to give the defendant,
"this poor scrap of colored humanity a fair, square deal." Leibowitz spoke for
three hours, often eloquently, but when he was done and the other summations had been delivered, the jurors quickly found Patterson guilty and, as in
the first trial, fixed a sentence of death in the electric chair.[55]

The Verdict's Aftermath

Surprised and shocked, Leibowitz told reporters that the jurors were "spitting
on the tomb of Abraham Lincoln." The day after the trial ended, the attorney
took the train to New York City, where he was greeted at Pennsylvania Station
by a lustily cheering, largely black crowd of 3,000. Buoyed by his reception
and still furious with the Decatur jury, Leibowitz denounced the jurors as
"bigots whose mouths are slits in their faces, whose eyes popped out at you
like frogs, whose chins dripped tobacco juice, bewhiskered and filthy." With
eight other clients still awaiting trial in Alabama, this intemperate statement
was a serious blunder that would hinder the later efforts by Leibowitz and
others to free the nine defendants.[56]

For the first time in his life, Leibowitz became an activist, speaking in
churches and at rallies that raised funds for the ILD. At the Salem Methodist
Episcopal Church in Harlem, he declared that he would sell his own house
and home, if need be, to save the nine boys. "I promise you," he told the
congregation, "that with the help of God, the Scottsboro boys will be free."[57]

His whole approach to the case was now far more radical than it had been
in January. After his Alabama experience, he thought it essential that the southern white attitudes and policies, which had made the Patterson verdict possible, be brought into the light and publicly challenged. For a time, he even

found kind words for the ILD, pointing out to a reporter that, without it, the nine Scottsboro defendants would all be in their coffins "buried back of the county jail."[58]

At the end of the Decatur trial, Leibowitz had shaken hands with Judge Horton, whom he summed up as "one of the finest jurists I have ever known." On June 22, Horton, in an exhaustive twenty-five-page opinion, set aside the jury's verdict as contradicted by the evidence and ordered a new trial for Haywood Patterson. There was, he observed, nothing in the record to corroborate the testimony of Victoria Price and there was much that contradicted it. "We should expect from this cloud of witnesses or from the mute but telling physical condition of the women or their clothes some one fact in corroboration of this story." But he had been unable to find any such fact. Horton's decision was very unpopular in Alabama, and in October he was pressured into withdrawing from the Scottsboro cases. In the following year, Judge Horton was overwhelmingly defeated when he ran for reelection in the Democratic primary.[59]

The Second Decatur Trial

The second Decatur trial of Haywood Patterson opened on November 20, 1933, and was in some respects very similar to the first. The chief witness for the prosecution was again Victoria Price, whose story was now backed up by Orville Gilley, who claimed that he had personally witnessed the rape of Victoria Price and Ruby Bates by Patterson and several other black hoboes. Dr. Bridges reiterated his testimony from the previous trial, but this time as a witness for the defense. As in April, Leibowitz challenged the indictment because the Jackson County grand jury that had brought it in 1931 had been recruited from lists from which the local blacks had been illegally excluded. When the names on the 1931 jury rolls were read out in court, however, Leibowitz was surprised to learn that they included the names of ten Negroes. Suspecting fraud, he hired a nationally known handwriting expert who, after examining the names in question, concluded that they were not entered at the same time as the other names, but were added to the lists later on. In short, the rolls had been tampered with and a forgery committed. As in the previous trial, however, Leibowitz's motion to quash the indictment was denied. Judge William Callahan, Horton's replacement, refused to believe that the jury commissioners had committed fraud or that an Alabama judge would have tolerated it if they had. Leibowitz drew comfort from the fact that the evidence of forgery had been placed on the record, which was now, he believed, in "a thousand per cent better shape" for an appeal to higher courts than it had ever been before.[60]

Unlike the moderate and flexible Horton, the new judge, William Callahan, was obviously biased against the defense. Callahan made it clear from the outset that he considered Patterson guilty and was determined to spend no more than three days on his trial. He refused to permit Leibowitz to question Victoria Price about her past conduct and jail terms and even declared off-limits all questioning about her conduct and whereabouts during the two days preceding the events on the train. He would cut short the defense counsel's interrogation of witnesses and he was sometimes more rigorous in his cross-examination of witnesses for the defense than were the prosecuting attorneys. He often glared at Leibowitz and spoke sarcastically to him. In his openly biased charge to the jury, Callahan even failed to mention that the jurors should vote to acquit the defendant unless they believed that his guilt had been proved "beyond a reasonable doubt." After Leibowitz ran to the bench and whispered in his ear, Callahan acknowledged his error and recited the correct form for acquittal to the jurors.

Leibowitz had been as feisty as ever at the trial. He was more successful than before in his exchanges with Victoria Price, forcing her into contradictory assertions and into statements that clashed with what she had said at earlier trials. But it was again to no avail. As in his first two trials, Patterson was found guilty and sentenced to die. As soon as his trial was over, a second Scottsboro defendant, Clarence Norris, was placed in the dock at the Decatur courthouse. His trial differed little from Patterson's, and he too was quickly found guilty by his jury and sentenced to death. Leibowitz and the other attorneys for the defense appealed first to the Alabama Supreme Court and then, when that tribunal upheld the Decatur verdicts, immediately appealed both decisions to the U.S. Supreme Court.[61]

Norris v. Alabama

The relationship between Leibowitz and the ILD had always been uneasy and it was to be shattered completely by the arrest on October 1, 1934, of two ILD agents in Alabama for trying to bribe Victoria Price. When ILD officials admitted to Leibowitz that they had authorized the bribe, he exploded in anger, accused the organization of "assassinating the Scottsboro boys," and demanded that no communist lawyer should have anything more to do with their cases. There followed a bitter struggle for the loyalty of the nine youths in which Leibowitz played a major role, first in organizing the American Scottsboro Committee as a moderate alternative to the ILD and then by enlisting the leading black ministers of New York City as his emissaries to the Scottsboro Nine. Meanwhile, the ILD fought back against Leibowitz and his allies chiefly by appealing to the defendants' parents.

In January 1935, the U.S. Supreme Court agreed to hear the appeals by Patterson and Norris of their 1933 convictions. To avoid jeopardizing their chances, the ILD and Leibowitz worked out a truce and a division of labor. It was agreed that Leibowitz, as the counsel for Norris before the court, would present the facts and that Walter Pollak and Osmond Frankel, as Patterson's representatives, would deal with the constitutional aspects.[62]

On February 15, 1935, Leibowitz, in his first and only appearance before the Supreme Court, accused officials in Jackson County of violating the rights of his client by totally excluding its black population from the county's jury rolls. Thomas Knight, representing Alabama, argued that the local officials had simply been careful and selective, but had not practiced exclusion on the basis of race. In reply, Leibowitz cited the evidence that he had so carefully placed in the case records at the three trials in Decatur. He charged that Alabama officials had engaged in forgery and fraud by adding surreptitiously to a 1931 jury roll the names of blacks, none of whom had been on the list of names at the time. When Chief Justice Charles Evans Hughes asked Leibowitz if he could prove his charge, the latter announced that he had brought the jury roll with him. Each of the justices then inspected the records that, according to Leibowitz, had been tampered with. Six weeks later, a unanimous Court ordered a new trial for Clarence Norris. A second decision handed down the same day dealt with Patterson's appeal, ordering the Alabama Supreme Court to reconsider the case. The opinion of the Court in *Norris* v. *Alabama* was given by Chief Justice Hughes, who accepted the contention of the appellants' attorneys that the systematic exclusion of blacks from the juries of Alabama had deprived the defendant of the equal protection of the laws as provided for by the Fourteenth Amendment.[63]

In hailing the decision (with considerable, if understandable, hyperbole) "as the culmination of the hopes and ambitions of 15 million Negro souls in America," Leibowitz even hoped that the defendants would not be retried. When Knight, now lieutenant governor, announced that the state intended to obtain new indictments of the Scottsboro Nine, Leibowitz appealed to Bibb Graves, Alabama's new governor, to "end the carousel of hate" by granting the defendants an unconditional pardon or at least appointing a fact-finding committee to review the case and recommend a course of action.[64]

Unfortunately, the state of Alabama was not yet ready to admit that it had been wrong. On November 13, 1935, all nine of the Scottsboro defendants were reindicted by a grand jury that for the first time since the days of Reconstruction included a black man. In late January 1936, there was another trial in Decatur with Judge Callahan again presiding in which another all-white jury again found Haywood Patterson guilty as charged. This time, Patterson was sentenced not to die but to "only" seventy-five years in prison. Eighteen months later, three more Scottsboro defendants were tried before Judge Callahan and found guilty after brief trials. Clarence Norris was for the third time found guilty and sentenced to death on July 15, 1937. Within the next nine days, both Andy Wright and Charlie Weems were found guilty and sentenced to prison terms of ninety-nine and seventy-five years, respectively.[65]

At the close of Weems's trial, Leibowitz gave vent to his anger at the repeated use by the prosecution in all the Scottsboro trials of blatant appeals to prejudice and at the rigid unwillingness of Decatur juries to acquit African-Americans even in the face of irrefutable evidence that they were innocent. "It isn't Charlie Weems on trial in this case," he complained. "It's a Jew lawyer and New York State." He declared himself "sick and tired of the sanctimony and hypocrisy of the state and people of Alabama." As historian Dan T. Carter has pointed out, this outburst came after four and one-half years of frustration for Leibowitz, who had won cases in New York even when there had been compelling evidence against his clients but who could not win in Alabama even though the evidence that his clients were innocent was overwhelming.[66]

Alabama's Grudging "Release" of the Scottsboro Nine

On July 24, 1937, the day that Weems was sentenced, the chief prosecutor of the case against him announced that the state was dropping its rape charges against the five remaining defendants. One of the five, Ozie Powell, was now facing assault charges for allegedly stabbing a deputy sheriff while in transit from one prison to another. The other four were to be immediately released. The state now admitted that Victoria Price must have been mistaken when she identified Willie Roberson, so afflicted with syphilis that he could scarcely walk, and the nearly blind Olen Montgomery as among the men who had jumped off the top of a boxcar to attack her and Ruby Bates. As for the other two youths, one had been thirteen and the other twelve when they had first been arrested and accused six and a half years earlier. The released youths were handed over to Leibowitz, who conveyed them in two automobiles to Nashville, from which they traveled by rail first to Cincinnati and from there to New York City.[67]

Negotiations between Alabama officials and various individuals purporting to speak on behalf of the Scottsboro defendants dated back to December 1936, when Lieutenant Governor Thomas Knight had come to New York City to offer Leibowitz a deal. At a public meeting in New York City on July 29, 1937, Leibowitz claimed that he had worked out a compromise with Alabama officials back in January, which provided for the release of all of the Scottsboro defendants within two years. He called on Attorney General Albert Carmichael to live up to their bargain, to "come forward like a man and a true American citizen" by saying to the governor of the state: "I have given my word . . . and I ask you to honor my promise." For whatever reason, the governor failed to act.[68]

Although four of the defendants were now free, the plight of the remaining five seemed worse than before. At the mercy of harsh and often racist guards, the imprisoned men began to think that their "friends," including Leibowitz, had sold them out to gain the release of the other four.

In 1937, Leibowitz appealed Patterson's conviction to the U.S. Supreme Court, arguing that by denying him a change of venue from the hopelessly biased Decatur setting, Judge Callahan had deprived the defendant of his right to due process of law under the Fourteenth Amendment. Unpersuaded, the justices refused without comment to review Patterson's conviction. With no hope at all of ever prevailing before Alabama judges and juries, and lacking any further constitutional basis for appealing to the federal courts, Leibowitz and his legal associates were at an impasse.[69]

The question of when and how Alabama would release the remaining five now rested entirely with the state's elected governors and various prison officials and parole boards. Four of the men were in fact released on parole during the 1940s. By 1947, Haywood Patterson, perhaps the most victimized of all the Scottsboro defendants, was the only one who had been neither released nor paroled. On the night of July 17, 1948, Patterson executed a daring escape from the prison farm in Kilby, Alabama. Traveling by freight train, he arrived a few days later in Detroit, where he was reunited with three of his sisters. In 1950, Patterson called attention to himself by coauthoring, with the New York–based writer Earl Conrad, his autobiography, *Scottsboro Boy*. Alabama attempted to extradite him, but when the governor of Michigan, G. Mennen Williams, refused to send him back, the Alabama authorities decided not to pursue him further. Unfortunately, Patterson's freedom was short-lived. In December 1950, he was accused of manslaughter following a barroom brawl in which the man he had fought with was stabbed to death. Following a mistrial, he was tried a second time, was found guilty, and sentenced to a prison term of six to fifteen years. He died of cancer in Michigan's state penitentiary in 1952 at the age of thirty-nine.[70]

Judge Leibowitz

While devoting much of his time over a five-year period to the Scottsboro trials and appeals, Leibowitz had also continued to take on other cases. He became increasingly reluctant, however, to defend professional criminals, refusing, for example, to defend either Lucky Luciano or Lepke Buchalter, even though the latter offered $250,000 to represent him, whatever the outcome. In 1939, Salvatore Gatti, a Leibowitz client, was convicted of murder because he had left his fingerprint on the murder weapon. Sentenced to die in the electric chair, Gatti was the only one among Leibowitz's 140 murder-case clients ever to be executed.[71]

Leibowitz, who had added greatly to his popularity and prestige via the Scottsboro cases, was now weary of being a defense attorney and eager to become either a prosecutor or a judge. A loyal organization Democrat, he supported the party's candidates for mayor against Fiorello H. La Guardia in 1933 and again in 1937 when La Guardia was the incumbent mayor. In 1939 he flirted with the idea of challenging William O'Dwyer for the Democratic nomination for district attorney in Kings County, but announced just before the filing deadline that he would support O'Dwyer. In 1940, the Kings County Democratic Party nominated Leibowitz for judge of the Kings County Court, one of the busiest criminal courts in the United States, and after winning easily in the primary, he was elected in November to a fourteen-year term, by a plurality of more than 400,000 votes.[72]

Leibowitz served as a judge for nearly thirty years, earning the nickname of "Sentencing Sam" by his toughness in dealing with convicted felons. When one elderly defendant complained that he could never at his age do the twenty years to which Leibowitz had sentenced him, Sam told him to "do the best you can." Having learned and applied many of the tricks of the trade while he was an attorney, Leibowitz had no tolerance at all for legal trickery now that he was a judge. "I'll give you a thousand years, if necessary," he told one hardened criminal who was refusing to answer his questions. He remained concerned, however, with justice. "Leibowitz," remarked one attorney who knew his work well, "is the toughest judge in the city of New York, but nobody gets sent away who is innocent." He also tempered his hard-line attitude on crime by advocating, long before it became fashionable, that prison inmates be allowed conjugal visits and by calling for special efforts to rehabilitate juvenile delinquents. Finally, Leibowitz played a notable role during the 1950s in exposing the corrupt dealings of bookmakers and gamblers with various New York City politicians and policemen. Thus, in his judicial career as in his work as a defense attorney, Leibowitz, while ambitious and tough-minded, was also a man of ideals and of high social purpose. In 1970, he retired from the bench, and on January 11, 1978, Samuel S. Leibowitz died, following a stroke.[73]

Notes

1. Quentin Reynolds, *Courtroom: The Story of Samuel S. Leibowitz* (New York: Farrar, Strauss, and Giroux, 1950), 20; Robert Leibowitz, *The Defender: The Life and Career of Samuel S. Leibowitz* (Englewood Cliffs, NJ: Prentice Hall, 1981), 1–2; Fred Pasley, *Not Guilty: The Story of Samuel S. Leibowitz* (New York: G.P. Putnam's Sons, 1933), 62.

2. David Frost, "Should the Death Penalty be Brought Back Quickly?" an interview of Samuel Leibowitz broadcast on the Metromedia Network on January 11, 1970, reprinted in David Frost, *The Americans* (New York: Stein and Day, 1970), 87–88; Leibowitz, *The Defender,* 2–3; Pasley, *Not Guilty,* 62.

3. Reynolds, *Courtroom,* 27; Pasley, *Not Guilty,* 64–65; Leibowitz, *The Defender,* 4.

4. Leibowitz, *The Defender,* 4–5; Pasley, *Not Guilty,* 65–66.

5. Leibowitz, *The Defender,* 6; Reynolds, *Courtroom,* 23; Pasley, *Not Guilty,* 66–68.

6. Alva Johnston, "Let Freedom Ring—II," *New Yorker,* June 11, 1932, 18; Reynolds, *Courtroom,* 24; Pasley, *Not Guilty,* 60.

7. Reynolds, *Courtroom,* 23–24; Leibowitz, *The Defender,* 10–11.

8. Johnston, "Let Freedom Ring—II," 18–19; Leibowitz, *The Defender,* 15–18; Pasley, *Not Guilty,* 70–71; Reynolds, *Courtroom,* 27.

9. Leibowitz, *The Defender,* 19–23; Pasley, *Not Guilty,* 72–77.

10. Pasley, *Not Guilty,* 75–76; Leibowitz, *The Defender,* 22.

11. "Held as Girl's Torturer," *New York Times,* April 30, 1920, 2; "Actor Guilty of Cruelty," *New York Times,* May 29, 1920, 18; Pasley, *Not Guilty,* 78–83.

12. Leibowitz, *The Defender,* 12–14, 20–25, 28, 51.

13. Johnston, "Let Freedom Ring—II," 22; Leibowitz, *The Defender,* 31–33; Pasley, *Not Guilty,* 83–93.

14. Alva Johnston, "Let Freedom Ring—I," *New Yorker,* June 4, 1932, 21.

15. Quoted by Reynolds, *Courtroom,* 417–418; Leibowitz, *The Defender,* 51, 108.

16. Johnston, "Let Freedom Ring—Part Two," 19–20; Pasley, *Not Guilty,* 108–116; John C. O'Brien, "Speedy Roundup in Gang Killings," *New York Sunday News,* December 27, 1925, 3;

"$500,000 Bail Ready, But 9 in Gang Killing Are Held," *New York Daily News,* December 30, 1925, 11; "Police Guard Court as Gunmen Are Held," *New York Daily News,* January 1, 1926, 6.

17. Leibowitz, *The Defender,* 144–147; Reynolds, *Courtroom,* 315–318.

18. Quoted in Leibowitz, *The Defender,* 106, 142; "the important thing" quote is in Reynolds, *Courtroom,* 418; ibid., 17, 33–34, 360, 417.

19. Johnston, "Let Freedom Ring—I," 22; Leibowitz, *The Defender,* 170–178.

20. Reynolds, *Courtroom,* 64–65, 80–82, 152–153, 160, 169.

21. Pasley, *Not Guilty,* 148–154; Leibowitz, *The Defender,* 50–51; Reynolds, *Courtroom,* 154, 207–209.

22. Reynolds, *Courtroom,* 35–62; Pasley, *Not Guilty,* 3–58; Leibowitz, *The Defender,* 54–76.

23. "Rule at Auburn Shifted, Dr. Christian in Charge," *New York Times,* December 15, 1929, 1, 20; "Convict Indicted in Auburn Killing," *New York Times,* January 8, 1930, 14; Leibowitz, *The Defender,* 82–83; Pasley, *Not Guilty,* 162.

24. "Pick Three Jurors for Auburn Trial," *New York Times,* February 19, 1930, 27; "Five Added to Becker Jury," *New York Times,* February 22, 1930, 17.

25. "Swear They Saw Becker Kill Chief," *New York Times,* March 4, 1930, 13; Pasley, *Not Guilty,* 174–186; Leibowitz, *The Defender,* 85–91; Johnston, "Let Freedom Ring—II," 22–23.

26. "Durnford Murder Denied by Becker," *New York Times,* March 8, 1930, 19; Leibowitz, *The Defender,* 92–95; Pasley, *Not Guilty,* 180–184.

27. "Says Guard Lied at Auburn Trial," *New York Times,* March 11, 1930, 16; "Auburn Jury Holds Max Becker's Fate," *New York Times,* March 12, 1930, 5; "Becker Acquitted; His Counsel Faints," *New York Times,* March 13, 1930, 3; Pasley, *Not Guilty,* 184–188; Leibowitz, *The Defender,* 96–99.

28. Quoted in Reynolds, *Courtroom,* 60; ibid., 62–63, 133, 153; Leibowitz, *The Defender,* 33–34, 62; Pasley, *Not Guilty,* 122.

29. Quoted in Pasley, *Not Guilty,* 121–122; Johnston, "Let Freedom Ring—II," 18–19.

30. Leibowitz, *The Defender,* 105; Johnston, "Let Freedom Ring—II," 18.

31. Pasley, *Not Guilty,* 201–203, 216–219, 221–225; Leibowitz, *The Defender,* 108–116; 148–165; "Leibowitz Indicted in Vice Case Inquiry," *New York Times,* September 30, 1931, 3; "Leibowitz Is Cleared," *New York Times,* August 26, 1932, 18.

32. As quoted in Leibowitz, *The Defender,* 166; ibid., 183; Pasley, *Not Guilty,* 118–119; Reynolds, *Courtroom,* 33, 359.

33. Dan T. Carter, "A Reasonable Doubt," *American Heritage Magazine,* October, 1968, 40–41; Dan T. Carter, *Scottsboro: A Tragedy of the American South* (Baton Rouge: Louisiana State University Press, 1979), 3–7; James Goodman, *Stories of Scottsboro* (New York: Random House, 1994), xi–xii, 3–4; " Jail Head Asks Troops as Mob Seeks Negroes," *New York Times,* March 26, 1931, 21.

34. Goodman, *Stories of Scottsboro,* 5.

35. Carter, *Scottsboro,* 7–13; Goodman, *Stories of Scottsboro,* 11–12, 17–18.

36. Carter, *Scottsboro,* 5–6; Goodman, *Stories of Scottsboro,* 7–10, 90–98.

37. Reynolds, *Courtroom,* 256–257; Carter, *Scottsboro,* 18–20; Goodman, *Stories of Scottsboro,* 5–10.

38. Carter, *Scottsboro,* 20–46; Goodman, *Stories of Scottsboro,* 13–15, 22–23; Reynolds, *Courtroom,* 257.

39. Carter, *Scottsboro,* 47–48; Goodman, *Stories of Scottsboro,* 6.

40. Carter, *Scottsboro,* Chapter 3; Goodman, *Stories of Scottsboro,* 32–38, 82–91; "Condemned Negroes Spurn 'Communist' Aid," *New York Times,* April 24, 1931, 4; "Quit Negroes' Defense," *New York Times,* January 5, 1932, 2.

41. Reynolds, *Courtroom,* 261; "New Trial Ordered by Supreme Court in Scottsboro Case," *New York Times,* November 8, 1932, 1.

42. Carter, *Scottsboro,* 181–183, Reynolds, *Courtroom,* 249–253; Goodman, *Stories of Scottsboro,* 103–104.

43. The Samuel Leibowitz quotation is in Leibowitz, *The Defender,* 190; Carter, *Scottsboro,* 183.

44. The Samuel Leibowitz quotation is in Carter, *Scottsboro,* 185; Leibowitz, *The Defender,* 189–195; Reynolds, *Courtroom,* 261–262; Goodman, *Stories of Scottsboro,* 104–105.

45. Carter, *Scottsboro,* 194–199; Reynolds, *Courtroom,* 262–263; Goodman, *Stories of Scottsboro,* 120–122.

46. Carter, *Scottsboro,* 199–203; Goodman, *Stories of Scottsboro,* 123–124; F. Raymond Daniell, "Fight for Negroes Opens in Alabama," *New York Times,* March 28, 1933, 6; F. Raymond Daniell, "Refuses to Quash Scottsboro Case," *New York Times,* March 29, 1933, 7; F. Raymond Daniell, "Pick Jury to Hear Scottsboro Case," *New York Times,* April 1, 1933, 34.

47. Goodman, *Stories of Scottsboro,* 125–127; Carter, *Scottsboro,* 206.

48. F. Raymond Daniell, "Evidence Assailed in Alabama Trial," *New York Times,* April 5, 1933, 40; Goodman, *Stories of Scottsboro,* 125–127; Carter, *Scottsboro,* 205–214.

49. Reynolds, *Courtroom,* 269–270; Goodman, *Stories of Scottsboro,* 138–140.

50. Carter, *Scottsboro,* 219–220; Goodman, *Stories of Scottsboro,* 128–130, 140, 144–145.

51. Quote in Carter, *Scottsboro,* 226; ibid., 221–225.

52. Reynolds, *Courtroom,* 271–272; Goodman, *Stories of Scottsboro,* 129–131; Carter, *Scottsboro,* 229–231.

53. F. Raymond Daniell, "Girl Recants Story of Negroes' Attack," *New York Times,* April 7, 1933, 3; Reynolds, *Courtroom,* 272–273; Goodman, *Stories of Scottsboro,* 131–132; Carter, *Scottsboro,* 222–235.

54. F. Raymond Daniell, "Warning by Judge at Alabama Trial," *New York Times,* April 6, 1933, 13; Goodman, *Stories of Scottsboro,* 130–132; Carter, *Scottsboro,* 223–224; Reynolds, *Courtroom,* 267, 273.

55. The Wright quotation and the quote of Leibowitz are both in F. Raymond Daniell, "New York Attacked in Scottsboro Trial," *New York Times,* April 8, 1933, 30; F. Raymond Daniell, "Jury Out Overnight with Scottsboro Case," *New York Times,* April 9, 1933, 1; F. Raymond Daniell, "Negro Found Guilty in Scottsboro Case," *New York Times,* April 10, 1933, 1; Carter, *Scottsboro,* 235–242.

56. Quoted in "Negroes in Riotous March Welcome Defender in Scottsboro Case," *New York Times,* April 11, 1933, 1; Carter, *Scottsboro,* 244.

57. Quoted in "Leibowitz in Harlem Stirs 4,000 by Plea," *New York Times,* April 14, 1933, 5; see also "Scottsboro Cause Wins O'Brien's Aid," *New York Times,* April 17, 1933, 4; Carter, *Scottsboro,* 243–246.

58. Quoted in Goodman, *Stories of Scottsboro,* 148; Reynolds, *Courtroom,* 275–276.

59. Quoted in Goodman, *Stories of Scottsboro,* 176–177; Carter, *Scottsboro,* 239, 264–273.

60. Reynolds, *Courtroom,* 281–283; Goodman, *Stories of Scottsboro,* 212–214; Carter, *Scottsboro,* 282–290.

61. Goodman, *Stories of Scottsboro,* 212–221; Carter, *Scottsboro,* 274–302; Reynolds, *Courtroom,* 285–287.

62. "Held as Bribers in Scottsboro Case," *New York Times,* October 2, 1934, 7; "Leibowitz Threatens to Quit Negro Case," *New York Times,* October 4, 1934, 8; "Reds Told to Drop Scottsboro Case," *New York Times,* October 11, 1934, 11; Carter, *Scottsboro,* 310–319; Goodman, *Stories of Scottsboro,* 239–243.

63. "U.S. Supreme Court Aids Two in Scottsboro Case," *New York Times,* January 8, 1935, 23; "Hits Alabama Jury Book," *New York Times,* February 16, 1935, 2; "New Trial Ordered by Supreme Court," *New York Times,* April 2, 1935, 1; Carter, *Scottsboro,* 319–324; Goodman, *Stories of Scottsboro,* 243–244, 249.

64. Quoted is in "Scottsboro Pardons Asked by Leibowitz," *New York Times,* May 1, 1935, 6; Reynolds, *Courtroom,* 295–296; Carter, *Scottsboro,* 325–328.

65. F. Raymond Daniell, "75 Years in Prison Set for Patterson," *New York Times,* January 24, 1936, 1; "Jury Again Dooms Scottsboro Negro," *New York Times,* July 16, 1937, 1; F. Raymond Daniell, "Scottsboro Jurors Give 99 Year Term," *New York Times,* July 22, 1937, 1; "Scottsboro Case Ends as Four Go Free; Two More Get Prison," *New York Times,* July 25, 1937, 1; Goodman, *Stories of Scottsboro,* 304–306.

66. Quoted in Carter, 373–374; ibid., 375–377; Goodman, *Stories of Scottsboro,* 306–307.

67. *New York Times,* July 25, 1937; F. Raymond Daniell, "Scottsboro Group Is Due Here Today," *New York Times,* July 26, 1937; Carter, *Scottsboro,* 376–377; Reynolds, *Courtroom,* 307–308.

68. "Leibowitz Bares Scottsboro Pact," *New York Times,* July 30, 1937, 8; Goodman, *Stories of Scottsboro,* 290–293, 300–301, 309–310; Carter, *Scottsboro,* 362–368, 378–395.

69. "High Court Weighs Scottsboro Case," *New York Times,* October 24, 1937, 11; "Justices Sustain Scottsboro Term," *New York Times,* October 26, 1937, 1; Goodman, *Stories of Scottsboro,* 349–350; Carter, *Scottsboro,* 379.

70. Goodman, *Stories of Scottsboro,* 286–293, 309–310, 367–381; Carter, *Scottsboro,* 399–414; Reynolds, *Courtroom,* 309–313.

71. Reynolds, *Courtroom,* 347–362.

72. James A. Hagerty, "McKee Aides Sure of Beating O'Brien," *New York Times,* October 13, 1933, 2; "Lehman Endorses Mahoney's Ticket," *New York Times,* October 17, 1937, 4; "Leibowitz Seeks Geoghan's Post," *New York Times,* May 21, 1939, Section 3, 5; "Solomon Blocks Brooklyn Fusion," *New York Times,* August 19, 1939, 24; "Leibowitz, Expert in Criminal Law," *New York Times,* November 6, 1940, 3; "Leibowitz Sworn as Judge in Kings," *New York Times,* December 22, 1940, 28.

73. Quotations are in "Jurist Before the Bar," *Time* (November 15, 1963): 70–71; Murray Schumach, "Samuel S. Leibowitz, 84, Jurist and Scottsboro Case Lawyer, Dies," *New York Times,* January 12, 1978, 84.

Selected Cases

Police Departmental Trials (1931)
Vice Scandals Cases

In 1930, Leibowitz was engaged by nine police officers to defend them in departmental hearings against charges that they had deliberately "framed" and falsely arrested thirty-two different women on charges of prostitution. These charges were advanced by Chile Mapocha Acuna, a petty criminal, who acknowledged that he had been a paid informant for the NYPD's vice squad for more than a year, starting in 1928. According to Acuna, the policemen had arrested the women without any significant evidence in order to extort money from them.

Leibowitz was soon able to locate witnesses who said that Acuna was himself a procurer and a convicted felon. One woman told Leibowitz that Acuna had employed her as a prostitute and another witness said that he had offered to install her in a Harlem bordello. According to another informant, members of the vice squad had once arrested Acuna for kidnapping. He was convicted and served a brief prison term, and he vowed afterward that he would get even.

At the departmental trial, Acuna said that in eight of the nineteen vice squad cases with which he had been involved, there was no real evidence at all against any of the women arrested. To rebut his charges, Leibowitz produced more than half a dozen witnesses. A prostitute testified that Acuna had brought her many clients but specifically denied his story that two of the accused policemen had come to her flat and had sex with her. Other witnesses attested to his scheme to frame some of the vice squad policemen. Character witnesses were brought forward in praise of Lieutenant Peter J. Pfeiffer, the highest ranking of the accused men. On February 16, 1931, Deputy Commissioner Rottenberg, the man in charge at the departmental hearing, dismissed the charges against five of the accused defendants, and in April 1931, after a few additional days of hearings, Rottenberg also dismissed the charges against the other four.

The People v. *Stein* (1931)
Bronx County Court

The dead body of Vivian Gordon, who had offered to tell investigators about a frame-up by New York City police officers, was found in Van Cortlandt Park in the Bronx at 7 A.M. on February 26, 1931. Gordon, a sexual adventuress and an associate of underworld figures, such as "Legs" Diamond, had been strangled with a length of clothesline. Because the courts and the police were already widely accused of corruption, civic leaders and editorial writers demanded that the killers of Vivian Gordon be brought to justice.

On April 9, the police arrested Harry Stein, an ex-convict with a long criminal record, for the murder of Gordon. On the day after his arrest, Stein secured the services of Leibowitz, who promptly announced that he would fight the case "every step of the way." He fought it first of all in the press, telling reporters that "this whole thing is a frame-up." When the case came to court in June 1931, Leibowitz pointedly asked of every prospective juror whether he would have the courage to vote "not guilty" if the police were trying to "railroad an innocent man."

The heart of the prosecution's case against Stein was the "confession" of Harry Schlitten, a professional chauffeur, who claimed that he had driven the car in which Vivian Gordon had been murdered. He claimed that he drove the car from midtown Manhattan to Van Cortlandt Park in the Bronx. According to Schlitten, it had been Stein and his accomplice, Sam Greenberg, who had strangled Gordon at approximately 2 A.M, on February 26.

With his case hanging in the balance, Leibowitz now set out meticulously to destroy the credibility of the state's star witness. He probed searchingly into Schlitten's motives for making a confession that could easily have landed him in the electric chair.

The lawyer scoffed at Schlitten's claim that he had come forward due to a guilty conscience, noting that he had confessed to taking part in a murder and, according to his own testimony, had never even asked who the victim was. Leibowitz got Schlitten to admit that the police had promised him immunity in exchange for his testimony against Stein and Greenberg. The attorney also pointed out that Schlitten had been interrogated for nearly seven hours before he had confessed, suggesting strongly that the police had beaten his story out of him.

Finally, Leibowitz charged that Schlitten had memorized his testimony. It was all too perfect—ten pages in which the witness had sounded more like a lawyer than the thug that he was. He had been letter perfect in his detailed narrative of an extremely complex chain of events. When asked to repeat his story, he had used virtually identical language and had told it in the same order as before. There were also statements that were less than credible. He was a chauffeur, but he needed help in renting a car. Did the jury believe that? He took part in a murder, but he never asked the victim's identity. Did the jurors believe that? This, concluded Leibowitz, was a memorized statement and "a cooked up story" devised by the police to get themselves off the hook.

After only three hours of deliberation, the jury voted to acquit Stein and Greenberg.

Powell v. *Alabama* (1932)
287 U.S. 45
Argued October 10, 1932; decided November 7, 1932

The first of the Scottsboro trials began on April 6, 1931, before the Circuit Court of Jackson County (Alabama) in Scottsboro, the county seat. By April 9, eight of the defendants had been found guilty by local juries and were sentenced to die in the electric chair by Judge Hawkins. The cases were appealed to the Alabama Supreme Court, which affirmed the decisions of the Circuit Court on March 24, 1932, by a five to one majority. The lone dissenter was Chief Justice John C. Anderson, who held that the defendants had not received a fair trial.

The attorneys for the accused, who included Walter Pollak, a leading constitutional lawyer, promptly appealed to the U.S. Supreme Court, which agreed to hear the case. When the case came before the Court in October 1932, the defense lawyers argued that the guilty verdicts were constitutionally invalid on three grounds: (1) the defendants' trials had not been "fair, impartial and deliberate," (2) Judge Hawkins had denied them their right to adequate counsel, and (3) the juries that tried them were drawn from a jury pool that contained no qualified members of their race.

Of these three counts, the Court decided to take up only the second one: the question of the adequacy of counsel. There were therefore two points at issue, one factual, the other constitutional. The factual question was whether the defendants had received adequate legal counsel. If the facts revealed that they had not, then this raised a constitutional question of whether this lack of adequate counsel infringed upon their right to "due process of law" as required by the Fourteenth Amendment.

In a seven-to-two decision, the Court reversed the judgment of the Alabama Court and remanded the cases back to that state's courts for retrial. In his opinion for the Court, Justice George Sutherland observed that it was not until the first day of their trials that a specific lawyer was appointed by the Circuit Court to represent the defendants. It was therefore clear that they had been denied their right to counsel. This is a right that is "fundamental in nature" and is an important part of "due process of law." Therefore, concluded Sutherland, the defendants were entitled to a new trial due to the failure of the court to fulfill its obligation. "A defendant charged with a serious crime," wrote Sutherland, "must not be stripped of his right to have sufficient time to advise with counsel and prepare his defense. To do that is not to proceed promptly in the calm spirit of enlightened justice, but to go forward with the haste of the mob."

The decision was not so expansive as it might have been. Sutherland was, after all, one of the Court's most conservative members. The decision did *not* assert, for example, that either the due process or the equal protection clause of the Fourteenth Amendment applied the "fair trial" requirements of the Sixth Amendment to the states. Instead, the "due process" requirement upon the state courts was left vague, and Sutherland dwelt at length on the unfortunate circumstances of the defendants as a factor in the decision. Perhaps the most that can be claimed for *Powell* v. *Alabama* was that the Court would not, in the phrase of Felix Frankfurter, "condone judicial murder."

Norris v. *State* (1934) and *Patterson* v. *State* (1934)
229 Ala. 234

After the U.S. Supreme Court ruled against it in *Powell* v. *Alabama*, the state moved quickly to again indict the Scottsboro defendants for rape. In 1933 Clarence Norris was tried for the second time and Haywood Patterson was put on trial twice. In each of these proceedings, the jury once again found the defendant guilty and sentenced him to die in the electric chair.

Leibowitz was chief defense counsel at all three trials. At each, he moved that the court quash both the indictment and the trial jury venire because both Jackson County and Morgan County had systematically excluded blacks from the juries that had indicted and tried the defendant. To demonstrate that the exclusion (in practice) of blacks from jury service had been due exclusively to their race, Leibowitz called a dozen black witnesses to the stand. Each of these men was fairly well educated and well established in the community, and each was an owner of property. Although all of these witnesses were well qualified to be jurors according to Alabama law, none had ever been called upon to serve on a jury. Leibowitz put Jackson County officials on the stand, and they freely admitted that they could not recall even a single instance of a black serving on either a grand or a petit jury.

Leibowitz also moved during each one of these trials that the Jackson County jury roll be brought into the courtroom to test whether any of the names listed on it belonged to a black. During Haywood Patterson's second trial at the Decatur courthouse in November 1934, officials of the county claimed to have identified the names of six black men on the current jury roll. After examining these entries, Leibowitz insisted that they were forgeries. He pointed out that the names of the blacks were not alphabetized like the other names on the jury roll, but in each case were at the bottom of the page, were written in a different color ink from the other entries, and had all been superimposed over a bright red line. To clinch matters, Leibowitz put a nationally known handwriting expert on the witness stand, and he testified that the names of the blacks on the jury roll had been written in recently, and not at the time that the rest of the document had been compiled.

The defense appealed the verdicts in the Norris and Patterson cases to the Alabama Supreme Court in June 1934. In the Patterson case, the court rejected the bill of exceptions filed by the defense on the ground of its not having been filed within the allotted period of ninety days from the final judgment of the trial court. (The question was whether the calendar began running at the time that the verdict was handed down or at the time of final sentencing five days later. The evidence suggests that both Thomas Knight, Alabama's attorney general, and Judge Callahan attempted to mislead the lawyers for the defense as to the actual deadline for filing their bill of exceptions.) This placed in doubt Patterson's right of appeal to the federal courts. If the Alabama Supreme Court never had to rule on the merits of the issues raised by the defense at Patterson's trial, then how could its decision on the case be appealed?

On June 28, 1934, the court unanimously rejected the motions that had been made to provide new trials for Patterson and Norris. On the jury selection issue, the Alabama Supreme Court ruled, again unanimously, that the absence of Negroes from the official lists of jurors resulted from the relative weakness of their qualifications rather than from their deliberate and systematic exclusion. Therefore, according to Alabama's highest court, the failure of Jackson County to include blacks on its jury roll had not deprived the black defendants of the equal protection of the laws.

Norris v. *Alabama* (1935)
294 U.S. 587

On January 8, 1935, the U.S. Supreme Court agreed to review the most recent rulings of the Alabama Supreme Court in the cases of Haywood Patterson and Clarence Norris. In his argument before the Court in mid-February, Leibowitz cited the testimony of defense witnesses at Norris's trial in Decatur as evidence that black men had been systematically excluded from serving on juries in Jefferson County. He also charged that the six names of Negroes that were listed on the county's jury roll were in fact forgeries. This falsification of the record, he added, was not only a crime against the defendants, but against the Supreme Court itself.

When Chief Justice Charles Evans Hughes asked whether Leibowitz could prove that there had been forgery, Leibowitz announced that he could prove it because he had brought the jury roll with him. At Hughes's request, the documents were brought into the Court and inspected in turn by each of the justices. Hughes was heard to exclaim that the forgery was "as plain as day." (It is very rare for the Supreme Court to directly scrutinize physical evidence as part of its deliberations.)

Writing for a unanimous Court (Justice James C. McReynolds did not take part in this opinion), Hughes credited the defense with having demonstrated that even though there were many black men in Jackson County who were fully qualified to serve on juries, none had actually been a juror there for decades. In addition, there was evidence that the jury rolls had been tampered with in order to conceal these facts. Norris's indictment and trial were therefore invalid because (as an African-American defendant), he had been denied the equal protection of the laws as guaranteed by the Fourteenth Amendment. "In view of the denial of the federal right, suitably asserted," concluded Hughes, "the judgment must be reversed and the cause remanded for further proceedings [to the Alabama courts]."

Patterson v. *State of Alabama* (1935)
294 U.S. 600

When Patterson's appeal came before the Supreme Court of Alabama, counsel for the state argued that the defendant's bill of exception had been filed after the deadline and therefore should not be considered by the court. The state's highest court accepted the state's contention, ignored the issues raised in the bill of exception, and affirmed the trial court's judgment. Before the U.S. Supreme Court, Alabama argued that the decision in the Patterson case rested entirely on a question of state appellate procedure and therefore no federal question was involved. There was, the state contended, no basis for intervention by federal courts.

In his decision for the Court, Chief Justice Hughes argued that the two cases were necessarily intertwined. The Alabama Supreme Court had announced both decisions on the same day, and it was impossible to prove that the decision in one case did not have an impact on the outcome of the other. Patterson had asserted the same rights as Norris and the evidence in both cases was the same. The federal question in Patterson's case was "precisely the same as that considered and decided in the Norris case."

The U.S. Supreme Court, declared Hughes, has the power to dispose of cases "as justice requires." To reverse the judgment against Norris while affirming the judgment of death against Patterson would be "anomalous and grave." The court, therefore, vacated the judgment of the Alabama Supreme Court and remanded the case to the state courts for further proceedings.

The Vera Stretz Trial (1936)
The Court of General Sessions (Manhattan)
March 20–April 3, 1936

In the early morning of November 25, 1935, Vera Stretz was arrested at Beekman Towers, a fashionable Manhattan hotel, for the shooting and killing of Dr. Fritz Gebhardt, her employer, who had also (until recently) been her lover. Gebhardt was an official of the German government who was stationed in New York for business reasons. He was educated, cultured, and appealing to women, and he and Stretz had had a passionate affair, even though she knew that he had a wife and children in Germany. A few days before the shooting, he had announced, according to Stretz, that he no longer considered himself as the type of man to get married. What he now wanted was for their relationship to go on as before—an offer that Stretz had declined.

Although Stretz freely admitted to the police that she had slain Dr. Gebhardt by firing four bullets into his body, she refused to tell them why she did it. After Leibowitz became her attorney, she confided to him that what had driven her to shoot her former lover was her fear that he would physically force her to perform oral sex. Leibowitz promptly informed the press that, having heard her story, he felt that "Dr. Gebhardt got what was coming to him."

As the trial opened, the prosecution depicted Stretz as a jealous and possessive lover who had become enraged at Gebhardt because he would not leave his wife. The killing, alleged prosecutor Miles O'Brien, had been a premeditated act of murder and Stretz deserved to go to the chair. Leibowitz made no opening statement, intending apparently to keep his strategy to himself and apparently hoping to keep the prosecution off-balance.

The key to the case would be Stretz's own testimony. Through his interrogation of Stretz on the witness stand, Leibowitz brought out facts (or her version of them) that were essential to his case for acquittal. She owned a gun, she explained, because she had lived for years in an unsafe neighborhood. The gun happened to be in Gebhardt's room because he had held it for safekeeping. She had gone to his room because Gebhardt suffered from abdominal pains and sometimes called her at night to apply compresses or a heating pad. When he called after midnight on the 25th of November, she went to him as before. In response to Leibowitz's questions, Stretz said that she did not have a bag with her and that her coat had no pockets. These bits of testimony laid a foundation for her claim that *her* gun was in *his* hotel room.

Leibowitz then forced (or seemed to force) from his client an account of what happened between her and Gebhardt on the night of the shooting. According to Stretz, Gebhardt raped her and then demanded oral sex. She reached for the gun that she had spotted at the top of a drawer that happened to be open. The gun went off when Gebhardt grabbed hold of her hand. Though struck by a bullet, he came at her menacingly and she shot him again and then (after a few seconds' pause) fired twice more, wounding him this time in the back.

All through her testimony, Stretz spoke in a barely audible voice and broke down repeatedly into outbursts of crying. Leibowitz in his summation depicted her as the innocent victim of a smooth, attractive man of the world. He also argued that premeditation had not been proved and that under the law anyone who has a "reasonable" fear of being attacked has the right not only to defend himself or herself, but even to kill the would-be attacker.

At the close of his summation, Leibowitz told the jury that it should not compromise, but either acquit his client or convict her of murder in the first degree. Judge Cornelius F. Collins took five hours to charge the jury as to its possible verdicts in this case and the legal points involved. "If you believe her story," he concluded, "acquit her." And that is precisely what the jury did. After deliberating for three hours and five minutes, it declared Vera Stretz "not guilty." To a number of observers, this had been Leibowitz's most brilliant performance yet.

The People v. *Irwin* (1938)
Court of General Sessions, Manhattan

On March 27, 1937, Mary Gedeon, her daughter, Veronica Gedeon, and a man named Frank Byrnes were all murdered in the house they shared at 316 East 50th Street in New York City. After investigating the crime for several days, the police settled on Robert Irwin, a former boarder in Gedeon's house, as their prime suspect. Irwin, who had briefly dated Veronica's sister Ethel, was an eccentric sculptor who had recently been released from a mental hospital after residing there for twenty consecutive months. The police soon gathered a great mass of incriminating evidence against Irwin, who had disappeared from his familiar haunts three months after the slaying.

The central issue in the case was whether Irwin was sane. In a pretrial proceeding in the Court of General Sessions on August 30, District Attorney William Copeland Dodge requested the court to create a lunacy commission to investigate the question of Irwin's sanity. Over the vehement protests of Leibowitz, Justice John J. Freschi agreed to appoint such a commission. It consisted of a prominent lawyer-editor, a neurologist, and a psychologist, but Leibowitz would not let Irwin appear before it. On March 24, 1938, the commission filed a 756-page report that concluded Irwin was sane both during and after the murders. The commissioners cited the statements in his confession indicating that Irwin had slain two of his victims out of a rational desire to avoid being found out.

Convinced, in his own words, that his client was "as crazy as a bedbug," Leibowitz set out to refute the commission's findings. He selected two psychiatrists who had never before testified in any criminal trial to talk with Irwin and assess his sanity. After questioning Irwin for many hours, both psychiatrists concluded that Irwin believed that he had superhuman powers and was convinced that, in committing the murders, he had simply carried out the decrees of God. (Irwin had told them of two eyes that glowed in the dark that had commanded him to complete the strangulation of Veronica Gedeon.) Both experts pronounced Irwin to be insane, both medically and legally.

Leibowitz's next move was to permit the press to interview Irwin and, as he hoped, their stories conveyed a clear impression of a man too addled to know right from wrong. After numerous postponements, the Irwin trial finally opened on November 7, 1938. A week later, Judge James G. Wallace proposed an arrangement to which both Leibowitz and the district attorney's office assented. It was agreed that Irwin would plead guilty to second-degree murder and would be imprisoned for life in Sing Sing prison. When he arrived there, Irwin received an exhaustive mental examination and was declared insane. He was transferred immediately to the state hospital at Dannemora, a facility for the criminally insane.

The People v. *Dooley* (1940)
Nassau County Court

On the morning of November 15, 1939, in Long Beach, New York, a local policeman, Alvin Dooley, shot and killed Louis F. Edwards, the town's mayor. He also shot and wounded police officer James Walsh, the mayor's bodyguard, who had recently succeeded Dooley as the president of the Policeman's Benevolent Association (PBA), the policeman's union in Long Beach. Dooley was angry at Edwards because the latter had used his influence to help unseat him as PBA head, a post that he had held for five years.

Dooley was indicted for murder in the first degree, and his trial took place in the Nassau County Courthouse in Mineola, Long Island, in late January and early February 1940. District Attorney Edward J. Nealy contended in his opening statement that the evidence would demonstrate that Dooley had shown premeditation, deliberation, and intent to kill. Dooley's attorney, Samuel Leibowitz, entered a plea of "not guilty," due to "temporary insanity." Dooley, argued the defense lawyer, could not be held responsible for the killing of the mayor and the wounding of Officer Walsh. The man who fired the shots was, in effect, another Alvin Dooley. A decent man had been temporarily transformed into a killer by forces beyond his control. To demonstrate his thesis, Leibowitz called to the witness stand Dooley's mother, his ten-year-old son, two of his fellow police officers, and eight other witnesses. Several testified that after he lost the PBA election, Dooley was a changed man, becoming bitter and morose, and drinking heavily. Two psychiatrists testified that on the day of the shooting, Dooley was in fact insane.

In his summation, Leibowitz admitted that the principal source of his client's disintegration was his own psychological weakness, but insisted that the mayor had played a key role in it as well. Not even in the days of Boss Tweed, maintained the lawyer, had there been so tyrannical and domineering a political organization as that of Mayor Edwards in Long Beach. It had been the mayor's petty maneuvering in the PBA election that had played a key role, argued Leibowitz, in the unhinging of Dooley. In fact, the defendant had suffered a series of minor setbacks during Edwards's mayoralty and he had reason to fear there might be more. "Blow, blow, blow, blow, blow," chanted Leibowitz, accompanying each word with a rap on the jury box rail. "That was the way this continuous persecution wore down Dooley's mind."

Given a choice among six possible verdicts by Judge Cortland A. Johnson, the jury deliberated for more than eleven hours before bringing in a verdict of first-degree manslaughter. On February 15 Judge Johnson sentenced Alvin Dooley to between ten and twenty years on the manslaughter charge and from five to ten years for committing a felony with a dangerous weapon, a sentence that struck some observers as excessively harsh.

Annotated Bibliography

Albraz, Nedda C. "Samuel Leibowitz." *Dictionary of American Biography.* Vol. 11. New York: Scribners, 1928, 447–448. Encapsulates Leibowitz's life and career.

Associated Press. "Samuel S. Leibowitz, Judge." *Associated Press Biographical Service,* Sketch 3753 (June 15, 1952): 1–2. Provides a swift summary of Leibowitz's life and work.

Basso, Hamilton. "Five Days in Decatur." *New Republic,* December 20, 1933, 161–164. This is by a journalist who covered the early Scottsboro trials.

Blaustein, Albert, and Robert L. Zagrando, *Civil Rights and the American Negro: A Documentary History.* New York: Trident Press, 1968. Contains a portion of Chief Justice Hughes's decision in *Norris* v. *Alabama,* 1935, 294 U.S. 587.

Carter, Dan T. "A Reasonable Doubt." *American Heritage Magazine.* October 1968, 40–43, 95–101. This is a clear and interesting account of the events and the controversy surrounding the trial of Haywood Patterson at Decatur, Alabama, in 1933.

———. *Scottsboro: A Tragedy of the American South.* Revised edition. Baton Rouge: Louisiana State University Press, 1979. This comprehensively researched and well-written book is the standard work on the subject.

Chalmers, Allan Knight. *They Shall Be Free.* Garden City, NY: Doubleday, 1951. Chalmers, a Protestant minister from the North, describes his attempts to assist the Scottsboro Nine by rallying moderate opinion in Alabama.

Crenshaw, Files A., and Kenneth A. Miller. *Scottsboro: The Firebrand of Communism.* Montgomery, AL: Brown Printing Company, 1936. Attacks the Scottsboro defendants and their allies from the North.

Endore, S. Guy. *The Crime at Scottsboro.* Hollywood, CA: Hollywood Scottsboro Committee, 1938. An eloquent plea for the release of the Scottsboro Nine that quotes at length from Judge Horton's decision in the second Patterson trial.

Frost, David. "Should the Death Penalty be Brought Back Quickly?" An interview of Samuel S. Leibowitz, broadcast on Metromedia, January 11, 1970. Reprinted in David Frost, *The American.* New York: Stein and Day, 1970. Leibowitz reminisces on his life and career and gives his views on public issues relating to criminal law.

Gist, William Gerry. *The Story of Scottsboro, Alabama.* Nashville, TN: Rich Printing Company, 1968. A history of the town by a resident that reprints some of the trial record and early newspaper accounts of the Scottsboro rape trials.

Goodman, James. *Stories of Scottsboro.* New York: Random House, 1994. This book views the case from a variety of viewpoints and is a useful supplement to Carter.

Hays, Arthur Garfield. *Trial by Prejudice.* New York: Covici, Freide Publishers [1935]. Hays studies five American law cases in which community prejudice played a key role.

Horne, Gerald. *Powell v. Alabama: The Scottsboro Boys and American Justice.* Danbury, CT: Franklin Watts, 1997. Relates the story of the first successful appeal by the Scottsboro defendants to the U.S. Supreme Court.

Howe, Irving, and Lewis Coser. *The American Communist Party: A Critical History.* Boston: Beacon Press, 1957. Argues that the party's attacks on the NAACP were harmful to the Scottsboro defendants.

Johnston, Alva. "Let Freedom Ring—I." *New Yorker,* June 4, 1932, 21–24.

———. "Let Freedom Ring—II." *New Yorker,* June 11, 1932, 18–23. Tells the story of Leibowitz's career as a defense attorney and analyzes his success in the handling of juries during his pre-Scottsboro career.

Jordan, J. Glenn. *The Unpublished Inside Story of the Infamous Scottsboro Case.* Huntsville, AL: White Printing Company, 1932. Insists that the Scottsboro Nine were given fair trails and were guilty as charged.

"Jurist Before the Bar." *Time,* November 15, 1963, 70–71. The article depicts Leibowitz as a judge who was harsh but fair.

Kelley, Robin D. *Hammer and Hoe: Alabama Communists During the Great Depression.* Chapel Hill: University of North Carolina Press, 1990. Relates the history of the Communist party of Alabama from 1929 to 1941.

200   SAMUEL S. LEIBOWITZ

Kirby, John B. *Black Americans in the Roosevelt Era: Liberalism and Race.* Knoxville: University of Tennessee Press, 1980. A study of how American liberals dealt with racial issues during the 1930s.

Klehr, Harvey. *The Heyday of American Communism: The Depression Decade.* New York: Basic Books, 1984. Includes a brief account of the Party's handling of the Scottsboro controversy.

Kunstler, William. "From Scottsboro to Goetz." *Village Voice,* March 26, 1985, 1, 13–20. Kunstler argues that many northern whites have in general become less sympathetic to blacks than whites were in the 1930s, when they viewed blacks as victims of a distant oppression.

Landsman, Steven. "History's Stories." *Michigan Law Review* 93 (May 1995): 1739–1764. Analyzes Goodman's book on Scottsboro and compares the trials in the case with other miscarriages of justice, such as the Dreyfus affair.

Leibowitz, Robert. *The Defender: The Life and Career of Samuel S. Leibowitz.* Englewood Cliffs, NJ: Prentice Hall, 1981. Provides unique material on his father's life and legal career through the year 1933.

Linder, Douglas O. "Without Fear or Favor: Judge James Edwin Horton and the Trial of the Scottsboro Boys." *The University of Missouri in Kansas City Famous Trials Website,* 1999. <www.law.umkc.edu/faculty/projects/finals/essayhorton.html>. According to Linder, many white southerners fought for justice in the case.

———. "An American Tragedy: The Trials of the Scottsboro Boys." *The Alabama Center for Justice Website,* 1999. <www.alabamacenterforjustice.com/bhm.htm>. Briefer version of the above article that provides links to Internet sites dealing with specialized aspects of the case.

Murray, Hugh T., Jr. "Aspects of the Scottsboro Campaign." *Science and Society* 35 (Summer 1971): 177–192. Murray argues that the ILD's campaign of mass agitation was just as important as the "courtroom dramatics" in saving the lives of the Scottsboro Nine.

———. "Changing America and the Changing Image of Scottsboro." *Phylon* 83 (1977): 82–92. Defends the Communists' role in the Scottsboro case.

———. "The NAACP versus the Communist Party: The Scottsboro Rape Cases, 1931–1932." In Bernard Sternsher, ed., *The Negro in Depression and War: Prelude to Revolution, 1930–1945.* Chicago: Quadrangle Books [1969]. A scholar's account crediting the Communists with saving the Scottsboro boys' lives when they were first arrested and tried in 1932.

Nolan, William A. *Communism Versus the Negro.* Chicago: Henry Regnery, 1951. Accuses the Communists of exploiting racial issues to the detriment of American blacks.

Norris, Clarence, and Sybil D. Washington. *The Last of the Scottsboro Boys: An Autobiography.* New York: Putnam, 1979. By the longest-lived of the Scottsboro Nine and the only one to receive a full pardon from the governor of Alabama.

Obermaier, Otto. "The Golden Years." *Litigation* 16 (Fall 1989): 1, 47–50, 63. Consists of brief, colorful profiles that depict Leibowitz and other renowned defense attorneys.

Obermaier, Otto, and Barry A. Bonner. "Those Were the Glory Days for Advocates." *National Law Journal* (May 31, 1998): 52–54. Presents additional facts about celebrated defenders, among them Leibowitz.

Ovington, Mary White. *The Walls Came Tumbling Down.* New York: Schocken Press, 1970. The Harlem social worker briefly describes the struggle between the Communists and the NAACP over Scottsboro.

Owen, Marie Bankhead. *The Story of Alabama: A History of the State.* 5 vols. New York: Lewis Historical Publishing, 1949. Includes a chapter on the case.

Owsley, Frank L. "Scottsboro, the Third Crusade: The Sequel to Abolition and Reconstruction." *American Review* 1 (June 1933): 257–285. A historian argues that the agitation over the Scottsboro trials was the work of northern capitalists bent on subjugating the South.

Pasley, Fred. *Not Guilty: The Story of Samuel S. Leibowitz.* New York: G.P. Putnam's Sons, 1933. In this early account by a contemporary journalist, there are some unique materials about Leibowitz's childhood and his law practice in the 1920s.

Patterson, Haywood, and Earl Conrad. *Scottsboro Boy.* Garden City, NY: Doubleday, 1979. A vivid account of Patterson's long ordeal and his escape from an Alabama prison.

Record, Wilson. *The Negro and the Communist Party.* New York: Atheneum, 1971. Argues that the Communists benefited from their association with the Scottsboro cause, but that the Party's tactics did harm to the defendants.

————. *Race and Radicalism: The NAACP and the Communist Party in Conflict.* Ithaca, NY: Cornell University Press, 1965. Traces the long history of conflict between the two organizations.

Reynolds, Quentin. *Courtroom: The Story of Samuel S. Leibowitz.* New York: Farrar Straus and Giroux, 1950. A popular and graphic account of Leibowitz's various trials. Includes three chapters on Scottsboro.

Schumach, Murray. "Samuel S. Leibowitz, 84, Jurist and Scottsboro Case Lawyer, Dies." *New York Times,* January 12, 1978, 84. Schumach's obituary provides some key facts and quotations.

"Scottsboro Case." *Guide to American Law.* Vol. 9. St. Paul: West Group [1998], 124–128. This is an excellent brief summary of the cases and their legal and institutional significance.

Scottsboro Defense Committee. *4 Free, 5 In Prison, On the Same Evidence: What the Nation's Press Says About the Scottsboro Case.* New York: Scottsboro Defense Committee, 1937. Pamphlet issued shortly after Alabama absolved four of the Scottsboro defendants.

————. *Scottsboro, The Shame of America: The True Story and The True Meaning of This Famous Case.* New York: The Committee, 1936. By the "umbrella organization" which brought together all the diverse groups who were working to free the Scottsboro defendants.

Smith, Beverly. "The Defense Never Rests." *American Magazine,* May 1938, 22–23, 174–178. This journalist's survey of Leibowitz's career as a defense lawyer was based largely on her interviews with him.

Tindal, George Brown. *The Emergence of the New South, 1913–1945.* Baton Rouge, LA: State Press, 1967. Contains an analysis of the case within the context of race relations and the political history of the South.

White, Walter F. *A Man Called White: The Autobiography of Walter White.* New York: Viking Press, 1948. Includes an account of the Scottsboro case and White's role in it.

————. "The Negro and the Communists." *Harper's Magazine,* December 1931, 62–72. The executive director of the NAACP here attacks the role of the ILD and the Communist Party in the defense of the Scottsboro Nine.

"Why Law Fails to Stop Teenage Crime—An Interview with Judge Leibowitz." *U.S. News and World Report,* January 14, 1955, 64–67. Leibowitz, while a sitting judge, expressed his hard-line views on crime and delinquency.

Zagrando, Robert, L. *The NAACP Crusade against Lynching, 1909–1950.* Philadelphia: Temple University Press, 1980. Notes briefly how the Communists outmaneuvered the NAACP in the early stages of the Scottsboro issue.

— Charles —
Hamilton Houston

(Schomburg Center for Research in Black Culture)

Chronology

1895   Born on September 3, 1895, in Washington, D.C., to William LePre Houston and Mary Ethel Hamilton Houston.

1911   Graduated from the M Street High School, Washington, D.C.

1915   Graduated *magna cum laude,* Phi Beta Kappa, from Amherst College, Amherst, Massachusetts; taught English at Howard University, Washington, D.C.

1916   Taught English at Dunbar High School (formerly known as the M Street High School).

1917   Enlisted in the United States Army; commissioned as a first lieutenant in the infantry; judge-advocate, United States Army.

1918   Resigned commission to attend artillery school; recommissioned as second lieutenant; served with the 351st Field Artillery in France and Germany.

1919   Discharged from United States Army in April; taught English at Dunbar High School under the end of the school year; entered Harvard Law School, Cambridge, Massachusetts, in September.

1922   Graduated *cum laude* from Harvard Law School; staff member, editorial board, *Harvard Law Review.*

1923   Received doctor of juridical science degree from Harvard Law School.

1924   Studied at the University of Madrid under a Sheldon Traveling Fellowship from Harvard Law School; admitted to the District of Columbia bar; entered private practice of law with William LePre Houston in the firm to be known as Houston and Houston; married Margaret Gladys Moran; adjunct instructor of law, Howard Law School; volunteer attorney, National Association for the Advancement of Colored People (NAACP), Washington, D.C.

1929   Appointed vice dean and associate professor of law, Howard Law School.

1932   Helped prepare brief in NAACP's successful lawsuit *Nixon* v. *Condon,* United States Supreme Court.

1933   Argued *Commonwealth of Virginia* v. *George Crawford* in NAACP's successful lawsuit, Loudon County, Virginia.

1935   Argued *Hollins* v. *Oklahoma* in NAACP's successful lawsuit, United States Supreme Court; resigned as vice dean at Howard Law School to become special counsel, NAACP; helped prepare brief in NAACP's successful lawsuit *Norris* v. *Alabama,* United States Supreme Court.

1936   Argued *Murray* v. *Maryland* in NAACP's successful lawsuit, Baltimore, Maryland.

1938   Argued *Missouri ex. rel. Gaines* v. *Canada* in NAACP's successful lawsuit, United States Supreme Court; argued *Hale* v. *Kentucky* in NAACP's successful lawsuit, United States Supreme Court; resigned as special counsel to the NAACP; rejoined the law firm of Houston and Houston.

1939   Divorced from Margaret Gladys Moran; remarriage to Henrietta Williams.

1944   Successfully argued *Steele* v. *Louisville and Nashville Railroad Company,* United States Supreme Court; successfully argued *Tunstall* v. *Brotherhood of Locomotive Firemen,* United States Supreme Court; birth of only child, Charles Hamilton Houston Jr.

1948   Successfully argued *Hurd* v. *Hodge,* United States Supreme Court.

1950   Death from coronary thrombosis, April 20, Washington, D.C.; posthumously awarded Spingarn Medal from the NAACP, June 25.

Biography

A year before his premature death in 1950 at the age of fifty-four, Charles Hamilton Houston encountered an ugly example of racism. This time, the victim was his little son, who had been born six years before his father's death. As related by Joseph Waddy, a partner in Houston's law firm and the godfather of Charles Hamilton Houston Jr.:

> I remember one time when his wife brought their son, little Charles, down to the office while she went off somewhere, and the little fella was playing around till Charlie had to go to the drugstore for something and he took the boy along. While Charlie was being taken care of, the boy climbed up on a stool by the soda fountain, and the man behind the fountain said to him, "Get down from there, you little nigger—you got no business here." When they got back to the office, we had to take Charlie into the back room and give him a sedative.[1]

It was one of the few occasions in which Houston would show his own feelings. In a life marked by strife in an ongoing battle for civil rights, he was usually self-controlled and preoccupied with his work to the point that his personal physician, Edward L. Mazique, said he never knew him to attend a social event.[2] But he was a man with a mission to fulfill and was driven by a fierce commitment to equal justice before the law.

Although he did not live to see the triumph of his famed protégé and former pupil Thurgood Marshall in *Brown* v. *Board of Education of Topeka* (1954), which outlawed de jure segregation in public education, he helped to make that victory possible. In his capacity as vice dean of Howard Law School, special counsel to the National Association for the Advancement of Colored People (NAACP), and as a lawyer in private practice, Charles Hamilton Houston was involved in nearly every major civil rights lawsuit in the 1930s and 1940s, and he either taught or encouraged virtually all of the black lawyers who fought to end legal discrimination in the United States.

If he remained an unsung hero—one of his lawyer friends said "he got less honor and remuneration than almost anyone else involved in this fight"[3]—he was appreciated by those who knew him best. According to his friends, he worked himself to death, but the work that he did would not be undone. "The school case was really Charlie's victory," remarked Marshall. "He just never got a chance to see it."[4]

At the end, Houston's biggest regret appeared to be personal. On a page in Rabbi Joshua Loth Liebman's best-selling *Peace of Mind* (1946), left at Houston's hospital bedside shortly before he died, he wrote a message for his son: "Tell Bo [Charles Hamilton Houston Jr.] I did not run out on him but went down fighting that he might have better and broader opportunities than I had without prejudice or bias operating against him, and in any fight some fall."[5]

Family Background

Houston, one of the best-educated black lawyers at the time of his graduation from Harvard Law School in 1923, came from a solidly middle-class
family of doers and achievers. Yet the "prejudice" and "bias" to which he
referred in the letter to his son meant that their lives would be constrained by
the boundaries imposed upon them by the society in which they lived. In
1896, one year after Houston's birth, the Supreme Court ruled in *Plessy* v.
Ferguson that segregation in public transportation was not a denial of the
guarantees afforded to all citizens of the states under the Fourteenth Amendment of "equal protection of the laws." The court reasoned that segregation
was legal as long as the facilities provided were "separate but equal," and
this decision would eventually put an official sanction on discrimination in
all aspects of life.

Houston's middle-class family chose not to view the United States solely
in terms of the limitations placed on blacks by the *Plessy* decision and other
forms of discrimination. Instead, they believed that success could be realized
by education, zeal, energy, and hard work. Members of his family worked and
had good jobs at a time when many blacks did not, which made Houston's
efforts on behalf of the excluded black masses even more noteworthy. Although Charles Hamilton Houston, as a black person, could not share fully in
the American dream and had incomplete access to the areas in which his brilliance could shine, his achievements nevertheless were remarkable.

One of the striking things about Houston's family was its emphasis on the
importance of education. According to family records, his paternal grandfather, Thomas Jefferson Hunn, was born into slavery in Kentucky in 1829.
Hunn and his mother and brothers were later bound to a cruel master in Missouri. He taught himself to read and write, much to the chagrin of his illiterate
master, and later escaped to the free state of Illinois. A short time afterwards,
he returned in the middle of the night to rescue his family, taking them to
Cairo, Illinois, where they remained for the duration of the Civil War.

Hunn changed his name to Houston to escape detection. He worked as a
conductor on the underground railroad between Missouri and Illinois. On one
occasion, he met General Ulysses S. Grant, whose Union troops were based
in Cairo. Houston quickly attached himself to Grant's army, became the
General's unofficial personal bodyguard, and saw action in the Civil War.[6]

The Quest for Educational Advancement

Thomas Jefferson Houston returned to Kentucky with his family at the end of
the Civil War. In 1866, he married Katherine Theresa Kirkpatrick, who had
also been an escaped slave. They had five children and moved frequently in
search of better educational facilities for them.

The family settled in Evansville, Illinois, in the late 1880s. The town had caught their attention because of its school system, but the schools were a disappointment to them. In 1890, Katherine Houston went to Washington, D.C., a city reported to have the best of the segregated school systems in the country. Leaving her husband and children behind, she was able to make a good living on her own as a hairdresser, summoning the rest of the family to join her the following year.

Thomas and Katherine Houston experienced upward mobility in Washington. He worked as a cabinetmaker and Baptist preacher, and she obtained employment as a hairdresser to the wives of several congressmen and other high government officials. Their eldest son, William LePre Houston, who was Charles Hamilton Houston's father, was a graduate of Howard Law School, a member of the adjunct faculty at Howard, one of the first black attorneys in Washington to head his own law firm, and a special assistant to the attorney general of the United States in 1937. His siblings included a physician who taught at Howard Medical School, another attorney, and a schoolteacher.[7]

The Nurturing of an Only Child

In 1891, William LePre Houston married Mary Hamilton, a schoolteacher from Ohio and the daughter of a free black man from South Carolina. She came from a mixed black, Indian, and white background and was raised as a Methodist. Their only child, Charles Hamilton Houston, was born on September 3, 1895. The younger Houston would follow neither the Baptist religion of his father nor the Methodism of his mother. In later years, he would refer to himself as an "in-between"; he was not a church goer.[8]

Mary Hamilton Houston was a working mother. Following her marriage, she learned hairdressing from her mother-in-law and worked for several affluent women in Washington, D.C. In order to provide her son with some of the cultural advantages she observed in the homes of the women for whom she worked, she set aside a portion of her income for his education. A proud woman, she always insisted that her employers refer to her by her married name, rather than by her first name.

Charles Hamilton Houston, doted upon by his parents and their families, was an excellent student. He went to a private nursery school, but to a public elementary and high school on account of a change in the family's finances. His education in the public school system was formidable, for he attended Washington's M Street High School (renamed the Dunbar High School in 1916 after the famed black poet Paul Lawrence Dunbar), which was the best black high school in the nation.

He took pride in his family background, regarding his paternal grandfather as his inspiration. The other heroes in his life were John Brown, the white man who led a raid at Harpers Ferry, Virginia, in 1859 to free slaves, and Frederick Douglass, the black abolitionist.[9]

Amherst College and a Teaching Job, 1911–1917

After graduating from high school, Houston turned down a scholarship at the University of Pittsburgh to attend the prestigious Amherst College, which he entered in the fall of 1911 at the age of sixteen. However, he did receive a scholarship at Amherst by the end of his first freshman semester. His college yearbook would state that "Charles was known as a hard worker who led a quiet life during his stay."[10] It did not state that he was one of the very few black students at Amherst.

If he made little time in college for social occasions, he made more than enough time for his studies. He had been at Amherst only a short time when he told his mother that he needed an extra room for a study. It was a request that she could not refuse, but she failed to mention it to her husband. When the elder Houston later visited the campus and went to his son's dormitory, he asked, "Whose room is this?" The unapologetic son replied, "This is my study."[11]

Houston put this study to good use. In 1915, he graduated *magna cum laude* from Amherst, where he was elected to Phi Beta Kappa. Selected as one of the six class valedictorians at the commencement, he elected to speak on Paul Lawrence Dunbar. Houston countered the initial objection that Dunbar was unknown to most of the students by asserting that everyone would know about him after the address.

A few months short of his twentieth birthday at the time of his graduation, he already made an imposing appearance: six feet tall, well-built, and handsome, with a light complexion and gray eyes. Despite his father's urging that he study law, he was uncertain about his future plans. Although displeased by his son's indecision, his father got him a one-year replacement job to teach English at Howard for the 1915–16 academic year. The following year, Houston returned to Dunbar High School to teach English.[12]

Army Service, 1917–1919

At this time in his life, he was described by his second cousin through marriage, William H. Hastie (later to be the first black appointed to a federal judgeship), as a "rather spoiled and self-centered only child, living a rather comfortable and somewhat secluded life and not very acutely or painfully disturbed by American racism."[13] This situation would change dramatically following Houston's service in the United States Army during World War I, which led him to his life's work.

America's entry in 1917 into what President Woodrow Wilson termed "the war to make the world safe for democracy" was greeted with a mixed reaction in the black community. Many blacks saw little need to support a country that violated their civil rights. Other blacks believed that the war provided them with an opportunity to show their patriotism and were eager to join the battle.

In 1917, Houston enlisted in the army and was sent to the Colored Officers' Training Camp at Fort Des Moines, Iowa. This training camp was itself a matter of controversy because it was segregated. But to white liberals like Joel E. Spingarn, chairman of the Executive Committee of the NAACP, and black spokesmen like W.E.B. DuBois, editor of the NAACP's *The Crisis,* it could be viewed as a step forward since it provided for the training of black officers, and they were solidly behind its establishment.

Houston was commissioned a first lieutenant in the infantry and was assigned to Fort Meade, Maryland. While there, he served a memorable stint as judge-advocate for the army in cases involving black soldiers. In one case, Houston angered the white officer in charge by finding that two black enlisted men were not guilty of disorderly conduct during a Thanksgiving furlough. Another case involved a black enlisted man who was found guilty of disorderly conduct and sentenced to one year of hard labor, in spite of Houston's own view that the charges were unfounded. Houston was so disillusioned by these events and by the attitude of several white soldiers toward black servicemen that he resigned his commission to go to artillery school. Recommissioned as a second lieutenant, he saw service with the 351st Field Artillery in France and Germany during the closing months of the war.[14]

The overt prejudice which he encountered for the first time in his hitherto sheltered life made a lasting impression on him. As he later wrote:

> I made up my mind that I would never get caught again without knowing something about my rights; that if luck was with me, and I got through this war I would study law and use my time fighting for men who could not strike back.[15]

Houston kept his word. It is unknown whether the other black officers who served with him regarded the war as a defining experience, but many of them achieved distinction in later years: Joseph L. Johnson, a Ph.D. and an M.D. from the University of Chicago, who later became dean at Howard University Medical School; Rayford Logan, another Ph.D., who was a noted historian; James Austin Norris, a Yale Law School graduate and a well-known tax attorney; and Hilary Robinson, a prominent architect in Washington, D.C.[16]

As he would do throughout his life, Houston kept his anger in check during his army years. On his return to the United States in 1919, Houston and another black officer went into the dining room of a train they were taking to Washington. Seated next to them was a white man who asked the waiter to find him another table when he noticed the black officers take the table near him. Houston told the man that they were officers who had just landed from overseas and hoped there would be no need to move. The man explained he was from the South and could not help his feelings. Houston and his fellow officer remained at their table and ate their meal, while the man moved to another table.[17]

Harvard Law School, 1919–1922

After his discharge in April 1919, Houston returned to teach English at Dunbar until the end of the school year. In September, he was off to Harvard Law School, where several of his law school classmates would regard him as "Supreme Court material."[18] Although he never achieved that position, he went on to argue some groundbreaking cases before the Court in the course of his distinguished career.

One of Houston's best friends at Harvard was a fellow black, Raymond Pace Alexander, who later became a judge in Philadelphia. They went to art galleries, museums, and theaters together during their law school days. Houston helped Alexander organize The Nile, a Harvard fraternity that was restricted to students of African ancestry and was one of the first attempts by black students to honor their racial heritage.

Houston's pride in his blackness was also manifest when he extended an invitation during his second year to Marcus Garvey to speak at Harvard. The controversial Garvey, who supported a back-to-Africa movement and was subsequently imprisoned for mail fraud, was ridiculed by black intellectuals like DuBois, but Houston typically preferred to take a more conciliatory position. Accepting the invitation, Garvey spoke to twenty-two students at Harvard in January 1921. Houston never changed his mind about the importance of the Garvey movement to the black community. He told an audience in 1934 that the Garvey movement "made a permanent contribution in teaching the simple dignity of being black. . . . For my purposes, it is immaterial whether he was a charlatan or fool."[19]

Graduate Work and a Fellowship, 1922–1924

In 1922, Houston graduated *cum laude* from Harvard, where he had been the first black student to be selected to serve on the editorial board of the *Law Review.* Encouraged to continue his studies by professor and future Supreme Court justice Felix Frankfurter and Law School dean Roscoe Pound, Houston received a Langdell Fellowship and stayed on at Harvard during the 1922–23 academic year to become the first black student there to receive the doctor of juridical science degree. He was one of the few lawyers of his time to earn this degree.

He took five courses for his doctoral degree and received an A in every one of them. His thesis was written under Frankfurter, a founding member of the American Civil Liberties Union, a member of the NAACP's Legal Advisory Committee, the only Jew on Harvard's law school faculty, and a crusader for social justice who passed on his zeal for reform to many of his students.

The two remained good friends, and Frankfurter provided an entry to Houston in Washington and in academic circles. In the early 1930s, it was Frankfurter, at the behest of Dean Houston of Howard Law School, who helped to

prevail upon Harvard to offer fellowships to promising black law school graduates. One of the students selected for a fellowship was Houston's own prized
pupil, Thurgood Marshall, who nevertheless passed up this opportunity to
study at Harvard in favor of starting his own law practice.[20]

After receiving his advanced law degree from Harvard, Houston continued
his studies for another year, attending the University of Madrid as the recipient of an $1,800 Sheldon Traveling Fellowship from Harvard. He saw a dif-
ferent world in Madrid and later in Italy and Morocco, which he also visited—a
world in which he could eat at any restaurant, sit where he wished when taking public transportation, move about freely without the possibility of harassment, and where the color of a person's skin had little to do with the rights he
or she enjoyed.[21]

The temptations were great to continue to enjoy this standard of living, and
Houston seriously considered becoming a diplomat. But he returned to his
home in Washington to practice law.

Law Firm of Houston and Houston

While Ivy League schools might seek out an outstanding black student, law
firms did not. Houston joined his father's practice in 1924, and the firm became known as Houston and Houston. In the same year, he married his childhood sweetheart, Margaret Gladys Moran.

His father, who had also been active in Republican party politics, had built
up a substantial practice in civil law, particularly in the representation of plaintiffs in personal injury cases. Mr. Houston had settled most of these cases out
of court, and had little, if anything, to do with race relations. Unlike his father,
the younger Houston was largely uninterested in making money and embarked
on his law career without having had the experience of struggling to support
his studies. This protected existence provoked the envy of even some of his
staunchest admirers, who could point out that "Charlie never had to work,"
and "he came into the firm never having had a job working for anybody."[22]
Although father and son had an affectionate relationship, there was friction
over the latter's indifference to money. As one associate of the Houston law
firm related:

> William L. Houston loved Charlie, there's no question about that, but he was con-
> stantly castigating him because Charlie was "wasting" his time trying to save the
> race. "You aren't going to get anywhere like that, you'll never make any money."
> And, of course, he didn't make any money to speak of. Charlie didn't even have a
> savings account until Juanita Kidd Stout [later to be a judge in Philadelphia] came
> to be his secretary. She insisted on deducting part of his money and putting it into a
> savings account. Throughout their relationship, Charlie would borrow money from
> his father and give his father an IOU. His father kept all those in a safe—he had this
> huge safe as tall as a filing cabinet. He was constantly reminding Charlie of the
> IOU's that he had. I'm sure they really didn't make any difference, and Charlie
> never really made any effort to pay them.[23]

Protected to a large extent by the financial largesse of his father, Houston was able to handle cases even when there was no fee involved, including landlord/tenant disputes and small business matters. He was nevertheless a perfectionist in his work and was fond of saying that each case, no matter how small, should be prepared with the same kind of diligence that it took to argue before the Supreme Court. While this quest for perfection propelled him to leave nothing to chance, it would drain him emotionally. Thurgood Marshall stated, "I have seen him writing a brief, and spending the whole day looking for one word—just the right word."[24] Houston's obsession with his work may also have been an acknowledgment of the difficult position in which any black lawyer was placed. He would later tell his students:

> When you get in a courtroom, you can't just say, "Please, Mr. Court, have mercy on me because I'm a Negro." You are in competition with a well-trained white lawyer, and you better be at least as good as he is, and if you expect to win, you better be better. If I give you five cases to read overnight, you better read eight. And when I say eight, you read ten. You go that step further, and you might make it.[25]

These rigorous standards were applied to himself. But he was compulsive about his work to such an extent that his family and friends were constantly apprehensive about his health.

A Part-Time Job at Howard Law School, 1924–1929

In 1924, Houston followed in the footsteps of his father by teaching at Howard Law School on a part-time basis. While teaching had never been a focus in his father's career, it became an all-consuming passion for his son. By the time he left Howard as its vice dean in 1935, he had helped to make it an accredited law school and trained a whole generation of lawyers who would carry on the struggle for equality in America.

Founded in 1866 by the First Congregational Society of Washington, D.C., Howard University was named after Oliver O. Howard, the Civil War general who headed the Freedmen's Bureau during Reconstruction. The university was largely funded by the federal government and had to rely on the generosity of Congress to meet its educational responsibilities. In the 1920s, it received a funding of barely over $217,000. Although its dental and medical schools were accredited at the time of their inception, its law school remained unaccredited. It had only a handful of twenty to thirty students who received degrees each year, and a generally undistinguished faculty.

At the time Houston joined the faculty at Howard, its law school was housed in a converted three-story building in a block of row houses occupied by black families in a section of Washington near the old federal courthouse. All the classes were held in the evening in order to accommodate its students, a majority of whom needed to finance their studies by working during the day. Even though it had educated most of the black lawyers in the country and was clearly the best of the black institutions offering a law degree, Howard was looked down upon by most of the residents in a city that had seven other law schools.[26]

This attitude was reflected in the treatment afforded to black attorneys in the nation's capital. Following the example of the American Bar Association, the District of Columbia's Bar Association barred nonwhites, arguing that, as a private, professional association, it had the right to restrict its membership. When Houston's former law school professor, Felix Frankfurter, petitioned the district's Bar Association to admit black lawyers, it denied his request, but did allow black students to use its excellent library.[27]

Unfazed by all these obstacles, Houston brought a commitment to teaching that came to surpass his interest in the private practice of law. He regarded teaching as not only a profession, but a way to mold the future. "There is an unlimited field in the law for young Negroes who are willing to make the fight," he told a schoolteacher who was considering applying to law school. "The lawyer is going to be the leader in the next step in racial achievement."[28]

In 1927, Houston accepted the directorship at Howard of a report on the status of the Negro lawyer in the United States. In order to gather data to complete the study, Houston traveled extensively in the South. His report not only presented a grim account of the limited opportunities available to the Negro lawyer, but noted that the training of this group lagged behind professional standards. According to Houston's calculations, there were only 1,230 Negro lawyers in the country, or one for every 9,535 Negroes. This important study was incorporated into Carter G. Woodson's *The Negro Professional Man and the Community, With Special Emphasis on the Physician and the Lawyer* (1934).[29]

Vice Dean at Howard Law School, 1929–1935

In the course of Houston's research, he was particularly struck by the need to upgrade the training of black lawyers. The chance to do something about this situation came in 1929, when he accepted a full-time appointment as vice dean at Howard Law School. His salary was $4,500 a year.

Houston may also have been bored by the routine nature of his law practice in view of his own rigorous academic training. A friend of his once noted that "he would not settle down in a place where he could not expand."[30]

In reality, there were limits to the opportunities for expansion available even for an outstanding black lawyer at this time, but the new vice dean acted as if nothing could stop him. Fortunately, he took up this position at a time when Howard, under the dynamic leadership of President Mordecai Johnson (the first black man to head the university), shared Houston's mission about the urgency of providing black law students with a first-rate education. Johnson gave Houston free rein in running the law school. "Mordecai Johnson turned Charlie loose and gave him full backing," remarked Oliver Hill, one of

Houston's students who later became a federal judge. "He got a whole lot of us off on the right start."[31]

In his capacity as vice dean, Houston had to make some tough decisions, including the phasing out of the evening school in favor of a full-time day program. This move was vehemently protested by the school's twenty-two night law students and drew sharp rebukes from the local press in the wake of charges that Houston was trying to "Harvardize" the law school. But the importance of a full-time day school was as obvious to Houston as it was to Johnson, a close friend of Supreme Court justice Louis D. Brandeis. "I can tell you most of the time when I am reading a brief by a Negro attorney," Brandeis told Johnson. "You've got to get yourself a real faculty out there or you're always going to have a fifth-rate law school. And it's got to be full-time and a day school."[32]

Houston plunged into the task of upgrading the law school. He raised the admissions standards, revamped the curriculum, hired five full-time faculty members, limited the number of part-time teachers, and instituted a lecture series that included Frankfurter, Roscoe Pound, and famed attorneys Arthur Garfield Hays and Clarence Darrow. Houston also replaced most of the white law teachers with black law teachers. This action was consistent with his belief that there were certain things that black people had to do for themselves. If the struggle for civil rights were to be led by black attorneys, it made sense for him to seek out a black faculty to teach them.

The results were impressive. "In six energy-filled years," wrote NAACP attorney Jack Greenberg, "[Houston] transformed it from a law school with a part-time faculty and student body into an accredited institution [in 1931] that became a West Point of civil rights, graduating an annual corps of lawyers rigorously trained to do battle for equal justice."[33]

"No Tea for the Feeble"

As a teacher, Houston left an indelible mark on his students. He was a hard taskmaster who prodded them on with his favorite slogan: "No tea for the feeble, no crepe for the dead." But his teaching meant more to him than the training of his students in the rigors of the law. He invariably reminded them that they had an obligation to give something back to society: "any [black] lawyer that was not a social engineer was a parasite on society."[34]

He understood that the role of the black lawyer would be difficult, but always advised his students to let no obstacles stand in their way to success. His views were expressed in a letter written to a young woman, a student at the University of Chicago, who was considering a career in law:

> You must not only be good but superior, and just as superior in all respects as time, energy, money and ability permit. . . . I wouldn't be stymied by the difficulties. You'll probably have both corns and scars anyway. You may as well acquire them in carrying out a program as getting bumped and stepped on, because you're so insignificant folks walk over you intentionally or unintentionally. . . . If you really

aim to be somebody big, you'll have to accept the fact that people will be digging into your background to see who you are and why. But if you are big enough the public won't care. More and more the American people are ignoring race. . . . The most important thing now, as fast as conditions are changing, is that no Negro tolerate any ceiling on his ambitions or imagination. Good luck and don't have any doubts, you haven't time for such foolishness.[35]

In later years, he was credited with starting what became known as the Houstonian school of jurisprudence, which was cited by the *Harvard Law Review* in 1995 as an example of legal activism that was taught not only at leading law institutions, but at Howard as well.[36] A definition of Houstonian jurisprudence was given by Margaret A. Haywood, who worked as a secretary at the Houston firm while attending law school and later became a senior judge of the Superior Court of the District of Columbia:

> I think it was the early commitment to use litigation to establish rights, rather than some of the other kinds of approaches such as sit-ins, or picketing, and so on. I think it is the use of the legal system to seek your rights and maintain them.[37]

Because Houston was so driven to have his students succeed, he sometimes lost his temper when they were unable to meet his standards. Thurgood Marshall recalled Houston's exasperation on one occasion in class when a student could not answer a question. According to Marshall, Houston angrily told the student:

> I have worked with you and worked with you and, damn it, you just don't have it. You need to be reeducated, and what I mean by reeducated is reeducated from the beginning. Repeat after me—A, B.[38]

At Howard, Houston did not confine his teaching to the classroom. On Saturdays, this Harvard Law graduate often took his students to learn some practical aspects of the legal system. These trips included visits to courtrooms, prisons, and insane asylums. "He was constantly challenging us, exposing us to things we wouldn't otherwise see," recalled Oliver Hill. "If he wanted to summon you to his office, he wouldn't just send someone down to get you. He would send registered mail to your home, return receipt. He said, 'I want to teach you that if you send notice of something, you have to have legal proof.'"[39]

A Volunteer Attorney for the NAACP

Houston was also active in civic affairs in Washington during this period. In 1925, he helped establish the National Bar Association, the black equivalent of the American Bar Association, when it became apparent that the latter would continue to bar black attorneys. In addition, he was one of the founders of the Washington Bar Association, the affiliate of the National Bar Association for the District of Columbia. From 1933 to 1935, he served as a member of the District of Columbia Board of Education.

But it was his work as a volunteer attorney with the NAACP in the 1930s that came to occupy a major portion of his attention, making heavy inroads into the time that he spent at Howard. This work would ultimately take him away from Howard, as the second major part of Houston's life began.

The NAACP had been established in 1909 by a group of black and white liberals seeking an end to discrimination in America. Houston litigated some important NAACP "venue" cases (criminal cases tried in Southern communities where black defendants were not likely to get a fair trial), as well as some of its earliest segregation cases. Since the NAACP was perennially short of funds, he frequently called on his law students, instead of paid legal assistants, for help.

The NAACP had been headed since 1929 by Walter White, who was only the second black to lead the organization. White relied heavily on Houston for advice. Houston recommended candidates for the Board of Directors and for legal committees, advised him on relations with the administration of Franklin D. Roosevelt (whose policies Houston felt were discriminatory toward blacks), and assisted White in shaping the NAACP's direction in the face of attacks from younger black intellectuals who demanded more direct action.

These intellectuals, as well as other members of the black community, were disturbed by the fact that the NAACP usually enlisted the aid of white attorneys. White made a notable reply to this criticism in 1934, when he told a convention of the National Bar that the NAACP would hire more black attorneys "when there were more Charlie Houstons."[40]

Houston was selected by the NAACP to undertake a series of trips throughout the South from 1934 to 1935 to document the unequal facilities in the segregated school systems. These trips were funded by the NAACP and the American Fund for Public Service, and Houston was paid at the rate of $5 per day, which was not always paid promptly. The data collected by Houston were significant and would be used to document to the courts the fallacy behind the "separate but equal" provision of *Plessy* in many of the school desegregation cases of the 1950s.[41]

Before leaving Howard in 1935, Houston handled two important cases for the NAACP: *Commonwealth of Virginia* v. *George Crawford* (1933) and *Hollins* v. *Oklahoma* (1935), a Supreme Court case. He also helped in the preparation for the NAACP of two famous Supreme Court cases: *Nixon* v. *Condon* (1932), in which the Court ruled for the second time that the all-white primary in Texas was unconstitutional; and *Norris* v. *Alabama* (1935), where the Court overturned the conviction of the nine black Scottsboro defendants accused of raping two white women on the grounds that the systematic exclusion of Negroes from the jury was a violation of the "equal protection" guarantees of the Fourteenth Amendment.

Commonwealth of Virginia v. George Crawford (1933)

The Crawford case was Houston's first legal triumph for the NAACP, and it was nearly as significant for what it revealed about racial attitudes in the

South as it was for its decision. George Crawford, a black ex-convict who had been twice convicted of larceny, was accused of murdering a socially prominent white widow and her maid in Loudoun County, Virginia, in 1932. He had worked for the widow as a chauffeur the previous year, and he was picked up in Boston after reports that he had been seen in the area where the killings took place. Although he had signed a confession while in police custody, he had an alibi witness who was willing to testify that Crawford was in Boston when the murders were committed. As a result, the NAACP decided to go to his aid after he was indicted by an all-white grand jury in Loudoun County.[42]

The NAACP was at first successful in getting a Boston judge to refuse to extradite Crawford because no blacks had served on the grand jury and were unlikely to be called as jurors in the trial. But the decision was overruled by the United States Court of Appeals for the First Circuit. The NAACP appealed to the Supreme Court, which declined to hear the case, and Crawford was extradited to Virginia for trial.

White assigned Houston the job of handling the defense, but thought that Crawford's chances would be improved if a white Virginia lawyer served as cocounsel. Although the NAACP had long relied on prominent white attorneys to argue their cases, Houston felt that the time had come to change this practice. Houston wrote White that "the men [at Howard] feel if Crawford could be defended by all Negro counsel it would mark a turning point in the legal history of the Negro" and that "as Dean of Howard University Law School for Negroes, it would not be consistent for me to serve with white counsel in the Crawford case."[43] Acquiescing, White accompanied Houston, along with three other black attorneys, to Virginia.

Unfortunately for Houston, he had delivered a highly charged speech to a group of Washington blacks just before the Crawford trial began, and his words came back to haunt him. In the speech, Houston had attacked the complacency of blacks in refusing to do something about their plight in the nation. "You've got to make every sacrifice, even to the point of having your own heads cracked," he told them, "until no Negro can be mistreated solely because he is a Negro, anywhere in the United States." Accordingly, when Houston arrived in town, he was greeted with a local headline: "Lawyer Advises Negroes to Crack Heads in Loudoun County."[44]

More bad news awaited the defense team. White was informed that Crawford and his alibi witness had lied to the NAACP and that Crawford's confession (he admitted acting as a lookout while another black man had committed the murders) was actually true. The NAACP nevertheless decided to go ahead with the case, focusing on the issue of the exclusion of blacks from grand juries.

These problems were further compounded when the Crawford defense team was openly threatened with death. During the first week of the trial, they took box lunches because both whites and blacks were afraid to feed them, and the judge and state police officers insisted on an early adjournment to permit them to reach the District of Columbia line before nightfall.[45]

Houston, ably assisted by Howard law professor Leon Ransom, put on an impressive performance before the reported 600 spectators, many of whom were blacks from Washington. The attitude of one of the white townspeople was noted by Walter White:

> One day I saw nearby a lanky Virginia farmer clad in overalls and manifestly in need of a shave and bath. A spirited passage at arms over a legal technicality was being waged between the prosecutor and Houston. The latter's greater familiarity with the law was so obvious that the court ruled in his favor. The Virginia farmer turned to his companion, nodding his head admiringly, and declared, "You got to give it to him. He knows what he's talking about even if he is a nigger."[46]

In his closing statement to the jury, Houston said that the state had not proved its case, but if the jury decided to believe Crawford's confession, the life of this "poor, homeless dog" should be spared so he could testify against the accomplice, if the latter were ever found. In a surprise decision, the jury returned a verdict of "guilty" with life imprisonment recommended, rather than the death penalty—a major win for Houston and the defense team in view of the race hatred in Loudoun County.[47]

The Crawford case was not an unmitigated victory for Houston, however, for his efforts were blasted as a sellout of his people. In the June 1934 issue of *The Nation,* Helen Broadman and Martha Gruening attacked the "abject surrender" of Houston in not appealing the sentence. The writers were associated with the International Labor Defense (ILD), a communist-sponsored labor organization that had been formed in 1925.

The following month, Houston replied to these charges in the magazine. He stated that he was following the wishes of his client in not seeking a retrial in which the death penalty was a possibility. Houston's response left his critics unsatisfied. On September 15, 1934, the *Black Liberator*, a leftist publication, termed the Crawford case the "worse [sic] betrayal that the N.A.A.C.P. leaders have ever perpetrated against the Negro masses."[48]

Houston fared no better with regard to his defense earlier in 1934 of ILD radical attorney Bernard Ades, who had been brought up before the Maryland bar on charges of professional misconduct. This time, he also made President Johnson of Howard unhappy by serving as the controversial Ades's lawyer. Even though Ades had engaged in certain questionable practices (he once had himself named as the beneficiary of client's will, without that client's consent), Houston was successful in preventing Ades from being disbarred. In explaining his position to Johnson, Houston wrote that Ades "had rendered significant service . . . in exposing certain discriminations which Negroes used to suffer in Maryland courts." But the ILD continued to attack Houston, awarding him a "bandanna" at the end of 1934 for being one of the "Uncle Toms" of that year for his conduct.[49]

A Conflict of Commitments, 1934–1935

Back in court in 1935, Houston scored another victory for the NAACP in *Hollins* v. *Oklahoma,* in which he was aided by the Court's earlier ruling in *Norris* v. *Alabama* that blacks could not be excluded from juries. The Hollins case involved a black man found guilty by an all-white jury of raping a white girl. In a per curiam decision in which the Court did not give a written opinion but cited the Norris ruling to uphold the same point, it ordered a new trial for him. *Hollins* was a personal triumph for Houston, who was assisted in the case by his father and Edward P. Lovett, one of his former students at Howard Law School. It marked the first time that the NAACP was represented exclusively by black attorneys in appealing a case to the Supreme Court.

Houston's legal work on behalf of the NAACP had taken him away from Howard for extended periods of time, sometimes to the dismay of his students. In 1934, a group of students threatened a strike because of the alleged racial prejudice of one of their two white law professors and the "absenteeism" of their dean. There were also complaints that Houston was more interested in his outside activities than in Howard. Although the strike was called off and the matters resolved, tensions continued between Houston and the administration.

In spite of his outstanding achievements at Howard in upgrading the law school, Houston was plagued by the rancor that followed him all his life. His title, vice dean, occasionally led him to joke. "Hell," he said, "considering the pennies they're paying me, why should anybody think I'm the dean?"[50] The office of dean was filled by Judge Fenton W. Booth, who had very little to do with the law school. Nevertheless, it was widely held that President Johnson had decided to pacify Congress (which provided funds for Howard) by naming a white figurehead as dean of the Law School.

If Houston held out any hope for being named dean, his hope was never realized, and many of his friends believed that he was very hurt by this slight. Thurgood Marshall later described this situation with his characteristic bluntness. "He [Booth] was barely doing anything," Marshall said. "He was just 'retired.' But he had one qualification—he was white."[51]

Special Counsel for the NAACP, 1935–1938

Houston resigned as vice dean on June 30, 1935, to accept the position as special counsel with the NAACP. He replaced Nathan Ross Margold, a white New York attorney, who had been appointed in 1930 to devise a strategy to combat segregation.

Margold had originally intended to launch an all-out attack on the unequal facilities and per capita expenditures in the public school system in the South on the grounds that such practices were a violation of the "equal protection"

clause of the Fourteenth Amendment. Although the Supreme Court continued to uphold the legality of segregation following the *Plessy* decision,
Margold believed that it was possible to convince the Supreme Court to change
its mind.

As much as he sympathized with Margold's approach, Houston felt it was
impractical. According to Houston, it would be too expensive to gather the
kinds of data the courts would accept to establish the existence of unequal
facilities, and it would be hard to find plaintiffs willing to risk the wrath of
their communities in seeking to end segregated schools. He also shared the
view of factions within the NAACP who felt that it was unrealistic to believe
that the courts would overturn *Plessy.*[52]

Houston convinced the NAACP to use the courts to attack the "separate but
equal" doctrine of *Plessy* as it applied to graduate and professional schools
throughout the country. In drawing upon his characteristic and impassioned
logic, Houston reasoned as follows: Inequality could easily be proved because Southern states had provided virtually no graduate training for blacks;
the building of separate graduate and professional schools would be so expensive that it would lead to economic pressure toward integration; and the admission of blacks to these graduate schools—whether to white schools or
separate schools built especially for them—would lead to educating more black
leaders. In addition, Houston concluded that judges would be reluctant to rule
against qualified black college graduates who wanted to further their education in integrated facilities, particularly in a setting where relatively few white
women were enrolled.[53]

Once this battle was won, Houston could focus on desegregating undergraduate education and eventually public and elementary schools as well. He
would whittle away at segregation on a piecemeal basis and use each court
victory as a precedent for another case, until segregation was no longer the
law of the land. It would be an uphill battle, but Houston knew that the law
was on the side of his clients and had faith that their cause would prevail. In
view of the language of the Constitution and its amendments, Houston had
always regarded *Plessy* as an aberration. He expressed these ideas in a speech
to a Young Women's Christian Association Conference in Philadelphia in
May 1935:

> The American Negro is the only subordinate, minority group that I know of whose
> legal rights outreach actual practice. The usual course of history is for a subordi-
> nate people to enjoy rights in fact long before their rights are given legal sanction.
> But the Thirteenth, Fourteenth and Fifteenth Amendments have given the Negro in
> theory and in law absolute equality of citizenship, so that the real problem of the
> Negro is not to obtain new rights but to obtain the effective enforcement of these
> he already has.[54]

In his three years as special counsel for the NAACP, Houston handled two
very important graduate school cases: *Murray* v. *Maryland* (1936) and *Missouri ex. rel. Gaines* v. *Canada* (1938). Furthermore, he brought cases to equal-

ize the salaries of black teachers in segregated schools. These latter cases were designed not only to help the teachers obtain equity, but to motivate them to be active participants in the struggles of the NAACP—a goal that Houston put on par with winning a case in court.

Murray v. Maryland (1936)

If Houston were to gain entry for blacks in graduate or professional schools, he needed plaintiffs who qualified for admission in every category but color. His former student, Thurgood Marshall, found such a plaintiff in Donald Gaines Murray, an Amherst graduate who was turned down by the University of Maryland Law School in 1935.

At the time Murray had applied to law school, Maryland had neither a separate law school for blacks nor a scholarship program to enable students of color to attend a law school outside the state. However, the state legislature hurriedly appropriated funds for such scholarships once his lawsuit was commenced.

The case was tried in Baltimore City Court in June 1935. Houston called Raymond Pearson, president of the university, to the stand and subjected him to grueling questions. He got Pearson to state that he had no objections to admitting Mexicans, Japanese, Indians, and Filipinos to the law school. But Pearson maintained that he would not admit black students because state policy was against it.

On June 25, 1935, the court ordered Pearson to admit Murray to the University of Maryland Law School. It was the first time that any American court had ordered an educational institution to admit a black student. As soon as the decision was announced, the attorney for Maryland said, "I wish to be quoted as saying that I hope Mr. Murray leads the class in the law school."[55] Nevertheless, Maryland appealed the decision to the Court of Appeals, which ruled in favor of the student in 1936.

According to the Court of Appeals, it was a violation of the equal protection clause of the Fourteenth Amendment to provide scholarships for blacks to attend out-of-state integrated law schools. In referring to Murray, the court said:

> Going to any law school in the nearest jurisdiction would, then, involve him in considerable expense even with the aid of one of the scholarships should he chance to receive one. And as the petitioner points out, he could not there have the advantages of study of the law of this state primarily, and of attendance on state courts, where he intends to practice.[56]

Houston was assisted in the Murray case by Thurgood Marshall, who in later years became the first black justice on the United States Supreme Court. A native of Baltimore, Marshall had decided not to apply to the University of Maryland Law School following his graduation from college because of its discriminatory admissions policy. Having harbored a personal resentment against the school for many years, he took particular delight in the Maryland court's ruling in favor of Murray. The future Supreme Court justice, who always paid homage to his mentor, played down his own important role in the case. "I worked the case out on the ground," he said, "and I drew the pleadings since there was some intricate old Maryland common law involved, but outside the leg work, I did very little. The court presentation was his doing. The fact is, I never was chief counsel in any case that Charlie took part in."[57]

Despite the triumph in *Murray*, Houston was realistic enough to know that it was premature to rejoice. In an article titled "Don't Shout Too Soon," written for the NAACP's *Crisis* in March 1936, Houston stated:

> Law suits mean little unless supported by public opinion. Nobody needs to explain to a Negro the difference between the law in books and the law in action. In theory the cases are simple: the state cannot tax the entire population for the exclusive benefit of a single class. The really baffling problem is how to create the proper kind of public opinion. The truth is there are millions of white people who had no real knowledge of the Negro's problems and who never give the Negro a serious thought. They take him for granted and spend their time and energy on their own affairs.[58]

Murray graduated from the University of Maryland Law School and entered the practice of law. He attended various NAACP events, but seldom participated in civil rights cases.[59]

There were four other Supreme Court cases between 1938 and 1950 that challenged segregation in graduate schools: *Missouri ex. rel. Gaines* v. *Canada* (1938), *Sipuel* v. *Oklahoma State Regents* (1948), *Sweatt* v. *Painter* (1950), and *McLaurin* v. *Oklahoma* (1950). In each case, the court ruled against segregation as a violation of Fourteenth Amendment rights. Together with *Murray*, these cases set the precedents for the *Brown* decision of 1954.[60]

Misssouri ex. rel. Gaines v. Canada (1938)

In some respects, the Murray case was a disappointment to Houston. He had really wanted to lose in Maryland so that he could take the case to the Supreme Court, where a favorable ruling would be binding throughout the country. The Gaines case in 1938 finally gave Houston the chance to confront the court with this issue, and it was to be his first major Supreme Court case.

Lloyd Lionel Gaines was a twenty-five-year-old St. Louis resident when he was rejected by the School of Law at the State University of Missouri. Gaines then sought the help of a local branch of the NAACP, which enlisted Houston to take the case to state court.

Unlike the situation in the Murray case, Gaines had the opportunity to apply for a scholarship to an out-of-state law school when he first applied for admission. Moreover, Missouri indicated that it was willing to build a separate law school for him in the event he refused to accept the scholarship.

Houston lost in the lower courts, and the Supreme Court agreed to hear the case in November 1938. His strategy was to argue that Missouri violated the

Plessy doctrine by its failure to provide Gaines with an equal-but-separate education and that it could not fulfill its obligation to him by sending him to an out-of-state law school. In essence, Houston was asking the court to enforce *Plessy* v. *Ferguson* on behalf of Gaines.[61]

Houston's argument before the Supreme Court led to another insulting experience for him when he went to the podium to begin his presentation. Justice James C. McReynolds, who was sitting to the left of Chief Justice Charles Evans Hughes, simultaneously began spinning his chair around so that his back was to Houston throughout the argument.[62]

In a seven-to-two decision (McReynolds joined Justice Pierce Butler in the dissent), the Supreme Court ruled that Missouri had to admit Gaines to law school or provide him with a separate law school within the state. As heartening as the decision was to Houston, he was later dismayed to find that very little had changed in the South as a result of the Gaines verdict. No Southern state admitted black students, and Missouri actually spent over $70,000 to build a separate law school for Gaines. The final irony was that Gaines disappeared, never attended law school, and was unable to benefit from the decision in his favor.[63]

Resignation of a Special Counsel, 1938

Another Supreme Court victory in 1938 for Houston was *Hale* v. *Kentucky,* in which the Court overturned a death sentence because blacks had been systematically excluded from the jury. The downside of these victories was that each success brought new demands on Houston's overextended schedule. His closest associates would insist that Houston never lay awake at night worrying about one crucial case—he worried about at least four at any given time.[64]

In order to relieve some of the pressure, in 1936 Houston had brought in Marshall as his assistant counsel in 1936 at a salary of $2,400 a year. Houston operated out of the New York office and dispatched Marshall to the South to seek plaintiffs for the graduate school cases, as well as white and black attorneys willing to litigate civil rights cases.

Sometimes they traveled to the South together in Marshall's beat-up 1929 Ford, which they turned into an office, with Houston typing out briefs in the back seat. Instead of taking lodgings, they either slept in the car or stayed at the home of friends. These economies were undertaken in view of the fact that the entire legal budget of the NAACP was approximately $8,000 a year— covering the salaries of two legal giants and a secretary.[65]

By 1938, the NAACP was again experiencing financial difficulties, and Houston resigned, with Marshall taking his place. The resignation was not unexpected by Houston's friends. "There was only enough money for one lawyer," said Oliver Hill. "Charlie knew he would go back to practice and earn money. So he left Thurgood as special counsel."[66]

The reasons for the resignation were probably more complicated than the NAACP's monetary problems. Houston had run into opposition within the NAACP: the radical wing felt he had ignored the masses in pursuit of a limited and narrow series of victories, and the conservatives were unhappy at his representation of leftists like Ades. In addition, Houston had come to feel frustrated by the very nature of the job that he had earlier undertaken with such enthusiasm. He expressed his thoughts in a letter to his father on April 14, 1938, a time when he still kept his affiliation with the NAACP but had moved back to Washington:

> I have had the feeling all along that I am much more of an outside man than an inside man. I usually break down under too much routine. . . . Certainly, for the present, I will grow much faster and be of much more service if I keep free to hit and fight wherever the circumstances call for action.[67]

Marshall, who would prove himself more adept than his mentor in handling the factions within the NAACP, described Houston in this period as "sick as hell, and still traveling like a maniac. I knew the internal strife . . . was driving him crazy. Charlie didn't like internal wars." Marshall joked with his wife that if he kept up Houston's schedule, he did not think he would make it to forty.[68]

The change in jobs for Houston came at a time when he sought greater financial security. He married Henrietta Williams, a secretary in his father's law office, in September 1939, a few weeks after his first marriage ended in divorce. His only child was born in 1944.

Return to Private Practice, 1938–1950

Houston's resignation from the NAACP meant a return to the private practice of law, and he rejoined his father's law firm. When he initially went to work full-time for the NAACP in New York, he was already separated from his first wife and lived modestly in a room at the Young Men's Christian Association in Harlem. But he had one luxury that he could not enjoy in Washington: the freedom to live in a nonsegregated city.

Upon his return to Washington, Houston could occasionally give away to his tightly controlled emotions, as on the day his little boy was called a "nigger" in the drug store. Benjamin Amos, an attorney in the Houston law office, recalled one similar outburst when Houston was obliged to buy a take-out lunch at a restaurant in Washington:

> At that time they had the Executive . . . at the corner of Fifth and F, and we had to go in there and stand by the fountain and watch [law] clerks, judges, and other whites belong[ing] to the court go in there, sit down, and eat. We'd have to stand there and take it out. This . . . day, Charlie, I, and a third person . . . got the lunch. We went up to the office, and he got inside and he couldn't stand it. . . . [He] said, "I just can't take it any longer," and threw the stuff on the floor in the center of the office . . . and burst into tears. [In that very emotional moment] for him, he said, "One day, we'll see these streets open and Negroes . . . go anywhere and eat."[69]

Houston helped to make his prophecy come true. He continued his crusade for justice until 1950, the year of his death. In spite of a demanding practice with his father, he resumed his part-time teaching at Howard and continued to handle cases for the NAACP without compensation. As before, there was no shortage of cases.

In the six years preceding his death, he won four groundbreaking cases in the Supreme Court: *Steele* v. *Louisville and Nashville Railroad Company* (1944), *Tunstall* v. *Brotherhood of Locomotive Firemen* (1944), *Hurd* v. *Hodge* (1948), and its companion case, *Urciolo* v. *Hodge* (1948).

These cases, together with the equally important decisions in *Hollins* v. *Oklahoma* (1935), *Missouri ex rel. Gaines* v. *Canada* (1938), and *Hale* v. *Kentucky* (1938), gave him a total of seven major victories in the United States Supreme Court. His only two losses were in *Fisher* v. *United States* (1946) and *Ex Parte Fisher* (1946). The latter cases involved Houston's unsuccessful efforts to prevent the execution of a convicted black murderer on the grounds of mental and emotional deficiencies.[70]

His last major effort was directed at going to court to obtain equal facilities for black schoolchildren in the District of Columbia. He worked closely with the Consolidated Parents Group, a local organization founded by a black barber named Garner Bishop. Upon first meeting Bishop in February 1948, Houston asked him how much money the group had in its treasury. When Bishop told him $14, Houston replied, "Well, you've got yourself a lawyer."[71]

Houston proceeded to formulate plans to file a series of lawsuits for equalization in the schools. In the process, he had an opportunity to learn firsthand about life in the inner cities, as well as to offer advice. As Bishop recalled:

> Charlie became us—a part of our group. There was no fake or make-believe about it. I'd come by his place and we'd sit up till three or four o'clock in the morning talking about everything. He wanted to find out about life in the gutter, and he found out plenty. Charlie would tell me I was too bitter. "You hate too bad," he'd say. "Just hate a little."[72]

Death of a Crusader, 1950

This extensive work took a heavy toll on Houston's health. At the end of 1949, he entered Freedman's Hospital in Washington, D.C., with a heart ailment. Bishop went to visit him, only to be upbraided by Houston's father for helping to cause his son's heart condition. The elder Houston lamented that "he won't let go," a reference to his son's unfailing devotion to the cause of his people.[73]

The end came in Freedman's Hospital on April 20, 1950, from an acute coronary thrombosis. Shortly before his death, Houston had summoned Bishop to his bedside. He told Bishop that there were few matters of more importance to him than the future of the children in Washington, D.C., and implored him to see Howard law professors George E.C. Hayes and James M. Nabrit Jr.

"Ask Hayes to take full charge . . . and ask Nabrit . . . to help him. [Tell] Hayes and Jim Nabrit they owe me and take your case."[74]

After Houston's death, Bishop sought out Nabrit, who had finished first in his class at Northwestern Law School in Chicago and would later become president of Howard. Nabrit turned him down about taking the equalization cases. As Bishop started to leave, Nabrit said that if Bishop would arrange for a group of plaintiffs to challenge segregation itself, he [Nabrit] would be pleased to handle it. The astonished Bishop then shook hands with his new lawyer. This case, which became *Bolling* v. *Sharpe* (1954), was part of the four school segregation cases (including *Brown* v. *Board of Education*) that led to the Supreme Court's ruling that segregation was unconstitutional.[75]

In death, Houston received many of the honors that had eluded him in life. Memorial services were held at Howard University's Rankin Chapel on April 26, four days after his death. The mourners included family members, associates, friends, civil rights activists, and Justices Tom Clark and Hugo Black of the United States Supreme Court. The Rev. A.F. Elmes, who had presided at the funeral of Houston's mother, delivered the eulogy. Judge William H. Hastie Jr., Houston's cousin and colleague, urged the mourners to continue the fight for justice, noting that Houston "stop[ped] only when his body could no longer keep pace with his will and his spirit."[76]

Hastie paid further tribute to Houston two months later in an article about him in the *Negro History Bulletin*. "He guided us through the legal wilderness of second class citizenship," Hastie wrote. "He was truly the Moses of that journey."[77]

On June 25, 1950, the NAACP posthumously awarded Houston its prestigious Spingarn Medal. The citation read as follows:

> In memory of a lifetime of gallant championship of equal rights for all Americans, of unselfish devotion to democratic ideals, of unwavering fidelity to the American dream of equal opportunity, the Spingarn Medal, presented annually to a Negro American for distinguished achievement, is this year awarded to the late Charles Hamilton Houston, stalwart defender of democracy, inspired teacher of youth, and leader in the legal profession.[78]

Houston's alma mater, Harvard Law School, dedicated the December 1984 issue of its *Law Review* to him, referring to him as "one of our most distinguished alumni, having played a key role in the civil rights litigation that culminated in *Brown* v. *Board of Education*."[79] Fourteen years later, the *Law Review* cosponsored a symposium on the life and legacy of Charles Hamilton Houston in honor of the seventy-fifth anniversary of the completion of his studies at Harvard Law School.[80]

There were numerous other accolades, but the tribute that Houston might have liked best had come years earlier from Thurgood Marshall. "It was Charlie Houston," he said, "who taught us the law."[81]

Notes

1. Quoted in Genna Rae McNeil, *Groundwork: Charles Hamilton Houston and the Struggle for Civil Rights* (Philadelphia: University of Pennsylvania Press, 1983): 186–187.

2. Interviewed in William Elwood, *The Road to Brown: The Untold Story of "The Man Who Killed Jim Crow"* (San Francisco: California Newsreel, 1989), videotape.

3. Charles Thompson, as quoted in Richard Kluger, *Simple Justice: The History of Brown v. Board of Education and Black America's Struggle for Equality,* 2 vols. (New York: Alfred A. Knopf, 1975), I: 351.

4. Quoted in Ken Gormley, "A Mentor's Legacy: Charles Hamilton Houston, Thurgood Marshall and the 'Civil Rights Movement." *ABA Journal* 78 (June 1992): 66.

5. Quoted in McNeil, *Groundwork,* 212.

6. Ibid., 15–16.

7. See Geraldine R. Segal, *In Any Fight Some Fall* (Rockville, MD: Mercury Press, 1975): 15–18; McNeil, *Groundwork,* 15–23.

8. Segal, *In Any Fight Some Fall,* 37.

9. Ibid., 15–18; McNeil, *Groundwork,* 24–30.

10. Segal, *In Any Fight Some Fall,* 23.

11. Quoted in McNeil, *Groundwork,* 31. This conversation was related to McNeil in an interview with Charles Hamilton Houston's aunt, Clotill Marconier Houston.

12. Segal, *In Any Fight Some Fall,* 23–24.

13. William H. Hastie, "Foreword," Segal, *In Any Fight Some Fall,* 6.

14. McNeil, *Groundwork,* 41–42; Segal, *In Any Fight Some Fall,* 6.

15. Quoted in McNeil, *Groundwork,* 42.

16. Ibid., 42–43.

17. Ibid., 45.

18. Segal, *In Any Fight Some Fall,* 29.

19. Quoted ibid., 38.

20. Carl T. Rowan, *Dream Makers, Dream Breakers: The World of Justice Thurgood Marshall* (Boston: Little Brown, 1993), 47.

21. Michael D. Davis and Hunter R. Clark, *Thurgood Marshall: Warrior at the Bar, Rebel on the Bench* (New York: Carol Communications, 1992), 53.

22. William B. Bryant, "Oral History: A Symposium on Charles Hamilton Houston," *New England Law Review* 27 (Spring 1993): 679; Margaret A. Haywood, "Oral History: A Symposium on Charles Hamilton Houston," *New England Law Review* 27 (Spring 1993): 617.

23. Haywood, "Oral History," 624.

24. Quoted in Rowan, *Dream Makers,* 46.

25. Quoted in Davis and Clark, *Thurgood Marshall,* 45. Houston's talk to his students was related by Thurgood Marshall.

26. Rayford W. Logan, *Howard University: The First Hundred Years, 1867–1967* (New York: New York University Press, 1967), 225–227, 314, 399; August Meier and Elliott Rudwick, "Attorneys Black and White: A Case Study of Race Relations Within the NAACP," *Journal of American History* 62 (1976): 918; Gormley, "A Mentor's Legacy," 63.

27. Meier and Rudwick, "Attorneys Black and White," 924.

28. Quoted in Mark Tushnet, "The Politics of Equality in Constitutional Law: The Equal Protection Clause, Dr. DuBois and Charles Hamilton Houston," *Journal of American History* 74 (December 1987): 901.

29. Carter Godwin Woodson, *The Negro Professional Man and the Community, with Special Emphasis on the Physician and the Lawyer* (Washington, D.C.: Association for the Study of Negro Life and History, 1934), 221.

30. Bryant, "Oral History," 680.

31. Quoted in Gormley, "A Mentor's Legacy," 64.

32. Quoted in Davis and Clark, *Thurgood Marshall,* 51–52.

33. Jack Greenberg, *Crusaders in the Courts: How a Dedicated Band of Lawyers Fought for the Civil Rights Revolution* (New York: Basic Books, 1994), 5.

34. Quoted in Oliver M. Hill Sr., "Oral History: A Symposium on Charles Hamilton Houston," *New England Law Review* 27 (Spring 1993) 673–674.

35. Quoted in Segal, *In Any Fight Some Fall,* 73–74.

36. "Legal Realism and the Race Question: Some Realism about Realism on Race Relations," *Harvard Law Review* 108 (May 1995): 1607–1624.

37. Haywood, "Oral History," 621.

38. Quoted in Douglas A. Aube, "Justice Thurgood Marshall," *New England Law Review* 27 (Spring 1993): 628.

39. Quoted in Gormley, "A Mentor's Legacy," 63–64.

40. Quoted in Meier and Rudwick, "Attorneys Black and White," 943.

41. Greenberg, *Crusaders in the Courts,* 5.

42. Kluger, *Simple Justice,* 1: 184–185.

43. Quoted in Meier and Rudwick, "Attorneys Black and White," 939.

44. Walter White, *A Man Called White* (New York: Arno Press and New York Times, 1969), 152–153.

45. Ibid., 152–154.

46. Quoted ibid., 155.

47. Kluger, *Simple Justice,* 1: 141.

48. Quoted in McNeil, *Groundwork,* 94, 102–104.

49. Ibid., 95.

50. Quoted in Rowan, *Dream Makers,* 67.

51. Quoted in Gormley, "A Mentor's Legacy," 63.

52. Tushnet, "The Politics of Equality in Constitutional Law," 897–900.

53. Herbert Hill and Jack Greenberg, *Citizen's Guide to Desegregation: A Study of Social and Legal Change in American Life* (Boston: Beacon Press, 1955), 58–59.

54. Quoted in Segal, *In Any Fight Some Fall,* 42.

55. Quoted in Davis and Clark, *Thurgood Marshall,* 87; see also Kluger, *Simple Justice,* 1: 235–238.

56. Quoted in Steven H. Hobbs, "From the Shoulders of Houston: A Vision for Social and Economic Justice," *Howard Law Journal* 32 (Fall 1989): 524.

57. Quoted in Davis and Clark, *Thurgood Marshall,* 90.

58. Quoted in McNeil, *Groundwork,* 139.

59. Greenberg, *Crusaders in the Court,* 63.

60. Joseph D. Martin Jr., "The Social and Educational Implications of the Murray Case and the Fourteenth Amendment," Ph.D. dissertation, University of Pittsburgh, 1989, 8–9.

61. Davis and Clark, *Thurgood Marshall,* 94.

62. Robert L. Carter, "In Tribute: Charles Hamilton Houston," *Harvard Law Review* 111 (June 1998): 2153–2154.

63. Greenberg, *Crusaders in the Court,* 63; Segal, *In Any Fight Some Fall,* 47.

64. Rowan, *Dream Makers,* 75.

65. Davis and Clark, *Thurgood Marshall,* 103.

66. Quoted in Gormley, "A Mentor's Legacy," 65.

67. Davis and Clark, *Thurgood Marshall,* 104; quoted in McNeil, *Groundwork,* 149.

68. Rowan, *Dream Makers,* 70; Davis and Clark, *Thurgood Marshall,* 76.

69. Quoted in McNeil, *Groundwork,* 186.

70. See William T. Coleman Jr., "In Tribute: Charles Hamilton Houston," *Harvard Law Review* 111 (June 1998): 2157, n. 7. Coleman omitted the *Urciolo* case in discussing Houston's Supreme Court victories. He listed *Ex Parte Fisher* (1948), but did not include it as a loss, presumably since the court denied certiorari.

71. Quoted in Kluger, *Simple Justice* 2: 652.

72. Quoted ibid.

73. Quoted ibid., 654.

74. Quoted in McNeil, *Groundwork,* 209–210.

75. Kluger, *Simple Justice* 2: 655–656; Jack Greenberg, "In Tribute: Charles Hamilton Houston," *Harvard Law Review* 111 (June 1998): 2166.

76. McNeil, *Groundwork,* 211.

77. William H. Hastie, "Charles Hamilton Houston, 1895–1950," *Negro History Bulletin* 13 (June 1950): 207.

78. Erwin N. Griswold, "Charles Hamilton Houston: Address by Dean," *Negro History Bulletin* 13 (June 1950): 212

79. "Dedication to Charles Hamilton Houston." *Harvard Law Review* 98 (December 1984): preface.

80. "In Tribute: Charles Hamilton Houston," *Harvard Law Review* 111 (June 1998): 2149.

81. Quoted in J. Clay Smith Jr., "The First Recipients of the Charles Hamilton Houston Medallion of Merit," *Howard Law Journal* 20 (1977): 11.

Selected Cases

Bountiful Brick Company et al. v. *Elizabeth Giles* (1927)
276 U.S. 154

Houston worked on this case in his third year of practice at the request of Samuel Horovitz, a former classmate at Harvard Law School. It was an opportunity for Houston to work in his first case before the United States Supreme Court.

Houston and Horovitz represented the Industrial Commission of Utah and Elizabeth Giles et al. Giles was the widow of Nephi Giles, who had been killed on his way to work in June 1925. His fatal accident had occurred when he was struck by a train when crossing railroad tracks that lay adjacent to his place of work. His employer knew about the use of this shortcut by some of its employees and consented to their use of it.

A lower court had ruled in favor of Elizabeth Giles by stating that the company was liable under the Utah Workmen's Compensation Act, but the company appealed to the United States Supreme Court. The company contended that the accident had been caused by Nephi Giles's negligence and his illegal intrusion on the railroad's property. Accordingly, it argued that there was an insufficient causal connection between the injury and employment.

The court upheld the lower court's ruling by stating that the employer, by consenting to the employee's trespass on the railroad right of way, cannot avail itself of such defense in a compensation hearing and that the employer was liable if the accident had occurred in the employer's premises or in close proximity thereto.

Nixon v. *Condon* (1932)
286 U.S. 73

Houston helped prepare the brief in this case, which was handled by several lawyers, including Nathan Ross Margold and Arthur Spingarn, on behalf of the NAACP.

L.A. Nixon, a black physician from El Paso, Texas, brought action against James Condon and another judge of elections in Texas to recover damages for their refusal to permit him to cast his vote at a primary election by reason of his race or color. It was not the first time that Nixon found it necessary to invoke the jurisdiction of the federal courts in vindication of privileges secured to him by the federal Constitution. He had gone to the Supreme Court in *Nixon* v. *Herndon* (1927), in which the court held that a Texas statute barring Negroes from participation in Democratic party primary elections was unconstitutional because it was a "direct and obvious infringement" of the equal protection clause of the Constitution.

Texas repealed the statute, substituting a measure authorizing the State Executive Committee of every political party to "prescribe the qualifications of its own members." The state's Democratic Party thereupon "prescribed" that "only whites" shall be eligible in its primaries. Since Dr. Nixon was once again denied the right to participate in the party primary of his choice, he returned to court with a constitutional challenge to the new statute.

In a five-to-four decision, the Court struck down the Texas statute on the grounds that the Democratic party was usurping state law by setting qualifications. It held that the inherent power to declare who should be members of the party resided in the state convention, and not in the committee and that the committee had no right to exclude Negroes since the state convention never declared its intention to take such action.

Commonwealth of Virginia v. *George Crawford* (1933)
NAACP Records, D52

Houston handled this case as a volunteer lawyer with the NAACP, and it was his first victory for the organization.

In 1932, George Crawford, a black ex-convict, was accused of murdering a socially prominent white widow and her maid in Loudoun County, Virginia. He was picked up by the police in Boston and signed a confession. However, he had an alibi witness prepared to testify that he had been in Boston when the killings took place.

The NAACP decided to enter the case after Crawford had been indicted by an all-white jury in Loudoun County. It subsequently learned that Crawford's confession was true and that he had acted as a lookout while another black man had committed the murders. Nevertheless, it decided to represent him and focus on the exclusion of blacks from grand juries.

In selecting Houston as Crawford's attorney, the NAACP asked him to work with a white attorney as cocounsel. Houston objected, maintaining that the presentation by a black attorney would be a turning point in the legal history of black people. The NAACP acquiesced, and Howard law professor Leon A. Ransom became Houston's cocounsel.

At the trial, Houston claimed that the state did not prove its case and asked the jury, if it believed Crawford's confession, to spare his life so that he could testify against the accomplice, if the latter were found. In a surprise decision, the jury spared Crawford's life, returning a verdict of "guilty" with life imprisonment recommended.

Since Crawford's life was spared, the case was an impressive victory for Houston in the racially charged atmosphere of Loudoun County, Virginia.

Hollins v. *Oklahoma* (1935)
295 U.S. 394

This case marked the first time that the NAACP employed black counsel exclusively before the United States Supreme Court. Houston served as chief counsel, assisted by William LePre Houston, his father, and Edward P. Lovett, one of his former students at Howard Law School.

Jess Hollins, a black man, had been tried in the District Court of Okmulgee County, Oklahoma. He was convicted of rape and sentenced to death. The decision was upheld by the Criminal Court of Appeals of the State of Oklahoma.

The United States Supreme Court agreed to take the case upon the argument made by the Houstons and Lovett in the petition for a writ of certiorari on the grounds that no black had ever served on a jury in Okmulgee County since 1907. The petition stated that blacks constituted approximately 17 percent of the county's population, and many of them had met the qualifications for jury service.

Charles Hamilton Houston made the oral argument, stating that the jury exclusion constituted an official policy of segregation. In a per curiam decision, the Court ruled in favor of Hollins and remanded the case for further proceedings to the lower court.

Murray v. *Maryland* (1936)
182 A. 590

Donald Gaines Murray, a black graduate of Amherst College and a resident of Maryland, was denied admission to the University of Maryland Law School in 1935. The case was first called to Houston's attention by Thurgood Marshall, and Houston worked on it on behalf of the NAACP.

At the time Murray had filed his lawsuit, Maryland had neither a separate law school for blacks nor a scholarship program that enabled black students to attend a law school outside the state. As soon as Murray brought suit, the state legislature promptly appropriated funds for such scholarships.

The case was tried in Baltimore City Court in 1935, and the court ordered that Murray be admitted to the law school. Maryland appealed the decision to the court of appeals, which ruled that it was a violation of the equal protection clause of the Fourteenth Amendment to provide scholarships for black students to attend out-of-state integrated law schools.

Murray attended the law school without any racial incidents, and his example became a key legal precedent in Marshall's subsequent successful Supreme Court case, *Sweatt* v. *Painter* (1950).

Hale v. *Kentucky* (1938)
303 U.S. 613

In 1936, Joe Hale, a black man, was indicted for murder in McCracken County, Kentucky. He pleaded not guilty, but was convicted and sentenced to death.

His attorneys, Houston and Leon A. Ransom, appealed the decision to the United States Supreme Court. They moved to set aside the verdict upon the ground that the jury commissioners, in the course of compiling the list from which the grand jury was drawn, had excluded all persons of African descent because of their race and color, thereby denying Hale the equal protection of the laws. In support of this motion, Houston and Ransom presented affidavits showing that the population of McCracken County was approximately 48,000, of which 8,000 were black, and that the assessor's books for the county contained the names of approximately 6,000 white persons and 700 black persons who were qualified for jury service. Nevertheless, no black person was ever called for jury duty by the county.

The Supreme Court reversed the conviction of Hale and held that the affidavits sufficed to show a systematic and arbitrary exclusion of blacks from the jury lists solely because of their race or color, constituting a denial of the equal protection of the laws guaranteed by the Fourteenth Amendment.

Missouri ex. rel. Gaines v. *Canada* (1938)
305 U.S. 337

Lloyd L. Gaines was a twenty-five-year-old resident of St. Louis, Missouri, who received a bachelor of arts degree from Lincoln University, an institution maintained by the State of Missouri for the higher education of black students. Lincoln University had no law school and Gaines applied to the law school of the University of Missouri, a state institution. Following his rejection, he sued S.W. Canada, the registrar of the university. Gaines met all the requirements for admission, and the NAACP entered the case on his behalf.

Missouri, which had no law school for blacks, offered to pay Gaines's expenses at any of the neighboring law schools that admitted blacks. The university also indicated that it was willing to build a separate law school for Gaines if he did not wish to go out of state for his legal education.

It was Houston's first major Supreme Court case, and he was assisted by several volunteer lawyers for the NAACP. Losing in the Circuit Court and in the Supreme Court of Maryland, he brought the case to the United States Supreme Court. His oral argument was shared with Sidney R. Remond, a Missouri attorney.

In its decision, the Court ruled that Missouri's refusal to admit Gaines to the state law school violated the equal protection clause of the Fourteenth Amendment. The Gaines decision did not imply that there was anything legally wrong with the "separate but equal" doctrine. Instead, it found that black students had a right of access to a "white" educational institution where no "separate but equal" facilities existed for them.

The irony of the decision was that Gaines vanished after the verdict was announced and never attended the law school.

New Negro Alliance v. *Sanitary Grocery Co.* (1938)
303 U.S. 552

The New Negro Alliance was a Washington, D.C., group that picketed and urged boycotts of commercial operations in the black community that refused to hire black workers. One of its targets was the Sanitary Grocery Company, which had failed to hire black clerks in several of its stores when positions were vacant. The alliance placed one person carrying a placard to patrol in front of one of the Sanitary Grocery stores. The placard urged blacks to stop shopping in a store where no blacks were employed.

The company obtained an injunction in the trial court in the District of Columbia prohibiting the alliance from picketing. The court held that the Norris-LaGuardia Act of 1932, which prohibited federal courts from issuing an injunction in any case arising from a labor dispute, was not applicable because the dispute was not a labor dispute within the meaning of the act.

The alliance appealed the decision to the United States Court of Appeals for the District of Columbia, which affirmed the ruling of the trial court. The Supreme Court took the case on appeal.

The Supreme Court ruled in favor of the New Negro Alliance by holding that the controversy at issue was a labor dispute as defined by the Norris-LaGuardia Act. Although Houston neither wrote the Supreme Court brief nor participated in the oral arguments, he played a major part in working with the alliance to appeal the case to the Supreme Court.

Teague v. *Brotherhood of Locomotive Firemen & Engineermen and Gulf, Mobile & Northern Railroad* (1940)
FEPC/RG228

Ed Teague, a black fireman with seniority, was displaced on his job with the Gulf, Mobile & Northern Railroad Company by a junior white fireman. The Brotherhood of Locomotive Firemen was the all-white bargaining representative of the International Association of Railway Employees under the provisions of the Railway Labor Act of 1926, as amended.

In January 1938, the brotherhood entered into a secret agreement with Gulf sanctioning the dismissal of certain black firemen in favor of white firemen. Litigation on behalf of Teague was undertaken by the Association of Colored Railway Trainmen and the Association of Railway Employees.

Teague was represented by Houston, Joseph C. Waddy, Joseph Settle, and F.O. Turnage, and they took the case to the District Court of the United States in Memphis, Tennessee. Their argument was that the secret agreement broke the railroad's individual contracts with Teague and other black firemen and violated or destroyed their vested seniority rights.

The District Court ruled that the right claimed by Teague was not specifically granted under the Railway Labor Act and did not present a federal question over which the court had jurisdiction. Teague's lawyers filed an appeal with the Circuit Court of Appeals, which had jurisdiction over the District Court for the eastern division of western Tennessee. The Circuit Court of Appeals upheld the ruling of the lower court.

Houston disagreed with the decision, but decided not to appeal to the United States Supreme Court because he felt that this case was not the best vehicle for a clear presentation of the fiduciary duty that the bargaining representatives had to the minority workers under the Railway Labor Act. He subsequently raised that issue in two other Supreme Court cases: *Steele* v. *Louisville & Nashville Railroad Company* (1944) and *Tunstall* v. *Brotherhood of Locomotive Firemen* (1944). Both cases were decided in favor of the black minority workers.

Steele v. *Louisville & Nashville Railroad Company* (1944) 323 U.S. 192

Bester William Steele brought suit against the Louisville & Nashville Railroad Company, Brotherhood of Locomotive Firemen and Engineermen, and others. The issue was whether the Railway Labor Act of 1944 imposed on a labor organization, acting as the exclusive bargaining representative of a craft or class of railroad employees, the duty to represent all the employees in the craft without discrimination because of their race; and, if so, whether the court had jurisdiction to protect the minority of the craft or class from the violation of such obligation.

Steele had been in a "passenger pool," to which one white and five black firemen were assigned. Following a reduction in the mileage covered by the pool, the railroad declared that all jobs in the pool were vacant. The brotherhood (which barred black firemen from union membership) replaced them with four white men. The latter were members of the brotherhood, and all junior in seniority to Steele.

Representing Steele, Houston filed suit in the State Court of Alabama, which ruled against his client. The United States Supreme Court granted certiorari, holding that the brotherhood was required to represent Negro firemen excluded from union membership without racial discrimination. It also ruled that Steele could seek relief in equity without first attempting to secure relief by administrative means under the Railway Labor Act.

Steele, a companion case to *Tunstall* v. *Brotherhood of Locomotive Firemen,* was Houston's second major Supreme Court victory after *Missouri ex. rel. Gaines* v. *Canada* (1938).

Tunstall v. *Brotherhood of Locomotive Firemen* (1944)
323 U.S. 210

Tom Tunstall, a Negro fireman, was employed by the Norfolk & Southern Railway. He brought suit against the Brotherhood of Locomotive Firemen, a labor union that was the designated bargaining representative for the craft of firemen of which Tunstall was a member. Tunstall argued that the brotherhood had discriminated against him and other black members of his craft in favor of white workers, deprived him of his existing seniority rights, removed him from the interstate passenger run to which he was assigned, and subsequently assigned him to more arduous and difficult work with longer hours in yard service.

Representing Tunstall, Houston filed suit in the United States Circuit Court of Appeals for the Fourth Circuit. The court ruled against his client. The United States Supreme Court granted certiorari, holding that the Railway Labor Act of 1944 imposed on a labor organization, acting as the exclusive bargaining representative of a craft or class of railway employees, the duty to represent all the employees in the craft without discrimination because of their race.

Tunstall was decided at the same time as *Steele* v. *Louisville & Nashville Railway Company.*

Kerr v. *Pratt* (1945)
149 F.2d. 212

Louise Kerr, a black woman, was refused admission to a library training class conducted by the Enoch Pratt Free Library of Baltimore, Maryland, to prepare persons for staff positions in the general library and its branches. She was a native of Baltimore who had graduated with a high average from the public high school in the city and later graduated from a public teachers' training school in the city. She had taken courses for three summers at the University of Pennsylvania and had taught in the Baltimore elementary public schools. She brought suit in the District Court of Maryland and lost, and the case was appealed to the Circuit Court of Appeals for the Fourth Circuit.

Houston took the case for the NAACP, presenting the oral argument in the circuit court. The brief was prepared by W.A.C. Hughes, a Baltimore attorney.

The city library was funded by the city, but managed by a private board of trustees funded by a private donor. The circuit court sought to determine whether refusal to receive a black woman as a member of the library training class violated her rights under the laws of the United States.

The court held that the board of trustees might be classified as representatives of the state to such extent that their action was subject to the constitutional restraints imposed by the Fourteenth Amendment and the Civil Rights Act of 1866, and ruled in Kerr's favor on the ground that she was excluded from the school because of her race.

Fisher v. *United States* (1946)
328 U.S. 463

Houston appealed the conviction of Julius Fisher, a black janitor who worked in a library in the District of Columbia, to the United States Supreme Court. Tried in the District Court of the United States for the District of Columbia, Fisher was convicted and sentenced to death for the murder of a white librarian at work on the morning of March 1, 1944.

At his trial, Fisher testified that he killed the librarian following her utterance of racial epithets directed at him about his janitorial work. He stated that he slapped her impulsively, ran up a flight of stairs to reach an exit, but turned back after seizing a stock of firewood to stop her screaming. He then dragged her to a lavatory and started to clean up her blood on the floor of the library. When he heard her screams again, he took out his knife and stuck her in the throat. He dragged her body down into an adjoining pump pit, where it was discovered the next morning.

In his original confession to the police, Fisher had made no mention of the librarian's use of insulting words. He mentioned them in his written confession and amplified their effect upon him during his testimony. At his trial, the court heard testimony from psychiatrists about the mental and emotional disabilities of Fisher, but to no avail.

In his argument to the Supreme Court, Houston took the position that Fisher's mental and emotional disabilities were of such a level at the time of the crime that he was incapable of deliberation and premeditation, even though he was then sane in the usual legal sense. The court rejected this argument, as Houston was unable to convince it that there should be a rule of criminal law in the District of Columbia that recognized mental deficiency short of insanity as a defense.

This decision was reached on June 10, 1946. In *Ex Parte Fisher*, 329 U.S. 688, decided on December 19, 1946, the Supreme Court denied Houston's request for a stay of execution.

In the course of his career, Houston won seven cases before the United States Supreme Court, and the Fisher cases were the only ones that he lost.

Urciolo v. *Hodge* (1948)
334 U.S. 24

Raphael G. Urciolo, a white real estate dealer, had sold three pieces of restricted property in the District of Columbia. These lots were sold to three black men, who occupied the premises, and were located in the same restricted area at issue in *Hurd* v. *Hodge* (1948).

Frederick E. Hodge and others sought to enforce these restrictive covenants and won their case in the trial court in the District of Columbia. The decision was upheld by the United States Court of Appeals for the District of Columbia, and Houston appealed to the United States Supreme Court, which agreed to hear the case.

Houston, who worked with NAACP attorneys to reverse the enforcement of these covenants, was assisted in the oral arguments by volunteer attorney Phineas Indritz of the Solicitor's Office in the Department of Interior. In addition, Spottswood W. Robinson III, a Howard Law School graduate and a future federal judge, worked on the case.

This case, which was tried together with *Hurd* v. *Hodge,* resulted in a victory for Urciolo. As in *Hurd,* the Supreme Court ruled that the restrictive covenants were a violation of Section I of the Civil Rights Act of 1866 and could not be enforced.

These cases were companion cases to the restrictive covenant cases of *Shelley* v. *Kraemer* (1948) and *McGhee* v. *Sipes* (1948). All these cases were decided by six of the nine members of the Supreme Court. Justices Stanley F. Reed, Robert H. Jackson, and Wiley B. Rutledge had to remove themselves from the cases because they owned property with deeds containing restrictive covenants.

Hurd v. *Hodge* (1948)
334 U.S. 24

James Hurd had purchased property in the District of Columbia in spite of the fact that there was a covenant specifying that "said lot shall never be rented, leased, sold, transferred or conveyed unto any Negro or colored person." The lot was located in the same restricted area at issue in *Urciolo* v. *Hodge* (1948).

Frederick E. Hodge and others sought to enforce these restrictive convenants and won their case in the trial court in the District of Columbia. The decision was upheld by the United States Court of Appeals for the District of Columbia, which rejected Hurd's contention that he was a Mohawk Indian and not a Negro. Houston subsequently appealed to the United States Supreme Court, which agreed to hear the case.

Houston, who worked with NAACP attorneys to reverse the enforcement of these covenants, was assisted in the oral arguments by volunteer attorney Phineas Indritz of the Solicitor's Office in the Department of Interior. In addition, Spottswood W. Robinson III, a Howard Law School graduate and a future federal judge, worked on the case.

This case, which was tried together with *Urciolo* v. *Hodge,* resulted in a victory for Hurd. As in *Urciolo,* the Court ruled that restrictive covenants in the District of Columbia could not be enforced in the federal courts because it would be a violation of Section I of the Civil Rights Act of 1866. This act stated that "all citizens of the United States shall have the same right, in every State and Territory, as is enjoyed by white citizens thereof to inherit, purchase, lease, sell, hold and convey real and personal property." In its decision, the court held that the District of Columbia is included in the phrase "every State and Territory."

Houston's oral arguments in *Hurd* and *Urciolo* drew on constitutional, statutory, common law, public policy, and social science materials and were his most extensively prepared cases.

These cases were companion cases to the restrictive covenant cases of *Shelley* v. *Kraemer* (1948) and *McGhee* v. *Sipes* (1948). All these cases were decided by six of the nine members of the Supreme Court. Justices Stanley F. Reed, Robert H. Jackson, and Wiley B. Rutledge had to remove themselves from the cases because they owned property with deeds containing restrictive covenants.

Annotated Bibliography

Abraham, Henry J. *Freedom and the Court: Civil Rights and Liberties in the United States.* 7th ed. New York: Oxford University Press, 1998. Study of the conflicts in a democratic society in its attempt to reconcile individual freedom with the rights of the community.

Aube, Douglas A. "Justice Thurgood Marshall." *New England Law Review* 27 (Spring 1993): 625–646. Marshall's recollections of Howard Law School, based on an interview with Professor Charles Ogletree Jr. of Harvard Law School, Washington, D.C., on January 29, 1992.

Auerbach, Jerold. *Unequal Justice: Lawyers and Social Change in Modern America.* New York: Oxford University Press, 1976. Critical study of America's elite lawyers and their response to social changes in the twentieth century.

Bell, Derrick A., Jr. *Race, Racism, and American Law.* 4th ed. Boston: Little Brown, 2000. Analysis of discriminatory practices in American law.

Berger, Raoul. *Government by Judiciary.* 2d ed. rev. Cambridge, MA: Harvard University Press, 1997. Assessment of the influence of the judicial branch of government in American law.

Bryant, William B. "Oral History: A Symposium on Charles Hamilton Houston." *New England Law Review* 27 (Spring 1993): 677–688. Bryant, a prominent attorney and the chief judge of the United States District Court for the District of Columbia from 1977 to 1982, had been one of Houston's law students at Howard Law School.

Burton, Alfred Gene, Jr. "Charles Hamilton Houston: Unsung Civil Rights Hero." *Illinois Bar Journal* 84 (August 1996): 434–435. Review of Houston's contributions to the civil rights movement.

Carter, Robert L. "In Tribute: Charles Hamilton Houston." *Harvard Law Review* III (June 1998): 2149–2155. Summary of Houston's career by one of his former Howard law students; Carter was a judge, United States District Court for the Southern District of New York.

Coleman, William T., Jr. "In Tribute: Charles Hamilton Houston." *Harvard Law Review* 111 (June 1998): 2155–2161. Discussion of Houston's legal talents by an attorney and colleague; Coleman was secretary of transportation in the administration of President Gerald R. Ford from 1975 to 1977.

Dalfiume, Richard M. "The 'Forgotten Years' of the Negro Revolution." *Journal of American History* 55 (June 1968): 90–106. Study of the early years of the civil rights movement.

Davis, Michael D., and Hunter R. Clark. *Thurgood Marshall: Warrior at the Bar, Rebel on the Bench.* New York: Carol Communications, 1992. Analysis of Marshall's career; discussion of the relationship between Houston and Marshall.

"Dedication to Charles Hamilton Houston." *Harvard Law Review* 98 (December 1984): preface. Issue dedicated to Houston, the first black editor of the *Harvard Law Review;* review of Houston biography by Genna Rae McNeil in the issue.

Diamond, K. Norman. "Exclusion of Negroes from State Supported Professional Schools." *Yale Law Journal* 45 (1936): 1296–1301. Study of the efforts of state-supported professional schools to exclude black students.

Douglas, William O. *The Court Years, 1939–1975: The Autobiography of William O. Douglas.* New York: Random House, 1980. Reminiscences by one of the Court's most prominent liberal judges.

Dunn, Frederick. "The Educational Philosophies of Washington, DuBois, and Houston: Laying the Foundations of Afrocentrism and Multiculturalism." *Journal of Negro Education* 62 (Winter 1993): 24–34. Discussion of the beliefs of Booker T. Washington, W.E.B. DuBois, and Houston on public education.

Dyson, Walter. *Howard University, the Capstone of Negro Education: A History: 1867–1940.* Washington, D.C.: Graduate School of Howard University, 1941. History of the founding of Howard Law School and its efforts to educate Black lawyers.

Elwood, William. *The Road to Brown: The Untold Story of "The Man Who Killed Jim Crow."* San Francisco: California Newsreel, 1989. Videotape. Highlights Houston's efforts in the 1930s and 1940s to end racial segregation in America.

Fairfax, Roger A. "Wielding the Double-Edged Sword: Charles Hamilton Houston and Judicial Activism in the Age of Legal Realism." *Harvard Blackletter Law Journal* 14 (Spring 1998):

17–44. A tribute to Houston and the work he undertook to insure the constitutional rights of African-Americans.

Foner, Philip S. *Organized Labor and the Black Worker.* New York: Praeger, 1974. Discussion of the efforts of black workers to end the discriminatory practices of organized labor.

Franklin, John Hope, and August Meier, eds. *Black Leaders of the Twentieth Century.* Urbana: University of Illinois Press, 1982. Edited collection of articles dealing with the major black leaders of the last century.

Goldman, Roger, with David Gallen. *Thurgood Marshall: Justice for All.* New York: Carroll and Graf, 1992. Analysis of Marshall's career, including the relationship between Houston and Marshall.

Gormley, Ken. "A Mentor's Legacy: Charles Hamilton Houston, Thurgood Marshall and the Civil Rights Movement." *ABA Journal* 78 (June 1992): 62–66. Discussion of Houston's influence upon Thurgood Marshall.

Greenberg, Jack. *Crusaders in the Courts: How a Dedicated Band of Lawyers Fought for the Civil Rights Revolution.* New York: Basic Books, 1994. A personal memoir and a history of the NAACP's Legal Defense and Educational Fund by the former director-general of the fund.

———. "In Tribute: Charles Hamilton Houston." *Harvard Law Review* 111 (June 1998): 2161–2167. Reflections on Houston's career with the NAACP.

———. *Race Relations and American Law.* New York: Columbia University Press, 1959. Study of the struggles in the fight for racial equality in the United States.

Griswold, Erwin N. "Charles Hamilton Houston: Address by Dean." *Negro History Bulletin* 13 (June 1950): 210, 212–213, 216. Comments on Houston's life by the successor to Dean Roscoe Pound at Harvard Law School.

Hastie, William H. "Charles Hamilton Houston, 1895–1950." *Negro History Bulletin* 13 (June 1950): 207–208. Houston's contribution to the civil rights movement.

Haywood, Margaret A. "Oral History: A Symposium on Charles Hamilton Houston." *New England Law Review* 27 (Spring 1993): 612–623. Haywood was an associate judge on the Supreme Court for the District of Columbia who worked as a secretary at Houston's law firm at an early stage in her career.

Higginbotham, A. Leon, Jr. "Reflections on the Impact of Charles Hamilton Houston—From a Unique Perspective." *New England Law Review* 27 (Spring 1993): 605–611. Tribute to Houston by a prominent black federal judge.

Hill, Herbert, and Jack Greenberg. *Citizen's Guide to Desegregation: A History of Social and Legal Change in American Life.* Boston: Beacon Press, 1955. This work, dealing with the end of segregation in public life, was dedicated to Charles Hamilton Houston, described as the "Moses of that journey."

Hill, Oliver W., Sr. "Oral History: A Symposium on Charles Hamilton Houston." *New England Law Review* 27 (Spring 1993): 659–676. Hill was a prominent attorney in Richmond, Virginia, who was one of Houston's law students in the first day class at Howard Law School.

Hine, Darlene Clark. "Black Lawyers and the Twentieth-Century Struggle for Constitutional Change." In *African Americans and the Living Constitution,* ed. John Hope Franklin and Genna Rae McNeil. Chicago: University of Chicago Press, 1995. Study of the leadership role of black lawyers in the enforcement of constitutional rights.

———. "Blacks and the Destruction of the Democratic White Primary, 1935–1944." *Journal of Negro History* 62 (January 1977): 43–59. The efforts to abolish the all-white Democratic primary in the South.

Hobbs, Steven H. "From the Shoulders of Houston: A Vision for Social and Economic Justice." *Howard Law Journal* 32 (Fall 1989): 505–547. Discussion of Houston's impact on changes in the American system of justice.

"In Tribute: Charles Hamilton Houston." *Harvard Law Review* 111 (June 1998): 2149–2179. Essays about Houston by Robert L. Carter, William T. Coleman Jr., Jack Greenberg, Genna Rae McNeil, and J. Clay Smith Jr.; essays prepared in conjunction with a symposium on Houston cosponsored by *Harvard Law Review,* February 1998.

Kellogg, Charles Flint. *NAACP: A History of the National Association for the Advancement of Colored People, 1909–1920.* Vol. 1. Baltimore: John Hopkins University Press, 1967. Study of the early years of the civil rights organization.

Kluger, Richard. *Simple Justice: The History of Brown v. Board of Education and Black America's Struggle for Equality.* 2 vols. New York: Alfred A. Knopf, 1975. A classic treatment of the struggle for civil rights in the United States.

Konvitz, Milton R. *A Century of Civil Rights.* New York: Columbia University Press, 1961. Evaluation of the struggle for civil rights.

———. *The Constitution and Civil Rights.* New York: Columbia University Press, 1947. The courts and their interpretations of the civil rights protections of the United States Constitution.

"Legal Realism and the Race Question: Some Realism about Realism on Race Relations." *Harvard Law Review* 108 (May 1995): 1607–1624. References to Houston's work in the legal fight to end racial discrimination.

Leonard, Walter J. "Charles Hamilton Houston and the Search for a Just Society." *North Carolina Central Law Journal* 22 (Spring 1996): 1–13. Summary of Houston's major contributions to end discrimination in American life.

Logan, Rayford W. *Howard University: The First Hundred Years, 1867–1967.* New York: New York University Press, 1967. Study of the founding of Howard University and the role that it took in the education of African-American students.

Martin, Joseph D., Jr. "The Social and Educational Implications of the Murray Case and the Fourteenth Amendment." Ph.D. dissertation, University of Pittsburgh, 1989. Unpublished dissertation on the case of *Murray* v. *Maryland* (1936); analysis of the legal strategies employed by Houston.

McCloskey, Robert G. *The American Supreme Court.* 3rd ed. Chicago: University of Chicago Press, 2000. Analysis of the role of the Supreme Court in American society.

McNeil, Genna Rae. "Charles Hamilton Houston." *Black Law Journal* 3 (Spring 1974): 123–131. Overview of the significance of his life.

———. "Charles Hamilton Houston: 1895–1950." *Howard Law Journal* 32 (Fall 1989): 467–477. Highlights of Houston's major achievements.

———. *Groundwork: Charles Hamilton Houston and the Struggle for Civil Rights.* Philadelphia: University of Pennsylvania Press, 1983. Well-documented biography of Houston; study began as a doctoral dissertation at the University of Chicago under the direction of prominent black historian John Hope Franklin.

———. "In Tribute: Charles Hamilton Houston." *Harvard Law Review* 111 (June 1998): 2167–2173. Discussion of Houston's legacy by one of his biographers.

Meier, August, and Elliott Rudwick. "Attorneys Black and White: A Case Study of Race Relations Within the NAACP." *Journal of American History* 62 (1976): 913–946. Study of conflicts between black and white lawyers within the NAACP.

Miller, Loren. *The Petitioners: The Story of the United States Supreme Court and the Negro.* New York: Random House, 1966. An account of the attempts of black people to enforce the guarantees of equality as set forth in the United States Constitution.

Nelson, Bernard H. *The Fourteenth Amendment and the Negro Since 1920.* Washington, D.C.: Catholic University Press, 1946. An examination of the Fourteenth Amendment and its application to the rights of black Americans.

Norton, Eleanor Holmes. "Black Legacy and Responsibility." *New England Law Review* 27 (Spring 1993): 689–692. Remarks about Houston made at a 1992 speech at the Association of American Law Schools' Minority Law Teachers Luncheon.

Reed, Michael Wilson. "The Contribution of Charles Hamilton Houston to American Jurisprudence." *Howard Law Journal* 30 (Fall 1987): 1095–1100. Discussion of Houston's role in the American judicial system in an issue of the *Journal* dealing with the bicentennial of the United States Constitution.

Reid, Herbert O. "Introduction." *Howard Law Journal* 32 (Fall 1989): x–468. Introduction to the articles about Houston's achievements in the Charles Hamilton Houston Commemorative Issue.

Robinson, Spottswood W., III, and William H. Hastie. "No Tea for the Feeble: Two Perspectives in Charles Hamilton Houston." *Howard Law Journal* 20 (1977): 1–9. Recollections of Houston at Howard Law School.

Ross, Barbara Joyce. *J.E. Spingarn and the Rise of the NAACP, 1911–1939.* New York: Athenaeum, 1972. Study of the formulative years of the civil rights organization.

Rowan, Carl T. *Dream Makers, Dream Breakers: The World of Justice Thurgood Marshall.* Boston: Little, Brown, 1993. Analysis of Marshall's career; Analysis of the relationship between Houston and Marshall.

Segal, Geraldine R. *In Any Fight Some Fall.* Rockville, MD: Mercury Press, 1975. A biography of Charles Hamilton Houston.

Smith, J. Clay, Jr. "The First Recipients of the Charles Hamilton Houston Medallion of Merit." *Howard Law Journal* 20 (1997): 10–19. Discussion of persons who received award in honor of Houston.

———. "Forgotten Hero." Review of *Groundwork: Charles Hamilton Houston and the Struggle for Civil Rights,* by Genna Rae McNeil. *Harvard Law Review* 98 (December 1984): 482–491. Discussion of book and laudatory remarks about Houston in issue dedicated to him.

———. "In Tribute: Charles Hamilton Houston." *Harvard Law Review* 111 (June 1998): 2173–2179. Account of Houston's influence at Howard Law School by a graduate of the class of 1967 and a professor of law at the school.

———. "Principles Supplementing the Houstonian School of Jurisprudence: Occasional Paper No. 1." *Howard Law Journal* 32 (Fall 1989): 493–504. Focus on Houston's efforts to use law to achieve efficient and orderly changes in American race relations.

Smith, J. Clay, Jr., and E. Desmond Hogan. "Remembered Hero, Forgotten Contribution: Charles Hamilton Houston, Legal Realism, and Labor Law." *Harvard Blackletter Law Journal* 14 (Spring 1998): 1–16. Emphasis on Houston's contributions in the area of labor law to protect the rights of minority workers.

Stout, Juanita Kidd. "Oral History: A Symposium on Charles Hamilton Houston." *New England Law Review* 27 (Spring 1993): 648–653. Recollections by a former secretary who worked at Houston's law firm at an early stage in her career; Stout was the first black woman to be popularly elected to the bench on Philadelphia's Municipal Court.

"The Talk of the Town: Notes and Comments." *New Yorker,* April 6, 1992, 23–24. Discussion of Houston's contributions as a lawyer and teacher; reflections on his influence on Thurgood Marshall.

Tushnet, Mark. *The NAACP's Legal Strategy Against Segregated Education, 1925–1950.* North Carolina: Chapel Hill Press, 1987. Account of the work of the NAACP in countering segregation in public education.

———. "The Politics of Equality in Constitutional Law: The Equal Protection Clause, Dr. DuBois, and Charles Hamilton Houston." *Journal of American History* 74 (December 1987): 884–903. Perspectives on the views of W.E.B. DuBois and Houston on the Fourteenth Amendment.

Ulmer, Sidney. "Supreme Court Behavior in Racial Exclusion Cases, 1935–1960." In *The Negro in Depression and War,* ed. Bernard Sternsher. Chicago: Quadrangle Books, 1969, 93–103. Discussion of opinions of the Supreme Court on cases dealing with the equal protection clause of the Fourteenth Amendment.

Vose, Clement. *Caucasians Only: The Supreme Court, the NAACP, and the Restrictive Covenant Cases.* Berkeley: University of California Press, 1959. Study of the efforts of the NAACP to end discrimination in housing.

Ware, Gilbert, ed. *From the Black Bar.* New York: G. Putnam, 1976. Edited collection of articles about black attorneys.

Ware, Leland. "A Difference in Emphasis: Charles Houston's Transformation of Legal Education." *Howard Law Journal* 32 (Fall 1989): 479–492. Houston's skills in transforming the American legal system to ensure equal treatment for all of its citizens.

White, Vibert L. "Charles Houston and Black Leadership of the 1930s and 1940s." *National Black Law Journal* 7 (Fall 1990): 331–347. Discussion of Houston's pivotal role among black leaders in fighting for equality.

White, Walter. *A Man Called White.* New York: Arno Press and New York Times, 1969. Autobiography of the executive secretary of the NAACP; account of Houston's work for the organization.

Woodson, Carter Godwin. *The Negro Professional Man and the Community, with Special Emphasis on the Physician and the Lawyer.* Washington, D.C.: Association for the Study of Negro Life and History, 1934. Study of the role of black professionals in the community; Houston contributed the section on black attorneys.

—Thurgood—
Marshall

(United States Supreme Court)

Chronology

1908	Born on July 2 in Baltimore, Maryland, to William ("Willie") Canfield Marshall and Norma Williams Marshall; originally named "Thorough Good," but changed his name to "Thurgood" in the first grade.
1925	Graduated from Douglass High School, Baltimore.
1929	Marriage to Vivian ("Buster") Burey, September, Philadelphia, Pennsylvania.
1930	Graduated *cum laude* from Lincoln University, Chester, Pennsylvania.
1933	Graduated first in class of six students, *magna cum laude,* from Howard Law School, Washington, D.C.; opened private practice in Baltimore.
1936	Assisted Charles Hamilton Houston with the successful arguments in *Murray* v. *Maryland;* joined the national legal staff of the National Association for the Advancement of Colored People (NAACP), New York, as assistant special counsel.
1938	Assisted Houston with brief in *Missouri ex. rel. Gaines* v. *Canada*; selected as chief legal officer of the NAACP.
1939	Admitted to practice before the United States Supreme Court.
1940	Became director-counsel of the NAACP Legal Defense and Education Fund.
1944	Argued *Smith* v. *Allwright* before the United States Supreme Court.
1946	Argued *Morgan* v. *Commonwealth of Virginia* before the United States Supreme Court.
1948	Argued *Shelley* v. *Kraemer* before the United States Supreme Court.
1950	Argued *Sweatt* v. *Painter* and *McLaurin* v. *Oklahoma State Regents* before the United States Supreme Court.
1951	Argued *Briggs* v. *Elliot* in Clarendon County, South Carolina; went to Korea and Japan on behalf of President Harry S. Truman and the NAACP to investigate complaints of discriminatory treatment of black soldiers.
1954	Argued *Oliver Brown et al.* v. *Board of Education of Topeka, Kansas (Brown* v. *Board of Education)* before the United States Supreme Court.

1955   Argued *Brown* v. *Board of Education II,* before the United States Supreme Court with regard to implementation of the 1954 decision; death of first wife, February; remarriage to Cecilia ("Cissy") Suyat, December.

1956   Birth of first son, Thurgood ("Goody") Jr.

1958   Birth of second son, John; argued *Cooper* v. *Aaron* before the United States Supreme Court.

1961·   Nominated and appointed to the United States Court of Appeals for the Second Circuit.

1965   Nominated and appointed solicitor general of the United States.

1967   Nominated and appointed associate justice of the United States Supreme Court.

1991   Retired as associate justice of the United States Supreme Court.

1992   Received Annual Medal of the American Bar Association.

1993   Died of heart failure at Bethesda Naval Hospital, January 24; buried at Arlington National Cemetery; release of Thurgood Marshall Papers (over objections of his family) by the Library of Congress, May 24.

Biography

Thurgood Marshall, the first African-American to be appointed to the Supreme Court, was a captivating raconteur. His stories, dealing with certain aspects of his life, were meant to illustrate a point. One of his favorites had to do with several white tourists who unwittingly entered an automated elevator in the Supreme Court that was reserved for the justices. When they stepped into the elevator, they saw Marshall and mistook him for the operator. "First floor, please," they called. In his best Southern accent, Marshall replied, "yowsa, yowsa," and pushed the button. The car reached the first floor, and he ushered them out. Marshall watched them walk down the hallway, as they slowly realized who he was.[1]

Marshall, a hefty 250-pound six footer with medium-sized glasses, a mustache, and a penchant for wearing off-the-rack suits that he had collected over several decades, could make an entirely different impression on other people. On the day in 1952 that he went to the Supreme Court for the first day of oral arguments in the landmark case of *Oliver Brown et al.* v. *Board of Education of Topeka, Kansas* (1954), he was accompanied in a cab by William T. Coleman, a young black attorney who went on to become secretary of transportation in the 1970s. Coleman recalled that when they reached the Supreme Court building, the driver turned to Marshall and said, "You never told me where you were going. I just knew."[2]

Rise to the Top

Marshall had the distinction of being one of the few Supreme Court judges whose fame preceded him to the Court. His victory in *Brown,* which overturned *Plessy* v. *Ferguson* (1896) and declared segregation in public education to be unconstitutional, assured his place in history as the man who won the case that is often regarded as the greatest moral triumph of the United States Supreme Court.[3] His rise to the highest court in the land followed a path that was unadorned with any major professional setbacks. Three years after his graduation at the head of his class at Howard Law School in 1933, he joined the national staff of the National Association for the Advancement of Colored People (NAACP) as assistant legal counsel. He became its legal counsel in 1938 and two years later was named to be the director-counsel of its Legal Defense and Education Fund. In 1961, he was named by President John F. Kennedy as a federal judge for the United States Court of Appeals for the Second Circuit. He was chosen to be solicitor general of the United States in 1965 by President Lyndon B. Johnson, who nominated him for the United States Supreme Court two years later. He went on to serve for twenty-four years as an associate justice until he retired from the Court in 1991, two years before his death.

This so-called Horatio Alger story was complicated by the fact that he was a member of a minority group, and he faced the kinds of obstacles that might have overwhelmed a lesser human being. In speaking of Marshall's work in the South, an attorney who argued cases against him noted that "it is a credit to him that he could be cordial when . . . there was no hotel, restaurant, or restroom open to him."[4]

Marshall had to spend these years avoiding the label of the "uppity" black man, displaying an enormous amount of self-discipline in this regard. As a young attorney trying cases for the NAACP, he took time to thank the presiding judges, making them feel that he was relying on their superior knowledge to help him prepare his work. He went out of his way to be gracious to opposing counsel, regardless of how they acted toward him.[5]

Nevertheless, his gracious demeanor did not shield him from the countless risks to his personal safety that he faced in the course of his work. During the twenty-five years he spent with the NAACP, he was nearly lynched with the help of the local police in Columbia, Mississippi, after an all-white jury acquitted his black clients; he was frequently forced to conceal his travel plans in his forays into the South so that his whereabouts would not be known to hostile segregationists; he was harassed by local law enforcement officials and arrested on trumped-up charges of drunken driving; he narrowly escaped being shot by a police chief in Dallas; and he endured repeated insults and threats to his life.[6]

A Man for All Seasons

Although his efforts resulted in clear-cut victories for African-Americans, Marshall was interested in protecting the rights of all citizens. During his tenure on the Supreme Court, he championed the right of women to have abortions, guarded the rights of Native Americans, protected the right of citizens to free speech, and fought for the right of death row prisoners to be spared a "cruel and unusual punishment" in his unmitigated opposition to capital punishment.

In a similar vein, he objected to being singled out as an African-American and was annoyed if queried about his "uniqueness." When a reporter called him to inquire how he planned to spend the newly designated holiday honoring the birth of Dr. Martin Luther King Jr., he retorted: "The same damn thing I do on every holiday—stay home." He then slammed down the phone in disgust.[7]

He had long avoided using the term "black" and once angrily replied to a question about whether the state of "black people" had improved during his tenure on the Supreme Court. "In the first place," he answered, "I am not a black people. I am an Afro-American. Now, do you want to rephrase the question?" When the question was rephrased, Marshall said it was irrelevant because both white and black people were better off at the present time.[8]

In spite of his vast achievements, Marshall was patronized by certain members of his profession. When he was named solicitor general in 1965, an unnamed government attorney referred to his performance as a federal judge and his qualifications to be solicitor general in highly unflattering terms in a magazine article:

> Thurgood's lack of knowledge was embarrassing [in some of his earlier tax cases as a judge]. I recall one case where a question he asked indicated that he didn't even understand the *concept* of a corporation. It was not a nice moment for anyone in that courtroom. But he has improved greatly, and he should have no trouble in this regard as a Solicitor. That office is staffed with the elite of the Justice Department, only ten men, but with excellent backgrounds, particularly in the business areas. So what Thurgood doesn't know they can teach him.[9]

Later in his career, Marshall felt that he was downgraded by the white legal community for lacking the intellectual attainments of other justices on the Supreme Court. Many of his suspicions were borne out in *The Brethren: Inside the Supreme Court* (1979), by Bob Woodward and Scott Armstrong. In the book, the authors claimed that Marshall was regarded by his fellow justices as being inattentive to details and too willing to rely on his law clerks in the preparation of cases. They further stated that Justice Abe Fortas, who was forced to resign from the Court in 1969 when it became known that he took money from a former client to run a charity, made derogatory comments about Marshall's intelligence—a view allegedly shared by Harry Blackmun, who replaced Fortas on the Court. According to *The Brethren*, Blackmun was impressed by all of its members except Chief Justice Warren E. Burger and Thurgood Marshall.[10]

An Advocate with Passion

Other accounts of Marshall's role on the Court directly contradict the views expressed in *The Brethren*. A key to understanding Thurgood Marshall was that he never pretended to be a legal scholar. His greatest asset was his ability to persuade, and few lawyers could ever equal him in the passion that he brought to his advocacy.

He had little patience with legal abstractions, viewing cases in terms of the effect that each decision would have on American society. Consequently, he never engaged in what lawyer Stuart Taylor referred to as "philosophical explorations or intellectual razzle-dazzle." In contrasting the common-sense legal arguments of Marshall with the erudite opinions of Justice Oliver Wendell Holmes, Taylor noted: "Marshall was no Holmes. But then, Holmes was no Marshall either."[11]

Marshall's law clerks on the Supreme Court (a majority of whom were white) shared the view of most people in regarding him as the most unpretentious of men. He kept his professional distance from his clerks, but they tended to be in awe of him. Former law clerk Mark Tushnet (who became a professor of law at Georgetown and wrote two books about Marshall) spoke about the "moral authority" that he brought to the Supreme Court's conference room whenever a case was discussed. He was fondly remembered by another law clerk, Paul Gerwirtz (who became a professor of law at Yale), as a man with the "heroic imagination" to think he could change "the ruthlessly discriminatory world" in which he lived, and "the courage and ability to do so."[12]

Marshall's colleagues on the Court had interesting recollections of his persuasiveness and his ability to regale them with stories of his experiences. In speaking of his influence, Associate Justice Antonin Scalia (arguably the most conservative member of the Court at the time of Marshall's tenure) made the following statement:

> Marshall could be a persuasive force by just sitting there. He was always in the conference a visible representative of a past that we wanted to get away from, and you knew that as a private lawyer he had done so much to undo racism or at least its manifestation in and through government. Anyone who spoke in conference on one of these race issues had to be looking at Thurgood when you're speaking. You know you're talking in the presence of someone sure about it. . . . He wouldn't have to open his mouth to affect the nature of the conference and how seriously the conference would take matters of race.[13]

A similar comment was made by Byron White, another conservative associate justice, who recalled that he was unprepared for the impact Marshall made on him:

> I guess I listened to him pretty carefully on race matters because I had known about Marshall before he became a judge and I knew his work on the Second Circuit and as S. G. [solicitor general], but I really wasn't prepared for the impact he would make. He spoke with such conviction. It was conviction that came out of experience. He could embellish his points with examples that would scare you to death, [in describing the] experience he had trying cases in the South.[14]

The "examples" that White referred to were Marshall's stories, which became his trademark. Nor were these stories necessarily repeated. Associate Justice Sandra Day O'Connor recalled that she never heard the same story twice during all the years she knew him on the bench.[15] Marshall told these stories in such a way that some listeners found them uproariously funny—as when he decided to take the next train out of a Southern town after being threatened by a stranger—but Justice White was closer to the truth when he stated that they "would scare you to death." Beneath his humor, Marshall had a message for his audience. He wished to remind them that there was a bitter heritage behind his stories—a heritage which must never be forgotten.

Family Background

Thurgood Marshall was born in Baltimore, Maryland, on July 2, 1908. His grandparents had lived in Baltimore for generations, and three of them were free blacks at the time of the Civil War. All of them were literate, proud, and ambitious.

His father was William ("Willie") Canfield Marshall, born in 1881 and the eldest of seven children of Thorney Good Marshall, a former slave, and Annie

Robinson, a free, blue-eyed, fair-skinned mulatto. Thorney Good Marshall had been brought to America by slave traders in the 1840s, was sold to a plantation owner on Virginia's eastern shore, and later escaped to freedom after the outbreak of the Civil War. Marshall, who described his paternal grandfather as "one mean man," was fond of discussing him. "His more polite descendants like to think he came from the cultured tribes in Sierra Leone," Marshall noted, "but we all know that he really came from the toughest part of the Congo."[16]

Marshall's mother, Norma Williams, was born in 1865, one of the six children of Isaiah Williams and Mary Fossett. Isaiah Williams, a mulatto who had fought in the Union navy during the Civil War, named his daughter after the heroine in the opera *Norma*, which he had seen during his service with the navy. Mary Fossett, a free young black woman at the time of her marriage to Isaiah Williams, later would teach at one of Baltimore's private academies for black students.

Thurgood Marshall's grandparents lived near each other in an integrated neighborhood, which was inhabited by Irish, German, and Russian immigrants, as well as black families. It was the kind of neighborhood in which upward mobility was possible. Thorney Good Marshall worked as a waiter and later opened a grocery store on the bottom floor of his house. Isaiah Williams took his earnings as a baker and also opened a grocery store. Williams's store was successful enough to enable him to open a second store, which catered to some of Baltimore's rich, white families.[17]

Marshall's father, a pale-skinned, blue-eyed man who could have passed for white, had more problems in adjusting to society. A rebellious youngster, he dropped out of high school and later went to work as a porter at the railroad station in Baltimore. When he met Norma Williams, he may not have been regarded as a suitable prospect for the young woman, who was attending a segregated teachers' college in Baltimore. But she became pregnant, and they were married in April 1905. Her mother insisted that her daughter finish college, and she graduated two months after her marriage. In September, their first child, Aubrey, was born.

Their second and last child, Thorough Good, was born three years later. The boy was named for his paternal uncle. The name lasted until the first grade, when the boy convinced his mother that it was too long and had her change it to "Thurgood."[18]

Early Years, 1910–1925

Baltimore would be Thurgood Marshall's home until he started working full-time for the NAACP in New York in 1936, but he lived in New York for four years as a child. In 1910, when he was two years old, his parents moved to a small apartment in Harlem, where Norma Marshall's older sister and her husband lived.

Willie Marshall, who joined his brother-in-law in working for the New York Central Railroad, felt that New York offered more economic opportunities than were available in Baltimore. Although he and his family enjoyed living in Harlem, they returned to Baltimore in 1914, when Norma Marshall's mother became ill.

Thurgood Marshall entered elementary school the same year that the family returned to Baltimore. Already known as a mischievous youngster, he was sent to the school where his mother was a substitute teacher in order that she could see that he behaved. He finally settled down a year before graduation and skipped to the eighth grade because of his high marks.[19]

After graduating from elementary school in 1921, Marshall entered Douglass High School, which had been Baltimore's first private school for black students. While the overcrowded school had no library, cafeteria, or gymnasium, it had a strong academic program. The family continued to believe that he needed help with discipline. It came from his father's younger brother, Cyrus Marshall, who taught mathematics at Douglass. "Any time that Thurgood would carry on in class, all you had to do was tell Cy Marshall," recalled a student, "and Thurgood's father would knock his head off."[20]

In spite of all these efforts, Marshall managed to get into trouble. When he became too disruptive in class, the principal sent him to the school's basement with a copy of the United States Constitution and orders that he could not return to the classroom until he had memorized a portion of it. "Before I left that school," he later told a reporter, "I knew the entire constitution by heart."[21]

For all his pranks, Marshall had a serious side. He joined the debate team and became its star performer. The debate coach was Gough McDaniels, a black graduate of Cornell University. McDaniels encouraged the loud, cocky youngster to do lengthy research projects on topics for debate. By the time he graduated, he was in the top third of his class, was never late to class, and was absent on only one school day.[22]

Marshall's later success was due in large part to the influence of his parents. Both of them took an active interest in the lives of the children. Their older son, Aubrey, was a graduate of Howard Medical School and became a cardiac physician, and their often defiant younger son would become the lawyer who ended segregation in public education in the United States.

Norma Marshall stressed the importance of education to her children, encouraging them to be independent thinkers. Willie Marshall, who became a steward at the exclusive, all-white Gibson Island Club on the outskirts of Baltimore, imparted a piece of advice to his son: "[If] anyone calls you 'nigger,' you not only got my permission to fight him—you got my orders to fight him."[23]

Willie Marshall enjoyed going to Baltimore courtrooms in his spare time and listening to the cases being tried. In the evening, he liked to engage both his sons in arguments, using his acquired "lawyer" tactics to get them to think logically. Although Willie Marshall, with his spirited temper and his fondness for alcohol, was out of work at various times in his life, his son remembered him with fondness and respect. "He never told me to become a lawyer," Marshall once said, "but he turned me into one. He taught me to argue, challenged my logic on every point, by making me prove every statement I made, even if we were discussing the weather."[24]

A Fun-Loving College Student, 1925–1930

Following his graduation from high school in January 1925, Marshall went to work full-time as a dining-car waiter to earn money for college. His choice was Lincoln University, in Chester, Pennsylvania. His brother was already a senior there, but the family owed the school money for Aubrey's junior year. However, Marshall who had earned enough from his railroad job to pay for a year's tuition, headed for Lincoln in September 1925.

Lincoln, known as the "black" Princeton, was an elite institution. It attracted a large number of the brightest black male students in the Northeast, and many of its graduates went on to professional studies. Marshall's classmates included Benjamin Nnamdi Azikawe, a future president of Nigeria; Langston Hughes, an already established poet who came to the University in his mid-twenties to complete his studies; and Cabell ("Cab") Calloway, a friend from high school who left after two years to embark on a career as a cabaret entertainer.[25]

The spirited Marshall joined Alpha Phi Alpha (an elite fraternity of mostly light-skinned boys) and was better known as a prankster than as a serious student. In his sophomore year, Marshall and twenty-five other students were suspended for two weeks for hazing freshmen. "He was a harum-scarum youth, the loudest individual in the dormitory," recalled one of his classmates, "and apparently the least likely to succeed."[26]

His mother had wanted him to become a dentist, but he had a fight with his biology teacher and failed the course. After the fiasco in biology, he became a humanities major and proudly asserted that he never cracked a book. The statement was borne out by comments made in later years by his fellow students, who remembered that he liked to spend all night playing poker and pinochle before examinations. He took the risk because, as he told his friends, he could get a passing grade without studying—a luxury that he would not allow himself at law school. [27]

Marshall was far from a student activist during his first two years at college. In 1927, he joined the majority of his fellow students in his sociology class (to the chagrin of Langston Hughes) in voting against a student proposal to integrate Lincoln's all-white faculty. According to Hughes, the reason for the class's opposition to the plan was that "favoritism" might occur if the black faculty member belonged to one of the competing fraternities on campus, in addition to their belief that "we are all doing well as we are" and that "students would not cooperate with Negroes."[28]

An Incident at Oxford, Pennsylvania, 1927

Marshall's carefree college days came to an abrupt end a few weeks after he voted against the faculty integration plan. One night, he and six other students went to see a movie in the neighboring town of Oxford, Pennsylvania. After purchasing their tickets, they were told by the usher that they were only allowed to sit in the balcony. They refused and seated themselves in the theater's orchestra, which was reserved for whites. There, Marshall recalled hearing someone say to him: "Nigger, why don't you just get out of here and sit where you belong?"[29]

Marshall was disturbed enough by the incident to write to his parents about it:

> You can't really tell what a person like that looks like because it's just an ugly feeling that's looking at you, not a real face. We found out that they only had one fat cop in the whole town and they wouldn't have the nerve or the room in the jail to arrest all of us. But the amazing thing was that when we were leaving, we just walked out with all those older people and they didn't do anything, didn't say anything, didn't even look at us—at least, not as far as I know. I'm not sure I like being invisible, but maybe it's better than being put to shame and not able to respect yourself.[30]

The students later succeeded in desegregating the theater. "I guess that's what started the whole thing in my life," he later said.[31] In the aftermath of the incident, Marshall had a change of heart about integrating Lincoln's faculty. He led a successful student referendum at Lincoln to put pressure on the administration to hire nonwhite teachers, and in 1930 the first black professor joined the faculty.[32]

Marriage and Graduation

Marshall met his first wife, Vivian ("Buster") Burey at a restaurant in Washington, D.C., in 1928. A freshman at the University of Pennsylvania, she came from a middle-class black family. Her father was a caterer for hotels, and during the summer he catered for several country clubs across the Delaware River in southern New Jersey.[33] As the romance blossomed, her family took her to Baltimore to meet his parents. The meeting (at least according to Marshall's version of it) went well until his father's brother, Fearless Mentor Williams, interjected his opinion of his nephew. "Young lady," he said to Vivian Burey, "you ought to be aware of Thurgood. He always was a bum, he is a bum, and always will be a bum."[34] In relating this story, Marshall was asked by a skeptical journalist whether his uncle was merely joking. "Hell no," Marshall replied. "He meant every word." As the journalist pressed him for more details, Marshall offered an explanation. "Because of my reputation," he said. "Hell, when Fearless died he didn't leave me a penny. He bequeathed $36,000 to Catholic Charities."[35]

In spite of the admonition, Vivian Burey married Marshall at the First African Baptist Church in Philadelphia in September 1929. The pretty eighteen-year-old bride was three years younger than her husband. The marriage, which lasted for over twenty-five years, was marred by her inability to have children. It ended with her death from cancer in 1955.

Vivian Burey proved to be a stabilizing influence, and Marshall did better work at Lincoln than his Uncle Fearless had expected. He settled down in his last two years after an injury had forced him to miss a semester. He graduated *cum laude* in January 1930.

On his college application to Lincoln, the sixteen-year-old Marshall had been asked: "What do you plan as your life's work?" His answer was "Lawyer." The young college graduate was now ready to follow that calling.[36]

Howard Law School, 1930–1933

Following his graduation from college, Marshall worked full-time as a waiter at the Gibson Island Club in the hope of earning enough money for law school. He wanted to attend the University of Maryland Law School, located a few blocks from the Marshall home in West Baltimore. However, this choice turned out to be unrealistic. Only two black students had graduated from the law school, and it had not admitted any black student since the 1890s. As a result, he did not even bother to apply there.

In spite of his earnings at the club, he could not afford the tuition at one of the northern law schools which admitted black students. The only alternative was Howard Law School, which had a modest tuition and was located within commuting distance in neighboring Washington, D.C.

Marshall began his studies at Howard in the fall of 1930, when the school was expanding its academic program and had abandoned its evening program in order to concentrate on the education of its full-time day students. The school was under the rigorous leadership of its vice dean, Charles Hamilton Houston, a Phi Beta Kappa graduate of Amherst College and the first black student to be selected to serve on the editorial board of the *Harvard Law Review.* As a teacher, Houston tolerated no nonsense from his students and expected them to share his commitment to the use of law as an instrument for social change. Marshall idolized Houston and became a serious student for the first time in his life. He would steadfastly maintain in later years that everything he knew about the law was pounded into him by this man.[37]

Marshall received excellent grades in his first year and was rewarded with a job in the school library. The job lengthened his school day to 8:00 P.M. and sometimes beyond, but it paid for his tuition and books. As before, he got up at five in the morning for his daily commute, walked a considerable distance to the station, caught the early train to Washington, and took the last train back to Baltimore.[38]

On many nights, Marshall stayed late in the library, where Houston often worked with NAACP members on cases seeking to end discrimination. It was only a matter of time before Marshall was given assignments to assist them in their research. His presence was noted by Walter White, the executive director of the NAACP:

> There was a lanky, brash young senior law student who was always present. I used to wonder at his presence and sometimes was amazed at his assertiveness in positions [taken] by Charlie [Houston] and the other lawyers. But I soon learned of his great value to the case in doing everything he was asked, from research on obscure legal opinions to foraging for coffee and sandwiches.[39]

Marshall became one of the survivors at Howard. The freshman class started out with thirty-five students. By the time of graduation, only six students remained. Marshall, who had finished first in his class at the end of every year, graduated *magna cum laude* in 1933. Before graduation, Marshall was offered a fellowship by Dean Roscoe Pound of Harvard Law School. The fellowship would have enabled him to earn a doctor of jurisprudence degree. But he was eager to start out on his own, so he turned it down.

Learning the Ropes, 1933–1935

Following his graduation from Howard, Marshall set up a small office on the fringe of downtown Baltimore, not far away from the University of Maryland Law School. He had intended to specialize in labor and antitrust law, but clients were scarce during these Depression years. The city's African-American population, which was heavily concentrated in domestic service and common labor, was hard hit by the economic downturn. More than 40 percent of Baltimore's black population was on relief, as compared to 13 percent of the white population.[40]

Marshall took whatever clients he could find and managed to hire a secretary at $7.50 per week. It was a hard struggle for both of them. "One day I'd bring two lunches, and the next day my secretary would bring two lunches," he recalled, "and sometimes we'd be the only people in the office for weeks at a time."[41]

It was lucky for Marshall that he knew how to relax and have fun—a needed diversion for him on innumerable occasions in the course of his professional life. "Once in a while, I got a good fee," he stated. "Then my secretary would immediately call her husband and I'd call Buster, and we'd get the biggest steak in town to celebrate."[42]

Marshall displayed tremendous vitality during this difficult period, embarking on a course of action that greatly improved his prospects. He learned how to maneuver his way within the white power system, courted the good will of the lawyers and judges he met with his personal charm and deferential manner, prepared his cases with care and dedication, honed his legal skills in court, and built up such a solid reputation that many white judges (including bigots) called upon him to represent black clients in order to protect themselves against possible charges of racial bias.[43]

But Marshall had a score to settle on another matter. In recalling this period in his life, he stated that the first thing he wanted to do when he got out of law school "was to get even with Maryland for not letting me go to its law school."[44]

A Role in *Murray* v. *Maryland* (1936)

Marshall did not have to wait long for his revenge. In December 1934, Donald Gaines Murray, a black graduate of Amherst, applied to the University of Maryland Law School and was rejected. A local attorney brought the matter to the attention of Houston. Aware that his former student was keenly interested in the case, Houston called upon Marshall for assistance.

Although Marshall would play down his part in the case later known as *Murray* v. *Maryland* (1936) by asserting that Houston did all the important work, he was more involved than he acknowledged. In April 1935, he helped Houston with a petition that they both filed in state court requesting that Murray be admitted to the law school. Two months later, the state judge ruled in favor of Murray, but Maryland appealed the decision.[45]

Marshall subsequently took two weeks off from his law practice to assist Houston with the brief. A hard taskmaster, Houston returned Marshall's first draft with the notation "It needs to be thoroughly reworked." Under the painstaking guidance of Houston, Marshall restructured his arguments to make them more compelling, focused on case law and investigations that initially had seemed only peripheral to the issue, and learned to appreciate the great value of attention to details.[46]

When the case was finally argued before the Court of Appeals in Maryland in 1936, Marshall joined Houston in the oral argument. Houston's presentation was far more polished, but his young associate got to the core of the case when he told the court, "What's at stake here is more than the rights of my client; it's the moral commitment stated in our country's creed." Their efforts were successful, and the court directed the University of Maryland to admit Murray to its law school.[47]

A Job at the NAACP

Marshall's three years as a solo practitioner came to an end in 1936 when Houston, who had resigned that year as vice dean at Howard and relocated to New York to become legal counsel to the NAACP, asked him to join the staff as assistant special counsel. The job was attractive to Marshall because of the chance for greater financial security. The NAACP had agreed to pay him $2,400 per year, and he accepted the offer.

In his new job as assistant special counsel, Marshall assisted Houston in many cases, including *Missouri ex. rel. Gaines* v. *Canada* (1938), a Supreme

Court case in which a black student gained admittance to the University of Missouri Law School. An unexpected opportunity opened up that same year with Houston's resignation as legal counsel. Marshall, who was thirty years old, was chosen to succeed him. In 1939—the same year he was admitted to practice before the Supreme Court—the NAACP set up the Legal Defense and Education Fund (or the Fund, as it came to be known) as a separate entity, and Marshall became its director-counsel the following year. He held that post until 1961, when he resigned from the NAACP to join the federal bench. At the time of his resignation, he had won twenty-nine of the thirty-two cases he had argued before the Supreme Court and had become known as "Mr. Civil Rights."[48]

Marshall's work for the NAACP frequently took him on trips to the South. During the 1940s and 1950s, he traveled 50,000 miles each year to obtain plaintiffs for future lawsuits and to encourage local black and white attorneys to represent the NAACP on a pro bono basis. He also investigated lynchings, filed lawsuits on behalf of black defendants, and argued cases in Southern courts. He sometimes handled over fifty lower court cases at a given time, in addition to his Supreme Court work and his administrative duties as director-counsel of the Fund. It has been remarked that the volume of his responsibilities was three to four times greater than the normal workload carried by a practicing attorney.[49]

During these years, Marshall made a lot of friends, as well as enemies. He faced a considerable amount of danger to his personal safety, but he tried to handle it in a nonconfrontational manner. He told his associates that he went to the South as a lawyer rather than as a demonstrator, adding that he learned to wrap his rights in cellophane and put them in his pocket.[50]

Part of Marshall's success in his work was due to his ability to attract—and keep—a core of dedicated lawyers at the Fund, as well as a group of unpaid volunteer attorneys. In discussing the kinds of skills he displayed during the NAACP's battle to end segregation during these years, one of his biographers noted the following:

> Thurgood Marshall was a great lawyer. His considerable courtroom skills, though they were not irrelevant to his greatness, were secondary. Those who know him understand his wisdom, the superb quality of his judgments about life and law. As general counsel in the NAACP's campaign against school segregation, he assembled a staff and a "kitchen cabinet" which presented him with the ingenious and innovative arguments that the litigation needed. Marshall then selected, almost always correctly and without hesitation, the set of arguments that would work best. But Marshall had another quality that contributed to—indeed, may have been the prerequisite to—his greatness. He was a great politician. Faced with conflicting demands from disparate elements in his constituency, Marshall was able to unite the constituency behind a program with which many had initially disagreed.[51]

Due to his heavy caseload, he argued only six of his thirty-two Supreme Court cases alone, and he made certain that proper credit was given those who assisted him. "I never hesitated to pick other people's brains—brains I didn't have," he stated.[52]

Brown v. *Board of Education,* 1950–1955

Prior to 1950, Marshall believed it would be futile to attack segregation in elementary and secondary schools. However, after winning two major victories in the Supreme Court that year on the admission of black students to graduate schools, he thought it might be possible to wage an all-out attack on segregation in public education. Several weeks after the Court's decisions were announced, he persuaded the NAACP to adopt a resolution stating that its priorities in the future would be "aimed at obtaining education on a non-segregated basis and that no relief other than that would be acceptable."[53]

The case that he selected to launch this attack was *Briggs* v. *Elliot.* It originated in Clarendon County, South Carolina, in 1950, when Harry Briggs Jr. and eighteen other parents went to the United States District Court to demand that the segregated schools in the county be brought up to the level of white schools. The plaintiffs were backed by the local branch of the NAACP, and Marshall went to South Carolina to represent them. At the trial, which began in May 1951, he not only asked for school equalization but also urged the court to strike down the South Carolina segregation statute on the grounds that it was a violation of the equal protection clause of the Fourteenth Amendment. The District Court ruled against him, and he appealed the decision to the Supreme Court.

By the time the case reached the Supreme Court in 1952, four other school segregation cases were argued at the same time. In addition to the South Carolina case, there were cases in Virginia, Delaware, Kansas, and the District of Columbia. The cases were consolidated and became known as *Oliver Brown et al.* v. *Board of Education of Topeka, Kansas.* The NAACP sponsored four of the cases, but decided not to handle the one in the District of Columbia. The latter raised a different issue because the Fourteenth Amendment's guarantee of "equal protection" of the laws was binding only on state jurisdictions.[54]

The writing of the brief led to controversy within the NAACP. Despite vigorous objections, Marshall decided not to assert that *Plessy* was bad law per se, but got around it by implication. Another controversial move was Marshall's decision to file a "Brandeis Brief," making use of studies by social scientists like Dr. Kenneth B. Clark showing the harmful effects of segregation on black children. This idea was first suggested by NAACP attorney Robert C. Carter, and Marshall supported it by maintaining that there was no reason not to use sociology, psychology, or anything else that might help to end segregation.[55] Marshall managed the different factions with characteristic skill. "You had to be impressed most by the firmness with which he was in charge," noted Attorney Charles Black, one of the NAACP's advisers. "He could be the next thing to autocratic," Black stated, "but he did it always in a nice way."[56]

At the time the oral arguments were made in December 1952, Marshall had the assistance of an integrated staff of excellent lawyers: Carter, his top assistant and a future federal judge, opened with the Brown argument; Marshall followed up with the South Carolina case; Spottswood W. Robinson, III, a Houston protégé from Howard Law School, did the Virginia case; and Marshall, with the assistance of Jack Greenberg (his future successor as director-counsel of the Fund) handled the Delaware case.[57] The lead opposing counsel was seventy-nine-year-old John W. Davis, a former solicitor general and the Democratic presidential candidate in 1924. He was regarded as the leading appellate lawyer in the country, who had argued approximately 140 cases before the Supreme Court. His admirers included Thurgood Marshall, who had sometimes cut classes at Howard to watch Davis argue before the high Court. At times, Davis was brilliant during the oral arguments in 1952 and the following year, but he met his match in Marshall. The case turned out to be his last hurrah. He died one year after Brown was decided.[58]

At the conclusion of the oral arguments in December, the Court was sharply divided. In June 1953, it directed the parties to return for a second round of oral arguments, instructing them to answer five questions. These questions primarily dealt with the intentions of the framers of the Fourteenth Amendment and whether the Court had the power to abolish segregation.

The Court also asked the Justice Department to participate in the reargument. Although President Dwight D. Eisenhower had misgivings about federally mandated integration, he allowed the Justice Department full discretion in its preparations for the brief. Philip Elman of the solicitor's general's office was given the job to write the brief by Attorney General Herbert R. Brownell Jr.[59]

The composition of the Court had changed dramatically by the time it was ready to reconsider *Brown* in December 1953. Three months earlier, Chief Justice Fred Vinson Jr. had died suddenly of a heart attack and been replaced by Earl Warren, governor of California. Marshall had figured correctly that Vinson had favored the other side. In speaking of the late chief justice, Marshall said: "We knew he was against us, but we managed to get it reargued. And then he died. The Lord was on my side."[60]

In November 1953, the NAACP responded to the five questions posed by the Court with a 256-page brief. Its main argument was that the Court had previously ruled that discrimination was unconstitutional, reminding the Court that if a state had "deprive[d] a Negro [of] a right which he would have freely enjoyed if he had been white, then that state's action violated the Fourteenth Amendment." Accordingly, the brief asserted that the Court had the right to abolish segregation in public education—a position echoed in Elman's brief for the Justice Department.[61]

In response to the question posed about the intentions of the framers of the Fourteenth Amendment about segregation, Marshall had an ingenious argument based on the work done by a group of leading scholars he had recruited in the fall of 1953 to research the question. Although he stretched the point by his selective use of the data regarding the writing of the Fourteenth Amendment, Marshall maintained in the brief that "the framers intended that the

Amendment would deprive the states of the power to make any racial distinction in the enjoyment of civil rights."[62]

The next hurdle was the oral arguments, which began in December 1953. In a stirring argument delivered at the conclusion of his rebuttal, Marshall implored the Court to enforce the Constitution of the United States of America with regard to equal treatment of all of its people:

> I got the feeling on hearing the discussion yesterday that when you put a white child in a school with a whole lot of colored children, the child would fall apart or something. Everybody knows that is not true.
>
> Those same kids in Virginia and South Carolina—and I have seen them do it— they play in the streets together, they play on their farms together, they go down the road together, they separate to go to school, they come out of school and play ball together. They have to be separated in school.
>
> There is some magic to it. You can have them voting together, you can have them not restricted because of law in the houses they live in. You can have them going to the same state university and the same college, but if they go to elementary and high school, the world will fall apart. . . .
>
> So whichever way it is done, the only way that this Court can decide this case in opposition to our position, is that there must be some reason which gives the state the right to make a classification that they can make in regard to nothing else in regard to Negroes, and we submit the only way to arrive at this decision is to find that for some reason Negroes are inferior to all other human beings.
>
> Nobody will stand in the Court and urge that, and in order to arrive at the decision that they want us to arrive at, there would have to be some recognition of a reason why of all the multitudinous groups of people in this country you have to single out Negroes and give them this separate treatment.
>
> It can't be because of slavery in the past, because there are very few groups in this country that haven't had slavery some place back in the history of their groups. It can't be color because there are Negroes as white as the drifted snow, with blue eyes, and they are just as segregated as the colored man.
>
> The only thing it can be is an inherent determination that the people who were formerly in slavery, regardless of anything else, shall be kept as near that stage as is possible, and now is the time, we submit, that this Court should make it clear that that is not what our Constitution stands for. [63]

Marshall was in Mobile, Alabama, on business for the NAACP on May 16, 1953, when he received a telephone call. The caller (never identified by Marshall) told him he might want to be in Washington, D.C., the following day. Concluding that the Court had finally reached a decision in *Brown*, he took the next plane to Washington.[64]

Since the Court had not announced that it would render its decision in *Brown* on May 17, 1954, some reporters began to think it unusual that the spectators that day included Attorney General Brownell; former Secretary of State Dean Acheson; black attorneys James M. Nabrit Jr. and George E.C. Hayes, who had handled the Washington, D.C., case; John W. Davis; and Thurgood Marshall. The reason for their presence became apparent at 12:52 P.M., when Chief Justice Warren picked up a document and said, "I have for announcement the judgment and opinion of the Court in *Oliver Brown* v. *Board of Education of Topeka*."[65]

Speaking for a unanimous Court, Warren started out by summarizing the cases' legal and historical background. It was not until he was two-thirds of the way through the fourteen-page opinion that the Court's opinion became clear. After noting that "we cannot turn the clock back to . . . 1896 when *Plessy* v. *Ferguson* was written," Warren made use of the sociological argument presented by Marshall and his staff in 1952 to state how segregation deprived black children of equal educational opportunities:

> To separate them from others of similar age and qualifications solely because of their race generates a feeling of inferiority as to their status in the community that may affect their hearts and minds in a way unlikely ever to be undone. . . . Whatever may have been the extent of psychological knowledge at the time of *Plessy* v. *Ferguson,* this finding is amply supported by modern authority. Any language in Plessy . . . contrary to this finding is rejected.[66]

In this conclusion, the Court refused to overturn the *Plessy* doctrine as being unconstitutional but contended that its application to public education was invalid:

> We conclude that in the field of public education the doctrine of "separate but equal" has no place. Separate educational facilities are inherently unequal. Therefore, we hold that the plaintiffs and others similarly situated . . . are, by reason of the segregation complained of, deprived of the equal protection of the laws guaranteed by the Fourteenth Amendment.[67]

Once the decision was announced, the justices filed out of the courtroom. Marshall was surrounded by reporters, but he turned first to Nabrit and Hayes and said, "We hit the jackpot."[68] When he was finished talking to reporters, Marshall impulsively picked up the son of Joe Greenhill, a white assistant attorney general in Texas who had taken his family on a visit to the Court that day. Marshall put the boy on his shoulders and ran down the corridor of the Supreme Court building with him. "He was having a good time, we were having a good time, and to hell with dignity," Joe Greenhill later said. "He just won a biggie."[69]

The day would always be a big one in Marshall's life. He later said that the decision was a turning point in the history of his people and "probably did more than anything else to awaken the Negro from his apathy to demanding his rights to equality."[70]

After the announcement of its decision, the Court asked the parties to return for rearguments to discuss the implementation of the ruling. The reargument took place in April 1955, and on May 31 the Chief Justice delivered the unanimous opinion on the Supreme Court. The Court's opinion ran only seven paragraphs and never mentioned the words "segregation" or "desegregation." It did specify that it was not going to usurp local prerogatives in the matter and urged that the parties go forward "with all deliberate speed" to carry out the Court's 1954 decision.

The Court failed to fix a date for the end of segregation, as Marshall had requested in the reargument made in April 1955. It also failed to require the defendant school boards to submit a desegregation plan within ninety days, as the government had urged in the Justice Department brief. But it did begin the process of integration in public education and changed the whole social fabric of American society in the process.[71]

Remarriage, 1955

Several months after his victory in *Brown*, Marshall learned that his wife had terminal cancer. It had been a troubled marriage, but he dropped many of his NAACP commitments to attend to her in the months prior to her death. She passed away on February 11, 1955, her forty-fourth birthday.

His second wife was Cecilia ("Cissy") Suyat, whom he married ten months later. Born in 1927 in Hawaii to parents of Philippine descent, she had gone to New York in 1947 to study stenography at Columbia University and later went to work as a secretary at the NAACP. She bore him two sons: Thurgood ("Goody") Jr., born in 1956, who went on to practice law, and John, born in 1958, who became a United States marshal.[72]

NAACP Activities, 1951–1961

Marshall's remarriage was one of many changes in this pivotal decade of his life. In 1951, he had gone to Korea and Japan on behalf of the NAACP to investigate complaints made by black soldiers of discriminatory treatment in court-martial convictions; he was able to win reduced sentences for twenty-two of the forty men convicted.[73]

A more controversial (albeit secret) role was his association with J. Edgar Hoover, director of the Federal Bureau of Investigation (FBI). During the 1950s, Marshall gave information to the FBI about the efforts of the Communist Party to infiltrate the NAACP. Although this period was a time when any alleged communist influence could have discredited the NAACP, the subsequent release of this information by the FBI in December 1996 took the public and the legal profession by surprise.[74]

In other respects, Marshall continued to work at his fast pace at the NAACP. A substantial part of his work now focused on litigating issues of compliance with the mandate in *Brown*. After 1954, he argued seven school cases before the Supreme Court on avoidance or resistance issues, including *Aaron* v. *Cooper* (1958), in which the Court ruled against the school board in Little Rock, Arkansas, by holding that its action in 1957 in resisting desegregation in its public schools was a violation of the law of the land. Marshall also worked on cases filed by the NAACP on the exclusion of black people from public facilities, and he won two Supreme Court cases—*Mayor and City Council of Baltimore City* v. *Dawson* (1955) and *Holmes* v. *City of Atlanta* (1955)—striking down racial restrictions.[75]

The civil rights movement in the 1950s gave Marshall and his staff another role to play. The Montgomery bus boycott, which began in December 1955, ended in triumph as the NAACP won a Supreme Court case, *Gayle* v. *Browder* (1956), declaring unconstitutional the Alabama law segregating passengers on public transportation. While Marshall was not pleased at the direct action tactics of the civil rights protesters (he preferred going to court as opposed to staging confrontations, which he felt could be counterproductive), he won two important Supreme Court cases—*Boynton* v. *Virginia* (1960) and *Garner* v. *Louisiana* (1961)—on the right to stage "sit-in" demonstrations at lunch counters in the South.[76]

Second Circuit Appointment, 1961

The election of President John F. Kennedy in 1960 changed the political landscape as far as Marshall was concerned. The Democratic Party sought to expand its base by appointing blacks to office, and Marshall's name came up in all discussions regarding nominees to the federal judiciary. It was not the first time Marshall had been considered for such a position. In 1949, President Harry S. Truman had wanted to appoint him to the federal bench, but backed down in the wake of opposition from black Democrats in Harlem, who objected to a nominee without any ties to their local party organization.[77]

As talk of a court appointment by Kennedy began to surface, Marshall realized that a judgeship would mean not only a rise in status, but a salary that would be considerably in excess of what he had received at the NAACP. Nevertheless, he had reservations about leaving his job. As he told a reporter from the *New York Times,*

> I had to fight it out with myself. By then I had built up a staff—a damned good staff—an excellent board, and the backing that would let them go ahead. And when one has the opportunity to serve his government, he should think twice before passing it up.[78]

He later followed up this statement with remarks made to a reporter from the *Washington Post.* "I've always felt that assault troops never occupy the town," he said. "I figured after the school decision, the assault was over for me. It was time to let newer minds take over."[79]

In 1961, the Kennedy administration offered him an appointment as a federal trial judge. Marshall told the president's brother, Attorney General Robert F. Kennedy, that he did not want to be a trial judge because "my fuse was too short." "It's that or nothing," Kennedy told him. But Marshall was unwilling to accept the offer. "Well, I've been dealing with nothing all my life," he said. "There's nothing new in that."[80] He stated that he wanted to serve only on the appellate court. When the Kennedy administration balked at the appellate court appointment on the grounds that too many Southern Democrats would be antagonized, Marshall went to work. He drummed up support in the black press and among civil rights leaders whose support had been crucial in

Kennedy's narrow election victory in 1960, and the president and his brother were forced to acquiesce.

On September 23, 1961, Marshall was nominated to the Court of Appeals for the Second Circuit, which covered New York, Connecticut, and Vermont. Aside from the Supreme Court, it was regarded as the most important Appellate Court in the federal system at that time. Marshall's appointment was held up in the Senate Judiciary Committee for eleven months, but he was finally confirmed by the Senate on September 12, 1962. By a vote of fifty-four to sixteen, he became the second black justice (the first was William H. Hastie, named to the Third Circuit by President Truman in 1949) appointed to the federal bench.[81]

Second Circuit Judge, 1961–1965

Marshall served on the Second Circuit from 1961 to 1965, and established a reputation as a solid though unspectacular appellate judge. At times, he had to plow his way through business and tax cases because of his unfamiliarity with technical details, but he took pains to master the intricacies of the cases, from tax to admiralty law. In philosophical terms, he favored letting the government exercise full discretionary powers in economic matters, while limiting its power to restrict First Amendment freedoms.[82]

While he enjoyed a cordial relationship with his fellow judges, he was criticized by some of them for his inability to sympathize with the prosecution in a number of cases and advised to examine litigation from the viewpoint of the government in order to gain a broader perspective.[83]

Nevertheless, his overall record was impressive. During his four years on the bench, he wrote 118 opinions, none of which was overturned, and some of his dissenting opinions were later adopted as majority opinions by the Supreme Court. Among his rulings were that loyalty oaths required of New York teachers were unconstitutional and that stringent protections be placed on the double jeopardy provisions of the Constitution.[84]

Solicitor General, 1965–1967

On July 8, 1965, Archibald Cox told Attorney General Nicholas de B. Katzenbach that he was resigning as solicitor general of the United States to rejoin the faculty at Harvard Law School. The job of solicitor general is a highly coveted position, for it consists of arguing the government's cases before the Supreme Court and determining the small number of the thousands of lower court federal cases that the government would appeal to the Court.[85]

On July 12, 1965, Marshall received a telephone call at a New York City restaurant from President Lyndon B. Johnson, who asked him to become the new solicitor general. An astonished Marshall told the president that he needed time to think about the offer, and Johnson told him to take all the time he needed. The next day, Johnson called back and asked for his decision. Marshall reminded the president that he had told him to take his time in considering the offer. "You've had it," Johnson snapped. In a voice breaking with emotion, Marshall told the president that he would be pleased to serve in that position.[86]

The job was a financial sacrifice for Marshall. He gave up a salary of $33,000 plus the security of a lifetime appointment on the federal bench for a position that only paid $28,500. But he realized that the job could be a stepping-stone to the Supreme Court, and he was willing to take the risk.

In contrast to his appointment to the Second Circuit, Marshall was quickly approved by the Senate Judiciary Committee and by the entire Senate on August 11, 1965. In taking his new position, he became the nation's thirty-third solicitor general and the third-highest-ranking lawyer (behind the attorney general and the deputy attorney general) in the government.

Although Marshall would refer to this position as "the best job I ever had," he faced some serious challenges. As he told journalist Carl Rowan in his unpretentious speaking manner,

> I got real shook up when I read that Cox had lain awake every night before a major case, sick to the point of wanting to vomit. I learned that other solicitors general had panicked at the thought of speaking for the country before those nine men. Even though I had been before the Court as a civil rights lawyer, my knees were knocking that first day when I put on that outrageous outfit and stood listening to Chief Justice Warren declare somberly, "The Court welcomes you." But I soon found out that I was dealing with, or against, people of pretty much the same abilities as I had, and I learned to relax.[87]

Marshall won fourteen of the nineteen cases he argued in which the government was a party or in which it had an interest as an amicus curiae. As might be expected, he won solid victories in civil rights cases, particularly in matters relating to the interpretation of the Civil Rights Act of 1964 and the Voting Rights Act of 1965. But he also was successful in cases involving civil suits, labor-management relations, corporate structures and mergers, and internal revenue violations—areas in which he supposedly had little interest.[88]

Associate Justice of the Supreme Court

At the beginning of 1967, Lyndon Johnson, having made up his mind to appoint Marshall to the Supreme Court, deftly planned his move. In February, he nominated Ramsay Clark as attorney general. Clark accepted the nomination with the knowledge that his father, Associate Supreme Court Justice Tom Clark, would have to give up his seat on the Court in order to avoid the appearance of a conflict of interest. The elder Clark (who was not averse to retiring) submitted his resignation on June 13.

The next day, Ramsay Clark went to see Marshall at his office. "The boss wants to see you," he told him. Marshall hurried to the White House and Johnson wasted no time in stating the purpose of their meeting. "I'm going to put you on the court," he said. "Well, thank you, sir," Marshall replied. Johnson and Marshall then went to the Rose Garden of the White House, where the president announced Marshall's appointment:

> He has argued nineteen cases in the Supreme Court since becoming Solicitor General. Prior to that time he had argued some thirty-two cases. Statisticians tell me that probably only one or two other living men have argued as many cases before the Court—and perhaps less than half a dozen in all the history of the Nation. . . .
>
> I believe he has already earned his place in history, but I think it will be greatly enhanced by his service on the Court. I believe he earned that appointment; he deserves the appointment. He is best qualified by training and by very valuable service to the country. I believe it is the right thing to do, the right time to do it, the right man and the right place.[89]

Afterwards, they returned to the Oval Office, where Marshall called his wife. Before the conversation could begin, the president grabbed the telephone: "Cissy—Lyndon Johnson," he said. "I've just put your husband on the Supreme Court."[90]

The confirmation hearings were bitter. The Senate held five days of hearings in July. Marshall was given a hard time by Southern Democrats, who grilled him about key decisions of the Warren Court and esoteric matters regarding the Thirteenth and Fourteenth Amendments. Marshall refused to be ruffled by the tone of the questions, and the Senate later confirmed him on August 30 by a vote of sixty-nine to eleven. The entire confirmation process had taken a total of seventy-eight days before the vote, which later led constitutional scholar Stephen Carter (a law clerk to Marshall on the Supreme Court) to complain that "no one has ever faced quite so vicious an onslaught as Thurgood Marshall, [who was] forced to sit through a demeaning constitutional history trivia quiz in order to demonstrate his intellectual acumen and gain Senate approval."[91]

Marshall took his seat on the Court in 1967, when the liberals were in the majority. Nevertheless, the Court, changing dramatically within two years, was later dominated by conservatives. At the time of Marshall's resignation in 1991, the liberals could usually muster only three votes and were overruled in most of the cases decided by the Court.

The election of President Richard M. Nixon in 1968 helped to bring about this transformation, notably when Warren resigned in 1969 and was replaced by Warren E. Burger. The new chief justice was far less liberal than Warren. He served until 1986, when he was succeeded by Associate Justice William H. Rehnquist, who was considered even more conservative.

As the Court shifted to a conservative stance, Marshall became more outspoken in his criticism of it. Although he gave no interviews in his first twenty years on the Court, he bluntly criticized the Court at public forums for backtracking on the rulings made in the Warren era. In 1987, he decided against participating in the celebrations marking the bicentennial of the United States Constitution; he was quoted as saying that if he had been present at the signing of the Constitution in 1987, he could have attended only "wearing breeches and serving tea." His harshest words on this subject were made in a speech delivered in May 1987 at the Hawaii meeting of the San Francisco Patent and Trademark Law Association, in which he blasted the "racist" founding fathers for failing to abolish slavery at the time the constitution was written and charged that the "government was defective from the start."[92] Four months later, he again made headline news. In the first interview that he gave as a Supreme Court justice, Marshall made blustering remarks about the treatment of blacks throughout American history and expressed disdain for President Ronald Reagan's record on civil rights.[93]

Marshall's outspokenness was further evident in his personal relationships with his judicial colleagues. Unlike the role he had assumed in the early part of his career, Marshall did not feel compelled to overcome his "outsider" status and took pride in asserting his own individuality. Refusing to conform to the norms expected of a federal judge, he made regular trips to racetracks and Atlantic City casinos. His staff made repeated efforts to get him to dress and act in a manner that was more in keeping with his position, but to no avail. As a result, it sometimes seemed that the prankster of years past had returned to the hallowed halls of the federal bench. He delighted in using salty language, sometimes addressing his judicial colleagues as "baby," including the austere chief justice, Warren Burger. "What's shakin', Chiefy baby?" was Marshall's favorite greeting to him.[94]

Although he shared a warm friendship with Associate Justice William J. Brennan, Marshall frequently stood alone on the Court—especially when the liberals were in the minority. In his full twelve terms, he rarely spoke in oral arguments, was not a consensus builder, and preferred to stake out his own positions in separate opinions rather than to sacrifice any of his beliefs in an effort to compromise with the majority. This choice was deliberate on his part. It enabled him to become part of the conscience of the Court, providing him with a platform that made it possible for him to speak passionately on behalf of the rights of blacks, women, the aged, the poor, and inmates on death row.[95]

During his tenure on the Court, Marshall wrote 363 dissenting opinions and 322 written opinions for the majority. His dissents, written after 1969 (as a member of the majority liberal wing from 1967 to 1969, he had concentrated on using his negotiating skills to convince the conservative minority to collaborate on the issuance of unanimous decisions), became so important to him that he asked prospective law clerks whether they liked to write dissenting opinions. "If they said no," Marshall stated, "they didn't get the job."[96]

At his retirement, he was the staunchest opponent on the Court of the death penalty. The final opinion of his career came in the last decision of the October 1990–1991 term in a case dealing with rights of a defendant on death row. In his dissent in *Payne* v. *Tennessee* (1991)—a decision that overturned two earlier rulings of the Court on capital punishment—Marshall wrote that "cast aside today [by the decision] are those condemned to face society's ultimate penalty," and he expressed apprehension that the majority would "squander the authority and legitimacy of this Court as a protector of the powerless."[97]

In the 1980s, Marshall began to be discouraged about his own role on the Court. During this period, President Ronald Reagan nominated three conservatives—Sandra Day O'Connor, Antonin Scalia, and Anthony Kennedy—all of whom were confirmed by the Senate. The final blow occurred in 1990 with the resignation of Associate Justice Brennan, his best friend on the Court and his closest liberal ally.

Since a Supreme Court judgeship is a lifetime appointment, Marshall had repeatedly said, "I was appointed to a life term, and I intend to serve it." But plagued by ill health and a sense of frustration at his inability to affect the outcome of the Court's decisions, he changed his mind.[98] For over a decade, there had been speculation on Capitol Hill about how long Marshall, who had been in failing health, could hold onto his seat on the Court. In 1976, he had suffered a mild heart attack and was hospitalized in later years for a series of illnesses. He was further plagued by failing hearing and a loss of vision due to glaucoma. A serious problem arose in 1987, when he was treated for a potentially dangerous blood clot in his right foot. Three years later, he was in the hospital again following a fall in the lobby of a Chicago hotel while attending a convention of the American Bar Association.[99]

His illnesses had led his critics to hope that he would be forced to resign. As early as 1970, President Nixon had asked for a medical report on him following his admission to Bethesda Naval Hospital for an appendectomy. When Marshall learned about the inquiry, he took his medical file from a hospital attendant and wrote in bold letters, "Not Yet!"[100]

As he approached his eighty-third birthday, he finally put the rumors to rest. On June 26, 1991, he took his colleagues on the Court by surprise at their final conference of the term by telling them that he would retire. His announcement stunned the other justices and led to a warm response. He received a bear hug and an "Oh, Thurgood" from Chief Justice Rehnquist, whom he greatly admired, despite their ideological differences. Justice O'Connor had another reaction. She wept at the news.[101]

The next day, he made the announcement at a press conference. When asked by a reporter why he was retiring, Marshall replied: "What's wrong with me? I'm old. I'm getting old and coming apart." When asked to assess his career on the Court, he offered the following comment:

> I don't know what legacy I left. It's up to the people. I guess you could say, "He did what he could with what he had." I have given fifty years to it, and if that is not enough, God bless them.[102]

Death of a Legend, 1993

Following his retirement, Marshall made only a few public appearances. Confined to a wheelchair and speaking hoarsely, barely above a whisper, he could still move an audience. In 1992, he spoke at an awards presentation at the American Bar Association annual meeting. He departed from his prepared text to delight the audience with a series of anecdotes, ranging from warm-up jokes to a poignant story about the early days of the civil rights movement. The story concerned a black laborer in Little Rock, Arkansas, who asked Marshall if he believed in life after death. When Marshall asked the man why he was so interested in reincarnation, the man replied that he only wanted to come back as a white man. "I saw some of my people just lost all hope," Marshall told the audience. He went on to state that the opportunity to give them hope had become central to his life's work.[103]

On January 14, 1993, eighteen months after his retirement, Marshall died at Bethesda Naval Hospital at the age of eighty-four. The cause was heart failure. He was buried at Arlington National Cemetery. Tributes to him came from all parts of the nation. But one of the most moving statements had already been made by Associate Justice O'Connor. Taking note of the occasion of his retirement from the Supreme Court, Justice O'Connor had written:

> I recall his unwavering commitment to the poor, the accused, and the downtrodden, and his constant, impassioned refutation of the death penalty. More than that, though, I think of the raconteur himself. Occasionally, at Conference meetings, I still catch myself looking expectantly for his raised brow and his twinkling eye, hoping to hear, just once more, another story that would, by and by, perhaps change the way I see the world.[104]

But Thurgood Marshall will not be remembered for his stories. His work was his legacy, and he arguably had more of an impact upon American society than any other lawyer in history.

Notes

1. Quoted in Michael D. Davis and Hunter R. Clark, *Thurgood Marshall: Warrior at the Bar, Rebel on the Bench* (New York: Birch Lane Press, 1992), 8; Bob Woodward and Scott Armstrong, *The Brethren: Inside the Supreme Court* (New York: Simon and Schuster, 1979; reprinted, New York: Avon Books, 1981), 64.

2. Glen M. Darbyshire, "Clerking for Justice Marshall," *ABA Journal* 77 (September 1991): 50; quoted in "Chronicle," *New York Times,* November 17, 1998, B7.

3. Stuart Taylor Jr., "Plain Truth from the People's Lawyer," *Legal Times,* July 1, 1991, 32.

4. Quoted in Mark V. Tushnet, *Making Constitutional Law: Thurgood Marshall and the Supreme Court, 1961–1991* (New York: Oxford University Press, 1997), 4–5.

5. Juan Williams, *Thurgood Marshall: American Revolutionary* (New York: Times Books, 1998), 80.

6. Ibid., 131–142; Davis and Clark, *Thurgood Marshall,* 105–119; Carl T. Rowan, *Dream Makers, Dream Breakers: The World of Justice Thurgood Marshall* (Boston: Little, Brown, 1993), 98–123.

7. Quoted in Darbyshire, "Clerking for Justice Marshall," 51.

8. Quoted in Neil A. Lewis, "Marshall Urges Bush to Pick 'The Best,'" *New York Times,* June 29, 1991, Section 1, 8.

9. Sidney E. Zion, "Thurgood Marshall Takes a New 'Tush-Tush' Job," *New York Times Magazine,* August 22, 1965, 70–71.

10. Williams, *Thurgood Marshall,* 369; Woodward and Armstrong, *The Brethren,* 214.

11. Stuart Taylor Jr., "Glimpses of the Least Pretentious of Men," *Legal Times,* February 8, 1993, 35.

12. Quoted ibid.

13. Quoted in Williams, *Thurgood Marshall,* 388–389.

14. Quoted ibid., 365.

15. Tushnet, *Making Constitutional Law,* 5.

16. Quoted in Davis and Clark, *Thurgood Marshall,* 30.

17. Williams, *Thurgood Marshall,* 19.

18. Ibid., 22, 26.

19. Ibid., 24–34.

20. Quoted ibid., 35.

21. Quoted ibid.

22. Quoted ibid., 36, 39.

23. Quoted in Davis and Clark, *Thurgood Marshall,* 30.

24. Ibid., 38.

25. Ibid., 43.

26. Quoted in Williams, *Thurgood Marshall,* 42.

27. Rowan, *Dream Makers,* 43.

28. Williams, *Thurgood Marshall,* 48.

29. Quoted in Davis and Clark, *Thurgood Marshall,* 44.

30. Quoted ibid., 45.

31. Ibid.

32. Williams, *Thurgood Marshall,* 49.

33. Howard Ball, *A Defiant Life: Thurgood Marshall and the Persistence of Racism in America.* New York: Crown Publishers, 1999, 42; Williams, *Thurgood Marshall,* 50.

34. Quoted in Rowan, *Dream Makers,* 44.

35. Quoted ibid., 44–45.

36. Williams, *Thurgood Marshall,* 39.

37. Juan Williams, "Marshall's Law," in *Thurgood Marshall: Justice for All,* ed. Roger Goldman, with David Gallen (New York: Carroll and Graf, 1992), 145.

38. Williams, *Thurgood Marshall,* 53, 59.

39. Quoted ibid., 53.

40. Davis and Clark, *Thurgood Marshall,* 69; Mark V. Tushnet, *Making Civil Rights Law: Thurgood Marshall and the Supreme Court, 1936–1961* (New York: Oxford University Press, 1994), 9.

41. Quoted in Davis and Clark, *Thurgood Marshall,* 70.

42. Quoted in Williams, *Thurgood Marshall,* 63.

43. Ibid., 68.

44. Quoted ibid., 76.

45. Davis and Clark, *Thurgood Marshall,* 90.

46. Tushnet, *Making Civil Rights Law,* 14–15.

47. Quoted ibid., 14.

48. See Davis and Clark, *Thurgood Marshall,* 105–119.

49. Ibid., 21.

50. Jack Greenberg, "War Stories: Reflections on Thirty-Five Years with the NAACP Legal Defense Fund," *Saint Louis University Law Journal* 38 (Spring 1994): 592.

51. Mark V. Tushnet, "Thurgood Marshall as a Lawyer: The Campaign against School segregation, 1945–1950," *Maryland Law Review* 40 (Summer 1981): 411.

52. Quoted in Davis and Clark, *Thurgood Marshall,* 109.

53. Williams, *Thurgood Marshall,* 198; quoted in Davis and Clark, *Thurgood Marshall,* 147.

54. See Randall W. Bland, *Private Pressure on Public Law: The Legal Career of Justice Thurgood Marshall, 1934–1991,* rev. ed. (Lanham, MD: University Press of America, 1993), 70–93.

55. Williams, *Thurgood Marshall,* 197.

56. Quoted ibid., 210.

57. Davis and Clark, *Thurgood Marshall,* 158.

58. Ibid., 151–152, 178.

59. Ibid., 168.

60. Quoted in Williams, *Thurgood Marshall,* 221.

61. Ibid., 222; Davis and Clark, *Thurgood Marshall,* 168–169.

62. Quoted in Williams, *Thurgood Marshall,* 222.

63. Quoted in Anthony C. Amsterdam, "Thurgood Marshall's Image of the Blue-Eyed Child in Brown," *New York University Law Review* 68 (May 1993): 231–232.

64. Williams, *Thurgood Marshall,* 225.

65. Quoted in Rowan, *Dream Makers,* 216.

66. Quoted in Bland, *Private Pressure on Public Law,* 82.

67. Quoted ibid.

68. Quoted in Williams, *Thurgood Marshall,* 226.

69. Quoted ibid., 227.

70. Quoted in Davis and Clark, *Thurgood Marshall,* 178.

71. Richard Kluger, *Simple Justice: The History of Brown v. Board of Education and Black America's Struggle for Equality,* 2 vols. (New York: Alfred A. Knopf, 1975), 2: 941.

72. Williams, *Thurgood Marshall,* 241–243.

73. Ibid., 168–173.

74. Neil A. Lewis, "Files Say Justice Marshall Aided F.B.I. in 50's." *New York Times,* December 4, 1996, B11.

75. Ralph S. Spritzer, "Thurgood Marshall: A Dedicated Career," *Arizona State Law Journal* 26 (Summer 1994): 363–364.

76. Ibid., 365.

77. Williams, *Thurgood Marshall,* 165–166.

78. Quoted in Davis and Clarke, *Thurgood Marshall,* 12.

79. Quoted ibid., 13.

80. Quoted in Williams, *Thurgood Marshall,* 292.

81. Davis and Clark, *Thurgood Marshall,* 240.

82. Tushnet, *Making Constitutional Law,* 18; Bland, *Private Pressure on Public Law,* 128–129.

83. Bland, *Private Pressure on Public Law,* 129.

84. Lisa A. Lunsman, "Justice Thurgood Marshall: A Retrospective," *University of West Los Angeles Law Review* 23 (Annual 1992): 67; Sidney E. Zion, "Thurgood Marshall," 69–71.

85. Davis and Clark, *Thurgood Marshall,* 246.

86. Williams, *Thurgood Marshall,* 313–314.

87. Rowan, *Dream Makers,* 290.

88. Ball, *A Defiant Life,* 190–192; Bland, *Private Pressure on Public Law,* 150–200.

89. Quoted in Williams, *Thurgood Marshall,* 11–12.

90. Quoted in Ball, *A Defiant Life,* 193.

91. Quoted ibid., 193–197.

92. Darbyshire, "Clerking for Justice Marshall," 48; "Marshall: U.S. Government Defective from Its Beginning," *Chicago Daily Law Bulletin,* May 6, 1987, 1.

93. Stuart Taylor Jr., "Marshall Ranks Reagan as Last on Civil Rights," *Chicago Daily Law Bulletin,* September 9, 1987, 1. Following Marshall's death in 1993, the public had an opportunity to learn more about his views. A series of interviews conducted in 1977 under the auspices of the Oral History Project at Columbia University was released a few days after his death. At the end of May 1993, the Library of Congress released (over the objections of his family) the papers that he had willed to it.

94. Ball, *A Defiant Life,* 202; quoted in Woodward and Armstrong, *The Brethren,* 64.

95. Geoffrey R. Stone, "Marshall: He's the Frustrated Conscience of the High Court," *National Law Journal* (February 18, 1980): 24.

96. Ball, *A Defiant Life,* 405–406; quoted in Davis and Clark, *Thurgood Marshall,* 7.

97. Quoted in Marcia Coyle and Marianne Lavelle, "High Court Loses a Voice: Justice Marshall's World View Passes from the Bench's Scene," *National Law Journal* (July 8, 1991): 29.

98. Quoted in Davis and Clark, *Thurgood Marshall,* 3; Andrew Rosenthal, "Marshall Retires from High Court; Blow to Liberals," *New York Times,* June 28, 1991, A1.

99. Henry J. Reske, "Marshall Retires for Health Reasons," *ABA Journal* 77 (August 1991): 14–15; "Marshall to Leave Court," *Chicago Daily Law Bulletin,* June 27, 1991, 1.

100. Quoted in Ball, *A Defiant Life,* 202–203.

101. Carl Rowan, "Justice Marshall: Candor on Court," *Legal Times,* December 14, 1987, 8; Linda Greenhouse, "Thurgood Marshall, Civil Rights Hero, Dies at 84," *New York Times,* January 25, 1993, A1.

102. Quoted in Davis and Clark, *Thurgood Marshall,* 382.

103. Quoted in Stephanie B. Goldberg, "Telling Stories: Marshall Recalls Civil Rights Struggle," *ABA Journal* 78 (October 1992): 40.

104. Sandra Day O'Connor, "Thurgood Marshall: The Influence of a Raconteur," *Stanford Law Review* 44 (Summer 1992): 1220.

Selected Cases

Smith v. Allwright (1944)
321 U.S. 649

Marshall argued this case, involving the constitutionality of the all-white primary in Texas, before the United States Supreme Court.

In 1940, Lonnie Smith, a black dentist who was also an officer of the Houston branch of the NAACP, tried to vote in a primary in which candidates for state and local offices were to be chosen. S.E. Allwright, a precinct election judge, and other election officials refused to give Smith a ballot. They maintained that a state Democratic Party convention resolution adopted in 1932 had limited membership in the party to white persons.

Marshall filed a brief in federal district court alleging that Allwright and other election officials had deprived Smith of his voting rights under the Fifteenth Amendment to the Constitution. The district court ruled against Smith, and a court of appeals affirmed the ruling. Marshall took the case to the United States Supreme Court. In the preparation of the case, Marshall was assisted by William H. Hastie, later to be the first black appointed to a federal judgeship, and by W.J. Durham, a local Texas attorney.

The case was presented to the Supreme Court in January 1944, and the decision was announced three months later. Speaking for the majority, Justice Stanley F. Reed held that the Fifteenth Amendment prohibits a party primary from being restricted to white persons. Accordingly, the southern Democratic Party, whose primaries were equivalent to the general election at that time, was no longer able to disfranchise black citizens.

The decision was praised by liberals as a major victory for the voting rights of African-Americans, although the poll tax and other restrictions of voting remained in force in the South at this time.

Morgan v. Commonwealth of Virginia (1946)
328 U.S. 373

Irene Morgan, a black woman from Baltimore, was convicted of violating a Virginia statute requiring the segregation of passengers of public motor carriers according to color. The statute specified that it was a misdemeanor for any passenger to refuse to change seats as required by a driver.

The incident arose when Morgan boarded a Greyhound bus in Gloucester County, Virginia. The bus passed through the District of Columbia, and went to Baltimore, Maryland, its final destination. There were both white and black passengers on the bus. Morgan refused the driver's request to move to a back seat so that the seat she occupied could be used by a white person.

She lost in the lower court and in the Court of Appeals of Virginia, and took her case to the United States Supreme Court. Morgan was represented by Marshall and William H. Hastie. Abram P. Staples represented the appellee.

In a seven-to-one ruling, the Court held for Morgan. It ruled that the Virginia statute relating to segregation of passengers of public motor carriers according to color, and making it a misdemeanor for any passenger to refuse to change seats as requested by the driver, violated the interstate commerce clause of the federal Constitution.

Sipuel v. Oklahoma State Regents (1948)
332 U.S. 631

Ada Lois Sipuel asked the Oklahoma branch of the NAACP to help her apply to law school. Roscoe Dunjee, a prominent black lawyer and newspaper publisher in Oklahoma, filed suit for Sipuel directing her admission to law school. The trial judge dismissed the case, saying that Sipuel could not challenge the segregation statute by using the procedure she selected. This decision was subsequently affirmed by the state Supreme Court.

Marshall took the case to the Unite States Supreme Court, challenging *Plessy* in his brief. In a per curiam opinion issued on January 12, 1948, the Court relied on the decision in *Gaines* v. *Murray* (1935), holding that the state had to provide Sipuel with a legal education on the same basis with applicants of any other group.

Following the decision, Marshall brought the case back to the Oklahoma Supreme Court. However, the court held that the ruling issued by the United States Supreme Court in *Gaines* meant that the university could create a separate law school for Sipuel. Within a matter of days, the regents created a law school for African-Americans. The school occupied three rooms in the state capitol and was staffed by three local attorneys.

Marshall returned to the United States Supreme Court and sought an order directing that Sipuel (whose married name was now Fisher) be admitted to the white law school. In *Fisher* v. *Hurst* (1948), the Court decided in a per curiam opinion that separate but equal was not an issue and ruled in her favor.

In June 1949, Ada Sipuel Fisher was admitted to the law school, but was segregated after her admission. She had to sit in back of the last row of seats, where there was a large wooden chair behind a wooden rail. Attached to a pole on the back of the chair was a large printed sign that said "Colored." The treatment continued until June 1950, when the *McLaurin* case was decided, and Fisher was finally able to sit with the rest of the students.

McGhee v. *Sipes* (1948)
334 U.S. 1

The case involved the use in Michigan of restrictive covenants stating that certain property "shall not be used or occupied by any person or persons except those of the Caucasian race." It was argued along with the companion case of *Shelley* v. *Kraemer.*

Orsel McGhee and his wife Minnie S. McGhee purchased certain restricted property in Michigan, and Benjamin J. Sipes and others brought suit in a lower court to enforce the covenant that the property should not be used or occupied by any person except those of the Caucasian race. The court ruled in favor of Sipes, and the judgment was affirmed by the Supreme Court of Michigan. An appeal was taken to the United States Supreme Court, and Marshall and Loren Miller presented the oral arguments on behalf of the McGhees.

In a landmark decision delivered by Chief Justice Fred R. Vinson Jr., the Court ruled that state courts cannot enforce antiblack restrictive covenants. While private individuals were free to sign contracts not to sell their houses to blacks, they cannot enforce these agreements in a court of law because such state action would be a violation of the equal protection clause of the Fourteenth Amendment.

Justices Stanley F. Reed, Robert H. Jackson, and Wiley B. Rutledge took no part in the decision or the consideration of the case. They owned property with deeds containing restrictive covenants.

Marshall made the oral argument in McGhee during the same week that he made the oral argument in *Sipuel* v. *Oklahoma State Regents* (1948).

Shelley v. *Kraemer* (1948)
334 U.S. 1

The case involved the use of restrictive covenants barring "people of the Negro or Mongolian Race" from owning residential property in St. Louis, Missouri. It was argued along with the companion case of *McGhee* v. *Sipes.*

In 1911, certain owners of property in St. Louis signed an agreement barring the sale of the property to "any person not of the Caucasian race." This restrictive covenant was to run until 1961. In 1945, a married black couple named J.D. and Ethel Lee Shelley (who were unaware of this restrictive covenant) received a deed to a portion of this property from Josephine Fitzgerald. Louis and Fern E. Kraemer, acting on behalf of the restrictive covenanters, attempted to block the Fitzgerald-to-Shelley sale, but lost on a technicality in a Missouri state circuit court. This decision was subsequently reversed by the Supreme Court of Missouri, which directed the lower court to order the Shelleys to vacate their property.

Marshall worked on this case with the assistance of Charles Hamilton Houston and William H. Hastie, as well as the support staff of the NAACP. In the earlier Supreme Court case of *Hurd* v. *Hodge* (1948), it was Houston who represented black clients in a challenge to the restrictive covenant laws in Washington, D.C.

The lawyers for Shelley made the case a constitutional issue by arguing that racial covenants were a violation of the equal protection clause of the Fourteenth Amendment. Since Marshall and Loren Miller had delivered the oral arguments in *McGhee,* the arguments in this case were made by St. Louis attorneys George L. Vaughn and Herman Willer.

Shelley and *McGhee* were argued during the same week that Marshall made the oral argument in *Sipuel* v. *Oklahoma State Regents* (1948). These cases were decided by six of the nine members of the Supreme Court. Justices Stanley F. Reed, Robert H. Jackson, and Wiley B. Rutledge had to remove themselves from the cases because they owned property with deeds containing restrictive covenants.

The Court adopted the same line of reasoning in this case and in *McGhee* v. *Sipes,* holding that state courts cannot enforce antiblack restrictive covenants. Chief Justice Fred M. Vinson Jr. delivered this landmark decision.

McLaurin v. *Oklahoma State Regents* (1950)
339 U.S. 637

Six African-American students applied for admission to several graduate programs at the University of Oklahoma at the end of 1948. The university regents decided not to create programs at the state's university for them, and they were rejected. George McLaurin, one of the six students, sued and obtained an order directing his admission. McLaurin, who wanted to obtain a doctoral degree in education, registered for four courses, which were promptly rescheduled to meet in a single classroom. This classroom had a small alcove on the side in which McLaurin was required to sit, surrounded by a rail on which there was a sign stating "Reserved for Colored." He was also assigned a special desk on the mezzanine floor of the library and informed that he could not use the desks in the regular reading room. In addition, McLaurin was directed to eat at a specifically designated table in the school cafeteria, at a different time from the white students.

Marshall, with the assistance of James M. Nabrit Jr., took this case to the Supreme Court and argued that the university had violated the equal protection clause of the Fourteenth Amendment. By the time the case was argued before the Supreme Court, the seating arrangements in the classroom were changed, and McLaurin was assigned to a seat in a row specified for colored students.

Marshall presented his oral argument on the same day that he argued *Sweatt* v. *Painter* (1950). In a unanimous opinion delivered by Chief Justice Fred M. Vinson, the Court ruled that the segregated arrangements provided for McLaurin were neither "equal" nor constitutional and that African-American students may not be segregated within a university after they have been admitted to its graduate school. The Court ordered McLaurin to be promptly admitted to full student citizenship and the equal protection of the laws.

Sweatt v. Painter (1950)
339 U.S. 629

Heman M. Sweatt was a black mail carrier in Houston, Texas, who had graduated from college in 1934. In the 1940s, he became active in a local branch of the NAACP and decided to become a lawyer. He applied to the all-white University of Texas Law School and was denied admission because of his race and color. Although there was a "colored" law school established by the state legislature at the Texas State University for Negroes in Prairie View, Texas, Sweatt refused to attend it and sought help from Marshall and the NAACP.

Sweatt lost in the state courts on the grounds that there were substantially equal facilities offered by the "colored" law school. In reality, this law school had no library, no accreditation, only three rooms, and a faculty consisting of three part-time law instructors.

Marshall, who was assisted by James M. Nabrit Jr., took the case to the Supreme Court, presenting an oral argument to the court on the very same day in April 1950 that he made an oral argument in *McLaurin*. His argument in *Sweatt* was that the Texas State University for Negroes was simply "inferior" and hence unequal.

Speaking for a unanimous Court on the same day that the *McLaurin* decision was announced, Chief Justice Fred M. Vinson Jr., did not hold that segregation per se was unconstitutional, but indicated that it was virtually impossible to comply with the separate but equal doctrine in the area of professional and graduate education.

Sweatt was admitted to the law school, but flunked out. Nevertheless, the case was an important legal victory in the fight to overturn *Plessy* v. *Ferguson* (1896).

Brown v. Board of Education I (1954)
347 U.S. 483

This decision overturned *Plessy* v. *Ferguson* (1896), in which the Court had held that separate facilities were constitutional as long as they were "separate but equal." *Brown,* one of the most important decisions ever handed down by the Supreme Court, became Thurgood Marshall's most famous case.

The case was a consolidation of four lower court cases in Kansas, South Carolina, Virginia, and Delaware respectively. Each case was based on the argument that segregated facilities in public education were a denial of the equal protection clause of the Fourteenth Amendment.

The lead case was brought by Oliver Brown against the Board of Education in Topeka, Kansas. Brown asked the Court to have his eight-year-old daughter Linda (who had to travel twenty-one blocks to an all-black school) admitted to a white school located five blocks from her home. In the South Carolina case, Harry Briggs Jr. and sixty-six black children challenged the allegedly unequal educational facilities in the state. The plaintiff in the Virginia case was Dorothy Davis and other black high school students who argued that their schooling was unequal to the education received by white students, and the Delaware case was brought by Ethel Belton and seven other black parents on similar grounds.

The NAACP sponsored the four cases, and Marshall argued the South Carolina and Delaware cases. There was a fifth case, *Bolling* v. *Sharpe,* which dealt with the segregated school facilities in the District of Columbia, but the NAACP decided not to sponsor the case because the Fourteenth Amendment's guarantee of equal protection of the laws was binding only on state jurisdictions.

The landmark nine-to-zero decision was announced on May 17, 1954. Chief Justice Earl Warren wrote the opinion, stating that "in the field of public education the doctrine of separate but equal has no place." As a result, segregation in public education was held to be unconstitutional.

Brown v. *Board of Education II* (1955)
349 U.S. 294

Following the 1954 *Brown* decision, the Court asked the parties to return for rearguments to discuss the implementation of the ruling. The rearguments took place in April 1955, and on May 31, Chief Justice Earl Warren delivered the unanimous opinion of the Supreme Court.

In the rearguments, Marshall had requested that the Court fix a date for the end of segregation in public education. Instead, the Court specified that it was not going to usurp local prerogatives in the matter, but urged that the parties go forward "with all deliberate speed" to implement the Court's 1954 decision.

Mayor and City Council of Baltimore v. *Dawson* (1955)
350 U.S. 877

The case, which involved state segregation of public recreational facilities, followed in the aftermath of the *Brown* decision. Dawson and other back citizens brought actions for declaratory judgments and injunctive relief against the enforcement of segregation in the use of public beaches and bathhouses maintained by officials of Maryland and the city of Baltimore. Marshall, Jack Greenberg, and Robert L. Carter took the case to the United States Court of Appeals for the Fourth Circuit. The court upheld Dawson, stating that the segregation of such facilities was an invalid use of Maryland's police power and violated the "equal protection" clause of the Fourteenth Amendment.

Baltimore officials appealed the case to the Supreme Court. In a per curiam decision, the Court affirmed the decision of the lower federal court.

Holmes v. *City of Atlanta* (1955)
350 U.S. 879

This case, following in the aftermath of the *Brown* decision, involved state segregation of public recreational facilities. At issue was the constitutionality of segregated golf courses in Atlanta. The case was argued by Marshall, with the assistance of Robert L. Carter and Atlanta attorney E.E. Moore. Since it was decided immediately after *Mayor and City Council of Baltimore* v. *Dawson* (1955), the Court remanded it to the lower court with directions to enter a decree conforming with the *Baltimore* decision, which had outlawed segregation in public beaches.

As a result of the *Brown* decision, lower courts began to invalidate segregation in public facilities, and the Supreme Court affirmed these decisions. But the task of the total elimination of segregation in public facilities would prove to be more difficult.

Cooper v. *Aaron* (1958)
385 U.S. 1

In May 1955, the United States Supreme Court ordered desegregation to proceed "with all deliberate speed." Seven days after the ruling, the Little Rock Arkansas School Board approved a desegregation plan.

On September 3, 1957, nine black students were scheduled to enter Central High, a previously all-white school. But on the night of September 2, Governor Orval Faubus dispatched units of the Arkansas National Guard to prevent the nine black students from entering the high school.

Faubus subsequently was enjoined by a United States District court from continued interference, and he removed the National Guard. Following its removal, rioting broke out in Little Rock and President Dwight D. Eisenhower felt obliged to take action. On September 26, he sent federal troops to Little Rock and federalized the state National Guard to protect the students. They attended Central High during the next year in the face of ongoing harassment.

In 1958, the Little Rock school board asked a federal judge for permission to discontinue desegregation, and defer all other action until 1960. The judge allowed them a two-year delay, and the decision was appealed. The Court of Appeals for the Eighth Circuit reversed, and certiorari was granted the petitioners, headed by William G. Cooper of the Little Rock school board.

In *Cooper* v. *Aaron,* the Supreme Court settled the Little Rock school issue. Richard C. Butler of Little Rock represented the petitioners. Marshall appeared for John Aaron, the respondent. J. Lee Rankin, solicitor general of the United States, filed an amicus curiae brief by invitation of the Court.

A unanimous Court ruled against the school board, holding that a state is unable to nullify federal law. It acknowledged that responsibility for public education is primarily the concern of the state, but such responsibility must be exercised consistently with federal constitutional requirements, as they apply to state action.

Boynton v. Virginia (1960)
364 U.S. 454

Bruce Boynton, a black Harvard Law student, was arrested on December 20, 1960, for refusing to move from a lunch counter reserved for whites at a Trailways bus station in Richmond, Virginia. Under Virginia's trespass law, it was a misdemeanor to stay on someone else's property after being asked to leave unless the person had a lawful excuse for remaining. Found guilty of violating the trespass law, Boynton appealed the decision to the Supreme Court. His appeal was sponsored by the Legal Defense Fund, and Marshall argued the case.

Marshall raised three points at the trial: segregation in a bus station violated the Interstate Commerce Act; segregation in a bus station interfered with interstate commerce; and the use of state power to enforce the restaurant owner's decision to discriminate was "state action" that was unconstitutional under the ruling in *Shelley* v. *Kraemer* (1948).

In a seven-to-two ruling, the Court reversed Boynton's conviction by holding that the restaurant owner's policy of refusing to serve a black patron violated the Interstate Commerce Act. Since the Court decided the case on statutory grounds, it avoided the more difficult question of "state action."

United States v. Rickenbacker (1962)
309 F. 2d 462

William F. Rickenbacker had been convicted in the District Court for the Southern District of New York for refusing to answer the 1960 census questionnaire. He had informed the grand jury that indicted him that he regarded the census questionnaire as an unnecessary invasion of his privacy. The district court imposed a suspended sentence of sixty days in prison, fined him $100, and placed him on probation for one day. Rickenbacker appealed the sentence to the Court of Appeals for the Second Circuit.

In delivering the unanimous opinion of the Court, Judge Thurgood Marshall found Rickenbacker's arguments to be without merit. He wrote that the gathering of the information required by the census was reasonably related to government purposes and functions, and that the census was neither arbitrary nor in violation of the Fourth Amendment guarantees for citizens to be secure in their homes.

New York v. *Galamison* (1965)
342 F. 2d 255

In 1964, Milton A. Galamison and approximately fifty other persons were prosecuted in Queens County, New York, for disrupting highway and subway traffic to the New York World's Fair in order to protest what they regarded as unequal treatment of African-Americans throughout the country. Two other defendants were prosecuted in New York County for staging a sit-in and demonstration at City Hall. All defendants subsequently appealed to the Second Circuit Court of Appeals on the grounds that the acts of protest and resistance were "under color of authority" of numerous laws providing for equal rights, including the guarantees of free speech and petition in the federal Constitution.

The Circuit Court ruled against the defendants, but Marshall dissented. He argued that since the litigation involved many separate offenses for a variety of acts, these acts could be decided only on a case-by-case basis.

Keyishian v. *Board of Regents of the University of the State of New York* (1965)
345 F. 2d 236

Marshall, in his capacity as a judge on the United States Court of Appeals for the Second Circuit, wrote the majority opinion in this First Amendment case involving the use of loyalty oaths.

Harry Keyishian and other faculty members of the State University of New York at Buffalo had refused to sign loyalty certificates pursuant to section 3022 of the Feinberg Law of 1949, which provided for the dismissal of public school teachers who refused to take the loyalty oath. The faculty members were dismissed, and Keyishian initiated a class-action suit in the Federal District Court for the Western District of New York challenging the constitutionality of the loyalty oaths. When a judge of the District Court refused to convene a three-judge panel to consider the case, the faculty members appealed to the United States Court of Appeals for the Second Circuit.

Speaking for the majority, Marshall held that the questions arising from the complaint were sufficient for the convening of a three-judge district court, and the second Circuit remanded the case to the district court with instructions to convene a three-judge panel. A panel subsequently found Section 3022 of the Feinberg Law to be constitutional, but the decision was later reversed by the United States Supreme Court in *Keyishian* v. *Board of Regents* (1967), when it held the section was vague and restrictive of free expression in violation of the due process clause of the Fourteenth Amendment.

United States ex. rel. Hetenyi v. *Wilkins* (2d Cir. 1965)
348 F. 2d 844

In this case, Marshall wrote the majority opinion for the United States Second Circuit Court of Appeals in New York, rendering an important decision on the issue of double jeopardy.

At that time, the principle of double jeopardy did not extend to state prosecutions. However, Marshall held in *Wilkins* that the Fifth Amendment protection against repeated prosecutions at the federal level also applied to the state because of the Fourteenth Amendment's guarantee of due process.

Marshall's opinion in *Wilkins* later became the law of the land in the Supreme Court case of *Benton* v. *Maryland* (1968). As a member of the Court at that time, he wrote the majority opinion.

Katzenbach and the United States v. *Morgan* (1966)
384 U.S. 641

Marshall argued this case before the Supreme Court in his capacity as solicitor general of the United States. The case involved the constitutionality of a provision of the 1965 Voting Rights Act.

The provision in question specifically granted the right to vote to Puerto Ricans (of whom 750,000 resided in New York), provided they had a sixth-grade education from a Puerto Rican school. However, New York State prohibited American citizens born in Puerto Rico from voting if they spoke only Spanish, even if they were literate. In November 1965, a three-judge federal district court upheld New York's action by declaring the provision of the Voting Rights Act to be unconstitutional.

Marshall brought the case to the Supreme Court, arguing that the government had no problem with requiring that voters be literate, but it was opposed to the English-only restriction. In a seven-to-two decision written by Justice William J. Brennan Jr., the Court upheld Marshall by stating that Congress, in passing the Spanish literacy section of the bill, had acted legally because it was "appropriate legislation . . . plainly adapted" to the enforcement of the equal protection clause of the Constitution.

Hoffa v. *United States* (1966)
385 U.S. 293

In 1965, James R. Hoffa, president of the International Brotherhood of Teamsters, and three other Teamster officials were convicted by a federal district court for criminal conspiracy in endeavoring to bribe two petit jurors with offers as high as $10,000. Hoffa and the officials were convicted and sentenced to prison terms. The convictions were later upheld by the United States

Court of Appeals for the Sixth Circuit, and the case was appealed to the Supreme Court.

At the time the case was argued, Marshall was solicitor general of the United States. Hoffa and the three other men maintained that the evidence obtained by the government was a violation of their constitutional rights because it involved the use of an informer.

The government's case was argued by Fred M. Vinson Jr., the assistant attorney general, and the legal brief was drawn up by Solicitor General Marshall, his assistant Nathan Lewin, and Department of Justice attorney Philip R. Monahan. They defended the government's use of testimony supplied by informers and accomplices, maintaining that the utilization by the government of "the services of an informant" is a practice "as old as law enforcement" and one which has been sanctioned by the courts from the beginning.

In a six-to-one decision, the Supreme Court upheld the convictions of the Teamster officials. Despite his stand on the use of informants by the government, Marshall opposed the use of electronic eavesdropping devices. On December 1, 1966, addressing the Association of Federal Investigators, he urged prosecutors to stop the use of all such devices. Basing his argument on the trend of decisions made by the Supreme Court against the use of eavesdropping devices, he warned that the government would lose cases unless this practice were stopped.

Benton v. Maryland (1969)
395 U.S. 784

Justice Thurgood Marshall wrote the majority opinion for the Supreme Court in a case which partly overturned *Palko* v. *Connecticut* (1937). In *Palko*, the court had rejected the claim that the double jeopardy guarantee in the Constitution was applicable to the states.

John Dalmer Benton had been indicted in Prince George's County and tried for burglary, housebreaking, and larceny. At the trial, the state did not press the housebreaking charge, and he was found not guilty on the larceny charge. However, he was convicted of burglary and sentenced to ten years in jail.

Both his indictment and conviction were subsequently set aside due to a technicality, and Benton was reindicted and retried on both the burglary and larceny charges. He was convicted on both charges. His sentence was fifteen years for burglary and five years for larceny, with the sentences to run concurrently.

Appealing to the Supreme Court, Benton argued that the larceny conviction should be reversed on double jeopardy grounds because he had been found innocent of larceny at his first trial. He further maintained that the burglary conviction could not stand because the jury was influenced by the testimony on the larceny count.

The Supreme Court announced its decision on June 23, 1969. Speaking for the six-to-two majority (one seat was vacant because Justice Abe Fortas had resigned two months before the decision was handed down), Justice Marshall held that the double jeopardy provision represented "a fundamental ideal in our constitutional heritage . . . that . . . should apply to the States through the Fourteenth Amendment" and that "[i]nsofar as it is inconsistent with the holding, *Palko* v. *Connecticut* is overruled."

This decision was announced on the last day of Earl Warren's sixteen-year tenure as Chief Justice of the United States.

New York Times Co. v. United States (1971)
403 U.S. 713

In June 1971, the *New York Times* and the *Washington Post* started to publish excerpts from the Pentagon Papers, a forty-three-volume history of American involvement in the Vietnam War. It had been commissioned by former secretary of defense Robert S. McNamara, and the papers were classified as top-secret documents. Daniel Ellsberg, a former Pentagon official who had participated in the study, had released these classified documents to the newspapers.

Citing national security concerns, the Justice Department obtained court orders halting the publication of the Pentagon Papers. On June 24, 1971, the newspapers challenged the injunctions before the Supreme Court.

The Court issued a per curiam order on June 30 overturning the injunctions and affirming the right of the newspapers to print the story. It was a six-to-three decision, with dissenting opinions by Justices Warren E. Burger, John Marshall Harlan, and Harry Blackmun.

In a separate concurring opinion, Marshall argued that Congress had refused to give the president power to stop newspapers from publishing the kind of information in the Pentagon Papers and that the Court had no right to overrule Congress in this regard.

Furman v. Georgia (1972)
408 U.S. 238

This case raised the issue of whether capital punishment constituted "cruel and unusual punishment," as outlawed by the Eighth Amendment. In a five-to-four decision, the Court invalidated the death penalty in Georgia, and presumably in all other states. However, only Justices Marshall and William J. Brennan Jr. argued that the death penalty was unconstitutional. The three other judges for the majority argued on the basis that Georgia had granted too much discretion to judges and juries, thus creating the potential for racial and other types of discrimination.

Marshall's opinion was the longest and most impassioned. He argued that the death penalty "fails upon the poor, the ignorant, and the underprivileged members of society" and stated that "the measure of a country's greatness is its ability to retain compassion in time of crisis."

The result of this decision was that no person was executed in the United States for nearly a decade.

Roe v. Wade (1973)
410 U.S. 113

"Jane Roe" was single, pregnant, and a resident of the state of Texas. Abortions were illegal in Texas unless they were performed in order to save the life of the woman.

Roe's lawyers asked the federal district court in Dallas to declare the Texas criminal abortion statute unconstitutional. They argued that the statute was an inherent deprivation of Roe's liberty without due process of the law and was in violation of the rights granted in the Fourteenth Amendment. The lawyers also asked the court to enjoin Henry Wade, the Dallas district attorney, from enforcing the statute. The federal district court ruled that the statute was unconstitutional, but did not issue an injunction against enjoinment. Both sides appealed the case, and it reached the United States Supreme Court.

In a seven-to-two majority opinion delivered by Justice Harry Blackmun, the Court recognized the right of a woman to have an abortion until the fetus had viability outside her body. The initial draft of the majority opinion had stated that abortions would be permitted only during the first three months of a pregnancy. But Justice William J. Brennan Jr. proposed that the three-month limit be replaced with a new standard: abortions could be performed until a fetus was "viable" outside the body. Marshall agreed with Brennan on this matter and advised Blackmun of his view. One of Marshall's arguments was that confining the right to have an abortion to the first three months of pregnancy might not serve the interests of women.

The arguments of Brennan and Marshall prevailed in this instance, and Blackmun rewrote his brief to reflect their views on viability.

United States v. Nixon (1974)
418 U.S. 683

On April 18, 1974, Special Prosecutor Leon Jaworski subpoenaed certain tapes of conversations recorded in the Oval Office that appeared likely to contain incriminating evidence against a number of high-ranking government officials in matters relating to the break-in of the Democratic Party headquarters at the Watergate Hotel in Washington, D.C., on June 17, 1972. On April 30, President Richard M. Nixon released edited transcripts of forty-three taped conversations and filed a motion to quash the subpoena. Federal district judge John J. Sirica denied the motion on May 20, ordering the president to surrender the tapes. Nixon appealed Judge Sirica's order to the United States Court of Appeals for the District of Columbia Circuit.

Acting upon the request of Jaworski, the Supreme Court agreed to expedite the decision by granting certiorari and bypassing the United States Court of Appeals. The issue in the case was whether Nixon could withhold the release of the subpoenaed tapes on the grounds of executive privilege.

At the time the case reached the Supreme Court, the four Nixon appointees to the Court—Lewis F. Powell, Harry Blackmun, William H. Rehnquist, and Chief Justice Warren E. Burger—appeared to favor the president's claim of executive privilege. Rehnquist subsequently recused himself from the case.

Marshall was particularly disturbed by Nixon's claim that only he could determine if it were in the national interest to release the tapes. When the first draft of the Court's opinion was circulated by Chief Justice Burger, Marshall sent him a strongly worded note objecting to Nixon's stance.

In the end, the Court rendered a unanimous opinion that the president had to release the tapes. The decision was announced on July 24, 1974, the same day that the House Judiciary Committee began hearings on whether to impeach the president. One month later, Nixon resigned as president.

Buckley v. *Valeo* (1976)
424 U.S. 1

This case challenged the Federal Elections Campaign Act of 1971 as amended in 1974, which sought to limit campaign spending in federal elections. The suit was brought by a group that included Senator James Buckley, who was running for reelection to the United States Senate from New York; a potential contributor; a candidate for president of the United States; and a coalition of groups including the Mississippi Republican Party, the Conservative Party of New York, and the New York Civil Liberties Union. The United States Court of Appeals for the District of Columbia upheld, with one exception, the substantive provisions of the act with respect to contributions, expenditures, and public disclosure. Buckley and the other plaintiffs appealed the decision to the Supreme Court.

In a per curiam opinion, the Court ruled all limitations on individual or candidate campaign spending to be unconstitutional. It sustained limits on the amount of money people may contribute to candidates and their campaign committees on the grounds that such limits only marginally restrict contributors' abilities to express political views.

Gregg v. *Georgia* (1976)
428 U.S. 153

After *Furman* v. *Georgia* (1972), many states enacted new death penalty statutes designed to meet the objections of the judges. In *Gregg* v. *Georgia,* the Court upheld Georgia's new death penalty statute and ruled that the death

penalty was not unconstitutional. The Court held that where proper procedures are followed and where the jury is provided with general rules for when
the death penalty can be invoked, no cruel and unusual punishment occurred.

Gregg v. *Georgia* was one of five cases dealing with southern states' death
penalty statutes that came under the scrutiny of the Supreme Court. The statutes were of two kinds: mandatory (adopted in Louisiana and North Carolina)
and mitigating (enacted in Georgia, Texas, and Florida). In the latter, the Court
allowed consideration of mitigating circumstances to determine whether life
imprisonment or the death penalty were to be the punishment. When the vote
was taken, only Justices Thurgood Marshall and William J. Brennan Jr. voted
against all five statutes.

In *Gregg,* Marshall maintained that "capital punishment is not necessary as
a deterrent to crime in our society" and that it was "an excessive penalty forbidden by the Eighth and Fourteenth Amendments."

Marshall's opposition to the death penalty placed him in a minority position on the court. From 1976 until his retirement in 1991, he wrote the majority opinion only four times in death penalty cases.

Regents of the University of California v. Bakke (1978)
438 U.S. 265

Allan Bakke, a thirty-two-year-old white male and an engineer by profession,
applied to the University of California Medical School at Davis in 1973. He
had an excellent academic record, but was denied admission. At the time that
he applied to the medical school, Davis had a policy of admitting one hundred
students each year, with sixteen places set aside for minority students. Since
Bakke's application was submitted late in the year, the only places left in the
entering class were those under the affirmation action program for which he
was ineligible. He then sued the medical school, claiming that by refusing to
consider him on racial grounds for the places designated for affirmative action, he was denied his constitutional rights to equal protection of the laws.

In a five-to-four decision, the Court ordered Bakke to be admitted to the
medical school. At the same time, it held that the Davis plan was unconstitutional because it created a category of admissions from which whites were
excluded solely because of race. The Court also held that affirmative action
plans were not necessarily unconstitutional and that a state university may
properly take race and ethnic background into consideration in order to get a
more diversified student body. However, the goal of the university may not be
to redress past misconduct by society or to ensure that more minority members become doctors.

Marshall wrote an emotional dissent in *Bakke,* contending that "it must be
remembered that, during most of the past 200 years, the Constitution as interpreted by this Court did not prohibit the most ingenious and pervasive forms

of discrimination against the Negro. Now, when a State acts to remedy the effects of that legacy of discrimination, I cannot believe that this same Constitution stands as a barrier."

After the *Bakke* decision, the Court dealt with a variety of affirmative action programs, sustaining most of them.

Harris v. *McRae* (1980)
448 U.S. 297

In 1976, Congress enacted the Hyde Amendment, which was named for pro-life Republican representative Henry Hyde of Illinois. The amendment barred the use of federal Medicaid funds for abortions, with exceptions made for cases of rape, incest, or when the life of the woman was at risk. The year that the amendment was enacted, Medicaid recipient Cora McRae, a twenty-four-year-old Brooklyn woman in her first trimester, was refused an abortion. McRae asserted that she had various health problems and that her pregnancy was detrimental to her health. She and the New York City Health and Hospitals Corporation went to court to enjoin the enforcement of the Hyde Amendment, and a federal district judge ruled in their favor. McRae had her abortion paid for by Medicaid, but the decision was appealed to the Supreme Court.

In a five-to-four decision, the Court upheld the Hyde Amendment. Marshall dissented, asserting that the denial of public assistance to poor women who needed abortions as a medically necessary procedure would have "a devastating impact on the lives and health of poor women" and criticizing the Court for "blinding itself" to the existence of the real world in which poor women lived.

His dissent was an indication that many of his most impassioned opinions came in cases dealing with the attempt of the government to regulate the lives of poor people.

Bowsher v. *Synar* (1986)
478 U.S. 714

This decision was one of the most closely watched cases during the 1986 term because it involved the constitutionality of the Balanced Budget and Emergency Deficit Reduction Act (also known as the Gramm-Rudman-Hollings Act). The act had set a maximum deficit amount for federal spending for each of the fiscal years from 1986 through 1991. In the event that the budget deficit exceeded the maximum stipulated by the act, the legislation provided that across-the-board cuts in federal spending were to be made. Since Congress preferred not to have to vote for cuts in federal programs, the automatic spending cuts were to be administered by the comptroller general of the United States, who was given the final word in ordering the president to trim spending and reduce deficits.

Representative Mike Synar filed a court challenge to the act on the grounds that it was unconstitutional and was later joined in the suit by eleven members of Congress. Named in the suit was Charles A. Bowsher, the comptroller general. A three-judge federal district court ruled against Bowsher, who took this case to the Supreme Court.

In a seven-to-two decision, the Court ruled that the act was unconstitutional on the grounds that it would violate the separation of powers doctrine because the comptroller general was, in effect, an officer of Congress, and only Congress had the power to remove him from office.

Marshall joined with Justice John Paul Stevens in concurring with the majority opinion.

Johnson v. *Transportation Agency of Santa Clara, California* (1987)
480 U.S. 616

The Santa Clara County Transportation Agency had adopted voluntarily an affirmative action program for hiring and promoting minorities and women. Paul Johnson, a white male who had worked for the county for fourteen years, applied for the vacant position of road dispatcher. At the time, there were no women holding the position. Johnson was passed over for promotion to the position in favor of county employee Diane Joyce, in spite of the fact that he scored higher in a civil service test than she did.

Johnson sued in federal district court, which held that the agency had violated Title 7 of the Civil Rights Act of 1964 by awarding the job to Joyce on the basis of her gender. The Court of Appeals for the Ninth Circuit reversed, and Johnson took the case to the Supreme Court.

In a six-to-three decision, the Court ruled against Johnson. Marshall voted with the majority in an opinion written by Justice William J. Brennan Jr. The court held that an agency, in an effort to end past discrimination in hiring and promotions, could voluntarily take race and gender into consideration.

Webster v. *Reproductive Health Services* (1989)
109 S. Ct. 3040

This case concerned the constitutionality of a Missouri statue regulating abortions. The statute prohibited the use of public facilities to perform abortions, outlawed public funding for abortion counseling, forbade public employees from performing nontherapeutic abortions, and required physicians to conduct viability tests prior to performing abortions.

The statute was challenged by Reproductive Health Services, a nonprofit corporation that offered abortion services to the public; Planned Parenthood of Kansas City; and five health professionals employed by Missouri. They took the case to a federal district court and named Missouri attorney general William L. Webster and other state officials in the suit. The relief they sought was to have the court declare the law unconstitutional and to issue an injunction preventing its enforcement.

The district court struck down the law and enjoined its enforcement. The decision was subsequently affirmed by the Court of Appeals for the Eighth Circuit. Missouri appealed to the United States Supreme Court.

In a five-to-four decision, the Court upheld the statute. Four of the justices who voted to uphold the constitutionality of the law—William H. Rehnquist, Byron R. White, Antonin Scalia, and Anthony M. Kennedy—wanted to overturn *Roe* v. *Wade* (1973). But the fifth justice—Sandra Day O'Connor—refused to go along with them.

The dissenters were Justices Marshall, William J. Brennan Jr., Harry Blackmun, and John Paul Stevens. The latter wrote a separate dissent, while Marshall and Brennan joined in Blackmun's dissent.

As a result of this decision, Marshall was concerned that the Supreme Court might eventually vote to overturn *Roe* v. *Wade*. His uneasiness on this matter continued until the time of his death.

Payne v. *Tennessee* (1991)
501 U.S. 808

This case overruled *Booth* v. *Maryland* (1986). In *Booth*, Justice Lewis F. Powell, speaking for the majority of the Court, held that sentencing juries in capital cases should not be told about the impact of a murder upon the victims of a crime and their survivors.

Payne v. *Tennessee* concerned a borderline retarded man who was convicted of killing a mother and her two-year-old daughter. At the trial, the prosecutor had referred in his closing arguments to the impact of the murder upon the victim's three-year-old son.

In a six-to-three decision, the Court ruled that the victim-impact statement could be heard by the jury. Marshall, a staunch opponent of the death penalty who had voted with the majority in *Booth*, vigorously dissented in this case.

He took issue with the court's reversal of the precedent established in *Booth*, arguing that neither the law nor the facts had undergone any change in the time that had elapsed between the two cases. However, he pointed out that the personnel of the Court had changed—a reference to the fact that Justices Lewis F. Powell and William J. Brennan Jr. had retired and been replaced by Justices Anthony M. Kennedy and David H. Souter.

The Court's decision was announced on the morning of June 27, 1991. That afternoon, Marshall announced his retirement from the Supreme Court.

Annotated Bibliography

Amsterdam, Anthony C. "Thurgood Marshall's Image of the Blue-Eyed Child in Brown." *New York University Law Review* 68 (May 1993): 226–236. Discussion of Marshall's arguments in *Brown* v. *Board of Education* (1954).

Aube, Douglas A. "Justice Thurgood Marshall." *New England Law Review* 27 (Spring 1993): 624–646. Overview of Marshall's legal career in an issue devoted to a symposium on Charles Hamilton Houston.

Ball, Howard. *A Defiant Life: Thurgood Marshall and the Persistence of Racism in America.* New York: Crown, 1999. A well-researched biography of Marshall and a thorough study of his achievements.

Band, Jonathan, and Andrew J. McLaughlin. "The Marshall Papers: A Peek Behind the Scenes at the Making of *Sony* v. *Universal*." *Columbia-ULA Journal of Law and the Arts* 17 (Summer 1993): 427–451. Discussion of information contained in Marshall's papers about the decision in the case of *Sony* v. *Universal.*

Bigel, Alan I. "Justices William J. Brennan, Jr. and Thurgood Marshall on Capital Punishment: Its Constitutionality, Morality, Deterrent Effect, and Interpretation by the Court." *Notre Dame Journal of Law, Ethics and Public Policy* 8 (Spring 1994): 11–163. An article on the views of Justices Brennan and Marshall on capital punishment; subsequently published as a book with the same title by University Press of America in 1997.

Bland, Randall W. *Private Pressure on Public Law: The Legal Career of Justice Thurgood Marshall, 1934–1991.* Rev. ed., Lanham, MD: University Press of America, 1993. A revised edition of a book first published in 1973, it presents an examination of Marshall's legal career, with emphasis on his work prior to his election to the Court and with added sections on the Burger and Rehnquist courts.

Blandford, Linda A. *Supreme Court of the United States, 1789–1980: An Index to Opinions Arranged by Justice.* Millwood, NY: Kraus, 1983. Reference guide on opinions of judges of the United States Supreme Court.

Branton, Wiley A. "Personal Memories of Thurgood Marshall." *Arkansas Law Review* 40 (Spring 1987): 665–670. Recollection of Marshall, in conjunction with the Justice Thurgood Marshall Symposium.

Brennan, William J., Jr. "Tribute to Justice Thurgood Marshall." *Arkansas Law Review* 40 (Spring 1987): 661–663. Tribute to Marshall, in conjunction with the Justice Thurgood Marshall Symposium.

Brennan, William J., Jr., et al. "In Tribute: Associate Justice Thurgood Marshall." *Journal of Supreme Court History* (Annual 1992): 1–25. Tributes to Marshall by Brennan, Sandra Day O'Connor, Robert L. Carter, Louis F. Claiborne, and Susan Low Block.

———. "A Tribute to Justice Thurgood Marshall." *Harvard Law Review* 105 (November 1991): 23–76. Tributes to Marshall upon his retirement from the United States Supreme Court, delivered by Brennan, Robert L. Carter, William T. Coleman Jr., Owen M. Fiss, A. Leon Higginbotham Jr., and Martha Minow.

Britain, John C. "The Culture of Civil Rights Lawyers: A Tribute to Justice Thurgood Marshall." *Connecticut Law Review* 35 (Spring 1993): 599–605. Discussion of Marshall's work in conjunction with the work of other civil rights lawyers.

Brown-Scott, Wendy. "Justice Thurgood Marshall and the Integrative Ideal." *Arizona State Law Journal* 26 (Summer 1994): 535–560. Exploration of Marshall's views on integration.

Carter, Robert L., et al. "Thurgood Marshall." *New York University Law Review* 68 (May 1993): 205–225. Testimonials to Marshall from Carter, Harry T. Edwards, Constance Baker Motley, William L. Taylor, Derrick A. Bell, Ronald L. Ellis, and Sherrilyn A. Ifill.

"Chronicle," *New York Times,* November 7, 1998, B7. Recollection of Marshall's trip in 1952 to deliver oral arguments in *Brown* case.

Clark, Ramsey, et al. "Remembrance of Justice Thurgood Marshall." *Hastings Constitutional Law Quarterly* 20 (Spring 1993): 493–519. Testimonials on Marshall by Clark, Kevin T. Baine, and J. Clay Smith Jr.

Cohen, Stephen B. "Thurgood Marshall: Tax Lawyer." *Tax Notes* 57 (November 2, 1992): 685–686. Assessment of Marshall's work on tax law, arguing that he had more comprehensive opinions on federal income taxation that any of the other judges on the United States Supreme Court.

Coltharp, Donna F. "Writing in the Margins: Brennan, Marshall, and the Inherent Weaknesses of Liberal Judicial Decision-Making," *St. Mary's Law Journal* 29 (Fall 1997): 1–46. Comparison and contrast of the philosophies of Justices Brennan and Marshall, with a critical assessment of their work.

Coyle, Marcia, and Marianne Lavelle. "High Court Loses a Voice: Justice Marshall's World View Passes from the Bench's Scene." *National Law Journal* (July 8, 1991): 1, 29. Favorable comments about Marshall upon his retirement from the United States Supreme Court.

Coyne, Randall. "Taking the Death Penalty Personally: Justice Thurgood Marshall." *Oklahoma Law Review* 47 (Spring 1994): 35–54. Account of Marshall's zeal in his opposition to the death penalty, in conjunction with a symposium on The Life and Jurisprudence of Justice Thurgood Marshall.

Darbyshire, Glen M. "Clerking for Justice Marshall." *ABA Journal* 77 (September 1991): 48–52. Fond recollections of clerking for Marshall by one of his law clerks on the United States Supreme Court.

Davis, Michael D., and Hunter R. Clark. *Thurgood Marshall: Warrior at the Bar, Rebel on the Bench.* New York: Birch Lane Press, 1992. A well-researched biography of Marshall and a thorough study of his achievements.

Fein, Bruce. "Yes: An Abuse of Discretion." *ABA Journal* 79 (September 1993): 48. Argument that it was a mistake for the Library of Congress to release Marshall's papers.

Fitzpatrick, Tracy B. "Justice Thurgood Marshall and Capital Punishment: Social Justice and the Rule of Law." *American Criminal Law Review* 32 (Summer 1995): 1065–1086. Examination of Marshall's views on capital punishment.

Futrell, J. William. "Thurgood Marshall: Environmental Lawyer." *Environmental Forum* 8 (September-October 1991): 40–42. Assessment of Marshall's work in environmental law.

Galloway, Russell W. "The First Decade of the Burger Court: Conservative Dominance (1969–1979)." *Santa Clara Law Review* 21 (Fall 1981): 891–956. Detailed view of the conservative decisions on the Burger court, including charts on voting patterns.

Gellhorn, Gay. "Justice Thurgood Marshall's Jurisprudence of Equal Protection of the Laws and the Poor." *Arizona State Law Journal* 26 (Summer 1994): 429–460. Overview of Marshall's decisions regarding the poor, and equal protection laws.

Goldberg, Stephanie B. "Telling Stories: Marshall Recalls Civil Rights Struggle." *ABA Journal* 78 (October 1992): 40–41. Brief account of Marshall's use of humor in relating stories about the civil rights struggle.

Goldman, Roger, and David Gallen, eds. *Thurgood Marshall: Justice for All.* New York: Carrol and Graf, 1992. Collection of articles on the life and accomplishments of Marshall.

Grana, Stephanie E. "Thurgood Marshall and the Fight for Life." *Southern University Law Review* 20 (Spring 1993): 1–20. Discussion of Marshall's unwavering opposition to the death penalty.

Grayson, Zebie A. "Marshall's Dream Deferred: Almost Four Decades After Brown, the Vestiges of De Jure Segregation Linger as the Implementation Process Continues." *Southern University Law Review* 20 (Spring 1993): 53–68. Account of segregation and Marshall's effort to combat it, as well as his interest in black colleges and universities.

Green, Bruce A., and Daniel Richman. "Of Laws and Men: An Essay on Justice Marshall's View of Criminal Procedure." *Arizona State Law Journal* 26 (Summer 1994): 369–402. Study of Marshall's view on criminal procedure, in an issue devoted to "Justice Thurgood Marshall: The Legacy of His Jurisprudence."

Greenberg, Jack. "War Stories: Reflections on Thirty-Five Years with the NAACP Legal Defense Fund." *Saint Louis University Law Journal* 38 (Spring 1994): 587–603. Reflections on the work of the NAACP Legal Defense Fund, with accounts of Marshall's work.

Greene, Linda S. "The Confirmation of Thurgood Marshall to the United States Supreme Court." *Harvard Blackletter Journal* 6 (Spring 1989): 27–50. Account of the bitter confirmation fight over Marshall's nomination to the Supreme Court.

Greenhouse, Linda. "Thurgood Marshall, Civil Rights Hero, Dies at 84." *New York Times,* January 25, 1993, A1. Detailed obituary that describes Marshall and his work.

Gross, Karen. "Justice Thurgood Marshall's Bankruptcy Jurisprudence: A Tribute." *American Bankruptcy Law Journal* 67 (Fall 1993): 447–477. Favorable assessment of Marshall's contributions to bankruptcy law.

Gwin, Carl R. "Comment." *Antitrust Bulletin* 42 (Spring 1997): 115–120. Response to article by William E. Kovaric in the issue about Marshall and antitrust enforcement.

Hale, F. Dennis. "Marshall Provided Key Votes, But Few Opinions, on Freedom of Speech and Press." *Communications and the Law* 16 (September 1994): 25–41. Discussion of Marshall's role on the Court in cases concerning freedom of speech and the press.

Hanna, Tassie, and Robert Laurence. "Justice Thurgood Marshall and the Problem of Indian Treaty Abrogation." *Arkansas Law Review* 40 (Spring 1987): 797–840. Marshall's position on Indian treaties, presented at the Justice Thurgood Marshall Symposium.

Hengstler, Gary A. "Marshalling His Views: Justice's Controversial Comments Break 20-Year Silence." *ABA Journal* 74 (March 1, 1988): 36. Report on Marshall's comments about public figures in his first interview as a justice of the United States Supreme Court.

Hester, Rena A. "Exit of a Guardian of the Right to Choose: Will the Choices of Young and Poor Women Follow?" *Southern University Law Review* 20 (Spring 1993): 27–52. View that Marshall's retirement from the Court had a negative effect on the right of young and poor women to obtain abortions.

Higginbotham, A. Leon, Jr. "The Ten Precepts of American Slavery Jurisprudence: Chief Justice Roger Taney's Defense and Justice Thurgood Marshall's Condemnation of the Precept of Black Inferiority." *Cardozo Law Review* 17 (May 1996): 1695–1710. Comparison of the views of Justices Taney and Marshall about the precept of "black inferiority."

Hill, Oliver E. "A Classmate's Recollections of Thurgood Marshall in the Earlier Years." *Howard Law Journal* 35 (Fall 1991): 49–52. Recollections of Marshall as a student at Howard Law School, in the Thurgood Marshall Commemorative Issue.

Hill, Ruth Johnson. "Mr. Justice Thurgood Marshall, 1908–1993: A Bio-Bibliographic Research Guide." *Southern University Law Review* 20 (Spring 1993): 113–139. Research guide on the life of Marshall.

Hollingsworth, P.A. "Tribute to Justice Thurgood Marshall." *Arkansas Law Review* 40 (Spring 1987): 671–675. Tribute to Marshall, in conjunction with the Justice Thurgood Marshall Symposium.

Jost, Kenneth. "No: More Respect for the Court." *ABA Journal* 79 (September 1993): 49. Argument that it was not a mistake for the Library of Congress to release Marshall's papers.

Kennedy, Randall. "Doing What You Can With What You Have: The Greatness of Justice Marshall." *Georgetown Law Journal* 80 (August 1992): 2081–2091. Assessment of Marshall, in conjunction with the symposium Honoring Justice Thurgood Marshall.

———. "Thurgood Marshall and the Struggle for Women's Rights." *Harvard Women's Law Journal* 17 (Spring 1994): 1–4. Discussion of Marshall's efforts on behalf of women's rights.

Kluger, Richard. *Simple Justice: The History of Brown v. Board of Education and Black America's Struggle for Equality.* 2 vols. New York: Alfred A. Knopf, 1975. Study of the civil rights movement, including Marshall's role in ending segregation in the United States.

Kovaric, William E. "Antitrust Decision Making and the Supreme Court: Perspective from the Thurgood Marshall Papers." *Antitrust Bulletin* 42 (Spring 1997): 93–114. Discussion of the United States Supreme Court's rulings, based on the papers of Marshall.

Kramer, Victor H. "The Road to City of Berkeley: The Antitrust Positions of Justice Thurgood Marshall." *Antitrust Bulletin* 32 (Summer 1997): 335–371. Marshall's positions on antitrust law, discussed in conjunction with *Fisher v. City of Berkeley.*

Laurence, Robert. "Thurgood Marshall's Indian Law Opinions. *Howard Law Journal* 27 (Winter 1984): 3–89. Discussion of Marshall's positions on American Indian law.

Lewis, Neil A. "Files Say Justice Marshall Aided F.B.I. in 50's." *New York Times,* December 4, 1996, B11. Evidence indicating that Marshall worked with the FBI in the 1950s over the threat of Communism in the NAACP.

———. "Marshall Urges Bush to Pick 'The Best.'" *New York Times,* June 29, 1991, Section 1: 8. Advice by Marshall on Supreme Court nominations.

"The Long-Distance Runner: A Roundtable on America's First Black Justice." *ABA Journal* 78 (June 1992): 70. Panel discussion of Marshall and his legacy.

Luney, Percy R., Jr. "Thurgood Marshall as Solicitor General: An Opportunity to Fulfill a Dream." *Harvard Blackletter Journal* 6 (Spring 1989): 18–26. Discussion of Marshall's work as solicitor general of the United States.

Lunsman, Lisa A. "Justice Thurgood Marshall: A Retrospective." *University of West Los Angeles Law Review* 23 (Annual 1992): 64–74. Assessment of Marshall's career.

Marcus, Maria. "Learning Together: Justice Marshall's Desegregation Opinions." *Fordham Law Review* 61 (October 1992): 69–104. Account of *Brown* v. *Board of Education* and its legacy.

Marshall, Thurgood. "Marshall: U.S. Government Defective from Its Beginning." *Chicago Daily Law Bulletin,* May 6, 1987, 1, 14. Summary of Marshall's speech denouncing the United States Constitution as a racist document.

———. "Remarks on the Death Penalty Made at the Judicial Conference of the Second Circuit." *Columbia Law Review* 86 (January 1986): 1–8. Transcript of Marshall's remarks about his opposition to the death penalty.

Mauro, Tony. "Back to Bakke." *California Lawyer* 14 (January 1944): 50–56. Discussion of *Regents of the University of California* v. *Bakke* (1978) and Marshall's dissenting opinion.

McCarthy, Jim. "ABA Honors Thurgood Marshall: Retired Justice Will Receive ABA Medal at Annual Meeting." *ABA Journal* 78 (August 1992): 104. Announcement of Marshall's selection in 1992 to receive the Annual Medal of the American Bar Association.

Mello, Michael. "Adhering to Our Views: Justices Brennan and Marshall and the Relentless Dissent to Death as a Punishment." *Florida State University Law Review* 22 (Winter 1995): 591–694. Commentary about the opposition of Justices Brennan and Marshall to capital punishment.

Minow, Martha. "Choices and Constraints: For Justice Thurgood Marshall." *Georgetown Law Journal* 80 (August 1992): 2093–2108. Discussion of the choices and constraints faced by Marshall as an associate justice of the United States Supreme Court, in conjunction with the symposium Honoring Justice Thurgood Marshall.

Moglen, Eben. "A Vigil for Thurgood Marshall." *Columbia Law Review* 93 (June 1993): 1061–1062. Reflections on Marshall's life.

Moran, Terence. "Plain Truths from the People's Lawyer." *Legal Times* (July 1, 1991): 23, 28. Editorial on Marshall's retirement from the United States Supreme Court and comments on his contributions to the American legal system.

Motley, Constance Baker. "Standing on His Shoulders: Thurgood Marshall's Early Career." *Harvard Blackletter Journal* 6 (Spring 1989): 9–17. Recollections of Marshall's early career and his influence on the life of Motley.

O'Connor, Sandra Day. "Thurgood Marshall: The Influence of a Raconteur." *Stanford Law Review* 44 (Summer 1992): 1217–1220. Account of Marshall's influence on O'Connor's thinking.

Oliveras, Michael A. "Mr. Justice Marshall, Dissenting: 'Meaningful Equality Remains a Distant Dream.'" *Southern University Law Review* 20 (Spring 1993): 21–25. Discussion of Marshall's role in fighting for equality in public education.

Percival, Robert. "Environmental Law in the Supreme Court: Highlights from the Marshall Papers." *Environmental Law Reporter* 23 (October 1993): 10606–10626. Information from Marshall's papers about the United States Supreme Court and environmental law.

Reske, Henry J. "A Court's Deliberations Revealed: Critics Charge Library's Release of Marshall Papers Thwarted the Justice's Intent." *ABA Journal* 79 (August 1993): 26–27. Information from Marshall's papers about the deliberations of the United States Supreme Court during his tenure there; criticism of the Library of Congress for the release of his papers.

———. "Marshall Retires for Health Reasons: First Black Justice Fought Discrimination as Litigator, Supreme Court Dissenter." *ABA Journal* 77 (August 1991): 14–15. Brief summary of Marshall's life following his retirement from the United States Supreme Court.

Rosenthal, Andrew. "Marshall Retires from High Court; Blow to Liberals." *New York Times,* June 28, 1991, A1. Effect of Marshall's retirement on Supreme Court's liberal minority.

Rowan, Carl T. *Dream Makers, Dream Breakers: The World of Justice Thurgood Marshall.* Boston: Little, Brown, 1993. Biography of Marshall focusing on his personality and his search for justice.

————. "Justice Marshall: Candor on Court, Meese, Life." *Legal Times,* December 14, 1987, 8. Marshall's candid comments about Attorney General Edwin Meese and other topics in one of his infrequent interviews.

Schotten, Peter. "Is the Constitution Still Meaningful? Public Reflections upon the Fundamental Law of the Land." *South Dakota Law Review* 33 (Spring 1988): 32–65. Discussion of Attorney General Edwin Meese's interpretation of the Constitution, in contrast to the interpretations of justices, with emphasis on the views of Justices Brennan and Marshall.

Sharpe, Calvin William. "'Judging in Good Faith': Seeing Justice Marshall's Legacy Through a Labor Case." *Arizona State Law Journal* 26 (Summer 1994): 479–493. Account of Marshall's dedication to the cause of labor.

Simons, Kenneth W. "Justice Thurgood Marshall: A Reminiscence." *Boston University Public Interest Law Journal* 3 (Spring 1993): 1–4. Tribute to Marshall after his death.

Smith, J. Clay, Jr., and Scott Burrell. "Justice Thurgood Marshall and the First Amendment." *Arizona State Law Journal* 26 (Summer 1994): 461–478. Marshall's views on the First Amendment freedoms.

Spritzer, Ralph S. "Thurgood Marshall: A Dedicated Career." *Arizona State Law Journal* 26 (Summer 1994): 353–367. Overview of Marshall's work and achievements.

Steiker, Carol S. "'Did You Hear What Thurgood Marshall Did for Us?'—A Tribute." *American Journal of Criminal Law* 20 (Winter 1993): 7–11. Appreciation of Marshall's work by minority groups in the country.

Steiker, Jordan. "The Long Road Up From Barbarism: Thurgood Marshall and the Death Penalty." *Texas Law Review* 71 (May 1993): 1131–1164. Tribute to Marshall for his opposition to capital punishment.

Stone, Geoffrey R. "Marshall: He's the Frustrated Conscience of the High Court." *National Law Journal* (February 18, 1980): 24, 34. Marshall's frustrations at the conservative decisions of the United States Supreme Court.

Taylor, Stuart, Jr. "Glimpses of the Least Pretentious of Men." *Legal Times,* February 8, 1993, 35–36. Account of Marshall's unpretentious nature.

————. "Marshall Ranks Reagan as Last on Civil Rights." *Chicago Daily Law Bulletin,* September 9, 1987, 1, 14. Summary of a Marshall interview in which he put President Ronald Reagan in last place among other presidents in terms of his record on civil rights.

————. "Marshall Sounds Critical Note on Bicentennial." *New York Times,* May 7, 1987, A1. Article on Marshall's criticism of the United States Constitution as a racist document.

————. "Marshall Unfinished Business." *Legal Times,* July 1, 1991, 22. Editorial about Marshall's retirement from the United States Supreme Court and the work that he left behind.

Tsosie, Rebecca. "Separate Sovereigns, Civil Rights, and the Sacred Text: The Legacy of Justice Thurgood Marshall's Indian Law Jurisprudence." *Arizona State Law Journal* 26 (Summer 1994): 495–533. Discussion of Marshall's rulings in the Supreme Court on issues affecting American Indians.

Tushnet, Mark V. *Making Civil Rights Law: Thurgood Marshall and the Supreme Court, 1936–1961.* New York: Oxford University Press, 1994. Marshall's efforts to secure civil rights through litigation, as well as the story of those lawyers and cases essential to secure equal justice before the law.

————. *Making Constitutional Law: Thurgood Marshall and the Supreme Court, 1961–1991.* New York: Oxford University Press, 1997. Discussion of Marshall's role in constitutional law during his tenure on the United States Supreme Court.

————. "The Supreme Court and Race Discrimination, 1967–1991: The View from the Marshall Papers." *William and Mary Law Review* 36 (January 1995): 473–545. Information in Marshall's papers about the Court and the efforts to end race discrimination in America, in conjunction with the symposium *Brown* v. *Board of Education* After Forty Years: Confronting the Promise.

————. "Thurgood Marshall and the Brethren." *Georgetown Law Journal* 80 (August 1992): 2109–2130. Discussion of Marshall's relationship with the other justices on the United States Supreme Court, in conjunction with the symposium Honoring Justice Thurgood Marshall.

————. "Thurgood Marshall and the Rule of Law." *Howard Law Journal* 35 (Fall 1991): 7–22. Overview of Marshall's legal philosophy.

————. "Thurgood Marshall as a Lawyer: The Campaign against School Segregation, 1945–1950." *Maryland Law Review* 40 (Summer 1981): 411–434. Story of Marshall's early work as a litigator on behalf of integration.

Uelmen, Gerald F. "Justice Thurgood Marshall and the Death Penalty: A Former Criminal Defense Lawyer on the Supreme Court." *Arizona State Law Journal* 26 (Summer 1994): 403–411. Discussion of Marshall's view in opposition to the death penalty and how his experiences as a criminal defense attorney influenced his thinking on this issue.

Wells, N. Douglas. "Justice Thurgood Marshall: 'Prophet with Honor': A Tribute." *Capital University Law Review* 22 (Summer 1993): 561–570. Tribute to Marshall after his death.

————. "Thurgood Marshall and 'Individual Self-Realization' in First Amendment Jurisprudence." *Tennessee Law Review* 61 (Fall 1993): 237–287. Analysis of Marshall's views on First Amendment freedoms.

Williams, Juan. "Marshall's Law," in *Thurgood Marshall: Justice for All,* ed. Roger Goldman, with David Gallen. New York: Carroll and Graf, 1992. Summary of Marshall's achievements.

————. *Thurgood Marshall: American Revolutionary.* New York: Times Books, 1998. Biography of Marshall based, in part, on interviews conducted with his friends, schoolmates, and law associates.

Williams, Karen Hastie. "Humanizing the Legal Process: The Legacy of Thurgood Marshall." *Harvard Blackletter Journal* 6 (Spring 1989): 90–94. Account of Marshall's zeal in having the legal process serve the public interest.

Woodward, Bob, and Scott Armstrong. *The Brethren: Inside the Supreme Court.* New York: Simon and Schuster, 1979; reprint, New York: Avon Books, 1981. Study of the inner workings of the United States Supreme Court from 1969 to 1976.

Zion, Sidney E. "Thurgood Marshall Takes a New 'Tush-Tush' Job." *New York Times Magazine,* August 22, 1965, 11, 68–71. Account of Marshall prior to his appointment as United States solicitor general in 1965.

-William M.-
Kunstler

(Courtesy of Ronald L. Kuby)

Chronology

1919   Born on July 7 New York City to Monroe Bradford Kunstler, M.D., and Frances Mandelbaum Kunstler.

1937   Graduated first in his class from DeWitt Clinton High School, New York City.

1941   Graduated Phi Beta Kappa from Yale University, New Haven, Connecticut; published first book, *Our Pleasant Vices* (a collection of sonnets), coauthored with Yale student William Vincent Stone; enlisted in United States Signal Corps.

1943   Married Lotte Rosenberger, in January in New York; birth of first child, Karin.

1946   Discharged from the army.

1948   Graduated from Columbia Law School, New York; worked as executive trainee at R.H. Macy's Department Store, New York; admitted to the bar.

1949   Cofounded law firm, Kunstler & Kunstler, in partnership with younger brother, Michael; birth of second child, Jane.

1954   Published *The Law of Accidents* and *Corporate Tax Summary.*

1961   Represented the Freedom Riders in Jackson, Mississippi; became personal trial attorney to Dr. Martin Luther King Jr.

1966   Cofounded Center for Constitutional Rights, New York.

1967   Won a major victory in *Hobson* v. *Hanson,* which ended the tracking and placement system in the public schools in the District of Columbia.

1970   Conclusion of Chicago Seven trial, Chicago, Illinois, in which all the defendants were found not guilty of conspiracy.

1971   Represented Attica prisoners, Auburn, New York, in negotiations with New York State's Department of Correctional Services.

1973   Defended Native Americans accused of illegally occupying Wounded Knee, South Dakota, the site of an Indian massacre in 1890.

1974   Divorced from Lotte Rosenberger Kunstler.

1975   Married Margaret L. Ratner, Esq.

1976   Birth of third child, Sarah.

1978   Birth of fourth child, Emily.

1982   Hired Ronald L. Kuby, a student at Cornell Law School, as a summer intern—the beginning of their longtime legal association.

1988   Won acquittal for Larry Davis, a young black man accused of wounding six policemen in a shoot-out in the Bronx, New York.

1989   Attacked by white police officers in a Brooklyn Court in retaliation for his defense of Larry Davis.

1990   Won acquittal for El Sayyid Nosair, an Arab identified by an eyewitness as the killer of Rabbi Meir Kahane of the Jewish Defense League; unsuccessful in efforts to win the acquittal of Yusef Salaam, a black fifteen-year-old accused of being one of the rapists of a white jogger in Central Park.

1993   Censured by a Manhattan appeals court for his derogatory comments to Acting State Supreme Court Judge Thomas B. Galligan.

1994   Represented Colin Ferguson (indicted for killing six white people in a Long Island railroad car) in a "black rage" defense, but later dismissed by his client, who unsuccessfully represented himself.

1995   Died of heart failure on September 4, in New York.

Biography

The critics of William Moses Kunstler—the flamboyant, controversial attorney who was called "the most hated lawyer in America"—might take note of a comment made by the late Supreme Court Justice Frank Murphy in *Bridges* v. *Wixon* (1945). "Only by zealously guarding the rights of the most humble, the most unorthodox and the most despised among us," he wrote, "can freedom flourish and endure in our land."[1]

Bill Kunstler transformed himself in the 1960s from a relatively undistinguished lawyer specializing in marriage, estate, and business law into one of the most important, unconventional attorneys in the twentieth century. His prominent (and protest-minded) clients included Dr. Martin Luther King Jr.; Malcolm X; the Freedom Riders; Abbie Hoffman; Jerry Rubin; Daniel and Philip Berrigan; the Black Panthers; Stokely Carmichael; H. Rap Brown; the Attica inmates; and members of the American Indian Movement. But he also defended an almost limitless number of anonymous and frightened people, without fanfare and without fee.

By the time of his death in 1995 at the age of seventy-six, he had more than lived up to the comment made about him at an earlier stage of his career. "Kunstler handles more big cases in a week," noted a young attorney in the late 1960s, "than I will in a lifetime." He participated in over two hundred federal district court cases, one hundred fifty federal appeals, and hundreds of New York State trials; argued six cases before the United States Supreme Court; and (according to attorney Gerald Lefcourt) had more social justice cases "than all the lawyers in the nation that ever lived combined."[2]

The controversial nature of Kunstler's practice tended to dwarf the major contributions that he made in the field of constitutional law. His six Supreme Court cases had far-reaching consequences, and one of his federal district court cases—*Hobson* v. *Hanson* (1967), which ended a tracking and placement system based on racially biased intelligence tests in the public schools of the District of Columbia—was described by him as "the most gratifying of my entire career."[3]

Kunstler was an upper-middle-class, Ivy League–educated lawyer who earned a Phi Beta Kappa key at Yale, where he majored in French literature; wrote nine nonfiction books and three collections of poetry; was an expert on Dylan Thomas; enjoyed opera and art (he often spent lunch breaks during his famous Chicago Seven case visiting the Chicago Art Institute); taught on an adjunct basis at Columbia University's School of General Studies, Cooper Union, and the New School for Social Research; had cameo roles in several motion pictures, including Spike Lee's *Malcolm X;* wrote poetry almost daily throughout his life; and liked to begin and end his courtroom summations with a literary quotation.[4]

If Kunstler had not led such a frenetic life in the course of championing the causes he cared about so passionately and defending the clients with whom he invariably bonded, he might have made his reputation as a writer. One of his manuscripts—an incomplete typewritten copy of *The Minister and the Choir Singer: The Hall-Mills Murder Case* (1964)—is housed in a special collection at the New York Public Library, perhaps incongruously alongside the works of twenty-three other writers, including Stephen Vincent Benet, Robert E. Sherwood, and John Steinbeck. A reference to this work (the only one of his books to be a best-seller) was made by Maurice N. Nessen, who had known Kunstler during their early years as colleagues at New York Law School. In introducing Kunstler at a forum at the New York County Lawyers' Association in 1971, Nessen reminisced: "He went on to write a book that I read and thought was going to be his greatest claim to fame."[5]

A Striking Personality

It was easy to spot Kunstler in court. A striking six-footer with a gravelly voice, chiseled features, glasses perched at the top of his head, a toothbrush in his pocket so that he would be prepared for jail if he were facing a contempt citation, a clenched fist raised defiantly over his head, and the dangling hair which became a symbol of both his unconventional approach to the legal system and the kinds of clients he tended to represent, Kunstler was described by *Esquire* as looking like "Lincoln on pot."[6]

Kunstler first attracted national attention in 1969, when he defended the Chicago Seven, a group of anti–Vietnam War protesters arrested the previous year for their demonstrations at the Democratic National Convention. It was at this trial that Kunstler adopted many of the practices that would become his trademark: attacking the presiding judge with gusto, identifying with the radical ideology of the defendants, using the trial to make political statements of his own, engaging in theatrics to attract attention, departing from the accepted standards of courtroom behavior, seeking publicity to give a positive spin on his clients, turning the tables on the prosecution by putting the legal system on trial, and employing humor as a tactic of the defense.[7]

After the trial, he became a hero of the counterculture, which questioned American values at a time when the country was polarized by issues like civil rights, race relations, and the Vietnam War. As the radical movement dissipated in the years that followed, Kunstler refused to abandon the cause. At the end of his life, he had become even more famous—or infamous—because of his defense of cop killers, Middle Eastern terrorists—and a deranged black man whose killing of six white people on a New York commuter train was justified by Kunstler as an example of "black rage."[8]

Kunstler relished all the attention he received and cherished his celebrity status, including the insults. A brilliant combination of showman and scholar, he seldom turned down a request for an interview. "Bill is one of the few lawyers," noted journalist Sidney Zion, "who knows how to talk to the press.

His stories always check out and he's not afraid to talk to you, and he's got credibility—although you've got to ask sometimes, 'Bill, is it really true?'"[9]

By many accounts, Kunstler was an extraordinarily warm, likable, and witty person—a view of him that contrasted sharply with his public persona. In the course of his career, he clashed with the Bar Association of the City of New York, managed to be held in contempt by so many judges that he had difficulty remembering the occasions, and considered himself a survivor because he was never stripped of his license. "If you hang around long enough and you don't get disbarred," he told a reporter in 1989, "they realize you won't go away."[10]

A "Radical" and His Clients

Would Kunstler take any person for a client? In 1970, he proclaimed that he was "not a lawyer for hire" and would defend only those "whom I love." Later on, he eagerly accepted clients—innocent or guilty—who he felt were victimized by the American legal system because they were members of an "oppressed" minority.* He surprised many of his friends by occasionally representing members of organized crime (who he felt were made scapegoats by the government), including reputed mobster John Gotti, for whom Kunstler in 1992 appealed a ruling that had barred Gotti's longtime lawyer, Bruce Cutler, from serving as his counsel—a civil rights matter, according to Kunstler, who never charged Gotti a fee for these services. But he preferred to draw the line on defending a suspect accused of rape, child abuse, or domestic violence. It also would have been highly unlikely for Kunstler to have defended the rights of a person with a right-wing ideology.[11]

His heavy caseload came at a price. He was frequently criticized by other lawyers for being unprepared and for "winging" it in court. There are many stories of how he failed to meet court deadlines, overlooked bail bonds for his clients, neglected to file papers, and displayed an impatience with facts. In 1994, Kunstler spoke at the twenty-fifth reunion of the participants in the Chicago Seven trial. When a reporter from the *Los Angeles Times* questioned him about his recollection of the testimony of Chicago Seven defense witness Paul Krassner, who had ingested three hundred micrograms of the hallucinogenic

---

*Legal expenses for most of these cases were borne, in whole or in part, by the Center for Constitutional Rights, a nonprofit organization in New York which Kunstler had cofounded in 1966 with attorneys Arthur Kinoy, Benjamin Smith, and Morton Stavis. These modest reimbursements included a payment to him of $100 per week for his expenses during the Chicago Seven trial. But he never received a fee from the center for any of his professional work and represented many (but not all) of his clients on a pro bono basis.[12]

drug LSD prior to testifying at the trial, Kunstler snapped, "These are details. I mean, the man was stoned out of his mind. That's all you need to know."*[13]

Kunstler was keenly aware of this type of criticism and could be candid about it. At the same time, he concluded that the balance sheet was clearly in his favor:

> I must admit some times the research was hasty, from the back seat of a car. But I think we lost very few of the ones I was associated with that came out of the [radical] movement. We didn't do so badly.[15]

A year before his death, Kunstler completed his autobiography, *My Life as a Radical Lawyer* (1994), written in collaboration with journalist Sheila Isenberg. The book, originally to be called *Loose Cannon,* was a remarkably frank account in which he admitted to promiscuity during his first marriage, a nearly fatal reaction on one occasion to drugs taken with his client, Lenny Bruce, and a painful recollection of his relationship with his younger brother, Michael. He strenuously objected to the title, which was chosen by the publisher. "That's not my title," he said in an interview in 1995. "I'm not sure lawyers who are still within the system have the right to call themselves radical." He had expressed the same sentiment in an interview he had given two years earlier to David Marshall, an attorney from England:

> I'm no radical lawyer. That's a label the press gave me. I'm the people's lawyer, an opponent of the government. My role is to be a constant threat.[16]

Kunstler's book included an unusually candid preface by collaborator Isenberg. She acknowledged that Kunstler "told me many stories that turned out to be untrue" and noted that she "checked key episodes with other sources, finally selecting from the sometimes mutable versions of his storytelling the account that strays least from the truth."[17]

Upper-Middle-Class Upbringing, 1919–1932

One indisputable fact in the life of William Moses Kunstler is that he gained his fame from representing clients whose socioeconomic backgrounds were vastly different from his own. He was born on July 7, 1919, to a well-to-do German-Jewish family in New York. His mother, Frances ("Fanny") Mandelbaum, was the stepdaughter of a successful physician, and met her future husband, Dr. Monroe Bradford Kunstler, when he joined her stepfather's practice. The family had hoped that the young physician would marry Dr. Mandelbaum's maiden sister, but he preferred Fanny and asked her to be his wife.

---

*In an article for *New York* in 1994, Krassner wrote that "Kunstler's account of my testimony bore no relation to the trial transcript." At the time of Kunstler's death the following year, his obituary in *The Nation* added an interesting detail to the story—that Krassner, out of deference to Kunstler, never mentioned that the latter also was stoned that day, having shared some hash with the defendants over lunch.[14]

The name Kunstler, which means "magician" in Yiddish, could have other connotations. On the very first day of the Chicago Seven trial, Kunstler introduced himself to Judge Julius Jennings Hoffman by saying, "That's 'Kunstler,' with a 'K,' your honor," a reference to the fact that many of his detractors liked to give it a pornographic spelling.[18]

Kunstler was the oldest of three children. He had a younger brother, Michael, and a sister, Mary. Michael was his brother's law partner for twenty-one years and carried the burden of the firm's caseload when the more famous brother became engaged in pro bono work. In 1976, Michael was grief-stricken over the suicide of his son, and he remained shattered emotionally until his own death eight years later at the age of sixty-two. Kunstler (who was unusually caring to his clients) acknowledged in his autobiography that he was too preoccupied with his own work to help Michael during the troubled last years of his brother's life.

> One of my major faults is that I'm too impatient with people to be a really good listener. I'm not very sympathetic, and I get bored with people who complain or agonize over their problems, as Michael was doing—as he was entitled to do. My way of dealing with emotional trauma has always been to avoid and deny. . . .
> To this day, I'm sorry I wasn't of more help to Michael. He needed someone to listen to him, and I just couldn't do it.[19]

Kunstler acknowledged that certain aspects of his childhood set him apart from several of his peers: he came from an eccentric family, and he could not remember a time when he did not feel "the desire to resist authority, oppose convention, and champion the underdog." Yet he was not unmindful of the opportunities available to him as a result of his background:

> I worked for what I have, but I was in a position to accumulate possessions because of what I was equipped with from the start. My father was a physician and my [paternal] grandfather had been a merchant. Being white, they had been able to accumulate goods and status. And, accordingly, I was always well fed; I was always warm in the winter and cool in the summer; and because of my background, I could get a Columbia and Yale education. Very few black people in this society get a chance to start with all these advantages.[20]

The strongest influence in his childhood was his maternal stepgrandfather, Moses Joseph Mandelbaum, known to his family as "Pa Moe." Mandelbaum, a physician, had married Kunstler's widowed grandmother, Hannah, in Albany, New York, when Kunstler's mother was two years old.

Following their marriage, the Mandelbaums moved to a brownstone on West 145th Street in New York City, where he established a successful practice as an ear, nose, and throat specialist. A nifty dresser and a ladies' man, Pa Moe lost all of his money in the stock market crash of 1929, but probably set an example to Kunstler by never losing his zest for life. Kunstler admiringly recalled that Pa Moe "maintained his spiffy appearance and *joie de vivre* and always looked prosperous," despite his financial reverses.[21]

Kunstler had more conflicting emotions about his father, whom he described as "a plodding sloppy man" with "wrinkled collars and nicotine-stained fingers." Dr. Kunstler initially had practiced with Pa Moe, but later opened his own office and became a successful proctologist. As a youngster, Bill particularly resented the fact that his father seemed more engrossed in his practice than in his family—a trait that Kunstler nevertheless admitted was characteristic of himself as well, particularly during his first marriage.[22]

From Rebel to Scholar to Soldier, 1932–1946

The Kunstler family led a life of comfort. In 1932, they moved to a spacious twelve-room apartment on Manhattan's fashionable Upper West Side. Their lives were enlivened by the antics of their oldest son, who enjoyed being different from everyone else and delighted in startling his parents and their friends. As Kunstler recalled,

> not a single day went by that I didn't misbehave in some way, large or small. In many ways, I am still that little boy who always must act outrageously so he can remain outside the mainstream.[23]

Kunstler claimed that one of his ways of misbehaving was to join the Red Devils, an interracial neighborhood gang. While he never became friendly with any of the Red Devils, he enjoyed the excitement that gang membership brought into his life.

> Although I ran with the gang, I never became close friends with any one boy. We broke windows, stole from penny gum machines, busted into warehouses, and attacked other kids. I rebelled against hanging out with the middle-class Jewish kids in the fancy high-rise apartment house where my family lived, and I reveled in my gang. There was no reason for it; I simply found the mixed gang more stimulating and exciting than the other group of kids—who were all exactly like me.[24]

After graduating from elementary school, Kunstler entered DeWitt Clinton High School's Manhattan Annex. It was then he decided to become a "scholar" and prove to his parents that he could make his mark in the world "even though I wasn't going to do it their way." At the time of his graduation in 1937, he was a straight A student and first in his class.[25]

Kunstler's excellent marks earned him admission to Yale University. His family had expected him to be a physician, but he struggled with his science courses and received a D in organic chemistry. In spite of his family's disappointment, he switched his major to French and never received a grade lower than A for the rest of his college career. By the end of his senior year, he was elected to Phi Beta Kappa.

While he was at Yale, he collaborated on a book with a fellow student, William Vincent Stone, to produce a volume of poetry entitled *Our Pleasant Vices*—a title borrowed from a line in Shakespeare's *King Lear.* It was printed with the help of Kunstler's paternal uncle, a trade magazine editor.

Three months after his graduation from Yale in June 1941, Kunstler enlisted in the United States Signal Corps. While he had intended to serve out a two-year tour of duty, he changed his mind when the country entered World War II following the Pearl Harbor attack on December 7, deciding to go to Officers' Candidate School. He later won a Bronze Star for his service with the Eighth Army in the Pacific, earning the rank of major after a postwar stint in the army reserves.

During the war, in January 1943, Kunstler married Lotte Rosenberger, a seventeen-year-old refugee from Nazi Germany and his fifth cousin. Their first daughter, Karin, was born at the end of the year, and their second, Jane, in 1949.[26]

Law School, 1946–1948

After Kunstler's release from the army in 1946, he had intended to study journalism. He may have been encouraged in this decision when several of his articles about his experiences in the Signal Corps appeared in the *Paterson Evening News,* which was published by a friend of his family. But he claimed that sibling rivalry dictated another choice when his brother, Michael (who had followed him to Yale), was accepted at Columbia Law School.

"Furious that my baby brother was now ahead of me," Kunstler wrote in his autobiography, "I dropped my plans to be a writer, forgot about journalism, and decided to go to law school—for no other reason than Michael was going." In actuality, there was another reason for his choice, and Kunstler proceeded to contradict himself (as he was prone to do on many other occasions) a few pages later in his book. "We were all on the road to success," he wrote, "[which was] something very important to me then." He went on to note that he was attracted to the legal profession because of its opportunities for status, prestige, and a reasonably high income.[27]

Although he was not the outstanding student at Columbia that he had been at Yale (he subsequently failed the procedural part of the bar examination on his first try), he steadied down after a shaky first year. But the life of a conventional law student did not suit Kunstler, who was drawn to areas outside the realm of his studies.

Finding he no longer had to rely on his family connections to get his writing into print, he wrote book reviews while in law school for many newspapers and magazines, including the *New York Herald-Tribune, Life, Saturday Review, Atlantic Monthly,* and the *New York Times.* In addition, he taught a course in writing at Columbia's School of General Studies, worked as a reader for the story department at Paramount Pictures, and collaborated with Michael on law course summaries known as "purples," which they sold to their fellow students at Columbia.

Kunstler pursued an accelerated course at Columbia, graduating in two years. He then worked briefly as an executive trainee at R.H. Macy's department store in New York. In December 1948, he was admitted to the bar and began his professional career.[28]

Law Practice, 1948–1956

He referred to himself as a "legal tradesman" during the early years of his law practice. His first office was in New York, where he went into partnership with his brother. The firm handled business and family law, the kinds of routine cases that were essential for the firm's financial success.

The practice proved too staid for Kunstler, and he quickly branched out into other activities. During the 1950s, he taught courses on trusts and estates at New York Law School; published two books, *The Law of Accidents* (1954) and *Corporate Tax Summary* (1954); served a stint as a radio talk show host on the ABC station WJZ (later WABC); wrote scripts dramatizing famous trials for the YMCA's radio station, WMCA; and reviewed books for various publications.[29]

Kunstler was not immune to the appeal of the comfortable life. He joined the exodus to suburbia in the 1950s, when he purchased a home in New York's affluent Westchester County, and became what he termed a "parlor liberal." He joined the National Association for the Advancement of Colored People (NAACP), the Urban League, and the American Civil Liberties Union (ACLU). He and his wife held meetings in their home, and he wrote letters to newspapers on civic matters and tried to influence local elections.[30]

Although his prosperous, soundly middle-class lifestyle would have satisfied many other attorneys of his generation, he felt unfulfilled and "bored out of my skull." An apt comment about this period in his life was made by writer Scott Spencer in an article in *Rolling Stone*. "It must have been the memory of how completely beside the point life can be," Spencer wrote, "that helped him endure the relatively low pay and high stress of his subsequent career as an attorney for the despised."[31]

Defense of William Worthy, 1956–1961

The tranquility of these early years was interrupted for a brief period in 1956, which helped launch him in another direction. Kunstler was retained on a pro bono basis by the ACLU to defend a black reporter named William Worthy, who worked for the *Baltimore Afro-American*. By going as a freelance reporter to Red China in 1956, the heyday of the anti-Communist period, Worthy had violated a United States government ban on travel to that country. Accordingly, his passport was confiscated by the government upon his return to the United States. Kunstler sued in the district court of the District of Columbia for the return of Worthy's passport, but the court ruled against his client.[32]

Six years later, Worthy was again in need of legal assistance. This time, he had visited Cuba, another country to which travel was prohibited, and was arrested when he arrived back in Miami, Florida. He was subsequently tried and convicted by a federal court in Miami under an obscure statute that made it a crime to return to the United States without a valid passport. Worthy faced a penalty of five years in jail or a fine of $5,000 or both.[33]

The ACLU once more called upon Kunstler to enter the case, and he appealed the decision before the Fifth Circuit in Atlanta in 1961. In his opening statement, he quoted the lines from Sir Walter Scott's poem, "The Lay of the Last Minstrel"—"Breathes there a man with soul so dead/Who never to himself hath said/This is my own, my native land." This dramatic opening was followed by his argument that there was no provision in the United States Constitution requiring a valid passport to be presented upon a person's return to his country. He asked the court to overturn Worthy's conviction. The circuit court invalidated the statute and ruled in favor of Worthy. Kunstler was delighted that he had made a change in the annals of American law. He recalled this case in his autobiography with the same kind of boyish enthusiasm that characterized his approach to life:

> This was the first time I had ever invalidated a statute. . . . Let the other lawyers draft wills and do real estate closings. I had *changed* the law! I had made a contribution! I felt an enormous thrill and a desire to do more of the same.[34]

Prolific Author, 1960–1964

Despite his desire for more stimulating legal work, Kunstler left himself little time for self-reflection. In addition to his full-time law practice and his work on *The Minister and the Choir Singer*, he managed to complete three more books in the early 1960s. They were *First Degree* (1960), a study of eighteen murder cases; *Beyond a Reasonable Doubt? The Original Trial of Caryl Chessman* (1961), an assessment of the conviction and execution of the California kidnapper; and *The Case for Courage* (1962). One of those ten was Clarence Darrow, one of Kunstler's heroes.

Freedom Riders, 1961–1964

It was while he was on a publicity tour for *Beyond a Reasonable Doubt?* in June 1961 that he received a telephone call that would change his life. The call was from the ACLU's Rowland Watts, who had originally called upon him in the Worthy case. This time, Watts asked Kunstler to fly to Jackson, Mississippi, to express the ACLU's "moral support" to black attorney Jack H. Young. A former postman who had studied law in the office of the only black lawyer in Mississippi at that time, Young was defending the Freedom Riders for the Congress of Racial Equality (CORE), one of the leading civil rights protest groups in the nation.[35]

The Freedom Riders were a group of white and black protesters from the North who had been organized under the auspices of CORE to desegregate the bus terminals and other places of public accommodation in the South. The telephone call, which came when Kunstler was in the midst of preparing the Worthy appeal, made him ponder what he wanted to do with the rest of his life:

> I told Rowland I needed some time to think about it and would call him back. I sat down on the bed and thought: Ever since the passport case, I had not been much interested in my law practice and had felt faint stirrings within me for more mean- ingful work, perhaps law on a grander scale. I recalled the words of Justice Oliver Wendell Holmes: "As life is action and passion, it is required of a man that he should share the passion and action of his time, at peril of being judged not to have lived." When Rowland asked me to go South, I was forty-two and decided that when I was old and looked back on my life, I didn't want to discover that I had merely existed.[36]

He arrived in Jackson on the night of June 15, 1961, and went to see Young early the next day. Kunstler had already been informed by Watts that four hundred Freedom Riders had been arrested in Mississippi and that Young was the only lawyer representing them. "I bring you regards from the ACLU," Kunstler told Young when they met. "I don't want regards," Young snapped. "I need lawyers." Young then instructed Kunstler to go down to the Grey- hound Bus Terminal, where a group of Freedom Riders was expected to ar- rive that same morning.[37] When Kunstler walked over to the bus terminal from Young's office, he noticed the presence of police officers and reporters. Shortly afterwards, the Freedom Riders (three young white women, a white man, and a black youth) arrived at the terminal and sat down at the lunch counter. When they refused a request by a police officer to move, they were promptly arrested.

Kunstler was visibly moved by the "total" commitment of "five frightened young people" who had dedicated themselves to the quest for "equality of all people." He spent the next few months commuting between Jackson and New York while working on filing habeas corpus petitions for their release from prison. His efforts were unsuccessful—an experience shared by other north- ern and southern lawyers working on behalf of the Freedom Riders, whose habeas corpus petitions were routinely rejected by the southern state courts.[38]

Realizing that bolder action was necessary, Kunstler wholeheartedly en- dorsed an idea first suggested to him by William L. Higgs, a Mississippi-born graduate of Harvard Law School and the great-grandson of the state's gover- nor at the time of the Civil War. Higgs found a little-known statute from the Civil Rights Act of 1866. This "removal statute," which was enacted to pre- vent the newly freed slaves from being tried in state courts by their former masters, required the federal courts to take an accused person from a state court when it was alleged that the defendant could not get a fair trial.[39] Kunstler proceeded to work with Higgs in petitioning the removal of the Freedom Rider cases to federal court. Soon other civil rights lawyers were calling them for advice on what Kunstler referred to as "the single most important procedural device we lawyers had during the early years of the Civil Rights movement."[40]

Three years later, Higgs and Kunstler got the support of Democratic Repre- sentative Robert Kastenmeier of Wisconsin, who had a provision inserted into the Civil Rights Act of 1964 regarding the removal of cases from state courts. Young and Carl Rachlin, the general counsel of CORE, were successful in getting the Supreme Court, in *Thomas* v. *Mississippi* (1965), to overturn a state court decision that had gone against the Freedom Riders. In a unanimous decision ending the use of local criminal statutes to enforce segregation in interstate carriers, the Supreme Court ordered the release of all the Jackson Freedom Riders. Although the decision was later watered down by the judges in *City of Greenwood* v. *Peacock* (1966), the Freedom Riders had won their day in court.[41]

Law Practice, 1961–1970

As requests for help came from all over the South, Kunstler moved to center stage. In 1961, he had already attracted the attention of Dr. Martin Luther King Jr., who asked Kunstler to be his personal trial attorney. Kunstler was known in liberal circles for his work on behalf of William Worthy, and King needed an attorney who would be prepared to handle the kinds of unpopular cases that an organization-minded lawyer might shun.[42] During his seven-year association with the famed civil rights leader (it ended when King was assassinated in 1968), Kunstler never became part of King's inner circle. But King called upon him to file many federal lawsuits during those years, and Kunstler remarked that he "never turned down calls from Martin, and was always thrilled to accept them."[43]

One of Kunstler's most potentially interesting assignments at this time never took place. In November 1963, the ACLU asked him to serve on the defense team for Lee Harvey Oswald, the alleged assassin of President John F. Kennedy. Oswald's murder by Dallas businessman Jack Ruby two days after Kennedy's death rendered that task unnecessary.

Kunstler did serve on a defense team in connection with the Kennedy assassination. After Ruby had been convicted for Oswald's murder, he sought Kunstler's help. It was not a pro bono case because Kunstler accepted a $2,500 fee from Ruby's family. Working with a group of lawyers, he was successful, in October 1966, in getting the Texas Court of Criminal Appeals to reverse Ruby's conviction on the grounds that the evidence used to convict him of Oswald's murder should not have been admissible. Ruby's subsequent death in January 1967, when he was awaiting a retrial, finally brought an end to Kunstler's role in the aftermath of the Kennedy assassination.[44]

Later in the 1960s, Kunstler had many other high-profile cases. He was one of the lawyers to handle the Reverend Adam Clayton's Powell's appeal in 1967 for the restoration of his congressional seat. The next year, he defended the Catonsville Nine, a group of antiwar protesters led by Catholic priests Daniel and Philip Berrigan, who had destroyed selective service records in Maryland. In 1969, he helped obtain the release from federal prison of Morton Sobell, who had been convicted of conspiring in espionage with accused atomic spies Julius and Ethel Rosenberg, both of whom had been put to death in 1953.[45]

Kunstler also handled a large number of cases in which he represented clients associated with the Movement, a group of radicals seeking to change the American political system. In taking these cases, he matched his own rhetoric to that of the Movement clients he represented. He warmly embraced the militant Black Panther Party's call to violence as a form of self-defense and angered large segments of the public for stating at a 1969 Panther rally in Oakland, California, that John Gleason, a white New Jersey policeman who had been killed by a mob two years before, had "deserved" to die. Gleason had shot Bobby Lee Williams, a member of the Black Panthers, after Williams had allegedly threatened him with a hammer; Gleason was in the process of fleeing an angry black mob when they stomped him to death.[46]

By the end of the 1960s, Kunstler had represented virtually every important black leader, including Malcolm X, H. Rap Brown, and Stokely Carmichael—all of whom had utterly rejected Dr. King's espousal of nonviolence. They trusted Kunstler more than any other lawyer because, as writer Victor Navasky noted, "they feel he can do it better than anyone else, that he won't patronize them or sell them out, [and] that he is on their side."[47] In light of Kunstler's later comments on the misconceptions about his radicalism, he may have misled the public by the vehemence of the rhetoric that he uttered in the course of his lifetime. Navasky, who conducted a lengthy interview with Kunstler in 1970, regarded him as "an essentially apolitical person who never thought systematically about social systems but identifies with the dreams of the oppressed minority."[48]

Chicago Seven Trial, 1969–1970

It was his role in the Chicago Seven trial that made Kunstler a household name. The case, *United States* v. *Dellinger* (1970), was one of the most notable trials in the twentieth century, but became better known for its courtroom theatrics than for the issues it sought to resolve.

Kunstler was the lead defense attorney for the Chicago Seven (originally the Chicago Eight, until one of the defendants was dropped from the case), a group of anti–Vietnam War protesters. They were arrested in August 1968 outside the Democratic National Convention in Chicago on orders issued by Mayor Richard B. Daley to break up the demonstrations. Although Chicago swarmed with thousands of protesters during the week of the convention, the eight defendants were the only ones brought to trial.

Kunstler maintained that each defendant represented a different aspect of the radical movement and that the reason that the government joined them in the lawsuit was to create the impression that the burgeoning antiwar movement was an integral part of the black power movement. In reality, five of the defendants had played a leading part in the demonstrations, two had served as marshals who tried to bring order to the scene, and one had replaced another speaker at the last moment, staying in Chicago for a brief period before leaving town.[49]

The indictment was based on their alleged violation of what was popularly known as the H. Rap Brown statute, named for one of the leading black activists of the 1960s. This statute, written into the Civil Rights Act of 1968, made it illegal for anyone to cross state lines with the intention of inciting a riot. The defendants were also charged with conspiracy in disrupting the convention, a controversial charge in view of the fact that they were not a cohesive group. One of the defendants—Abbie Hoffman—even quipped that they could not agree on anything, including lunch.[50]

There was keen interest in the trial because the confrontations between the Chicago police and the demonstrators during the convention week had been featured on both national and local television. Every night the viewing public had an opportunity to watch Mayor Daley's police use tear gas and beat up the protesters on the streets of Chicago. Many people undoubtedly sided with the law enforcement officials because of the protesters' widely publicized threats to disrupt both the city and the convention, but the Chicago Crime Commission investigating the disturbances later concluded that there had been "unrestrained and indiscriminate police violence."[51]

The trial began on September 28, 1969, and lasted until the end of February 1970. It was tried in Chicago's federal court before Judge Julius Jennings Hoffman, who was known to have excellent control of the courtroom. One of Kunstler's not-so-affectionate names for Hoffman was "Julie," and the two matched wits throughout the trial.

Since Kunstler believed that his clients were "political" victims of the American legal system, he strongly suspected that the government was using unfair tactics against them.* As a result, he pursued the case with a furor seldom unleashed in a courtroom. His conduct led the *New York Times* to accuse him of turning the trial "into a chaos of deliberate insults and purposeful disruption" and "becoming nearly as outrageous as his clients."[52]

Kunstler had been asked to take the case by two of the defendants who were his former clients, Abbie Hoffman and Jerry Rubin, both of whom were identified with the youth culture and its radical "yippie" movement. At the time they approached him, Kunstler was preparing for trial on behalf of the

---

*His suspicions were borne out in the late 1970s, when he obtained documents under the Freedom of Information Act revealing not only that there was collusion between the judge, prosecutors, and Federal Bureau of Investigation (FBI) agents during the trial, but that the government had videotaped key legal meetings of the defense and instigated secret communications with several of the jurors. In addition, he learned that FBI director J. Edgar Hoover had informed several of the bureau's top aides in October 1968 that "approximately twenty principal leaders and activists of various New Left Organizations" would be charged under the H. Rap Brown statute, an action that "should seriously disrupt and curtail the activities of the New Left."[52]

Panthers 21, a group of Black Panthers charged with conspiracy to blow up a number of sites in New York City. Unable to make up his mind about which case to take, Kunstler tossed a coin with attorney Gerald Lefcourt, who was also working on the Panthers 21 trial. Lefcourt wound up getting the Panthers, and Kunstler went to Chicago.[54]

The other defendants represented a broad spectrum of the New Left counterculture: David Dellinger, a pacifist Quaker who at the age of fifty-four was more than twenty years older than the other defendants; John Froines, a Bard College chemistry professor; Lee Weiner, a doctoral student and instructor at Northwestern University; Bobby Seale, the only nonwhite defendant and the chairman of the Black Panther Party; and Tom Hayden and Rennie Davis, members of the militant Students for a Democratic Society. At one point in the proceedings, Hoffman ordered a defiant Seale to be gagged and chained to his chair—a spectacle that lasted until the Judge severed him from the trial.[55]

Kunstler's cocounsel was Leonard Weinglass, an attorney from Newark, New Jersey, who was asked to enter the case by Tom Hayden, a former client. A detail-oriented attorney who did much of the research for the case, Weinglass had never previously tried a case outside of New Jersey.[56]

The prosecution team was headed by Thomas Foran, United States Attorney for the Northern District of Illinois, and Assistant United States Attorney Richard Schultz. The hostility exhibited in the courtroom between the prosecution and defense lawyers remained long after the trial had been completed. In 1988, Foran refused an interview about Kunstler with reporter Sam Howe Verhouvek, because Foran "did not want to participate in anything that would give William Kunstler publicity."[57]

The trial degenerated into what former United States Attorney Ramsey Clark called a "legal atrocity." Judge Hoffman could barely contain his contempt for the defendants, and the feeling was mutual. One day in open court, Abbie Hoffman referred to the judge as "the laughingstock of the world."[58] The defendants proved adept at demonstrating their disdain for the American legal system. Their antics included wearing judicial robes in court and then discarding them and jumping on them, blowing kisses to the spectators, doing handstands and pole vaulting over the railing, refusing to stand when the judge entered the courtroom, hurling insults at both the judge and the prosecutors, talking out loud to themselves and to the witnesses, displaying a Viet Cong flag in court, trying to hold a birthday party in the midst of the trial, munching on jelly beans, collecting litter on the defense table, and keeping joints of marijuana under a copy of an underground newspaper from Berkeley, California.[59]

The marijuana had been sent by mail to the defendants from one of their admirers. Fearing that it would be detected, Kunstler announced its presence in the courtroom and requested instructions from Judge Hoffman on what to do with it. "Mr. Kunstler," the judge told him, "you're a resolute attorney. I'm sure you'll know how to dispose of it." Kunstler replied, "Your Honor, it will be burned tonight."[60]

While Weinglass was more subdued, Kunstler lived up to his reputation as the kind of lawyer who "did not just represent people in the trenches, he jumped into the trenches with them." Judge Hoffman hardly appreciated this trench warfare and sentenced the defendants and their lawyers on 159 counts of contempt as soon as the jury started to deliberate. The sentences ranged from two months and eight days to four years and thirteen days—the latter sentence for Kunstler.[61]

Although case law limited judges to sentences of no more than six months without a jury trial, Hoffman maneuvered his way around the law by limiting each sentence to the maximum or less but running the sentences consecutively. In reacting to his sentence, Kunstler gave one of the most impassioned speeches in his life, concluding it by indulging in a rare form of self-depreciation:

> I have tried with all my heart faithfully to represent my clients in the face of what I consider—and still consider—repressive and unjust conduct toward them. If I have to pay with my liberty for such representation, then that is the price of my beliefs and my sensibilities. . . .
> I have the utmost faith that my beloved brethren at the bar, young and old alike, will not allow themselves to be frightened out of defending the poor, the persecuted, the radicals and the militant, the black people, the pacifists, and the political pariahs of this, our common land. . . .
> [Other lawyers must] stand firm, remain true to those ideals of the law which, even if openly violated here and in other places, are true and glorious goals. . . . Never desert those principles of equality, justice, and freedom without which life has little if any meaning.
> I may not be the greatest lawyer in the world . . . but I think that I am at this moment, along with Len Weinglass . . . the most privileged. We are being sentenced for what we believe in.[62]

The jury announced its verdict in February 1970, acquitting all the defendants on the more serious charge of conspiracy but finding five of them—Davis, Dellinger, Hayden, Hoffman, and Rubin—guilty of violating the H. Rap Brown statute. Judge Hoffman imposed the maximum sentences of five years and fined each of them $5,000.

Despite Hoffman's ruling, neither the defendants nor their attorneys served any time in jail or paid a fine. The criminal contempt convictions for violation of the H. Rap Brown statute were reversed by the appellate court in November 1972. While the court cited certain legal errors in the procedural matters relating to the trial, it concluded that "the demeanor of the judge and the prosecutors would require reversal if other errors did not." The government did not appeal this ruling.[63]

The contempt citations were reversed by the circuit court of appeals on the ground that the defendants were entitled to a jury trial. It took place in December 1973, and the judge threw out most of the citations. Even though he had the option of imposing fines or sentences on the remaining ones, he held that such an action on his part would serve no useful purpose.[64]

Charting a New Course

The conclusion of the Chicago Seven trial left Kunstler to ponder his future. In looking back at this time in his life, he made a brutally candid comment to the press:

> There I'd been, in the goldfish bowl, people poised with microphones and pens at my every word. And then suddenly I was back in Westchester, going to the drugstore, taking out the laundry. And I said to myself, have I reached my high point, is it going to be all downhill from here? I was afraid it would all dry up, that I'd be back with my brother again, just earning a living, riding the commuter train. I would have shriveled up and died.[65]

His apprehensions were unwarranted. In the years that followed, he was seldom out of the news. "I enjoy the spotlight, as most humans do, but it's not my whole *raison d'être*," he said in a speech two years before his death. "My purpose is to keep the state from becoming all domineering, all powerful, and that's never changed."[66]

These years brought personal changes in his life. In 1974, he and his wife were divorced, and the following year he married Margaret L. Ratner, a Columbia Law graduate who was twenty-six years his junior. They had two daughters: Sarah, born in 1976, and Emily, born in 1978. At the time of his remarriage, Kunstler had two grown daughters from his first marriage. Karin Kunstler Goldman became an attorney and Jane Kunstler Drazek, a physician.

He later had a new law associate named Ronald L. Kuby, a pony-tailed graduate of Cornell Law School who had earlier worked for Kunstler's law practice in 1982 as an intern during a summer break. These two legal soul mates were dedicated to pro bono work. In spite of their prominence in the profession, they never had more than a combined income of $150,000 during the thirteen years they worked together, and a substantial portion of it came from speaking fees.[67]

Attica, 1971

In professional terms, the highlights of Kunstler's practice in the 1970s were Attica and Wounded Knee. The first enhanced his reputation as a scoundrel, and the second added to his luster as a hero. Both made national headlines.

In 1971, Kunstler served on a citizens' negotiating committee attempting to reach a settlement during a riot at Attica, an overcrowded maximum security prison in upstate New York. The prison, which was built to accommodate 1,600 men, housed 2,200 inmates at the time of the riot. The demands of the prisoners included improved medical care, translators for Latino inmates, more black and Hispanic guards, and better educational programs.

The riot began on September 9, 1971, when 1,281 inmates launched an attack against the guards (one of whom died two days later of club wounds), took dozens of them as hostages, and obtained control of the prison yard.

Kunstler was arguing a case in Florida when he was notified by telegram that the rioting inmates wanted him to come. Arriving the next day, he joined a team of negotiators, including Russell G. Oswald, Commissioner of New York State's Department of Correctional Services, various elected officials from the state, members of the press, and an urban affairs adviser to Governor Nelson A. Rockefeller.[68]

Upon his arrival in Attica, Kunstler accepted the offer of the inmates to serve as their lawyer. Knowing the tense nature of the situation, he earnestly sought to win their confidence. As he later wrote:

> I wanted them to know I was not just another lawyer with a briefcase saying, 'I'll do the best I can.' I wanted them to know that I was willing to go to the wire for them.[69]

Nevertheless, he and the other members of the committee were unable to work out a settlement after four difficult days of negotiation. As the talks broke down, Governor Rockefeller ordered state troopers to retake the prison. The riot was put down, but twenty-nine inmates and ten hostages were killed, making it the bloodiest prison uprising in American history.[70] Kunstler was his usual outspoken self in his criticism of Rockefeller, whom he called a "murderer" for failing to go to Attica and meet with the negotiating committee. William F. Buckley Jr., the editor of the conservative *National Review,* promptly called for Kunstler's disbarment, expressing the wish that the lawyer would "experience the isolation which he has earned from the civilized community."[71]

Wounded Knee, 1973

The Wounded Knee episode had more positive results. Kunstler defended Russell Means and Dennis Banks of the American Indian Movement (AIM), a group formed in 1968 by Native American leaders to improve the impoverished conditions of their kinfolk. The men were accused of illegally occupying Wounded Knee, South Dakota (on the state's Pine Ridge Reservation), the site of an Indian Massacre in 1890.

Members of the AIM had occupied Wounded Knee on February 27, 1973 as a way of commemorating the 1890 massacre and demanding improvements in the Native American reservations throughout the nation. The occupation, which lasted seventy-one days, ended on May 8, when government representatives agreed to investigate the situation. The government failed to honor its promise, instead indicting several hundred Native Americans, including Means and Banks, for illegally occupying Wounded Knee.[72]

Kunstler and the other defense attorneys moved to dismiss the charges against Means and Banks on the grounds of prosecutorial and FBI misconduct: a conspiracy to commit perjury and to cover up the subornation of perjury by a last-minute prosecution witness, suppression of an FBI statement exposing the perjury of another prosecution witness, the unconstitutional use of military personnel and equipment at Wounded Knee, and an attempt by the government to cover it up illegally.[73] Although Kunstler and presiding Judge Fred Nichols exchanged harsh words—at one point, Kunstler was cited for contempt and spent three nights in the town jail after he too vehemently protested the judge's order removing American Indian observers from the courtroom—the judge dismissed the charges against the defendants. At the conclusion of the trial, Judge Nichols delivered a lecture to the prosecutor that sounded as though it had been written by Kunstler. Nichols blasted the "incidents of misconduct" by government agents and concluded that "this case was not prosecuted in good faith or in the spirit of justice."[74]

"Celebrity Sociopaths," 1986–1995

The type of clients Kunstler came to represent in the last decade of his life were referred to by the *New Yorker* as "celebrity sociopaths" and caused the *National Review,* his long-time critic, to remark: "What cause was furthered by defending such clients . . . is difficult to say." But he also had his admirers. In January 1994, Kunstler received a letter from Sol Wachtler, former chief judge of the New York Court of Appeals, who had been sent to prison for his harassment of Joy Silverman, his former lover:

> You might be interested to know, if you didn't already know, that amongst me and my fellow prisoners you are a folk hero. There isn't a murderer, rapist, arsonist or major drug dealer who doesn't think of you as a great man. That includes the harasser of Joy Silverman.[75]

Among his most controversial clients in this stage of his career were Larry Davis, a young black man accused of wounding six policemen in a shootout in a Bronx, New York, apartment in 1986; El Sayyid Nosair, an Arab identified by an eyewitness as the killer of Rabbi Meir Kahane, of the militant Jewish Defense League, in 1990 at a New York hotel; Yusef Salaam, a black fifteen-year-old accused of being one of the rapists of a white female jogger in New York's Central Park in 1989; and Colin Ferguson, an allegedly deranged black man indicted for killing six white people in a crowded Long Island railroad car in 1993.*

---

*One controversial client whom Kunstler did not represent was Tawana Brawley, a sixteen-year-old black girl who alleged that she was raped and sodomized by six white men in 1987 in Wappingers Falls, New York. State investigators later concluded that her story was a hoax, and Kunstler's comments on the case drew widespread criticism. "It makes no difference anymore whether the attack on Tawana Brawley really happened," he said. He justified his position by stating that "a lot of young black women are treated the way she said she was treated," and he hoped that her attorneys would seize upon this issue to "grab the headlines and launch a vigorous attack on the criminal justice system."[76]

Kunstler, working with attorney Lynne Steward on the Davis case, and with Kuby on the Nosair trial, helped to devise a strategy that led to the acquittal of both defendants. His work in these two cases and others during the last decade of his life led one reporter to write how "impressed" he was that Kunstler was able to

> win one surprising against-the-odds, impossible victory after another in highly publicized cases he militantly politicized, often using—as he did in the Nosair case—wildly conjectural conspiracy theories backed by dubious—or no—evidence. In the Nosair case, for instance, Kunstler proclaimed in his opening argument that the defense would prove that a conspiracy of Jews—factional enemies within the Jewish Defense League—murdered Kahane. The judge refused to allow the scant evidence Kunstler had to back this up into the case, called the theory "pure speculation." But the jury acquitted anyway.[77]

In the Davis case, Kunstler convinced the jury in 1988 that Davis had actually been a victim of the so-called drug-dealing, corrupt police officers he shot, who had conspired to assassinate him when he tried to go straight. After Davis's acquittal, Kunstler (who was strongly opposed to the death penalty) told a reporter from the *Village Voice* that "any black guy that shoots six cops and put fear of God in police officers, I think is great."[78]

Kunstler was less successful with Salaam, who was found guilty in 1990, and Colin Ferguson. Since Ferguson was clearly identified as the shooter by fellow passengers on the railroad, Kunstler and Kuby offered the "black rage" defense: an already unbalanced Ferguson was pushed over the edge by American racism. Ferguson rejected the defense and dismissed his lawyers. In 1994, he represented himself by trying to convince the jury that a Caucasian male was the actual killer.[79]

The *National Review* later referred to this case in its obituary on Kunstler. "Ferguson was so unbalanced," it noted, "that he defended himself." The magazine found solace that "Mr. Kunstler goes before a Judge whose system he cannot subvert."[80]

Kunstler paid a heavy price for his defense of these clients. He began to receive frequent death threats, menacing phone calls, and hate mail. After the Nosair trial, he was picketed at his house by members of the Jewish Defense Organization and felt obliged to place a letter of apology on the doorstep of every home on his block. The worst incident was a reprisal for the Larry Davis acquittal. Kunstler was attending a hearing in a Brooklyn court in 1989 when a fight broke out in the back of the courtroom. In the melee that followed, he was attacked by white police officers. As one of them delivered a kick in the ribs, he told Kunstler: "This is for Larry Davis." His injuries were so severe that Kunstler's left knee required surgery, and it bothered him for the rest of his life.[81] Kunstler took these episodes in stride. "I'm more loved and more hated than I ever was," he told a reporter in 1992. But he frequently was called upon to display real courage in the face of these incidents, and his acquaintances were convinced that he feared for the safety of his family.[82]

Kunstler's zeal for his clients remained undiminished. As a pretrial hearing in the Yusef Salaam case in 1990, he vigorously protested a ruling by Acting Manhattan State Supreme Court Judge Thomas B. Galligan. "You have exhibited what your partisanship is," Kunstler shouted. "You shouldn't be sitting in court. You are a disgrace to the bench." The judge held Kunstler in contempt and sentenced him to thirty days in jail or a fine of $250 (later paid by a friend). The sentence remained on the books, and Kunstler was publicly censured by a Manhattan appeals court in 1993 for his comments to Judge Galligan.[83]

He ran into trouble again the following year, when Southern District Judge Gerard Goettel imposed a Rule 11 Sanction under the Federal Rules of Civil Procedures for bringing a frivolous lawsuit. In addition to imposing the sentence, Judge Goettel delivered a stern rebuke:

> Mr. Kunstler is apparently one of those attorneys who believe that his sole obligation is to his client and that he has no obligations to the court or in the processes of justice. Unfortunately, he is not alone in this approach to the practice of law, which may be one reason why the legal profession is held in such low esteem by the public at this time.[84]

Kunstler was vindicated in March 1995, when the United States Court of Appeals for the Second Circuit reversed Judge Goettel. In an opinion written by Judge Wilford Feinberg, the court found that the sanction was unjustified and imposed in a manner that suggested "a personal attack" against Kunstler and "perhaps, more broadly, against activist attorneys who represent unpopular clients or causes." Kunstler, who had also had a Rule 11 Sanction imposed upon him in 1989, was pleased that this time the court had recognized that "lawyers are sometimes attacked by judges, federal and state, simply because they represent persons who are not favored by the Establishment."[85]

Final Curtain

Kunstler was plagued by ill health prior to his death. In the early 1990s, he was diagnosed with cancer of the bladder. He had a pacemaker implanted on August 7, 1995, but two days later gave a stand-up comedy performance at Carolyn's Comedy Club in New York. A few weeks after his performance, on September 4, 1995, Kunstler died of heart failure in his sleep. He was seventy-six years old. He left an estate estimated at less than $400,000, the bulk of which came from the valuation on the Greenwich Village townhouse that he had purchased for a modest price in 1979.[86]

His funeral service was private, but a memorial service two months after his death at the Cathedral of St. John the Divine in New York was attended by more than one thousand people. The service began with Dakota Indian chants and the beating of drums. It ended with the smoking of a ceremonial Indian pipe similar to the one Kunstler had received over two decades before from the members of the AIM who occupied Wounded Knee. The services were picketed by Mordechai Levy, a member of the Jewish Defense Organization. When a heated exchange arose between Levy and several of the mourners, Norman Siegel, the executive director of the New York Civil Liberties Union, noticed the confrontation and rushed to defend Mr. Levy's right to speak. The scene was witnessed by two Spanish women on a double-decker sightseeing bus. One turned to the other and said in Spanish, "That's how it is in America."[87]

The laudatory comments in the media following Kunstler's death were at odds with the way that the American public had generally perceived him during his lifetime. Noting this dichotomy, *Fortune*'s Daniel Seligman called attention to the "relentless sappiness of the American press when it passes judgment on people of the left." Seligman referred to Kunstler as an "outrageous egomaniac."[88] On a more personal level, the widow of a man whose alleged killer was defended by Kunstler and Kuby was puzzled at the reaction in the media to Kunstler's death. In a letter to the *New York Law Journal* in October 1995, Maggie Pack wrote the following:

> William Kunstler defended Joe Gordon, the man who murdered my husband, Daniel. In spite of the compelling evidence against Mr. Gordon, the team of Mr. Kunstler and Ron Kuby set about trying to convince the jury that Daniel had been killed not by Mr. Gordon, but by his 16-year-old son. The district attorney kept the case on track, however, presenting clear-cut evidence of Mr. Gordon's guilt and winning a conviction.
>
> When I heard Mr. Kunstler had died, I felt sadness I did not anticipate. I've read that he was a brilliant civil rights lawyer, an advocate for outcasts, a man who upheld the rights of the accused, if also a bit of a showoff and a publicity-seeker. But nowhere have I read that what he sometimes did during his career was attempt to derail the truth to gain his clients' acquittals.
>
> It is one thing to fight against preconceived notions of guilt, and quite another thing to do battle for a defendant who really is guilty. Do we really believe that upholding a defendant's civil rights extends to keeping a criminal from going to jail? Why do we make it possible for defense lawyers to invent defenses to protect dangerous and evil people who really do exist and who have done terrible things? Is that what is meant by the right to a fair trial?[89]

An entirely different appraisal of Kunstler was given two months after his death in an article in the *New York Law Journal* by Gustin L. Reichbach, a Brooklyn civil court judge. Noting that "Bill's celebrity tends to overshadow the enormous range of his advocacy skills," Reichbach wrote:

> At a time when the legal profession is increasingly narrowly specialized, Bill Kunstler's range of achievements included unlikely acquittals in seemingly hopeless criminal trials, civil litigator and master of procedural strategy, and appellate advocate including constitutional appeals in the U.S. Supreme Court and the highest courts in many states.[90]

Reichbach predicted that Kunstler would eventually occupy a position in the second half of the twentieth century—similar to the one held by Clarence Darrow in the first half of the century—as the greatest champion of the disadvantaged and vilified. "Indeed, while the parallels are striking," Reichbach argued, "a fair appraisal suggests that Kunstler's victories were won over

considerably more varied legal terrain and were of far greater lasting constitutional impact than Darrow's."[91]

William Moses Kunstler must have always felt that his accomplishments
would outlive his reputation. One of his prized possessions was a letter addressed to his oldest daughter at the time of her birth from one of his Yale
professors. "Take good care of your father," the professor wrote. "He is going
to do great things." Kunstler kept the letter all those years and gave it to his
daughter a short time before he died.[92]

One of the "great things" Kunstler did was to use his formidable talents to
defend, as the late Supreme Court Justice Frank Murphy had phrased it, "the
most humble, the most unorthodox and the most despised among us." In a law
journal article one year after Kunstler's death, an attorney discussed working
with him on a case involving a Native American who was in trouble with the
law. "He never asked whether he would get paid," the attorney recalled. "He
just said he would do it because the accused needed to be defended."[93]

Notes

1. Ron Rosenbaum, "The Most Hated Lawyer in America," *Vanity Fair,* March 1992, 68;
quoted in *Bridges* v. *Wixon* 326 U.S. 135 (1945), 166.

2. Quoted in Victor S. Navasky, "Right On! With Lawyer William Kunstler," *New York
Times Magazine*, April 19, 1970, 90; David J. Langum, *William M. Kunstler: The Most Hated
Lawyer in America* (New York: New York University Press, 1999), 354; Charlie Rose WNET
Program, Gerald Lefcourt, "Remembrance of William Kunstler," September 5, 1995 (transcript
#1458).

3. Gerald Lefcourt, "In Memorium: Mouthpiece," *New York State Association of Criminal
Defense Lawyers* 3 (September/October 1995): 9; quoted in F. Peter Hodel, Sid Lerner, and Hal
Drucker, "Chatting with Bill Kunstler over General Noriega's Cookies," *New York Law Jour-
nal,* September 18, 1995, 2.

4. William M. Kunstler, with Sheila Isenberg, *My Life as a Radical Lawyer* (New York:
Birch Lane Press, 1994), 34, 65–70, 96, 402; Langum, *William M. Kunstler,* 45–46, 338.

5. Maurice N. Nessen (moderator), "Attica: Its Causes, Implications, and Lessons," Special Forum, Evening, *New York County Lawyers Association* 3 (November 23, 1971): 4.

6. Quoted in Navasky, "Right On!" 91.

7. Kunstler, *My Life,* 21.

8. See, for example, Sheila Isenberg, "Preface," Kunstler, *My Life*, ix–xii; Rosenbaum,
"The Most Hated Lawyer in America," 55.

9. Quoted in Navasky, "Right On!" 89–90.

10. Quoted in Elliot Pinsley, "At 70, The Cause Is Still Supreme for Kunstler: Despite Tide
of Conservatism, He Remains Consistent Defender of the Left," *New Jersey Law Journal* 124
(September 7, 1989): 21.

11. Quoted in "A Lawyer for Hire," *American Bar Association Journal*, 56 (June 1970):
552; Pinsley, "At 70, The Cause Is Still Supreme," 5; Kunstler, *My Life,* 340–341, 343–347;
Charlie Rose WNET Program, Alan Dershowitz, "Remembrance of William Kunstler," September 15, 1995 (transcript #1458).

12. Kunstler, *My Life,* 15; Langum, *William M. Kunstler,* 132–133, 235.

13. Navasky, "Right On!" 89; Elliot Pinsley, "William Kunstler's Cause and Effects: Leftist
Lawyer Still Pushing 'People's Law,'" *Legal Times,* August 14, 1989, 12: 16; quoted in Paul
Krassner, "Abbie Hoffman and Jerry Rubin, Together Again," *New York,* December 12, 1994,
22.

14. Krassner, "Abbie Hoffman and Jerry Rubin," 22; "William Kunstler," *Nation,* September 25, 1995, 300.

15. Quoted in Pinsley, "William Kunstler's Cause and Effects," 17.

16. Quoted in Dennis Bernstein and Julie Light, "The Life and Times of William Moses Kunstler," *Z Magazine,* October 1995; quoted in David Marshall, "William Kunstler—a 'Loose Cannon'?" *New Law Journal* 143 (November 26, 1993): 1164.

17. Isenberg, "Preface," Kunstler, *My Life,* xi.

18. Quoted in Kunstler, *My Life,* 17.

19. Ibid., 266.

20. Quoted ibid., 49; quoted in Nat Hentoff, "Playboy Interview: William Kunstler," *Playboy,* October 1970, 12.

21. Kunstler, *My Life,* 50.

22. Ibid., 52.

23. Ibid., 57.

24. Ibid., 58.

25. Ibid., 61.

26. Ibid., 71–75; Langum, *William M. Kunstler,* 42.

27. Kunstler, *My Life,* 82, 86.

28. Ibid., 83–87.

29. Ibid., 94–95; Langum, *William M. Kunstler,* 47–50.

30. Kunstler, *My Life,* 95; "Defending the Despised," *People Weekly,* September 18, 1995, 225.

31. Quoted in Scott Spencer, "William Kunstler: 1919–1995," *Rolling Stone,* October 19, 1995, 89.

32. William M. Kunstler, *Deep in My Heart* (New York: William Morrow, 1966), 119–120; Kunstler, *My Life,* 95–97.

33. William M. Kunstler, *Trials and Tribulations* (New York: Grove Press, 1985), 125; David Stout, "William Kunstler, 76, Dies; Lawyer for Social Outcasts," *New York Times,* September 5, 1995, B16.

34. Kunstler, *My Life,* 97.

35. Kunstler, *Deep in My Heart,* 3–4, 24–33.

36. Kunstler, *My Life,* 102.

37. Quoted ibid., 102–103.

38. Kunstler, *Trials and Tribulations,* 88; Kunstler, *Deep in My Heart,* 86.

39. Kunstler, *Deep in My Heart,* 50–51.

40. Kunstler, *My Life,* 106.

41. Randall Coyne, "Defending the Despised: William Moses Kunstler," *American Indian Law Review* 20 (Spring 1995): 259.

42. Kunstler, *My Life,* 108–109; Kunstler, *Trials and Tribulations,* 50.

43. Kunstler, *My Life,* 111.

44. Ibid., 153–160.

45. Ibid., 184–190, 192–193; 90, 91, 93, 94.

46. Quoted in Navasky, "Right On!" 30; Langum, *William M. Kunstler,* 97–98.

47. Navasky, "Right On!" 91.

48. Ibid., 90.

49. Kunstler, *My Life,* 4; Langum, *William M. Kunstler,* 102

50. Kunstler, *My Life,* 3–45; quoted in Langum, *William M. Kunstler,* 104.

51. Quoted in William E. Leuchtenburg, *A Troubled Feast: American Society Since 1945* (Boston: Little, Brown, 1973), 208–209.

52. Quoted in Hentoff, "Playboy Interview," 6; David Margolick, "Still Radical After All These Years; at 74, William Kunstler Defends Clients Most Lawyers Avoid," *New York Times,* July 6, 1993, B1.

53. Kunstler, *My Life,* 13; Langum, *William M. Kunstler,* 119, 104.

54. Kunstler, *My Life,* 14.

55. Ibid., 4, 7–10.

56. Mike Ervin, "The Progressive Interview: Leonard Weinglass," *Progressive* 60 (May 1996): 34.

57. Sam Howe Verhouvek, "Profile: William M. Kunstler," *Los Angeles Daily Journal,* August 12, 1988, 1.

58. Quoted in Ervin, "Progressive Interview," 35; quoted in Eric Pace, "Jerry Rubin, 56, Flashy 60's Radical Dies: 'Yippies' Founder and Chicago 7 Defendant," *New York Times,* November 30, 1994, B13.

59. Hentoff, "Playboy Interview," 7; Kunstler, *My Life,* 21–22; Langum, *William M. Kunstler,* 100–128.

60. Quoted in Kunstler, *My Life,* 27–28.

61. Quoted in Stout, "William Kunstler, 76, Dies," B6.

62. Quoted in Kunstler, *My Life,* 39.

63. Quoted in Langum, *William M. Kunstler,* 120.

64. Ibid., 119–124.

65. Quoted in Connie Bruck, "William Kunstler: Actor Without a Stage," *American Lawyer* 2 (August 1980): 26.

66. Quoted in Stout, "William Kunstler, 76, Dies," B6.

67. Margolick, "Still Radical After All These Years," B1; Langum, *William M. Kunstler,* 342.

68. Langum, *William M. Kunstler,* 187–215; Kunstler, *My Life,* 214–227.

69. Kunstler, *My Life,* 218.

70. William M. Kunstler, "Back to Attica," *Nation,* March 25, 1991, 364; Clyde Haberman, "No Solace for Widow of Attica," *New York Times,* February 22, 2000, B1.

71. William F. Buckley, Jr., "Kunstler," *National Review,* November 5, 1971, 1258.

72. Coyne, "Defending the Despised," 270.

73. Ibid., 268.

74. Ibid., 266.

75. "The Death of a Revolutionary," *New Yorker,* September 18, 1995, 40; Adam Freedman, review of *My Life as a Radical Lawyer,* by William M. Kunstler, with Sheila Isenberg, *National Review,* December 31, 1994, 65; quoted in Lefcourt "In Memorium: Mouthpiece," 8.

76. Frank Tippett, "Tawana Brawley: Case vs. Cause: How a Rape Investigation Has Fired Up a Political Movement," *Time,* June 20, 1988, 22; quoted in Langum, *William M. Kunstler,* 182.

77. Rosenbaum, "The Most Hated Lawyer in America," 70.

78. Quoted ibid., 70.

79. Sophfronia Scott Gregory, "Black Rage: In Defense of a Mass Murderer," *Time,* June 6, 1994, 31; John T. McQuiston, "Adviser to L.I.R.R. Suspect Threatens to Quit," *New York Times,* February 7, 1995, B8.

80. "William Kunstler, RIP," *National Review,* September 25, 1995, 19.

81. Rosenbaum, "The Most Hated Lawyer in America," 70; Langum, *William M. Kunstler,* 307–308.

82. Quoted in Margolick, "Still Radical After All These Years," B1; Charlie Rose WNET Program, Alan Dershowitz, "Remembrance of William Kunstler" (transcript #1458); Langum, *William M. Kunstler,* 330.

83. Kunstler, *My Life,* 391–393.

84. Quoted in Deborah Pines, "Bases for Sanctioning Lawyers Clarified in Ruling for Kunstler," *New York Law Journal,* March 3, 1995, 1, 12.

85. Ibid., 1.

86. Langum, *William M. Kunstler,* 353, 232; Kunstler, *My Life,* 77.

87. Quoted in Richard Perez-Pena, "1,000 Honor Kunstler, Defender of Their Faith," *New York Times,* November 20, 1995, B11.

88. Daniel Seligman, "Radical Chic Forever," *Fortune,* October 16, 1995, 245.

89. Maggie Pack (Armonk, New York), letter to the editor, *National Law Journal* (October 2, 1995): A18.

90. Gustin L. Reichbach, "Bill Kunstler: An Appreciation," *New York Law Journal,* November 13, 1995, 2.

91. Ibid.

92. Quoted in Langum, *William M. Kunstler,* 39.

93. Bruce H. Ellison, "William Kunstler: A People's Lawyer," *South Dakota Law Review* 41 (Spring 1996): 230.

Selected Cases

Christ v. Paradise (1949)

Kunstler's first case following his admission to the bar in December 1948 was handled by the New York law firm of Kunstler & Kunstler, which he co-founded with his brother Michael. Their client was Royal Christ, who sued the Paradise Taxi Company for damages received in an automobile accident. This negligence case was taken on a contingency fee basis and was settled for $1,500 shortly before it was to be tried. The firm of Kunstler & Kunstler received $500 for its work in handling the case.

United States v. Worthy (1961)
328 F. 2d 386

A black journalist, William Worthy Jr., ignored a law which banned travel to Communist China and had his passport confiscated in 1956 upon his return to the United States. Six years later, he went to Cuba, another country to which travel was prohibited, and was arrested in Miami International Airport for returning to the United States without a valid passport.

Worthy was tried and convicted in 1961 by a federal court in Miami under an obscure statute that made it a crime to return to the United States without a valid passport. Following the verdict, Kunstler appealed the decision to the United States Court of Appeals for the Fifth Circuit in Atlanta, arguing that the statute under which Worthy had been convicted was unconstitutional. The court overturned the conviction, holding that the statute was unconstitutional because there was no provision in the United States Constitution requiring a person to return to this country with a passport.

People v. Wansley (1962)

On December 8, 1961, a sixteen-year-old black boy of limited intelligence named Thomas Carlton Wansley was arrested in Lynchburg, Virginia, and charged with the rape and robbery of a fifty-nine-year-old church matron. The robbery charge stemmed from the allegation made by the church matron that her assailant stole $1.47 from her pocketbook. When the prosecution tried Wansley on February 7, 1962, the victim admitted that she was unable to identify her assailant. The only evidence presented by the prosecution was a jailhouse oral "confession." By the end of the day, the all-white jury returned a guilty verdict, and the judge sentenced Wansley to death.

Before the sentence could be carried out, the case was brought to the attention of Dr. Martin Luther King Jr., who was conducting a civil rights protest in Danville, Virginia, sixty miles south of Lynchburg. Kunstler, who was traveling with King at the time, volunteered to go to Lynchburg. Kunstler worked with Arthur Kinoy and Leonard Holt to obtain a stay of execution and won an appeal primarily due to the absence of a trial record. Kunstler eventually represented Wansley at two trials and in ten appeals, incurring the wrath of the townspeople in Lynchburg wherever he made an appearance on behalf of his client.

In the mid-1980s, Wansley was freed by the Virginia Parole Board after nearly twenty years in prison. Although Kunstler's reputation grew nationally after the 1962 trial, he never abandoned his client. Kunstler kept in touch with Wansley after his release and took pride in the fact that his former client became a productive member of society.

Shuttlesworth v. *Moore* (1962)
369 U.S. 35

Fred Shuttlesworth, the former pastor of the Bethel Baptist Church in Birmingham, and several other black citizens were arrested in 1958 for violation of a local ordinance on the breach of the peace. The alleged breach of peace occurred when they refused to sit in the back of a segregated bus in the city. Although there was no evidence against them for disorderly conduct, they were found guilty in the circuit court of Jefferson County, Alabama, and fined $100 each. Shuttlesworth failed to pay the fine.

The men appealed the decision to the United States Supreme Court. On January 8, 1962, the Court refused to overturn Shuttlesworth's conviction due to a technicality. At the time the Court reached its decision, Shuttlesworth had begun to serve ninety-two days in the Birmingham city jail for the 1958 offense. While he was languishing in jail, Kunstler and two black Birmingham attorneys took the unusual step of filing a writ of habeas corpus directly with the United States Supreme Court. The Court ordered Shuttlesworth's release in February 1962.

COFO v. *Rainey* (5th Cir. 1964)
339 F. 2nd 898

Kunstler, Arthur Kinoy, and Morton Stavis had been appointed general counsel to the Council of Federated Organizations (COFO) in 1964, when it set up a voter registration drive for Mississippi. In the course of this voter registration drive, two young white men, Michael Schwerner and Andrew Goodman, and one young black man, James Earl Chaney, disappeared.

To find out what happened to them, Kunstler and other attorneys filed a suit in the name of COFO against Lawrence A. Rainey, the sheriff of Mississippi's Neshoba County, where the young men had vanished.

The case was tried in the summer of 1964 before local federal judge Sidney Mize, who was known as a segregationist. Mize dismissed the case on a technicality when the plaintiffs did not appear in court, as ordered. Judge Mize's ruling was overturned in December, but by that time the bodies of Cheney,

Goodman, and Schwerner had already been found under a dam site outside Philadelphia, Mississippi.

The State of Mississippi never brought charges against anyone for the murders of these three civil rights workers, but the federal government later tried seven people for violating their civil rights. Five men were convicted and sentenced to ten years each in prison. Their sentences were subsequently reduced, so none of them served out the full ten-year term.

Dombrowski v. Pfister (1965)
380 U.S. 479

This Supreme Court case dealt with the issue of when a person may seek to litigate in federal rather than state court and seek federal court intervention in state judicial proceedings.

Kunstler, Arthur Kinoy, and four other attorneys represented Dr. James A. Dombrowski, the executive director of the integrationist Southern Conference Leadership Fund, and two white law partners, Ben Smith and Bruce Walter, who had been very active in civil rights protests. They were accused of violating Louisiana's antisubversive statute in 1963. The charges against them were brought by James W. Pfister, chairman of the Louisiana Joint Legislative Committee on Un-American activities.

Although Dombrowski lost in federal court, Kunstler and the other lawyers asked a three-judge federal court to enjoin the charges against the men on the grounds that the antisubversive laws were a violation of the First Amendment of the Constitution. The court ruled against them by a vote of two-to-one. The sole dissenter, Federal Judge John Minor Wisdom, argued that "the distinguishing feature of this case is the contention that the State under the guise of combating subversion, is in fact using and abusing its laws to punish the plaintiffs for their advocacy of civil rights for Negroes. If those contentions are sound, unquestionably the plaintiffs have a right to relief in the federal court."

Kunstler and the other attorneys appealed the decision to the Supreme Court. Kinoy, delivering the oral argument, succeeded in getting the Court to void major sections of the antisubversive statute. The decision established the important principle that a federal court could halt a racially motivated state criminal proceeding without waiting for the outcome of said proceeding, if the criminal prosecution was unconstitutional.

Carmichael et al. v. Allen et al. (N.D. Ga., 1967)
267 F. Supp. 985

Stokely Carmichael brought suit, as an individual, as chairman of the Student Nonviolent Coordinating Committee, and on behalf of all black residents of Atlanta, Georgia, against Ivan Allen Jr., mayor of Atlanta, and other local and state officials. The lawsuit arose when Carmichael was arrested under a Georgia criminal statute and an Atlanta city ordinance for disorderly conduct in making a speech that allegedly threatened an insurrection against the state. The speech was made on September 6, 1966, in the Summerhill area of Atlanta, following the shooting of a black man by a white police officer. The last time the criminal statute had been invoked was in the 1930s, when Angelo Herndon, a black communist organizer, was indicted under it.

At his trial, Carmichael gave an account of his speech and told the court he had stated that "we were tired of these shootings, these incidents that occurred, and that we would mount a protest and tear up and turn inside out the city until these incidents have stopped." Kunstler was part of a team representing Carmichael. The team argued that the Georgia riot statute conflicted with the freedom of speech protections in the First Amendment and that the statute wrongly could be used to punish words rather than actions. The United States District Court for the Northern District of Georgia, ruling for the plaintiff, invalidated both statutes on the grounds that they were unconstitutional insofar as they were so vaguely and broadly written that they could be construed as to prohibit conduct and punish offenders for conduct protected by the First Amendment.

Hobson v. *Hanson* (D.D.C. 1967)
269 F. Supp. 401

Jules Hobson, a social security economist who had a daughter in the public schools in Washington, D.C., brought a class action suit against the district's school system on the grounds that its tracking system was based on a white-oriented intelligence test. The suit was brought against members of the school board and the federal district judges who had appointed them.

Kunstler tried the case with attorney William L. Higgs. They argued that public school children were unfairly tracked for their entire school career on the basis of a Stanford-Binet IQ test taken in the third grade. Students who did poorly on these tests were placed in classes studying domestic science and automobile maintenance. Circuit Court Judge J. Skelly Wright ruled in favor of the plaintiff and ordered the IQ test to be revamped. As a result, many black students were able to take college-track courses. The district appealed the decision to a seven-judge panel of the District of Columbia Circuit, which affirmed Judge Wright's decision.

Kunstler referred to this ruling as the most gratifying decision of his entire career.

McSurely et al. v. *Ratliff et al.* (E.D. Ky. 1967)
282 F. Supp. 848

Alan McSurely and four other plaintiffs were accused of violating Kentucky's sedition law and indicted in Pike County, Kentucky. At issue was the constitutionality of this sedition law, which was passed in 1920 in the aftermath of World War I and the Bolshevik Revolution in Russia.

The plaintiffs were members of organizations that investigated conditions in Pike County to inform the people of their rights and to help local citizens organize. Thomas B. Ratliff and the other defendants were law enforcement officers in Kentucky.

State officials seized books, posters, and pamphlets from the plaintiffs at the time of their arrest. The criminal prosecution of the plaintiffs rested on the theory that they were engaged in a communist conspiracy to overthrow the government of Kentucky and its subdivision, Pike County.

Kunstler headed a team of lawyers for the plaintiffs. They argued that Kentucky's sedition law was unconstitutional. In a decision rendered by the United States District Court for the Eastern District of Kentucky, the court held for the plaintiffs. It found the Kentucky sedition law unconstitutional on the grounds that it was too broad and vague; unduly prohibited freedom of speech, freedom of the press, and the right of assembly; failed to distinguish between advocacy of idea and advocacy of action; penalized the advocacy of an unpopular political belief; and contained no requirement of criminal intent.

Powell v. *McCormack* (1969)
385 U.S. 486

In 1967, the House of Representatives refused to let black congressman Adam Clayton Powell Jr. take his seat. Powell, who represented the Eighteenth Congressional District in New York City's Harlem, had been accused of misconduct by Congress. John McCormack was the Speaker of the House of Representatives.

Kunstler joined a team of lawyers to represent Powell before the House Judiciary Committee and later in federal court. Their argument was that Powell met all three qualifications necessary to be a congressman (United States citizenship, minimum age of twenty-five, and residency in his district), and Congress had no authority to prevent an elected official from taking his oath of office. Kunstler wrote a certiorari petition to the United States Supreme Court, which agreed to hear the case in 1969. The case was argued before the court by Arthur Kinoy and Herbert Reid. The Court ruled in favor of Powell, rejecting the argument that Congress's determination to exclude a member of Congress for misconduct is within Congress's political domain and should be considered a political question.

Powell won his case, but never returned to Congress. He was defeated in the Democratic primary by Charles Rangel, who won in the general election against the Republican candidate.

United States v. *Moylan* (4th Cir. 1969)
417 F. 2d 1002

This case arose in 1968 when a group of nine anti–Vietnam War protesters, led by two Roman Catholic priests, Daniel Berrigan and his brother Philip Berrigan, broke into the draft board in Canonsville, Maryland, removed 378 draft files, and later burned them with napalm in an adjacent parking lot. The protestors were indicted by the federal government for this action.

Kunstler represented the defendants in a federal jury trial. Arguing that the actions of the Canonsville Nine were justified because of their opposition to the Vietnam War, he asked the jury to nullify a law which made it a crime to destroy government property. The judge instructed the jury to enforce the law, and it returned a verdict of guilty. Kunstler's appeal to the court of appeals and to the United States Supreme Court was denied.

United States v. *Sinclair* (E.D. Mich. 1971)
321 F. Supp. 1074

John Sinclair, Lawrence Robert "Pun" Plamondon, and John Waterhouse Forest were charged with being leaders of the White Panther Party (a Detroit-based group of antiwar activists and political revolutionaries who modeled themselves after the militant Black Panther Party). They were charged with conspiring to bomb the Central Intelligence Agency building in Ann Arbor, Michigan. They key evidence against the men was based on tapes made of conversations they allegedly had with employees of the Cuban embassy.

Kunstler and coattorney Leonard Weinglass moved to suppress the tapes on the grounds that said tapes had been obtained without a legal search warrant. The government admitted that it had wiretapped without having secured search warrants, but claimed that it had the right to tap the phones of any person who the attorney general of the United States (acting on behalf of the president) felt was a national security threat. This national security exemption was a right asserted by President Richard M. Nixon.

Federal District Judge Damon J. Keith ruled that the wiretaps were obtained illegally, but the government appealed the decision. This case was later consolidated with *United States* v. *United States District Court* (1972).

Palmer v. *Thompson* (1971)
403 U.S. 217

In the early 1960s, Jackson, Mississippi, closed its five municipal pools after a federal court issued an order to integrate them. The order was challenged by local black citizens, but it took nearly a decade for the case to reach the United States Supreme Court.

Kunstler and Paul Rosen, an attorney from Detroit, Michigan, argued that the city's action in closing the pools was a violation of the equal rights protection of the Fourteenth Amendment. In a five-to-four decision, the Court ruled that Jackson (which had desegregated its public parks, golf courses, auditoriums, and city zoo) had the right to close its public swimming pools on the grounds that to integrate them would create a threat of violence in the city.

United States v. *Dellinger* (7th Cir. 1970)
472 F. 2d 340

This famous case of the Chicago Seven, lasted from September 1969 until February 1970. It made Kunstler, the lead attorney for the defense, a household name. He was assisted in the case by Leonard Weinglass. They represented David Dellinger, Rennie Davis, John Froines, Tom Hayden, Abbie Hoffman, Jerry Rubin, and Lee Weiner. The eighth defendant had been Bobby Seale, but he was severed from the case after he was gagged and tied for disruptive behavior, on orders of the presiding judge, Julius Jennings Hoffman.

The defendants had gathered in Chicago at the time of the Democratic National Convention in 1968 to protest the government's policies on Vietnam and were indicted for conspiring to disrupt the convention and for crossing state lines with the intention of inciting a riot. The defendants were acquitted on the conspiracy charge, but five of them—Davis, Dellinger, Hayden, Hoffman, and Rubin—were found guilty of inciting a riot. Before the jury's verdict was read, Judge Hoffman sentenced the defendants and their lawyers on 159 counts of contempt. Kunstler received the longest contempt sentence, a term of four years and thirteen days. The sentences were appealed, and neither Kunstler, Weinglass, nor any of the defendants served time in prison.

United States v. *United States District Court* (1972)
407 U.S. 297

The case concerned the scope of executive power regarding domestic surveillance and the extent to which the Fourth Amendment protects individual rights. It arose out of a ruling made by Federal District Judge Damon J. Keith that wiretaps obtained by the government without a search warrant were illegal. This case was consolidated with *United States* v. *Sinclair* (1971).

The government was represented by Robert G. Mardian (later indicted for illegal wiretapping in the Watergate investigations that led to President Richard M. Nixon's resignation in 1974). The district court was represented by Kunstler and Buck Davis, a Detroit lawyer. They argued that a warrant for wiretapping must be issued by a court, and there could be no national security exception to that requirement. By an eight-to-zero vote, the Court ruled in favor of Judge Keith, and the earlier case of *United States* v. *Sinclair* was dismissed because the government was not able to use the wiretaps as evidence. Associate Justice William H. Rehnquest (later elevated to Chief Justice) abstained from the vote because he had been instrumental in framing the national security exemption when he was deputy attorney general under President Nixon.

Holder v. Banks (1974)
417 U.S. 187

Arthur Banks, a black actor, had received a five-year prison sentence in the 1970s in Indiana for resisting the draft. It was the maximum sentence allowed under federal law, and he was sent to prison in Terre Haute. While in prison, Banks led a demonstration to the warden's office to protest conditions in the facility. After the demonstration, he was allegedly beaten in his cell by prison guards. When Banks fought back, he was indicted on charges that he assaulted a federal corrections officer.

Kunstler agreed to represent Banks at his trial, but federal judge Cale J. Holder barred him from appearing in the case on the grounds that Kunstler had engaged in a pattern of pretrial publicity that had diminished the prospect of obtaining a fair and impartial jury. Kunstler then filed a petition for a writ of mandamus with the United States Court of Appeals for the Seventh Circuit, which reversed Judge Holder's ruling and permitted Kunstler to represent Banks. Holder, in turn, appealed the decision to the United States Supreme Court.

The Supreme Court initially agreed to hear the case, but later declined to review the court of appeals' decision that Kunstler could represent Banks. Banks returned to prison, but the government decided not to try him on the assault charge.

United States v. Peltier (1976)
422 U.S. 531

In 1975, two FBI agents were murdered when they entered the Pine Ridge Indian Reservation in South Dakota. A grand jury indicted four Native Americans, including Leonard Peltier, for the murder. Peltier fled to Canada before he could be tried, but was later found by authorities and extradited. At his trial in Fargo, North Dakota, he was convicted by the jury of both murders. He received a double life sentence.

Kunstler was trying another murder case at the time of the trial and was unable to represent Peltier. After the conviction, Kunstler became the lead counsel on numerous appeals, writs, and motions to obtain a retrial. It was Kunstler's belief that the government had fabricated and hidden evidence, in addition to suborning perjury, in order to convict Peltier. In 1992, Kunstler turned the appeal over to Ramsey Clark, a former United States attorney general. Nevertheless, Kunstler continued to work on behalf of Peltier, sending a letter about the case to First Lady Hillary Rodham Clinton in 1993. Kunstler was disappointed at her response, but hoped he would live to see the release of Leonard Peltier. When Kunstler died in 1995, Peltier was still in prison.

People of the State of New York ex rel. Little v. *Ciuros* (1978)
406 N.Y.S. 2d 449

In the 1970s, Joan Little, a young black woman, was arrested in North Carolina for stealing a television set and articles of clothing. Unable to raise bail, she was in jail awaiting trial when her white jailer allegedly entered her cell one night and demanded sexual favors from her. She killed him by stabbing him with an ice pick, which she had found in the jail, and managed to escape.

Little was later captured and indicted for first-degree murder. The story made headline news, and women from all parts of the country raised money for her defense. One of her lawyers was Morris Dees, head of the Southern Poverty Law Center, but he was forced off the case by Judge Hamilton Hobgood. Kunstler was summoned to replace Dees, but the judge also barred Kunstler from representing her. When the trial took place, she was acquitted of the murder charge, but fled the state because she still owed jail time.

Little was subsequently found by the police in Brooklyn, New York. Kunstler and his second wife, attorney Margaret L. Ratner, represented Little in an attempt to resist extradition. The case was brought against William Ciuros, New York City Commissioner of Correction.

Kunstler and Ratner argued that Little would be in danger from prison guards in North Carolina because she had killed her jailer. The New York Court of Appeals denied her application resisting extradition. The court held that Little's claim that she would be subjected to unconstitutional treatment may not be invoked in the asylum state for the purpose of preventing extradition except in the most unusual circumstances.

Little served her time in North Carolina without incident and returned to live in New York.

People v. *Smith* (1984)
63 N.Y. 2d 41

Lemuel Smith, a thirty-nine-year-old black man, was serving a twenty-five-to-life sentence at the Green Haven Correctional Facility in upstate New York for murdering two Albany bookstore owners. While in prison, he was accused of murdering Donna Payant, a prison guard whose body was found in a landfill twenty-five miles from Green Haven on May 16, 1981. It was alleged that Smith, who served as an assistant to a Catholic chaplain in the prison, had lured the victim to the chaplain's office, strangled her, wrapped her body in a plastic bag, and disposed of it outside the prison grounds.

At the time of the murder, New York had abolished the death penalty, with one exception: an inmate serving a life sentence would automatically receive the death sentence if convicted of a murder. Smith's mother, in an effort to spare her son's life, asked Kunstler to take the case. Smith had earlier told his mother that he did not want to be represented by a public defender.

In his appeal, Kunstler argued that Smith had been framed by a corrupt group of drug-dealing prison guards. Nevertheless, Smith was convicted and sentenced to death. Kunstler then appealed the death sentence, working with Ronald L. Kuby and Mark Gombiner on the case. Kuby wrote the brief, which contended that it was unconstitutional to mandate the death penalty without allowing a hearing on mitigating factors.

In 1984, New York's Court of Appeals overturned Smith's sentence and invalidated the death penalty statute. New York appealed to the United States Supreme Court, which declined to hear the case.

New York later reinstated the death penalty. Although Smith was not put to death, he was subsequently retried for Payant's murder. He was convicted and received the maximum sentence of twenty-five-to life.

Williams v. *State* (1985)
312 S.E. 2d 40

Wayne Bertram Williams was a young black man who was accused of murdering two black men in Atlanta. In the course of his trial in 1983, he was found guilty of their murder and also was linked to the unsolved murders of ten of the twenty-seven black children who had been killed in the city during the years 1979–81. He was never tried for the Atlanta child murders, but the prosecution contended at the trial that there were striking similarities between the killing of the two men and the ten children.

Kunstler was asked by writer James Baldwin to appeal Williams's conviction. Although reluctant to represent an alleged child killer, Kunstler became part of the defense team. His decision to take the case was made because he had come upon information linking members of the Ku Klux Klan to the child murders. It was Kunstler's belief that the prosecution decided to make Williams a scapegoat because it feared that a race war would erupt in Atlanta if the Klan was charged with the murders.

In 1985, the defense team filed the first of its habeas corpus petitions for Williams. The petition was denied, but Kunstler continued to work on the appeal. Kunstler's last appeal, which was made a short time before his death, was also unsuccessful.

O'Prey v. *Ward* (1987)

Raymond O'Prey was a married white policeman in New York City and the father of three children. He had served on the force for twenty-six years at the time of the lawsuit.

O'Prey headed a troupe of jazz-dancing police officers (both men and women), who performed in their uniforms at various functions. At a performance at New York City's Little Red School House, where one of Kunstler's younger daughters was a student, Kunstler and O'Prey met. The police officer complained about the discriminatory treatment the troupe had received from members of the New York City Police Department. Kunstler later brought a civil rights action in federal court against Police Commissioner Benjamin Ward for the Police Department's alleged harassment of O'Prey.

The case was to be tried before Judge Kenneth Conboy, a former deputy police commissioner. Judge Conboy prevailed upon the parties to settle out of court. O'Prey received his settlement and retired at full pension. In gratitude, O'Prey had his detective shield mounted on a plaque and sent it to Kunstler. It was engraved: "To William Moses Kunstler, honor to a good man." Kunstler's plaque—an unlikely tribute from a white police officer—hung in his office.

Texas v. *Johnson* (1989)
491 U.S. 397

On August 22, 1984, Gregory Lee Johnson and others participated in a march outside the Republican National Convention in Dallas, Texas, to protest the policies of President Ronald Reagan and the practices of several Dallas-based defense-industry corporations. In the course of the march, one of the approximately 100 fellow protesters grabbed an American flag from a building pole outside a targeted defense-industry building and gave it to Johnson. The demonstration ended in front of the Dallas City Hall, where Johnson doused the flag with kerosene and set it on fire. His fellow demonstrators then began to chant: "America, the red, white, and blue, we spit on you." The rest of the demonstration was uneventful, and no one was hurt nor threatened.

Johnson was convicted of desecrating the flag in violation of a Texas law that prohibited the desecration of a "venerated object." The decision was appealed by the American Civil Liberties Union in Texas state courts until the highest court ruled that Johnson's conviction was unconstitutional. The state appealed to the United States Supreme Court. The Supreme Court brief for Johnson was prepared by David Cole, a lawyer from New York's Center for Constitutional Rights, and the oral argument was made by Kunstler. The main thrust of Kunstler's argument was that Johnson's intention in burning the flag was to exercise his right of free speech under the First Amendment. The Court ruled in favor of Johnson, and flag burning was held to be a right protected under the Constitution.

In re Kunstler (4th Cir. 1990)
914 F. 2d 505

In 1988, Kunstler and two other lawyers were fined by a North Carolina federal court under Rule 11, which provides for sanctions against attorneys who file "frivolous" lawsuits. The sanctions arose from the actions of the three attorneys in filing a lawsuit against Judge Joe Freeman Britt and several other state officials in North Carolina. The lawsuit was filed to stop the alleged harassment of a defense committee formed to represent two Native Americans, Timothy Jacobs and Eddie Hatcher, who had been indicted for kidnapping.

The federal court ordered Kunstler and the two attorneys to pay $120,000, which was subsequently reduced to $43,000 due to the efforts of attorney Morton Stavis, who fought the decision until he died in 1992. The reduced fine was ultimately paid by New York's Center for Constitutional Rights.

United States v. *Eichman* (1990)
496 U.S. 310

In 1989, Congress passed the Flag Protection Act, which made it a crime to desecrate the American flag. The act was worded to be sufficiently different from the Texas statute prohibiting the desecration of a "venerated object"—a statute that the United States Supreme Court struck down in *Texas* v. *Johnson* (1989).

On the day that the Flag Protection Act was passed, a number of young people, including Shawn D. Eichman, burned United States flags at a political demonstration on the steps of the United States Capitol. At another demonstration led by Mark John Haggarty in Seattle, American flags were also burned. Both groups of demonstrators were arrested and charged with violation of the Flag Protection Act.

The demonstrators moved to dismiss the charges on the grounds that the act violated the First Amendment. The federal district courts agreed, citing *Texas* v. *Johnson,* and the government appealed to the United States Supreme Court.

The two cases were consolidated for argument before the Supreme Court. Kunstler, who had argued the case in the Washington, D.C., court, and David Cole, of New York's Center for Constitutional Rights, both wanted to present the oral argument before the Supreme Court. The lawyers left the decision to their seven remaining clients (Gregory Lee Johnson, the respondent in *Texas* v. *Johnson,* had also been charged, but the government dropped its case against him), and they chose Kunstler by a four-to-one vote. The brief was prepared by Cole.

Arguing the case on May 14, 1990, Kunstler maintained that burning the flag was exactly the type of speech that the First Amendment was designed to protect. Kunstler won the case as the Court declared the Flag Protection Act unconstitutional.

Cabey v. *Goetz* (1996)

On December 22, 1984, Bernhard Goetz, a white man, shot four black youths in the subway in New York City. The shooting occurred when one of the youths asked Goetz for money. Fearing that he was about to be mugged, Goetz pulled out a gun and shot at all of them. Three of the youngsters escaped serious injury, but one of them—Darrell Cabey—was badly hurt. Although

Goetz was subsequently acquitted of attempted murder in 1986, he was sentenced to six months in prison for the illegal possession of a gun.

Kunstler and Ronald L. Kuby later represented Darrell Cabey, the injured youth, in a civil suit against Goetz. Cabey had been paralyzed from the waist down and suffered brain damage as a result of the shooting. Cabey was a resident of the Bronx, and the lawyers insisted that the civil suit be tried in that borough because it had the reputation of being sympathetic to minority groups in the city.

Kunstler and Kuby sued Goetz for $50 million in a lawsuit that dragged on in the courts for years. On April 24, 1996—six months after Kunstler's death—the six-member jury, consisting of four blacks and two Hispanics, found that Goetz had acted recklessly and deliberately inflicted emotional distress on Cabey. It awarded Cabey $43 million. Goetz had very limited assets, and Cabey was unlikely to see anywhere near that amount. In such cases, the court usually will garnish 10 percent of the defendant's wages for twenty years.

Annotated Bibliography

Adams, Edward A. "Constitutional Rights Center: 13 Years of Unpopular Causes." *New York Law Journal,* June 23, 1989, 1. Discussion of the Center for Constitutional Rights and its work.

———. "Kuby Battles On for Use of Kunstler's Name." *New York Law Journal,* December 12, 1996, 1. Dispute between Ronald L. Kuby and Kunstler's widow, Margaret L. Ratner, about the use by Kuby of the firm's name, Kunstler and Kuby.

———. "Kunstler Colleague Deprived of Right to Use Firm Name." *New York Law Journal,* December 19, 1996, 1. A ruling prohibiting Kuby from using the firm name.

"An Advocate's Passions." Reprint from *Sacramento Bee.* In *Los Angeles Daily Journal,* September 14, 1995, 6. Reprint on the editorial page of favorable assessment of Kunstler.

Allen, Charlotte. Review of *My Life as a Radical Lawyer,* by William M. Kunstler. *Wall Street Journal,* October 13, 1994, A18. Critical account of Kunstler, but an acknowledgment of his literary skills in his court presentations.

Allon, Janet. "Neighborhood Report: Lower Manhattan; Remembering Abbie, Jerry and Chicago." *New York Times,* December 3, 1995, Sec. 13: 8. Recollection of the Chicago Seven trial.

Altman, James M. Review of *My Life as a Radical Lawyer,* by William M. Kunstler. *New York Law Journal* (January 24, 1995): 2. Assessment of Kunstler's autobiography.

Anderson, Cerisse. "Kunstler Loses 3rd Mistrial Bid in Jogger Case: Judge Again Rejects Attempt to Vacate Salaam Conviction." *New York Law Journal,* August 20, 1991, 1. Unsuccessful attempt by Kunstler in Yusef Salaam case.

———. "Libel Claim against Kunstler by Bernhard Goetz Is Dismissed." *New York Law Journal,* March 15, 1995, 16. Account of Goetz's unsuccessful libel suit against Kunstler.

Bernstein, Dennis, and Light, Julie. "The Life and Times of William Moses Kunstler." *Z Magazine,* October 1995 1–13. <http:\\zena.secureforum.comZnet\zmag\zmag.cfm>. An interview with Kunstler published after his death.

Buckley, William F., Jr. "Kunstler." *National Review,* November 5, 1971, 1258. Criticism of Kunstler for statements he made about Governor Nelson A. Rockefeller of New York in connection with the Attica uprising.

Bruck, Connie. "William Kunstler: Actor Without a Stage." *American Lawyer* 2 (August 1980): 24–26. Critical account of Kunstler's career.

Coyne, Randall. "Defending the Despised: William Moses Kunstler." *American Indian Law Review* 20 (Spring 1995): 257–279. Appraisal of Kunstler's career, with emphasis on his work on behalf of Native Americans.

"The Death of a Revolutionary," *New Yorker,* September 18, 1995, 39–40. Article on Kunstler following his death, with comment that he lived according to his principles.

"Defending the Despised." *People Weekly,* September 18, 1995, 225. Assessment of Kunstler's career.

Eisler, Kim Isaacs. "William Kunstler in Lynchburg: The Real Measure of the Man." *Legal Times,* September 11, 1995, 41–42. Account of Kunstler's defense of Thomas Carlton Wansley, a black teenager accused of rape in Lynchburg, Virginia.

Ellison, Bruce H. "William Kunstler: A People's Lawyer." *South Dakota Law Review* 41 (Spring 1996): 229–235. Summary of Kunstler's law career, with emphasis on his work on behalf of Native Americans.

Ervin, Mike. "The Progressive Interview: Leonard Weinglass." *Progressive* 60 (May 1996): 34–36. Weinglass discusses his work and the Chicago Seven trial.

Frank, Cheryl. "Subway Shootout: Goetz Case Just Beginning." *ABA Journal* 71 (April 1985): 18. Kunstler's role in the case against Bernhard Goetz for the shooting of four black youngsters on a New York City subway train in 1984.

Freedman, Adam. Review of *My Life as a Radical Lawyer,* by William M. Kunstler with Sheila Isenberg. *National Review,* December 31, 1994. Critical assessment of Kunstler's autobiography.

Friedman, Leon. "A Provocative Lawyer Who Challenged Rules: William M. Kunstler." *National Law Journal* (September 18, 1985): A21. Obituary on Kunstler and assessment of his work.

Gregory, Sophronia Scott. "Black Rage: In Defense of a Mass Murderer." *Time,* June 6, 1994, 31. Account of Kunstler and Ronald L. Kuby's strategy in Colin Ferguson case.

Haberman, Clyde. "No Solace for Widow of Attica." *New York Times,* February 22, 2000, B1. A summary of the Attica uprising in 1971 and the failure to compensate the widow of a prison guard.

Hentoff, Nat. "Playboy Interview: William Kunstler." *Playboy,* October 1970, 1–16. Kunstler recalled his childhood and spoke about the Chicago Seven trial.

Hodel, F. Peter, Sid Lerner, and Hal Drucker. "Chatting with Bill Kunstler over General Noriega's Cookies." *New York Law Journal,* September 18, 1995, 2. A discussion by Kunstler of his views and attitude toward the legal profession.

Hoffman, Jan. "Defense Lawyers Increase Their Use of the Press." Reprint from *New York Times.* In *Los Angeles Daily Journal,* May 6, 1994, 10: 9. The usefulness of press coverage to Kunstler and other defense lawyers.

———. "The Next Generation, New Kunstlers." *New York Times,* September 18, 1995, B1. Focus on Kunstler's two youngest daughters.

Kalish, Jon. "Kunstler's Short, Happy Acting Career." *New York Law Journal,* November 18, 1992, 2. Column about Kunstler's appearance in the movie *Malcolm X.*

Kifner, John. "Silver Protest Reunion for Yesteryear's Yippies." *New York Times,* October 30, 1994, Sec. 1: 43. Gathering to commemorate the twenty-fifth anniversary of the Chicago Seven trial.

"Klan Link Is Cited in Child Killings." *New York Times,* October 10, 1991, A20. Evidence linking the Ku Klux Klan to the murders of ten children in Atlanta in the early 1980s after Kunstler's client, Wayne Williams, had been linked to the murders.

Krassner, Paul. "Abbie Hoffman and Jerry Rubin Together Again." *New York,* December 12, 1994. Recollections of the Chicago Seven trial by friends of the late Hoffman and Rubin.

Kunstler, William M. . . . *And Justice For All.* Dobbs Ferry, NY: Oceana Publications, 1963. A study of ten unpopular defendants, who were allegedly victimized by racial, religious, or political prejudice.

———. "Back to Attica." *Nation,* March 25, 1991, 364. Recollection of the 1971 Attica uprising.

———. *Beyond a Reasonable Doubt? The Original Trial of Caryl Chessman.* New York: William Morrow, 1961. An examination of the trial of a famed kidnapper who was executed in San Quentin, California, in May 1960 after nearly twelve years on death row.

———. "The Bill of Rights—Can It Survive?" *Gonzaga Law Review* 26 (Fall 1990): 1–11. Apprehensions about the survival of the Bill of Rights, delivered at the William O. Douglas Lecture Series.

———. "By Hook or By Crook." *Hamline Law Review* 8 (October 1985): 611–624. Criticism by Kunstler of the trial of Native American Leonard Peltier.

———. *The Case for Courage.* New York: William Morrow, 1962. Study of ten lawyers over a two-hundred-year span and their roles in handling some of the most explosive cases of their time. Lawyers studied are Andrew Hamilton, John Adams, William Henry Seward, Reverdy Johnson, John Peter Altgeld, Clarence Seward Darrow, William Goodrich Thompson, Homer Stille Cummings, Harold R. Medina, and Joseph Nye Welch.

———. *Corporate Tax Summary.* New York: Oceana Publications, 1960. A short text designed for lay readers on corporate tax law.

———. *Deep in My Heart.* New York: William Morrow, 1966. A personal account of his involvement in the civil rights struggle in the South beginning in the late 1950s.

———. "Exposing the Storm: Constitutional Objections in the Persian Gulf War." *St. John's Law Review* 66 (Fall 1992): 655–686. Kunstler expressed his objections to the Persian Gulf War at a symposium on this topic.

———. *First Degree.* New York: Oceana Publications, 1960. A study of eighteen first-degree murder cases (including the Leopold and Loeb case), with a discussion of the causes of murder.

———. *Hints and Allegations: The World in Poetry and Prose, According to William M. Kunstler.* New York: Seven Stories Press, 1994. A collection of over 100 sonnets, each accompanied by a context-setting note.

———. "Keynote Address." *New York University Review of Law and Social Change* 15 (June 1987): 429–433. Kunstler's speech at a symposium on Federal and State Methods of Repressing Political Activism.

————. *The Law of Accidents*. Dobbs Ferry, NY: Oceana Publications, 1954. A short text designed for lay readers on negligence law.

————. *The Minister and the Choir Singer: The Hall-Mills Murder Case*. New York: William Morrow, 1964. Account of a sensational 1922 murder case in New Jersey that resulted in the acquittal of the defendants. It was Kunstler's only book to become a best-seller. He sold the movie rights for $25,000, which he used to buy his home in Mamaroneck, New York. The movie was never made.

————. "Remarks in Accepting the New York State Association of Criminal Defense Lawyers' Thurgood Marshall Practitioner's Award," Mouthpiece: *New York State Association of Criminal Defense Lawyers* 7 (March/April 1994): 16–17. Recollections of some of the highlights of his life in a speech dedicated to his clients and their quest for equal justice.

————. "Silencing the Oppressed: No Freedom of Speech for Three Behind the Walls of the First Amendment Issue." *Creighton Law Review* 26 (June 1993): 1005–1025. Article on First Amendment rights.

————. *Trials and Tribulations*. New York: Grove Press, 1985. A collection of sonnets concerning political events. Each poem is preceded by a prose description of the subject covered.

Kunstler, William M., with Sheila Isenberg. *My Life as a Radical Lawyer*. New York: Birch Lane Press, 1994. Kunstler's autobiography; he had preferred the title *Loose Cannon*.

Kunstler, William M., and William Vincent Stone. *Our Pleasant Vices*. New Haven, CT: privately printed, 1941. A collection of sonnets written by Kunstler and Stone when they were undergraduate students at Yale University.

Langum, David J. *William M. Kunstler: The Most Hated Lawyer in America*. New York: New York University Press, 1999. First biography of Kunstler, written by a professor of law at the Cumberland School of Law, Samford University, in Birmingham, Alabama.

"A Lawyer for Hire." *American Bar Association Journal* 56 (June 1970): 552. Criticism of Kunstler for his views on attorneys and clients.

Lefcourt, Gerald. "In Memoriam," Mouthpiece: *New York State Association of Criminal Defense Lawyers* 3 (September/October 1995): 7–9. Laudatory comments about Kunstler, made at the association's annual dinner in 1994, when he received the Thurgood Marshall Award.

Leuchtenburg, William E. *Troubled Feast: American Society Since 1945*. Boston: Little, Brown, 1973. Analysis of problems after World War II.

Lynd, Staughton. Review of *My Life as a Radical Lawyer*, by William M. Kunstler. *Los Angeles Daily Journal*, October 4, 1994, 7. Review of Kunstler's autobiography.

Margolick, David. "Still Radical After All These Years; at 74, William Kunstler Defends Clients Most Lawyers Avoid," *New York Times*, July 6, 1993, B1. Account of Kunstler and his radical clients.

————. "Verbal Sparks Fly During Ethics Debate at Harvard University." Reprint from *New York Times*. In *Los Angeles Daily Journal*, March 26, 1982, 5. Debate at Harvard; participants included Kunstler and Roy Cohen.

Marshall, David. "William Kunstler—a 'Loose Cannon'?" *New Law Journal*, 143, November 26, 1993, 1164. Assessment of Kunstler by an English lawyer.

McMorris, Frances A. "Kunstler Censured for Comments to Trial Judge." *New York Law Journal*, December 29, 1993, 1. Action against Kunstler for statements made to Acting Judge Thomas B. Galligan of the Manhattan State Supreme Court.

————. "William M. Kunstler Censured Publicly for Calling Judge a Name." *National Law Journal* (January 10, 1994): 2. Action against Kunstler for statements made to Judge Thomas B. Galligan.

McQuiston, John T. "Adviser to L.I.R.R. Suspect Threatens to Quit." *New York Times*, February 7, 1995, B8. One of Colin Ferguson's legal advisers threatened to quit and Kunstler and Ronald L. Kuby asked judge to stop the trial.

Morgan, Bryan. Review of *My Life as a Radical Lawyer*, by William M. Kunstler. *Colorado Lawyer* 24 (October 1995): 2325–2326. Assessment of Kunstler's autobiography.

National Institute Conference. "The Supreme Court and Daily Life: Who Will the Court Protect in the 1990s?" *New York University Review of Law and Social Change* 18 (March 1990): 5–13. Kunstler's comments as a participant in the conference.

Navasky, Victory S. "Right On! With Lawyer William Kunstler." *New York Times Magazine*, April 19, 1970, 31, 88–93. Analysis of Kunstler's views and his approach to the legal profession.

Needle, Jeffrey. Review of *My Life as a Radical Lawyer,* by William M. Kunstler. *Trial* 31 (April 1995): 82–83. Assessment of Kunstler's autobiography.

Nessen, Maurice N, moderator. "Attica: Its Causes, Implications, and Lessons." Special Forum, Evening, *New York County Lawyers Association* 3 (November 23, 1971): 1–108. Discussion by Kunstler and other attorneys of Attica uprising in 1971.

Pace, Eric. "Jerry Rubin, 56, Flashy 60's Radical Dies; 'Yippies' Founder and Chicago 7 Defendant." *New York Times,* November 30, 1994, B13. Obituary of Jerry Rubin and an account of the Chicago Seven trial.

Pack, Maggie (Armonk, New York). Letter to the editor, *National Law Journal* (October 2, 1995): A18. Letter by widow about Kunstler's defense of a man found guilty of killing her husband.

Perez-Pena, Richard. "1,000 Honor Kunstler, Defender of Their Faith." *New York Times,* November 20, 1995, B11. Coverage of memorial service for Kunstler at the Cathedral of St. John the Divine in New York.

Pines, Deborah. "Bases for Sanctioning Lawyers Clarified in Ruling for Kunstler." *New York Law Journal,* March 3, 1995, 1, 12. Discussion of Kunstler's exoneration in 1995 under a Rule 11 Sanction of the Federal Rules of Civil Procedure, and the implication of the decision in sanctioning lawyers.

Pinsley, Elliot. "At 70, The Cause Is Still Supreme for Kunstler: Despite Tide of Conservatism, He Remains Consistent Defender of the Left." *New Jersey Law Journal* 124 (September 7, 1989): 4. Discussion of Kunstler's devotion to leftist causes.

————. "William Kunstler's Cause and Effects: Leftist Lawyer Still Pushing 'People's Law.'" *Legal Times,* August 14, 1989, 12: 16–17. Discussion of Kunstler's devotion to leftist causes.

"Publicity Key to Kunstler's Career." *Chicago Daily Law Bulletin,* March 16, 1987, 1. Comments on Kunstler's effective use of publicity in his lawsuits.

Reichbach, Gustin L. "Bill Kunstler: An Appreciation." *New York Law Journal,* November 13, 1995, 2. An evaluation of Kunstler's work, and a comparison with Clarence Darrow.

Reidinger, Paul. Review of *My Life as a Radical Lawyer,* by William M. Kunstler. *ABA Journal* 80 (December 1994): 106. Assessment of Kunstler's autobiography.

Rose, Charlie. WNET program: "The Chicago Seven, Revisited." October 28, 1994, transcript #1236. Panel discussion with Kunstler, David Dellinger, Tom Hayden, and Bobby Seale.

————. "Remembrance of William Kunstler," September 5, 1995, transcript #1458. Panel discussion on Kunstler with Gerald Lefcourt and Alan Dershowitz.

Rosen, Jeffrey. Review of *My Life as a Radical Lawyer,* by William M. Kunstler. *Chicago Daily Law Bulletin* September 22, 1994, 2. Assessment of Kunstler's autobiography.

————. Review of *My Life as a Radical Lawyer,* by William M. Kunstler. *New York Times,* September 18, 1994, Sec. 7: 16. Assessment of Kunstler's autobiography.

Rosenbaum, Ron. "The Most Hated Lawyer in America." *Vanity Fair,* March 1992, 68–94. Discussion of the controversy surrounding Kunstler and his work.

Ryan, James. "Film: The Comeback Kid Tries Again." *New York Times,* January 14, 1996, Sec. 2: 11. Article about actor Richard Dreyfus and his movie *Mr. Holland's Opus,* in which the leading character was allegedly based on Kunstler.

Seligman, Daniel. "Radical Chic Forever," *Fortune,* October 16, 1995, 245–246. Criticism of the favorable comments made about Kunstler following his death.

Sherman, Rorie. "'Black Rage' Rises Again as Defense; 1946 Precedent Found in Railroad Killing Case." *National Law Journal* (April 25, 1994): A6. Comments on the Colin Ferguson case and the "black rage" defense.

Spencer, Scott. "William Kunstler: 1919–1995." *Rolling Stone,* October 19, 1995, 89. Discussion of Kunstler, his work, and his admirers.

Stout, David. "William Kunstler, 76, Dies; Lawyer for Social Outcasts." *New York Times,* September 5, 1995, B6. Obituary of Kunstler, with emphasis on his clients.

Tippett, Frank. "Tawana Brawley: Case vs. Cause: How a Rape Investigation Has Fired Up a Political Movement," *Time,* June 20, 1988, 22. Account of attempt by Brawley's advisers to turn case into a national protest.

Verhouvek, Sam Howe. "Profile: William M. Kunstler." *Los Angeles Daily Journal,* August 12, 1988, 1. Highlights of Kunstler's professional career.

Weber, Bruce. "May It Please the Audience: Kunstler Does Comedy." *New York Times,* August 10, 1995, B3. Column on Kunstler's performance at a comedy club in New York.

"William Kunstler." *Economist* 336 (September 16, 1995): 121. Obituary noting his accomplishments and skills in the courtroom.

"William Kunstler." *Nation,* September 25, 1995, 299–300. Obituary praising his dedication to his clients.

"William Kunstler, RIP." *National Review,* September 25, 1995, 19. Obituary criticizing his work.

Williams, Lena. "Revolution Redux?" *New York Times,* March 28, 1993, Sec. 9: 1. Discussion of Kunstler's two youngest daughters and their political views.

Wise, Daniel. "Kunstler Disciplinary Hearing Takes on Conciliatory Tones," *New York Law Journal,* November 16, 1992, 1. The disciplinary hearing dealing with Kunstler's remarks to Acting Judge Thomas B. Galligan of the Manhattan State Supreme Court.

—Ruth—
Bader Ginsburg

(United States Supreme Court)

Chronology

1933   Born on March 15, in Brooklyn, New York, to Celia and Nathan Bader.

1950   Graduated in June from James Madison High School in Brooklyn; Celia Bader died on the day before Ruth's graduation.

1954   Graduated Phi Beta Kappa and *summa cum laude* from Cornell University in Ithaca, New York; married Martin D. Ginsburg.

1955   Daughter Jane born on July 21.

1956–1958   Both Ruth and her husband attended Harvard Law School at Cambridge, Massachusetts.

1959   Graduated from Columbia University Law School tied for first in her class; admitted to the New York State bar.

1959–1961   Served as law clerk to Edmund L. Palmieri, U.S. District Court Judge for the Southern District of New York.

1961–1963   Served as research associate and then as associate director of the Columbia Law School Project on International Procedure; did legal research in Sweden for six months.

1963   Joined the faculty of the Rutgers University Law School, where she continued to teach until 1972; became full professor and was granted tenure in 1969.

1965   Son James born on September 8; published *Civil Procedure in Sweden,* a book she coauthored with Anders Brezelius.

1971   Coauthored ACLU's brief in *Reed* v. *Reed,* helping to win a key victory in which, for the first time, the Supreme Court overturned a state law on grounds of sex discrimination.

1972   Cofounded the Women's Rights Project and served for the next eight years as its codirector and chief litigator; joined the faculty of Columbia University Law School, where she taught until 1980.

1973   Argued and won *Frontiero* v. *Richardson,* her first case before the Supreme Court.

1974   Her coauthored textbook, *Text, Cases, and Materials on Sex-Based Discrimination,* was published.

1979   Nominated by President Carter to the United States Court of Appeals for the District of Columbia, where she served until 1993.

1993   Nominated to the U.S. Supreme Court by President Clinton on June 14; confirmed by the Senate on August 3; sworn in on

August 10 as the 107th justice of the United States Supreme Court; the American Bar Association gave Ginsburg its annual Margaret Brent Women Lawyers of Achievement Award.

1996   Wrote the majority opinion in *United States* v. *Virginia*, requiring the Virginia Military Institute to admit qualified women students, thereby completing the gender integration of the nation's military academies.

1999   Operated on successfully for colon cancer and returned to work in time for the opening of the October 1999 session of the Supreme Court.

Biography

On June 14, 1993, at a ceremony held in the White House Rose Garden, President Bill Clinton introduced Ruth Bader Ginsburg to the assembled media and guests as his first nominee for the U.S. Supreme Court. For thirteen years, Ginsburg had sat on the U.S. Court of Appeals in Washington D.C., and before that she had been the chief advocate of gender equality before the federal courts, winning five out of the six cases that she argued before the U.S. Supreme Court. The president hailed Ginsburg for her "pioneering work in behalf of the women of this country," noting that her achievements in the advancement of woman's rights had been found comparable by some experts to those of Thurgood Marshall in the field of civil rights. Ginsburg then made a short speech in which she linked her appointment to the advances made by women in the legal profession. At the close, she paid homage to her late mother, Celia Amter Bader, "the bravest and strongest person I have known who was taken from me too soon. I pray that I may be all that she would have been had she lived in an age when women could aspire and achieve, and daughters are cherished as much as sons."[1]

Origins

Ruth Bader Ginsburg* was born on March 15, 1933, in the Flatbush section of Brooklyn. Her parents, Nathan and Celia Bader, were both the children of Jewish immigrants who had arrived in New York City during the early 1900s. Celia's family had originated in Central Europe and Nathan's parents had come over from Russia. When Ruth was one year old, her only sibling, her six-year-old sister Marilyn, died of meningitis.[2]

Flatbush in the 1930s was an ethnically mixed area in which Jewish immigrants and their children mingled freely with families of Irish and Italian extraction. Although far from poor, the Baders were essentially of the lower middle class. Nathan Bader was a furrier and clothier who had worked in various shops and had for brief periods owned such a shop himself. Up to the time of Ruth's fourth birthday, she and her parents shared a single house with her uncle and aunt, and their son, Richard, who became her closest childhood friend and playmate.[3]

As was the case with many Jewish parents of the period, the Baders believed strongly in the value of learning and were as one in encouraging their only child to do well in school. Of the two, however, her mother was by far the more important influence upon the future lawyer and judge. Celia Amter had done extremely well in school as a child and adolescent, but her family had

---

*Her name at birth was Joan Ruth Bader, but when she was five, her mother changed it to Ruth Joan Bader because there were two other girls named Joan Ruth in her kindergarten class.

subscribed to the view then prevalent among the poor that college was only for boys. After graduating from high school at the early age of fifteen, she worked briefly in the garment district so that her brother could attend Cornell University. Once married, Celia, like most women in her day, was expected to have no career other than being a housewife and mother. Determined that her daughter have the education and the career that she had been denied, Celia did everything she could to encourage Ruth to have high ambitions and to apply herself diligently to her studies. Even before the little girl entered kindergarten, she would often spend whole afternoons with her mother at the public library. Their local library branch was located above a Chinese restaurant, and in later years Ruth would associate her love of reading with the smell of Chinese cooking.[4]

Throughout her childhood, Ruth was called "Kiki," a nickname bestowed on her as a baby by her older sister, Marilyn. She spent several summers during her childhood in the countryside of upstate New York at a "sleepaway" camp for Jewish youngsters. Ruth also received religious instruction after school and at age thirteen was confirmed at the East Midwood Jewish Center.[5]

Ginsburg attended Public School 238 in Brooklyn from 1938 to 1946. At school she was both accomplished and popular. As an eighth grader, she edited the *Highway Herald,* a mimeographed student newspaper. An editorial that she wrote for the paper revealed a precocious interest in politics and law. Entitled "Landmarks of Constitutional Freedom," her essay identified five great documents in the history of human freedom: the Ten Commandments, the Magna Carta, the English Bill of Rights, the Declaration of Independence, and the Charter of the United Nations. Each one of these, wrote the young editor, had by its very existence played a major role in the shaping of history.[6]

At her junior high school graduation Ruth received an award for "outstanding achievement and service to the school" and joined with another girl in delivering the valedictory speech. She went on to James Madison High School, where she continued to excel as a student while taking part in a wide array of extracurricular activities. "Kiki" was a cheerleader, a baton-twirler, and the treasurer of the Go-Getters, a pep club that held rallies to cheer on Madison's sports teams and to sell tickets to their games. "She was popular, personable, serious," recalled one classmate. "She belonged to all the right groups. She studied without giving the impression of studying." Ruth played the cello in the orchestra, acted in school plays, belonged to Arista (the honor society), and was features editor of the school newspaper.[7]

During Ruth's first year of high school, her mother was diagnosed as having cancer of the cervix. While saying little at school of her mother's illness, Ruth did what she could to comfort her. Knowing that she loved to see her daughter study, Ruth would do her homework whenever possible in her ailing mother's bedroom. Celia Bader died in June 1950 on the day before her daughter's graduation from high school. Ruth, who ranked sixth in the graduating class and had been scheduled to take part in the Forum of Honor at graduation, was unable to attend, and her teachers brought to her home her diploma and the awards that she had won. "So much of my childhood was unhappy," Ginsburg once observed. "I grew up with the smell of death."[8]

A Student at Cornell

Celia Bader left nearly $8,000 to her daughter and urged in her will that Ruth use the money to continue her education. In September 1950, Ruth began her first semester at Cornell University in Ithaca, New York. Having won scholarships from the university and from New York State, she was able to give most of her mother's legacy to her father. Ruth met the rest of her expenses by doing part-time clerical work.[9]

At Cornell in the 1950s, the female students, who comprised some 20 percent of the student body, were supervised far more strictly than the men. For example, the female students, but not the males, were required to live in dormitories on the campus grounds and were expected to be in their rooms at night by 10:30. Like nearly all college students of the period, Ruth Bader simply accepted the prevailing double standard as part of the natural order of things. "I did not think of myself as a feminist," Ginsburg has said of her college years. Indeed, she cannot recall ever hearing woman's rights discussed during her years at Cornell, whether in the classroom or even in conversation among students. (She did, however, belong to a campus student government body called the Woman's Self-Governance Association.)[10]

Although not yet a feminist, Ruth Bader, remembering her mother's hopes for her future, was consciously preparing herself to become something more than a wife and mother. The intensity of her ambition made her somewhat unusual among the female students at Cornell, for most of whom, as Ginsburg would later observe, "the most important degree to earn was the MRS and it didn't do to be seen reading and studying." To avoid seeming out of step with her peers, Ruth became a sort of "closet grind," seeking out Cornell's most obscure and little-used libraries where she would put in long hours of study.[11]

Although some of the male students regarded her as "scary-smart," Ruth was popular and enjoyed an active social life. She was admitted to a Jewish sorority and attended many social gatherings and sports events. On a blind date during her first semester in college, she met her future husband, Martin Ginsburg, a Cornell sophomore and the scion of an affluent family in Long Island. The two of them differed markedly in their personalities, for Martin was outgoing and talkative while Ruth was shy and rarely made small talk. Despite these differences in temperament, Ruth and Martin became sweethearts. They took most of their classes together, and in Ruth's junior year, they announced their engagement. Part of Martin's appeal for Ruth may well have been his earnest support for her goals and ambitions. "Martin," she would later recall, "was the only boy I knew who cared that I had a brain."[12]

Among Cornell's faculty, the person who influenced Ruth Bader most was Robert E. Cushman, a professor of government and a noted expert on the Constitution. She took some of the courses that he taught, became his research assistant, and regarded him as both mentor and friend. In later years, Ginsburg said that Cushman had improved her prose style through his sharp critiques of the papers that she had written while a student in his classes.

Cushman also influenced her by his total opposition to all attempts to curb freedom of thought and speech, whatever their ideology or motivation. The early 1950s were an anxious time in which political leaders such as Senator Joseph R. McCarthy (R-WI) succeeded in persuading millions of Americans that the nation was in grave danger from its disloyal citizens and their liberal "dupes," all of whom were accused of serving the cause of Communism, both at home and abroad. Under Cushman's tutelage, Ginsburg became aware of the important work being done by activist lawyers who were defending basic rights against the excesses of McCarthyism. Her admiration for these defenders of free speech seems to have played a role in her eventual decision to become a lawyer. It impressed her "that a lawyer could do something that was personally satisfying and at the same time work to preserve the values that have made this country great."[13]

It was not so much idealism, however, that drew Ruth Bader toward the law, as it was her growing belief that her talents were better suited to the legal profession than to any other line of work. As an attorney, she believed, her ability to write well and to analyze problems clearly could be of great value. When Ruth confided to her father that she was thinking seriously of studying law, he warned her that she might not be able to make a living as a lawyer and urged that she become a teacher instead. To Martin Ginsburg, however, his fiancée's interest in a legal career made abundant sense. After he and Ruth had begun to think about marriage, they decided it would be a good idea if they went into the same profession. They settled finally on the law because it seemed to be the only field in which both would be truly comfortable.[14]

In June 1954 Ruth Bader graduated from Cornell, first in her class and *summa cum laude,* with High Honors in government and Distinction in all subjects, and was elected to two different honor societies: Phi Beta Kappa and Phi Kappa Phi. Later that month she married Martin Ginsburg, who had just completed his first year at Harvard Law School. In September, Martin's studies were interrupted when he was drafted into the U.S. Army.

The newly wedded Ginsburgs would spend the next two years in Lawton, Oklahoma, where Martin was stationed as a junior officer at Fort Sill and Ruth found work at the local Social Security office. When she became pregnant, her superiors demoted her to a lesser job, an affront that she would view ever afterward as a typical instance of how women can be oppressed when it is exclusively men who make the decisions and rules. On July 21, 1955, Ruth gave birth to her first child, a daughter they named Jane. For the next year, she was a full-time housewife for the first and only time in her life.[15]

The Ginsburgs at Harvard

After Martin was discharged from the army in the autumn of 1956, he resumed his studies at the Harvard Law School, and Ruth also enrolled there, one of the nine women to be admitted that year out of an entering class of over 500. The female law students were then viewed as oddities by both the professors and the male students. The professors seemed to call on the outnumbered women to answer questions more frequently than they did the men. For some on the faculty, according to Ginsburg, it was simply "fun and games" and "let's call on the women for comic relief." Women were still at that time excluded from the periodicals room at the Harvard Law Library. On one occasion, Ruth needed to go there to check a source in an article that she was editing for the law review. She was denied admission and a male staff member had to be sent over to check the reference. "There was [at Harvard] no outrageous discrimination," recollects Ginsburg, "but an accumulation of small instances."[16]

At the beginning of each new academic year, Erwin N. Griswold, the dean of the Harvard Law School, would hold a dinner party at his home to which he would invite all the new female students and an equal number of law school faculty. He would ask each of the women in turn to justify her occupying a place at the law school that might otherwise have gone to a qualified male. When it was her turn, according to Ginsburg, her reply was far from "liberated." Studying law, she timidly ventured, would help her to understand her husband's work better and might lead to part-time employment for herself.[17]

Despite these and other petty incidents, Ginsburg thrived at Harvard. So intensely did she pursue her studies that a fellow student called her "Ruthless Ruthie." She achieved outstanding grades and made the law review for which she did proofreading and fact-checking. By the end of her second year at Harvard Law, she was ranked among the top ten students in her class. When her husband was stricken with testicular cancer, a life-threatening disease, Ruth copied the notes taken by other students in his classes, so that Martin would be able to study even in the hospital. When Martin recovered, he was able to take his final exams and to graduate on schedule. One of her male classmates would later tell her: "You set a standard too high for any of us to achieve . . . your law review work was always done; you were always beautifully dressed and superbly groomed; and you had a happy husband and a lovely young daughter."[18]

These achievements were made possible by a marriage that was ahead of its time in that Martin shared equally with Ruth the domestic burdens that were typically assumed only by wives. Discovering that her cooking was all but inedible, Martin taught himself to cook and in time became quite skillful at it. "My husband," Ruth admitted, "is a master chef while I am at most a bare pass." Martin and Ruth also alternated in looking after Jane, so that each would have time to study. "A supportive husband who is willing to share duties and responsibilities," Ginsburg has observed, "is a must for any woman who hopes to combine marriage and a career."[19]

After receiving his law degree in June 1958, Martin Ginsburg accepted an attractive job offer from a law firm in New York City. As a result, Ruth transferred to Columbia Law School. Jane was then three and the Ginsburgs were determined to hold their family together. At Columbia, as at Harvard, Ginsburg was an outstanding student: winning a Kent Fellowship, making the law review, and finishing in a tie for first place in the graduating class of 1959.[20]

From Law Clerk to Scholar

In spite of Ginsburg's outstanding record as a law student, no New York law firm offered her a job. By the late 1950s, these firms were beginning to employ Jewish lawyers, but, as Ruth Ginsburg herself has noted, "to be a woman, a Jew, and a mother to boot, that combination was a bit much." Her motherhood, she has remarked, was probably the biggest obstacle to getting hired by law firms "because they would fear that I wouldn't be able to give my full mind and time to my legal work."* One of her former professors at Harvard recommended her for a clerkship to U.S. Supreme Court Justice Felix Frankfurter, but the latter, while acknowledging that her record was impressive, was not ready to hire a female clerk. Learned Hand, another revered and important judge, also refused to consider Ginsburg (or any woman) for a clerkship. Finally, another of her former professors persuaded Judge Edmund L. Palmieri of the U.S. District Court in the Southern District of New York to take her on as a clerk. Eager to prove herself, Ginsburg worked longer hours than any of the other court clerks, came in on Saturdays, and took work home. After she had worked for Palmieri for two years, several New York law firms asked her to work for them, due, in large measure, to the judge's assessment of Ginsburg as one of the best clerks that he had ever had.[21]

Ginsburg passed on these offers, however, and went to work instead for the Columbia Law School Project on International Procedure, first as a research associate and later as associate director. When offered an assignment to study firsthand the judicial system of Sweden, the ambitious Ginsburg eagerly accepted it, because it would give her the opportunity both to write a book and also to broaden herself by living on her own for several months in a foreign country. After being tutored in Swedish for several months, she journeyed to the University of Lund, where she studied Swedish law for four months in 1962 and for another two-month stint in the following year.[22]

---

*Justice Sandra Day O'Connor, the first woman to sit on the United States Supreme Court, had ranked third in her Stanford University Law School graduating class in 1952 (the future Chief Justice, William Rehnquist, was first), and she too was unable to land a job at a private law firm even though she was neither Jewish nor (at that time) a mother.

While in Sweden, Ginsburg became aware of the ongoing controversy in that country over sex roles. Although in the main committed to the principle of the equality of the sexes, the Swedes were divided over how far they should go in conferring identical rights and responsibilities on everyone, regardless of gender. By the 1960s, the opportunities open to the women of Sweden were on the whole greater than those available to women in American society. At a time when barely 3 percent of American lawyers were women, Ginsburg found that in Sweden "women were all over the legal profession." There were many female judges, for example. She had even seen a judge presiding over a case while in her eighth month of pregnancy. [23]

In 1963, Ginsburg joined the faculty of the Rutgers University Law School in Newark, New Jersey, just the second woman ever appointed there, and only the twentieth woman ever appointed to a professorship of law in the United States.* In her early years at Rutgers, she taught courses on the federal courts, court procedure, and the conflict of laws. In 1965, when she had been at Rutgers for less than two years, Ginsburg become pregnant for the second time. Recalling how her first pregnancy had resulted in a demotion, she feared that if the administrators at the law school knew of her condition, they might not renew her contract. Resolving to say nothing about her pregnancy to her colleagues, she concealed it by wearing clothes borrowed from her mother-in-law that were a size too big for her. On September 8, 1965, Ginsburg gave birth to her second and last child, James Thomas, and was able to return to work at the beginning of that year's fall semester.[24]

During her first five years at Rutgers, Ginsburg's scholarly publications were almost entirely in the areas of Swedish law and comparative court procedure. In that brief span, she produced four books, one of them concerning economic regulation in the Common Market nations while the others all dealt with the Swedish legal system. Two of the latter works Ginsburg coauthored with Professor Anders Brezelius of the University of Lund. *Civil Procedure in Sweden* was published in 1965 and *The Swedish Code of Judicial Procedure* appeared three years later. She also produced eight articles at this time, four of them on Swedish law. In later years, Ginsburg would assess her work in comparative law as one of her two most significant legal activities. She served as editor of the *Journal of Comparative Law* from 1966 to 1972 and has lectured over the years at many foreign universities. In 1969, Ginsburg was awarded an honorary doctorate of law by the University of Lund for her contributions to the study of Swedish law.

Ginsburg was promoted to associate professor in 1966 and upgraded to full professor and granted tenure in 1969. The dean of the law school would later

---

*Eva Hanks, the first woman to teach at Rutgers Law School, was hired in 1962, one year before Ginsburg.

recall her as "pleasant, hard-working, agreeable, conscientious, and a solid scholar." She would later remark that during her first years at Rutgers, she had felt less than fully welcome, citing her experience as an example of what pioneering woman lawyers were at that time encountering in a profession that was still dominated and controlled by men.[25]

From Scholar to Activist

It was during her last three years at Rutgers that Ginsburg began her transformation from a quiet, apolitical professor into a deeply committed and highly vocal advocate for woman's rights. Up to then, she had never even considered making a legal specialty of either woman's rights or sex discrimination. Ginsburg has said that it was her students who "helped put the idea into [her] head." Perhaps inspired by the rapid, accelerating growth of the national woman's movement, a group of female law students at Rutgers requested of Ginsburg in the autumn of 1968 that she give a seminar at the law school on women and the law. She spent the next month in the library reading every case and article that she could find on the subject. Astonished at how little had been written about the legal status of women, but also irate at the large amount of sexual discrimination that had been sanctioned by American law, Ginsburg resolved to devote her career to the cause of "equal justice for men and women under the law."[26]

From her reading, Ginsburg learned that the common law, judicial decisions, the statutes of legislatures, and administrative decrees had all relegated women to an inferior position. Some states still restricted the right of women to make contracts, serve on juries, act as trustees, and sue in court. In addition, federal and state laws normally tolerated gender bias by private institutions, providing no remedy, for example, when educational institutions excluded women or when businessmen dismissed female employees for becoming pregnant. The gender lines in the law appeared to Ginsburg to be "senseless." In Arizona, for example, it was required by law that the state's governor be a male, and in Wisconsin the law permitted male barbers to cut the hair of both sexes while female hairdressers or barbers could have only females as customers. "How," she wondered, "have people been putting up with such arbitrary distinctions? How have I been putting up with them?"[27]

The courts routinely sanctioned unequal treatment, the judges often expressing their paternalistic concern and chivalrous attitudes toward the "ladies." There were "protective" labor laws that prohibited the employment of women for night work, imposed a workday shorter than that allowed to men, or even excluded women altogether from certain occupations. Well-intentioned reformers, such as Louis Brandeis and Florence Kelley, had fought for some of these laws, but Ginsburg felt that economic regulations that singled out women worked nearly always to their detriment. In Michigan, for example, there was a law against the employment of women as bartenders, and one of the key factors in passing it had been the lobbying of male bartenders bent on protecting their jobs.[28]

Ginsburg was fully converted to feminism in 1969 when she read *The Second Sex,* a pioneer feminist tract by Simone de Beauvoir that was first published in 1949. She found the book "staggering" and was altogether convinced by De Beauvoir's arguments that woman's inferior status in society was caused not by the decrees of nature but by "a culture created and controlled by men" that defined women as emotional and passive in temperament and their proper role in society as exclusively domestic and maternal. Looking back on her own life, she now believed that her setbacks in the workplace formed part of a social pattern that denied to women opportunities that were routinely available to men. According to some of her colleagues at Rutgers, Ginsburg was a changed woman after reading *The Second Sex.* "There was a passion that all of a sudden gripped her," recalled Eve Hanks, one of her colleagues at the time. "She was so excited and talked to lots of colleagues about the book. She sort of caught fire. . . . She had found her goal or passion starting with that book."[29]

Impressed by recent advances, Ginsburg had high hopes for significant change in the coming decade. "Activated by feminists of both sexes," she wrote in 1970, "courts and legislatures are beginning to recognize claims of women to full membership in the class of *people* entitled to due process, and to life and liberty, and the equal protection of the laws." She noted, for example, that many of the lower state and federal courts were applying the Fourteenth Amendment's equal protection clause to overturn obsolete gender-based laws. In addition, new federal measures promised to give women greater opportunities. The Equal Pay Act of 1963 made it national policy that women receive as much pay as men for the same work, and Title VII of the Civil Rights Law of 1964 barred major employers from discriminating against either employees or job applicants because of their sex. Since these laws were seldom enforced, it was up to the woman's movement and its legal advocates to make them effective. "I have a talent," Ginsburg remembered thinking at the time, "to contribute to this cause. This is so right."[30]

Ginsburg was also encouraged by what she described as "the awakening consciousness [of the woman students] in the law schools." By 1970, 7.8 percent of the nation's law students were women, as compared with 4.3 percent only four years earlier. Due to this trend and the growing influence of feminist ideas, lectures and textbooks were being "purged" of "sexist" references and stereotypes. In the new courses that were being given on the legal status of women in America, according to Ginsburg, there were normally two broad themes: how women had been held "in their place" by laws that supposedly protected them, and how the law might now be used to move society toward gender equality and greater independence for women.[31]

Although optimistic about the prospects of the woman's movement, Ginsburg urged its leaders to pursue a course of moderation and pragmatism. Since little could be achieved in the end without broad public support, it was essential that the feminists engage their opponents in dialogue rather than shouting matches. In her eagerness to limit conflict and tumult, Ginsburg contended that the woman's movement should in the short run stress its less controversial goals, leaving the high-intensity issue of abortion, for example, to be dealt with more gradually and primarily through the political process rather than the courts.[32]

By 1969, Ginsburg's feminism had become the focus of her academic career. As a professor, she would now specialize in studying the effect of American law upon woman as well as developing and teaching lecture courses and seminars on the subject. She also helped woman law students at Rutgers to establish a new journal, the *Women's Rights Law Journal,* and assisted them in organizing one of the first academic conferences on women in the law, which was held in May 1970. Of the dozens of articles that she has written since 1970, virtually all have dealt with one aspect or another of gender equality and the status of women in American law.[33]

The "Grandmother Brief"

Ginsburg had been an active member of the New Jersey branch of the American Civil Liberties Union since joining the Rutgers faculty. In the late 1960s, the New Jersey affiliate of the ACLU began to send her cases "of a kind the affiliate had not seen before: teachers forced out of the classroom when their pregnancy began to show, women whose employers provided health insurance with family coverage only for male employees, and parents whose school-age daughters were excluded from publicly funded educational programs open only to boys." (What was new, of course, was not the abuses themselves, but the fact that the women were summoning the courage to bring lawsuits.)

These cases were referred to Ginsburg not because she was (at least at first) especially interested in them, but because she was both a qualified lawyer and a woman, and sex discrimination was thought of as a woman's issue. In the first of her ACLU cases, Ginsburg successfully challenged a New Jersey law that required the dismissal of any schoolteacher who became pregnant while providing no assurance that the teacher would be rehired after her pregnancy ended.[34]

Ginsburg's ties to the ACLU led to her involvement with the case of *Reed* v. *Reed* (1970), a landmark case and a turning point in the U.S. Supreme Court's handling of sex equality issues. The case had originated in Idaho in 1970 when Sally Reed applied to become the administrator of her late son's estate. Richard Lynn Reed, a minor, had died intestate on March 29, 1967. Sally Reed's claim was rejected because of an Idaho law stating, "Where there are several persons equally entitled to administer the estate of a person dying intestate, *males must be preferred to females.*"[35]

There ensued a series of appeals in which the lawyers for Sally Reed insisted that the statute violated the equal protection clause of the Fourteenth Amendment and was unconstitutional. After Idaho's highest court ruled that the law was constitutional, the ACLU appealed to the U.S. Supreme Court. Impressed by her work on woman's rights cases in New Jersey, Melvin Wulf, the legal director of the ACLU, now added Ginsburg to the team of lawyers working on the case. She became the principal author of the organization's amicus curiae brief, on which she collaborated with Wulf. (Ginsburg and her colleagues later referred to the ACLU's *Reed* brief as "the grandmother brief" because many of the arguments presented in it were also used in other sex discrimination lawsuits.) Allan R. Derr, who had represented Sally Reed in the Idaho courts, was retained as cocounsel and argued the case before the high court.[36]

In their brief, Ginsburg and Wulf asserted that under the equal protection clause of the Fourteenth Amendment, all classifications by sex were "suspect" and should be given the same "strict scrutiny" that the federal courts were already giving to classification by race or ethnicity. By this standard, a classification by sex could be valid only if it were necessary to achieve "a compelling state interest." Were this doctrine applied by the courts, it would place the burden of proof upon the measure's advocates to demonstrate that it was rational rather than following the practice then current of requiring its opponents to show that it was without any "rational basis."[37]

Until 1971, the Supreme Court had applied the less rigorous doctrine of "rational basis" in sex equality cases, whereby government policies that treated men and women differently would routinely be upheld unless they were found to be "wholly irrational or arbitrary." As a fallback position, Ginsburg and Wulf also argued that the statute (under which Sally Reed had been denied the right to administer the estate of her deceased son) was lacking even in "the rational basis" claimed for it by the Idaho Supreme Court. The biological differences between the sexes were totally unrelated to the duties performed by an administrator. Many contemporary women, the brief's authors pointed out, in Idaho as elsewhere in America, had as much or more education and business experience as men. If ever there had been a basis for arguing that women as a class were necessarily less able than men to manage estates, such a claim was no longer even plausible. Thus, in automatically preferring men to women, the Idaho law and the judicial decision based on it were arbitrary and irrational, and had denied to Reed "the equal protection of the laws."[38]

On November 22, 1971, a unanimous Court found in favor of Sally Reed, reversing the ruling of the Idaho Supreme Court. "To give a mandatory preference to members of either sex," wrote Chief Justice Warren Burger, "is to make the very kind of arbitrary choice forbidden by the Equal Protection clause of the fourteenth Amendment." It was the first time, as many observers noted, that the U.S. Supreme Court had ever overturned a state law on grounds of sex discrimination. While the Court did not adopt the "strict scrutiny" standard, it did pronounce all measures that classify by sex to be "subject to scrutiny." The *Reed* decision drew heavily on the material presented in the ACLU brief, and its language would later prove useful to Ginsburg in arguing other woman's rights cases before the Court. "With the Reed decision," Judge Stephanie K. Seymour has said, "the genie was out of the bottle. . . . Rights, once set loose, are very difficult to contain; rights consciousness—on and off the court—is a powerful engine of legal mobilization and change."[39]

The Women's Rights Project

In 1971, while *Reed* v. *Reed* was still pending in the Supreme Court, a number of ACLU lawyers, with Ginsburg taking the lead, were urging the organization to create a permanent organization to coordinate and lead the legal battle for woman's rights. The ACLU's National Board, approving the proposal toward the end of the year, established the Women's Rights Project (WRP). The ACLU agreed to contribute space and office services at its New York City headquarters and an initial grant of $50,000 to the project.* The parent body chose Ginsburg and Barbara Feigen-Fasteau, a practicing lawyer and the co-founder of *Ms.* magazine, as codirectors. The former would oversee research and litigation and the latter was to manage day-to-day operations.[40]

The goal of the WRP was to establish precedents through litigation that would end all discrimination by government on the basis of sex. In addition, the organization provided training to attorneys in the law of sex discrimination and educated women and women's organizations as to their rights. Ginsburg and the other WRP attorneys argued that the law should be sex neutral. They dismissed as a "stereotype" the idea that husbands are always and necessarily the breadwinners for their families and that their wives are always dependent upon them for their survival. Decision-makers must be shown, Ginsburg once wrote, "how the notion that men are this way (frogs, snails, puppy dog tails) and women are that way (sugar, spice, everything nice) ends up hurting both sexes."[41]

In January 1972, Ginsburg shifted her academic base from Rutgers, where she had taught for eight years, to Columbia University's School of Law. The federal government and the rapidly growing woman's movement were both at that time pressuring the law schools to hire more women. As a result, there was intense competition among the leading law schools for the top female talent in the field. When Ginsburg agreed to come to Columbia, according to a story in the *New York Times,* the administrators there were "gleeful" at having landed so distinguished a scholar. Beginning at her new post with the same rank—full professor—that she had achieved at Rutgers, she was the first woman ever hired by Columbia Law to a full-time position higher than lecturer, as well as the first ever to receive tenure.[42]

---

*Some of the funding for the WRP's fund-raising mailings came from Hugh Hefner's Playboy Foundation, moving some militant feminists to outraged protest. One woman shouted at Ginsburg over the phone: "Do you know what's on those envelopes? The bunny!"

Ginsburg's academic work fit in neatly with her activities for the ACLU. Her contract with Columbia permitted her to devote half her time to the Women's Rights Project. A seminar that she conducted on women in American law, the first course ever given on the subject at Columbia, required her students to do research and to draft briefs for the WRP. According to legal historian Ruth Cowen, Ginsburg's law review articles and the textbook that she coauthored with two other professors of law were factors in opening the eyes of judges to the realities of sex discrimination. For the next eight years, Ginsburg would continue to divide her time between the classroom and the courts. In 1973, she became a general counsel of the ACLU and in the following year she was appointed to the organization's national board of directors. In a 1991 interview with historian Linda Kerber, Ginsburg recalled that "in the early 1970s everything was coming together: the Equal Rights Amendment, the Women's Rights Project, the casebook, litigation . . . it was really exhilarating . . . but we were always tired."[43]

Ginsburg's Legal Strategy

As the WRP's chief litigator, it was Ginsburg who organized the cases, found the plaintiffs, often drafted the briefs and other legal documents, and frequently acted as counsel in appellate proceedings before the federal courts. She would also confer with other ACLU attorneys who were preparing briefs and oral arguments in sex discrimination cases. Ginsburg played a major role in most of the important sex discrimination cases that were heard by the U.S. Supreme Court during the 1970s. Of the six cases that she argued personally before the Court, Ginsburg prevailed in five. She viewed the statutes that she was challenging as atypical and anomalous in an age of rapid change and attributed much of her courtroom success to being in the right place at the right time. The continuing influx of women into the labor force, according to Ginsburg, had dramatically altered American culture, and the courts were beginning to reflect these changing realities.

An important aspect of Ginsburg's leadership in the legal campaign for woman's rights was her careful selection of cases. She charted a strategy intended to persuade the courts that laws that discriminated between men and women—even those that were meant to help women—were based on unfair and inaccurate stereotypes and were also for the most part unconstitutional. According to legal scholar Ruth Cowan, Ginsburg tried to select cases that were "maximally suited to a favorable response—each serving as a foundation for its immediate successor and each taking the reasoning one step closer to constitutionally guaranteed sex equality." Ginsburg once explained her "incremental," step-by-step strategy with a quote from the onetime Supreme Court justice Benjamin Cardozo: "Justice is not to be taken by storm. She is to be wooed by slow advances."[44]

Ginsburg realized that arguments that called for justice to both sexes were more likely to gain the approval of male judges than a stridently one-sided appeal for woman's rights. Hence, most of the cases taken by the WRP, roughly two out of every three, were filed on behalf of male plaintiffs. "Instead of presenting gender-equality cases as situations in which injustices against women had to be rectified," wrote Supreme Court historian Christopher Henry, "Ginsburg chose to present gender equality as a more comprehensive struggle, a popular cause that pitted powerless women *and* men against egregious, capricious, and arbitrary acts of their own government." She rejected the proposal of colleagues that the WRP challenge as unfair to women the special opportunities given to Vietnam veterans. No such lawsuit could succeed, Ginsburg warned, and if it were lost, it would set a precedent for the rejection of other gender equality claims by the courts.[45]

Martin D. Ginsburg, Ruth's husband, a leading tax lawyer, was also interested in the problem of sex discrimination, particularly as it related to questions of taxation. In 1972, the two Ginsburgs joined forces to represent William E. Moritz, an unmarried man residing in Denver, Colorado, who was paying the home care expenses of his elderly, infirm mother. Under federal law at that time, only daughters and married sons were allowed a tax deduction for the expense of caring for a sick parent. In *Moritz* v. *Internal Revenue,* a case that was heard in the Tenth Circuit Court of Appeals, this rule was challenged. The Ginsburgs coauthored the brief and also divided the oral argument between them. The challenged provision was found unconstitutional by the circuit court, which held that the classification based on sex lacks justification when placed under the scrutiny required by *Reed.* This was the first time ever, according to Ruth Ginsburg, that a court had struck down a segment of the Internal Revenue code.[46]

Another early victory for Ruth Ginsburg was in *Struck* v. *Secretary of Defense* (1972). This lawsuit challenged a U.S. Air Force rule requiring the immediate discharge of all unmarried officers who became pregnant. Captain Susan Struck, who had become pregnant while serving in Vietnam, decided to go to court when her superiors threatened her with dismissal unless she agreed to an abortion. Her petition argued that the Air Force's decision to dismiss her was unconstitutional because it violated her right to bear a child and limited her freedom of religion. (As a religious Catholic, Struck would not consider abortion.)

After the Ninth Circuit Court of Appeals rejected the Air Force captain's petition, Ginsburg, who had consulted previously with Struck's attorneys, prepared petitions and briefs for an appeal to the U.S. Supreme Court. Her documents argued that the Constitution required the federal government to treat the pregnancy of an employee exactly the same as it treated every other kind of temporary disability among its workers. To do otherwise was to discriminate against women since it is only they who become pregnant. Ginsburg accused the Air Force of rank discrimination in seeking the dismissal of Susan

Struck, but not of the man who had impregnated her. Even drug addicts and alcoholics, she noted, were not threatened with dismissal from the service as Struck had been.

The U.S Supreme Court accepted Struck's petition for certiorari in 1972. Soon afterward, the Air Force announced that it was changing its policy. Unmarried officers who became pregnant would no longer face automatic dismissal, and Susan Struck would be allowed to remain in the service. As a result, the judgment of the lower court, which had upheld the Air Force's rule, was vacated. "The outcome in Struck," Ginsburg later observed, "indicated the beginning stage of change in the direction of more equitable employment practices regarding child-bearing women."[47]

The Frontiero Case

Ginsburg first appeared before the United States Supreme Court in the case of *Frontiero* v. *Richardson* (1973). In 1970 Sharon Frontiero, a married lieutenant in the Air Force, applied for the increased housing and medical benefits that are provided to persons in the military with dependents. Her application was rejected because, under laws that had been enacted by Congress, the wife of a male member of the armed services was automatically defined as his dependent (even if her income exceeded his), thereby qualifying him for added benefits, while the husband of a woman in the military could not qualify as *her* dependent unless he received over half of his support from her earnings. In other words, a married woman in the military had to earn at least three times what her husband did before she could qualify for the same amount in added benefits as was awarded automatically to every married serviceman.

In December 1970, Sharon Frontiero and her husband Joseph filed suit against the Department of Defense in federal court in the Middle District of Alabama. They argued that the provision in federal law that "required different treatment for female and male members of the uniformed services had arbitrarily and unreasonably discriminated" against them and had thereby violated the due process clause of the Fifth Amendment to the U.S. Constitution. The district court rejected their claim, and the Frontieros immediately filed a direct appeal to the U.S. Supreme Court.[48]

At this point, Ginsburg and the WRP became involved with the case, which seemed a promising vehicle for challenging classifications by gender in federal law. After the appeal was filed, Ginsburg drafted the jurisdictional statement, and when the Supreme Court noted probable jurisdiction, she again joined with Melvin Wulf in drafting an amicus curiae brief. In it, they argued that the challenged law was unconstitutional because in discriminating against women, it violated the due process clause of the Fifth Amendment that implicitly guaranteed to each person the equal protection of the laws.[49]

As in their *Reed* brief, Ginsburg and Wulf called for the strict scrutiny by the courts of all classifications by sex, but also argued that even under the less rigorous rational basis standard, the discrimination suffered by Sharon Frontiero was still unconstitutional. It was not, they asserted, "rational" for the government to act as though husbands were always and inevitably the sole significant earners for their families. They presented national economic data to demonstrate that millions of married women contributed appreciably to the support of their families and that there was even a sizable minority who, like Sharon Frontiero, earned more than their husbands.

The brief also argued that the case at hand was a good example of how supposedly "benign" classifications in the law that were designed to favor women as housewives or as "the weaker sex" could actually work against their interests as wage earners, breadwinners, and citizens. The laws that the Frontieros were challenging were intended to benefit the wives of servicemen, but had done harm to the interests of married women in the armed services. As a result, married servicemen were, in effect, being paid more than their female counterparts who were thereby denied the equal protection of the laws.[50]

On January 17, 1973, the Supreme Court heard oral argument in the case of *Frontiero* v. *Richardson.* Speaking for the ACLU, Ginsburg added her arguments for reversing the Alabama court. Earlier in the day, she had been so nervous that she had not eaten lunch for fear that she might throw it up in court. But as she began to speak, her stage fright vanished. "Suddenly, I realized," Ginsburg would later recall, "that here before me were the nine leading jurists in America, a captive audience. I felt a surge of power that carried me through."[51]

In her ten-minute statement, Ginsburg argued that the justices should embrace "strict scrutiny" because recent rulings by the lower federal and state courts showed that they were confused by the *Reed* ruling and were in need of guidance from the Court in the form of clear doctrine. Although *Reed* remained an important turning point in the quest for equality, many judges were still issuing rulings of the kind that had in the past contributed to keeping women in a subordinate and inferior position. "In asking the Court to declare sex a suspect criterion," said Ginsburg, "*amicus* argues a position forcibly stated by Sarah Grimke, noted abolitionist and advocate of equal rights for women. She spoke not elegantly, but with unmistakable clarity. She said, 'I ask no favor for my sex. All I ask of our brethren is that they take their feet off our necks.'"[52]

On May 14, 1973, the Supreme Court ruled eight-to-one that the military could not provide benefits to male servicemen that it did not provide to their female counterparts. Therefore, the challenged federal laws permitting the differential treatment of military personnel solely on the basis of sex were declared unconstitutional. In his written opinion, Justice William J. Brennan, joined by Justices Thurgood Marshall, William O. Douglas, and Byron R. White, adopted Ginsburg's position, declaring that "classifications by sex, like classification based on race, alienage, and national origin, are inherently suspect and must therefore be subjected to close judicial scrutiny." But with only four of the justices opting for Brennan's position, it fell one vote shy of adoption.[53]

Although it amounted to less than a total victory for their cause, the leaders of the woman's movement hailed the *Frontiero* decision as of major importance in their ongoing struggle to end sex discrimination. Ginsburg was among the prominent women who applauded the decision to the news media. "It will," she predicted, "spell the beginning of reforms in hundreds of statutes which do not give equal benefits to men and women."[54]

In the wake of the *Frontiero* ruling, Ginsburg and Brenda Feigen-Fasteau coauthored a report on the legal status of women under federal law. The actual research was done by a team of fifteen Columbia law students and was sponsored by the Equal Rights Advocacy Project. According to the report, most of the federal code discriminated against women as earners and as citizens. To make federal law "consistent with the equal rights principle," wrote Ginsburg and Feigen-Fasteau, required, first of all, that Congress make changes in the wording of the laws so that, wherever possible, words referring to only one sex are replaced by "sex-neutral" terms (e.g., "child-rearing" rather than "child-bearing"). There would also have to be substantive changes in the code's content so that it would no longer "project images of distinct spheres of action for men and women." For example, women should be subject to the draft if men are, and women in the labor force who become pregnant should be treated the same as any other worker who is temporarily disabled.[55]

Kahn v. *Shevin*

Ginsburg's second appearance before the high court was in February 1974 in *Kahn* v. *Shevin,* the only Supreme Court case that she ever lost. Mel Kahn, the appellant in the case, was challenging Florida's policy of giving to widows, but not to widowers, a small reduction in their annual property tax. He alleged that this practice discriminated against him solely because he was male, thereby depriving him of the equal protection of the laws. After the Supreme Court of Florida rejected his claim, the Florida branch of the ACLU took over Kahn's case and appealed it to the U.S. Supreme Court, which accepted jurisdiction.

Ginsburg was dismayed when the *Kahn* appeal went on the Supreme Court's docket because she thought it quite unlikely that the Court would reverse the Florida court's decision. Historically, taxation was an area in which the Court had normally given much leeway to the states. Moreover, the reduction (even if quite meager in scope) of property taxes for widows could most readily be viewed as a "favor" to needy women.

Although victory seemed a remote prospect, Ginsburg agreed to write the ACLU's brief for *Kahn* v. *Shevin* and also to present Kahn's case before the Supreme Court. According to her, the Florida law assumed that a woman would suffer more damage economically from the loss of her husband than would a man from the loss of his wife. Such a notion, she claimed, was founded on the stereotype that men are self-sufficient while women are dependent upon the men in their lives. "Such one-eyed, sex-role thinking," stated Ginsburg, "no longer accords with reality for much of the population." She also contended that the Court's *Reed* and *Frontiero* decisions had already ruled out all legislative line-drawing on the basis of sex stereotypes.

On April 24, 1974, the Court rejected Kahn's appeal by a six-to-three vote. In his majority opinion, Justice William O. Douglas upheld the finding of the Florida Supreme Court that in this instance, to classify by gender was valid because it had "a fair and substantial relation to the object of the legislation— to reduce the disparity between the earnings of a man and a woman." In support of his reasoning, Douglas cited Census Bureau data that, according to him, showed that the national disparity in earnings between the sexes was, if anything, widening.[56]

The Social Security Cases

Ginsburg also challenged government policy in the field of Social Security, where widowers were excluded from benefits that were available to widows. Here again, the policy that was challenged seemed actually to favor women since it was men whose claims were being denied. It was Ginsburg's contention, however, that most, if not all, classifications by gender did harm to both sexes and especially to women, since laws of this kind reinforced conventional stereotypes that defined women as inevitably dependent and passive beings. "To turn the Court in a new direction [of gender equality]," as Ginsburg would later recall, "it first had to gain an understanding that legislation designed to protect women could have the opposite effect."[57]

In *Weinberger* v. *Wiesenfeld* (1975), Ginsburg represented Stephen Wiesenfeld, a widower whose wife had died while giving birth to their first child. After her death, he had applied for Social Security child-care benefits so that he could stay home with his infant son, but his claim was rejected. At that time a widow with children was entitled to benefits (described as mothers' insurance benefits by the statute) based on her late husband's Social Security taxes, but a widower was not eligible unless he could prove that he had been dependent economically on his late wife. "The law," Ginsburg wrote in a journal article, "assumed that fathers, of course, would prefer full-time gainful employment to rocking cradles."[58]

Ginsburg had selected the case because she saw in it an opportunity to challenge the traditional stereotypes on which laws that discriminated by sex were often based. In her brief, she argued that "the rigid sex-role allocation reflected in the statute did not correspond with reality for millions of people." Wives were not always the caregivers of the family nor were husbands always the breadwinners. The sharp line drawn between the sexes by the Social Security law was yet another instance of "double-edged" discrimination. To deny Stephen Wiesenfeld the benefits earned by his now dead wife was to deprive both husband and wife of the equal protection of the laws. "When [Paula Wiesenfeld] died, her social insurance provided less protection to her family than the social insurance of a wage-earning man. . . . The payout to her survivors was subject to a deep discount."[59]

The Court held unanimously that the challenged sections of the Social Security laws violated "the right to equal protection secured by the Due Process Clause of the Fifth Amendment" and were therefore unconstitutional. Justice Brennan agreed with Ginsburg's contention that the Social Security laws were discriminating "unjustifiably" against female wage earners by requiring them to pay Social Security taxes at the same rate as male workers but affording them less protection for their families. Six of the justices also accepted Ginsburg's contention that the line drawn in the law between widows and widowers was founded on an "archaic and overbroad generalization not tolerated under the Constitution, namely, that male workers' earnings are vital to their families' support, while female workers' earnings do not significantly contribute to families' support."[60]

After their victory in *Wiesenfeld,* Ginsburg and her colleagues decided to challenge the constitutionality of other Social Security measures that treated the sexes differently. At one point, WRP attorneys were arguing five different Social Security cases in various courts. In essence, Ginsburg and company were seeking the destruction of the double standard in the Social Security code by presenting judges with cases that departed from the usual patterns of family life, hoping to persuade them that the challenged provisions of law were unconstitutional. The plaintiffs in these cases were invariably men, widowers who were seeking the same benefits that went automatically to widows.[61]

One such case, *Califano* v. *Goldfarb* (1977), found its way to the Supreme Court in October 1976. Ginsburg again represented a widower, defending his right to receive benefits on precisely the same basis as many widows receive them—from the taxes paid into Social Security by a deceased spouse. This time, the facts were far less sympathetic to her client than in the Wiesenfeld case. Leon Goldfarb already had a pension and his wife, Hannah, had been a part-time worker who had never been the family's breadwinner. Moreover, unlike the earlier case, there was no child for the justices to be concerned about. A male senior citizen, who was retired but not in dire need, could not hope to evoke the same degree of sympathy as a widowed father with an infant son to raise.

On the surface, the Social Security code appeared to disadvantage only men, but Ginsburg emphasized that the discrimination in the law was in fact "double-edged." As in *Wiesenfeld,* Ginsburg argued that women were required to pay Social Security taxes at the same rate as men, but received less protection for their families. She also argued that such "statutory gender lines . . . underestimate women's contributions to family support, overestimate men's, and place an official *imprimatur* on categorization of women as second-class workers."[62]

Ginsburg prevailed again, but this time by the narrow margin of five to four. In an opinion joined by three other justices, Justice William Brennan concluded that the sex-based distinction created by the challenged section of the Social Security code was in violation of the due process clause of the Fifth Amendment. Brennan's opinion drew on some of the points made by Ginsburg in her brief, notably her claim that the government's policy was conditioned by "archaic and overbroad generalizations."[63]

Craig v. Boren

Ginsburg again wrote a brief for a male plaintiff in *Craig* v. *Boren,* which came before the Supreme Court in 1976. The case concerned an Oklahoma law that permitted girls to purchase 3.2 beer at the age of eighteen, but required males to be twenty-one before they could legally do so. Curtis Craig, a nineteen-year-old college student, and Carolyn Whitener, a beer vendor, challenged the law in court, arguing that the statute was unconstitutional because it discriminated against young men, thereby depriving them of the equal protection of the laws. After a federal district court in Oklahoma found the challenged law constitutional, Ginsburg decided to become involved. When the U.S. Supreme Court accepted jurisdiction in the case, she filed a "friend of the court" brief. In it she argued that in addition to discriminating against men, the Oklahoma statute was "on deeper inspection, yet another manifestation of traditional attitudes and prejudices about the expected behavior and roles of the two sexes in our society . . . [defining] men as society's active members, women as men's quiescent companions, members of the other or second sex."[64]

In December 1976, the high court reversed the decision of the district court. By a seven-to-two vote, the Supreme Court found the challenged law unconstitutional because it denied to Oklahoma's young men the equal protection of the laws. Influenced apparently by Ginsburg's brief, five of the justices also established a new standard for evaluating gender-based classifications, holding that no such measure could be constitutional unless it advanced "an important government objective" and was "substantially related" to that objective. This is the doctrine known as "intermediate scrutiny" or "heightened scrutiny," and since *Craig* v. *Boren,* it has often been invoked in sex equality cases. With its ruling in *Boren,* as Ginsburg would later recall, the Supreme Court acknowledged that the familiar stereotype of the "passive girl-active boy" dichotomy could not legitimately be made the basis of laws.[65]

Jury Service Cases

Ginsburg also appeared before the Supreme Court in two cases dealing with the issue of women's service on juries. In *Edwards* v. *Healy* (1975), she was opposing counsel when Governor Edwin Edwards of Louisiana challenged the 1973* ruling of a federal district court that it was unconstitutional for Louisiana to permit women to be exempted from jury services on a basis unavailable to men. The governor and the state's lawmakers regarded the policy that the court had rejected as benign and as chivalrous toward women since females (as homemakers and mothers) were allowed a choice that was denied to males. In 1961, the Supreme Court had upheld the constitutionality of a similar law in *Hoyt* v. *Florida*. "While she [the female citizen of Florida] had the privilege to serve on a jury," observed Ginsburg of the Hoyt decision, "service was not imposed upon her as a duty."[66]

In *Edwards*, Ginsburg argued that in making their service on juries voluntary, Louisiana was in fact discriminating against women, who were being told, in effect, that they were not really "essential in community decision-making roles." Moreover, since few of their sex volunteered, women who were either facing lawsuits or on trial were often faced with all-male juries.

Edwards v. *Healy* became moot when a new constitution was adopted in Louisiana that required women to serve on juries on the same basis as men. In *Taylor* v. *Louisiana*, a case that had been argued in tandem with *Edwards*, the Supreme Court ruled unconstitutional the state law that restricted jury service by women to volunteers.** The ruling was based not on the equal protection clause, but on the Sixth Amendment's requirement that in criminal trials there be an impartial jury. The majority did, however, observe: "it is no longer tenable that women as a class may be excluded or given automatic exemptions . . . if the consequence is that criminal jury venires are almost totally male."[67]

Ginsburg dealt again with the jury service question in *Duren* v. *Missouri* in 1979, her last appearance before the Supreme Court. Her argument was essentially the same as in *Edwards*, and once again, she helped persuade the Court to find unconstitutional the jury service law of a state that had made it too easy, and therefore too common, for women to exempt themselves from serving on juries. The Duren case was unusual for Ginsburg because it was a criminal procedure case and her client was a convicted thief and murderer who bore no resemblance at all to the model citizens that she had represented in the past. In her brief, Ginsburg pointed out that an all-male jury had convicted Billy Duren in a county where women made up 54 percent of the population but averaged less than 15 percent of jury venires. In an eight-to-one decision, the Court reversed the judgment of the Missouri Supreme Court on the ground that the "systematic exclusion" of women from the jury selection process had deprived Duren of his right to an "impartial jury."[68]

---

*Ginsburg had been co-counsel in the earlier case, *Healy* v. *Edwards*, which is discussed on pages 398–399 of this chapter.

**Edwards* and *Taylor* were before the Court at the same time and both challenged the same statute. Although Ginsburg played no direct role in *Taylor*, legal historian Adele Markowitz thinks that her brief and argument in *Edwards* probably influenced the *Taylor* decision.

Litigator and Role Model

"By any standards," wrote Adele Markowitz in 1989, "Ginsburg had achieved a great deal." Her victories resulted in the elimination of many of the distinctions between men and women that had formerly resided in the law. "Her greatest asset as a litigator," concluded Markowitz, "was knowing how to pick cases and frame her arguments so that they would appeal to individual members of the court on an intuitive level." Through her incremental strategy, she brought a majority of the Supreme Court around to the view "that sex-based classifications required a heightened level of scrutiny."[69]

As a result of her courtroom triumphs, Ginsburg became, in the words of a feature story that appeared in the *Washington Post* in 1993, "an institution—mentor, role model, and heroine for the first generation of feminist lawyers." Kathleen Peratis, who had worked closely with Ginsburg on the Women's Rights Project and had named her daughter Ruth in Ginsburg's honor, credited her with having "infected dozens and dozens of women lawyers with her vision of social justice." Eleanor Holmes Norton, long a leading figure among civil rights lawyers and an outspoken black feminist, describes Ginsburg as "the navigator in the journey that took women, after more than 100 years, into the safe harbor of the Constitution." There are also male lawyers who acknowledge her influence on them. "She was always a role model for me," said Gerard Lynch, a law professor, "as someone [who] while being an academic, could have an impact on the world."[70]

Outside the Courtroom

Ginsburg was also a role model for many woman lawyers because her feminism and active career had not prevented her from having a happy marriage and a normal family life. Both she and her husband participated actively in the raising of their two children. Ruth has remarked (only partially in jest) that she owed her success as a lawyer to her children who, on discovering that "daddy cooks ever so much better than mommy, phased me out of the kitchen early." In the 1970s Martin Ginsburg began to acquire his own library of books on tax law so that he could do more of his work at home. On most evenings the whole family dined together. During his childhood, according to James Ginsburg, "a night did not go by when my mother did not check to see that I was doing my schoolwork. She was always there when I wanted her to be—and even when I didn't." Both of the Ginsburg children became successful professionals. James, perhaps influenced by his parents' passion for serious music, became a producer of classical music recordings, while his elder sister Jane followed directly in the footsteps of her father and mother by becoming a professor at Columbia University Law School.[71]

Martin Ginsburg, one of the nation's leading authorities on federal tax law, is both a law professor at Georgetown University and a partner at the Washington law firm of Fried, Frank, Harris, Shriver and Johnson. He has advised government agencies on tax matters and has a number of wealthy clients, among whom the best known is H. Ross Perot, the Texas billionaire who twice ran for president during the 1990s. By 1993, due primarily to Martin's lucrative law practice, the Ginsburgs reported a net worth of over $6 million, the largest family fortune among the current members of the Supreme Court.[72]

"He is," Ginsburg has said of her husband, "my best friend and biggest booster." The Ginsburgs have maintained over the years an active and highly cultured lifestyle. They go often to art museums and both are enthusiastic opera fans. In 1996, they traveled to Glyndebourne, England, where they attended an opera festival. They frequently travel both in America and overseas, often for the purpose of delivering lectures. They have also found time for outdoor sports such as golf, water-skiing, and horseback riding. A family friend once quipped that Ruth Ginsburg played golf the same way that she decided cases: "she aims left, goes right, and ends up down the center."[73]

For a crusading lawyer, Ginsburg has always struck journalists and other observers as remarkably soft-spoken and reticent. She usually speaks slowly and selects her words with care. "Even her conversation seems footnoted," according to journalist Elaine Shannon. Although her prose is articulate, forceful, and clear, it too is carefully and cautiously worded. She has little of the overt glamour that attaches itself to a feminist like Gloria Steinem, and her writing possesses virtually none of the flamboyance of language of such colorful jurists as Antonin Scalia or William Brennan. "[Ginsburg] has learned," writes *Time* commentator Margaret Carlson, "to be unafraid of dead air time." She has been known to say very little at parties until the conversation turns to a topic she cares about, such as art or law, and then she becomes very animated and lively. Ginsburg does not laugh or smile easily. When her daughter Jane was a child, she kept a little book that she called "Mommy Laughs" in which she kept track of the rare occasions when her mother smiled.[74]

Ginsburg's appearance accords well with her generally austere personality. Petite at barely five feet tall and slender, she has been described as "birdlike" and as resembling "an exquisite figurine." She wears glasses and her hair is usually tied straight back in a bun or ponytail. Although the suits and dresses that she wears are usually quite conventional, she often sports a suntan and usually wears tasteful costume jewelry. Her offices at the Supreme Court are likewise orderly and sober, and she is the only one among the nine current justices to prefer abstract to representational art in adorning the walls of her chambers.[75]

She is also a thorough perfectionist who sets high standards for herself as well as for others. Extremely hardworking, Ginsburg often labors until three in the morning. On her evenings out, she carries a small flashlight in her purse so that she can read and write even in taxicabs and during theater intermissions. First as an attorney and later as a judge, Ginsburg has put her assistants and law clerks through exacting apprenticeships, criticizing in great detail their briefs and memos when these have fallen short of her standards. On the bench, she is often highly critical of attorneys who come into her courtroom less than well prepared, and she has even corrected the typographical errors in the written opinions of her Supreme Court colleagues.[76]

Ginsburg also has her warmer and lighter side. She and her husband periodically hold elaborate banquets for dozens of their friends, relatives, and colleagues. Their friends insist that when out of the public spotlight, she laughs often and has a rich sense of humor. Ginsburg also takes an interest in the lives of her law clerks and aides, and every year holds a reunion dinner for the lawyers who worked for her in the past. Finally, there is in Ginsburg's approach to the law, both as lawyer and as judge, a strong emphasis upon its human dimension. She tends, according to the legal scholar Jeffrey Rosen, to view each case that she deals with "from the bottom up," considering the circumstances and motives of the various plaintiffs and defendants and the likely effect upon their lives of particular judicial decisions.[77]

Nomination to the Supreme Court

On December 15, 1979, President Jimmy Carter nominated Ruth Bader Ginsburg for a seat on the nation's second highest court, the U.S. Court of Appeals for the D.C. Circuit. She easily won approval in 1980 and served as judge for the next thirteen years. To the surprise of some observers, the former woman's movement activist became a moderate and cautious judge who was respectful of precedent and deferred carefully to the decisions of the Supreme Court. One study of her judicial record found that she sided more frequently during the 1980s with the judges appointed by President Reagan than with those chosen by Carter. She also became the personal friend of Robert Bork and Antonin Scalia, two of the most conservative judges on the D.C. Circuit. When a reporter asked Scalia with which liberal law professor he would prefer to be marooned on a desert island, Mario Cuomo (the New York governor who had taught at the law school of St. John's University) or Lawrence Tribe of Harvard Law School, he replied "Ruth Bader Ginsburg."[78]

On March 19, 1993, Associate Supreme Court Justice Byron White announced that after thirty-one years as a member of the Court, he would be retiring within the next few months. President Clinton, who was seeking to position both his administration and the Democratic Party at the center of the nation's political spectrum, pledged that in selecting White's successor (the first Supreme Court nominee by a Democratic president in twenty-five years), he would be guided not by ideology but by the need to find the best possible person for the job. Having mishandled some important appointments during its early months, the Clinton administration was determined, in the words of the president, to "hit a home run" this time around. He was seeking someone, said Clinton, who combined "a big heart" with judgment and experience. He also pledged not to select anyone who was not "pro-choice" on the question of abortion rights.[79]

Clinton took nearly three months to make his decision, making this one of the longest nominating processes in the history of the Supreme Court. He considered forty-two different candidates, including New York State's governor, Mario Cuomo, and two members of his own cabinet. In early June, the *New York Times* reported that Judge Stephen Breyer of the Second Circuit Court of Appeals appeared likely to be Clinton's choice. Breyer's prospects were damaged, however, when it was revealed that he had never paid Social Security taxes for a woman who had been his one-day-per-week housekeeper for thirteen years.[80]

Even before Breyer's eclipse, prominent people were urging Clinton to select Ginsburg. In mid-May, the *New Republic* called her a "distinguished candidate" who if she were added to the Court "could revive the flame of principled liberalism for decades to come." Senator Daniel Patrick Moynihan (D-NY) brought to the president's attention the comment made in 1988 by Erwin N. Griswold, Ginsburg's former dean at Harvard Law School and one of the nation's leading constitutional lawyers, that Ginsburg had done for gender equality what Thurgood Marshall had achieved in the realm of civil rights. Ginsburg's husband, Martin, also promoted her candidacy, soliciting letters to the president from his fellow tax lawyers as well as key figures in the academic, legal, and feminist establishments.[81]

Clinton decided to nominate Ginsburg as Justice White's successor on June 13, following a ninety-minute interview at the White House in which the president and the judge achieved an immediate rapport. According to members of his staff, Clinton felt comfortable with Ginsburg, was impressed by her achievements, and "fell in love with her life story." He announced his decision at a White House press conference on the following day. The president gave three reasons for nominating Ginsburg: her achievements as an attorney on behalf of American women, her thirteen-year record as a "fair-minded" judge, and his hope that she would be a "consensus builder" on the Supreme Court as she had been formerly on the D.C. Circuit Court of Appeals. Calling Ginsburg "too intelligent for labels like liberal or conservative," Clinton predicted that she would help the members of the Court to find common ground on the great legal questions of the day.[82]

Clinton's selection of Ginsburg, who was widely viewed as a moderate liberal, also reflected his own political centrism as well as his need for a safe choice at a time when he could not afford to make a risky one, due to his decline in the opinion polls. Clinton's strategy was quickly proven right. Ginsburg was acceptable to most liberals because of her achievements as a feminist lawyer and was less objectionable to conservatives than most other liberal jurists, due to the stress that she had placed upon precedent and procedure as a federal judge. Moreover, Ginsburg's credentials as a scholar, attorney, and judge insured that no one would think her unqualified. The *New York Times* applauded Ginsburg's nomination and the American Bar Association's judicial panel unanimously rated her "well-qualified," its highest rating. Many members of Congress from both parties hailed Ginsburg's nomination, predicting that she would be easily and speedily confirmed.[83]

Ginsburg did have her critics, however. Many at the conservative end of the political spectrum objected to her pro-choice position on abortion and suspected that, once on the Court, she would resume her activist ways. Certain liberals were also less than enthusiastic. In a commentary published in the *Washington Post,* Nat Hentoff gave Ginsburg only "one cheer," depicting her as a once-passionate advocate who had become an excessively cautious judge, and at times even a markedly conservative one. Alan Dershowitz, the noted attorney and Harvard Law School professor, assessed her as "a thoroughly ordinary judge" and added that lawyers who had appeared before her in court had found her to be "schoolmarmish, demanding, and a nit-picker." Dershowitz also scoffed at the claim that Ginsburg's achievements as a lawyer had been comparable to those of Thurgood Marshall, claiming that all she had done in the 1970s was to "argue voguish cases from the safety of a fancy New York office building, and never risked her life in the South."[84]

The Judiciary Committee Hearings

The U.S. Senate Judiciary Committee held hearings on the president's nomination for the Supreme Court from July 20 to 23, 1993. Like some of the other recent nominees to the Court, Ginsburg (who had studied the videotapes of several confirmation hearings) refused to discuss how she might rule as a member of the high court on issues and cases about which she had not yet spoken or written. She declined, for example, to reveal whether she thought the death penalty constitutional, saying only that she had an open mind as to its constitutionality. While applauding "diversity" and denouncing "rank discrimination" against homosexuals, she steadfastly refused to give any "hint, forecast, or preview" as to how she might vote on specific government policies and law cases, such as the denial of benefits to homosexuals, affirmative action programs, or government censorship of pornographic literature. When Ginsburg was asked how she differed from Justice White, the judge whom she would replace on the Court, she answered that she did not have his athletic skills and that White "is very tall and I am rather small."[85]

When it came to the question of abortion rights, however, Ginsburg spoke out with clarity and fervor. Women, she insisted, would never be the equals of men if denied the right to choose whether or not to take their pregnancies to term. "It's a decision that she must make for herself," declared Ginsburg, "and when government controls that decision for her, she's being treated as less than a fully adult human responsible for her own choices." With this statement, Ginsburg became the first Supreme Court nominee ever to support abortion rights at a confirmation hearing.[86]

At the hearings, as previously in her writings and lectures, Ginsburg rejected the notion that the U.S. Constitution must always be interpreted according to the intentions of the Framers. Like many of her predecessors on the Court, she viewed the Constitution as an evolving document that had continually been adapted to changing times. She distinguished between the immediate aims of the Founders and their long-term aspirations for the nation. They had, she said, intended "to create a more perfect union that would become ever more perfect with time." Thus, through a combination of judicial interpretation, constitutional amendment, and laws enacted by Congress, "'We the People' had grown ever larger" and now encompassed people whose ancestors had been slaves and women who had long been excluded from the political community. Although she frankly admitted that the authors of the Fourteenth Amendment, ratified in 1868, had not intended that it apply immediately to women, Ginsburg maintained that the passage of the Nineteenth Amendment in 1920, granting women the right to vote, had undeniably established that adult women were "full citizens" entitled just as much as were men to the equal protection of the laws. It was not until the 1970s, however, that the federal courts had recognized this basic change in the position of women under the Constitution.[87]

Ginsburg had always adhered to liberal values and goals, but had tempered these beliefs as a judge on the court of appeals by her emphasis on procedure and precedent and by her commitment to the doctrine of judicial restraint. Once confirmed as a justice of the Supreme Court, she told the Judiciary Committee, she would be neither a liberal nor a conservative, but would cast her vote in each case on the basis of the facts and the law, deciding the case before her "without reaching out to cases not yet seen." In a lecture in March 1993, Ginsburg declared that "the judiciary's greatest figures—Learned Hand is perhaps the best example in this century—have been notably skeptical of all party lines; above all, they have exhibited a readiness to reexamine their own premises, liberal or conservative, as thoroughly as those of others. They set a model I strive to follow."[88]

Doctrines, she believed, should emerge from particular decisions, not the other way around. "Generally," observed Ginsburg at one of her confirmation hearings, "change in our society is incremental. . . . Real change happens one step at a time." To her, the performance of the Supreme Court on sex equality issues during the 1970s was a prime example of how courts can cautiously assist in the solution of social problems. "The Court," Ginsburg had written in 1988, "was neither out in front of, nor did it hold back social change. Instead, it functioned as an amplifier—sensitively responding to, and, perhaps, moderately accelerating the pace of change." This, she maintained, is how courts should function—by "measured motions" rather than by issuing rulings so sweeping that they cause "a backlash too forceful to contain."[89]

Ginsburg admitted, however, that there are times when the courts, and especially the U.S. Supreme Court, must make decisions for which neither the public nor its elected officials are fully prepared. Judicial intervention becomes necessary, she maintained, whenever "political avenues become blind alleys." A good example was the unanimous ruling in *Brown* v. *Board of Education* (1954), the history-making case in which the Supreme Court had declared unconstitutional the policy of racial segregation in public schools. But in *Brown*, Ginsburg argued, the Court had been right to act boldly because many African-Americans in the southern and border states were disfranchised, barred from participation in the political process. Even this landmark decision was not "altogether bold." The way had been paved for it, Ginsburg pointed out, by a long series of verdicts against segregation that had been won "incrementally" in the Supreme Court by Thurgood Marshall and other lawyers employed by the NAACP. Each one of these victories, she noted, would serve in turn as a precedent for the cases that were taken up after it. Finally, the decision in *Brown* had not attacked racial segregation in every part of southern life, but dealt only with the public schools.[90]

According to Ginsburg, the ruling of the Supreme Court in *Roe* v. *Wade* (1973) was far more drastic than its decision in *Brown*. In *Roe,* the Court in a seven-to-two decision had struck down all state laws that limited in any way the access of women to abortions during the first trimester (initial three months) of pregnancy and had also prohibited placing any restriction upon abortion during the second trimester (months four through six) except for those designed to protect the pregnant woman's health. Although a staunch advocate of abortion rights, Ginsburg thought the Court's ruling in *Roe* defective. First of all, it was far from "a measured motion." Unlike *Brown*, it had not been preceded by a gradual forward movement via a long series of cases, but had suddenly and sweepingly "displaced virtually every state abortion law then in force."[91]

The court's second mistake in *Roe* lay, according to Ginsburg, in making "the right to privacy," a phrase that appears nowhere in the Constitution, the sole basis of abortion rights. Even though, as she testified at her confirmation hearing, Ginsburg believed that there was a constitutional right to privacy and that it did protect a woman's right to have an abortion, she thought that it would have been far wiser had the justices based their abortion rights decision not on privacy alone, but also on the equal protection clause of the Fourteenth Amendment. A woman's right to terminate her pregnancy, she argued, might well be crucial in deciding whether she could compete economically and participate in general in the life of her time. "No one," Ginsburg once remarked, "is for abortion. People are for a woman's right to shape her life's course."[92]

These strategic errors by the Court, according to Ginsburg, had halted a political process that was "moving in a reform direction." By 1973, roughly one-third of the states had liberalized their abortion laws. *Roe*, she contended, had reversed the trend, energizing all the foes of legalized abortion while fostering complacency in the pro-choice camp. The resulting backlash had brought about the passage of measures restricting and regulating abortion in various ways, including the refusal of Congress and many state legislatures to fund abortions for poor women. Ginsburg suggested that abortion might not have become so divisive a national issue if the Court had gone no further than to simply find unconstitutional the Texas abortion law that had been challenged by "Jane Roe." In acting more boldly than the situation required, the Court had probably prolonged and intensified the conflict over abortion, which as of the early 1990s had been raging for more than two decades.[93]

Like the confirmation hearings of other recent Supreme Court nominees, Ginsburg's were nationally televised, but in stark contrast to what the viewing public had witnessed when the Judiciary Committee had delved into the views and character of Clarence Thomas in 1991, there was scarcely any rancor or blatant partisanship in the committee's interrogation of Ginsburg. Most of the hearings' first three days were taken up with her responses to the questions asked by members of the committee, but Ginsburg was treated far more gently than most other recent nominees to the Court. In general, a friendly and genial tone prevailed in the hearing room, and it seemed obvious from the outset that the president's nominee would be endorsed by the committee and would soon be confirmed by the Senate. "Back slapping," noted Senator Howell Heflin (D-AL), "has replaced back-stabbing."[94]

The absence of bitter controversy, according to Walter Goodman, the television critic of the *New York Times,* had scaled down the hearings to "a one woman show" in which Ginsburg had lectured to the committee's members on the constitutional order and on the place of the judiciary within it. Testifying without notes, she had displayed a remarkable knowledge of constitutional case law. "Although no reviewer has suggested," Goodman wrote, "that Judge Ginsburg is a showstopper, she grows on you. There was something moving about the slight figure alone at the big table, with her husband, children, and grandchildren basking behind her."[95]

At various times in the hearings, Republican senators Orrin Hatch (R-UT) and Arlen Specter (R-PA) became impatient with Ginsburg over her refusal to state her views on constitutional issues that she had not previously written about. In the Judiciary Committee's final report on her nomination, Senator Larry Pressler (R-KN) was also critical, complaining of her unwillingness to discuss more thoroughly the legal questions relating to American Indians that he had raised during the hearings. In spite of these minor clashes, the Judiciary Committee voted unanimously on July 29 to approve Ginsburg's nomination to the Supreme Court. On the Senate floor, only Jesse Helms (R-NC) spoke against her joining the Court, citing her support of abortion and predicting that as a justice she would support "the homosexual agenda." On August 3, 1993, the full Senate voted to confirm Ginsburg by a vote of ninety-six-to-three.[96]

Member of the Supreme Court

From almost the minute of her accession to the U.S. Supreme Court, Ginsburg has been thoroughly at home there. "In her first term," wrote Linda Greenhouse of the *New York Times* in June 1994, "[Ginsburg] took the bench every morning with a smile and, by all accounts, enjoyed herself immensely." Like her old friend, Justice Antonin Scalia, she soon proved a persistent and prob-ing questioner during oral argument, asking seventeen questions in the first hour of her first day on the Court. During the 1993–1994 term of the Supreme Court, Ginsburg wrote nine opinions for the Court, ten concurring opinions, and eight dissents for a total of twenty-seven, a figure far higher than usual for a first-year justice. "She has," wrote the *Legal Times* of Ginsburg's first three months as a justice, "given a clinic on how to hit the ground running." (It should, however, be noted that, according to the *New York Times* review of the Court's 1993–1994 term, only one of her opinions for the Court came in an important case, *Barclay's Bank* v. *Franchise Tax Board,* a case concerning California's taxation of foreign-based corporations.[97]

During Ginsburg's first term on the Court, she seemed at the center of its ideological spectrum, voting more frequently with Justice Anthony Kennedy, a moderate conservative, than she did with Justice Harry Blackmun, who was then the Court's most liberal member. But, even in that first year, in every case decided by a vote of five-to-four, Ginsburg invariably aligned herself with the Court's three most liberal justices: Blackmun, David Souter, and John Paul Stevens. Since then, Ginsburg has emerged as a left of center justice who usually votes with the Court's more liberal justices.[98]

In cases dealing with religion, Ginsburg, like other liberal justices, both past and present, maintains that the First Amendment requires a "wall of sepa-ration" between church and state. She therefore voted with the majority in *Kiryas Joel Village Board of Education* v. *Grumet* (1994), a case in which the Court decided by a margin of six-to-three that it was unconstitutional for New York state to create a special school district to accommodate the demands of a community of ultra-Orthodox Satmar Jews. Ginsburg has dissented in cases where the Court has condoned a measure of cooperation between organized religion and state or local government. She filed a dissenting opinion, for example, in *Agostini* v. *Fulton,* a 1997 case in which the Court ruled that it was constitutional for New York City to have public school teachers provide tutoring to students in Catholic parochial schools.[99]

On issues of criminal justice there are limits to Ginsburg's liberalism. She does not, for example, believe, as did such liberal justices of the past as Wil-liam Brennan and Harry Blackmun, that the death penalty is always unconsti-tutional because it can never be anything other than "cruel and unusual punishment." In fact, during her first year on the Court, Ginsburg voted to sustain the death penalty law of the state of California. On the other hand, she has dissented from decisions of the high court that deny stays of execution to people who have been convicted of murder. In 2001, she supported the idea of a national moratorium on executions, observing that she had never heard of anyone receiving the death penalty that was well represented in court.[100]

Ginsburg has gone further than most of the justices in protecting the right of citizens under the Fourth Amendment to be spared "unreasonable searches and seizures." She dissented in 1996 when the Court held in *Kilgore* v. *Penn-*

sylvania that "probable cause" of suspect contraband in a car was sufficient to warrant a search. In 1995 in the case of *Ohio* v. *Robinette,* she joined an eight-to-one majority, which ruled that the Supreme Court of Ohio had erred in holding that under the federal and Ohio constitutions, it was unlawful for a police officer who had detained a motorist for speeding to search his car without first informing him that he was free to go. Although Ginsburg concurred in the high court's finding, she wrote a separate opinion in which she urged states that provide "protection more complete than the Constitution demands, to be. clear about their ultimate reliance upon state law." In short, she has envisaged using the Fourth Amendment and other portions of the Bill of Rights as a floor rather than a ceiling in protecting the rights of the citizen.[101]

Ginsburg and the other liberal justices have defended statutes that impose racial and gender preferences (known collectively as "affirmative action") on government, business, and education in order to increase the number of women and persons from racial and ethnic minorities who succeed in life and become affluent, prominent, and powerful. In this area, it has been the more conservative justices who have applied the "strict scrutiny" standard that views all such preferences as "inherently suspect."[102]

Perhaps the most important such case to be heard while Ginsburg has been on the Court was *Adarand Construction* v. *Pena* in 1995. Adarand was a construction contractor who submitted the low bid on a government project, but lost out to a Hispanic contractor who was given preference as a member of a socially disadvantaged group. Adarand filed a lawsuit, alleging that the Department of Transportation had discriminated against him on racial grounds, thereby violating "the equal protection component" of the Fifth Amendment's due process clause. In a five-to-four opinion written by Justice O'Connor, the Supreme Court applied the strict scrutiny standard and remanded the case back to the Court of Appeals for further consideration. "In my mind," wrote Justice Clarence Thomas in a separate concurring opinion, "government sponsored racial discrimination based on benign prejudice is just as noxious as discrimination inspired by malicious prejudice. In each instance, it is racial discrimination, pure and simple." [103]

Ginsburg wrote a separate dissent in *Adarand* in which she quoted with approval Justice Stevens's assertion that "'large deference is owed by the Judiciary to Congress's institutional competence and constitutional authority to overcome historic racial subjugation.'" Citing as proof the results of recent scholarly studies, Ginsburg insisted that "the lingering effects of discrimination are still evident in our workplaces, markets, and neighborhoods. Given this history, Congress surely can conclude that a carefully designed affirmative action program may help to realize, finally, the equal protection of the laws the Fourteenth Amendment has promised since 1868." Ginsburg also maintained that review by the Court "can ensure that preferences are not so large as to trample unduly upon the opportunities of others." She drew comfort from the fact that the claim of Justices Scalia and Thomas that racial preferences are never justified, either constitutionally or morally, was not adopted by the Court. "I see today's decision as one that allows our precedent to evolve, still to be informed by and responsive to changing conditions."[104]

Ginsburg has also tended to defer to Congress on issues of federalism involving the division of authority between the federal government and the states. In this area the nation has in general witnessed a vast strengthening of federal authority and power since the 1930s. Ginsburg shares the views of most liberals that new attempts by Congress to solve social and economic problems are legitimately derived from the powers conferred on it by the Constitution, particularly the commerce clause, which gives Congress the power to regulate commerce among the several states. She has resisted recent decisions by the U.S. Supreme Court that attempt to strengthen the states by rolling back the authority of Congress. She dissented, for example, from the Court's decision in *U.S.* v. *Lopez* in 1995 that had struck down a federal law criminalizing the possession of a firearm within 100 feet of a school. Ginsburg was also in the minority in 1997 when the Court in another five-to-four vote declared unconstitutional a section of the gun control law of 1993, the Brady Act, that required of local sheriffs (in states that did not pass laws implementing the act) to conduct background checks of people who wanted to buy firearms.[105]

The VMI Case

Ginsburg's specialty as an attorney and scholar had, of course, been sex discrimination. Yet, even though the Court heard several such cases during her first term as a justice, she wrote no opinions on any of them. This surprised and disappointed some of the leaders of the woman's movement many of whom had long regarded Ginsburg as an important ally in the struggle for woman's rights.[106]

In 1996 the case of *U.S.* v. *Virginia* reached the Supreme Court. This was a lawsuit filed by the U.S. Department of Justice, which challenged the exclusion of women from the Virginia Military Institute (VMI), a highly regarded, state-managed military academy that had for many decades prepared young men to become officers in the U.S. Army. After the justices voted seven-to-one to declare unconstitutional the males-only policy at VMI, Chief Justice William Rehnquist chose Ginsburg to write the opinion of the Court. (Justice Thomas recused himself because his son was then attending VMI.)

The opinion that she wrote in the VMI case remains Ginsburg's most famous and controversial action as a member of the Supreme Court. By permitting the exclusion of women as a class from a highly regarded state supported training program for military officers, Virginia was, she concluded, violating the equal protection clause of the Fourteenth Amendment. Citing the previous rulings of the Court, Ginsburg, who had successfully argued some of these cases while still an attorney, maintained that it was no longer permissible under the U.S. Constitution for governments at any level to permit women to be deprived of opportunities for education or employment solely because of their sex. To be constitutionally acceptable, Ginsburg insisted, a government policy that treats the sexes differently must have "an exceedingly persuasive justification." (This phrase was used originally by Justice Sandra Day O'Connor in 1982 in the case of *Mississippi University for Women* v. *Hogan.*) "Women seeking and fit for a VMI quality education cannot be offered anything less under the Commonwealth's obligation to afford them genuinely equal protection."[107]

Critics, including Justice Scalia in his dissent, have described the VMI decision as a classic instance of the Supreme Court imposing the values of its members upon society. "Today," wrote Scalia, "change is forced upon Virginia, and reversion to single sex education is prohibited nationwide not by democratic processes, but by order of this court." Some observers of the Court see the VMI opinion as a virtual enactment by judicial fiat of the Equal Rights Amendment. To Ginsburg, however, the decision simply codified changes in society that had already taken place. West Point, Annapolis, and other military academies had, after all, been admitting women for several years when the decision in *U.S.* v. *Virginia* was handed down.[108]

Bush v. Gore

The presidential election in the year 2000 was one of the closest in the history of the nation. On November 8, the day after the balloting, neither Vice President Albert S. Gore, the Democratic candidate nor George W. Bush, the governor of Texas, the Republican nominee, had amassed enough electoral votes to become the next president. The election now hung on the vote count in Florida, the only state where the outcome of the balloting was still in doubt. The candidate who carried Florida would win the presidency.

The initial count of the Florida vote put Bush ahead of Gore by 1,784 votes out of the nearly 6 million votes cast in the state. Before Bush could be officially certified the winner, however, Gore's attorneys filed motions in the Florida courts calling for manual recounts in four predominantly Democratic counties. In the ensuing weeks, individual ballots were scrutinized and fought over by Florida election officials and by representatives of the two presidential candidates. On December 8, the Supreme Court of Florida, in response to motions filed by Gore's attorneys, ordered a manual count in Miami-Dade County of the 9,000 "undervotes" (ballots on which the vote-counting machines had failed to detect a vote for president). The court also ordered manual recounts in every county in the state where the undervotes had not yet been counted.

The attorneys representing George Bush and his running mate, Richard Cheyney, filed an emergency application for a stay of the recount with the U.S. Supreme Court. On December 9, the Court issued the stay and granted certiorari. Three days later, on December 12, the high court ruled by a vote of seven-to-two that the methods being used in various Florida counties were so lacking in uniformity that they were unconstitutional under the due process and equal protection clauses of the Fourteenth Amendment. The Court also voted five-to-four that there must be no further recount of the ballots in Florida, thereby effectively making Bush the next president. The five-person majority consisting of Chief Justice William Rehnquist, and Justices Antonin Scalia, Clarence Thomas, Sandra Day O'Connor, and Anthony Kennedy, declared it impossible to devise a method of recounting the disputed ballots that would both meet constitutional standards and be completed by December 12th. The five-justice majority considered that date the deadline for certifying the outcome of the vote, because after that, the makeup of a state's slate of electors could be challenged in Congress.

Two other justices, Stephen Breyer and David Souter, agreed with the majority that the lack of uniformity in the recount raised serious questions relating to due process and equal protection and were part of the seven-member majority that found unconstitutional the recount as it was being conducted in Florida. They argued, however, that these constitutional flaws could have been remedied and the recount continued. Moreover, contended Breyer and Souter, the majority was attaching too much importance to the December 12 "deadline" as the electors would not be meeting in their home states until December 18th, and Congress would not need to request a final certification by Florida of its election results until December 27. Souter and Breyer therefore dissented from the Court's second ruling, ordering that there be no further attempt to recount the presidential vote in Florida.

The remaining two justices, Ginsburg and John Paul Stevens, dissented on both of the rulings in *Bush* v. *Gore*. They saw little to criticize in the conduct of the Florida Supreme Court. "There is no cause here to believe'" wrote Ginsburg, "that the members of Florida's high court have done less than 'their mortal best to discharge their oath of office.'" The admittedly imperfect remedy of the Florida Supreme Court was surely no worse than leaving uncounted ballots that had been legally cast. Moreover, she pointed out, the federal courts typically defer to the state high courts when it comes to the interpretation of state law. "Were the other members of this court as mindful as they generally are of our system of dual sovereignty," she wrote, "they would affirm the judgment of the Florida court."[109]

Conclusion

The career of Ruth Bader Ginsburg exemplifies the struggle of women, both before and during the rise of the modern woman's movement, to participate fully in their professions and in public life as the colleagues and equals of men. Her rise to prominence was in part due to the growth of that movement amid the turmoil and ferment of the 1960s and to its accelerating expansion during the 1970s. As a feminist lawyer and legal scholar, Ginsburg advanced the principle of gender equality as the best possible formula for improving the status and condition of women. As the chief litigator and strategist for the ACLU's

Women's Rights Project, she represented plaintiffs, many of them men, who claimed that they had suffered discrimination on account of their sex. Except for programs of affirmative action, which she has (apparently with some reluctance) supported as a necessary remedy for the discrimination suffered by women and minorities in the past, Ginsburg has always rejected the idea that women should be granted special privileges by the government and the courts. Where more radical feminists, such as Catherine MacKinnon, have called for the restructuring of society in favor of women, Ginsburg has remained true to the equal rights feminism that she first embraced during the 1970s.[110]

As a judge from 1979 to the present, Ginsburg has seemed, more than ever, an ideological moderate, a cautious jurist who has stressed process and continuity, and has usually justified on narrow grounds her votes on the cases that came before her. The contrast between her former role as an advocate and her judicial decision-making has led some observers to conclude that there have really been *two* Ruth Bader Ginsburgs: the feminist heroine and the careful, dispassionate jurist. But there is an important strand of continuity between the two phases of Ginsburg's career. Both as an attorney and as a judge, she has usually functioned as a case-by-case gradualist who believed that if the courts decided correctly the vexed and complicated disputes that came before them, they would help society to gradually advance toward ever greater justice and freedom.

Notes

1. Richard L. Berke, "Clinton Names Ruth Ginsburg, Advocate for Women, to Court," *New York Times,* June 15, 1993, A1; Ginsburg's tribute to her mother is in "Transcript of President's Announcement and Judge Ginsburg's Remarks," *New York Times,* June 15, 1993, A24; Holly Idelson, "Clinton's Choice of Ginsburg Signals Moderation," *Congressional Quarterly* 51 (June 19, 1993): 1569, 1599.

2. U.S Senate Committee on the Judiciary, *Hearings on the Nomination of Ruth Bader Ginsburg to be Associate Justice of the Supreme Court of the United States*, 103rd Congress, 1st scss., July 20–23, 1993 (hereinafter cited as *Confirmation Hearings*), 57; Elaine Shannon, "Justice for Women," *Vogue,* October 1993, 472; Linda Bayer, *Ruth Bader Ginsburg* (Philadelphia: Chelsea House, 2000), 14, 16; Rebecca Mae Salokar, "Ruth Bader Ginsburg," *Women in Law: A Bio-Bibliographical Sourcebook,* ed. Rebecca Mae Salokar and Mary L. Volcansek (Westport, CT: Greenwood Press, 1996), 79.

3. Christopher Henry, "Ruth Bader Ginsburg," *The Justices of the United States Supreme Court: Their Lives and Major Opinions,* ed. Leon Friedman and Fred Israel, 5th edition, vol. 6 (New York: Chelsea House, 1997), 1861; Salokar, "Ruth Bader Ginsburg," 78–79; Bayer, *Ruth Bader Ginsburg,* 16; Bill Hewitt, "Feeling Supreme," *People,* June 28, 1993, 50; Carmen Bredeson, *Ruth Bader Ginsburg: Supreme Court Justice* (Berkeley Heights, NJ: Enslow Publishers), 15.

4. David Margolick, "Trial by Adversity Shapes Jurist's Outlook," *New York Times,* June 25, 1993, A19; Elinor Porter Swiger, *Women Lawyers at Work* (New York: Julian Messner, 1978), 55–56; Shannon, "Justice for Women," 472; Angela Hunt, "Meet Our New Supreme Court Justice," *Glamour,* October 1993, 116–117.

5. Eleanor Ayer, *Ruth Bader Ginsburg: Fire and Steel on the Supreme Court* (New York: Dillon Press, 1994), 12, 16; "Ruth Bader Ginsburg," *Biography Today* (January 1994): 49; Bayer, *Ruth Bader Ginsburg,* 14–15; "Ruth Bader Ginsburg," *Current Biography Yearbook* 55 (1994): 214.

6. Bayer, *Ruth Bader Ginsburg,* 18–21; Ayer, *Ruth Bader Ginsburg,* 14; Margolick, "Trial by Adversity," A19.

7. "Ruth Bader Ginsburg," *Biography Today,* 50; Sara Fritz, "Nominee Called Trailblazer Who Kept Low Profile," *Los Angeles Times,* June 15, 1993, A16.

8. Quotation of Ginsburg is in Swiger, *Women Lawyers at Work,* 56; Jennifer S. Thomas, "Ruth Ginsburg: Carving a Career Path Through Male-Dominated Legal World," *Congressional Quarterly* 51 (July 17, 1993): 1876–1877; Bayer, *Ruth Bader Ginsburg,* 47.

9. Swiger, *Woman Lawyers at Work,* 56; Ayer, *Ruth Bader Ginsburg,* 19.

10. Linda Kerber, *No Constitutional Right to Be Ladies: Women and the Obligations of Citizenship* (New York: Hill and Wang, 1998), 201–202; Margolick, "Trial by Adversity," A20.

11. Quote of Ginsburg is in Stephanie Goldberg, "The Second Woman Justice," *American Bar Association Journal* 79 (October 1993): 42; Thomas, "Carving a Career Path," 1876.

12. Quote is from Bayer, *Ruth Bader Ginsburg,* 29; Ayer, *Ruth Bader Ginsburg,* 19; "Ruth Bader Ginsburg," *Biography Today,* 50; Margolick, "Trial by Adversity," A19; Neil A. Lewis, "Rejected as a Clerk; Chosen as a Justice," *New York Times,* June 15, 1993, A1.

13. Ginsburg quote is in Lynn Gilbert and Gaylen Moore, *Particular Passions: Talks with Women Who Have Shaped Our Times* (New York: C.N. Potter, 1981), 156; Swiger, *Women Lawyers at Work,* 56–57.

14. Lewis, "Rejected as a Clerk," A1; Hewitt, "Feeling Supreme," 49; Gilbert and Moore, *Particular Passions,* 156.

15. "Ginsburg-Bader," *New York Times,* June 24, 1954, 34; Margolick, "Trial by Adversity," A19; Swiger, *Women Lawyers at Work,* 54; *Confirmation Hearings,* 58; Shannon, "Justice for Women," 392.

16. Ginsburg's observations about Harvard are in Gilbert and Moore, *Particular Passions,* 158; Margaret Carlson, "The Law According to Ruth," *Time,* June 28, 1993, 38; Ruth Bader Ginsburg, "The Equal Rights Amendment Is the Way," *Harvard Women's Law Journal* 1 (Spring 1978): 20.

17. Kerber, *No Constitutional Right to Be Ladies,* 202; Carlson, "The Law According to Ruth," 38; Hewitt, "Feeling Supreme," 49.

18. Her classmate's tribute to Ginsburg is in Margolick, "Trial by Adversity," A19; Hewitt, "Feeling Supreme," 50.

19. Quote of Ginsburg's tribute to her husband is in Swiger, *Women Lawyers at Work,* 54; Gilbert and Moore, *Particular Passions,* 157; Carlson, "The Law According to Ruth," 38.

20. Cynthia Fuchs Epstein, *Women in Law,* 2d ed. (Urbana: University of Illinois Press, 1993), 54; *Confirmation Hearings,* 58; Carlson, "The Law According to Ruth," 38.

21. Quote on motherhood as "obstacle" is in Gilbert and Moore, *Particular Passions,* 158; Lewis, "Rejected as a Clerk," A1; Goldberg, "The Second Woman Justice," 41; Swiger, *Women Lawyers at Work,* 58; Richard L. Ellis, "Sandra Day O'Connor," *The Oxford Companion to the Supreme Court of the United States,* ed. Kermit L. Hall et al. (New York: Oxford University Press, 1992), 604; "Sandra Day O'Connor," *Current Biography Yearbook* 43 (1982): 298.

22. Gilbert and Moore, *Particular Passions,* 158; Bayer, *Ruth Bader Ginsburg,* 45.

23. Ruth Bader Ginsburg, "Comparative Side Glances," in Kenneth M. Davidson, Ruth Bader Ginsburg, and Herma Hill Kay, *Text, Cases, and Materials on Sex-Based Discrimination* (St. Paul: West Publishing, 1974), 937–948; Ibid., 927; Ruth Bader Ginsburg, "The Equal Rights Amendment Is the Way," 20.

24. Tracy Schroth, "At Rutgers, Ginsburg Changed," *New Jersey Law Journal* 134 (June 21, 1993): 32; Gilbert and Moore, *Particular Passions,* 152; Carlson, "The Law According to Ruth," 38.

25. Swiger, *Women Lawyers at Work,* 51; *Confirmation Hearings,* 59, 66–67, 92–93.

26. The "students helped" quote is in Ruth Cowan, "Women's Rights Through Litigation: An Examination of the American Civil Liberties Union Women's Rights Project," *Columbia Human Rights Law Review* 8 (1977): 378; Ruth Bader Ginsburg, "The Treatment of Women by the Law: Awakening Consciousness in the Law Schools," *Valparaiso University Law Review* 5, no. 3 (Spring 1971): 480–488; Kerber, *No Constitutional Right to Be Ladies,* 202; Deborah L. Markowitz, "In Pursuit of Equality: One Woman's Work to Change the Law," *Women's Rights Law Reporter* 11, no. 2 (Summer 1989): 75.

27. The "arbitrary distinctions" quote is in Gilbert and Moore, *Particular Passions,* 153; Ruth Bader Ginsburg, "Sex and Unequal Protection: Men and Women as Victims," *Journal of Family Law* 11, no. 2 (1971): 347–349; Shannon, "Justice for Women," 472; Markowitz, "In Pursuit of Equality," 73; Fred Graham, "Lessons in the Law of Lib," *New York Times,* November 28, 1971, Sec. 4: 8.

28. Ruth Bader Ginsburg, "The Status of Women," *American Journal of Comparative Law* 20 (1972): 590–591; Ruth Bader Ginsburg, "Men, Women, and the Constitution," *Columbia Journal of Law and Social Problems* 10 (1973): 101; Hunt, "Meet Our New Supreme Court Justice," 117.

29. Kenneth M. Davidson, Ruth Bader Ginsburg, and Herma Hill Kay, *Text, Cases and Materials on Sex-Based Discrimination* (St. Paul, MN: West Publishing), xi; quote from Eve Hanks is in Schroth, "At Rutgers, Ginsburg Changed," 32; Margolick, "Trial by Adversity," A19.

30. The "activated by feminists" quote is in Ruth Bader Ginsburg, "Introduction, 'Women and the Law—A Symposium,'" *Rutgers Law Review* 25 (1970): 3; the "I have a talent" quote is in Shannon, "Justice for Women," 372.

31. Ruth Bader Ginsburg, "Treatment of Women by the Law," 481–487; "More Law Courses on Women's Rights Backed at Parley," *New York Times,* October 22, 1972, 83.

32. Ruth Bader Ginsburg, "Introduction, 'Women and the Law,'" 10–11.

33. Epstein, *Women in Law,* 54; Kerber, *No Constitutional Right to Be Ladies,* 202; there is a bibliography of Ginsburg's writings up to 1993 in *Confirmation Hearings,* 59–64.

34. Margolick, "Trial by Adversity," A19; "In Her Words: Ginsburg on Abortion, the Confirmation Process, Equal Rights," *Congressional Quarterly* 51 (June 19, 1993): 1572–1573; Ruth Bader Ginsburg with Barbara Flagg, "Some Reflections on the Feminist Legal Thought of the 1970s," *University of Chicago Legal Forum* (1989): 11.

35. *Reed* v. *Reed* 404 U.S. 71 (1971), 71–74; ACLU, *Amicus Curiae Brief for Appellant in Reed* v. *Reed* (1971), 7; the quotation of the Idaho statute appears in Ruth Bader Ginsburg, "Introduction to 'Women and the Law,'" 9; "Court Will Rule on Birth Control Ban," *New York Times,* March 2, 1971, 22.

36. Cowan, "Women's Rights Through Litigation," 383, 387; Markowitz, "In Pursuit of Equality," 78; Epstein, *Women in Law,* 138.

37. Cowan, "Women's Rights Through Litigation," 379; ACLU, *Amicus Brief in Reed,* 5; Carol Pressman, "The House That Ruth Built: Justice Ruth Bader Ginsburg, Gender, and Justice," *New York Law School Journal of Human Rights* 14 (1998): 320.

38. Pressman, "The House That Ruth Built," 322; Markowitz, "In Pursuit of Equality," 79; ACLU, *Amicus Brief in Reed,* 7.

39. "Court Unanimously Strikes Down an Idaho Law Giving Men Preference Over Women," *New York Times,* November 23, 1971, 1; Burger's statement is in *Reed* v. *Reed* 404 U.S. 71 (1971), 76; "First No to Sex Bias; Victory for Ms. Sally Reed," *Time,* December 6, 1971, 71; quote of Judge Seymour is in Martha Craig Daughtry, "Women and the Constitution, Where We Are at the End of the Century," *New York University Law Review* 75 (April 2000): 9.

40. Epstein, *Women in Law,* 138; Cowen, "Women's Rights Through Litigation," 383; Kerber, *No Constitutional Right to Be Ladies,* 195; the "bunny" quote is in David Von Drehle, "Redefining Fair With a Simple Careful Assault," *Washington Post,* July 19, 1993, A8.

41. Gilbert and Moore, *Particular Passions,* 153; Karen O'Connor, *Women's Organizations' Use of the Courts* (Lexington, MA: Lexington Books, 1980), 119.

42. Kerber, *No Constitutional Right to Be Ladies,* 202–203; Epstein, *Women in Law,* 227–228; Carlson, "The Law According to Ruth," 38; Lesley Oelsner, "Columbia Law Snares a Prize in the Quest for Women Professors," *New York Times,* January 26, 1972, 39.

43. *Confirmation Hearings,* 59; Epstein, *Women in Law,* 232; Cowan, "Women's Rights Through Litigation," 384–385; O'Connor, *Women's Organizations' Use of the Courts,* 129; Ginsburg's "coming together" statement is in Kerber, *No Constitutional Right to Be Ladies,* 204.

44. Lewis, "Rejected as a Clerk," 1A; Gilbert and Moore, *Particular Passions,* 153; Hewitt, "Feeling Supreme," 50; Cowan, "Women's Rights Through Litigation," 389; *Confirmation Hearings,* 82–83; Ginsburg's quotation of Cardozo is in Joyce Murdock and Deb Price, *Courting Justice: Gay Men and Lesbians v. the Supreme Court* (New York: Basic Books, 2001), 419.

45. O'Connor, *Women's Organizations' Use of the Courts,* 125–126; Henry, "Ruth Bader Ginsburg," 1864; Goldberg, "The Second Woman Justice," 40; "Men's Rights," *New Yorker,* July 15, 1993, 32.

46. *Moritz* v. *Commissioner of Internal Revenue,* 469 F. 2d 466 (10th Cir. 1972), certiorari denied, 412 U.S. 906 (1973); *Confirmation Hearings,* 84–85; Markowitz, "Women's Rights Through Litigation," 382; Fred P. Graham, "No Relief For the Chauvinist Pigs," *New York Times,* April 9, 1972, Section 4, 9.

47. Fred P. Graham, "It Would Help If It Happened to a Man," *New York Times,* October 29, 1972, Section 4, 10–11; "Air Force Mother Loses Plea," *New York Times,* May 6, 1972, 41; Fred Graham, "Justices to Weigh Pregnancy Issue," *New York Times,* October 25, 1972, 8; "Air Force Drops Effort to Oust Woman Captain," *New York Times,* December 2, 1972, 31; *Struck* v. *Secretary of Defense,* certiorari granted 409 U.S. 947; judgment vacated, 409 U.S. 1071 (1972); The "outcome in *Struck*" quotation is in *Confirmation Hearings,* 85.

48. *Confirmation Hearings,* 86; ACLU, *Amicus Curiae Brief in Frontiero* v. *Richardson* (1973), 3–4; *Frontiero* v. *Richardson, Secretary of Defense* 411 U.S. 677 (1973), 677–678.

49. Daughtrey, "Women and the Constitution," 9; ACLU, *Amicus Brief in Frontiero,* 20–21.

50. ACLU, *Amicus Brief in Frontiero,* 20–27, 30–43.

51. Swiger, *Women Lawyers at Work,* 52.

52. ACLU, *Amicus Brief in Frontiero,* 19–20; Ginsburg's quotation of Sarah Grimke is in Pressman, "The House That Ruth Built," 326.

53. *Frontiero* v. *Richardson,* 683–690; the "close judicial scrutiny" quote is from Brennan's opinion on page 688; Ruth Bader Ginsburg, "Let's Have E.R.A. as a Signal," *American Bar Association Journal* 63 (1977): 72–73; Markowitz, "In Pursuit of Equality," 84–85.

54. Quote of Ginsburg is in "Sex Equality: Impact of a Key Decision," *U.S. News & World Report,* May 28, 1973, 69.

55. Ruth Bader Ginsburg and Brenda Feigen-Fasteau, *The Legal Status of Women Under Federal Law: Report of the Columbia Law School Equal Rights Advocacy Project* (1974), 1–4, 10–15, 202–213.

56. Quote of Ginsburg is in Markowitz, "In Pursuit of Equality," 86; the statement of Justice Douglas is from his opinion in *Kahn* v. *Shevin* 416 U.S. 351 (1974), 351–352; Ruth Bader Ginsburg, "Let's Have E.R.A. as a Signal," 72.

57. Ginsburg and Flagg, "Some Reflections," 14; Henry, "Ruth Bader Ginsburg," 1866; Ginsburg, "Let's Have E.R.A. as a Signal," 72; Markowitz, "In Pursuit of Equality," 85–86; Cowan, "Women's Rights Through Litigation," 390–391.

58. The Ginsburg quote is from Ruth Bader Ginsburg, "From No Rights to Half Rights to Confusing Rights," *Human Rights* 7 (May 1978): 46; *Weinberger* v. *Wiesenfeld* 420 U.S. 636 (1975); George Pieler, *"Weinberger* v. *Wiesenfeld,"* Columbia Human Rights Law Review 8 (1977): 413–433; Markowitz, "In Pursuit of Equality," 88.

59. The quotes from Ginsburg are from Markowitz, "In Pursuit of Equality," 88–89; Ginsburg, "Let's Have E.R.A. as a Signal," 72.

60. Quotation is from Justice Brennan's opinion in *Weinberger* v. *Wiesenfeld,* 643; Ruth Bader Ginsburg, "Gender and the Constitution," *University of Cincinnati Law Review* 44 (1975): 14.

61. Cowan, "Women's Rights Through Litigation," 403, 412; Pieler, *"Weinberger* v. *Wiesenfeld,"* 426–427; Markowitz, "In Pursuit of Equality," 90.

62. The Ginsburg quotation is from Markowitz, "In Pursuit of Equality," 91; Gilbert and Moore, *Particular Passions,* 154–155; *Califano* v. *Goldfarb* 430 U.S. 199 (1976).

63. Henry, "Ruth Bader Ginsburg," 1867; the quote from Brennan's opinion is in *Califano* v. *Goldfarb,* 217.

64. "Men's Rights," 32.

65. Ibid. *Craig* v. *Boren* 429 U.S. 190 (1976), 190–199; Markowitz, "In Pursuit of Equality," 95; Pressman, "The House That Ruth Built," 327–329.

66. *Edwards* v. *Healy* 421 U.S. 772 (1975), 772; *Hoyt* v. *Florida* 368 U.S. 57 (1961), 57–62; Ginsburg's characterization of *Hoyt* is in Ginsburg, "Sex and Unequal Protection," 355.

67. The quote is from the majority opinion in *Taylor* v. *Louisiana* 419 U.S. 522 (1975), 537; Ginsburg, "Let's Have E.R.A. as a Signal," 72; Ginsburg, "From No Rights to Half Rights to Confusing Rights," 14; Markowitz, "In Pursuit of Equality," 86–87.

68. *Duren* v. *Missouri* 439 U.S. 357 (1979), 357–361; Henry, "Ruth Bader Ginsburg," 1867–1868.

69. Eva Rodriguez, "Ginsburg Tailored Radical Arguments to Fit Mainstream," *Legal Times* 16 (June 21, 1993): 16; Markowitz, "In Pursuit of Equality," 97.

70. Gerard Lynch quote appears in Guy Gugliotta and Eleanor Randolph, "A Mentor, Role Model and Heroine of Feminist Lawyers," *Washington Post,* June 15, 1993, A14; Epstein, *Women in Law,* 108; "Prepared Statement of Kathleen Peratis," *Confirmation Hearings,* 408–409; "Prepared Statement of Eleanor Holmes Norton," *Confirmation Hearings,* 12.

71. Jeffrey Rosen, "The New Look of Liberalism on the Court," *New York Times Magazine,* October 5, 1997, 63; "Transcript of President's Announcement and Judge Ginsburg's Remarks," A24; Swiger, *Women Lawyers at Work,* 58–59; Hewitt, "Feeling Supreme," 50; "Ruth Bader Ginsburg," *Current Biography Yearbook,* 216.

72. Epstein, *Women in Law,* 345; *Confirmation Hearings,* 54, 97; Janet MacLachlan, "Mr. Ginsburg's Campaign for Nominee," *National Law Journal* 15 (June 28, 1993): 33.

73. Rosen, "The New Look of Liberalism on the Court," 64; Carol Saline and Sharon J. Wohlmuth, *Mothers and Daughters* (New York: Doubleday, 1997), 50; her friend's comment on Ginsburg's golf game is in Margolick, "Trial by Adversity," A19.

74. Carlson, "The Law According to Ruth," 40; Swiger, *Women Lawyers at Work,* 50, 57; Shannon, "Justice for Women," 472; Ayer, *Ruth Bader Ginsburg,* 64.

75. Rosen, "The New Look of Liberalism on the Court," 63; Swiger, *Women Lawyers at Work,* 56; Mary Lynn Kotz, "Ruth Bader Ginsburg's Interest in Modern Art," *Art News* 98 (October 1999): 168–169.

76. Rosen, "The New Look of Liberalism on the Court," 96; Stephanie Goldberg, "Those Heady ACLU Years," *ABA Journal* 79 (August 1993): 18; Carlson, "The Law According to Ruth," 38, 40.

77. Rosen, "The New Look of Liberalism on the Court," 63–64; "Ruth Bader Ginsburg," *Current Biography,* 216; MacLachlan, "Mr. Ginsburg's Campaign for Nominee," 33; Bayer, *Ruth Bader Ginsburg,* 86–88.

78. Henry, "Ruth Bader Ginsburg," 1869–1873; Laura A. Kiernan, "Feminist Picked for U.S. Court of Appeals Here," *Washington Post,* December 16, 1979, A1; the Scalia story is in Carlson, "The Law According to Ruth," 40.

79. Henry Julian Abraham, *Justices, Presidents, and Senators: A History of the U.S. Supreme Court Appointments from Washington to Clinton,* revised edition (Lanham, MD: Rowman and Littlefield, 1999), 316–317; "White Announces He'll Step Down From High Court," *New York Times,* March 20, 1993, A1; David S. Broder, "For the High Court, a Practicing Politician," *Washington Post,* March 31, 1993, A19.

80. Ruth Marcus, "President Asks Wider Court Hunt," *Washington Post,* May 6, 1993, A1; Richard L. Berke, "A Slow Search to Find a High Court Nominee," *New York Times,* June 10, 1993, A24; Richard L. Berke, "Favorite for High Court Failed to Pay Maid's Taxes," *New York Times,* June 13, 1993 I, 1.

81. Abraham, *Justices, Presidents, and Senators,* 366; "The Borking of Bill," *New Republic* 208 (May 17, 1993), 7; Stephen Labaton, "The Man Behind the High Court Nominee," *New York Times,* June 17, 1993, A1.

82. Clinton's stated reasons for appointing Ginsburg are in "Transcript of President's Announcement and Judge Ginsburg's Remarks," *New York Times,* June 15, 1993, A24; Anne Devroy and Ruth Marcus, "After 87 Days, Tortuous Selection Process Came Down to Karma," *Washington Post,* June 15, 1993, A11; Abraham, *Justices, Presidents, and Senators,* 368.

83. "Mr. Clinton Picks a Justice," *New York Times,* June 15, 1993, A26; Stephen Labaton, "Senators See Easy Approval for Nominee," *New York Times,* June 16, 1993, A22; Joan Biskupic, "Quick Confirmation of Ginsburg Sought," *Washington Post,* June 16, 1993, A1; Neil A. Lewis, "High Court Nominee Is Given Bar Association's Top Rating," *New York Times,* July 14, 1993, A14.

84. Mickey Kaus, "Moderate Threat," *New Republic,* July 12, 1993, 6; Nat Hentoff, "One Cheer for Judge Ginsburg," *Washington Post,* July 3, 1993, A23; Dershowitz's comment is in Carlson, "The Law According to Ruth," 40.

85. Ginsburg's reference to Justice White is in *Confirmation Hearings,* 231; ibid., 130–131, 144–145, 192–193, 267; Joan Biskupic, "Ginsburg Hearings Elicit Sketchy View," *Washington*

Post, July 26, 1993, A6; Michael Comiskey, "The Usefulness of Senate Confirmation Hearings for Judicial Nominees: The Case of Ruth Bader Ginsburg," *P.S.* 27 (June 1994): 224–226.

86. Ginsburg's statement on abortion is in *Confirmation Hearings,* 207; Joan Biskupic, "Ginsburg Endorses Right to Choose Abortion," *Washington Post,* July 22, 1993, A1.

87. Ginsburg's "we the people" statement is in *Confirmation Hearings,* 119; her comment on the Nineteenth Amendment is on page 221; Ruth Bader Ginsburg, "Speaking in a Judicial Voice," *New York University Law Review* 67 (December 1992): 1185–1188.

88. *Confirmation Hearings,* 51–52; Ginsburg, "Speaking in a Judicial Voice," 1209; Ginsburg's statement on "the judiciary's greatest figures" is in Henry, "Ruth Bader Ginsburg," 1873.

89. Ginsburg's statement on "real change" is in *Confirmation Hearings,* 122; Ginsburg remark on Court as "amplifier" is in Ruth Bader Ginsburg, "Remarks on Women Becoming Part of the Constitution," *Journal of Law and Inequality* 6 (1988): 24; Jeffrey Rosen, "The Book of Ruth," *New Republic* 209 (August 2, 1993): 31.

90. The "political avenues" quote is in Ginsburg's testimony, *Confirmation Hearings,* 168; Ginsburg, "Speaking in a Judicial Voice," 1206–1208; Rosen, "The New Look of Liberalism on the Court," 64.

91. *Roe* v. *Wade* 410 U.S. 113 (1973); Davidson, Ginsburg, and Kay, *Sex-Based Discrimination,* 360–361; Elizabeth Frost-Knappman and Kathryn Cullen-DuPont, *Women's Rights on Trial* (Detroit: New England Publishing, 1997), 177–184.

92. *Confirmation Hearings,* 149–150, 208; Ginsburg, "Speaking in a Judicial Voice," 1200–1204; Rosen, "The New Look of Liberalism on the Court," 65.

93. Ginsburg, "Speaking in a Judicial Voice," 1205–1209; Davidson, Ginsburg, and Kay, *Sex-Based Discrimination,* 353; Rosen, "The Book of Ruth," 30.

94. Senator Heflin's statement is in *Confirmation Hearings,* 94; Joan Biskupic, "Quick Confirmation of Ginsburg Sought," *Washington Post,* June 16, 1993, A1; Linda Greenhouse, "An Absence of Suspense Is Welcomed," *New York Times,* July 25, 1993, Section 4, 3.

95. Walter Goodman, "A Judicious TV Image With a Flair for Detail," *New York Times,* July 22, 1993, C16; Eva M. Rodriguez, "Ginsburg Hits Home Run in Game She Already Won," *Legal Times* 16 (July 26, 1993): 6.

96. U.S. Senate Committee on the Judiciary, *REPORT Together with ADDITIONAL VIEWS (To Accompany the Nomination of Ruth Bader Ginsburg to be an Associate Justice of the U.S. Supreme Court),* 103d Congress, 1st session (August 5, 1993): 3–4, 46; *Confirmation Hearings,* 282–291; Linda Greenhouse, "Senate, 96–3, Easily Affirms Judge Ginsburg as a Justice," *New York Times,* August 4, 1993, B8.

97. Linda Greenhouse, "Parting Snapshots for the Supreme Court Yearbook," *New York Times,* July 8, 1994, B7; "Winner," *Legal Times,* December 27, 1993, 5; Christopher Smith et al., "The First-Term Performance of Ruth Bader Ginsburg," *Judicature* 78, number 2 (September–October, 1994): 74–80.

98. Smith et al., 'The First Term Performance," 74, 78; Linda Greenhouse, "Fierce Combat on Fewer Battlefields," *New York Times,* July 8, 1994, section 4, 1; Abraham, *Justices, Presidents, and Senators,* 320–321.

99. *Board of Education of Kiryas Joel Village* v. *Grumet* (1994), 512 U.S. 687; *Agostini et al.* v. *Felton et al.,* 521 U.S. 203, Ginsburg's dissent is on 255–260.

100. Smith et al., "The First Term Perfomance," 78; *Tuilaepa* v. *California* (1994), 512 U.S. 967; "Ginsburg Backs Ending Death Penalty," A.P. News, April 9, 2001. *Cases in the News* <http://www.truthinjustice.org/ginsburg.htm>.

101. *Pennsylvania* v. *Kilgore* (1996), 116 S. Ct. 2485; *Ohio* v. *Robinette* (1996), 519, U.S. 33. The Ginsburg quote is ibid, 44.

102. *Adarand Constructors, INC* v. *Pena, Secretary of Transportation et al.* (1995), 515 U.S. 200, 204–205.

103. Ibid., 234–237. The quotation from Justice Thomas is on 241.

104. Ginsburg's dissent is in ibid., 271–276.

105. *United States* v. *Lopez* (1995), 514 U.S. 549; *Printz* v. *United States* and *Mack* v. *United States* (1997), 521 U.S. 898.

106. Smith et al., "The First Term Performance," 80.

107. *United States* v. *Virginia* (1996), 518 U.S. 515. The quotation of Ginsburg is at 557; *Mississippi University for Women* v. *Hogan* (1982), 458 U.S. 718.

108. See Scalia's dissent, Ibid., 566–603. The quote is at 570; Rosen, "The New Look of Liberalism," 65.

109. *George W. Bush et al.* v. *Albert Gore Jr. et al.* (2000), 531 U.S. 98; Linda Greenhouse, "An Awareness of Hazards, *New York Times,* December 13, 2000" A1, A26; The Ginsburg quotes are from her dissenting opinion, published in the *New York Times,* December 13, 2000, A25.

110. Rosen, "The Book of Ruth," 20, 29; Markowitz, "In Pursuit of Equality," 76, 96–97.

Selected Cases

Reed v. *Reed* (1971)
404 U.S. 71

This decision marked the first time in the history of the U.S. Supreme Court that it declared a state law unconstitutional for discriminating against women.

The case originated with Sally and Cecil Reed of Boise, Idaho, a divorced couple whose adopted son, Richard Lynn Reed, committed suicide at the age of sixteen. The boy had been in the care of his mother until he reached adolescence, when, as required by Idaho law, his father was given custody. Sally Reed, who blamed her ex-husband for Richard's suicide, was determined to prevent him from administering their deceased son's estate (which consisted in toto of less than $1,000). Since Richard had left no will, both parents petitioned the Probate Court of Ada County for the letters of administration that would make one or the other the sole administrator of the estate. The court chose Cecil Reed to be the administrator, citing an Idaho statute that said that whenever a man and a woman were equally entitled to administer an estate, the man was to be preferred.

Sally Reed won a reversal of the probate court's ruling in an Idaho district court. Her ex-husband appealed to the state's Supreme Court, which reversed the lower court's judgment and reinstated the original order. The central issue in these proceedings was Sally Reed's claim that the provision of state law on which the probate court had based its ruling was unconstitutional because it violated the equal protection clause of the Fourteenth Amendment. Noting that the U.S. Supreme Court had never struck down a state law for treating men and women differently, Idaho's highest court declared the challenged statute to be constitutional. The ACLU now persuaded Sally Reed and her attorney, Allan R. Derr, that they should appeal to the U.S. Supreme Court. It was agreed that Derr would present the oral argument if the Court accepted the case, but the ACLU's lawyers would prepare the jurisdictional statement and the legal brief. Ruth Bader Ginsburg and Melvin Wulf wrote the brief. Ginsburg and Wulf argued that the Court should invalidate the Idaho law because it violated the equal protection clause. As in the case of the nation's blacks, they maintained, discrimination against women was widespread and severe, and was based, ultimately, on a physical characteristic that they were powerless to change. Therefore the Court should adopt the principle of "strict scrutiny" for all classifications by sex just as it had already done for classifications by race, religion, and ethnicity.

The ACLU's *Reed* brief also argued that the challenged Idaho statute had no "rational basis" because it was based on an out-of-date stereotype that women lacked the ability and experience to participate as equals in the workaday world, whereas, in modern America, millions of women were highly educated and gainfully employed.

The brief seems to have influenced the Court, which held unanimously that the challenged section of the Idaho probate code was unconstitutional. "To give a mandatory preference to members of either sex," wrote Chief Justice Warren Burger for the Court, "merely to accomplish the elimination of hearings on the merits, is to make the very kind of arbitrary legislative choice forbidden by the Equal Protection Clause." While Burger did *not* declare all laws that discriminated between men and women to be inherently suspect, he did call for the application of "careful scrutiny" to classifications by sex. In the future, laws that treated men and women differently would be viewed as constitutional by the Court only if a majority of the justices concluded that the measure in question had "a rational relationship to the purpose of the legislation."

Struck v. *Secretary of Defense*
460 F. 2d 1372 (1972)
Certiorari granted 409 U.S. 947; judgment vacated, 409 U.S. 1071.

The issue raised by *Struck* was whether the military services (and by extension other federal government agencies) were required by the Constitution to treat pregnant employees the same as they did personnel with other forms of temporary disability.

Captain Susan R. Struck, a trained nurse, joined the United States Air Force as a commissioned officer on April 8, 1967. While serving in Vietnam in early 1970, Struck, who was not married, became pregnant. The Air Force had for several years followed the policy of discharging servicewomen who became pregnant. Once her superiors learned of her condition, they transferred Struck to McChord Air Force Base in Tacoma, Washington. There she was told that unless she agreed to have an abortion, she would be dismissed from the service.

Struck, a Roman Catholic, refused to consider abortion, but was determined to remain in the Air Force. In late October, the Secretary of the Air Force approved an order that Captain Struck be discharged from the service "for moral or administrative reasons" on October 28. But her attorneys succeeded in obtaining one "temporary"·stay after another from the federal courts. On December 3, Struck became the first Air Force servicewoman ever to give birth while on active duty. She immediately gave up the child for adoption and, after a brief respite, reported for work.

But her legal battle to stay in the Air Force continued. Struck, advised now by the ACLU, sought a permanent injunction to keep the Air Force from dismissing her. In seeking to discharge women who became pregnant, argued Struck and her attorneys, the Air Force was discriminating flagrantly and unconstitutionally against them. How, they asked, could it be constitutional for the military to hold that unmarried servicemen who father children can stay while servicewomen who give birth to a child must go?

Struck's claims were rejected and the right of the Air Force to discharge her was affirmed in 1971 by a federal district court in the state of Washington and in 1972 by the U.S. Court of Appeals for the Ninth Circuit. The Women's Rights Project decided to appeal the case next to the U.S. Supreme Court, and Ginsburg drafted a petition for certiorari. After the Court agreed to hear Struck's appeal, Ginsburg also wrote the Petitioner's Brief, which argued that the Air Force had acted arbitrarily, and therefore unconstitutionally, in seeking Struck's dismissal from the service. If the reason was moral, argued Ginsburg, then it was inconsistent for Struck's superiors to have taken no action against the father of her child, who was also an Air Force officer. If the reason was administrative, then the Air Force should explain how time lost to pregnancy differed from time lost due to other temporary disabilities, including alcoholism and drug addiction, neither of which, under Air Force regulations, was grounds for automatic dismissal.

Before the Court could hear Struck's appeal, the Air Force, acting on the recommendation of Solicitor General Erwin N. Griswold, changed its policy. Pregnant servicewomen could now apply for a waiver that, if granted, would permit them to remain in the Air Force. Susan Struck applied immediately for such a waiver, received it, and was able to continue her career in the military. Since the case was now moot, it was never argued before the Supreme Court. Ginsburg would later say that the outcome in *Struck* was an important first step in winning more equitable treatment for pregnant women in the labor force. By 1990, all the armed services were permitting servicewomen who gave birth to remain in their ranks.

Moritz v. *Commissioner of Internal Revenue* (1972)
469 F. 2d 466; certiorari denied 412 U.S. 906 (1973)

Ginsburg wrote of this case that it was "the fraternal twin to Reed." In *Moritz,* a federal Court applied the equal protection principle on behalf of a male citizen and against the federal government. This was also the first time that a federal court had declared unconstitutional a provision of the Internal Revenue Code.

Charles E. Moritz, a resident of Denver, Colorado, was a full-time book editor, a job that required him to work long hours and to go frequently on business trips. Since 1958, Moritz's mother had been living with him and he had contributed more than half of her support. She was elderly, confined to a wheelchair, and her faculties were impaired. In 1961, Moritz hired a woman to take care of his mother, and this person was still in his employ in 1968.

In that year, Moritz attempted to deduct his mother's home care costs on his tax return, but was told by the IRS that he was not eligible for such a deduction. Under federal law, a woman who was both gainfully employed and single could deduct the expense of caring for elderly parents from taxable income, but a man who had never been married could not. The home care deduction could be taken only by women, widowers, divorcées, or a husband whose wife was incapacitated or in an institution. When Moritz appealed to the tax court, it ruled in favor of the IRS.

Moritz now appealed the United States Tax Court's ruling to the U.S. Court of Appeals of the Tenth Circuit. Ruth Bader Ginsburg and Martin D. Ginsburg, her husband, were cocounsel, collaborating on Moritz's brief and dividing oral argument between them. In its ruling, the court of appeals drew on the Supreme Court's decision in *Reed v. Reed*, noting the finding in that case that all classifications "based on sex are subject to scrutiny under equal protection principles." Writing for the court, Judge William Holloway concluded that "the challenged distinction" made by the statute (Section 214 of the Internal Revenue Code) was "a special discrimination premised on sex alone which cannot stand." Therefore, Moritz was entitled to the income tax deduction he had claimed, and the decision of the tax court was reversed. The Department of Justice attempted to appeal the decision to the Supreme Court, but the justices rejected the petition for certiorari.

Frontiero v. Richardson (1973)
411 U.S. 677

Frontiero involved a challenge to federal laws that automatically extended to married men in the military additional fringe benefits for their wives, but denied these extra benefits to married servicewomen unless they could prove that their husbands were dependent upon them for at least half of their support.

The plaintiff was First Lieutenant Sharon Frontiero, who had joined the Air Force at the age of twenty-one in 1968. In the following year, while stationed at Maxwell Air Force Base in Montgomery, Alabama, she had married Joseph Frontiero, a civilian who, as a Navy veteran and a full-time college student, was receiving a monthly stipend under the G.I. Bill of Rights. In 1970, Lieutenant Frontiero applied for the housing, medical, and dental benefits to which she thought her husband entitled as the spouse of an officer in the Air Force.

When her application for the added benefits was rejected, Sharon Frontiero filed suit in a federal district court in Alabama against the Department of Defense, which she accused of discriminating against her because of her sex and of depriving her of property without due process of law (Elliot Richardson, the defendant named in the lawsuit, was Secretary of Defense). On April 6, 1972, the district court rejected her claims, declaring that the Air Force had acted lawfully when it refused to grant her husband the disputed benefits. The court noted that Joseph Frontiero was not in fact his wife's dependent because his veteran's benefits accounted for over half of his income. Finally, the three-judge panel affirmed the constitutionality of the Defense Department's policy of simply presuming that the spouses of servicemen were their dependents while demanding proof that servicewomen's spouses were financially dependent on their wives.

The case was appealed to the Supreme Court. Ginsburg was the principal author of the jurisdictional statement and also, after the Court agreed to hear the appeal, of the ACLU's amicus curiae brief. As in *Reed,* the ACLU team urged the justices to endorse "strict scrutiny" of all sex-based classifications in the law. The brief also noted that the Court, in its *Reed* ruling, had held specifically that "administrative convenience could not be used to justify sex-based classification."

By an eight-to-one vote, the Court ruled that women in the military were entitled to dependency benefits for their husbands on the same basis as such benefits were granted to servicemen for their wives. Four of the justices (Brennan, Douglas, White, and Marshall) declared all statutory classification based on sex to be "inherently suspect." Four other members of the Court (Powell, Stewart, Burger, and Blackmun) concurred that the challenged statutes were unconstitutional, but did not concede that every sex-based classification was suspect. Only Justice Rehnquist upheld the ruling of the lower court and the constitutionality of the statute.

The Court's decision in *Frontiero* would lead in future years to questioning of the constitutionality of dozens of state and federal laws that differentiated between men and women solely on the basis of sex. Many statutes that had stood for decades would be reconsidered and declared invalid by the courts.

Healy v. *Edwards* (1973)
363 F. Supp. 1110

As of 1972, the constitution of the state of Louisiana exempted women from serving on juries unless they declared in writing that they wanted to be jurors. As a result, the percentage of women on jury venires in the state seldom reached even 5 percent. In 1973, Marcia Healy, an active member of the ACLU, was the original plaintiff in a class action lawsuit brought in federal district court that alleged that her exemption from jury service left her less than a full citizen and deprived her of the equal protection of the laws.

Healy was joined in her lawsuit by other plaintiffs who, among them, represented three distinct classes: (1) females who contended that their right to serve on juries had been abridged, (2) female litigants in civil cases who alleged that they were being denied a jury of their peers, and (3) male potential jurors who complained that their obligation to serve on juries was being made more onerous than necessary by the exemption of women from this aspect of citizenship.

In 1961, in *Hoyt* v. *Florida,* the U.S. Supreme Court had upheld a state law virtually identical to the challenged Louisiana statute. In *Hoyt,* the Court majority had held that since "woman was still the center of home and family life," it was fitting for a state to give her special treatment. Therefore, the exemption of women as a class from jury service had a "rational basis" and did not violate the Fourteenth Amendment.

In spite of the *Hoyt* precedent, the three-judge district court found for the plaintiffs in *Healy* v. *Edwards*. The exemption of women from jury service, ruled the court, deprived female litigants of equal protection and amounted to a denial of due process to all litigants. The challenged provisions of Louisiana law were therefore in violation of the federal Constitution and were null and void.

The state of Louisiana appealed the Healy decision to the U.S. Supreme Court, and oral argument was heard in October 1974. While the case was still pending, the state of Louisiana adopted a new constitution in which women were required to serve on juries on the same basis as men. The Supreme Court now vacated the order of the district court and instructed its judges to consider whether the issues raised in *Healy* were now moot.

On the docket of the Supreme Court, *Healy* had been paired with *Taylor* v. *Louisiana,* another suit that challenged the exemption of women from jury service, but brought this time on behalf of a criminal defendant. While the court never voted on *Healy,* it ruled by an eight-to-one vote in *Taylor* that, in the interests of securing fair trials, women must have equal opportunities to serve on juries. It now became established doctrine that women must be counted in determining whether juries represent "a fair cross-section of the community."

Kahn v. Shevin (1974)
416 U.S. 351

In *Kahn,* the Court upheld a challenged Florida law, first enacted in 1885, that provided an annual property tax exemption of $500 to widows, but not to widowers. The outcome represented a setback to the cause of gender equality in the courts.

The case originated with Mel Kahn, a widower in Florida who had applied to the Dade County tax assessor for the $500 exemption, but was informed that he was ineligible. Kahn filed suit in Dade County Circuit Court, charging that he had been denied equal treatment solely because he was a man. The court ruled in his favor, but the Florida Supreme Court reversed that decision, holding that in granting the exemption to widows, but not to widowers, the state had been properly concerned about reducing "the disparity between the economic capabilities of a man and a woman."

Kahn appealed to the U.S. Supreme Court where Ginsburg argued his case, joined on the brief by Melvin Wulf. The Court ruled by a six-to-three vote that the challenged statute was constitutional. Justice Douglas delivered the opinion of the Court (joined by Chief Justice Burger, and by Justices Stewart, Blackmun, Powell, and Rehnquist). According to the majority, the Florida law reasonably implemented "the state's policy of cushioning the financial impact of spousal loss upon the sex for whom that loss imposes a disproportionately heavy burden."

Justice Brennan filed a dissenting opinion in which Justice Marshall joined, and Justice White wrote a dissent of his own. Both dissents protested that an impoverished widower would be denied the tax exemption while a widow who was well-off would receive it.

The outcome in *Kahn* suggested that gender-based distinctions might survive judicial scrutiny if the Court saw them as compensating women for the disadvantages they suffered from in competing economically with men.

Weinberger v. Wiesenfeld (1975)
420 U.S. 636

Stephen Wiesenfeld, a mathematician and computer expert, married Paula Polotschek, a schoolteacher, in November 1970. For the next year and a half, Paula's earnings were the couple's principal source of income. On June 5, 1972, Paula Wiesenfeld died in childbirth, leaving Stephen with sole responsibility for their newborn son.

Shortly after Paula's death, Stephen Wiesenfeld applied as a widower for Social Security benefits both for himself and for his young son. He was awarded benefits for his child, but he himself was ineligible under the Social Security law. In February 1973, Stephen Wiesenfeld filed suit in federal court in New Jersey. He argued in his lawsuit that it was unconstitutional for the Social Security Administration to deny him benefits solely on the basis of his sex. The court agreed to Wiesenfeld's request for summary judgment against the federal government, holding that the different treatment of men and women mandated by the Social Security laws was unconstitutional. These laws, said the court (adopting as doctrine an argument made by Ginsburg in her brief), discriminated against female wage earners by affording them less protection for their families than that provided to the families of men.

The Department of Health, Education, and Welfare appealed the decision to the United States Supreme Court, which accepted probable jurisdiction. On March 14, 1975, the Court voted by eight-to-zero to affirm the lower court's ruling. According to the majority opinion of Justice Brennan, the Social Security Administration had violated the due process clause of the Fifth Amendment in providing survivors' benefits to widows with children while denying them to widowers in the same position: single persons with children to raise.

This was the first time that the Court had insisted on equal treatment in a sex discrimination case when it entailed great expense to the government. It was estimated that implementing the Wiesenfeld decision would cost the government $20 million a year.

Craig et al. v. Boren (1976)
429 U.S. 190

Curtis Craig, a male college student, and Carolyn Whitener, the proprietress of the *Honk 'n Holler* and a licensed vendor of 3.2 percent beer, were jointly the plaintiffs in this lawsuit against the state of Oklahoma. At issue was the constitutionality of a state law permitting the sale of 3.2 beer to girls of eighteen, but requiring that males be at least twenty-one before they could legally purchase such "near-beer." This distinction, alleged Craig and Whitener, amounted to gender-based discrimination because it deprived Oklahoma males between the ages of eighteen and twenty-one of the equal protection of the laws.

A three-judge district court in Oklahoma rejected the claims of the two plaintiffs. The challenged law, said the district court, met the constitutional test imposed by *Reed* v. *Reed* (1971). The Supreme Court in that famous turning-point decision had ruled that a gender-based classification could be constitutional if it advanced an important governmental objective and did so in a rational way. The objective of the law in question, said the district court, was to make the roads of Oklahoma safer, which was clearly an important goal. Moreover, the court found persuasive the statistics used by Oklahoma to demonstrate the rationality of the statute. According to the state's figures, only about .18 percent of women of eighteen to twenty years of age had been arrested in the past year for drunken driving, while among men in the same age group, the percentage was 2 percent, about ten times as high. Therefore, concluded the district court, the classification by sex was a rational means for advancing an important government objective.

When the U.S. Supreme Court heard the case, the justices were agreed that Craig who was now twenty-one, no longer had standing in the case. But Whitener, the other plaintiff, still had standing to sue, according to a majority of the justices. Her interests were affected by the law because it was forcing her to choose between economic injury if she obeyed it and legal sanctions if she didn't. Moreover, ruled the Court, she was entitled to advocate in court the rights of third parties who desired access to her market.

The key question in the case, the justices agreed, was whether the gender-based differential in the Oklahoma law denied to males eighteen and twenty years of age the equal protection of the laws. By a seven-to-two margin, the Court ruled that it did so discriminate and reversed the ruling of the district court. In his majority opinion, Justice Brennan denied that the statistics presented by Oklahoma justified the classification by gender imposed by the state's law. The fact that 2 percent of males in Oklahoma whose ages were between eighteen and twenty-one had been arrested for drunk driving meant that 98 percent of the men in that age group had not been. Therefore, reasoned Brennan, sex could not serve as an accurate proxy for the regulation of drinking and driving. Given the absence of a clear connection between the stated objective of safer roads and the law in question, the Court ruled by seven to two that the sex-based differential imposed by the statute was "an invidious discrimination" that denied to Oklahoma males in the affected age group the equal protection of the laws.

Fred Gilbert, Craig's original attorney, argued *Craig* v. *Boren* before the Court. Ginsburg's role was confined to preparing an amicus brief and advising Gilbert as to strategy. Her most important contribution was to devise the

concept of "heightened scrutiny" as the standard for testing the constitutionality of all classifications by gender. She advanced this concept in her *amicus*
brief and persuaded Gilbert to use it in his oral presentation. The references
to this concept in Brennan's majority opinion and the concurring opinion of
Justice Powell make *Craig* an important case in American legal history. The
Court had, in *Craig,* declared officially that a gender-based classification in
the law would only be constitutional if it advanced an important governmental goal and was "substantially related" to the achievement of that statutory
objective.

Califano v. *Goldfarb* (1977)
430 U.S. 199

After the death of his wife, Hannah, Leon Goldfarb, a retired federal employee, applied for Social Security "survivors benefits." He had paid no Social Security taxes himself, but his late wife had done so for over twenty-five
years. His application was rejected because, under federal law, a widow was
automatically eligible to receive benefits based on her late husband's earnings, but a widower could not receive such payments on the basis of his deceased wife's earnings unless he was receiving at least half of his support
from her at the time of her death. The question for the federal courts was
whether this gender-based distinction violated the equal protection principle
(implied by the due process clause of the Fifth Amendment).

Urged on by Ginsburg and her Woman's Rights Project, Goldfarb sued for his
benefits in District Court for the Eastern District of New York. The three-judge
panel found in his favor, adopting the argument of Ginsburg, Goldfarb's attorney in the case, that the denial of benefits to widowers amounted also to invidious discrimination against female wage-earners because their Social Security
taxes bought less protection for their families than that given to male workers.
The Department of Health, Education, and Welfare (HEW) appealed the decision and the United States Supreme Court accepted probable jurisdiction.

By a five-to-four margin, the high court upheld the ruling of the district
court. Justice Brennan (joined by Justices White, Marshall, and Powell) held
that in treating widows differently from widowers, the Social Security laws
had violated the equal protection principle of the Constitution. Brennan maintained that sex-based classification in the law was justifiable only when there
was an important objective at stake and the means adopted were clearly related to that goal. HEW Secretary Joseph Califano's defense of the gender-
based distinction amounted, said Brennan, to no more than "administrative
convenience," which the court had in earlier cases rejected as a justification
for gender-based distinctions.

Justice Stevens filed a separate concurring opinion in which he argued that
the relevant discrimination in the case was against surviving male spouses
rather than deceased female wage earners. Justice Rehnquist filed a dissent

(joined by Chief Justice Burger and Justices Stewart and Blackmun). Rehnquist pointed out that administrative convenience was of greater weight when it came to social insurance than it was in other areas of policy because of the large scale and high expense of social insurance programs. (The government would have to pay an additional $500 million a year if Goldfarb won the case.) Moreover, it remained true that women, on average, earned less than men. The current distinction, concluded Rehnquist, in the treatment of surviving spouses by the Social Security Administration rested upon "a ground of difference having a fair and substantial relation to the object of the legislation." To Rehnquist, therefore, it remained constitutional for federal law to treat the Social Security claims of widows more indulgently than it treated those of widowers.

United States v. *Virginia* (1996)
518 U.S. 515

Virginia Military Institute (VMI) is part of the state system of higher education in Virginia. Through its vigorous and demanding curriculum and behavior code, it has gained prestige and importance as a trainer of leaders both for the U.S. military and in American life generally. Even while other military academies were beginning to admit woman students, VMI (like Citadel, a state-run military academy in South Carolina) remained an all-male institution.

In 1990, the Department of Justice, under President George H.W. Bush, challenged the constitutionality of VMI's continued refusal to enroll female students. In the following year, a federal district court found for VMI, but that decision was reversed by the Court of Appeals for the Fourth Circuit, which ruled that in excluding women from VMI, the State of Virginia was providing opportunities to men that it was not providing to women. The court held, however, that the best available remedy was not to admit women to VMI, but to set up a program that would permit women to develop their leadership skills as effectively as male students had done at VMI. Soon afterward the Virginia legislature did in fact set up a special leadership program for women at Mary Baldwin College. When the case came back to the circuit court, it ruled that the single-sex policy at VMI was now constitutional.

In 1995, the Department of Justice appealed the circuit court's decision to the U.S. Supreme Court, which accepted probable jurisdiction. In 1996, the high court reversed the lower court's ruling. In a seven-to-one decision, the justices declared Virginia's policy of permitting the exclusion of women from VMI to be in violation of the equal protection clause.

Ruth Bader Ginsburg, who had first gained renown as an attorney in gender discrimination cases, was the author of the Court's opinion. In it, she reviewed the various precedent-setting decisions by the Court in sex discrimination cases, some of which she had argued herself. Ginsburg reminded her colleagues that when government at any level classifies by sex, it is constitutional only when the objective is important and the means adopted are clearly related to that objective.

Moreover, discriminatory measures must have an "exceeding persuasive justification" and must not rely on "overbroad generalizations" regarding the supposed difference between men and women. While there are and must always be inherent differences between the sexes, Ginsburg observed, they could not constitutionally be used to justify "artificial constraints on an individual's opportunity." The supposed goal of educational diversity was not advanced by a policy that provided a unique opportunity only to men. As for the parallel program for women at Mary Baldwin College, Ginsburg dismissed it as "but a pale shadow" of the education provided at VMI that had over the years produced so many effective leaders.

Chief Justice Rehnquist agreed with the Court's conclusion, but objected in his own written opinion to some of the language used by the Court, which seemed to him to set a higher constitutional standard for sexual classifications than were warranted by the Court's prior decisions. The sole dissenter was Justice Antonin Scalia, who viewed *United States* v. *Virginia* as a prime example of the Court imposing its values on society. Citing studies that showed single-sex colleges to be educationally superior, Scalia concluded that in maintaining VMI as an all-male entity, Virginia was pursuing a policy that was constitutional because it was "substantially related to an important government objective."

Annotated Bibliography

Abraham, Henry Julian. *Justices, Presidents, and Senators: A History of the U.S. Supreme Court Appointments from Washington to Clinton.* Rev. ed. Lanham, MD: Rowman and Littlefield Publishers, 1999. A historical survey dealing primarily with the nomination and confirmation process that also touches briefly on the background and the impact on the Court of the various justices.

Ayer, Eleanor H. *Ruth Bader Ginsburg: Fire and Steel on the Supreme Court.* New York: Dillon Press, 1995. A biography written for school-age children that is useful and accurate.

Baer, Judith. *Women in American Law from the New Deal to the Present.* 2d ed. New York: Holmes and Meier, 1996. Baer regards Ginsburg's legal victories of the 1970s as of little value to the cause of women's liberation.

Barry, Dawn Bradley. *The 50 Most Influential Women in American Law.* Los Angeles: Contemporary Books, 1996. This is a collection of brief profiles of the most notable American woman lawyers both past and present.

Bayer, Linda. *Ruth Bader Ginsburg.* Philadelphia: Chelsea House, 2000. A biography of Ginsburg written for high school students.

Bredeson, Carmen. *Ruth Bader Ginsburg: Supreme Court Justice.* Berkeley Heights NJ: Enslow Publishers, 1995. A well-written children's biography.

Carlson, Margaret. "The Law According to Ruth." *Time,* June 28, 1993, 38–40. A colorful account of Ginsburg's career by a commentator on public affairs.

Comiskey, Michael. "The Usefulness of Senate Confirmation Hearings for Judicial Nominees: The Case of Ruth Bader Ginsburg." *P.S.* 27 (June 1994): 224–226. Comiskey analyzes Ginsburg's testimony at the hearings on her nomination to the Supreme Court.

Coogan, Peter W., and Ruth Bader Ginsburg. "Men, Women and the Constitution: The Equal Rights Amendment." *Columbia Journals of Law and Social Problems* 91 (1973): 73–110. Joint lecture by two constitutional lawyers on the E.R.A., its prospects for becoming law, and the consequences for society, should it become law.

Cowan, Ruth. "Women's Rights Through Litigation: An Examination of the American Civil Liberties Union Women's Rights Project." *Columbia Human Rights Law Review* 8 (1977): 373–412. This is a seminal study of the impact of the Women's Rights Project that includes a statistical breakdown of its work and brief summaries of its most significant court cases.

Daughtry, Martha Craig. "Women and the Constitution: Where We Are at the End of the Century." *New York University Law Review* 75 (April 2000): 1–25. Daughtry argues that the progress of woman's rights via the courts suggests that an Equal Rights Amendment may no longer be needed.

Davidson, Kenneth M., Ruth Bader Ginsburg, and Herma Hill Kay. *Text, Cases, and Materials on Sex-Based Discrimination.* St. Paul, MN: West Publishing Company, 1974. Authoritative law-school textbook that describes in detail how the law and the courts have treated American women over the years.

Ellis, Richard L. "O'Connor, Sandra Day." In Hall et al., ed. *Oxford Companion to the Supreme Court of the United States,* 604–605. New York: Oxford University Press, 1992. Brief essay that assesses O'Connor's impact on the Supreme Court.

Epstein, Cynthia Fuchs. *Women in Law.* 2d ed. Urbana: University of Illinois Press, 1993. A sociological study of woman lawyers that refers often to Ginsburg's life and career.

Feigen, Brenda. *Not One of the Boys.* New York: Knopf, 2000. A memoir by the codirector (with Ginsburg) of the Women's Rights Project in the 1970s.

Freeman, Jo. *The Politics of Women's Liberation.* New York: David McKay, 1975. A contemporary study of the women's movement by a political scientist.

Fritz, Sara. "Nominee Called Trailblazer Who Kept Low Profile." *Los Angeles Times,* June 15, 1993, A16. A journalist's view of Ginsburg's career written after her nomination to the Supreme Court.

Frug, Mary Jo. *Women and the Law.* Westbury, NY: Foundation Press, 1992. A casebook that explores the role of the law in maintaining the subordination of women.

Gilbert, Lynn, and Gaylen Moore. *Particular Passions: Talks with Women Who Have Shaped Our Times.* New York: C.N. Potter, 1981. Contains Ginsburg's own recollections of her life and career up to 1980.

Gilman, Elizabeth E., and Joseph M. Micheletti. "Justice Ruth Bader Ginsburg." *Seton Hall Constitutional Law Journal* 3 (1994): 657–661. An analysis of Ginsburg's first year on the Supreme Court.

Ginsburg, Ruth Bader. "Comparative Side Glances." In Davidson, Ginsburg, and Kay, *Text, Cases, and Materials on Sex-Based Discrimination,* 937–948. A brief comparison of how women are treated by the law in different nations.

———. "The Equal Rights Amendment is the Way." *Harvard Women's Law Journal* 1 (Spring 1978): 19–26. Argues that the advocates of the Equal Rights Amendment should promote the ratification of the amendment as written rather than modify it to meet the objections of its critics.

———. "From No Rights to Half Rights to Confusing Rights." *Human Rights* 7 (May 1978): 13–14, 46–48. While admitting that the United States Supreme Court had recently improved its record on gender equality, Ginsburg charged that the justices remained hesitant and contradictory on these issues.

———. "Gender and the Constitution." *University of Cincinnati Law Review* 44 (1975): 1–42. In this essay, Ginsburg discusses the various legal remedies for gender discrimination, and defends affirmative action as essential to equal opportunity.

———. "In Her Words: Ginsburg on Abortion, the Confirmation Process, Equal Rights." *Congressional Quarterly* 51 (June 19, 1993): 572–574. A compendium of Ginsburg statements on the legal system and on woman's rights.

———. "Introduction, 'Women and the Law—A Symposium.'" *Rutgers Law Review* 25 (1970–1971): 1–11. Reviews recent progress towards gender equality and list the key items on the feminist agenda.

———. "Let's Have E.R.A. as a Signal." *American Bar Association Journal* 63 (1977): 70–73. Ginsburg argued here that if the Equal Rights Amendment were ratified, the courts would become more consistent and enlightened on issues of sex discrimination.

———. "Remarks on Women Becoming Part of the Constitution." *Law and Inequality: A Journal of Theory and Practice* 6 (1988): 17–25. Says that the legal gains for women since the 1970s were due to the "interplay among the people, the political branches, and the courts."

———. "Sex and Unequal Protection: Men and Women as Victims." *Journal of Family Law* 11, no. 2 (1971): 347–362. A speech that Ginsburg delivered in 1971, arguing that sex discrimination not only victimizes women, but also does harm to many men.

———. "Some Thoughts on the 1980s Debate Over Special Versus Equal Treatment for Women." *Journal of Law and Inequality* 4 (1986): 143–151. Argues that women's gains of recent decades will be jeopardized if they demand special treatment.

———. "Speaking in a Judicial Voice." *New York University Law Review* 67 (December 1992): 1185–1209. The most complete statement of Ginsburg's judicial philosophy.

———. "The Status of Women." *American Journal of Comparative Law* 20 (1972): 585–591. Briefly compares the position of women in the law of various modern nations.

———. "The Treatment of Women by the Law: Awakening Consciousness in the Law Schools." *Valparaiso University Law Review* 5, no. 3 (Spring 1971): 480–488. This article portrays the position of women in American law as of 1971 and discusses as well the growing feminism among female law students.

Ginsburg, Ruth Bader, and Brenda Feigen-Fasteau. *The Legal Status of Women Under Federal Law: Report of the Columbia Law School Equal Rights Advocacy Project* (1974). The authors combine feminist advocacy and practical suggestions with a clear and concise summary of federal laws and rules regarding the treatment and status of women.

Ginsburg, Ruth Bader, with Barbara Flagg. "Some Reflections on the Feminist Legal Thought of the 1970s." *University of Chicago Legal Forum* (1989): 9–21. In this speech, Ginsburg and Flagg defend Ginsburg's work and ideas against the criticisms of latter-day feminists with more radical views.

"Ginsburg, Ruth Bader." *Current Biography Yearbook 1994,* 213–217. Provides an accurate summary of Ginsburg's life and career up to 1993.

"Ginsburg, Ruth Bader." *Biography Today,* January 1994, 49–50. A brief, useful account.

Goldberg, Stephanie. "The Second Woman Justice." *American Bar Association Journal* 79 (October 1993): 42–43. A biographical profile that includes several pithy quotations from Ginsburg.

————. "Those Heady ACLU Years." *American Bar Association Journal* 79 (August 1993): 18. Attempts to convey the mood among the lawyers of the Women's Rights Project during the 1970s.

Hall, Kermit L., et al., eds. *The Oxford Companion to the Supreme Court.* New York: Oxford University Press, 1992. Contains concise reliable articles on some of the important gender-related cases and issues that Ginsburg dealt with as a scholar, attorney, and judge.

Harrington, Mona. *Women Lawyers: Rewriting the Rules.* New York: Knopf, 1994. Views Ginsburg's work as a litigator for equal rights in the 1970s as part of a wider, continuous movement to equalize power in American life.

Henry, Christopher. "Ruth Bader Ginsburg." *The Justices of the United States Supreme Court: Their Lives and Major Opinions,* 5th ed., ed. Leon Friedman and Fred Israel. New York: Chelsea House, 1997, vol. 6, 1860–1873. A scholarly and interpretive essay on Ginsburg's life and career both as advocate and as appeals court judge.

Hewitt, Bill. "Feeling Supreme." *People,* June 28, 1993, 50. Contains some revealing quotations and anecdotes.

Hunt, Angela. "Meet Our New Supreme Court Justice." *Glamour* 91 October 1993, 116–117. Interview with Ginsburg shortly after she became a member of the Court.

Idelson, Holly. "Clinton's Choice of Ginsburg Signals Moderation." *Congressional Quarterly* 51 (June 19, 1993): 1569, 1599. A report on the politics involved in President Clinton's nomination of Ginsburg to the Supreme Court.

Ingber, Stanley. "O'Connor, Sandra Day." In Kermit L. Hall, ed. *The Oxford Companion to the Supreme Court of the United States,* 604–605. A brief assessment of O'Connor's impact on the Court.

Kanowitz, Leo. *Women and the Law: The Unfinished Revolution.* Albuquerque, NM: University of New Mexico Press, 1970. Kanowitz argues that sex discrimination, while still pervasive in the law as of the late 1960s, is on its way out.

Kaus, Mickey. "Moderate Threat." *New Republic,* July 12, 1993, 6. Kaus thinks Ginsburg is a radical in moderate's clothing.

Kerber, Linda K. *No Constitutional Right to Be Ladies: Women and the Obligations of Citizenship.* New York: Hill and Wang, 1998. This is a thoroughly researched study of the changing status and condition of women under the constitution of the United States.

Kotz, Mary Lynn. "Ruth Bader Ginsburg's Interest in Modern Art." *Art News* 98 (October 1999): 168–169. Notes that of the nine Supreme Court justices as of 1999, Ginsburg was the only one to prefer modern abstract art to more conventional forms of painting and sculpture.

Lewis, Neil A. "Rejected as a Clerk; Chosen as a Justice." *New York Times,* June 15, 1993. Contains some interesting anecdotes and sidelights.

Maclachlan, Janet. "Mr. Ginsburg's Campaign for Nominee." *National Law Journal,* June 28, 1933, 33–34. Recounts the efforts of Martin Ginsburg to mobilize his fellow tax-lawyers in support of his wife's appointment to the Supreme Court.

Margolick, David. "Trial by Adversity Shapes Jurist's Outlook." *New York Times,* June 25, 1993, A19. A journalist's feature article that contains numerous biographical details.

Markowitz, Deborah L. "In Pursuit of Equality: One Woman's Work to Change the Law." *Women's Rights Law Reporter* 11, no. 2 (Summer 1989): 73–97. A highly informative history of the Women's Rights Project during the 1970s based in part on interviews with Ginsburg.

"Men's Rights." *New Yorker,* July 15, 1993, 32. This article briefly depicts the odd but important case of *Craig* v. *Boren* (1976).

Murdock, Joyce, and Deb Price. *Courting Justice: Gay Men and Lesbians v. the Supreme Court.* (New York: Basic Books, 2001). A study of how the U.S. Supreme Court has dealt with homosexuals and their demands for equal treatment by the law.

O'Connor, Karen. *Women's Organizations' Use of the Courts.* Lexington, MA: Lexington Books, 1980. Discusses, among other women's organizations, the Women's Rights Project, the ACLU-sponsored group that Ginsburg headed during the 1970s.

"O'Connor, Sandra Day." *Current Biography Yearbook 1982,* 297–301. Good, brief account of O'Connor's life.

Perry, Barbara Ann. *The Supremes: Essays on the Current Justices of the Supreme Court of the United States.* New York: Peter Lang, 1999. Provides brief, vivid profiles of the nine justices as of 1999.

Pieler, George. "*Weinberger* v. *Wiesenfeld.*" *Columbia Human Rights Law Review* 8 (1977): 413–433. A detailed, scholarly analysis of one of Ginsburg's victories before the Supreme Court.

Pressman, Carol. "The House That Ruth Built: Justice Ruth Bader Ginsburg, Gender, and Justice." *New York Law School Journal of Human Rights* 14 (1998): 311–337. Summarizes Ginsburg's life and career and analyzes some of the cases that she argued before the Supreme Court.

Roberts, Steven V. "Two Lives of Ruth Bader Ginsburg." *U.S. News and World Report,* June 28, 1993, 20–22, 24–26, 28. A clear statement of the "Two Ginsburgs" thesis.

Rodriguez, Eva. "Ginsburg Tailored Radical Arguments to Fit Mainstream." *Legal Times,* June 21, 1993, 1, 16–17. Contains quotes from law professors as well as lawyers and judges with whom she has worked as an attorney and appeals court judge.

Rosen, Jeffrey. "The Book of Ruth." *The New Republic* 209 (August 2, 1993): 19–20, 29–32. Contrasts Ginsburg's equal rights approach to feminism with the more radical approach of the "difference" theorists.

———. "The New Look of Liberalism on the Court." *New York Times Magazine,* October 15, 1997, 60–65, 86, 90, 96–97. A portrayal of Ginsburg as an "incremental" liberal on an increasingly conservative Supreme Court.

Saline, Carol, and Sharon J. Wohlmuth. *Mothers and Daughters.* New York: Doubleday, 1997, 47–51. A joint interview with Ruth Ginsburg and her daughter, Jane, who is, as her mother was, professor of law at Columbia.

Salokar, Rebecca Mae. "Ruth Bader Ginsburg." *Women in Law: A Bio-Bibliographical Sourcebook.* Edited by Rebecca Mae Salokar and Mary L. Volcansek. Westport, CT: Greenwood Press, 1996, 78–87. Salokar provides a concise and readable overview that draws its facts almost entirely from the newspaper articles written at the time of Ginsburg's appointment to the Supreme Court.

Schafran, Lynn Hecht, et al. *Women Changing the Law for Women: A Case Chronology 1970–2000.* New York: Association of the Bar of the City of New York & NOW Legal Defense Fund, 2000. A summary of the important women's rights and gender discrimination cases from the 1970s through the 1990s.

Schroth, Tracy. "At Rutgers, Ginsburg Changed." *New Jersey Law Journal* 134 (June 21, 1993): 32–33. Describes Ginsburg's "conversion" to feminism.

Shannon, Elaine. "Justice for Women." *Vogue,* October 1993, 392–393, 472–473. A portrait of Ginsburg based largely on interviews; provides useful biographical information.

Smith, Christopher, et al., "The First-Term Performance of Justice Ruth Bader Ginsburg." *Judicature* 78, number 2 (September–October, 1994): 74–80. Incisive analysis of Ginsburg's first year as a Supreme Court Justice.

Strossen, Nadine. "The American Civil Liberties Union and Women's Rights." *New York University Law Review* 66 (1991), 1940–1961. Sees Ginsburg's activities in the 1970s as illustrating the ACLU's consistent commitment to women's liberty and equality both inside and outside its ranks.

Swiger, Eleanor Porter. *Women Lawyers at Work.* New York: Julian Messner, 1978. Biographical essays, each dealing with a pioneer woman lawyer of the 1970s.

Thomas, Jennifer S. "Ruth Ginsburg: Carving a Career Path Through Male-Dominated Legal World." *Congressional Quarterly* 51 (July 17, 1993): 1876–1877. Brief, anecdotal summary of Ginsburg's career.

U.S. Senate Committee on the Judiciary. *The Nomination of Ruth Bader Ginsburg to be Associate Justice of the Supreme Court of the United State.* 103d Congress, 1st session, July 20–23, 1993. Contains biographical material as well as Ginsburg's views on the role of law, the Constitution, and many other matters. It also includes her summaries of her ten most important cases as an attorney and a virtually complete bibliography of her writings up to 1993.

———. *REPORT Together With ADDITIONAL VIEWS (To accompany the nomination of Ruth Bader Ginsburg to be an Associate Justice of the U.S. Supreme Court).* 103d Congress, 1st session, August 5, 1993. The Committee's final report on the Ginsburg nomination with some added comments by senators who criticized her somewhat even while voting to confirm her appointment.

Van Drehle, David. "Conventional Roles Hid a Revolutionary Intellect." *Washington Post,* July 18, 1993, A1. One of the best journalistic portrayals of Ginsburg's early life and career.
————. "Redefining Fair With a Simple Careful Assault." *Washington Post,* July 19, 1993, A8. Argues that Ginsburg played a key role in advancing the equality of the sexes before the law.
Walsh, Amy. "Ruth Bader Ginsburg: Extending the Constitution." *John Marshal Law Review* 32 (Fall 1998): 197–225. Walsh depicts Ginsburg's career as a largely successful struggle against sexual discrimination via the nation's courtrooms.

—Ralph—
<u>Nader</u>

(Public Citizen Group)

Chronology

1934	Born on February 27 in Winsted, Connecticut, to Nathra and Rose Nader.
1951	Graduated from The Gilbert School in Winsted.
1955	Graduated Phi Beta Kappa from Princeton University, Princeton, New Jersey.
1958	Received law degree from Harvard University, Cambridge, Massachusetts; admitted to the Connecticut bar.
1959	Completed six-month stint in United States Army as a cook at Fort Dix, New Jersey.
1964	Took job as consultant on automobile safety at the Labor Department in Washington, D.C.
1965	Published *Unsafe at Any Speed.*
1966	General Motors president James M. Roche issued a public apology to Nader for the investigation of him that had been ordered by officials of the firm.
1967	Played a crucial role in winning passage by Congress of automobile safety and meat inspection laws.
1968	"Nader's Raiders" investigated the Federal Trade Commission.
1969	Founded the Center for the Study of Responsive Law, a public interest think tank in Washington, D.C.
1970	Established his first Public Interest Research Group.
1971	Founded Public Citizen and launched his Congress Project.
1977	Several Nader associates were appointed to significant positions in the administration of Jimmy Carter.
1978	The House of Representatives rejected Nader's proposal for a consumer protection agency, probably his most important defeat.
1980	Resigned as president of Public Citizen and announced that he was now going to put greater emphasis upon organization at the local level.
1986	Suffered from a temporary loss of morale due to the death of his brother and to the partial paralysis of his face by Bell's palsy.
1988	Led the successful campaign for Proposition 103 in California, which rolled back the automobile and casualty insurance rates in that state.

1989   Joined with political conservatives to block a pay raise for members of Congress.

1992   Ran in the New Hampshire presidential primary of both major parties.

1993   Began to actively oppose GATT, NAFTA, and other policies and institutions that advanced the globalization of economic life.

1996   Nominated for the presidency by the Green Party, he campaigned only halfheartedly and received barely 1 percent of the total vote.

2000   Again ran for president on the Green Party ticket, but this time more actively and seriously. He received 3 percent of the national vote, which, due to the extreme closeness of the election, may have decided the outcome in favor of George W. Bush.

2001   Published *The Best of Ralph Nader,* the latest of the more than two dozen books that he has authored.

Biography

The incident which first elevated Ralph Nader to national fame is by now, and has been for some time, the stuff of legend. On March 22, 1966, at a nationally televised hearing of a United States Senate subcommittee, James M. Roche, the president of General Motors, admitted that his company had employed private detectives to spy on Nader, the author of *Unsafe at Any Speed,* a book that blamed American auto companies for the high and rising accident rate on the nation's highways. Although Roche denied that he had authorized the hiring of the detectives, he apologized to the young attorney. The accounts in the media in succeeding days presented the dramatic, inherently appealing spectacle of a lone idealist confronting the nation's most powerful corporation and getting it to back down. Hailed as a hero, Nader now embarked on his controversial, multifaceted career as a self-appointed advocate for the interests of consumers and citizens, and as a critic of established institutions, especially the nation's most powerful corporations.[1]

Nader's Origins

Ralph Nader was born on February 27, 1934, in Winsted, Connecticut, a small town of 10,000 people in the foothills of the Berkshire Mountains, about thirty miles from Hartford near the state's border with Massachusetts. His parents, Nathra and Rose Nader, were both immigrants from Lebanon. Nathra had come to America in 1912 at the age of nineteen and had settled in Newark, New Jersey, where he eventually established a successful food store. While on a visit to Lebanon in 1924, he met and married Rose Bouziane, a nineteen-year-old schoolteacher. The couple would have four children: Ralph; their other son, Shafeek, who was their eldest child and the only one to receive an Arab-style name; and two daughters, Claire and Laura.

They lived for five years in Danbury, Connecticut, where Nathra ran a food store. Then they moved on to Winsted, where three of their children were born. Acquiring a large, run-down diner in Winsted, Nathra and Rose renamed it the Highland Arms and managed in time to transform it into one of the best-regarded restaurants in town.[2]

Nathra might have fared even better as a restaurant owner had he not been in the habit of passionately debating controversial issues with his customers. At Nathra's place, said one resident of Winsted, "you pay ten cents for a cup of coffee and you also get a dollar's worth of talk." In a democracy, according to the largely self-educated Nathra, it was every citizen's duty to take a position on public questions and oppose anything that was unjust. Citizens should seek not only their own welfare, but also that of every member of society. "When I went past the Statue of Liberty," he once said, "I took it seriously." Although an admirer of the American system, Nathra was often critical of the ways in which it was, as he saw it, used and abused. According to him, the big interests and the big forces in both business and government were always combining to thwart the average person. It seems obvious that these attitudes, which Nathra strove to impress upon his children, rubbed off on his younger son and helped to shape Ralph's destiny both as a consumer advocate and as a crusader against Big Business.[3]

The town of Winsted was perhaps as well-suited as any community could be to the type of active citizenship believed in and practiced by the Naders. The town was so compact that all its public agencies and institutions were clustered near one another within easy walking distance of the Nader home, and many of the townspeople were on a first-name basis with their elected officials. Nathra, his eldest son Shafeek, and Ralph (once he reached high school) often attended meetings of the elected town council and the town meetings at which all of Winsted's residents were allowed to speak and vote. At these gatherings, the Naders would raise questions about policy. They would demand to know, for example, why tax revenues were being spent as they were. Nathra campaigned successfully for better sewers and Shafeek persuaded the town council to build a community college. Despite these successes, the Naders and their incessant agitation irritated some of the townspeople. "The family could have been popular in town," observed a local newspaper editor, "except that they always had something to say about everything."[4]

Ralph Nader grew up in a ten-room house that was described by journalist Hays Gorey as "large, roomy, cheerful, bright, and neat." The family spoke both Arabic and English. After dinner each night, Rose, but especially Nathra, would lead the children in discussions both of current events and of the rights and wrongs of American society. With each family member stating his or her views on each question, the discussions would turn into competitive free-for-alls that would go on until bedtime. "When the Naders sat around the table growing up," Mark Green, Nader's longtime associate, told journalist Ken Auletta, "it was like the Kennedys. Except that the topic was not power but justice."[5]

According to Nathra Nader, "the family was like a bank. You put in work and you take out education." The Naders were Eastern Orthodox Christians, but Rose and Nathra sent their children to a Methodist Sunday school. All four of the Nader children attended The Gilbert School in Winsted, a private high school where the tuition was free. One of Ralph's classmates was his next-door neighbor and friend, David Halberstam, who later would win fame and the Pulitzer Prize as a journalist covering the early stages of American involvement in the Vietnam War. The teenage chums argued politics, followed the New York Yankees, and played baseball and basketball together. All four of the Nader children also helped out in the restaurant, working at the counter or as a cashier. In return, Rose and Nathra saw to it that each attended a first-rate college, and all four went on to do graduate work. Shafeek attended Boston University Law School for a time, but withdrew to work with his father at the restaurant. Both of Ralph's sisters went on to earn Ph.D.s: Claire in political science at Columbia University and Laura in anthropology at Harvard.[6]

For as long as Ralph could remember, his parents had been urging him to become a lawyer. "We made Ralph understand," Nathra would later recall, "that working for justice in the country is a safeguard of our democracy." When he was five, Nathra took him to visit the local courthouse. The boy was impressed that here was a place where people who were treated unfairly could go and, if they made their case well enough, could obtain justice. After that visit, he often went to the courthouse after school to listen to the arguments of the rival attorneys. While still in elementary school, Ralph decided that he would become a lawyer in the belief that this career would give him his best chance of helping people.[7]

Ralph, who never dated in high school and seldom went to movies, was already a voracious and serious reader. By the time he was fourteen, he had read all of the classic muckraking exposés, including those by Lincoln Steffens, Upton Sinclair, and George Seldes. These books undoubtedly reinforced his belief, acquired initially from his father, that American life was rife with corruption and injustice. While in high school, Ralph also read many volumes of the *Congressional Record,* which fascinated him with its display of the people's representatives clashing in debate over the problems of the nation. His preoccupation with things factual was becoming so marked now that he soon stopped reading poetry and novels altogether.[8]

At Princeton and Harvard Law School

After graduating from The Gilbert School in June 1951, Ralph attended the Woodrow Wilson School of Public Affairs at Princeton University. At a time when social conformity was the norm, he stood out as something of a rebel. Nader refused to wear the white buck shoes favored by nearly all the Princeton students of that era, and on one occasion, he attended class in a bathrobe. He also tried, but failed, to arouse his fellow students against the spraying of the trees on campus with DDT, which, he pointed out, had resulted in the death of many birds. The editors rejected his letter to the student newspaper protesting the practice on the grounds that if the spraying were dangerous to humans, the biology and chemistry departments at the college would have spoken out against it.

Nader spent most of his time at Princeton reading on a wide variety of subjects. After being locked in several times when the college library closed for the night, he was finally given his own key. Nader also managed to learn enough Russian, Chinese, and Spanish so that by the time of his graduation, he could converse in five different languages. A government and economics major, he graduated *magna cum laude* in June 1955 and was elected to Phi Beta Kappa.[9]

Ralph Nader was admitted to Harvard Law School in the autumn of 1955. In the previous month, his family's restaurant business had been for a time shut down when a local river overflowed its banks, flooding the streets of Winsted and several other Connecticut towns. Suddenly in need of funds, Ralph took out student loans, worked at a series of part-time jobs, and sold the 1949 Studebaker that remains to this day the only car he ever owned.

He felt ill at ease in the Harvard milieu. For someone like himself who had grown up in a small town in a semirural setting, Cambridge seemed "too cramped and vertical." Moreover, his father's influence and his own earnest and voluminous reading had made him too much of an idealist to accept the approach to the law taken by most of his professors. "If you were worried about issues of right and wrong and justice and injustice, you were considered soft intellectually." The great majority of Harvard law students were, Nader decided, just as conformist as Princeton undergraduates, bent only on achieving wealth and power. The law school was simply "a high priced tool factory," producing hired advocates for corporate law firms and corporations.[10]

Ralph's unhappiness at Harvard led him frequently to miss classes and to study less industriously. "At Princeton," wrote Nader biographer Charles McCarry, "he had been a student among the idlers; at Harvard he became an idler among the students." So restless did he become that on one occasion, he dropped everything to go to Mexico, remained there for several weeks, and returned with a deep suntan. He managed to remain in good standing, however, by offering shrewdly devised excuses to faculty members and administrators and by cramming industriously before examinations.

To Nader, at twenty-two, such Harvard Law icons as Oliver Wendell Holmes and Louis D. Brandeis seemed "staid, dry," and far from heroic. Brandeis, he complained, had become "a people's lawyer" only after acquiring his first million. "Who the hell says that a lawyer has to be like that?" Nader aspired instead to become what he called "a public service lawyer," a lawyer without clients, whose goal would be not making lucrative fees but advancing the public good. "I always thought that he would be terrific," observed his college and law school roommate Ted Jacobs, "because he didn't have the same set of values as everyone else."[11]

Nader joined the *Harvard Law Record,* the student newspaper, during his first year at the law school and a year later became its editorial manager. He was now beginning to write articles of a muckraking kind. In one of his exposés, he characterized poverty among America's long-suffering migrant workers as virtually no different from that of people living in Third World nations. Another of his articles depicted the poverty and ill health suffered by reservation Indians that Nader had witnessed firsthand while traveling through some of the western states during the summer of 1956. His hard-hitting pro-Indian article struck a chord with groups that were championing the Native Americans' cause. As a result, hundreds of reprints were sold, leaving the *Record* with a modest profit.

The publication's editorial board selected Nader as its president for the coming academic year, but when his plan to transform the rather bland *Record* into a national journal of reform met with resistance, he resigned as president. After an absence of three months, however, he rejoined the *Record*'s staff, surely one of the few occasions on record of Nader accepting defeat.[12]

It was also during his law school years that Nader first became aware of the issue of automobile safety. As a frequent hitchhiker, he had often seen the horrendous damage done to life and limb by accidents on the highway. Once, while hitchhiking between Winsted and Cambridge, Nader encountered a wreck in which an eight-year-old girl was decapitated when she was flung forward just as the glove compartment in her parents' car sprang open as a result of its collision with another car. Appalled at the apparent indifference of many drivers to the deaths and injuries occurring on the nation's roads, Nader decided to look into what was known about automobile accidents, their causes, and their results. Gathering data from the engineering libraries of Harvard and MIT, he was encouraged to look into the legal aspects by an article in the *Harvard Law Review* in 1956 by Professor Harold Katz, who argued that automobile companies might be held liable under the law for deaths and injuries that were traceable to "negligent" car design.

Nader decided to write his third-year essay (a requirement for all Harvard law students) on the legal aspects of automobile design. Among his most important sources of information were the committee hearings on automobile safety held by Representative Kenneth Roberts (D-AL), who was a pioneer on this issue at a time when few were interested in it. Nader received an A for his paper and summarized its findings in an article published in the *Harvard Law Record* under the title "American Cars: Designed for Death." In early 1959, Nader's piece "The Safe Car You Can't Buy," ran in the *The Nation,* his first article for a national publication.[13]

Nader received his law degree in June 1958, but lingered at Harvard for a few months as the research assistant of one of his former professors. After being admitted to the Connecticut bar, he was hired for $75 a week by George Athanson, a Hartford lawyer, who put him to work on accident cases, divorce cases, and the drawing up of wills. Nader conducted a sort of legal aid clinic on the side, devoting nearly as much of his time to people who couldn't afford to pay him as he did to the clients who paid him fees. To avoid being drafted, Nader decided to enlist in a reserve program under which he served in the army for six months, spending them as a cook at Fort Dix, New Jersey. Shortly before his stint in the military ended, he purchased at bargain prices at the PX the twelve pairs of shoes and the forty pairs of cotton socks that he would wear for years to come.[14]

For the next five years, Nader struggled to find his place in the scheme of things. He opened a law office in Hartford, but showed little enthusiasm for routine legal work. He taught an occasional course on American history or government at the University of Hartford, but spent far more of his time traveling to

Europe, Asia, Africa, and Latin America while writing articles on the social conditions and politics of the countries he journeyed through that were published in the *Atlantic Monthly* and the *Christian Science Monitor.*

When not abroad, Nader would lobby in Connecticut and elsewhere for reforms that he believed in. His experience earlier as a lawyer for poor people, who were often unable to bear the cost of a lawsuit, led him to champion the idea of the ombudsman, an official whose job is to protect the individual from the mistakes and excesses of government. As both the practice and the word had originated in Scandinavia, Nader while in Europe had gone to that region so the he could learn more about it. Although it is possible that he was the first American to use the term "ombudsman," the idea did not really become popular in the United States for several years, and by then, Nader had gone on to other things.

The issue that had most concerned him since his days at Harvard was automobile safety. In the early 1960s, he delivered speeches on the subject to New England civic groups and testified in favor of stricter regulations on car designs before committees of the legislatures of both Connecticut and Massachusetts. On learning that Nader was a resident of Connecticut, one Bay State legislator asked him: "Well, what the hell are you doing in Massachusetts?" In 1963, Nader lobbied in Connecticut for legislation that would have required safety equipment in every automobile that was registered in the state, but the bill was never passed.[15]

The Auto Safety War

After these rebuffs, Nader decided that it was time to take his personal battle for safer automobiles to Washington. "I had watched years go by and nothing happened," he said; "I decided that what it took was total commitment." He packed one suitcase and hitchhiked his way to the nation's capital, rooming at first in a YMCA before moving into a furnished room in one of the city's poorest neighborhoods. He began his crusade by making contacts among journalists, congressional staff members, and minor officials in the executive branch. At the time, Nader struck many of the people he spoke with as an oddball and monomaniac, obsessed with the problem of making cars safer. "Ralph," remarked one congressional aide, "is a basically sound fanatic."[16]

Nader had been acquainted with urbanologist Daniel Patrick Moynihan since April 1959, when both men had published articles on automobile safety, an issue with which each had remained deeply concerned. Both articles had made essentially the same argument that many of the deaths and injuries resulting from car crashes were due to faulty car design and could be averted in the future if Congress passed a law making safety features mandatory and requiring automakers to follow regulatory guidelines in the design of their cars. Moynihan, who had served as the Assistant Secretary of Labor for policy planning since 1961 in the administrations of both John F. Kennedy and Lyndon

B. Johnson, offered Nader a job as a staff consultant to the Labor Department on highway safety at $50 a day, and he eagerly accepted it.* He was given the job of writing a report on the highway safety activities of the federal government that was intended to serve as authoritative background information on the issue for federal officials and members of Congress. A year later, Nader completed his 232-page study, "A Report on the Context, Condition, and Recommended Direction of Federal Activity in Highway Safety."[17]

In January 1965, Nader had also begun to work as an unpaid consultant for the Senate Subcommittee on Government Reorganization that was chaired by Senator Abraham Ribicoff (D-CT), an arrangement that was kept secret at the time because Nader was still employed at the Labor Department. The subcommittee was preparing to hold hearings on automobile safety, a subject of growing interest on Capitol Hill. Told by a mutual acquaintance of Nader's familiarity with the subject, the subcommittee's chief counsel, Jerome Sonosky, invited him to lunch and, after conversing with him for three hours, informed Ribicoff that they had "struck gold." Nader would play a key role in the committee's investigation from behind the scenes, furnishing data and suggesting lines of inquiry. "I didn't need anyone else," Sonosky later recalled. "He had everything." From behind an open door in the committee room, Nader fed questions to Sonosky, who passed them along to senators on the panel. It was at Nader's suggestion that Senator Robert Kennedy (D-NY) asked of James Roche, president of General Motors, how much of its profits the company was spending on making its cars safer. This question drew from Roche the damaging admission that after earning profits of $1.7 billion in 1964, General Motors had budgeted just a bit more than $1 million or .06 of 1 percent of its earning for safety research in 1965.[18]

Aware that the auto companies had for years followed the practice of quietly recalling their defective cars, Nader suggested that the subcommittee's staff should reveal this to the public. When the top automobile company executives made clear their continuing opposition to government regulation, Ribicoff demanded that each of the four major companies—General Motors, Ford, Chrysler, and American Motors—provide the committee with a complete list of all the product warnings that they had sent to their dealers since 1960. A few weeks later, he publicly announced that there had been 426 recall campaigns involving over 8 million cars over the past five years. This development, noted Washington journalist Elizabeth Drew, indicated "less than superb quality control and a disturbing degree of casualness about whether the customer found out, [and] left another gaping hole in the industry's fenders."[19]

---

*Moynihan's job offer was made before Nader left for Washington, but, according to the latter, he had already decided to go to Washington before receiving it.

In April 1965, Nader resigned from the Labor Department. Already under contract with Richard Grossman, a small New York publisher, to write a book on unsafe cars, he spent most of the next six months working on it. Titled *Unsafe at Any Speed: The Designed-In Dangers of the American Automobile,* the book was a hard-hitting, impressively researched attack on the American automobile industry. It argued that in stressing "power," "style," and cost-cutting rather than safety in the design of their car models, the automobile companies were knowingly and callously producing cars that were unsafe (or less safe than they might have been) in order to increase their profits. Particularly unsafe, according to Nader, was the Corvair, a model produced by the Chevrolet division of General Motors. Carrying its engine at the rear of the chassis, this car, asserted Nader and the various experts that he cited, had a tendency to skid out of control and turn over on sharp turns. While working on the book, Nader had on occasion acted as an informal adviser to some of the plaintiffs who were suing General Motors because they had been injured while riding in a Corvair.

At Grossman's urging, Nader held a press conference in which he challenged the automobile companies to debate, but they did not respond. Although the book was favorably reviewed in some newspapers, other papers refused even to mention it in their columns for fear of losing their advertising revenue from the automakers. As a result, the book was no more than a modest success during the first four months it was on sale.

Nader's book drew much of its material about the lack of safety in American-made cars from the work done by small groups of researchers at Cornell, the University of California at Los Angeles, and a handful of other universities. It was from their published research that he learned of "the second collision," when vulnerable flesh and bone collide with the hard, protruding surfaces inside badly designed automobiles. He was also indebted to Moynihan's 1959 article, "Epidemic on the Highways," which contained several of the major ideas presented in Nader's book. Although Moynihan was more willing than Nader to acknowledge the role played by bad driving in causing road accidents, both writers viewed American automobiles as unsafe and blamed their manufacturers for the flaws in their design. Both noted the finding of the accident researchers that most of the fatalities in highway accidents occurred at relatively low speeds. They were also in accord in criticizing the automakers for the emphasis on speed in their advertising, and both called on Congress to require by law and through federal regulation that the industry produce safer cars.[20]

Both Nader and Moynihan viewed highway accidents as a problem of growing seriousness, but Nader's tone was far angrier and his denunciations of the auto industry, and various other institutions and groups, far more pointed. He wrote of "bringing the industry to justice," thereby suggesting that the leading auto executives were criminals. The book was also critical of the nation's medical, legal, and engineering professions for having done nothing, by and large, to halt the carnage on the highways. He denounced as well the insurance industry and the auto safety establishment for failing to demand of the automakers that they make safer cars. He even castigated the relative handful of academic researchers who had devoted their lives to the study of automobile accidents, attacking them for failing to alert the general public to research findings that could have saved thousands of lives.[21]

Thanks in part to the publication of *Unsafe at Any Speed* and two other books on the subject—William Haddon et al., *Accident Research* and Jeffrey A. O'Connell and Arthur Myers, *Safety Last*—there was increasing pressure for automobile safety legislation, and by the end of 1965, three different congressional committees were investigating the problem, all of them bent on passing new legislation. More than half the state legislatures were also considering bills to require that the automobile companies produce safer cars. In his State of the Union address in January 1966, President Lyndon Johnson called attention to the auto safety problem and promised to propose a new highway safety law. In mid-February, he described "highway carnage" as a national problem second only to the Vietnam War, renewing his pledge that legislative action would seek an end to "this mounting tragedy." The urgency of the issue for politicians rested largely on the growing number of highway accidents, a decade-long trend, which in 1965 had resulted in 49,000 deaths (a new record) and more than 1,500,000 other injuries.[22]

With automobile safety now at the top of the national agenda, Nader swung into action, launching, according to Drew, "a one man-lobbying operation probably unprecedented in legislative history." From the lecture platform, in newspaper interviews, and in testimony before congressional committees, he called repeatedly for the rejection of half-measures and for the enactment of rigorous, mandatory safety standards to be enforced by federal officials and for criminal penalties for the auto executives responsible for producing cars that failed to meet the standards. With the automobile companies now claiming to be deeply interested in safety, Nader received page-one coverage when he accused Ford and General Motors of producing unsafe seat belts out of their "lust for profits." Nor did he spare foreign auto companies. He declared that Volkswagens had a tendency to instability that "made the driver's task harder" and even criticized the vaunted Rolls Royce, terming it "the most overrated of cars" and charging that its current model had defective door locks. When an auto manufacturer maintained that auto buyers should remain free to choose their own interior styles, Nader responded that his copy of the Constitution "nowhere asserts a civil liberty to go through the windshield."[23]

The Great Blunder of General Motors

Even more important than Nader's lobbying in persuading senators and congressmen to support auto safety legislation was the sudden, highly public revelation that General Motors had pried into the young lawyer's personal life in what amounted to an attempt to intimidate and silence him. Nader had first come to the attention of General Motors executives when they learned that a lawyer by that name was advising (though not representing) some of the Corvair owners who were suing their company. When an article by Nader criticizing the Corvair as an unsafe car was published in the liberal periodical *The Nation* in early October 1965, the company decided to have him investigated by a detective agency.

Their interest in Nader intensified after the publication of his book on the last day of November 1965. General Motors invited him to visit the General Motors Technical Center in Warren, Michigan, and Nader accepted the invitation. When he visited the facility in mid-January, a high-ranking General Motors executive repeatedly suggested that Nader take a job with the company. After they failed to co-opt him, General Motors officials engaged a second, more aggressive detective agency to dig up everything it could about him.

Aware that he was being followed, and alerted by friends who had been questioned about him by detectives, Nader gave an interview to the *New York Times,* published on March 6, 1966, in which he charged that private detectives in the employ of General Motors had been following and harassing him for weeks. He claimed that investigators had approached dozens of his acquaintances to ask whether he was homosexual, politically radical, or anti-Semitic. Finally, Nader accused the corporation's hirelings of harassing him with late-night telephone calls and of using attractive women as lures in an attempt to discredit him by involving him in scandal.[24]

At first the company's spokesmen dismissed Nader's charges as "absurd," but on March 9, General Motors released a statement admitting that it had initiated a "routine investigation" to determine whether Ralph Nader was acting on behalf of litigants or their attorneys in any of the more than 100 lawsuits then pending against the company by people injured in accidents while riding in Corvairs. All of these plaintiffs were claiming that the accidents in which they were injured were due to the car's faulty design. The company spokesmen denied, however, that the investigation had involved any harassment or intimidation of Nader. On the following day, Ribicoff announced on the Senate floor that his subcommittee would hold hearings on the Nader–General Motors matter on March 22. At that hearing, the president of General Motors, James M. Roche, confirmed that the company had hired the detectives, but insisted that it had been the company's legal department and not he that had authorized the investigation, and blamed whatever excesses that had occurred on the detectives. Acknowledging that there had "apparently been some harassment," he apologized to Nader for any pain or embarrassment that he might have been caused, but repeated the company's denial of telephone calls late at night and attempts at sexual entrapment by the hired detectives. Another witness at the hearing, Vincent Gillen, the head of the detective agency that had investigated Nader, admitted following the young attorney and asking his friends the prying questions to which Nader had alluded in his March 5 interview, but denied the rest of his charges.[25]

In his own testimony, Nader denounced General Motors' investigation of him as "an invasion of the self." He charged that spying on people's private lives was widespread in corporate America and was often used by powerful business firms to cow their critics into silence. Automobile industry employees, for example, were kept from criticizing the companies that employed them by the industry's "far-flung apparatus of private detectives and security agents." Moreover, existing law did not hold corporate executives responsible for the consequences of their decisions: "I am responsible for my actions, but who is responsible for those of General Motors. An individual's capital is basically his integrity. He can lose only once. A corporation can lose many times and not be affected." When asked why he was campaigning for safer cars, Nader noted with some irritation that nobody would ask him this if he was seeking to prevent cruelty to animals, but since he was "seeking to prevent cruelty to humans, my motivations are constantly inquired into."[26]

After the witnesses had been heard, Senators Ribicoff and Kennedy denounced General Motors and declared that Nader had been vindicated. "You and your family can be very proud," Ribicoff told him. "They [the detectives] have put you through the mill and they haven't found a damn thing wrong with you." The young lawyer was hailed in the press as the David who had bested the corporate Goliath and was compared with the hero of *Mr. Smith Goes to Washington,* a celebrated 1939 movie about a naive idealist who prevails over corrupt businessmen and venal politicians. Nader's confrontation with General Motors had instantly given him fame, credibility, and a heroic underdog image. His book became a best-seller and he was now well-positioned both to continue his crusade for safer automobiles and to campaign on other consumer issues as well. In revealing to the public that General Motors could be arrogant and had made use of dubious methods in defending its interests, the hearing had played into and accelerated the demand for regulation of the auto industry.[27]

The Passage of the Auto Safety Law

Nader also participated in the legislative struggle from behind the scenes. He and other advocates of regulation got in touch with Washington columnist Drew Pearson and gave him the names of those congressmen and senators who claimed to support their cause, but were secretly trying to weaken or even kill the legislation. In his widely read, nationally syndicated column, Pearson exposed the backsliders to the public. In similarly backdoor fashion, Nader had his ally, Senator Vance Hartke (D-IN), propose on the Senate floor nine amendments to the highway safety bill that were designed to toughen its demands upon the auto industry. Some of Nader's ideas, as modified by Hartke, were taken into account. But the Senate on June 24, 1966, by a vote of sixty-two to fourteen, rejected his most controversial proposal: that the automakers be subject to criminal penalties if they produced cars that fell short of the federal standards. On the same day, the Senate approved the bill itself by a final vote of seventy-six to zero.

Countering Nader's influence was Lloyd Cutler, a prominent Washington attorney and veteran lobbyist for some of the nation's largest corporations. Having acknowledged by the end of April that some form of regulation was inevitable, the automobile companies had hired Cutler to represent them in negotiations with the Commerce Committees of the Senate and House. In a scene Elizabeth Drew likened to "a Mack Sennett farce," Nader and Cutler sat in separate anterooms outside the chamber while the Senate's final version of the bill was being worked out. An aide would bring the latest revision either to Cutler, representing the companies, or to Nader, who was given the job of representing the public. When either of them approved a proposed change, it was shuttled at top speed to the adjoining anteroom for the perusal of the other.[28]

The House was considering its own version of automobile regulation, which was in some ways tougher on the industry than the Senate's bill. After Nader's proposal for criminal penalties was rejected, the House passed its bill on August 17 by the margin of 313 to zero. A conference committee then ironed out the differences between the Senate and House versions, and the bill's final version was sent on to President Johnson. He signed it on September 9 at a ceremony to which all who had figured prominently in the passage of the act were invited, including Ralph Nader.

Known as the National Traffic and Vehicle Safety Act, the new law required that the secretary of commerce devise safety standards for all motor vehicles to go into effect by January 31, 1968. To enforce the standards, the act created a National Traffic Safety Agency (NTSA), which was given the power to recall vehicles that it considered defective. The measure also provided that the states were to be encouraged to develop safety programs of their own. Although he already harbored doubts that the act's provisions were strong enough, Nader was quoted as saying, "President Johnson has launched the nation on a great life saving program."[29]

The new law's passage marked the first time that automobile transport had been subjected to federal regulation, and the news media gave Nader much of the credit for the act's passage. He had won, said a *Washington Post* editorial, "through his book . . . his determination and his seemingly limitless energy . . . a one-man lobby for the public prevailed over the nation's most powerful industry." A few weeks later, the Junior Chamber of Commerce voted Nader one of the "ten outstanding young men" for 1966.[30]

To Nader, however, the passage of a new law did not, in and of itself, constitute meaningful reform. Genuine reform, he has often pointed out, is actually a three-step process: the exposure of a problem to public view, the enactment of a new law, and finally, its implementation. With the enactment of the traffic safety law, Nader, the aggressive activist, assumed the role of a watchdog and critic of the NTSA*, the regulatory agency created by the new law. As early as January 1967, he accused the new body and its chief, William Haddon, of "considerably weakening" its regulations and charged that the agency had already developed "a protective attitude" toward the automobile industry, Nader may simply have been trying to prod the Bureau in the direction of stricter standards and more aggressive enforcement, but his criticisms seemed unfair and unduly suspicious to the administrators involved.[31]

Over the next three decades, Nader would remain active in promoting regulations designed to make automobiles safer and more "crashworthy." More than any other individual, he has been responsible for the universal adoption of compulsory seat belts, and also in winning widespread acceptance for air bags.[32]

Nader's Lawsuit Versus General Motors

In mid-November 1966, Nader had filed a lawsuit against General Motors, Detective Vincent Gillen, and Fidelifacts, Inc., a nationwide investigative firm from whom Gillen held a franchise for greater New York. Alleging harassment, intimidation, and the invasion of his privacy, Nader's lawsuit asked for $26,000,000 in compensatory and punitive damages. After pointing out that Gillen and General Motors had already admitted publicly to following him, keeping tabs on him, and prying aggressively into his personal life, Nader also repeated the allegations that the defendants would never admit to and which to this day have never been proved: that they had harassed him over the telephone late at night and employed women to accost him "for purposes of entrapment and extortion."

When Gillen was incautious enough to tell a reporter that he would refer Nader to a psychiatrist, Nader bought a second lawsuit against the detective for $100,000 for doing damage to his reputation. Faced suddenly with financial ruin, Gillen turned on his former client, presenting hard evidence in the form of written documents and tapes that he had been instructed by General Motors to ferret out something, anything, that could be used to discredit Nader, whom they viewed as a threat to their profits. Gillen produced a tape of a phone conversation between him and Richard Danner, a lawyer and former FBI agent who had been hired by General Motors specifically to act as a go-between in arranging for the investigation of Nader. "They [General Motors] want," said Danner on the tape, "to get something, somewhere, on this guy to get him out of their hair and to shut him up."[33]

---

*The name of the NTSA was changed in November 1966 to National Highway Safety Agency, and when absorbed by the new Department of Transportation in 1967, it was renamed the National Highway Safety Bureau.

Since it seemed likely that Nader would win the case once it came to trial, General Motors' lawyers repeatedly filed motions to postpone its being heard. After three years, Nader's lawsuit was still pending, and the end was not in sight. On the other hand, the corporation's top executives realized that the various delays and procedural moves were resulting in fresh headlines that could only do additional damage to the company's reputation. Since it seemed to be in the interests of both parties, an out-of-court settlement was arrived at in August 1970. Under its terms, General Motors paid to Nader the sum of $425,000, of which his share came to nearly $300,000, with the rest going to his attorney, Stuart Speiser. In an accompanying statement, the company insisted that it was not conceding that it had either invaded Nader's privacy or done anything else that had been charged in the lawsuit.[34]

Nader's Public Interest Crusades

During the three years that his lawsuit had been pending, Nader had fully established himself as a public interest lobbyist, a permanent defender of what he believed to be in the public interest and a foe of the arbitrary exercise of power by large institutions. No longer confining himself to a single issue, he spoke out on a number of problems, all of them relating in some way to "safety"—the right of people to go their way unharmed by the technological hazards that surround and threaten them. "A great problem of contemporary life," wrote Nader in *Unsafe at Any Speed,* "is how to control the power of economic interests which ignore the harmful effects of their applied science and technology [which amount to] man-made assaults on the human body." People injured by defective products, he has always insisted, have the right to generous compensation, and manufacturers are under an obligation, both moral and legal, to produce a safe commodity.*[35]

In his continual search for new problems and issues, Nader carefully studied the daily press, the *Federal Register,* and journals of medicine and engineering. He also obtained useful intelligence from "whistleblowers," disgruntled employees of private businesses or government agencies who, whether out of conscience or for other, less creditable reasons, secretly informed Nader of the mistakes and wrongdoing of the institutions that employed them.

He would then release the information about the budding scandal to his contacts in the media or would have one of his allies in Congress make a

---

*Nader has always opposed and lobbied against the idea of placing limits on either the monetary awards to plaintiffs in damage suits or the amount of money that can go to their attorneys. He has argued that "tort reform" of this and other kinds is simply a means devised by insurance companies, and by corporations generally, to protect their profits by restricting the rights of injured parties to seek redress in court.

speech about it. Accusations of wrongdoing and/or incompetence were, of course, news, and stories would appear soon afterward in the *New York Times,* the *Washington Post,* and other newspapers. Congressional committee hearings would follow at which Nader was often among the witnesses called. He would then write a muckraking article, based largely on the facts developed at the hearings, that would run in either or both the *New Republic* and *The Ladies' Home Journal.* Thus Nader was able to combine the roles of publicist and lobbyist. Not only did he lead in developing new issues, but he also played an important role in winning public support for proconsumer reforms.[36]

The end result was often new legislation. "In those days," Nader would later recall, "I could get through practically anything I wanted." In addition to the auto safety legislation, he was chiefly responsible for the following series of measures: the Wholesome Meat Act (1967), the Natural Gas Pipeline Safety Act (1968), the Wholesale Poultry Act (1968), the Radiation Control for Health and Safety Act (1969), and the Coalmine Health and Safety Act (1969). He figured significantly as well in getting Congress to create the Occupational Health and Safety Administration (OSHA) in 1970 and the Consumer Product Safety Commission in 1972. Nader also participated in successful battles to strengthen environmental laws and to widen the reach and utility of the Freedom of Information Act (1974).[37]

Perhaps the most remarkable of Nader's lobbying efforts was his role in bringing intrastate meatpacking, which had formerly been regulated only by the states, under federal supervision. Although this campaign, involving the plants that processed one-fourth of the nation's meat, was begun by others, notably by Nick Kotz, an investigative reporter for the *Des Moines Register,* Nader made contributions to it that were crucial to its success. Through the legwork of Kotz, he gained access to a secret report, compiled a few years earlier by the U.S. Department of Agriculture, that described conditions in the state-supervised meatpacking plants in every state, detailing numerous instances of extreme laxity and grotesquely bad sanitation. He released a summary of it to his friends in the press, who wrote articles that shocked their readers with accounts of conditions that seemed every bit as bad as those described in *The Jungle,* the famous muckraking novel by Upton Sinclair that had been instrumental in the passage of the Meat Inspection Act of 1906. Among other stomach-turning details, the secret report described how diseased, even cancerous carcasses were made into sausages and how rats and insects made themselves at home in the meatpacking plants.[38]

Aled Davies, the leading meat-industry lobbyist, credited Nader with having focused public opinion on the issue during the second half of 1967. First, Nader joined with other consumer advocates in stimulating and organizing a national campaign of letter writing to members of Congress. He then went on a ten-city speaking tour and at each stop contacted the local newspapers and urged them to give greater coverage to the meat inspection issue. Soon stories began appearing in midwestern cities about the shocking conditions in the

local slaughterhouse and meatpacking plants. Nader also popularized the issue by writing two muckraking articles for the *New Republic.* He was the star
witness at the hearings of the Senate Agriculture Committee chaired by Senator Walter Mondale (D-MN). He also helped to persuade three federal meat
inspectors to appear before the committee, where their testimony confirmed
the reality of the dreadful conditions in many of the state-regulated plants that
had been described in the press.

President Johnson had called in February 1967 for the extension of federal
standards of meat inspection to the states, but the White House and the Department of Agriculture at first favored keeping state compliance voluntary.
With public concern mounting, however, thanks at least in part to Nader, the
administration shifted its position to endorse the Mondale-Montoya bill, which
provided for mandatory compliance by the states with federal meat-inspec-
tion standards. The Wholesome Meat Act passed the Senate by a vote of 89 to 2
on December 6 and was approved by the House on the same day by a margin
of 336 to 28. The president signed the bill on December 15, and at the signing
ceremony, Nader met Upton Sinclair, probably the individual most responsible for the passage of the Meat Inspection Act in 1906. The novelist, who
was now eighty-nine, had been just twenty-eight when the earliest measure
was enacted. "I sort of felt," he would later recall, "that two historic consumer
ages were meeting—Upton Sinclair and I were together in the White House.
'Maybe this time,' I thought, 'the work will have some effect.'"[39]

Nader's favorable treatment by the press (and to a lesser degree, by television) was probably the most important single factor in his early success in his
public interest crusades. One reason for this was that Nader's activities made
good copy, for he would allege that the public was in great danger from some
hazard that no one else in the public eye was talking about, and he would
accuse corporation executives and public officials of wrongdoing. He always
had something new to say and furnished many in the press with contacts whom
they could interview and leads that they could look into. In addition, Nader's
language was vivid and the reporters found that his facts usually checked out.
Nader stories, observed Ben Bradlee, executive editor of the *Washington Post,*
were of great interest to politicians and "often had wonderful results."[40]

Part of Nader's appeal for both the press and the public rests on their per-
ception that he is fundamentally unselfish and concerned only with advancing
his aims. A key aspect of this appeal is his ascetic life style. Nader lived for
more than two decades in a one-room efficiency apartment in northwestern
Washington that he rented initially at $80 a month while sharing a single pay
phone with four other tenants. In 1968, *Newsweek* reported that Nader's social life consisted almost entirely of occasional dinners out with "issue-ori-
ented" friends, most of them journalists or congressional aides. Once, in Paris
during a lecture tour, he somehow found himself booked into a luxury hotel
suite, but he immediately exchanged it for a simple room. To this day, he owns

no car, uses no credit card, watches little television, and goes to no more than two movies a year.[41]

Nader's earnestness is also displayed in his approach to matters of health and diet. He has lectured friends about their need for exercise and will not visit a home where there are pets, which he regards as a potential source of dangerous infections. A smoker in college, he gave up tobacco in his twenties and in 1969 petitioned the Federal Aviation Agency to ban smoking from all interstate flights. Having warned the public repeatedly about the danger to its health from hot dogs ("fatfurters"), hamburgers ("shamburgers"), and Coca-Cola, three famous staples of the American way of life, he has for the past four decades consumed none of these widely loved products.

In his appearance, too, Nader, although tall and good-looking, has always looked like a man with no interest at all in either glamour or comfort. His dark suits often seem slightly too large for his thin body. "If Hollywood were casting the role of Ralph Nader," wrote Nader biographer Robert Buckhorn, "Ralph Nader would never get the job. Six foot four, sad eyed, shy and slightly stooped, Nader could easily pass for a small-town basketball coach . . . but a flamboyant crusader . . . a man who could humble the all-powerful General Motors? Never."[42]

So ascetic has been Nader's lifestyle that there seems to be little or no room in it for romance. Even his friends are said to be unsure whether he has ever dated or, if he has, whom. On being told that a young woman was interested in seeing him socially, Nader replied that it wouldn't be fair to date her since he would never consider marriage. He regards the career that he has chosen, that of a full-time "people's lawyer" or "professional citizen," to be too demanding on his time to permit him to function well in the dual role of husband and father.[43]

What has mattered most to Nader, obviously, is his work. Throughout his career, he has routinely labored for eighteen hours a day, allowed himself no more than a very occasional day off, and has rarely gone on vacation. For Nader, his work is his principal recreation. As he once told journalist Jack Newfield:

> I happen to like what I do very much. I actually find the act of staying up until dawn researching a memorandum pleasurable. It's just that I would rather work twenty hours a day on something that gives me real satisfaction than three hours a day on an alienating job that bores me. So I don't have to go to a discotheque at night to relax.[44]

In spite of his fame and the many publicized crusades and controversies in which he has been involved, Nader has always remained a highly private, even secretive man. During his early years in Washington, he kept his home address secret and gave out the number of the pay phone at his boarding house only to a handful of reporters and friends. When he granted an interview, he would meet the reporter at some out-of-the-way hotel or restaurant. People he has worked with, such as Mark Green, his longtime associate, and Daniel

Moynihan, have told of Nader's fears that the office phones might be tapped or the entire office bugged. One reason for his fear that enemies might be breaching his security was Nader's need to keep secret the identities of his numerous informants, many of whom were employed by the very government agencies and business corporations whose secrets they had been divulging to Nader. Apparently, he sees himself as engaged in a desperate struggle with the great corporations in which, Nader believes, it can be taken for granted that each side will, if it can, spy on the other.[45]

Nader's Message

Even while clinging to his privacy, Nader has made innumerable public statements over the years. In addition to his frequent appearances before congressional committees, he has also been in great demand as a lecturer. In the early 1970s when his influence was at its peak, he was delivering 150 lectures per year. He spoke at that time before trade and professional associations and civic groups, but found his most frequent and receptive audiences on college campuses. On some days he would visit as many as four different colleges. At each stop, he would speak for over two hours, largely without notes, and would invariably end the session by answering questions from the audience for at least a half hour afterward.[46]

In speeches, articles, and numerous books, Nader has argued that there is a constantly growing need to hold big business and big government, the nation's two largest concentrations of power, accountable for their acts. His second major theme is that such accountability can be fully achieved only if growing numbers of rank-and-file Americans take an interest in public affairs and become organized both as consumers and citizens. They would thus create a new constituency, "a countervailing force," that would put pressure upon politicians and bureaucrats to act in the public interest.

Nader urges his audiences to be active and aggressive both as consumers and as citizens. "With freedom goes duty," he states; "otherwise it's just license." He tries to convince them that being a "professional citizen" could actually be fun by recounting tales of his own audacious confrontations with authority. He insists that citizens can challenge even the most powerful institutions and, if smart enough and determined enough, make things happen. James Fallows, a former associate, has observed of Nader that "his mission in life is to get people active on the assumption that if they are passive, everything else will be bad because unchecked power will be abused."[47]

According to Nader, most of what is wrong with modern America is due to the power and greed of corporate enterprise. He believes that the quality of life in America has been undermined by a long series of evils, every one of them caused by the operations of Big Business. In his public statements and writing over the years, he has blamed the major corporations for air and water pollution, for the "trauma" on our highways, and for what he regards as too slow a pace in the development of new technologies. He accuses the great companies of overcharging, misleading, and manipulating the consumer and, in general, using their dominant position within the economy to sell their goods on a "take it or leave it" basis.

Nader also blames the corporations for much of the violence in American life. In addition to the immediate violence of industrial accidents and explosions (many of which he believes to be avoidable if the firms involved would take proper precautions), there is the long-range violence of air and water pollution, which, in Nader's view, has been caused primarily by the neglectful, shortsighted policies of industrial companies. He accuses General Motors, for example, of preferring to maximize its profits rather than correct its defective products. "Industry," he once wrote, "infiltrates the bodies of millions of people with its contaminants. Its violence is all-pervasive, whatever its various motivations may be."[48]

Nader believes that businessmen who defraud consumers or put them unnecessarily at risk are criminals who belong in jail. He has frequently complained that street crime is punished far more severely than business crime, even though, in his opinion, the latter is by far the more destructive of the two: "If there are criminal penalties for the poor and deprived when they break the law, then there must be criminal penalties for the automobile [and other] companies when their executives knowingly violate [or even fail to implement] standards designed to protect citizens from injuries and systematic fraud." He remains convinced that such wrongdoing by business is widespread and commonplace. "Scratch the image of any industry," Nader has written, "and unsavory practices become visible."[49]

Nader contends that our economy is so thoroughly dominated by large corporations that it is no longer capitalistic, but actually a system of "corporate socialism." The most powerful of the corporations operate in controlled markets and exercise virtually unchecked power. They are also, he claims, favored by government at all levels, which grants tax breaks and subsidies to major firms and allows them to acquire valuable resources at bargain prices. Should a corporate giant, due to its own mismanagement, be threatened with bankruptcy, the federal government can be relied upon to bail it out. Worst of all, according to Nader, is the ability of the corporate giants in our "seller-sovereign" system to pass along to consumers many of the costs resulting from their operations. These include high prices, shoddy goods, and the damage to the environment and to people's health that is being done every day by air and water pollution.[50]

According to Nader, there either is, or can be, a technological answer to virtually any problem. In the tradition of Louis Brandeis, he thinks that small enterprises innovate more than large ones. He also believes that large firms have often used their market power and political influence to obstruct the use of new technologies. "We can build a car that won't pollute the air," said Nader in 1967. "The question is whether we can overcome the resistance of the auto industry and the oil industry to get it built."[51]

Nader has advocated three different strategies for the curbing of corporate power. First, he has called on the federal government to strengthen competition by blocking mergers and vigorously enforcing the antitrust laws. Second, although he has long been a critic of the federal regulatory commissions, Nader has also advocated that new regulatory bodies be created in order to curb pollution and protect the consumer. To facilitate regulation, he has endorsed the proposal of Mark Green that the federal government charter the most powerful of the corporations. Finally, Nader has also promoted the idea that consumers should organize cooperatives in order to gain better terms from public utilities, insurance companies, and other large-scale firms. "If one way fails," said Nader in 1972, "we'll try another and keep trying until the job is done."[52]

Observers of Nader have often wondered what his ultimate goal is. Early in his career, he said that his objective was "nothing less than the qualitative reform of the Industrial Revolution." Whether he believes in capitalism and simply wants to make it work more justly or is in fact a socialist of some kind remains a much-disputed issue. While some of his statements over the years suggest the former view, other of his comments can be cited that point to the latter. Nader does on occasion state that he believes in capitalism *but* he also wants to break up existing concentrations of power, to empower workers and consumers, and to somehow persuade average Americans to completely transform their whole approach to life.[53]

Nader's Raiders

By the end of the 1960s, Nader had fully arrived as a public figure. Certainly, his idealistic principles and his evident willingness to live by them fit in well with the spirit of that reformist decade. In January 1968, a cover story in *Newsweek* called him "the Consumer Crusader" and depicted him as the very symbol of the consumer's movement. In the following year, the *New Republic* selected him as the first recipient of its Public Defender award. Eager to participate in a Ralph Nader crusade, thousands of college and law school students were sending him their résumés. A few would-be volunteers somehow obtained his address and turned up at Nader's door, bent on doing something to make the country healthier and more honest.[54]

In the summer of 1968, Nader's career entered a new phase when he recruited seven unpaid volunteers to assist him in investigating the Federal Trade Commission (FTC), a federal regulatory agency that is supposed to insure that businesses compete fairly and that consumers are not deceived or cheated. Of the volunteers, six men and one woman, all had attended the law schools of either Harvard or Yale, and all were in their twenties. Three were in their first year of law practice while the others were still students. Labeled "Nader's

Raiders" by a *Washington Post* reporter, the seven volunteers spent the summer months at the headquarters of the FTC in Washington, interviewing its officials and examining its files.

The Nader Report on the Federal Trade Commission, which was written by three of the Raiders, was published in book form in January 1969. It charged that the FTC had failed to protect consumers and that, instead of regulating the corporations, the commissioners had often collaborated with them. The authors of the report also claimed that alcoholism, indolence, absenteeism, and a lack of commitment to their regulatory mission were widespread among the FTC's employees. The newspaper accounts of the report led President Richard Nixon to ask the American Bar Association to look into the charges. When the bar association's inquiry largely confirmed the findings of the *Nader Report,* the president appointed Casper Weinberger to head the FTC, and he proceeded to reorganize the agency so that it now became far more active and aggressive in its oversight of business firms.[55]

In May 1969, Nader founded the Center for the Study of Responsive Law. Located in Washington, D.C., the center was established as a sort of think tank at which lawyers could confer with other professionals with the purpose of making the legal system more responsive to the interests of ordinary citizens. In addition to a few permanent staff members, the center became the base of operations for the dozens of student interns (his Raiders) employed by Nader each summer to work on special projects. "Now," wrote journalist Jack Newfield, "the Lone Ranger has a posse."[56]

Most of the interns were law students, but some were from medical and engineering schools. Although they were paid no more than $300 a month, there were more than fifteen applicants for every opening. Most of those finally selected were studying at elite institutions, many of them at Ivy League schools. At the center, they were divided into teams, each of which would study a particular topic in depth and would then write a report that in most cases was published soon afterward in book form. Each of these works was intended to be a muckraking exposé that would lay the groundwork for reform by revealing the abuses and failings of both business and government. Among the subjects covered were environmental pollution, industrial hazards, property tax abuses, nursing home abuses, antitrust laxity, the monopolistic control of land and water, and the United States Congress.[57]

Some of the Raiders' books were well received, and some contributed to the enactment of new reforms. Others were considered superficial and biased by reviewers or were unable to arrive at any definite prescription for the problems that they dealt with. Nader was accused in some quarters of taking credit for the work of others since each of the published studies was labeled as "the Nader Report" on its subject. One of his critics, banker Walter Wriston, charged that Nader, in associating himself with the work of novice authors of whose accuracy he could not really be sure, had franchised his name as though he were "a fried chicken stand."[58]

Of all the studies sponsored by the center, the most ambitious by far was the Ralph Nader Congress Project. Nader had decided on the project when he discovered that several of the laws that he had proposed and fought for, although passed in both houses of Congress by overwhelming majorities, were being nullified by meager appropriations and halfhearted enforcement. When he announced the Congress Project in 1971, Nader accused the legislators of deceiving the public by passing measures that pretended to solve major problems, but often amounted to little more than empty gestures. Congress, he declared, has "become a surrogate for special interests and has passed out of the control of the people. . . . Many of its most important operations—from campaign financing to committee deliberations—have been and still are kept from public scrutiny." By revealing to the voting public how Congress writes the laws and sets policy, Nader hoped to recall the institution to its democratic mission.[59]

So ambitious was the project that Nader, who was its sole source of funds, felt obliged to deliver additional lectures in order to meet its bills. A detailed questionnaire was sent to every member of Congress. More than a thousand volunteer researchers were employed, descending in ones or twos on the district or state, respectively, of each representative and senator, except for those who were retiring. They conducted interviews with each legislator's constituents and did other basic research on his or her life and career. The material that they gathered was given to student interns at the center, who would make use of it in preparing profiles (each from twenty to forty pages long) of 484 incumbent senators and representatives. The project also included plans for thirteen book-length studies of congressional committees and eleven additional volumes on specialized topics, such as the role of seniority in Congress and the methods employed by congressmen in raising funds.

Although Nader spent $400,000 on the project, all of it money that he had earned himself, in the end it proved only a limited success. The questionnaire, consisting of 633 questions, antagonized many legislators who simply refused to fill it out. The profiles were published in nine volumes, in time for the November 1972 elections. But few incumbents were defeated, and subsequent opinion polls showed that most voters continued to think well of their own congressmen while despising Congress as an institution. Moreover, the project had severely weakened Nader's ties both to Congress and to the press. Many congressmen and senators thought it unfair that their careers should be critically written about while those of their opponents were not. To the Washington press corps, Nader and his followers seemed to be poaching on their preserve, since Congress was already well-covered by the press.[60]

The Nader Network

In July 1970, Nader, using funds from his General Motors settlement, had established his own "public interest law firm" in Washington, D.C. Intended to serve as "the action arm" of Nader's movement, the Public Interest Research Group (PIRG) had at its founding a total of fourteen members: ten recent law graduates, three experienced attorneys, and one law professor on sabbatical leave. Although the members of PIRG were drawn from the top-ranked graduates of the nation's best law schools, they were paid salaries of just $4,500 a year. Unlike conventional law firms, PIRG did not have specific clients, but filed petitions and sued corporations and government agencies on behalf of whatever Nader and his followers regarded as in "the public interest." To cite one notable example, two PIRG attorneys joined forces with local activists in organizing opposition in West Virginia towns to the pollution of the local air by three chemical plants owned and managed by Union Carbide. Like others who practice "public interest law," Nader believes that what is needed is not so much the passage of new legislation as the enforcement of laws that already exist. "I am trying to tell people that if they can just organize to make the establishment obey its own rules, they will have created a peaceful revolution of tremendous proportions."[61]

Nader was also taking steps to set up student and citizen organizations to lobby at the local level for environmental regulation and consumerist reform. By the end of 1972, his organizers could report that there were Public Interest Research Groups on 138 college campuses with a total membership of 400,000. The Student PIRGs and the Nader-inspired citizen groups both employed lawyers, economists, and other professionals as sources of expert advice and also as spokespeople for their positions.

On the college campuses, the PIRGs have been funded through a check-off system in which the university, once a majority of students has voted to approve the plan, adds three dollars to tuition and then transfers the proceeds to public service groups on campus. The adoption of this plan by dozens of colleges across the country has increased Nader's influence among college students and permitted the training of hundreds of undergraduates in the basic techniques of public advocacy. In addition, student dollars have been used to provide employment to dozens of "public interest lawyers" and other trained professionals who advise the student PIRGs on how to deal with local issues and problems. As a result, Nader-style consumerism has gained and kept a foothold in dozens of communities.[62]

Public Citizen

In 1971, Nader founded Public Citizen, Inc., a nonprofit lobbying organization that has over the years both watched over and raised funds for a diverse array of public service organizations. While drawing some of its funds from philanthropic foundations, it was the first of Nader's institutions to raise money directly from the general public, making use of both newspaper advertisements and direct-mail solicitation. Within a year of its founding, Public Citizen had 62,000 members and raised over a million dollars. By 1998, the organization described itself as having the support of 150,000 people in its ongoing "fight for safer drugs and medical devices, cleaner and safer energy, a cleaner environment, fair trade, and a more open and democratic society."[63]

In 1971, Nader established the Litigation Group, another of his public interest law firms, but placed this time under the Public Citizen umbrella. Its stated objective was and is to bring both government agencies and private parties into compliance with the law. Unlike PIRG, the new firm de-emphasized research and social action in favor of public interest litigation and the provision of legal advice and counseling to Nader-affiliated organizations. To head the new firm, Nader hired Arthur Morrison, a Harvard Law alumnus and an experienced litigator. The Litigation Group would over the years bring numerous class action suits on behalf of consumers. By the end of the year 2000, it had also pleaded more than forty cases before the United States Supreme Court, winning over 60 percent of them.[64]

Over the years, Nader has founded, organized, and raised money for an ever widening array of consumer and citizen organizations. These include the Health Research Group (1971), Congress Watch (1973), Critical Mass Energy Project (1974), and many others too numerous to mention. By 1985, the number of groups he had founded totaled twenty-four, and he is constantly establishing new ones. He has described himself as a "Johnny Appleseed" of the consumer and citizen movements, seeing it as his role to get new groups started, but insisting that each organization learn to function on its own without relying on him or any other outsider.[65]

In order to finance the groups that he has either founded or helped found, Nader has raised hundreds of thousands of dollars each year. His own earnings as lecturer and writer, which for the past three decades have averaged a quarter of a million dollars per year, have permitted him to finance some of the groups himself. He has also proven adept at attracting grants from liberal foundations (usually the smaller ones) and has gleaned contributions from labor unions and individuals, including a few sympathetic business leaders. The dues collected annually by Public Citizen from its members, amounting roughly to $1 million per year, and the fees collected from college students by the campus-based PIRGs have also helped to pay for the activities of people employed by Nader-connected groups.[66]

Those who have worked for Nader over the years have unanimously found him to be a tough taskmaster. Accustomed to working eighteen-hour days, seven days a week, he has never seen why his colleagues and underlings cannot do the same. Nader's thrift and hatred of waste have contributed to his payment of low salaries to his full-time coworkers, and he complains loudly if more was spent on a project than he expected. Some of his employees say that they were made to feel guilty if they went to a movie or took a weekend off. "When you get to feeling you have to take a day off every week," remarked one former aide, "you shouldn't work for Ralph anymore."[67]

Nader's Decline

By the early 1970s Nader was coming under increasing attack and, since then, the number and intensity of his critics have continually grown. His bitter invective and angry accusations against corporations and their executives drew the fire of many business leaders and political conservatives who accused him of seeking the destruction of the free enterprise system. Even some of his former allies have criticized Nader, accusing him of hypocrisy in demanding openness from government and industry while practicing secrecy in his own activities, and in denouncing bureaucracy while building an institutional framework of his own that is so elaborate and diverse that some writers have described it as a conglomerate and others as an empire.[68]

By the mid-1970s, Nader's romance with the press had cooled and his influence with the United States Congress was also declining. With various consumer protection measures already in effect, his issues no longer seemed either as urgent or as popular as in the recent past. Representatives and senators were also irritated by Nader's unwillingness to compromise and by his readiness to attack them ferociously whenever they deviated even slightly from his ideas. Toward the decade's end, several popular magazines reported Nader's influence to be on the wane. When the crusading activist asked to be booked as a guest on *Tomorrow,* a late-night television show broadcast every weeknight by NBC, Tom Snyder, the show's host, turned him down. "Nader," said Snyder, "is yesterday's news."[69]

Since the consumer movement has never included in its ranks more than a tiny fraction of the American people, its legislative victories have depended upon a favorable political climate. By the late 1970s the climate had changed, and very few of the proposals of Nader and other consumer advocates were being enacted. Part of the reason for the growing resistance to federal regulation was the vigorous counterattack by business against the environmental and consumer movements. While there were only 71 full-time corporate lobbyists in Washington as of 1970, there were 4,000 eight years later. In addition, business firms set up hundreds of political action committees. Some companies also financed conservative think tanks to defend the good name of big business while criticizing activists such as Nader and the regulatory programs of the federal government.[70]

The declining influence of both Nader and of the consumer movement in general was dramatically demonstrated by the rejection of his proposal for a consumer protection agency, a new department with the sole mission of reviewing the conduct of all federal agencies on consumer issues. Nader, who had first proposed such an agency in 1970, campaigned vigorously for it at each new session of Congress, only to see it fail in the end. On February 8, 1978, the House of Representatives voted on his idea for the last time, when it was defeated by a margin of 227 to 189. Although the measure was backed both by President Jimmy Carter and by the Democratic leadership of the House, 101 Democrats voted "No." Some of the defecting Democrats said they had voted against the bill because they were angry with Nader, who had put them under pressure by attacking them in their home districts.[71]

Paradoxically, Nader saw his influence with Congress decline rapidly during the presidency of Jimmy Carter, a man whom he had once viewed as an ally and had spoken of warmly during the presidential campaign of 1976. He had visited Carter at the latter's home in Plains, Georgia, and the two men had immediately hit it off. After becoming president, Carter appointed more than twenty environmental and consumer activists to office, several of them Nader loyalists, including Michael Pertschuk, who was chosen to head the FTC, and Joan Claybrook, who became the National Highway Traffic Safety Administrator. These former activists soon learned that it is far more difficult to bring about change from within government than to criticize it from the outside. Dissatisfied with their performance, Nader denounced these old allies as though they were the enemy. He even called on Claybrook to resign, but she refused, informing an interviewer from *People* magazine that she still considered Nader a friend because they were still on the same side. As for Carter, Nader scoffed at him as "a sheep in wolf's clothing," denounced him as "a betrayer of the consumer," and when he ran for reelection in 1980 refused to endorse either him or Ronald Reagan, his Republican opponent.[72]

The national political climate became even less hospitable for Nader-style activism with the election in 1980 of Reagan to the presidency. Reagan, a convinced free-market conservative, was committed to reducing the role of government in people's lives and in particular to cutting sharply the regulation of business by the federal government. Nader found that the policies he believed in were no longer popular and that the press had moved on to other issues. Nader quipped that a consumer activist, lobbying in Washington in the Reagan era, was equivalent to the golfer who was told that the course he must now play on was in the Amazon jungle.

In the 1980s, the enforcement of consumer and environmental regulations was weakened and some of the old rules were simply abandoned. Nader now had to struggle even to hold the ground that had been won in the past. According to Morton Mintz, a veteran *Washington Post* reporter who in previous years had often written about Nader, "there were simply no new consumer initiatives to report." Business lobbyists were more numerous and united than ever, while organized labor, which had often supported Nader's efforts, was itself declining both in the size of its membership and in its political influence. Poll results showed that a majority of the public still wanted to be protected from unsafe consumer products, but that to most Americans big government was now more suspect than big business.[73]

The conservative trend in national policy-making led Nader to place greater emphasis on organization at the local level. In October 1980 he resigned as president of Public Citizen, and at the organization's tenth anniversary gathering in 1981, he called on the assembled activists to help local citizen groups to gain control of publicly owned resources, such as the airwaves and the public lands. By 1985, Nader-connected activists were taking the lead in several cities in setting up Citizen Utility Boards (CUBs), private civic groups that monitor the performance of local utility companies. Another of Nader's grassroots ventures in the 1980s was Buyers Up, a cooperative purchasing organization through which local groups of small business owners join forces with homeowners in order to wrest lower prices from the suppliers of heating oil.[74]

Nader's public activism was obstructed during 1986 by setbacks that he suffered in his personal life. Early in the year, he was afflicted with Bell's palsy, a condition that paralyzes the facial nerve, which for a time distorted the left side of his face, making it appear as though he had suffered a stroke. In October, his brother, Shafeek, died of prostate cancer, and Nader, who has always been close to the family, took the news hard. He moved in with his parents and withdrew from all his public activities for three months.[75]

Nader's Resurgence

After this hiatus, his morale restored, Nader returned to the wars. In Winsted, he had found another cause worth fighting for. Joining forces with his sister Claire, he opposed the plan of the local school board to close the Mary P. Hinsdale elementary school that all four of the Nader children had once attended, and replace it with a larger and more modern building. Ralph characterized his former school as "an old friend, a part of one's community roots." He and his sister Claire tried to rally the voters against the proposed new building, arguing that it would be cheaper to alter and improve the old school, but to no avail. Their proposal was rejected twice by the voters. Ralph was bitter in defeat, describing the demolition of the old schoolhouse as "a loss to ignorance, stubbornness, and political ego-tripping." In reply, the town's mayor observed: "people are getting quite fed up with the Naders telling them how to live."[76]

In 1988, Nader played a leading role in a controversial referendum in California in which several citizen initiatives were on the ballot, all of them dealing with the problem of the rapid rise in the cost of automobile insurance and other kinds of property and casualty insurance. Nader went on a two-week speaking tour of the state in support of Proposition 103, an initiative requiring the state's insurance companies to reduce their premiums on all their automobile, property, and casualty policies by at least 20 percent. This measure was of course opposed by the insurers, who gave their backing to two relatively moderate proposals and spent $43 million in trying to sway the voters to support their position. In the event, the Nader-backed proposal won, albeit by a narrow margin, even though the companies had outspent their various opponents by more than two to one.[77]

Nader's resurgence continued in the early months of 1989 when he played a conspicuous role in getting Congress to reject a proposed salary increase of 51 percent for its own members as well as other high officials of the federal government. Nader became the most noticeable and effective opponent of what he termed "the Salary Grab Act" by going on every radio and television talk show that would put him on the air. "Armed with his telephone," remarked *Wall Street Journal* reporter David Rogers, "Mr. Nader can reach radio talk show audiences from Massachusetts to Florida to Texas in a single afternoon." Researchers in Nader's employ, pointing to the travel and other "perks" and privileges enjoyed by members of Congress, questioned whether they really deserved a raise in pay. When it became clear that an overwhelming majority of the public opposed the pay raise, the House of Representatives rejected it by a margin of 380 to 48. Many members of Congress felt that they had no choice but to vote "No"—if they wanted to keep their jobs, and several of them expressed bitterness and anger about Nader's role in blocking the measure.[78]

In the 1990s, Nader's growing concern over the size and power of multinational corporations caused him to oppose both the principle of "free trade" and to such international arrangements as the General Agreement on Tariffs and Trade (GATT) and the North American Free Trade Agreement (NAFTA). On these issues, Nader's stance made him the ally of political nonconformists, such as H. Ross Perot, the billionaire entrepreneur from Texas, who has twice run for president, and Patrick Buchanan, the conservative commentator who has also been a third-party presidential candidate.

An increasingly globalized economy, Nader predicted, would result in huge profits for multinational firms but would do harm to blue-collar workers, family farmers, and to the owners of small businesses. Another important reason for his opposition to GATT and NAFTA was Nader's belief that the globalization of commerce and industry was likely to undermine not only the wages of American workers, but also the consumer and environmental laws that he had worked so long and hard to promote. "What's really at work," he wrote, "in all of these agreements is the yearning by multinational firms to break free from the constraints of national sovereignty." Where the business is worldwide but government is not, the result, he warned, must be to make business "accountable to no one and nothing outside of itself."[79]

To Nader's dismay, President Bill Clinton, although a Democrat, proved as much, or perhaps even more, of a supporter of international trade agreements as his Republican predecessors. Nader referred mockingly to the president who had moved his once aggressively liberal party toward the center as "George Ronald Clinton," "the bully coward in the bully pulpit," and as "the ultimate Democratic-Republican hybrid." The two major parties, complained Nader, were both "indentured to big business," and as a result, the voters were denied all meaningful choice. Here again, he blamed the corporations, accusing them of undermining and corrupting the system by delivering, via their political action committees, campaign contributions to both major parties that were so large that they amounted really to "legalized bribery." He charged that "big business has been on a collision course with American democracy, and American democracy has been losing."[80]

To protest the conservative trend in American politics, Nader campaigned in February 1992 as a write-in candidate in the presidential primaries of both parties in New Hampshire. He issued a manifesto calling for the empowerment of the people, a sharp reduction in military spending, and the adoption by the nation of a government-run "single-payer" system of universal health care, such as existed in Canada. Again deploring the lack of meaningful political choice, Nader declared himself "the none of the above candidate" and proposed that there be an official none-of-the-above option on electoral ballots.[81]

Four years later, the Green Party, an organization that describes itself as "an environmental, anti-nuclear and social justice movement," nominated Nader for the presidency. He was an unusual candidate, refusing either to join the party that had nominated him or to endorse its platform. "I don't believe in belonging to a party," he said, "because I am a citizen advocate first and foremost." He rejected all campaign contributions and spent less than $5,000 of his own money on the campaign. Nader was on the ballot in twenty states, but received barely 1 percent of the total presidential vote.[82]

In the year 2000 Nader was again nominated by the Greens, but campaigned far more seriously and actively than in his previous runs.* Hoping to be on the ballot in every state, he hired twenty-five full-time organizers. Nader's agenda in the campaign was essentially a recycling of his favorite concepts. He again called for an end to "corporate welfare," the tax breaks and subsidies that, according to Nader, allowed big companies to "privatize profits and socialize risks." He echoed the complaint of many parents that there was too much sex and violence in television programming, recorded music, and Hollywood films, and blamed the major media corporations. His wariness of foreign trade was another theme of Nader's campaign, and in April, he addressed a crowd of protesters in Washington, D.C., many of them union members, that shared Nader's misgivings over the increasing globalization of the American economy.[83]

---

*In June, Nader filed the official statement of wealth and earnings, which is required by federal law of all candidates for national office who are raising and spending significant amounts of money. It revealed that he was worth $4 million, much of it invested in technology stocks, causing not a few lifted eyebrows among political observers. It was pointed out that although Nader was a critic of corporations in general and was at best ambivalent about new technologies, he was not averse to investing in the stock of companies at the cutting edge of technological change. In his own defense, Nader maintained that he still devoted more than 80 percent of his earnings to his organizations and social movements and challenged critics to find any other candidate for office who gave away that much of his income.

It was obvious to all, of course, that Nader had no chance of winning the election. His goal was to win at least 5 percent of the vote, the minimum necessary for the Green Party to be partially reimbursed by the Federal Election Commission for the costs of its campaign. Moreover, in drawing votes away from their presidential candidate, Nader was seeking to compel the Democrats to move further to the left. He denied that he was a "spoiler," remarking, "You can't spoil a spoiled system."[84]

On Election Day, Nader received slightly more than 2.6 million votes, less than 3 percent of the national total, but he seems nevertheless to have decided the outcome. The presidential election of 2000 was one of the closest of all time. In the popular vote, Vice President Albert Gore, the Democratic candidate, received roughly 500,000 votes more than his Republican opponent, George W. Bush, the governor of Texas, but Bush managed to carry enough states to garner 271 electoral votes, one more than the minimum needed to win the presidency. Had Gore won just one more state, he rather than Bush would have become the next president.

In the end, the election was decided in the state of Florida, where the race was so close that the nation was uncertain for more than a month which of the two candidates would be its next president. Nader received more than 90,000 votes in the state, half of which, opinion polls indicated, would have gone to Gore had Nader not been on the ballot. In the wake of Gore's narrow defeat, many liberals and Democrats were bitterly angry with Nader and vowed that they would have nothing to do with him in the future. "He's dead politically," said Garry Sellers, once one of Nader's Raiders. "People won't return his phone calls. He's alienated his closest friends." Nader remained unrepentant, however, insisting that Gore had lost due to his lackluster campaign and a stance on the issues that made him indistinguishable from Bush. "The Democrats," Nader warned, "must find their progressive roots or see their party wither away."[85]

The Ideals of Ralph Nader

Although obviously an ambitious man and highly successful as a writer and lecturer, Nader has always preached, and always lived by, his concept of the public citizen—a person who devotes a high proportion of his time and energy to working for the "public good." While eager to exercise power, Nader has never seriously aspired to public office, instead working tirelessly for such lofty public purposes as safe products, the curbing of corporate power, and a clean environment. In pursuit of these goals, he has inspired and taken the lead in organizing an impressive network of locally based citizen groups that have attempted to bring people together so that they can jointly deal with their economic and political problems. Nader has often said that the point that he is striving to make is "that individuals still count." As he put it, "there remains a very critical role for citizen action and the development of citizenship that will improve the quality of life in this country."[86]

Nader also sees himself as a "people's lawyer"—an attorney who does not want paying clients but seeks to shield the powerless from the oppressive or harmful actions of corporations and other large institutions. "Lawyers," he has said, "should represent systems of justice." Nader has criticized the lawyers who defend the great corporations as "high priced prostitutes" and as "men whose agility of mind is matched only by their viscosity of conscience." He has done as much perhaps as anyone to promote "public interest law" and has attracted many young lawyers to this specialty, inspiring them, at least for a time, to serve their consciences rather than their pocketbooks.[87]

Although he remains a controversial figure, few would deny that Nader is the most extraordinary advocate for the consumer in all of American history. Throughout his long career, he has exposed and fought the business practices that, he believes, cheat consumers, as well as the production and sale of commodities that in his view are unsafe. He has had a major impact on public policy, helping to win passage for dozens of laws, most of them in the areas of consumer rights, product safety, and environmental protection. Most of all, Nader has constantly preached and tirelessly put into practice his own gospel of "public citizenship," urging people to join forces in demanding accountability from business, government, and established institutions generally. He has personally conceived the ideas for, and taken the lead in creating, as many as fifty different consumer and citizen organizations, many of which have been functioning for decades. In a nation in which materialism and self-seeking are commonly the norm, Ralph Nader has been and remains a combative idealist who refuses to accept social injustice or to make peace with the status quo.

Notes

1. This incident is more fully discussed on pages 423 to 425 of this chapter.

2. Patrick Anderson, "Ralph Nader, Crusader; or The Rise of a Self-Appointed Lobbyist," *New York Times Magazine,* October 29, 1967, 111; David Bollier, *Citizen Action and Other Big Ideas: A History of Ralph Nader and the Modern Consumer Movement* (Washington, DC: Public Citizen, 1991), Chapter 1, 1; Charles McCarry, *Citizen Nader* (New York: Saturday Review Press, 1972), 30–31; Robert F. Buckhorn, *Nader: The People's Lawyer* (Englewood Cliffs, NJ: Prentice Hall, 1972), 39.

3. The quotation of Nathra Nader is in McCarry, *Citizen Nader,* 31; Hays Gorey, *Nader and the Power of Everyman* (New York: Grosset and Dunlap, 1975), 183; Buckhorn, *Nader,* 39–40; "Nathra Nader Is Dead; Restaurateur Was 98," *New York Times,* July 9, 1991, D19.

4. Quote is in McCarry, *Citizen Nader,* 37; Mark Litwak, *Courtroom Crusaders* (New York: Morrow, 1989), 222–225; Gorey, *Nader and the Power of Everyman,* 156–157, 175–176, 186; Charlotte Libov, "A Consumer Activist Candidly Studies His Hometown," *New York Times,* August 21, 1988, Section 23, 2.

5. Ken Auletta, "Ralph Nader, Public Eye," *Esquire,* December 1983, 482; Gorey, *Nader and the Power of Everyman,* 165, 172–173; McCarry, *Citizen Nader,* 32, 37; Buckhorn, *Nader,* 40, 42.

6. The Nathra Nader quote is in McCarry, *Citizen Nader,* 37; Gorey, *Nader,* 170–171.

7. The Nathra Nader quote is in Buckhorn, *Nader,* 40; Litwak, *Courtroom Crusaders,* 225; Anderson, "Ralph Nader, Crusader," 111.

8. McCarry, *Citizens Nader,* 34–40; Buckhorn, *Nader,* 40.

9. McCarry, *Citizen Nader,* 41–46; Bollier, *Citizen Action,* Chapter 1, 1; Auletta, "Ralph Nader, Public Eye," 487; "Dante and Turrets and DDT," *New York Times,* March 3, 1996, Section 13, 9, Buckhorn, *Nader,* 45.

10. The "if you were worried" is in Bollier, *Citizen Action,* chapter 1, 2; the "high priced tool factory" statement is in Auletta, "Ralph Nader, Public Eye," 487; McCarry, *Citizen Nader,* 47–49.

11. Ted Jacobs's statement is quoted in Auletta, "Ralph Nader, Public Eye," 482; Nader's quotes are from McCarry, *Citizen Nader,* 50–52.

12. McCarry, *Citizen Nader,* 53–56; Buckhorn, *Nader,* 45.

13. Harold A. Katz, "Liability of Automobile Manufacturers for the Unsafe Design of Passenger Cars," *Harvard Law Review* 69 (1956): 863–73; Buckhorn, *Nader,* 6, 45; Ralph Nader, "The Safe Car You Can't Buy," *The Nation,* April 11, 1959, 310–313.

14. Auletta, "Ralph Nader, Public Eye," 483; Buckhorn, *Nader,* 35, 45; McCarry, *Citizen Nader,* 58.

15. Buckhorn, *Nader,* 46; McCarry, *Citizen Nader,* 58–64; Anderson, "Ralph Nader, Crusader," 112.

16. The Nader quote is in Anderson, "Ralph Nader, Crusader," 112; McCarry, *Citizen Nader,* 64; Elizabeth B. Drew, "The Politics of Auto Safety," *Atlantic Monthly,* October 1966, 98; Bollier, *Citizen Action,* Chapter 1, 1.

17. McCarry, *Citizen Nader,* 71–78; Anderson, "Ralph Nader, Crusader," 25, 112; Drew, "The Politics of Auto Safety," 98; Daniel Patrick Moynihan, "Epidemic on the Highways," *Reporter* 20 (April 30, 1959): 16–22; Nader, "The Safe Car You Can't Buy," 310–313.

18. The Sonosky quote is in McCarry, *Citizen Nader,* 18; Buckhorn, *Nader,* 6–8; Litwak, *Courtroom Crusaders,* 202–204.

19. Drew, "The Politics of Auto Safety," 99–100; McCarry, *Citizen Nader,* 82–83.

20. Ralph Nader, *Unsafe at Any Speed: The Designed-In Dangers of the American Automobile,* 2d ed. (New York: Grossman Publishers, 1972), 58–65, 90–100, 125–128, 228–232, 326–335.

21. Moynihan, "Epidemic on the Highways," 118–122; Nader, *Unsafe at Any Speed,* xci–xciii, 77–80; "Lawyer Charges Auto Safety Lag," *New York Times,* November 30, 1965, 68; Bollier, *Citizen Action,* Chapter 1, 2–3.

22. William Haddon et al., *Accident Research: Methods and Approaches* (New York: Harper and Row, 1964); Jeffrey A. O'Connell and Arthur Myers, *Safety Last: An Indictment of the Auto Industry* (New York: Random House, 1966); "Steps to Curb Highway Death," *New York Times,* February 13, 1966, Section 4, 2; Drew, "The Politics of Auto Safety," 95, 98; "Auto Safety Goes Into High Gear," *Newsweek,* February 21, 1966, 77; "The Nader Caper," *Newsweek,* March 21, 1966, 77.

23. Drew, "The Politics of Auto Safety," 99–100; Auletta, "Ralph Nader, Public Eye," 482; John D. Morris, "Volkswagen Called Unsafe," *New York Times,* April 15, 1966, 20; John D. Morris, "Rolls Royce Latches Criticized by Nader," *New York Times,* May 5, 1966, 1; McCarry, *Citizen Nader,* 84.

24. Walter Rugaber, "Critic of Auto Industry's Safety Standards Says He Was Trailed and Harassed," *New York Times,* March 6, 1966, 94; Walter Rugaber, "G.M. Apologizes for Harassment of Critic," *New York Times,* March 23, 1966, 1, 32; Thomas Whiteside, *The Investigation of Ralph Nader: General Motors Versus One Determined Man* (New York: Pocket Books, 1972), 12–31; Buckhorn, *Nader,* 9–22; McCarry, *Citizen Nader,* 13–17.

25. Whiteside, *The Investigation of Ralph Nader,* 32–54, 71–92, 102–105 (the statement quoted is on page 103); McCarry, *Citizen Nader,* 19–28; Buckhorn, *Nader,* 22–32; Litwak, *Courtroom Crusaders,* 217–220; James Ridgeway and David Sanford, "The Nader Affair," *The New Republic,* February 18, 1967, 16–18; "Nader Again," *Newsweek,* February 27, 1967, 85–88.

26. "Testimony of Ralph Nader," as presented in Whiteside, *The Investigation of Ralph Nader,* 203–210 (the "integrity" quote is on page 206); Buckhorn, *Nader,* 31–32.

27. Ribicoff's statement is in Buckhorn, *Nader,* 33–34: Whiteside, *The Investigation of Ralph Nader,* 65–71; McCarry, *Citizen Nader,* 28–29.

28. Drew, "The Politics of Auto Safety," 200–202; McCarry, *Citizen Nader*, 85–86; John D. Morris, "Auto Safety Bill Voted by Senate," *New York Times*, June 25, 1966, 1.

29. Nader quoted in John D. Morris, "President Signs Car Safety Bills," *New York Times*, September 10, 1966, 1, 12; "House Approves Auto Safety Bill for 1968 Models and Used Cars," *New York Times*, August 18, 1966, 1.

30. The *Washington Post* editorial was quoted in Drew, "The Politics of Auto Safety," 202; "Jaycees Salute Vietnam Hero in Rating Top Ten Young Men," *New York Times*, January 9, 1967, 4.

31. McCarry, *Citizen Nader*, 86–106; Anderson, "Ralph Nader, Crusader," 25.

32. Bollier, *Citizen Action*, Chapter 5, 8–11.

33. Danner is quoted in Whiteside, *The Investigation of Ralph Nader*, 103; "Spartan Life: Invasion of Privacy Suit," *Newsweek*, November 28, 1966, 88; Douglas Robinson, "Nader Sues GM for $26 Million," *New York Times*, November 17, 1966, 35.

34. Buckhorn, *Nader*, 154–155; Craig R. Whitney, "GM Settles Nader Suit on Privacy for $425,000," *New York Times*, August 14, 1970, 1, 62.

35. Nader quote is from Nader, *Unsafe at Any Speed*, xci–xcii; Anderson, "Ralph Nader, Crusader," 25, 103; Ralph Nader, Introductory Remarks at conference The Future of Tort Litigation in California, Santa Clara College, March 11, 1989, *Santa Clara Law Review* 29 (1989): 516–525. See also Ralph Nader, "The Assault on Injured Victims' Rights," *Denver University Law Review* 64 (1988): 625–639, and Ralph Nader, "The Corporate Drive to Restrict Their Victims' Rights," *Gonzaga Law Review* 22 (1986/87): 15–29.

36. Mark V. Nadel, *The Politics of Consumer Protection* (Indianapolis: Bobbs-Merrill, 1971), 180–84; "Meet Ralph Nader," *Newsweek*, January 22, 1968, 65–67; Anderson, "Ralph, Nader, Crusader," 103–104, 111.

37. Nader quote is from interview by William Greider, published as "Ralph Nader," *Rolling Stone*, November 5–December 10, 1987, 116; Litwak, *Courtroom Crusaders*, 221; McCarry, *Citizen Nader*, 155.

38. McCarry, *Citizen Nader*, 321; Anderson, "Ralph Nader, Crusader," 106; Max Frankel, "Johnson Welcomes Upton Sinclair Back to White House," *New York Times*, December 16, 1967, 1; Ralph Nader, "We're Still in the Jungle," *New Republic*, July 15, 1967, 11–12; Ralph Nader, "Watch That Hamburger," *New Republic*, August 19, 1967, 15–16.

39. McCarry, *Citizen Nader*, 114–125; "Crusader Widens Range of His Ire," *Business Week*, January 25, 1969, 128–130.

40. Ben Bradlee quote is in Bollier, *Citizen Action*, Chapter 4, 9; "Meet Ralph Nader," 67; Anderson, "Ralph Nader, Crusader," 111; Wesley J. Smith, "Nobody's Nader," *Mother Jones*, July/August, 1996, 61–62; James Dao, "Nader Is Running Again, This Time With Feeling," *New York Times*, April 15, 2000, A1, A10.

41. Auletta, "Ralph Nader, Public Eye," 487; McCarry, *Citizen Nader*, 117, 133–134, 139; Buckhorn, *Nader*, 53.

42. Buckhorn, *Nader*, 35; Gorey, *Nader and the Power of Everyman*, 25–26; Thomas N. Whiteside, "A Countervailing Force, 1," *New Yorker*, October 8, 1973, 50–52.

43. Gorey, *Nader and the Power of Everyman*, 151; Anderson, "Ralph Nader, Crusader," 111; McCarry, *Citizen Nader*, 130.

44. Quoted in Jack Newfield, "Nader's Raiders: The Lone Ranger Gets a Posse," *Life*, October 3, 1969, 56A.

45. McCarry, *Citizen Nader*, 74, 127; Anderson, "Ralph Nader, Crusader," 25; Nadel, *The Politics of Consumer Protection*, 180.

46. Whiteside, "A Countervailing Force, 1," 46–47, 56; Buckhorn, *Nader*, 69.

47. Fallows is quoted in Connie Bruck, "Will Reaganism Revive Nader?" *American Lawyer* 3 (May 1981), 31; Nadel, *The Politics of Consumer Protection*, 179; Whiteside, "A Countervailing Force, 1," 56; Buckhorn, *Nader: The People's Lawyer*, 236–239; McCarry, *Citizen Nader*, 139.

48. Whiteside, "A Countervailing Force, 1," 50–51; Buckhorn, *Nader*, 55, 98, 151.

49. Quote is from Ralph Nader, "Business Crime," *New Republic*, July 1, 1967, 7–8; Buckhorn, *Nader*, 38; McCarry, *Citizen Nader*, 85.

50. Ralph Nader, "A Citizen's Guide to the American Economy," *New York Review of Books*, September 2, 1971, 15–16; Ralph Nader, "No More Bailouts," *Mother Jones*, September/October 1990, 22–23; Gorey, *Nader and the Power of Everyman*, 81; Buckhorn, *Nader*, 238.

51. Quote is in Anderson, "Ralph Nader, Crusader," 103; Ralph Nader, "Inventions and Their Uses," *New Republic,* July 22, 1967, 34.

52. Robert G. Vaughn, "Ralph Nader," in Justin Winkler ed., *Makers of Modern Culture: The Twentieth Century* (New York: Facts on File, 1979), 378–379; Nader, *Unsafe at Any Speed,* xc; Gorey, *Nader and the Power of Everyman,* Chapter 4; Buckhorn, *Nader,* 49; Whiteside, "A Countervailing Force, 1," 51–52.

53. Quoted by Buckhorn, *Nader,* 48; Martha May, "Ralph Nader and the American Tradition of Consumer Activism," in *American Reform and Reformers: A Biographical Dictionary,* ed. Randall Miller and Paul Cimbala (Westport, CT: Greenwood Press, 1996), 392; Jennifer Scarlott, "Ralph Nader," in *Leaders from the 1960's: A Biographical Sourcebook of American Activism,* ed. David DeLeon (Westport, CT: Greenwood Press, 1994), 332–333.

54. "Meet Ralph Nader," 65–67; Jonathan Rowe, "Ralph Nader Reconsidered," *Washington Monthly* 17 (March 1985): 16–17; Gorey, *Nader and the Power of Everyman,* 61.

55. David Sanford, "Rocking the Foundations," *New Republic,* November 29, 1969, 17–18; John D. Morris, "FTC: New Help for the Consumer," *New York Times,* April 27, 1969, Section 4, 9; Nadel, *The Politics of Consumer Protection,* 184.

56. Buckhorn, *Nader,* 73–83; Newfield, "Nader's Raiders," 56, 56A.

57. Bollier, *Citizen Action,* Chapter 2, 1–3; Buckhorn, *Nader,* 89.

58. Nadel, *The Politics of Consumer Protection,* 182–183; Buckhorn, *Nader,* 83–91.

59. Nicholas Wade, "Nader's Congress Project," *Science* 178 (October 13, 1972): 142–146; Gorey, *Nader and the Power of Everyman,* 254–257; Whiteside, "A Countervailing Force, 1," 44.

60. Gorey, *Nader and the Power of Everyman,* 257–267.

61. Quote is in Buckhorn, *Nader,* 49; "Ralph Nader Becomes an Organization," *Business Week,* November 28, 1970, 86; McCarry, *Citizen Nader,* 203–205.

62. "Ralph Nader Becomes an Organization," 87; Thomas Whiteside, "A Countervailing Force, 2," *New Yorker,* October 15, 1973, 99; "Oregon Students Back Nader Idea," *New York Times,* November 22, 1970.

63. "More About Public Citizen," Statement posted on the website, *Public Citizen* <http:www.citizen.org>, 1999), 1; "Ralph Nader Urges You to Become a Public Citizen," full-page ad, *New York Times,* September 12, 1971, Section 4, 5.

64. Litwak, *Courtroom Crusaders,* 241–247; Gorey, *Nader and the Power of Everyman,* 247–248; Public Citizen Litigation Group, "Annual Report," *Public Citizen Litigation Group* website <http:www.citizen.org/litigation/annualrep/annrep99.htm>.

65. Bollier, *Citizen Action,* Chapter 2, 1–3; "Ralph Nader," in *American Social Leaders,* ed. William McGuire and Leslie Wheeler (Santa Barbara, CA: ABC-CLIO, 1993), 343; Linda Charlton, "Ralph Nader's Conglomerate Is Big Business," *New York Times,* January 29, 1978, Section 4, 3.

66. Buckhorn, *Nader,* 145–146; Bollier, *Citizen Action,* Chapter 4, 9; Frances Serra, "Consumer Organizations Over Nation Hurt by a Loss of Grants," *New York Times,* July 8, 1975, 16.

67. Quote is from Whiteside, "A Countervailing Force, 1," 72; Connie Bruck, "Will Reaganism Revive Ralph Nader?" 30; McCarry, *Citizen Nader,* 133.

68. Gorey, *Nader and the Power of Everyman,* 135; Bollier, Chapter 2, 2; Bob Hernandez, "The Lurking Danger of Naderism," *New York Times,* March 30, 1972, 37.

69. Gorey, *Nader and the Power of Everyman,* 135–136, 148, 154–155; "Nader Woos *Tomorrow* Show But Snyder Says He's Yesterday's News," *Esquire,* July 4, 1978, 12; "Is Nader Fading?" *Newsweek,* June 28, 1976, 60; "Is Nader Losing His Clout?" *U.S. News and World Report,* December 19, 1977, 18.

70. Bollier, *Citizen Action,* Chapter 3, 8; Thomas A. Stewart, "The Resurrection of Ralph Nader," *Fortune,* May 22, 1989, 108.

71. Bruck, "Will Reaganism Revive Nader?" 32; Ralph Nader, "Swiss Cheese," *New Republic,* November 22, 1969, 12; John D. Morris, "House Panel Approves a Bill for a Consumer Agency," *New York Times,* September 24, 1971, 81; Frances Serra, "Veto Is Feared," *New York Times,* May 14, 1975, 1; Adam Clymer, "Defeat for Consumer Drive," *New York Times,* February 10, 1978, 16.

72. Bollier, *Citizen Action and Other Big Ideas,* Chapter 3, 7; James Q. Wilson, *American Government: Institutions and Policies,* 4th ed. (Lexington, MA: D.C. Heath, 1989), 276; Charles

Mohr, "Carter Denies Knowing of Payments," *New York Times,* August 9, 1976, 13; Seth S. King, "Consumer Aides Find U.S. Jobs Frustrating," *New York Times,* November 14, 1977, 1; "Nader Criticizes Carter and Reagan Candidacies," *New York Times,* April 15, 1980, Section 1, Part 2, B14.

73. Mintz's statement is in Stewart, "The Resurrection of Ralph Nader," 108; Bollier, *Citizen Action,* Chapter 3, 8; Jonathan Rowe, "The Most Dangerous Man in America," *Rolling Stone,* November 16, 1995, 86.

74. Bruck, "Will Reaganism Revive Nader?" 34; Stewart, "The Resurrection of Ralph Nader," 106; Michael de Courcy Hinds, "Nader Expanding Consumer Efforts," *New York Times,* September 27, 1981, 31; Michael de Courcy Hinds, "A Subdued Nader Works to Organize Consumers," *New York Times,* April 27, 1982, 20.

75. Stewart, "The Resurrection of Ralph Nader," 108; Anthony Ramirez, "Consumer Crusader Feels a Chill in Washington," *New York Times,* December 31, 1995, Section 3, 3.

76. Nick Ravo, "School Ralph Nader Couldn't Save Is Razed," *New York Times,* July 9, 1988, 29.

77. Richard B. Schmitt and Sonia Steptoe, "California's Voter's Shake Up Insurers," *Wall Street Journal,* November 10, 1988, B1; Robert Reinhold, "Car Insurance Industry Fights Consumer Revolt in California," *New York Times,* August 16, 1988, Section 1, 1; Stewart, "The Resurrection of Ralph Nader," 106.

78. David Rogers, "Congress's Pay Raise Slated for Next Week Stirs a Spirited Debate," *Wall Street Journal,* February 1, 1989, A1; Bernard Trainor and David E. Rosenbaum, "Nader's Crossed Line," *New York Times,* February 3, 1989, A12; Michael Oreskes, "Pay Increase Plan Killed in Congress," *New York Times,* February 8, 1989, A1, D24; Douglas A Harbrecht, "The Second Coming of Ralph Nader," *Business Week* (March 6, 1989), 28.

79. Ralph Nader, "Drop the GATT," *Nation* 259 (October 10, 1994), 368–369; Bollier, *Citizen Action and Other Big Ideas,* Chapter 8, 4; Ralph Nader and Michael Waldman, "Off Track," *New Republic,* June 3, 1991, 17.

80. Nader's "hybrid" comment is in Smith, "Nobody's Nader," 61; the quote on Big Business is in Dao, "Nader Is Running Again," A1, A10; Tish Durkin, "The Un-Candidate," *New York Times Magazine,* October 20, 1996, 48.

81. Elizabeth Kolbert, "In Nader's Campaign, White House Isn't the Goal," *New York Times,* February 18, 1992, 1, 16; Scarlott, "Ralph Nader," 335; May, "Ralph Nader and the American Tradition of Consumer Activism," 393.

82. Durkin, "The Un-Candidate, 51; "Nader Wants to Keep His Finances Out of Presidential Race," *San Jose Mercury News,* September 14, 1996; James Dao, "Nader is Running Again, This Time With Feeling," *New York Times,* April 15, 2000, A10.

83. *Fighting for People and Democracy,* a Green Party campaign brochure of the year 2000; Ralph Nader, interview with Tim Russert, *Meet the Press,* NBC, June 25, 2000; Sam Howe Verhovek, "Unlike '96, Nader Runs Hard in '00," *New York Times,* July 1, 2000, A8.

84. Nader, interview with Tim Russert; Verhovek, "Unlike '96, Nader Runs Hard," A8.

85. The Sellers quote is in James Dao, "Angry Democrats, Fearing Nader Cost Them Presidential Race, Vow to Retaliate," *New York Times,* November 9, 2000, B3; Nader quote is in James Warren, "Nader Dismisses Critics, Sees Green Days Ahead," *Chicago Tribune,* November 9, 2000, Section 1, 9; James Dao, "Nader Falls Short of the 5% Needed for the Green Party to Get Federal Campaign Funds," *New York Times,* November 8, 2000, B5.

86. The quote is in Buckhorn, *Nader,* 37; Smith, "Nobody's Nader," 61; Litwak, *Courtroom Crusaders,* 232; Gorey, *Nader and the Power of Everyman,* 116.

87. The "viscosity of conscience" quote is in Anderson, "Ralph Nader, Crusader," 110; "Ralph Nader," *Contemporary Authors* 77–80, 390; Irwin Molotsky, "Behind Nader, a Generation at the Ready," *New York Times,* September 9, 1985, B8; Whiteside, "Countervailing Force," 2, 99–100.

Selected Cases

Ralph Nader v. General Motors et al. (1968)
57 New York Misc. 2d 301

Nader charged that General Motors and three other defendants had conducted a campaign of intimidation against him. As a result, his right to privacy under the common law had been violated in four distinct ways. His telephone had been·wiretapped and his phone conversations spied on. People in the employ of General Motors had also followed him. In addition, private detectives whose questions had cast aspersions on his character had interviewed people who knew him. Finally, he accused the corporation and people in its employ of causing him to be accosted by women who made illicit proposals to him and of having him harassed and threatened by late-night telephone callers.

According to Nader, these facts furnished different causes of action. The first of these accused the defendants of invading his privacy in several different states. The second cause of action made the same claims as the first, but placed these hostile and invasive acts only in New York State. The third cause of action relied on the same facts as the first two, but alleged that conduct of the defendants had deliberately caused him mental anguish. Finally, Nader added a fourth cause of action that rested on the claim that the defendants had damaged him economically by seeking to limit the sales of *Unsafe at Any Speed* and by blocking the publication of articles that he had written that were critical of the automobile industry.

The lawyers for General Motors replied that "the right to privacy" had never been enforced in either the District of Columbia or New York State courts. Therefore, the first and second causes of action should be dismissed. The Supreme Court of New York County denied General Motors' motion on the grounds that "the right to privacy was a constitutional right fully recognized by the federal courts as well as in the courts of the states."

In 1970, more than three years after he had filed his lawsuit, Nader and General Motors negotiated an out-of-court settlement whereby the company agreed to pay him more than $425,000.

Ralph Nader et al. v. Earl J. Butz, Secretary of Agriculture, et al. (1972)
474 F. 2d 426
See also: Ralph Nader et al. v. Earl Butz et al. (1974)
372 F. Supp. 175

In 1971, the U.S. Department of Agriculture announced a more than 5 percent increase in its price supports for milk and milk products. This announcement came less than two weeks after the department had declared that there would be no increase in these price supports for the next twelve months. This sudden reversal aroused Nader's suspicions.

Basing his claims to standing on the fact that he was both a drinker of milk and a taxpaying citizen, Nader filed a complaint in the District Court of Washington, D.C., alleging that the March 25 policy shift had been unlawful because it was based not on economic factors, as was required by law, but on political considerations. According to Nader and the three nonprofit organizations who were his coplaintiffs in the lawsuit, the Nixon administration had raised the price support level for milk partly because of pressure on the administration from members of Congress and also because of the large contributions made by dairy product interests to the president's reelection campaign.

In *Nader et al.* v. *Butz,* the plaintiffs sought a judgment from the courts, declaring illegal the price support increase and an injunction against the continuance of the increase over the next twelve months.

Judge William B. Jones dismissed the lawsuit on the ground that the setting of price support levels for the new market year, 1972–73, had rendered the previous year's actions moot. This judgment was reversed on appeal by Judge Spottswood Robinson of the D.C. circuit's court of appeals, who remanded the case back to the district court. In 1974, Judge Jones heard the case of *Nader* v. *Butz* for the second time. He ruled that none of the plaintiffs had valid standing to sue and again found for the defendant.

The revelations of corruption in *Nader* v. *Butz* made it the first great political scandal of the Nixon administration. When it was heard in court, depositions and testimony revealed a corrupt linkage between the price of milk and the activities of political fund-raisers. The case contributed to the ever widening controversy over the tactics used by Nixon and his staff in the election of 1972, which culminated finally in Nixon's resignation from the presidency.

Ralph Nader et al. v. *Richard G. Kleindienst et al.* (1973)
375 F. Supp. 1138

Nader and the other plaintiffs brought a class action suit against the attorney general of the United States, the U.S. attorney for the District of Columbia, the Clerk of the House of Representatives, and the secretary of the Senate. The plaintiffs were asking the court to declare that these officials had not enforced the Federal Corrupt Practices Act (FCPA) and to issue a writ of mandamus to require them to do so.

Nader laid claim to standing in the case as a voter, and Public Citizen claimed it as an organization that represented voters. The nonenforcement of the FCPA, they argued, deprived all citizens of information that they needed if they were going to vote intelligently with respect to the issues of the day.

All four defendants moved for dismissal of the suit on the grounds that none of the plaintiffs had standing to sue since their stake in the case was no greater than that of all other citizens. Moreover, the clerk of the House of Representatives and the secretary of the Senate insisted that the FCPA imposed no enforcement duties upon them at all. The attorney general and the

U.S. attorney for Washington, D.C., argued that any action or inaction on their part to enforce the FCPA was solely within their discretion and was not subject to judicial review.

Speaking for the court, Judge William Bryant ruled that Nader and Public Citizen did have standing to sue, but he also accepted the claim of the attorney general that he and the other federal prosecutors had absolute discretion. He thus dismissed the case for failure to state a claim upon which relief could be granted.

Campaign Clean Water, Inc. v. *Russel E. Train, Administrator, Environmental Protection Agency* (1973)
489 F. 2d 492
and *Train, Administrator, Environmental Protection Agency* v. *Campaign Clean Water, Inc.* (1975)
420 U.S. 136

In 1972, Congress enacted several amendments to the Water Pollution Control Act of 1970. One such measure provided, over the president's veto, for $18 billion in federal grants for the construction of sewage plants. Shortly after his reelection in 1972, President Nixon instructed Russel Train, administrator of the Environmental Protection Agency (EPA), to reduce his agency's expenditure on sewage plants to $2 billion for the fiscal year of 1973 and to $3 billion in fiscal 1974. The president's orders to Train required him to spend only 45 percent of the amount that Congress had appropriated for the construction of sewage treatment facilities. This was one of several instances in which Nixon had impounded a sizable portion of the funds appropriated by Congress for various programs.

In 1973, Campaign Clean Water, a Virginia environmental organization, challenged the Nixon impoundments in court, working closely on the case with Nader's Public Citizen Litigation Group. The plaintiff asked the court to declare that the administration lacked the discretion under the law to allot less than the full amount voted by Congress. The Virginia lawsuit also requested injunctive relief from the court, asking that Administrator Train be required to allot the full amount that had been appropriated by Congress for new sewage treatment facilities.

Train moved to dismiss the case on the grounds that the courts lacked jurisdiction over some of the matters raised in the suit and also because the complaint had failed to state a claim upon which relief could have been granted. The district court denied Train's motion to dismiss and granted in part the motion of the plaintiff for summary judgment. (See 361 F. Supp. 689.)

This decision was appealed to the U.S. Court of Appeals for the Fourth Circuit. There the issue was whether the administration had exceeded the limits of its discretion by impounding more than half of the funds appropriated by Congress for sewage treatment plants.

It its decision, the appeals court agreed with nearly all of the rulings in the case by the district court, but denied the latter's finding that the mere fact of withholding 55 percent of the appropriated funds proved that Administrator Train had violated the spirit, intent, and letter of the act and had abused his executive discretion. It therefore remanded the case back to the district court for further consideration. But in 1975, the Court of Appeals for the Fourth Circuit vacated its previous ruling, holding now that the EPA's administrator had no authority to allot less than the full amount appropriated by Congress.

Ralph Nader et al. v. Robert H. Bork, Acting Attorney General of the United States (1973)
366 F. Supp. 104

The mounting nationwide uproar over the Watergate scandal led the U.S. Congress, in 1973, to authorize the attorney general to appoint a special prosecutor to deal with all aspects of the scandal. The Department of Justice then issued a regulation stipulating that the special Watergate prosecutor would be removable from office only for "extraordinary improprieties" and could not be dismissed by the president, but only by the attorney general. On May 17, 1973, Attorney General Elliot Richardson appointed Professor Archibald Cox of Harvard Law School as special Watergate prosecutor.

Later that year, Cox's aggressive pursuit of Watergate evidence caused President Nixon to order Attorney General Richardson to dismiss the special prosecutor. Richardson resigned rather than comply with Nixon's order. When the deputy attorney general, William Ruckelshaus, also refused to dismiss Cox, he was immediately fired by Nixon. Solicitor General Robert Bork now assumed the duties of acting attorney general, dismissing Cox and rescinding the Department of Justice's regulation that had ruled out dismissing him.

Soon after these events, Nader, joined by three congressmen as coplaintiffs, sued the acting attorney general in the federal District Court of the District of Columbia. The plaintiffs asked for a declaratory judgment and an injunction requiring that Cox be permitted to resume his post and remain in command of the ongoing investigation.

Defendant Bork maintained that none of the plaintiffs had standing to sue. While concluding that Nader lacked standing, Judge Gerhard Gesell held that the three congressmen were in fact interested parties who could rightfully challenge in court the legality of actions by the president that might prevent Congress from learning relevant facts about Watergate. As members of the House of Representatives, they were necessarily in need of such facts, since they might have to consider whether the president should be impeached.

Judge Gesell denied the injunctive relief bought by the plaintiffs, however, observing that there was now a new Watergate special prosecutor (Leon Jaworski) and that the public interest would not be served by disrupting his ongoing investigation. But the judge also declared that the dismissal of Cox had been an illegal act. In so ruling, observed Gesell, he was seeking to keep the administration from repeating its illegal conduct, so that the Watergate inquiry could go on and the facts in the case could be uncovered and acted upon.

Nader et al. v. Butterfield (1974)
373 F. Supp. 1175

Nader and the Aviation Consumer Action Project (ACAP) were seeking declaratory relief against the administrator of the Federal Aviation Administration (FAA). To establish standing to sue, Nader pointed out that he was a frequent airline passenger and the ACAP argued that it was a nonprofit organization concerned with the health of airline passengers and employees.

The plaintiffs were challenging the legality of action taken by the FAA on March 29, 1973, when it, in effect, approved (without either public hearing or advance notice) a policy allowing x-ray machinery in airport terminals for the purpose of inspecting the carry-on luggage of the passengers. Nader and ACAP were seeking summary judgment against the new policy on the grounds that, in allowing the x-ray procedures, the FAA had failed to comply with two federal laws. First, the rule-making requirements of the Administrative Procedures Act had not been followed by the FAA. Under that act, a federal regulatory agency could adopt a new rule that materially affected people's rights and obligations only if the affected persons were given notice of the change and opportunity to respond to it at a public hearing. Since both sides conceded that no such procedure had been followed, Judge Barrington Parker conceded Nader's point that the FAA had acted illegally and granted the motion of the plaintiffs for summary judgment.

Nader and the ACAP also claimed that before the FAA could authorize the use of x-rays in airport security programs, it was required by the National Environmental Policy Act (NEPA) to submit an environmental impact statement (EIS). The agency denied that NEPA was applicable because the risk of doing harm to people by the x-raying of baggage was negligible. Judge Parker concluded, however, that the FAA would have to submit a more through analysis and rationale before the court could accept its claim that no EIS was required.

Nader v. Allegheny Air Lines (1975)
512 F. 2d 527

In early April 1972, Nader agreed to attend two fund-raising events in Hartford, Connecticut, both scheduled for April 28, on behalf of CCAG, a Connecticut consumer group. On April 25, he purchased a ticket for flight 864 on Allegheny Airlines, which was scheduled to take off from Washington at 10:15 A.M. on April 28 and land in Hartford one hour later. Although he arrived on time at the Allegheny Airlines Terminal at National Airport on the 28th, Nader was denied a seat on the plane because it was already filled to capacity. As a result, he was unable to attend one of the Hartford events and arrived late at the other.

Nader and CCAG, the Connecticut group at whose rally he had been scheduled to appear, jointly sued the airline for compensatory and punitive damages, alleging that the airline had been guilty of "fraudulent misrepresentation." The District of Columbia district court judge, Charles J. Richey, ruled in favor of the plaintiff and required Allegheny Airlines to pay compensatory damages of $10 to Nader and of $51 to CCAG. The judge also ordered the airline to pay punitive damages of $25,000 apiece to Nader and to CCAG.

In 1973, this ruling was reversed by the court of appeals on the grounds that in overbooking Flight 864, Allegheny Airlines had violated no law or federal guidelines. Moreover, the policy of overbooking was commonplace in the airline industry and was viewed approvingly by the Civil Aeronautics Board. In 1978, *Nader* v. *Allegheny Airlines* reached the U.S. Supreme Court, which affirmed the appeals court ruling in favor of the airline.

Ralph Nader et al. v. *John C. Sawhill et al.* (1975)
514 F. 2d 1064

On December 19, 1973, the Cost of Living Council (CLC), acting without holding a hearing, amended its price regulation on domestic crude petroleum to permit an immediate one-dollar per barrel increase in the price charged for "old" oil. The CLC justified its decision on two grounds. First, the increase was in line with its established policy of gradually moving the domestic ceiling price for petroleum nearer to the world price. A second reason for the price rise was to provide an incentive for increased production by American oil producers.

On July 9, 1974, appellants Nader et al. filed suit against the CLC in the federal district court of the District of Columbia. They attacked the CLC's decision to permit a higher price for domestic oil as "arbitrary, capricious, an abuse of discretion, in excess of statutory authority, and otherwise not in accordance with law." Nader and the other plaintiffs contended that the price spreads referred to by the CLC posed no threat to the American people, and even if they had posed a threat, there were other measures that might more properly have been taken.

The CLC's action, argued the plaintiffs, was also flawed because it did not follow the procedures required by the law. They also claimed that the departure from the normal rule-making process was a unilateral decision made not by the CLC, but by its general counsel. The issue before the court was whether the agency's decision had been based on a consideration of all relevant factors and whether there had been a clear error in judgment.

After examining the record, including the internal memoranda and the affidavits of CLC officials, the court, speaking through Judge Edward Tamm, found that it had been the CLC, and not its general counsel, that had approved the price increase for domestic crude oil. The court also decided that the agency had, in fact, considered all relevant factors in making its decision. The CLC had clearly demonstrated, said the court, that its decision to raise the price of crude petroleum was not an error in judgment.

Nader and Friends of the Earth v. *Nuclear Regulatory Commission and the United States of America* (1975)
513 F. 2d 1045

The plaintiffs had previously petitioned the Nuclear Regulatory Commission (NRC) to shut down as unsafe twenty nuclear power plants that had been licensed for operation in various parts of the nation. They had argued that the core-cooling system in use at these utilities was still an unproven technology. In rejecting their claim, the NRC replied that the challenged system in combination with the other safety measures mandated by federal law provided "reasonable assurance" that nuclear reactors would pose no serious danger to the public's health and safety.

The members of the commission described the guarantees sought by Nader and the Friends of the Earth as unrealistic, tantamount to demanding that nuclear power be completely risk-free. They also disputed the content of the petition, claiming that several of the engineers and scientists cited by the petitioners did not in fact subscribe to their view of the problem.

The question before the court, observed Judge Spottswood Robinson, was whether, in rejecting the petition, the NRC had been "arbitrary and capricious" and had acted at variance with the law. Judge Robinson declared that the commission had not violated its own rules and had acted rationally and in accordance with law. He noted that a substantial body of expert opinion had been consulted by the NRC and that most of the experts supported its view that the existing safety measures in place at the nation's atomic-powered plants provided "reasonable assurance" of protection to the health and safety of the public.

Bowsher, Comptroller General of the United States, v. *Synar, Member of Congress et al.* (1986)
478 U.S. 714

In order to eliminate the federal budget deficit, Congress enacted the Balanced Budget and Emergency Deficit Control Act of 1985 (also known as Gramm-Rudman-Hollings after the three senators who sponsored it). The act set ambitions goals for deficit reduction and provided for across-the-board cuts if the targets were not going to be met. The size of the deficit was to be progressively reduced and was required to reach zero by the 1991 fiscal year. The comptroller general, an official responsible to Congress rather than the president, was to be entrusted with the responsibility of specifying the required cuts in federal spending to the president, who, in turn, was required under the act to carry them out. The law also provided for a fallback procedure that was to go into effect should the comptroller general be removed from the process as a result of court decisions.

No sooner was the act passed than several congressmen, led by Representative Michael Synar (D-OK), challenged its constitutionality in federal district court in the District of Columbia. Also joining Synar's lawsuit was the National Treasury Employees Union, whose members were likely to suffer losses of income and benefits if the Gramm-Rudman-Hollings law were carried out.

Prominent in the handling of Synar's court challenge was the Public Citizen Litigation Group, a public interest law firm founded by Ralph Nader. Alan B. Morrison, the man Nader had recruited to head the firm in 1972, argued the case for Synar et al., first as appellants before the district court and then as the appellees before the U.S. Supreme Court.

The district court ruled that Section 251 of the challenged law, mandating the direct involvement of the comptroller general in the reduction of the deficit, was unconstitutional. Since only Congress could remove him, reasoned the court, it was not acceptable for the comptroller to perform functions belonging to the executive branch. This violated the separation of powers as imposed by the U.S. Constitution.

The comptroller general appealed the ruling to the U.S. Supreme Court, however, where it was affirmed seven to two. The high court majority, speaking through Justice Warren Burger, declared the challenged section of the Balanced Budget Act to be in violation of the separation of powers, which it regarded as of "crucial" importance to the constitutional order. "We conclude," Burger wrote, "that the District Court correctly held that the powers vested in the Comptroller-General under Section 251 violate the command of the Constitution that the Congress play no direct role in the execution of the laws."

Annotated Bibliography

Anderson, Patrick. "Ralph Nader, Crusader; or The Rise of a Self-Appointed Lobbyist." *New York Times Magazine,* October 29, 1967, 25, 103–104, 106–108, 110–112. A first-class, highly informative portrait of Nader at the start of his career.

Armstrong, Richard. "The Passion That Rules Ralph Nader." *Fortune,* May 1, 1971, 144–147, 319–327. An assessment of Nader, which argues that his goal of smashing corporate power is incompatible with a market system.

Auletta, Ken. "Ralph Nader, Public Eye." *Esquire,* December 1983, 481–487. An excellent article based largely on interviews with Nader and his closest aides.

Bauer, David. "Raiders of the Past." *National Law Journal* (October 19, 1981): 1, 26–27. A description of the later career paths followed by the young lawyers who had once worked for Nader.

Blum, Andrew. "Raiders at 20 Look Forward." *National Law Journal* (January 8, 1990): 24–26. Report on Nader's operation that found consumerism to be in vogue again.

Bollier, David. *Citizen Action and Other Big Ideas: A History of Ralph Nader and the Modern Consumer Movement.* Washington, DC: Public Citizen, 1991. This is the most comprehensive account of the activities of Nader and his organizations.

Booth, Richard. "The Outsiders Move Inside." *Newsweek,* January 2, 1978, 32–34. Depicts the troubled tenures of reformers turned government officials in the Carter presidency.

Brimelow, Peter, and Leslie Spencer. "Ralph Nader Inc." *Forbes,* September 17, 1990, 117–122. Brimelow and Spencer charge that Nader is secretly partisan, beholden to the trial lawyers, and secretive in his operations while demanding openness from business and government.

Bruck, Connie. "Will Reaganism Revive Nader?" *American Lawyer* 3 (May 1981): 24–25, 28, 30–34. Provided excellent quotations from Nader and his collaborators, both past and present.

Buckhorn, Robert. *Nader: The People's Lawyer.* Englewood Cliffs, NJ: Prentice Hall, 1972. Organized topically, focusing on Nader's efforts to enlist and organize support in various sectors for his ongoing struggles against Big Business.

Burt, Dan M. *Abuse of Trust: A Report on Ralph Nader's Network.* Chicago: Regnery Gateway, 1982. Burt charges Nader and his organizations with violating dozens of state laws and IRS regulations and with practicing secrecy while demanding public accountability from major institutions.

Celsi, Teresa. *Ralph Nader: The Consumer Revolution.* Brookfield, CT: New Directions, Millbrook Press, 1991. A well-done biography of Nader written for high school students.

Cockburn, Alexander, and James Rodriquez. "Citizen Nader." *Rolling Stone,* August 23, 1979, 45–49. An interview in which Nader expresses his disillusionment with President Carter and calls for a new third-party movement.

Collier, Bernard Law. "The Story of a Teenage Nader Raider." *New York Times Magazine,* March 14, 1971, 30–32, 72–73, 76, 78–79. Follows one of Nader's Raiders as she investigates and writes about the treatment of the elderly in nursing homes.

"Consumer Protection: Gains and Setbacks." *Editorial Research Reports* (February 17, 1978): 3–20. A description of the consumer movement written just as it was beginning to decline.

Creighton, Lucy Black. *Pretenders to the Throne: The Consumer Movement in the United States.* Lexington, MA: Lexington Books, 1976, Chapter 5. Creighton believes Nader to be the most effective and important leader of the consumer movement, but considers his goals unattainable.

Drew, Elizabeth B. "The Politics of Auto Safety." *Atlantic Monthly,* October 1966, 95–102. A vividly written account of Nader's first great breakthrough as a public interest lobbyist.

Durkin, Tish. "The Un-Candidate." *New York Times Magazine,* October 20, 1996, 48–51. An updated profile of Nader written during his "campaign" in 1996.

Duscha, Julius. "Stop! In the Public Interest." *New York Times Magazine,* March 21, 1971, 4, 6, 12, 14, 16, 19. A brief, colorful portrayal of Nader and his cohorts as self-appointed guardians of the public good.

Frost, David. "Can Don Quixote Whip the Telephone Company into Shape?" in *The Americans.* New York: Stein and Day, 1970, 108–112. A typical Nader interview. He denounces corporations, deplores the public's apathy, and warns of defective cars and baby food.

Glass, Gene V. "Nadir Is to Nader as Lowest Is to . . ." *National Review,* July 8, 1977, 776–777. Portrays Nader as boorish and arbitrary toward the targets of his investigations.

Gorey, Hays. *Nader and the Power of Everyman.* New York: Grosset and Dunlap, 1975. A sympathetic depiction of Nader's background, viewpoint, lifestyle, and public interest activism.

Greider, William. "How Far Can a Lone Ranger Ride?" *Ramparts,* March 1974, 21–23, 52–55. A brilliantly written exploration of the theory and practice of Nader-style activism, or what Greider terms "sophisticated guerilla warfare."

———. "Ralph Nader." *Rolling Stone,* November 5–December 10, 1987, 115–116, 118. In an interview with Greider, Nader laments Reagan's presidency, decries the ill effects of economic change, and calls again on his countrymen to become active citizens.

Haddon, William, et al. *Accident Research: Methods and Approaches.* New York: Harper and row, 1964. An influential work by a pioneer in the field of automobile safety.

Holdsworth, Robert D. *Public Interest Liberalism and the Crisis of Affluence: Reflections on Nader, Environmentalism, and the Politics of a Sustainable Society.* Boston: G.K. Hall, 1980. Holdsworth criticizes Nader's approach to the environment as too consumer-oriented and therefore as unlikely to be sustainable in the long run.

Ignatius, David. "Stages of Nader." *New York Times Magazine,* January 18, 1976, 9, 44–45, 51–55. Ignatius sees Nader as evolving first into a litigator and lobbyist, then into an economic reformer bent on restructuring the American economy.

Katz, Harold A. "Liability of Auto Manufacturers for the Unsafe Design of Passenger Cars." *Harvard Law Review* 69 (1956): 863–873. An important article that Nader read while at Harvard that confirmed his interest in the subject of automobile safety.

Kinsley, Michael. "My Life and Hard Times with Nader's Raiders." *Seventeen,* September 1971, 148–149, 204. An amusing piece about Kinsley's futile effort to live up to the Nader ideal.

Lazarus, Simon. *The Genteel Populists.* New York: Holt, Rinehart and Winston, 1974. Views Nader as the greatest master of "political theatrics" in his time, but argues that his methods could never significantly alter the distribution of power.

Litwak, Mark. *Courtroom Crusaders.* New York: Morrow, 1989, 202–247. Stresses the legal aspects of the work done by Nader and his Raiders.

May, Martha. "Ralph Nader and the American Tradition of Consumer Activism." In *American Reform and Reformers: A Biographical Dictionary,* ed. Randall Miller and Paul Cimbala. Westport, CT: Greenwood Press, 1996, 384–394. Views Nader as part of a long tradition of consumer advocacy. A fine bibliography.

McCarry, Charles. *Citizen Nader.* New York: Saturday Review Press 1972. An interesting book, but written in an ironic tone. Stresses Nader's eccentricity and views his anger as often overwrought.

———. "A Hectic, Happy, Sleepless, Stormy, Rumpled Week on the Road with Ralph Nader." *Life,* January 21, 1972, 45–46, 50–55. His first biographer describes one of Nader's lecture tours on the college circuit.

"Meet Ralph Nader." *Newsweek,* January 22, 1968, 65–67, 70, 73. A portrait of Nader at the beginning of his career.

Nadel, Mark V. *The Politics of Consumer Protection.* Indianapolis: Bobbs-Merrill, 1971. An informative work that includes extensive sections on Nader, his methods, and his movements.

"Nader, Ralph." *Contemporary Authors,* vols. 77–80, 389–390. Contains a biographical summary and a bibliography of Nader's early writings.

"Nader, Ralph." *Current Biography Yearbook, 1986,* 402–405. A compact, serviceable summary.

Nader, Ralph. "A Citizen's Guide to the American Economy." *New York Review of Books,* September 2, 1971, 14–18. Nader's economic ideas, consisting mainly of his analysis of the manifold ways in which the great corporations dominate the system and do harm to the American people.

———. "The Great American Gyp." In *Consumerism: Search for the Consumer Interest,* ed. David A. Aaker and George S. Day, 3d ed. New York: Free Press 1978, 39–52. Describes the forces and techniques that are available to the consumer movement in its fight to curb the excesses of the great corporations.

————. Interview with Tim Russert on *Meet the Press,* NBC, June 25, 2000. Took place during Nader's third-party campaign for president.

————. "Law Schools and Law Firms." *New Republic,* October 11, 1969, 20–23. Calls on the legal profession to put the public interest before its fealty to their clients.

————. "Protecting the Consumer: Towards a Just Economy." *Current* (December 1968): 15–23. Proposes a ten-step program to reform the economic system, stressing litigation and more extensive regulation by federal agencies.

————. "The Safe Car You Can't Buy." *Nation,* April 11, 1959, 310–313. An early essay on the auto-safety issue.

————. *Unsafe at Any Speed: The Designed-In Dangers of the American Automobile,* 2d ed. New York: Grossman Publishers, 1972. An exposé of the automobile industry that also presents several of Nader's key ideas, including his strategy for reform.

Nader, Ralph, and Wesley J. Smith. *No Contest: How The Power Lawyers Are Perverting Justice in America.* New York: Random House, 1996. Nader and Smith contend that lawyers who have worked for major corporations have betrayed the public interest.

Nader, Ralph, and William Taylor. *The Big Boys: Power and Position in America.* New York: Pantheon Books, 1986. Nader and Taylor are surprisingly positive in assessing some of the nation's top business leaders.

Newfield, Jack. "Nader's Raiders: The Lone Ranger Gets a Posse." *Life,* October 3, 1969, 56A, 56B. Newfield portrays Nader and his Raiders as a new and rising force in American politics.

O'Connell, Jeffrey, and Arthur Myers. *Safety Last: An Indictment of the Auto Industry.* New York: Random Houst, 1966. A critique of the automobile makers written independently of Nader, but deals with some of the same themes as *Unsafe at Any Speed* and comes to similar conclusions.

Pertschuk, Michael. *The Revolt Against Regulation: The Rise and Pause of the Consumer Movement.* Berkeley: University of California Press, 1982. Defends Nader's confrontational approach as often essential in defending the public against the excesses of business.

Reynolds, Alan. "What Does Ralph Nader Really Want?" *National Review,* February 28, 1975, 219–223. Claims that Nader is often wrong in his accusations and underestimates the value of a free market.

Rowe, Jonathan. "The Most Dangerous Man in America." *Rolling Stone,* November 16, 1995, 85–92. An interview in which Nader again declares the corporations to blame for the nation's ills and calls for a new political coalition to counter their influence.

————. "Ralph Nader Reconsidered." *Washington Monthly* 17 (March 1985): 12–21. A ringing defense of Nader's ideas and of his role in American life and politics.

Sanford, David. *Me and Ralph: Is Nader Unsafe for America?* Washington, DC: New Republic Book Company, 1976. By a former associate who accuses Nader of hypocrisy and charges that often neither he nor his followers know what they are talking about.

Scarlott, Jennifer. "Ralph Nader." In *Leaders from the 1960s: A Biographical Sourcebook of American Activism,* ed. David DeLeon, Westport, CT: Greenwood Press, 1994, 330–336. A skillful summary of Nader's career that views him as combining traditional values with populist radicalism.

Smith, Wesley J. "Nobody's Nader." *Mother Jones,* July/August 1996, 61–62. An updated sketch by Nader's sometime collaborator.

Speiser, Stuart M. *Lawsuit.* New York: Horizon Press, 1980, Chapter 1. The lawyer who represented Nader in his lawsuit against General Motors tells the story of the case.

Stewart, Thomas A. "The Resurrection of Ralph Nader." *Fortune,* May 22, 1989, 106–116. An important article chronicling Nader's resurgence in the late 1980s.

Toledano, Ralph de. *Hit and Run: The Rise—and Fall?—of Ralph Nader.* New Rochelle: Arlington House, 1975. Contends that Nader is secretly bent on gaining control of industry and replacing private enterprise with economic collectivism. No source notes or bibliography.

TRB. "Saint Ralph." *New Republic,* December 9, 1985, 4. An admirer's view of Nader.

Vaughn, Robert G. "Ralph Nader." In ed. Justin Winkler, *Makers of Modern Culture: The Twentieth Century.* New York: Facts on File, 1979, 378–379. A brief, incisive summary of Nader's major ideas.

Vidal, Gore. "The Best Man/72." *Esquire,* June 1971, 102–105. Vidal urged Nader to run for president as the candidate of a new third party committed to radical change.

Wade, Nicholas. "Nader's Congress Project." *Science* 178 (October 13, 1972): 142–146. Wade noted the ambivalence of the political science professors toward this ambitious Nader project.

Whiteside, Thomas. "A Countervailing Force, 1." *New Yorker,* October 8, 1973, 50–111. An in-depth interview and portrait of Nader.

———. "A Countervailing Force, 2." *New Yorker,* October 15, 1973, 46–101. A long and perceptive portrait of Nader on one of his lecture tours by a journalist who traveled with him for several weeks.

———. *The Investigation of Ralph Nader: General Motors Versus One Determined Man.* New York: Pocket Books, 1972. A well-written account of the incident that launched Nader's career.

Wilson, James Q. *American Government: Institutions and Policies,* 4th ed. Lexington, MA: D.C. Heath, 1989, 432–441. Wilson sees Nader as a major instance of the policy entrepreneur, a private citizen who mobilizes support for new laws "at the cost of small identifiable segments of society."

—Morris —
<u>Dees</u>

(Southern Poverty Law Center)

Chronology

1936	Born on December 16 in Shorter, Alabama, to Morris Seligman Dees Sr. and Annie Ruth Frazer Dees.

1936   Born on December 16 in Shorter, Alabama, to Morris Seligman Dees Sr. and Annie Ruth Frazer Dees.

1953   Married first wife, Beverly Crum Dees, April 15; graduated from Sidney Lanier High School, Montgomery, Alabama, June.

1958   Received A.B., University of Alabama School of Commerce and Law, Tuscaloosa, Alabama.

1960   Received LL.B., University of Alabama School of Law, Tuscaloosa, Alabama; entered into partnership with Millard Fuller for general practice of law, Montgomery, Alabama; started book publishing business partnership with Millard Fuller.

1964   Dissolved law partnership with Millard Fuller.

1969   Entered into partnership with Joseph J. Levin Jr. for general practice of law; sold publishing company to Times Mirror, Inc., for $6 million; successfully represented Annie Ruth Smith and Mary Louise Smith in *Smith* v. *YMCA*.

1971   Dissolved law partnership with Joseph J. Levin Jr.; cofounded (with Joseph J. Levin Jr.) Southern Poverty Law Center, Montgomery, Alabama; volunteered in George F. McGovern's Democratic presidential campaign.

1973   Successfully represented three black defendants known as the Tarboro Three in a rape case, Tarboro, North Carolina.

1976   Served as national finance director in Jimmy Carter's Democratic presidential campaign.

1980   Served as consultant in Edward M. ("Ted") Kennedy's Democratic presidential campaign.

1981   Established Klanwatch program in the Southern Poverty Law Center; successfully represented plaintiffs in *Vietnamese Fishermen's Association* v. *Knights of the Ku Klux Klan*.

1984   Served as consultant in Gary Hart's Democratic Presidential campaign.

1987   Obtained $7 million judgment against the United Klans of America for the murder of Michael Donald; received Trial Lawyer of the Year Award from Trial Lawyers for Public Justice; received Young Lawyers Distinguished Service Award from the American Bar Association.

1989   Obtained $950,000 judgment against the Ku Klux Klan for attacking a peaceful black demonstration in Forsythe County, Georgia.

1990   Successfully represented the family of Mulugeta Seraw and won a $12.5 million award against Thomas Metzger and White Aryan Resistance.

1991   Published his autobiography, *A Season for Justice: The Life and Times of Civil Rights Lawyer Morris Dees,* with Steve Fiffer.

1993   Published *Hate on Trial: The Case Against America's Most Dangerous Neo-Nazi,* with Steve Fiffer; successfully litigated to stop the governor of Alabama from flying the Confederate flag over the state capitol.

1996   Published *Gathering Storm: America's Militia Threat,* with James Corcoran.

1997   Successfully litigated to stop the reintroduction of prison chain gangs in Alabama.

1998   Obtained $37 million judgment against the Christian Knights of the Ku Klux Klan for bombing the Macedonia Baptist Church, South Carolina.

Biography

As a teenager growing up in rural Alabama in the early 1950s, famed trial lawyer Morris Seligman "Bubba" Dees Jr. ran a variety of business ventures. One of his many projects involved buying pigs from his neighbors. The going price for young pigs weighing up to 80 pounds was $5. The young man would then fatten the pigs to over 210 pounds and sell them at a profit of $40 per head. Although his efforts drew derisive comments from his schoolmates, Dees revealed a lack of concern as to how people felt about him that would be characteristic of him throughout his life:

> A few of my high-school classmates laughed at my entrepreneurial ventures. Some of my friends from old wealthy Montgomery families had never worked a day in their lives. They found it comical that Bubba was hauling scraps from their lunchroom for his pigs. I was too busy to worry about what people thought. I was more concerned that someone might beat me to the garbage.[1]

His entrepreneurial skills paid off handsomely. By the time he graduated from the University of Alabama Law School in 1960, he was on his way to becoming a millionaire. He juggled his law and business careers until 1969, when he made enough money to forgo the latter and concentrate on the former. The pursuit of money would take a back seat to protecting the rights of the have-nots in Southern society, whose cause he embraced as fervently as if it were his own.

A Fearless Lawyer

Dees brought his business skills to the practice of law. His aggressive tactics, willingness to face challenges, and his fearlessness in going after what he wanted have made him one of the most distinguished civil rights attorneys in the country. But they have also led him to confrontations with the Ku Klux Klan and other white supremacist groups and have put both his professional career and his life at risk.

He seemingly had a knack for incurring the wrath of Southern society and appeared to relish taking cases that few lawyers would handle. Several of his early victories—forcing the Young Men's Christian Association (YMCA) in Montgomery, Alabama, to desegregate its facilities; winning freedom for three black North Carolina death row inmates accused of raping a white woman; and helping to gain the acquittal of Joan Little, a black woman charged with murdering her white jailer in North Carolina—gained him more notoriety than acclaim. He had reason to fear for his professional life in both the YMCA and the Little cases. In the former, he was threatened with disbarment if he continued the case, and he had to withdraw as counsel from the Little case when he was accused of subornation of a witness and threatened with arrest.[2]

A particularly telling incident in his life took place in December 1984. At that time, Dees had moved up to first place on the hit list of a hate group known as The Order following the murder in June of Denver talk show host Alan Berg, who had ridiculed bigotry during his broadcasts. Dees, who had no connection to Berg but also had incurred the wrath of The Order, had been warned by the Federal Bureau of Investigation that he was on the hit list, and he hired two bodyguards to protect his home. When the outside guard informed Dees that he had spotted an armed man wearing a paramilitary uniform, the lawyer was forced to take refuge in a dark closet with Ellie, his fourteen-year-old daughter. "Why do you do the cases you do, Daddy?" she said to him. "Why can't you just practice regular law?"[3]

Dees, who has received numerous death threats and was once challenged to a duel by Louis Beam, the Grand Dragon of the Texas Knights of the Ku Klux Klan, continued to surround himself with bodyguards. While on a tour in 1996 in conjunction with the publication of his book *Gathering Storm: America's Militia Threat,* Dees referred to his bodyguards and the heightened security measures undertaken at the Southern Poverty Law Center (SPLC), which he cofounded in 1971:

> This is not for show. I would like to say I don't live in fear because we've been in this for so long. But we have a very sophisticated security system, not only for ourselves, but for our property and employees.[4]

He has always been at the center of controversy. "In certain circles below the Mason-Dixon Line," wrote Ken Englade in the *ABA Journal,* "one name is virtually guaranteed to get a reaction: Morris Dees." While he is vastly admired by many people, he is also fiercely disliked and is seldom out of the spotlight. His success in winning multimillion-dollar verdicts against groups like the Klan was the subject of a made-for-television movie, *Line of Fire: The Morris Dees Story* (aired on January 21, 1991, by NBC), but may have added to the dispute about him by giving credibility to the accusation that he craves attention. Although his ability to raise substantial sums of money for the SPLC has made him the envy of certain civil rights leaders whose organizations are often strapped for funds, several of his critics have dubbed it "Poverty Palace" and the "Southern Affluent Law Center."[5]

Dees is as striking outside of court as he is in it. A lanky man with blond hair and blue eyes, he speaks in a beguiling Southern drawl and was described by one interviewer as telling "story after story, barely completing one before beginning the next." Nevertheless, he is less forthcoming about his personal life, a reticence that is understandable in view of the constant threat to his safety. In his autobiography, *A Season for Justice: The Life and Times of Civil Rights Lawyer Morris Dees* (1991), he revealed little about his four younger siblings, hardly mentioned his three children, and in regard to his third wife, Mary Farmer—who ran an abortion clinic that he partially financed—omitted any reference to her whatsoever. The same fate later befell his fourth wife, Elizabeth Breen Dees, who was omitted from the 1998 reprint of his autobiography.[6]

If his goal was to make a lot of money and lead a life on his own terms, Dees has succeeded. From the profits made in his business, he bought the Rolling Hills Ranch, a sprawling two-thousand-acre compound in Mathews, Alabama, complete with stables, tennis courts, and a pond. In 2001, he relocated to Montgomery, where he resides with his fifth wife, Susan Starr Dees. He draws a salary from the SPLC, but neither he nor the center accepts any fees from clients.[7]

Tolerant Parents in the Segregated South

Some of the maverick qualities in Dees were inherited from his family. His Baptist paternal grandfather named Dees's father for Morris Seligman, a Jewish merchant in Montgomery who had befriended him. The family had originally come from Scotland, migrating from coastal North Carolina to central Alabama early in the eighteenth century. Dees's father dropped out of high school in order to support his family, beginning what his son termed "the hard life of a cotton farmer." When Dees was born on December 16, 1936, in Shorter, Alabama, his father was working as an overseer on a cotton plantation. Four years later, the elder Dees left his job and became a tenant farmer.[8]

The son grew up in the segregated South, where blacks were relegated to second-class citizenship. Dees attended segregated schools and never took a class with a black person from the time he entered the first grade in 1942 until he graduated from law school in 1960. He recalled that the message he got from white men in his community was that "my skin color automatically made me better than the black man." In describing the attitude of whites toward blacks in 1945 in the small southern town where he lived, Dees referred to a statement made in 1865 by Colonel Samuel Thomas, the Director of the Freedmen's Bureau in Mississippi:

> Men who are honorable in their dealings with their white neighbors will cheat a Negro without a single twinge of their honor; to kill a Negro they do not deem murder; to debauch a Negro woman they do not think fornication; to take property away from a Negro they do not deem robbery. . . . They still have the ingrained feeling that black people at large belong to the whites at large.[9]

When Dees explained how a boy who grew up in the segregated South could become a champion of civil rights, he cited the influence of his parents. His mother, Annie Ruth Frazer, was the daughter of a hard-drinking tire salesman from Montgomery who belonged to the Ku Klux Klan, and her grandfather had fought for the Confederacy. While Annie Ruth Dees and her husband believed in segregation, their treatment of blacks differed from the Southern norm. "Mamma felt that her Christian faith," her son wrote, "demanded she act kindly to all God's children." He frequently found his mother sitting at the family's breakfast table with some of the black women from the community to help them fill out requests for welfare relief. As he noticed his mother's actions, he realized how differently she behaved from her neighbors:

> The white wives of plantation owners and even the wives of smaller farmers and tenant farmers would rarely take the time to do paper work for black folks, and certainly wouldn't let them sit down at the family table. But Momma, who believed everybody should get along with everybody else, was the white go-between.[10]

In his recollection of his father, Dees mentioned that he remembered him drinking out of the same dipper as the black field hands. Another childhood memory was a day when Dees was five years old and refused to get off a mule he was riding. After being gently prodded by a field hand named Wilson to get off, the boy snapped: "You black nigger, you can't tell me what to do." Unknown to the boy, his father was standing behind the mule, and he proceeded to give his son the first whipping in his life. "Don't you ever call anybody a 'black nigger,'" he told him. "You mind Wilson. You do what he says."[11]

Although Dees was strongly influenced by the example of his parents in their attitude toward Southern black people, he later approached this issue with a boldness that eluded them. In 1963, he led a white Sunday school in prayers for four black girls who were killed when a black church was bombed in Birmingham, Alabama. As he prayed in silence in front of a church pew, the congregation walked out on him. He realized that he had come very far from his parents' views on the matter of race. He believed that his mother would have prayed silently for the girls and might have sent the family a check. But neither parent would have wanted him to create a scene.[12]

Growing Up on the Outskirts of Society

The Great Depression added to the family's economic difficulties. Until they were able to rent a comfortable home with a screened porch, they lived in a series of homes without either indoor plumbing or electricity. The new home was remembered by Dees as the place where his mother read to him and his younger sister every afternoon. But the family soon learned that their lease had been terminated by the owners. "This wasn't the first time we had to give up a farm," Dees recalled; the incident "reinforced the lack of control we have over our lives and the difference between us and the plantation owners." In 1948, the father was finally able to purchase a one-hundred-and-ten-acre farm in Mount Meigs, which had a population of four hundred and was located ten miles north of Montgomery. Unfortunately, most of the land was unsuitable for farming.[13]

Mount Meigs was considered a "civilized community with a better-educated group of folks." Some people in Mount Meigs even felt that Dees's paternal uncles were jealous of their brother's moderate success. Nevertheless, the stigma of being on the outskirts of society was exceedingly painful to the son:

> We weren't in the same league with these folks, who considered their family trees as valuable as any stand of lumber. Our genealogy and our bank account didn't measure up, but if anyone had asked my parents if we were poor they would have said no. We certainly weren't as poor as many of the people in the county. And we

would never have fallen into the class of people described by the horrible term "white trash." But we were *wealthy poor,* and in some ways that's worse than being dirt poor because you deceive yourself that you can keep up with the Joneses, or in our case the McLemores, the Scotts, and the Handeys.[14]

Despite his financial problems, Dees's father appeared to be an enterprising man. He was described by his wife as a man with "a lot of git-up-and-git," and he had many well-connected friends. After he met Alabama's governor, James E. ("Jim") Folsom, through a friend, Folsom used to visit the Dees home on Sunday afternoons, telling stories over a bottle of whiskey. The elder Dees took his son to Folsom's first inauguration in 1946 and later introduced him to state judge George C. Wallace at Folsom's second inauguration in 1954 with the prophetic statement, "Bubba, this is Judge Wallace. He's gonna be governor someday."[15]

This politically astute father tried to steer his son in the direction of a secure livelihood. But the son, who enjoyed speaking at Baptist summer youth revivals and had a knack for swaying an audience, wanted to be either a Baptist preacher or a farmer. His father was against both ideas. "Why don't you go to law school, Bubba?" he said. "If you get a law degree, you won't have to worry about nothing because boll weevils don't get into those law books. You won't have to worry about the rain or the price of cotton. You'll have it made."[16]

His father's best friend had a brother, Charles Pinkton, who was a successful attorney, and the elder Dees felt he understood how to make money in that profession: an attorney practiced law for a while, kept on the lookout for meeting people with business or political connections, and used these contacts to get state business, an appointment to office, or a judgeship. The result of all these endeavors was to have a guaranteed source of income for life.[17]

In speaking of his boyhood years, Dees acknowledged that "from an early age, I started doing anything and everything I could to make certain I'd have the financial security my parents never achieved." He was valedictorian in junior high school, where he made extra money by delivering newspapers and selling homegrown watermelons to his neighbors. By the time he graduated from Sidney Lanier High School, he had invented a chicken plucker, tended his own cabbage patch, and run a chicken, pig, and cattle operation that netted him $5,000 a year—all at a time when his father's debts amounted to over $30,000. Dees was named Star Farmer of Alabama by the Future Farmers of America and awarded a scholarship to Auburn University.[18]

A First "Client," 1952

Since this constant hustling for money "didn't always sit well with Daddy," his father tried to point him in other directions. In 1952, he brought his sixteen-year-old son his first "client," a black man named Clarence Williams who worked as a field hand on the Dees farm. The son later said that the Williams case "influenced me to want to become a lawyer."[19]

Williams got into trouble with the law because of an automobile accident. He had been driving near Mount Meigs when his tire rod broke, causing him to hit his head on the dashboard as his car ran off the road. Williams got out of the car, became dizzy, and staggered along the road as a sheriff arrived at the scene of the accident. He arrested Williams for driving while intoxicated, resisting arrest, and assault. Although Dees told the local justice of the peace that Williams was innocent of all charges against him, his "client" was fined $250. The verdict was a surprise to Dees, who believed wholeheartedly in Williams's innocence.[20] It was not until twenty years later that Dees learned that a justice of the peace received a fee from the state only if he or she found the defendant guilty. Dees promptly filed a class action suit that resulted in ending the practice. He then paid a visit to Williams to tell him the outcome of the lawsuit.[21]

School Years, 1952–1956

At the time Dees "represented" Williams, he had been taking vocational courses in high school with the intention of becoming a farmer. But the Williams case so angered him that he found a book with the speeches of Thomas Jefferson and Abraham Lincoln and memorized them. Practicing in back of a cotton wagon when he was certain that nobody was listening, he made up his own speeches about the concepts of equal justice that he had been studying in his United States history classes. "I was kind of playing being a lawyer, standing here in the cotton wagon," he noted.[22]

The budding lawyer's aspirations nearly ended in April 1952, when he eloped with Beverly Crum, a sophomore at the Sidney Lanier High School. It was two months before his own school graduation. Fortunately, the young bridegroom had saved enough money for college. His family responsibilities—he and his first wife would have two boys in the first three years of their marriage—delayed his college graduation, but did not impede his determination to finish his studies. He graduated from the University of Alabama at Tuscaloosa in 1958, and two years later from its law school.

Dees was no ordinary student. Three months after he began college, his mother sent him a birthday cake. The next year, he and Millard Fuller, a fellow student whom Dees had met at a Young Democrats meeting, established the "'Bama Birthday Cake Service," sending cakes to the students from their families. Each month, they sold 350 cakes (custom-made at a local bakery) for a profit of $3 a cake. Before graduation from college, they expanded their business by selling fund-raising products to clubs and organizations. They invested some of their profits in real estate by buying run-down buildings near the campus, renovating them by themselves, and renting them out to students. By the time Dees and Fuller graduated from law school, they had combined assets in excess of $250,000.[23]

In 1957, Dees had postponed going to law school for six months in order to work on the gubernatorial campaign of George C. Wallace. At this stage of his career, Wallace was a populist and had the support of most of the few blacks who voted. But Wallace was defeated by John Patterson, the segregationist candidate, and vowed never to be "out-segged" again. While Dees reportedly once toyed with the idea of running for governor of Alabama, he stated that this campaign convinced him that a political career was not for him:

> I didn't like the back room dealing and ass kissing I'd seen during the campaign. I didn't like the notion that after working for four years, fickle voters could turn you out. In short,. I'd learned firsthand that politics wasn't for me. I wanted to control my own destiny.[24]

While Wallace and Dees took distinctly different paths in later years, they had an unusual association with each other. In 1961, Dees's father died suddenly in an automobile accident, and the following year the newly elected Governor Wallace made Annie Ruth Dees a justice of the peace. Wallace's help to Mrs. Dees may explain the fact that Dees, who sued Governor Wallace many times in connection with alleged violations of the civil rights laws, maintained a cordial relationship with him. In 1968, Dees was put in an embarrassing situation when a newspaper editor saw him in Wallace's office and it was alleged that Dees gave Wallace some fund-raising advice in connection with the latter's presidential bid that year. This incident was not well publicized, but it helped to alienate Dees from liberal groups in Montgomery.[25]

Law and Business, 1960–1964

After passing the Alabama bar in 1960, Dees and Fuller formed a law partnership in Montgomery. They decided to combine the practice of law with business. By taking "little bitty nothing cases" referred to them by other attorneys, they made $12,000 at the end of their first year of practice, a sum considerably higher than what most first-year lawyers made in the early 1960s.[26]

Although the law partners were doing well financially, Dees harbored old resentments. He was angry that some of his father's wealthy friends did not give him any major business and came to him only when they had a "hopeless" case. One such case involved Earl Thornton, who had asked Dees to collect a $10,000 debt owed to him by a tenant farmer. Thornton was an employee of the Alabama Cotton Warehouse, which reputedly charged farmers like Dees's father high prices for storing their cotton. Dees managed to track down the farmer and collect the debt, but was offered only $200 by Thornton. The young lawyer, who had already decided that he would lower the regular fee in this type of collection case to $2,500, was so furious that he tore up the money into small pieces in front of a startled Thornton.[27]

Dees's father was aghast to learn from Thornton what his son had done. "What are you, crazy or something?" he said to Dees. "If it wasn't for those people, we wouldn't have been able to eat many a time." The son did not accept that line of reasoning. "That's you, and I'm me," he replied. "I don't owe him anything. I don't mind being nice or busting my butt for him. But I expect to be paid for it."[28]

The business dealings of Messrs. Dees and Fuller blossomed to such an extent that they sometimes had scant time for their law practice. In 1963, they compiled and published *Favorite Recipes of Home Economics Teachers,* which they sold to chapters of Future Homemakers of America. The two lawyers, who had set up their own book company, subsequently published other cookbooks and within two years became the largest publisher of cookbooks in the country and millionaires as well.

It was the zenith of their financial success. In 1964, Fuller wearied of the business and sold out to Dees for $1 million. Fuller proceeded to give his profits to several humanitarian charities and went on to found Habitat for Humanity International, a nonprofit organization based in Georgia that builds housing for the poor.[29]

Before Dees had a similar change of heart about his commitments, he admitted that he was too busy making money to pay much attention to the civil rights movement. Ironically, so much of the early movement had been centered in his own backyard: Montgomery was Martin Luther King's base of operations until 1960, and the place where the refusal by Rosa Parks to change her seat in December 1955 sparked the city's famous 381–day bus boycott.

Early Interest in Civil Rights, 1955–1969

The whirlwind of violent events taking place in the South made it increasingly difficult for Dees to avoid taking sides. The 1955 lynching in Money, Mississippi, of fourteen-year-old Emmett Till (his "crime" was saying "Bye, baby" to a white woman) had made Dees "seriously" examine "the Southern way of life" and prompted him to write a letter to a Tuscaloosa newspaper, which published it. In his sophomore year at the University of Alabama in 1956, he witnessed a mob chant "Nigger go home" to Autherine Lucy, who sought to be the first black student to enroll there. One week later, when Dees spoke to his Baptist Sunday school about it, he was quickly dismissed by the church's minister as superintendent of the Married Students Sunday School. His reaction to the 1963 bombing of a black church in Birmingham led him to speak out once again in his own church to a congregation that did not want to hear him.[30]

Dees' boldest action at this time occurred in 1965, when he drove black friends from Montgomery to the civil rights march in Selma. Even though he did not participate in the march, he soon detected a marked coolness toward him in town, and he was taken aback when two of his father's brothers (one of them, Lucien Dees, kept a country store that had one price for whites and a higher one for blacks) went to his office to ask him to change his last name.[31]

But the road to his "salvation" was not a direct one. In 1961, he and Fuller had defended Claude Henley, a neighbor and a member of the Ku Klux Klan.

Henley was accused of joining in an attack on the Freedom Riders, who had been dispatched to the South under the auspices of the Congress of Racial Equality (an interracial direct action group founded in 1942) to test the Supreme Court's ruling outlawing segregation in bus terminals. According to Fuller, he and Dees agonized over whether to represent Henley, but concluded that "it would be bad for business if rising young lawyers and businessmen spoke out for social justice and equality." As Dees left the courtroom after the prosecutors agreed to drop the charges against Henley, he was approached by two of the riders. "How can you represent people like that?" one of them asked. "Don't you think that black people have rights?" Dees noted that he felt the anger of a black person for the "first time" in his life.[32]

Fuller said that their fee was paid by the Klan and the White Citizens' Council. But Henley was the last Klansman the firm would ever represent.[33]

In the following years, Dees came to be regarded as sympathetic to the civil rights movement and to First Amendment issues. He did occasional work for the American Civil Liberties Union (ACLU), including representing Gary Dickey, a student editor at a local university who was suspended for writing an editorial critical of Governor Wallace. In 1967, Dees took the case to federal courts and won. Two years later, he returned to federal court on behalf of the Reverend William Sloane Coffin, a well-known anti–Vietnam War protester who was denied the right to speak before a student group at Auburn University. The case was another victory for the right of freedom of speech, but a harrowing one for the attorney. When Dees went to his office the morning after Sloane had delivered his speech, he found that the building had been vandalized and the letters "KKK" written all over the wall. It was the first— but not the last—time the Klan would strike.[34]

In characteristic fashion, Dees did not take this incident lightly. He called his former client Claude Henley to his office, pulled out a shotgun from behind the drapes, and told him to call Robert ("Bobby") Shelton, the Imperial Wizard of the United Klans of America. "Bobby," Dees said on the telephone, "I'm going to blow this son of a bitch's head right off of his god damn neck. You don't fuck with me now."[35]

As his reputation grew, Dees received more offers to participate in civil rights cases. In 1968, Fred D. Gray, the black attorney who represented Dr. Martin Luther King Jr. during the Montgomery bus boycott, was seeking an attorney with "some ties to the white community" for a pending lawsuit and asked Dees to assist him. The lawsuit was an attempt to block the sale of $5 million in state bonds to build a branch of Auburn University in Montgomery. Dees agreed to serve as cocounsel. They argued that the building of the branch would divert funds from the all-black Alabama State College in Montgomery and it would not welcome minority students. In a decision that was a particularly bitter one for Gray, a federal panel ruled that a state could build colleges as long as its doors were open to all—a decision that the Supreme Court later affirmed without an opinion.[36]

At this point in his life, Dees was described by writer Jack Bass as a "millionaire businessman" who had "a law degree, and little experience." But as Bass conceded, "Dees displayed an intuitive grasp of constitutional protection of civil rights and civil liberties, deep-seated feelings about injustice, and determination."[37]

In the midst of the struggle to find his identity in these convoluted years, Dees, stranded in an airport on a stormy night in February 1968, discovered Clarence Darrow. At the time, Dees was on his way to a business meeting in Chicago when a snowstorm closed the city's O'Hare airport, forcing his plane to land in Cincinnati for an overnight stay. Dees picked up a copy of Darrow's autobiography, *The Story of My Life,* at an airport newsstand. He was fascinated by Darrow's life and his decision to forsake the business world in order to fight for the rights of the powerless. In the course of reading the book, Dees remembered a verse from Ecclesiastes in the Bible: "To every thing there is a season, and a time to every purpose under the heavens . . . a time to keep silent, and a time to speak." Although he had heard this verse many times before in church, this time it took on a new meaning. Dees vowed he would have his "season for justice" (which he took for the title of his own autobiography), but it would take another year before he was able to make good on this pledge.[38]

Dees sold his publishing business in 1969 to the Times Mirror Corporation for $6 million. Prior to the sale, he may have overextended himself by seeking to establish a trade book company focusing on a sex education library for teenagers, in addition to marketing a projected aerospace encyclopedia to capitalize on the public's interest in the space program. Dees admitted that he owed a bank $2 million and "our collateral was as weak as well-water." Fortunately, he was helped through this crisis when a favorable article about his company appeared in the *Reporter of Direct Mail Advertising,* the major trade publication of the mail sales industry, and there was an upturn in his business.[39]

As the negotiations were in progress, there were other changes in his life. His marriage to Beverly Crum Dees ended in divorce and he married Maureene Buck, a former beauty queen from Georgia, who was an editor at his publishing company. Their marriage, which ended in a "bitter" divorce twelve years later, produced one daughter.[40]

While loath to discuss his family life, Dees made a revealing statement in 1990 about the professional and personal strains involved in being a trial lawyer:

> Most good lawyers get all the facts. They don't leave any stone unturned. That is just a given.
>   You live your case from the day you get it until it is over with. The person who becomes a great trial lawyer has a mind for details. He or she is a perfectionist in every way. Trial lawyers make poor family members.
>   If anything separates a great trial lawyer from an average lawyer, it is that the great trial lawyer deals with the totality of the case. He makes it all consuming. To win big, to take those chances and be on the cutting edge, you can't leave the case lying on your conference table when you go home. Last night, I woke up about

4:30 in the morning, and I was just lying there thinking. I thought about something in a case and wrote myself a note and brought it to work this morning. It occupies your subconscious, even if it doesn't occupy your conscious, at all times.[41]

Smith v. *YMCA* (1969)

The buy-out deal with Times Mirror required Dees to work at the company for at least one more year, but it did not stop him from taking on a major adversary: the Montgomery branch of the YMCA. According to *Time,* this case made him the second most hated man in Alabama, ranking only behind Judge Frank M. Johnson Jr., who ruled against the YMCA and was known as a foe of segregation.[42]

In 1969, two black cousins, Annie Ruth Smith and Mary Louise Smith, decided to file suit to integrate the facilities at the YMCA after their two children had been turned down for its two-week summer camp program. A friend of the Smiths asked Dees to bring a class action suit to end racial discrimination at the YMCA.

Dees was skeptical about the lawsuit. The YMCA was a private organization, and civil rights suits had been based on public, not private, discrimination. But he was very impressed by the resolve of the prospective clients (he would later learn that Mary Louise Smith had been fined and arrested for refusing to give up her seat on a bus two months before the famous Rosa Parks incident), and he decided to take the case.

Dees, who enlisted the aid of Gray in prosecuting the case, was aware that virtually all of Montgomery's most prominent citizens, including the mayor, served on the YMCA's board of directors. Also, he had few of the investigative resources that would become available to him after he cofounded the SPLC. Nevertheless, he was able to find a secret City Recreation–YMCA Coordinating Committee Agreement showing that the YMCA had received city monies, and he maintained that the agreement belied the YMCA's argument that it was strictly a private organization.

The case was argued before Judge Johnson. In a sweeping decision that effectively ended all segregation in Alabama, Johnson ruled that the YMCA had violated the equal protection clause of the Fourteenth Amendment "by operating segregated branches and by excluding Negroes from certain activities." He ordered the YMCA to integrate all its facilities on the grounds that it had become a de facto city recreation department.

Johnson awarded legal fees of $25,000 to Dees and Gray. At the judge's suggestion, they turned it over to the YMCA to provide membership dues and camp scholarships to children of all races.[43]

The victory in the YMCA was a hard-fought one for Dees. Three weeks after he had commenced the suit, Beverly Crum Dees received an anonymous phone call inquiring if her ex-husband had ever done anything illegal as an attorney. As the case progressed, Dees became convinced that his opponents were trying to smear him, and at one point they indicated to him that he would be disbarred unless he dropped the case.[44]

Origins of the SPLC, 1970–1971

Dees was finally able to sever his ties with Times Mirror in 1970, and he plunged full force into the work of the law partnership he had entered into with Joseph L. Levin Jr. in Montgomery the previous year. The son of a prominent debt collection attorney, Levin had grown weary of practicing law with his father. During their first year of practice, Levin and Dees handled several important pro bono cases: they defended a high school English teacher dismissed for teaching a Kurt Vonnegut story, they represented a woman in the military who had been discriminated against due to her sex, and they brought a class action suit against the *Montgomery Advertiser* for the paper's refusal to print a news story about a black couple in its society pages.[45]

Their law firm evolved into the Southern Poverty Law Center (SPLC), which they incorporated into a not-for-profit legal and educational foundation in 1971. Levin became the legal director of the SPLC, and Dees was originally named its chief counsel and executive director. His title was later changed to chief trial counsel. The SPLC has endured in the South as a bastion for protecting the rights of the poor, educating the public about the need for tolerance, and alerting the nation to the threat of hate groups.

The SPLC's multimillion-dollar endowment was made possible by the fundraising skills of Dees. In 1972 he obtained the mailing list used that year by the presidential campaign of Democratic senator George McGovern. Having volunteered earlier in 1971 to work for the presidential hopeful, Dees wrote a seven-page solicitation letter, which was vetoed by the staff on the grounds that it was too long. Dees sent the letter off anyway, paying for the postage with his own money, and it drew an unprecedented response rate of 15 percent. In addition, Dees expanded the campaign's mailing list, which proved enormously helpful to the SPLC when the list became available to him.[46]

Dees subsequently worked in the presidential campaigns of Democrats Jimmy Carter in 1976, Edward M. ("Ted") Kennedy in 1980, and Gary Hart in 1984. He reportedly deserted Carter in 1980 because the president had declined to name him as his attorney general following the election victory in 1976. Dees denied this report, maintaining that he never wanted to be attorney general.[47]

Tackling the Ku Klux Klan

In 1981, he created another controversy, but this time within the SPLC. In spite of opposition from many of his colleagues, he set up the Klanwatch program to monitor the activities of the Ku Klux Klan, the terrorist organization established in the South after the Civil War. Until this point, the SPLC had concentrated on litigating capital punishment cases and had published several well-known manuals for death penalty lawsuits.

His critics at the SPLC pointed out that the Klan, whose members wore hoods and white sheets to conceal their identity, was no longer a threat in the country and had only an estimated 10,000 members in the early 1980s. But Dees insisted that the civil rights movement had created a backlash and that the Klan loomed as a potent threat.[48]

The Klan's response to the Klanwatch program was not subtle. In 1983, it sent its own message to the SPLC when three Klan members burned it down. The arsonists were apprehended and drew up to fifteen years in prison sentences. The SPLC was rebuilt at a cost of $1 million, and featured a state-of-the art electronic security system. It now resembles a two-story fortress, with its darkened windows and permanently locked front doors. In order to gain entry, a visitor must talk to a faceless voice over a public address system.[49]

While stunned by the incident, Dees proved resilient. He made use of the firebombing and the subsequent rebuilding of the SPLC to seek additional contributions. In one instance, he sent out a two-page letter and an 18-minute videocassette to prospective supporters, who were urged to watch the tape and "come inside our new building, meet our people, see the sophisticated equipment used to track white supremacist activities, relive some successful and tragic moments of our past, and dream with us of the future." The effort was successful. The SPLC's endowment was doubled in the next eight years.[50]

Court Victories

By most accounts, the SPLC has been an unqualified success. Since the SPLC first attracted national attention in the Joan Little case in 1975, it has litigated an astonishing number of precedent-making cases. As for some of Dees's own notable achievements in this area, he brought a lawsuit that opened the Alabama police to black and female troopers, and he helped to institute a successful state action to split the Alabama legislature into single-member districts, thereby ensuring the election of the first black lawmakers since Reconstruction.[51]

Dees became most famous for his battles against the Klan and other white supremacist groups, and his court victories included the following: an injunction in 1981 against the Texas Knights of the Klan for harassing and intimidating a group of Vietnamese fishermen in Galveston Bay, Texas; a $7 million judgment in 1987 against the United Klans of America for the murder of a nineteen-year-old black man named Michael Donald in Mobile, Alabama; a criminal contempt decree against the Carolina Knights in 1987 that was designed to protect black people in North Carolina from violence; a $950,000 judgment against the Klan in 1989 for attacking a peaceful black demonstration in predominantly white Forsythe County, Georgia; and a $12.5 million award in 1990 against Thomas Metzger and other leaders of the California White Aryan Resistance for the murder of Mulugeta Seraw, an Ethiopian immigrant in Oregon.[52]

In spite of the magnitude of these victories, Dees insists that he is fully in accord with the freedom of expression rights in the First Amendment. "The Klan has a right to exist," he noted after the proposed settlement in the Forsythe County case was announced. "This is not just an attempt to put the Klan out of business." This latter statement led to a quip by *Time:* "Maybe not, but at this pace, he is not going to leave them with the price of a sheet."[53]

Much of the SPLC's success is due to the sophisticated technology Dees has assembled as a result of the substantial amounts of money he has raised for its work. In committing himself to both a case and a cause, Dees spares no expense to win. One of his favorite tactics is to hire jury selection experts, like Cathy E. Bennett, who had pioneered new strategies for picking and persuading juries. Bennett advised Dees in trials against the Klan and the White Aryan Resistance.[54]

The advantages of this kind of massive assistance can make the difference between winning and losing. In the 1973 case of the Tarboro Three, in which three black men were accused of raping a white woman in Tarboro, North Carolina, Dees retained seasoned local attorneys, paid for exhibits, and secured the services of a photographer to take aerial pictures of the area in which the alleged rape took place in order to discredit the accuser's testimony. When Dees' cocounsel, Larry Diedrick, saw the $400 bill for the photographs, he told Dees, "This case proves one thing. A poor person doesn't have a chance."[55]

But having the resources of the SPLC behind him should not obscure the fact that Dees is an extraordinarily gifted attorney. In a perceptive article for the *Maryland Journal of Contemporary Legal Issues* in 1992, Wilburn L. Chesser identified several of Dees's most notable trial skills:

- has sufficient moral courage to win
- spends the time and money necessary for a case
- identifies strong witnesses through his investigative work
- inspires the witnesses to continue despite a hostile atmosphere in court
- appeals to a sense of justice in overcoming a reluctant witness's fear of testifying
- instinctively knows when to depose a witness and when to call a witness to the stand
- files the action in the jurisdiction or court most likely to produce a favorable result
- hires consultants and psychologists
- spends time polling local residents to identify the juror profile most likely to be sympathetic to his client
- relies on his interpersonal talents to maintain the strength of a client during the trial
- extends his dedication beyond the typical attorney-client responsibilities.[56]

Dees relied on all these skills in the Donald and Seraw cases, his most famous lawsuits. He made a distinctive argument by citing the doctrine of vicarious liability, which holds a corporation or an organization responsible for the actions of its agents, in order to convince the respective juries that the incitement of violence by the Klan and the White Aryan Resistance was responsible for the deaths of each of these two young black men.[57]

The Murder of Michael Donald, 1981

The Donald case, which he tried in 1987, captured the attention of a nation stunned by the violence of the Klan, the quiet dignity of Beulah Mae Donald, the grieving mother, and the dramatic plea for forgiveness by one of Michael Donald's murderers at the end of the trial. The poignancy of Donald's death was also captured in a haunting photograph of Mrs. Donald at her son's funeral. She had insisted that the coffin be kept open "so that the world could know."[58]

The murder itself was senseless. Michael Donald, the youngest of seven children of Beulah Mae Donald, was picked off the street in Mobile on March 20, 1981, by two members of Unit 90 of the United Klans of America, the most powerful Klan group in America. The killing was in retaliation for the failure of a mixed jury in Mobile to reach a verdict in a case involving a black man accused of killing a white policeman. At a meeting of Unit 90 held earlier that evening, Bennie Jack Hays, the sixty-four-year-old titan of the United Klans, said to the members, "If a black man can get away with killing a white man, we ought to be able to get away with killing a black man."[59]

The murderers were James ("Tiger") Knowles, age seventeen, and Henry Francis Hays, the twenty-six-year-old son of Bennie Jack Hays. They left the meeting and randomly abducted Michael Donald, a technical student who worked part-time in the delivery room of a local newspaper. Donald was forced into Henry's car, where he begged them, "Please don't kill me." He tried to escape when the car stopped, but was caught and hit more than 100 times with a tree limb. When he stopped moving, they wrapped a rope around him. Hays shoved his boot in Donald's face and pulled on the rope. Before they strung him up to a tree, they cut his throat.[60]

Hays and Knowles were found guilty in separate trials in state court in 1983. Although there were few references to the Klan in either of the trials, Dees suspected its involvement. In 1984, he suggested to Mrs. Donald that she file a civil action against the members of Unit 90, the United Klans of America, and several of its leaders, including Imperial Wizard Shelton, under the Ku Klux Klan Act of 1871, which made it a federal offense to deprive a person of his civil rights.

The suit was filed in federal court in June 1984 by Dees and Michael Figures, a thirty-nine-year-old black state senator in Alabama who was Mrs. Donald's lawyer. It was filed on behalf of Michael Donald's family and the National Association for the Advancement of Colored People in connection with its representation of "all black citizens of Alabama." However, the case was not tried until February 1987, almost three years later.

The trial took place in Mobile, Alabama, and the strategy of Dees and his investigators at the SPLC was to convince the all-white jury that the death of Michael Donald was not simply the act of two Klansmen. Instead, it was the Klan that was civilly liable for the killing on the grounds that its pattern of violence against black people incited Knowles and Hays to commit the murder. In order to prove the Klan culpable, the SPLC tracked down former Klansmen, including many members who were in the witness protection program, and persuaded them to testify against the Klan. The witnesses talked.[61] His role in getting them to give evidence was described by Frank Judge in an article in the *American Lawyer* as guiding them "as easily as a preacher hearing a sinner's repentant cries for salvation." Dees had his own explanation:

> How did we get 'em to talk? I think it was just how you convince anybody to do anything: You show them the rightness of your cause. You try to give them the bigger picture of life in front of them. One day they're not going to be on this earth, and they're going to look back, and they're going to say, "What did I do to help my fellow man? I did a lot of bad things in the Klan and maybe this is an opportunity to do a little good." They got to live with themselves. You talk to people about what life's all about.[62]

A dramatic point in the trial came when Dees received word that Tiger Knowles wanted to see him. In the tiny cell where Knowles was being held when court was not in session, he announced that he would like to make a statement in court. Dees agreed to let him speak. "Everything I said is true," Knowles proclaimed in court. "I was acting as a Klansman when I done this. I hope that people learn from my mistake." As tears filled Knowles's eyes, he turned to Beulah Mae Donald and said:

> I can't bring your son back, but I'm sorry for what happened. God knows if I could trade places with him, I would. I can't. Whatever it takes—I have nothing. But I will have to do it. And if it takes me the rest of my life to pay it, any comfort it may bring, I hope it will. I will.[63]

There were few dry eyes in the court when Knowles was finished speaking. Beulah Mae Donald, who had been rocking in her seat, stopped and looked at Knowles. "I forgive you," she said softly.[64]

Disputing Knowles's assertion that he had acted on behalf of the Klan, the defense lawyer tried to counter the agency theory of liability by arguing that there was no evidence that Shelton or the United Klans organization was involved in Michael Donald's murder. The jury thought otherwise. It took just four and a half hours to announce its $7 million award to the plaintiffs.

Six weeks after the trial, Mrs. Donald received the deed to the Klan's only sizable asset, its $225,000 national headquarters in Tuscaloosa. She sold the building and used the money in 1989 to buy a house. She died less than one year later.[65]

The Murder of Mulugeta Seraw, 1988

The Seraw case gave Dees the opportunity to sue Thomas Metzger and other leaders of White Aryan Resistance (WAR), a loosely knit group of several thousand white supremacists and militaristic skinheads who advocate racial separatism and anti-Semitism. The suit, which was the subject of Dees's second book, *Hate on Trial: The Case Against America's Most Dangerous Neo-Nazi* (1993), was brought on behalf of the family of Mulugeta Seraw, a twenty-seven-year-old black college student from Ethiopia who lived in Portland, Oregon.

On the night of November 13, 1988, Seraw was driven home by two Ethiopian friends and dropped off at the curb. They were spotted by three skinhead members of a local gang called the East Side White Pride, who were wearing their traditional garb of military jackets and steel-toed boots. Although the skinheads knew neither Seraw nor his two friends, they blocked the car's path. One of them smashed the car windows with a baseball bat, and another skinhead took the baseball bat and attacked Seraw with repeated blows to his head. By the time the police arrived on the scene in response to a neighbor's call, Seraw was unconscious, his body twisted and blood flowing from his crushed head. He was pronounced dead at a local hospital six hours later.[66]

The civil lawsuit, *Berhanu* v. *Metzger,* was instituted by the SPLC and the Anti-Defamation League of B'nai B'rith on behalf of the family of the murdered man. Engedaw Berhanu, the victim's uncle and plaintiff in the case, had flown in from San Francisco to identify the body.

Defendant Metzger did not know the victim, had never authorized his murder, and was 1,500 miles away at the time of the killing. But Dees again relied on the theory of vicarious liability in attempting to prove that the skinheads had been incited by agents of WAR and that this incitement led to the death of Mulugeta Seraw.[67]

While Dees had originally filed the case in federal court, he moved it to Oregon state court. As he told the *National Law Journal:*

> We chose state court because Oregon discovery rules are quite different than the federal rules. You can do trial by ambush in Oregon. You have no interrogatories, no production of evidence; you don't have to give the names of witnesses or give the other side your documents.[68]

As a surprise witness, Dees produced twenty-one-year-old David Mazzella. Dees alleged that Mazzella had been sent by Metzger to organize the East Side White Pride. Mazzella had originally issued a statement three days after the killing stating that the local skinheads had nothing to do with the murder. It was Dees who had persuaded Mazzella to testify. In the course of his seven hours of testimony, Mazzella admitted he was with the skinheads several hours before the attack and referred to himself as the "direct link" between Metzger and the skinheads.

The jury, returning a verdict of $12.5 million in damages to the family of the deceased, rejected Metzger's argument that he was not responsible for Seraw's death. It also dismissed the argument made in a friend-of-the-court brief by the Oregon chapter of the ACLU that the suit may have violated Metzger's First Amendment rights under the constitution.[69]

Public Recognition

In spite of the national attention that Dees received as a result of the cases, his greatest satisfaction was found elsewhere. He told a reporter in 1991 that his "proudest achievement" was the creation of the Civil Rights Memorial, built in 1989 in the plaza of the headquarters of the SPLC. Dedicated to forty black and white people who died in the struggle for civil rights, it has become the largest tourist attraction in Montgomery.[70]

Following the Metzger verdict, Dees turned his attention to the militia movement, which he referred to in the title of his third book as a *Gathering Storm* (1996). The book was published on the first anniversary of the Oklahoma City bombing, in which a federal office building was destroyed and 168 people were killed. Timothy McVeigh, who had ties to the militia movement, was later found guilty of fire bombing the building, sentenced to death, and executed. Six months before the April 1995 bombing in Oklahoma City, Dees had written a letter to Attorney General Janet Reno warning her of the danger posed by the growing number of radical militia groups in the country.[71]

Dees has taken considerable pride in several recent notable cases handled by the SPLC. In 1993, it won a case that prevented the governor of Alabama from flying the Confederate battle flag over the state capitol. The flag had been raised by Governor George C. Wallace back in 1963 to symbolize Alabama's opposition to racial integration. Another important victory occurred in 1997, when the SPLC succeeded in blocking the reintroduction of prison chain gangs in Alabama. In 1998, Dees obtained "one of the most satisfying court victories in my career" when the SPLC won a lawsuit on behalf of the Macedonia Baptist Church in South Carolina against the Christian Knights of the Ku Klux Klan. The suit was commenced after the Klan had burned the church in June 1995 in an alleged effort to provoke racial warfare. Instead, the verdict resulted in a $37 million judgment against the Klan.[72]

Morris Dees has garnered many prestigious honors and awards in the course of his legal career, including two citations he received in the aftermath of his victory against the Klan for the murder of Michael Donald. In 1987, he was named Trial Lawyer of the Year by the Trial Lawyers for Public Justice and received the Young Lawyers Distinguished Service Award from the American Bar Association. He holds numerous honorary degrees from schools including Hebrew Union College–Jewish Institute of Religion in Ohio, Wesleyan University in Connecticut, and Howard University in Washington, D.C. Between 1972 and 1976, he was a visiting instructor at the John F. Kennedy

School of Government at Harvard, and he has taught at various law schools throughout the country.

A more unusual honor was bestowed upon him at Direct Marketing Day in New York in 1991, when he received a Special Humanitarian Award for raising millions of dollars at the SPLC for "the principles of justice and fair play." Acknowledging that "I'm not ashamed to say I'm a salesman," Dees wryly noted, "I've used other talents at the center, like being a lawyer, but without my direct-marketing skills, I wouldn't have the money to do it with." Seven years later, he was inducted into the Hall of Fame of the Direct Marketing Association.[73]

In response to a question once posed to him by an interviewer about how he felt about his work, Dees replied, "I don't foresee ever quitting practicing law. There is nothing else I really want to do."[74]

Notes

1. Morris Dees with Steve Fiffer, *A Season for Justice: The Life and Times of Civil Rights Lawyer Morris Dees* (New York: Charles Scribner's Sons, 1991), 71.

2. Ibid., 103–105, 108–127, 152–153, 162–178; Stephen E. Rendahl, review of *Hate on Trial: The Case Against America's Most Dangerous Neo-Nazi,* by Morris Dees and Steve Fiffer, *North Dakota Law Review* 69 (Spring 1993): 368.

3. Dees, *A Season for Justice,* 3; Morris Dees, "Remember Me by My Clients: They Make My Life Worthwhile," *Trial* 26 (April 1990): 65.

4. Quoted in Kevin Sack, "A Son of Alabama Takes on Americans Who Live to Hate," *New York Times,* May 12, 1996, E7.

5. Ken Englade, "Today's Unsung Heroes: Profiles of Lawyers Who Help the Disadvantaged," *ABA Journal* 74 (November 1, 1988): 62; Michael Leahy, "Poetic Justice: L.A. Lawyer Plays Real-life Attorney . . . and It's Not Easy," *TV Guide,* January 19–25, 1991, 39; John Egerton, "Poverty Palace: How the Southern Poverty Law Center Got Rich Fighting the Klan," *Progressive* 52 (July 1988): 14–17.

6. Quoted in Robert E. Shapiro, "Interview of Morris Dees," *Litigation* 16 (Summer 1990): 6; Dees, *A Season for Justice,* 35, 55, 68, 78, 82, 129, 278. For a reference to Mary Farmer, see Tucker Carlson, "With Friends Like Dees . . ." *Weekly Standard* 1 (May 20, 1996): 25; Dees, *A Season For Justice* (reprint edition, 1998), 340–351.

7. Drew Jubera, "Profile: Civil Rights Lawyer Morris Dees, Jr.," *Los Angeles Daily Journal,* January 26, 1990, 1, 10; Bill Shaw, "Morris Dees," *People Weekly,* July 22, 1991, 50–54; information furnished to author by Southern Poverty Law Center, July 2001.

8. Dees, *A Season for Justice,* 52–53.

9. Quoted ibid., 63.

10. Ibid., 64.

11. Ibid., 63.

12. Ibid., 88.

13. Ibid., 55.

14. Ibid., 56.

15. Jubera, "Profile," 10; Dees, *A Season for Justice,* 80.

16. Dees, "Remember Me by My Clients," 64.

17. Dees, *A Season for Justice,* 58.

18. Ibid., 70.

19. Ibid., 71; Dees, "Remember Me by My Clients," 64.

20. Dees, *A Season for Justice,* 58–61; Dees, "Remember Me by My Clients," 65.

21. Dees, *A Season for Justice,* 140; Dees, "Remember Me by My Clients," 64–65.

22. Dees, *A Season for Justice,* 61; Dees, "Remember Me by My Clients," 64.

23. Englade, "Poverty Palace," 15; Millard Fuller and Diane Scott, *Love in the Mortar Joints: The Story of Habitat for Humanity* (Piscataway, NJ: Association Press, 1980), 38–42.

24. Dees, *A Season for Justice,* 81; John Egerton, *Shades of Gray: Dispatches from the Modern South* (Baton Rouge: Louisiana State University Press, 1991), 217.

25. Dees, *A Season for Justice,* 88–90; Jack Bass, review of *A Season for Justice,* by Morris Dees with Steve Fiffer, *Los Angeles Daily Journal,* August 6, 1991, 7; Jack Bass, *Taming the Storm: The Life and Times of Judge Frank M. Johnson, Jr. and The South's Fight Over Civil Rights* (New York: Doubleday, 1993), 383; Egerton, *Shades of Gray,* 223–224.

26. Dees, *A Season for Justice,* 82.

27. Ibid., 83.

28. Ibid.

29. Fuller and Scott, *Love in the Mortar Joints,* 39.

30. Dees, *A Season for Justice,* 76–83.

31. Sack, "A Son of Alabama," E7.

32. Dees, *A Season for Justice,* 84–85; Egerton, *Shades of Gray,* 217.

33. Egerton, "Poverty Palace." 15.

34. Dees, *A Season for Justice,* 94, 99–100.

35. Ibid., 100–101.

36. Ibid., 98; Fred Gray, *Bus Ride to Justice: Changing the System by the System: The Life and Works of Fred D. Gray* (Montgomery: Black Belt Press, 1995), 274–291; Bass, *Taming the Storm,* 388.

37. Bass, *Taming the Storm,* 385.

38. Dees, *A Season for Justice,* 95–97.

39. Ibid., 97–102.

40. Ibid., 99, 198; Egerton, *Shades of Gray,* 226.

41. Shapiro, "Interview of Morris Dees," 48.

42. Dees, *A Season for Justice,* 110, 123–124.

43. Bass, *Taming the Storm,* 385; Robert F. Kennedy Jr., *Judge Frank M. Johnson, Jr.: A Biography* (New York: G.P. Putnam's Sons, 1978), 80–81.

44. Dees, *A Season for Justice,* 104–105; Herbert Mitgang, review of *A Season for Justice,* by Morris Dees, *New York Times,* July 19, 1991, C25.

45. Dees, *A Season for Justice,* 130–131.

46. Ibid., 135–137.

47. Egerton, *Shades of Gray,* 224.

48. Egerton, "Poverty Palace," 17.

49. Ibid.; Vicky Quade, "Klan Buster: How the Southern Poverty Law Center Smashed the United Klans of America," *Barrister* 15 (Summer 1988): 14.

50. Quoted in Stuart Elliott, "A Marketer of Civil Rights Who Has Made a Difference," *New York Times,* May 15, 1991, D20.

51. Dees, *A Season for Justice,* 5, 14, 132.

52. Ibid.; Morris Dees and Ellen Bowden, "Hate: Taking Hate Groups to Court," *Trial,* 31 (February 1995): 24.

53. "The High Cost of Klanning," *Time* 132 (November 7, 1988): 37.

54. Bruce Lambert, "Cathy E. Bennett, Who Pioneered Jury Selection Method, Dies at 41," *New York Times,* June 12, 1992, D20; David Margolick, "For a Faltering Pioneer in Jury Selection, the Smith Case Provides New Inspiration," *New York Times,* November 22, 1991, A28.

55. Dees, *A Season for Justice,* 158.

56. See Wilburn L. Chesser, review of *A Season for Justice,* by Morris Dees, *Maryland Journal of Contemporary Legal Issues* 3 (Spring 1992): 302–303.

57. Barbara Reynolds, "You Have a Right to Hate, But Not the Right to Hurt," *USA Today,* June 3, 1991, A11.

58. Jesse Kornbluth, "The Woman Who Beat the Klan," *New York Times Magazine,* November 1, 1987, 29.

59. Quoted ibid., 26.

60. Ibid.

61. Frank Judge, "Slaying the Dragon," *American Lawyer* 9 (September 1987): 83–89.

62. Ibid., 88.

63. Quoted in Dees, *A Season for Justice,* 329.

64. Quoted ibid.

65. Ibid,, 330–332.

66. Morris Dees and Steve Fiffer, *Hate on Trial: The Case Against America's Most Dangerous Neo-Nazi* (New York: Villard Books, 1993): 3–7.

67. Walter Goodman, "Free Speech and the Right to Hate," *New York Times,* February 5, 1992, C20.

68. "Finding the Forum for a Victory: Successful Strategies from 10 of the Nation's Top Litigators," *National Law Journal* 13 (February 11, 1991), S3.

69. "White Supremacist Leaders Penalized for Inciting Death," *New York Times,* October 23, 1990, B6.

70. Quoted in Shaw, "Morris Dees," 54. See also D. Michael Cheers, "Dedicate Memorial to 40 Who Died in Civil Rights Struggle," *Jet* 77, November 20, 1989, 4–16; and William Knowlton Zinsser, "I Realized Her Tears Were Becoming Part of the Memorial," *Smithsonian* 22 (September 1991): 32–40.

71. Morris Dees with James Corcoran, *Gathering Storm: America's Militia Threat* (New York: HarperCollins, 1996): 6–7.

72. Dees, *A Season for Justice,* reprint edition, 338.

73. Quoted in Elliott, "A Marketer of Civil Rights," D20; information furnished to author by the Southern Poverty Law Center, July 2001.

74. Quade, "Klan Buster," 48.

Selected Cases

Dickey v. *Alabama State Board of Education* (N.D. Ala. 1967)
273 F. Supp. 613

Gary Dickey, a white Vietnam veteran, had been student editor of the newspaper at Troy State University in Alabama. He had been suspended for writing an editorial criticizing Governor George C. Wallace. The president of the university, Ralph Adams, was a friend of Wallace and justified the suspension by stating that the university had received state funds and should refrain from criticizing the legislature and the governor. In his statement, Adams referred to the *Birmingham News,* which he said was owned by Jews and was never critical of Jewish people.

Dees handled the case on a pro bono basis for the Montgomery chapter of the American Civil Liberties Union. The case was heard by Judge Frank M. Johnson Jr., who viewed the action of the university as a violation of Dickey's First Amendment rights to freedom of speech. In ruling for Dickey, Judge Johnson held that a state cannot force a college student to forfeit his constitutionally protected right of freedom of expression as a condition of his attending a state-supported institution.

Alabama State Teachers' Association v. *Alabama Public School and College Authority* (N.D. Ala. 1968)
289 F. Supp. 784

The Alabama State Teachers' Association, an all-black organization, filed suit to stop the building of a branch of Auburn University in Montgomery, Alabama. The association believed that the branch at Auburn would drain away funds from Alabama State, an all-black college, and that it would not welcome minority students.

Fred D. Gray, a prominent black civil rights attorney who had represented Dr. Martin Luther King Jr. in the Montgomery bus boycott of 1955, enlisted Dees's help in the lawsuit against the Alabama Public School and College Authority. In preparation for trial, Dees interviewed principals at thirty-five predominantly white high schools and was informed that their students were actively recruited by Auburn. The principals at Montgomery's three predominantly black schools indicated that their students were never contacted by the university.

The case was heard by a three-judge federal panel, which included the liberal Judge Frank M. Johnson Jr. It ruled in favor of the university on the grounds that a state could build new colleges as long as its doors were open to all students.

Brown v. *Invisible Empire, Knights of the Ku Klux Klan* (N.D. Ala., filed November 3, 1980)
No. 80–HM–1449–S

This case evolved from a series of incidents involving the Ku Klux Klan in Decatur, Alabama. In 1978, a mentally retarded black man named Tommy Lee Hines was arrested for a series of black-on-white rapes in Decatur. Hines denied taking part in the rapes, and the black community felt that an innocent person had been picked up by the police in their haste to solve the crimes. Following Hines's arrest, blacks staged a sit-in in the courthouse and erected a tent at City Hall.

Hines was convicted by an all-white jury. On May 26, 1979, a protest march was held in Decatur to mark the first anniversary of his arrest. Although a police line had been created to enable the marchers to pass through the streets, a group of 100 robed Klansmen led by Alabama officials of the Louisiana-based Invisible Empire, Knights of the Ku Klux Klan, broke through the line and attacked the marchers. In the melee that followed, shots were fired and two blacks and two Klansmen were wounded.

Four Klansmen were subsequently arrested: three for assaulting a police officer and another for discharging a weapon. Curtis Robinson, a black man who had been watching the march, was arrested for shooting David Kelso, a Klan leader. Robinson admitted shooting Kelso, but stated that he acted in self-defense.

Dees was asked by the Director of Alabama Legal Services in Decatur to have the Southern Poverty Law Center (SPLC) defend Robinson. Although the SPLC had concentrated on death penalty cases prior to this time, Dees agreed to take the case.

At the trial, Dees made use of a videotape of the riot showing Kelso provoking Robinson with a club before the latter drew his gun. Nevertheless, an all-white jury convicted Robinson. The judge acted upon the jury's recommendation and gave Robinson two years' probation.

In spite of the setback, Dees was determined that the Klan be held accountable for its attacks on the marchers. The *Brown* case was filed in 1980 on behalf of the Southern Christian Leadership Conference (SCLC), and the Klan was sued for violating the civil rights of the marchers. The case led to the criminal conviction of ten persons, the cessation of Klan paramilitary activity in Alabama, and a civil settlement that called for the defendants to pay monetary damages and to take a race relations seminar taught by Dr. Joseph Lowery, president of the Southern Christian Leadership Conference. In 1989, the court issued a final order approving the consent decree.

This case ended the Invisible Empire as a viable group in Alabama. Bill Wilkinson, its national leader, resigned after he exhausted the group's money in defense of the lawsuit. His group filed for bankruptcy.

Vietnamese Fishermen's Association et al. v. *The Knights of the Ku Klux Klan* (1981)
518 F. Supp. 993

Louis Beam, the Grand Dragon of the Knights of the Ku Klux Klan in Texas, responded to a call in January 1981 for help from an American fishermen's group operating out of the Kemah-Seabrook area of Texas, on the west shore of Galveston Bay. They wanted to stop a group of fishermen, who emigrated from Vietnam, from fishing in Galveston Bay and competing with them in the sale of fish.

On February 14, 1981, Beam addressed a rally in Santa Fe, Texas. He brought with him thirteen men in military garb whom he referred to as his "security force." In his speech, Beam said he would give the government ninety days to rectify the problem with respect to the Vietnamese fishermen. The ninety-day period would have been one day before the opening of the spring shrimping season on May 15, 1981. In the event that the government did not take action, Beam said it "may become necessary to take laws into our own hands." He added that it was necessary to "fight fight fight" and see "blood blood blood" if this country were to survive.

Before the rally ended, Beam demonstrated how to burn a boat. A cross propped up with the aid of a pickup truck was also burned at the rally.

When the shrimping season began on May 15, 1981, a "boat ride" was held in the waters surrounding the Kemah-Seabrook area. Although the boat was owned by a local fisherman, several persons on it wore robes of the Ku Klux Klan, others wore hoods, and most were visibly armed. The boat was equipped with a small cannon, and an effigy of a Vietnamese fisherman hung from the rear deck rigging. The cannon was fired before the end of the ride.

The rally and boat ride were not the only incidents. Other Vietnamese-owned and operated boats were burned by the Klan members, who also pointed pistols at the fishermen and members of their families.

Learning about the initial threats to the Vietnamese fishermen, Dees had offered to help them. On April 16, 1981, the Southern Poverty Law Center filed a lawsuit on behalf of the Vietnamese Fishermen's Association seeking to enjoin the Ku Klux Klan from harassing and intimidating Vietnamese fishermen in the exercise of their legal right to fish in Galveston Bay.

Judge Gabrielle McDonald of the United States District Court for the Southern District of Texas granted a preliminary injunction on May 14, 1981. When the fishing season began the next day, the Vietnamese blessed their fleet and entered Galveston Bay.

On August 7, 1981, the court turned the temporary injunction into a permanent injunction.

Vietnamese Fishermen's Association et al. v. *The Knights of the Ku Klux Klan et al.* (1981)
518 F. Supp. 1017

This proceeding was decided on July 16, 1981, approximately three weeks before the United States District Court for the Southern District of Texas granted a permanent injunction against the Knights of the Ku Klux Klan for their harassment and intimidation of members of the Vietnamese Fishermen's Association. The proceeding was instituted on behalf of the Knights of the Ku Klux Klan to disqualify Judge Gabrielle McDonald, a black district judge, from the case on the grounds that she had demonstrated a personal bias or prejudice against the Klan in favor of the Vietnamese Fishermen's Association.

The matter at issue was the fact that Judge McDonald had instructed her law clerk to inquire of Morris Dees, counsel for the Fishermen's Association, whether said plaintiffs would be intimidated or in any way adversely affected in the presentation of their case if Louis Beam, Grand Dragon of the Ku Klux Klan in Texas, or any other member of the Ku Klux Klan wore Klan robes at the court hearing. According to the defendants, this inquiry on the part of Judge McDonald, without benefit of a motion by the plaintiffs, evidenced sympathy and sensitivity toward the plaintiffs' personal feelings and conversely showed bias and prejudice against the defendants.

In his testimony at the hearing presided over by Judge McDonald, Beam stated: "I no more have the opportunity and confidence that I could get any fairer trial here in front of you than you would feel were you to go before a Ku Klux Klansman who was judge as a defendant." He further testified that he had been in the Klan for twelve years and that he considered that blacks were prejudiced against the Klan and that this prejudice was strictly unfounded.

Judge McDonald dismissed the defendant's motion, holding that mere allegations of the personal bias of a judge are insufficient to require disqualification.

Vietnamese Fishermen's Association et al. v. *The Knights of the Ku Klux Klan et al.* (1982)
543 F. Supp. 198

When the United States District Court for the Southern District of Texas converted the preliminary injunction against the Knights of the Ku Klux Klan to a permanent injunction, it limited the lawsuit to the request by the Vietnamese Fishermen's Association and the State of Texas for an injunction against the Klan's military operations within the state.

These military operations became known to the Klanwatch project of the Southern Poverty Law Center when it was investigating the activities of Louis Beam, the Grand Dragon of the Ku Klux Klan in Texas. Klanwatch investigators obtained evidence that Beam was operating several secret camps that trained hundreds of Klan military operatives. Beam identified the group of persons who received this training as the Texas Emergency Reserve.

The defendants conceded that the Texas Emergency Reserve was the military arm of the Ku Klux Klan. The evidence revealed that most of its members were past, present, and former members of the Ku Klux Klan. The Texas Emergency Reserve had participated in a boat ride on March 15, 1981, to intimidate the Vietnamese fishermen, and it had trained at various locations within the State of Texas.

Dees represented the plaintiffs in court. It was Dees who convinced Texas Attorney General Mark White to enter the case in opposition to the paramilitary training in the state.

The court sought to determine whether an injunction enjoining the defendants from conducting military operations was necessary and appropriate in order to protect the plaintiffs' federal civil rights, and whether it could enjoin defendants from conducting military training camps within the state of Texas pursuant to a Texas statute that barred private armies.

The court ruled for the plaintiffs. Judge Gabrielle McDonald held that the defendants' military operations and training operations were outside the scope of the First Amendment; that an injunction against the defendants' military activities did not violate the Second Amendment; that the plaintiffs had standing to seek enforcement of Texas statute prohibiting, *inter alia,* private armies; that the state of Texas was entitled to intervene to enforce state statute; and that the defendants' conduct violated state law.

Beulah Mae Donald, as Executor of the Estate of Michael Donald, Deceased* v. *United Klans of America et al.
(S.D. Ala., filed June 14, 1984)
No. 84–0725–CS

Michael Donald was picked off the street in Mobile, Alabama, on May 20, 1981, and killed in retaliation for the failure of a mixed jury in Mobile to convict a black man accused of killing a white policeman. It was a random shooting solely because Donald was black.

Donald's killers acted at the behest of Bennie Jack Hays, the South Alabama Grand Titan of the United Klans of America—a group led by Robert Shelton, its Imperial Wizard. The United Klans of America was the principal Klan organization in the 1950s and 1960s, responsible in 1963 for the bombing of the Sixteenth Street Baptist Church that led to the death of four black girls, the murder in 1963 of white civil rights worker Viola Liuzzo during a protest march, from Selma to Montgomery march; and numerous other crimes during the civil rights movement. The contributions of its swelling membership enabled it to build a 7,500-square-foot office building in Tuscaloosa County in 1979, from which the group operated a nationwide Klan program.

Donald's murder had been particularly brutal. His killers were seventeen-year-old James ("Tiger") Knowles and twenty-six-year-old Henry Hays, the son of Bennie Jack Hays. They beat him with a tree limb, slit his throat and hung his body from a tree in a predominantly black Mobile neighborhood.

In 1963 the Federal Bureau of Investigation and the United States Justice Department arrested Knowles and Henry Hays. Knowles testified against Hays and accepted a life sentence. Hays received the death penalty and was executed on June 6, 1997. He became the first white to be put to death for killing a black in Alabama since 1913.

The matter might have ended with the conviction of Knowles and Hays, but Dees and SPLC attorneys were determined to take action against the United Klans of America on the grounds that Bennie Jack Hays, Tiger Knowles, and Henry Hays had acted as conspiratorial agents to perpetuate the history of Klan violence. In 1984, the SPLC filed suit for the Donald family, seeking $10 million in damages against the United Klans of America and other members of the Klan. Robert Shelton, the Imperial Wizard of the United Klans of America, was also named as a defendant.

On February 12, 1987, a federal jury awarded $7 million in damages against the United Klans of America and six of its members. The only asset of the United Klans of America was its real estate. Lawyers from the SPLC were able to get title to its real estate transferred to the Donald estate. Only a small amount of the $7 million was collected because none of the defendants had money, but the lawsuit effectively bankrupted the United Klans of America.

.In the course of its investigation for the trial, the SPLC uncovered new evidence that it presented to the Mobile County district attorney. In 1987, the district attorney obtained indictments against Frank Cox and Bennie Jack Hays for their part in Michael Donald's murder. Cox was convicted and sentenced to life imprisonment. Hays died before he could be tried.

United States v. *Handley* (1985)
763 F. 2d 1401

Roger David Handley was one of nine defendants in this lawsuit before the United States Court of Appeals, Eleventh Circuit. The defendants were members or former members of the Invisible Empire, Knights of the Ku Klux Klan, who were allegedly involved in a clash with police and black marchers in Decatur, Alabama, on May 26, 1979. Several people were injured.

After the incident, black leaders, both national and local, called upon President Jimmy Carter and the FBI to investigate and prosecute the Klan. The FBI's investigation failed to develop sufficient evidence to support federal criminal charges against the Klansmen, and the government closed the investigation in October 1979. However, the SPLC obtained the redacted FBI report on May 22, 1980. It later sued under the Freedom of Information Act to obtain the full FBI file, but was unsuccessful.

On November 3, 1980, the SPLC filed a civil suit against the Klan and the Klan's "agents, servants, employees and assigns, et al.," on behalf of a putative class of persons who claimed that the Klan had violated their civil rights in Decatur. Morris Dees represented the civil plaintiffs.

Lloyd Letson, a former Klansman, testified at a hearing on behalf of the civil plaintiffs on October 20, 1982. He had originally been a defendant, but the plaintiffs voluntarily dismissed him from the suit in return for his testimony about the alleged Klan conspiracy at the Decatur incident. Henry Frohsin, an assistant United States attorney, attended the hearing to represent an FBI agent who was to testify. Frohsin obtained a transcript of Letson's testimony and sent it to the Justice Department in Washington. The department reopened its investigation on December 7, 1982.

The SPLC subsequently took approximately ninety depositions of Klansmen and turned the evidence over to the FBI. This evidence resulted in federal criminal indictments charging ten top Alabama Invisible Empire members with a criminal conspiracy to violate the civil rights of the Decatur marchers. These indictments came just six days before the statute of limitations was to expire.

The ten defendants (who were also defendants in the SCLC's civil suit) sought to suppress depositions obtained in the civil action. The United States District Court for the Northern District of Alabama granted the defendants' suppression motion, and the government appealed.

In *United States* v. *Handley* (1985), the United States Court of Appeals reversed the decision of the District Court. The Court of Appeals ruled that depositions taken in a civil rights action were admissible in civil rights prosecution over defendants' claims of Fifth Amendment privilege, where there was no evidence of governmental involvement in the actual taking of these depositions.

Handley, the lead defendant, was the Grand Dragon of the Invisible Empire, Knights of the Ku Klux Klan in Alabama, and this lawsuit effectively ended the Invisible Empire as a viable group in Alabama.

Marshall v. *Bramer* (6th Cir., 1987)
828 F. 2d 355

Robert Marshall and Martha Marshall were a black couple whose home was firebombed twice after they moved into Sylvania, an exclusively white community of seventy-five homes located near Louisville in Jefferson County, Kentucky. Blacks who had lived there in the past had been targets for harassment. At the time the Marshalls bought their house in 1985, no blacks were living in Sylvania.

When the community learned that a black family had purchased a house, there was a Ku Klux Klan meeting in Jefferson County. The Klan also posted approximately 150 "Join the Klan" signs and distributed hundreds of Klan leaflets in Sylvania.

The first arson occurred on July 29, 1985, the night that the Marshalls and their two children moved into the house. Around bedtime, Martha Marshall saw a pickup truck drive by and heard someone shout "Nigger!" At 3:00 A.M., a firebomb was thrown into the house, causing a considerable amount of damage.

Defendants Carl Ray Bramer and Billy Wayne Emmones pleaded guilty to the firebombing. The other defendants were "John Doe, and unknown defendants K-1 through K-50, Ku Klux Klan members and others who participated in the event set out in this complaint and those whose names are unknown at this time." Alex Young, who was a Jefferson County police officer at the time of the arson, was named as a nonparty-appellant.

Shortly after the first arson, the local media revealed that Young belonged to the Klan. When Young admitted that he was a Klan official, the Marshalls subpoenaed him to obtain a list of members of his local Klan group, which was known as the Confederate Officers Patriot Squad (COPS). Young moved to quash the subpoena, but the United States District Court for the Western District of Kentucky ruled against him. The court held Young in contempt for failure to comply with the subpoena.

Young appealed the decision to the United States Circuit Court of Appeals. The Southern Poverty Law Center represented the Marshalls, and Dees was one of a team of lawyers involved in the case. The court of appeals held that evidence of the involvement of a white supremacist organization in firebombing the Marshalls' house justified the order requiring the nonparty member of an organization to produce the list. According to the court, the First Amendment freedom of association rights of members of an organization did not entitle a nonparty member to refuse to disclose the membership list.

Exposure of COPS led to the dismissal of officer Alex Young. Although the SPLC was unable to tie the group to the arson, it did learn the names of all enforcement personnel involved in COPS.

This case was a companion to *In re The Courier-Journal* v. *Marshall* (1987), in which the court ruled that a newspaper could not have access to the list of Klan members.

In re The Courier-Journal v. *Marshall* (6th Cir. 1987) 828 F. 2d 361

Robert Marshall and Martha Marshall were a black couple whose home was firebombed twice after they moved into the exclusively white community of Sylvania, in Jefferson County, Kentucky. Because the Ku Klux Klan was active in the community, the Marshalls listed named and unnamed Klan members as defendants in the federal complaint they filed against the Klan.

Shortly after the first arson, the local media revealed that Alex Young, a Jefferson County police officer, belonged to the Klan. When Young admitted that he was a Klan official, the Marshalls subpoenaed him to obtain a list of members of his local Klan group. Young moved to quash the subpoena, but the court ordered him to reveal the information. However, it held that only the law firms involved in the suit could have access to the deposition's contents.

The *Courier-Journal* had been covering the Marshalls' case, and its publisher brought a motion to vacate the protective order as violative of the First Amendment right of the press of access to judicial proceedings, especially proceedings of intense public concern.

The Southern Poverty Law Center represented the Marshalls. Oral arguments were made by Dees, J. Richard Cohen, legal director of the center, and Alexander R. Sussman of New York.

The court ruled against the newspaper. It held that a news organization did not have First Amendment right of access entitling it to see the membership lists of local white supremacist organizations and documents containing members' names, which were the fruit of discovery in a civil rights suit against members of that organization, even though approximately two dozen local law enforcement officers allegedly were members of that organization.

This case was a companion case to *Marshall* v. *Bramer* (1987), in which the court ruled that the Marshalls had the right to obtain a list of members of the local Ku Klux Klan.

Person v. *Miller* (4th Cir. 1988)
854 F. ed 656

In June 1984, the SPLC filed a suit on behalf of Bobby L. Person, a black citizen of the United States and of the State of North Carolina, seeking to enjoin Glen Miller and his group, the Christian Knights of the Ku Klux Klan (CKKKK), from harassing blacks and running paramilitary operations. An ex-Green Beret, Miller had founded the CKKKK in the early 1980s, enrolling ex-military enlisted men and officers. He formed a paramilitary army in the Carolinas and Virginia that reached over 2,000 in number and terrorized minorities in those regions.

A court-ordered settlement was reached in January 1985, and Miller agreed to cease harassment of blacks and to cease paramilitary operations. Miller changed the name of the CKKKK to White Patriot Party after the entry of the court's order in January 1985. However, the Klanwatch project of the SPLC obtained photographs showing that Miller had violated the court order by using active-duty military personnel from the United States Army to train his Klan paramilitary army. Klanwatch turned over the evidence of active-duty military involvement to Secretary of Defense Casper Weinberger, and several soldiers were later dismissed. Secretary Weinberger subsequently issued an order forbidding military personnel from participating in white supremacist groups.

The decision to turn over evidence to Weinberger did not deter the SPLC from seeking redress in the court. In April 1986, Dees and SPLC's legal director, Richard Cohen, moved to cite Miller and the White Patriot Party for criminal contempt of court by violating the January 1985 order. Afterward they filed several amendments to the original complaint and moved to add various parties as defendants, including Stephen Miller (no relation to Glen Miller), who was second in command of the White Patriot Party.

Dees was initially authorized by the court to prosecute the contempt action. However, counsel for Stephen Miller moved in June 1986 to have Dees disqualified on the ground that he would be a material witness at trial and that his appointment as prosecutor violated both the North Carolina Rules of Professional Conduct and Stephen Miller's right to be prosecuted by an impartial prosecutor, as guaranteed by the due process clause of the United States Constitution. Since there was some question whether counsel for an interested party could prosecute a related criminal contempt action, the court ordered that the prosecution would be under the "direct supervision and control" of Sam Currin, United States attorney for the Eastern District of North Carolina. At the same time, Dees was appointed to assist Currin.

The trial produced evidence uncovered by Klanwatch that Miller had purchased thousands of dollars' worth of stolen military hardware and had planned to use the items to start a major racial disturbance. After a week's trial, a federal jury convicted both Glen Miller and Stephen Miller of criminal contempt. Glen Miller was sentenced to the maximum one year in jail, and Stephen Miller received a prison sentence of six months.

The defendants appealed the conviction. In *Person* v. *Miller,* the United States Court of Appeals for the Fourth Circuit upheld the conviction in 1988. Since the federal government joined in the lawsuit, the plaintiffs-appellees were Bobby L. Person and the United States of America.

The court held that the United States government did not have to prove that the defendants had engaged in or ordered any acts threatening immediate danger in order to establish that the defendants violated the North Carolina civil disorder statute in criminal contempt of the district court order prohibiting violation of said statute. The court stated that prosecution had only to provide that the prohibited activities were engaged in with intent of further civil disorder at some point in time.

In the aftermath of the lawsuit, Stephen Miller and four former White Patriot Party members conspired to rob a business to obtain funds to purchase rockets to kill Dees and blow up the Southern Poverty Law Center. Glen Miller also issued a written threat to kill Dees and, with three other former White Patriot Party members, set out in a van loaded with explosives and automatic weapons to carry out the assassination. The FBI arrested the group in a predawn raid.

Stephen Miller and his codefendants later received long prison sentences. Glen Miller received a five-year sentence, but later became a government witness against other violent white supremacists. As a result, the White Patriot Party ceased to exist.

United States v. *White* (11th Cir. 1988)
846 F. 2d 678

This appeal to the United States Court of Appeals, Eleventh Circuit, consisted of six consolidated criminal cases, involving eight defendants, in which the United States sought the reversal of the district court's suppression of evidence.

The defendants sought to suppress depositions and other fruits of discovery obtained in civil action based upon a confrontation between black marchers and the Ku Klux Klan in Decatur, Alabama, on May 26, 1979.

Following several appeals and reversals on technical points in this matter, the court of appeals ruled for the government. It held that law of the cases doctrine, which mandates that the appellate court decision on issues be followed in all subsequent trial proceedings in the same case applied in this instance. The court of appeals also stated that a witness who testifies at any proceeding instead of asserting Fifth Amendment rights loses the privilege of invoking said amendment.

McKinney et al. v. *Invisible Empire, Knights of the Ku Klux Klan et al.*
(11th Cir., December 12, 1989)
No 89–8092 slip op.

The Southern Poverty Law Center brought this class action suit on behalf of sixty plaintiffs against the Invisible Empire, Knights of the Ku Klux Klan, the Southern White Knights, and approximately a dozen Klan leaders and members. Damages and injunctive relief were sought.

In February 1987, the two groups had brutally assaulted over fifty peaceful black and white demonstrators in all-white Forsyth County, Georgia. The demonstration was in honor of Dr. Martin Luther King Jr.

The Atlanta federal court awarded the sixty plaintiffs $940,000. The Invisible Empire was forced to turn over all of its assets, its name, trademarks, and office equipment to the plaintiffs, in addition to paying them $37,000. It was also ordered to destroy its membership and publication subscription lists, which included 10,000 names.

The Southern White Knights, a Georgia-based Klan group, was likewise forced to destroy its list. In another part of the settlement, all noncash assets given to the plaintiffs by the Invisible Empire were turned over to the Raleigh, North Carolina, branch of the National Association for the Advancement of Colored People.

Berhanu v. *Metzger* **(October 25, 1990)**
No. A8911–07007, Oregon, Multnomah County Circuit Court

The action was brought as a Klanwatch civil suit by Dees on behalf of the family of Mulugeta Seraw, a twenty-seven-year-old black college student from

Ethiopia. In 1988, Seraw was beaten to death with a baseball bat in Portland, Oregon, by three members of East Side White Pride, a local skinhead group that advocated racial separatism and anti-Semitism.

The Portland police arrested the three skinheads, and Dees instituted a wrongful death suit. Named in the lawsuit were Thomas Metzger, individually and as president of White Aryan Resistance (WAR), his son John Metzger, and skinheads Kenneth Mieske and Kyle Brewster. John Metzger was an official of WAR, and Mieske and Brewster were two of the skinheads involved in Seraw's murder.

The Metzgers, whose operation was based in Fallbrook, California, argued that they were 1,200 miles away from the scene of the crime and were acquainted with neither the victim nor the killers. At the trial, Dees produced twenty-one-year-old David Mazzella, who told the jury that he had been sent by Thomas Metzger to organize East Side White Pride. Testifying for seven hours, Mazzella stated that he was with the skinheads several hours before the attack. He also referred to himself as the "direct link" between Metzger and the killers.

The jury held that the Metzgers, acting through Mazzella, were also responsible for Seraw's murder. It awarded damages in the amount of $12.5 million to Engedaw Berhanu, acting on behalf of the estate of Seraw. It was the largest award in Oregon history.

The court rejected the argument made in the amicus curiae brief of the Oregon chapter of the American Civil Liberties Union that the suit may have violated the First Amendment rights of the Metzgers. In 1993 the defendants appealed the verdict to the Oregon Court of Appeals, which denied review, and in 1994 to the United States Supreme Court, which denied certiorari.

Annotated Bibliography

Bass, Jack. Review of *A Season for Justice: The Life and Times of Civil Rights Lawyer Morris Dees,* by Morris Dees with Steve Fiffer. *The Los Angeles Daily Journal,* August 6, 1991, 7. Review of Dees's autobiography.

———. *Taming the Storm: The Life and Times of Judge Frank M. Johnson, Jr. and the South's Fight Over Civil Rights.* New York: Doubleday, 1993. Discussion of the role of Judge Johnson in liberalizing Southern law and his decisions in some of the cases litigated by Dees.

Blum, Bill. Review of *A Season for Justice: The Life and Times of Civil Rights Lawyer Morris Dees,* by Morris Dees with Steve Fiffer. *ABA Journal* 77 (June 1991): 104. Review of Dees's autobiography.

Berry, Jason. Review of *Hate on Trial: The Case Against America's Most Dangerous Neo-Nazi,* by Morris Dees and Steve Fiffer. *New York Times Book Review,* March 21, 1993, 7, 27. Review of book on Dees's prosecution of Thomas Metzger of the White Aryan Resistance.

Bradford, Janet E. Review of *A Season for Justice: The Life and Times of Civil Rights Lawyer Morris Dees,* by Morris Dees with Steve Fiffer. *Legal Times* (July 29, 1991): 46. Review of Dees's autobiography.

Carlson, Tucker. "With Friends Like Dees . . ." *Weekly Standard* 1 (May 20, 1996): 23–27. Discussion of Dees's legal victories against hate groups.

Carmody, Cris. "Civil Rights Lawyer Becomes Author." *Chicago Daily Law Bulletin* June 3, 1991, 1. Discussion of Dees's autobiography, *A Season for Justice.*

Cheers, D. Michael. "Dedicate Memorial to 40 Who Died in Civil Rights Struggle." *Jet,* November 29, 1989, 4–16. Story about the Civil Rights Memorial at the Southern Poverty Law Center.

Chesser, Wilburn L. Review of *A Season for Justice: The Life and Times of Civil Rights Lawyer Morris Dees,* by Morris Dees with Steve Fiffer. *Maryland Journal of Contemporary Legal Issues* 3 (Spring 1992): 301–303. Review of Dees's autobiography and discussion of his work.

Clark, Jan. Review of *Hate on Trial: The Case Against America's Most Dangerous Neo-Nazi,* by Morris Dees and Steve Fiffer. *Kentucky Bench and Bar* 58 (Winter 1994): 41–42. Review of book on Dees's prosecution of Thomas Metzger of the White Aryan Resistance.

———. Review of *A Season for Justice: The Life and Times of Civil Rights Lawyer Morris Dees,* by Morris Dees with Steve Fiffer. *Kentucky Bench and Bar* 58 (Winter 1994): 41. Discussion of Dees's autobiography and work.

Copeland, Anna. "Until Justice Rolls Down like Waters." *Omni* 16 (February 1994): 29. Discussion about Dees and the work of the Southern Poverty Law Center.

Curriden, Mark. "Hitting the Klan—Civilly: Alabama Lawyer's Suits Cost Violent Extremists Plenty." *ABA Journal* 75 (February 1989): 19. Discussion of Dees's success in winning huge sums of money from the Ku Klux Klan and other white supremacist groups.

Davis, Johanna. Review of *Hate on Trial: The Case Against America's Most Dangerous Neo-Nazi,* by Morris Dees and Steve Fiffer. *National Trial Lawyer* 5 (September 1993): 85–86. Review of book about Dees's prosecution of Thomas Metzger of the White Aryan Resistance.

Dees, Morris. "McVeigh vs. Kaczynski: Similar, Yet So Different." *USA Today,* April 18, 1996, A13. A comparison and contrast by Dees of terrorists Timothy McVeigh and Theodore Kaczynski.

———. "Remember Me By My Clients: They Make My Life Worthwhile." *Trial* 26 (April 1990): 64–69. Recollection by Dees about his work in fighting the Ku Klux Klan and the clients that he represented in court.

Dees, Morris, and Ellen Bowden. "Hate: Taking Hate Groups to Court." *Trial* 31 (February 1995): 24. Dees discusses his work in suing white supremacist groups for conspiracy.

Dees, Morris, with James Corcoran. *Gathering Storm: America's Militia Threat.* New York: HarperCollins, 1996. Study by Dees and Corcoran on the growth of the American militia movement.

Dees, Morris, with Steve Fiffer. *A Season for Justice: The Life and Times of Civil Rights Lawyer Morris Dees.* New York: Charles Scriber's Sons, 1991, 1998. Dees's autobiography; updated version contains a brief epilogue that highlights his major work from 1991 to 1998.

Dees, Morris, and Steve Fiffer. *Hate on Trial: The Case Against America's Most Dangerous Neo-Nazi*. New York: Villard Books, 1993. Dees and Fiffer discuss the trial of Thomas Metzger of the White Aryan Resistance for the murder of a black college student from Ethiopia in 1988.

Egerton, John. "Poverty Palace: How the Southern Poverty Law Center Got Rich Fighting the Klan." *The Progressive* 52 (July 1988): 14–17. Discussion of the large financial settlements obtained by Dees and the Southern Poverty Law Center.

————. *Shades of Gray: Dispatches from the Modern South.* Baton Rouge: Louisiana State University Press, 1991. Account of changes in the South in the twentieth century, and a discussion of the work of the Southern Poverty Law Center.

Eisler, Kim I. Review of *Hate on Trial: The Case Against America's Most Dangerous Neo-Nazi,* by Morris Dees and Steve Fiffer. *Legal Times,* March 29, 1993, 47. Review of book about Dees's prosecution of Thomas Metzger of the White Aryan Resistance.

Elliott, Stuart. "A Marketer of Civil Rights Who Has Made a Difference." *New York Times,* May 15, 1991, D20. Discussion of the accomplishments of Dees and his successful strategy in the work of the Southern Poverty Law Center.

Ellis, David. "Suits Against White Sheets." *Time,* October 1, 1990, 31. Account of efforts by Dees to take legal action against the Ku Klux Klan.

Englade, Ken. "Today's Unsung Heroes: Profiles of Lawyers Who Help the Disadvantaged." *ABA Journal* 74 (November 1, 1988): 60–64. Discussion of the work of several lawyers, including Dees, whose work revolves around helping disadvantaged groups in American society.

Films for the Humanities and Sciences. *Hate on Trial: Challenging the First Amendment.* 3 videos, 1997. Three-part program on the trial of white supremacist leader Thomas Metzger and his son for the murder of a black college student from Ethiopia in 1988.

"Finding then Forum for a Victory: Successful Strategies From 10 of the Nation's Top Litigators." *National Law Journal* 13 (February 11, 1991), S3. Suggestions by leading attorneys, including Dees, on how to win court cases.

Flynn, Wayne. Review of *A Season for Justice: The Life and Times of Civil Rights Lawyer Morris Dees,* by Morris Dees with Steve Fiffer. *Forum* 73 (Fall 1993): 47–48. Review of Dees's autobiography.

Frantz, Douglas. "The Rhetoric of Terror." *Time,* March 27, 1995, 48–51. Account of the rise of white supremacist groups and their incendiary language.

Fuller, Millard, and Diane Scott. *Love in the Mortar Joints: The Story of Habitat for Humanity.* Piscataway, NJ: Association Press, 1980. Account by former law partner of Dees about their association and Fuller's later work in establishing Habitat for Humanity.

Gannon, Julie. "'We Can't Afford Not to Fight': Morris Dees Takes Bigotry to Court." *Trial* 33 (January 1997): 18–23. Discussion of Dees's efforts to fight bigotry in the American court system.

Gidari, Albert. Review of *Hate on Trial: The Case Against America's Most Dangerous Neo-Nazi,* by Morris Dees and Steve Fiffer. *Federal Bar News and Journal* 40 (November–December 1992): 662–663. Review of Dees's book about his prosecution of Thomas Metzger of the White Aryan Resistance.

Goodman, Walter. "Free Speech and the Right to Hate," *New York Times,* February 5, 1992, C20. Discussion of Bill Moyers's television program "Hate on Trial" WNET about the trial of Thomas Metzger of the White Aryan Resistance, and Dees's prosecution of him.

Gray, Fred. *Bus Ride to Justice: Changing the System by the System: The Life and Works of Fred D. Gray.* Montgomery: Black Belt Press, 1995. Details of the life and work of attorney Gray, who represented Dr. Martin Luther King Jr. during the Montgomery bus boycott of 1955.

Harrington, James. Review of *A Season for Justice: The Life and Times of Civil Rights Lawyer Morris Dees,* by Morris Dees with Steve Fiffer. *Texas Bar Journal* 56 (June 1993): 616. Review of Dees's autobiography.

Hathaway, Geoff. Review of *A Season for Justice: The Life and Times of Civil Rights Lawyer Morris Dees,* by Morris Dees with Steve Fiffer. *Bench & Bar of Minnesota* 49 (November 1992): 31–32. Review of Dees's autobiography.

"The High Cost of Klanning." *Time,* November 7, 1988, 37. Discussion of Dees's success in winning big settlements against the Ku Klux Klan.

Imahara, Kathryn K., and Stewart Kwoh. Review of *Hate on Trial: The Case Against America's Most Dangerous Neo-Nazi,* by Morris Dees and Steve Fiffer. *Trial* 29 (October 1993): 80–82. Review of Dees's book about his prosecution of Thomas Metzger of the White Aryan Resistance.

Jubera, Drew. "Profile: Civil Rights Lawyer Morris Dees, Jr." *Los Angeles Daily Journal,* January 26, 1990, 1, 10. Account of Dees's accomplishments and the work of the Southern Poverty Law Center.

Judge, Frank. "Slaying the Dragon." *American Lawyer* 9 (September 1987): 83–89. Discussion of Dees's work against the Ku Klux Klan.

"Klan Marches to Show Contempt for Civil Rights Lawyer." *Atlanta Journal Constitution,* March 10, 1991, E41. Report of march by Ku Klux Klan to demonstrate its opposition to the work of Dees.

Kennedy, Robert F., Jr. *Judge Frank M. Johnson, Jr.: A Biography.* New York: G.P. Putnam's Sons, 1978. Story of Judge Johnson's impact upon the Southern legal system and an account of Dees's association with him.

Koniak, Susan P. Review of *Gathering Storm: America's Militia Threat,* by Morris Dees with James Corcoran. *Michigan Law Review* 95 (May 1997): 1761–1798. Discussion of Dees's book on the growth of the American militia movement.

Kopel, David B. "The Militias Are Coming." *Reason* 28 (August 1996): 57–60. Account of the rise of the militia movement in America and the problems resulting from its growth.

Kornbluth, Jesse. "The Woman Who Beat the Klan." *New York Times Magazine,* November 1, 1987, 26–30, 36–39. Article on Beulah Mae Donald and her case against the Ku Klux Klan in the killing of her son, Michael Donald.

Kovach, Bill. Review of *A Season for Justice: The Life and Times of Civil Rights Lawyer Morris Dees,* by Morris Dees with Steve Fiffer. *New York Times Book Review,* June 30, 1991, Sec. 7, 27. Review of Dees's autobiography.

Lambert, Bruce. "Cathy E. Bennett, Who Pioneered Jury Selection Method, Dies at 41." *New York Times,* June 12, 1992, D20. Obituary on Bennett, who helped Dees select juries in cases involving the Ku Klux Klan and the White Aryan Resistance.

Leahy, Michael. "Poetic Justice: L.A. Lawyer Plays Real-Life Attorney . . . and It's Not Easy." *TV Guide,* January 19–25, 1991, 16–17. Actor Corbin Bernsen, former attorney, played Morris Dees in the NBC television movie *Line of Fire.*

Lewis, Mark F. Review of *Hate on Trial: The Case Against America's Most Dangerous Neo-Nazi,* by Morris Dees and Steve Fiffer. *Florida Bar Journal* 67 (May 1993): 82. Review of Dees's book about his prosecution of Thomas Metzger of the White Aryan Resistance.

Line of Fire: The Morris Dees Story. National Broadcasting System, 1991. A made-for-television movie on Dees's career.

Margolick, David. "For a Faltering Pioneer in Jury Selection, the Smith Case Provides New Inspiration." *New York Times,* November 22, 1991, A28. Article on jury selection specialist Cathy E. Bennett, who helped Dees pick juries in cases involving the Ku Klux Klan and the White Aryan Resistance.

Mass, Alan H. Review of *Hate on Trial: The Case Against America's Most Dangerous Neo-Nazi,* by Morris Dees and Steve Fiffer. *New York Law Journal* (March 17, 1993): 2. Review of Dees's book about his prosecution of Thomas Metzger of the White Aryan Resistance.

McManuss, James G. "Rich White Man Took a Stand for Justice." *National Catholic Reporter* 27 (August 30, 1991): 17. Account of Dees's determination to fight for underprivileged groups in society after he amassed a personal fortune.

Mitgang, Herbert. Review of *A Season for Justice: The Life and Times of Civil Rights Lawyer Morris Dees,* by Morris Dees with Steve Fiffer. *New York Times,* July 19, 1991, C25. Review of Dees's autobiography.

Mohr, Anthony J. Review of *A Season for Justice: The Life and Times of Civil Rights Lawyer Morris Dees,* by Morris Dees with Steve Fiffer. *Los Angeles Lawyer* 16 (June 1993): 54. Review of Dees's autobiography.

Polski, Perry M. Review of *A Season for Justice: The Life and Times of Civil Rights Lawyer Morris Dees,* by Morris Dees with Steve Fiffer. *University of West Los Angeles Law Review* 23 (Annual 1992): 377–381. Review of Dees's autobiography, and discussion of his work.

Pruitt, Paul M., Jr. Review of *A Season for Justice: The Life and Times of Civil Rights Lawyer Morris Dees,* by Morris Dees with Steve Fiffer. *Journal of Southern History* 59 (May 1993): 422–424. Review of Dees's autobiography, and his relationship to the civil rights movement in the South.

Quade, Vicki. "Klan Buster: How the Southern Poverty Law Center Smashed the United Klans of America." *Barrister* 15 (Summer 1988): 12–16. Interview with Dees about his work in the fight against the United Klans of America.

"Racism: Shall We Overcome?" *U.S. Catholic* 55 (December 1990): 28–34. Interview of Dees regarding his attitude on race prejudice in the United States.

Reaves, Lynne. "Klan in Court: Rights Suit Spurs Indictment." *ABA Journal* 70 (August 1984): 36. Discussion of Dees's work against the Ku Klux Klan for the murder of Michael Donald.

Reedy, Gary S. Review of *Hate on Trial: The Case Against America's Most Dangerous Neo-Nazi,* by Morris Dees and Steve Fiffer. *Advocate (Idaho)* 36 (October 1993): 19. Review of Dees's book about his prosecution of Thomas Metzger of the White Aryan Resistance.

Rendahl, Stephen E. Review of *A Season for Justice: The Life and Times of Civil Rights Lawyer Morris Dees,* by Morris Dees with Steve Fiffer. *North Dakota Law Review* 69 (Spring 1993): 361–368. Review of Dees's autobiography and discussion of his work.

———. Review of *Hate on Trial: The Case Against America's Most Dangerous Neo-Nazi,* by Morris Dees and Steve Fiffer. *North Dakota Law Review* 69 (Spring 1993): 361–368. Review of Dees's book about his prosecution of Thomas Metzger of the White Aryan Resistance, with a discussion of Dees's work.

Review of *Hate on Trial: The Case Against America's Most Dangerous Neo-Nazi,* by Morris Dees and Steve Fiffer. *Texas International Law Journal* 28 (Spring 1993): 435. Review of Dees's book about his prosecution of Thomas Metzger of the White Aryan Resistance.

Review of *A Season for Justice: The Life and Times of Civil Rights Lawyer Morris Dees,* by Morris Dees with Steve Fiffer. *Harvard Law Review* 106 (May 1993): 1704. Review of Dees's autobiography.

Reynolds, Barbara. "You Have a Right to Hate, but not the Right to Hurt." *USA Today,* June 3, 1991, A11. Discussion of Dees's beliefs about First Amendment freedoms and hate groups.

Rutledge, Bruce. Review of *A Season for Justice: The Life and Times of Civil Rights Lawyer Morris Dees,* by Morris Dees with Steve Fiffer. *Barrister* 18 (Summer 1991): 4–5. Review of Dees's autobiography.

Sack, Kevin. "A Son of Alabama Takes on Americans Who Live to Hate." *New York Times,* May 12, 1996, E7. Discussion of Dees's work against hate groups in the South.

"Scalping the Skinheads." *Time,* November 5, 1990, 37. Dees's actions in court against the Skinhead movement.

Schroeter, Leonard W. Review of *A Season for Justice: The Life and Times of Civil Rights Lawyer Morris Dees,* by Morris Dees with Steve Fiffer. *Trial* 27 (September 1991): 71–72. Review of Dees's autobiography, with a discussion of his work.

Shapiro, Robert E. "Interview of Morris Dees." *Litigation* 16 (Summer 1990): 6–13, 46–47. Analysis of Dees and his impact on the legal profession.

Shaw, Bill. "Morris Dees." *People Weekly,* July 22, 1991, 50–54. Summary of Dees's life and his work with the Southern Poverty Law Center.

Stasiulis, Stanley P. Review of *A Season for Justice: The Life and Times of Civil Rights Lawyer Morris Dees,* by Morris Dees, with Steve Fiffer. *Illinois Bar Journal* 79 (December 1991): 646–647. Review of Dees's autobiography and discussion of his work.

"White Supremacist Leaders Penalized for Inciting Death." *New York Times,* October 23, 1990, B6. Article about the trial of Thomas Metzger and other leaders of the White Aryan Resistance.

Willwerth, James. "Making War on WAR." *Time,* October 22, 1990, 60–61. Description of efforts by Dees to sue the White Aryan Resistance.

Zeskind, Leonard. Review of *Gathering Storm: America's Militia Threat,* by Morris Dees with James Corcoran. *Nation,* October 28, 1996, 20–24. Discussion of Dees's book and other works dealing with "white racist counterculture."

Zinsser, William Knowlton. "I Realized Her Tears Were Becoming Part of the Memorial." *Smithsonian* 22 (September 1991): 32–40. Account of the civil rights memorial at the site of the Southern Poverty Law Center.

Index

About the Authors

Diana Klebanow studied at Bard College, graduated with honors in history from Brooklyn College, and received a Ph.D. in history from New York University, where she was the recipient of the Alumnae Association Award for Excellence in History. She is an adjunct professor of political science at the Brooklyn Center of Long Island University and teaches in the law program at August Martin High School in Jamaica, New York. Her earlier book, *Urban Legacy: The Story of America's Cities* (1977), was coauthored with Franklin L. Jonas and Ira M. Leonard.

Franklin L. Jonas received a Ph.D. in history from New York University and has taught at the college level for nearly four decades. Over that span, he has specialized in American history, but has taught a wide variety of courses, including several in political science, public policy, and sociology. He has been the recipient of three research grants and has several publications to his credit. He has been teaching at the Brooklyn Center of Long Island University since 1965. His first book, *Urban Legacy: The Story of America's Cities* (1977), was coauthored with Diana Klebanow and Ira M. Leonard.